sport, culture, and society

sport, culture,

EDITED BY

JOHN W. LOY, Jr., and GERALD S. KENYON

UCLA   University of Wisconsin

and society

A READER ON THE SOCIOLOGY OF SPORT

MACMILLAN PUBLISHING CO., INC.
NEW YORK

COLLIER MACMILLAN PUBLISHERS
LONDON

preface

Those who have been giving some thought to the sociological implications of sport are not surprised to hear or read of its considerable economic import, of its increasing national and international political significance, of its strong influence upon styles of dress, or even of its power to control the lives of those committed to it. Neither are they surprised to learn that Americans spend $40,000,000 a year on bowling balls; that the U.S. Lawn Tennis Association paid the Davis Cup players $9,000 per year as "amateurs"; or even that game stoppages in commercially televised sport are not always determined by the actual occurrence of rule infractions. Such information, and much more, is easily obtainable by anyone interested in digging it out.

Facts such as these may be interesting and certainly attest to the pervasiveness of sport and its place in the lives of people throughout the world. But to the social scientist the facts themselves are largely trivial; it is discovering an explanation for them that excites the mind. The many possibilities of accomplishing just that have been alluded to for well over half a century. However, other than a few minor forays, only recently has there been an other-than-token interest in explaining sport within a sociological context. Now, for the first time, researchers from several countries and with different backgrounds are undertaking a wide variety of studies and are publishing their findings. Unfortunately, results have been reported not in any one periodical, but rather in a wide array of publications, from *The American Journal of Sociology* to *The Research Quarterly*. Thus, there seems to be a need to bring together in one place representative samples of contemporary work. This, in part, is what we have attempted to do in *Sport, Culture, and Society*.

Basically, we set out to draw from two general research traditions, physical education and the social sciences, despite certain limitations of the literature. Physical education research, which in this country alone goes

87956

back over 75 years, contains very little sport sociology. The research-oriented physical educator has been concentrating, for the most part, upon either physiological or perceptual-motor aspects of exercise and sport. Particularly in the United States, it has been the social scientists—sociologists, anthropologists, and social psychologists—who have recognized sport as a fertile ground for study. However, they have been less interested in the explanation of sport and more interested in the use of sport as a social system within which various theories can be put to test. Indeed, we doubt that many of the writers whose work is reprinted here consider themselves sport sociologists. Nevertheless, we consider their research as part of the body of knowledge of the sociology of sport.

The writings we have selected were chosen on the basis of several criteria. We have tried to include some works which were primarily theoretical and others which provided empirical tests of certain propositions. As much as possible (sociologists have a high affinity for baseball) we have varied the subject matter, and have endeavored to present different methodological orientations. Finally, and foremost, we have tried to include selections which describe and explain the interrelationships between sport and society at a variety of levels.

In brief, the book has five parts. Part One, "The Sociology of Sport: An Emerging Field," consists of our efforts to provide a historical and a contemporary perspective of the sociology of sport. Part Two, "Frames of Reference," presents readings which detail different orientations to the field, and which illustrate beginning attempts both to define key concepts unique to it and to employ them in various conceptual frameworks. Part Three, "Sport and Social Organization," encompasses four sections of readings, treating sport as a subsystem of more inclusive social systems. Section One deals with some antecedents of modern sport, and Section Two considers sport as a subsystem of ethnic cultures, preliterate and modern. Sections Three and Four provide articles which focus on the role of sport in modern societies. In the former, emphasis is placed on the relationships between sport and basic social institutions such as the polity, whereas in the latter, stress is on the relationships between sport and certain fundamental social processes such as stratification. In Part Four, "Sport and Small Groups," there are selected references treating sport from a small group perspective, first at the micro-social system level, with attention centered on the problems of individual adjustment and team effectiveness, and second at the subculture level, where the small sport group is considered in terms of certain occupational subcultures. Finally, Part Five consists of a selected list of articles and books related to the material contained in the previous four parts.

A basic assumption underlying our selection of articles was that sport can be considered as both a dependent and an independent variable. When investigating sport as a dependent variable, the sport sociologist becomes interested in explaining sport in terms of other social systems or subsystems. In so doing, he becomes interested in questions such as, "How do athletes

or fans become 'socialized' into sport?" "How and why do new sports originate, while others die?" "What accounts for the adoption of new training
techniques and equipment?" On the other hand, sport considered as an independent variable becomes a potential factor in explaining, at least in part,
the nature of other social systems. In this case, the questions become: "What
is the political function of contemporary international sport?" "To what
extent does involvement in sport provide the means for achieving status or
social position?" "To what extent does the degree of involvement in sport
influence the economy?" Reducing the distinction to the level of personality, we have "Is achievement in sport a function of personality?" as opposed
to "Is personality a function of success in sport?" Thus the dual considerations
of sport as either a dependent or independent variable provides the sport
sociologist with almost endless possibilities for research. We have tried to
give examples of several such possibilities in our selection of readings.

Although the book may be useful for more than one purpose, it would
seem to us that its primary function should be as a basic reader for an introductory course in the sociology of sport. We believe it will also be useful
to various courses in sociology and in the social foundations of physical education. Many of the papers included will undoubtedly appeal to the general
reader as well. More than anything else, however, it is our wish that the book
may in some small way motivate students to become seriously interested
and active in the sociology of a most fascinating aspect of contemporary
times—sport.

J. W. L.
G. S. K.

acknowledgments

We are indebted to Dr. Elisabeth Kenyon for her invaluable assistance in translating the article by Lenk and the article by Klein and Christiansen, and to Dr. John M. Harkin for his translation of the article by Lüschen. Gratitude is expressed also to Mr. Wesley White, who retrieved the many articles which were considered for inclusion in this volume.

J. W. L.
G. S. K.

contents

PART FIVE

further readings in the sociology of sport

sport, culture, and society

the sociology of sport: an emerging field

The notion that sport and related phenomena might be studied using the theoretical frameworks and the empirical tools of the social sciences is not new. Over the years a number of books and articles have appeared in various parts of the world, written by psychologists, sociologists, anthropologists, historians, and physical educators. What follows is meant to show briefly some aspects of the genesis of a new field from a few almost unrelated writings to the beginnings of a subdiscipline.

SPORT SOCIOLOGY IN HISTORICAL PERSPECTIVE

Interest in the nature and function of play, games, and sports has been shown by physical educators and social scientists alike. In the case of the former, it is not surprising as the subject matter was their medium. Thus, the idea that exercise and sports were important for reasons other than physiological has been expressed by many of the early leaders in physical education. In the United States alone, statements have been made for many years attesting to the role of sport in character formation, group solidarity, and the like (Hetherington, 1910; Williams, 1930; Nash, 1931).[1] Numerous accounts by physical educators have appeared condemning certain forms and "abuses" of sport in the community. Thus, sport and physical activity were seen as the means for inculcating some self-evident morality. Later, when the work week was becoming shorter, the contribution of physical education to preparing for leisure was frequently alluded to. From a professional point of view then, the physical educator has long recognized some of the relationships between sport and society. Yet few in physical

[1] Complete references for writers cited in introductory statements are given at the end of the volume.

1

education have devoted much of their career to the subject. With the possible exception of Cowell's work [2] serious empirical studies have not been popular, at least in the United States.

Equally interested in the social significance of sport, but motivated by a desire to understand rather than modify behavior, were a variety of social scientists, from psychologists to anthropologists. Some have reflected upon their casual observations of sport over the years, often within a theoretical framework of sorts. Others have carried out empirical studies. But seldom has either the social scientist or the physical educator used anything like a consistent set of concepts to describe the phenomenon of his interest. Where writers *have* used like terms, their meanings were often unalike. However, despite the semantic difficulties of the past one hundred years or more, three concepts have emerged to which most writers and researchers have addressed themselves—the concepts of "play," "game," and "sport." At this point, we present a brief historical account of results obtained from treating each.

Serious work addressed to the concept *play* largely preceded that addressed to the concepts "game" and "sport." Moreover, efforts to explain the nature and function of play have been several, mostly by psychologists or social psychologists. The results have since become relatively well known. For example, Spencer (1873) wrote about play as the use of accumulated energy in unused "faculties." Groos (1898) proposed that play of children was practice for life. G. Stanley Hall's (1920) recapitulation theory explained play as due to the fact that ontogeny repeats phylogeny. For McDougall (1918) play was the primitive expression of the "instincts." Many others, from Freud to Dewey, also have had something to say about play. Today, however, we find that it is considered to be much more complex than early theorists suggested (Piaget, 1951).

Although psychologists have been concerned with the play of individuals, it is not surprising to find that sociologists and anthropologists have been more interested in play in a collective sense, i.e., *games*. A number of early accounts have appeared, describing the nature of games found in non-European societies (Tylor, 1879). Interest in documenting the game forms of a wide variety of cultural groups continues to the present day. (Stumpf and Cozens, 1947; Goellner, 1953; Jones, 1967; Salter, 1967).

Attempts to explain the function of games in society have been several. For Simmel, writing in 1917, play and games were a part of a "world of sociability"—an artificial world—in which "social game" has the double sense of the game being played in a society (as its external medium), and with the help of game "people 'play' 'society'" (Wolff, 1964, pp. 49–50).

Max Weber conceived of the game as having an important function in society, using feudalism as an example.

> In feudal ideology the most important relations in life are pervaded by personalized ties, in contrast to all factual and impersonal relationships, which

[2] For example, see Charles C. Cowell, "The Contributions of Physical Activity to Social Development," *Research Quarterly*, 31 (May, 1960), 286–306; a review of literature which includes five of his own reports.

are regarded as plebeian and specifically devoid of dignity. This contrast has several aspects. Originating in an army of warriors for whom the battle between individuals was decisive feudalism made skillful handling of weapons the object of its military education; it had little use for mass discipline to perfect a collectively organized military effort. As a result the feudal style of life incorporated the *game* as an important means of training that inculcated useful abilities and qualities of character. The game was not a "pastime" but the natural medium in which the physical and psychological capacities of the human organism came alive and became supple. In this form of "training" the spontaneous drives of man found their outlet, irrespective of any division between "body" and "soul" and regardless of how conventionalized the games often became. The knightly strata of medieval Europe and Japan regarded the game as a serious and important aspect of life that had a special affinity with spontaneous artistic interests and helped bar the way to all forms of utilitarian rationality. The artistocratic sentiment of these feudal strata found its expression in pomp and circumstance, in utensils and equipment that displayed the splendor of the household. From this standpoint luxury is not a superfluous frill but a means of self-assertion and a weapon in the struggle for power. (Bendix, 1960, p. 364)

More from the point of view of social psychology, George Herbert Mead (1934) showed how play and games provide a medium for the development of the "self" in children.

The child responds in a fairly intelligent fashion to the immediate stimuli that come to him, but they are not organized. He does not organize his life as we would like to have him do, namely, as a whole. There is just a set of responses of the type of play. The child reacts to a certain stimulus, and the reaction is in himself that is called out in others, but he is not a whole self. In his game he has to have an organization of these roles; otherwise he cannot play the game. The game represents the passage in the life of the child from taking the role of others in play to the organized part that is essential to self-consciousness in the full sense of the term. (p. 152)

Two more recent conceptualizations of game are those of Erving Goffman (1961) and Eric Berne (1964). For Goffman, in his sociology of interaction writings, the game becomes a "situated activity system" or "focused gathering." For Berne, a social psychiatrist, the various forms of human interaction can all be considered as games, with each one capable of being played in "adult," "parent," or "child" fashion.

Although the concepts "play" and "game" have seen rather extensive treatment, much less attention has been paid to *sport*. The word is not new, but sport as we usually think of it today has a much shorter history than either play or game. Nevertheless, Veblen had already formed some strong opinions by 1899. In his *Theory of the Leisure Class*, he saw sports as a reversion to barbarian culture. Whether they were engaged in by the leisure class or the working class, they were "marks of an arrested spiritual development" (Veblen, 1934, p. 253). As for college sport, he said:

These manifestations of the predatory temperament are all to be classed under the head of exploit. They are partly simple and unreflected expressions of an attitude of emulative ferocity, partly activities deliberately entered upon with a view to gaining repute for prowess. Sports of all kinds are of the same general character, including prize-fights, bull-fights, athletics, shooting, angling, yachting, and games of skills, even where the element of destructive physical efficiency is not an obtrusive feature. Sports shade off from the basis of hostile combat, through skill, to cunning and chicanery, without its being possible to draw a line at any point. The ground of an addiction to sports is an archaic spiritual constitution—the possession of the predatory emulative propensity in relatively high potency. A strong proclivity to adventuresome exploit and to the infliction of damage is especially pronounced in those employments which are in colloquial usage specifically called sportsmanship. (p. 255)

By the turn of the century "sport" was becoming of some concern to the academician. In 1903 Patrick wrote on the psychology of football. At this time William Graham Sumner was lecturing on "folkways" and "mores" at Yale University. In his book *Folkways*, published in 1906, he devoted a chapter to "popular sports, exhibitions, and drama." In 1910, Steinitzer's critique of sport, *Sport and Kultur*, was to be the forerunner of a series of debates published in the Polish journal *Ruch* in 1911 (Wohl, 1966). In 1912, there appeared in *The American Journal of Sociology* an article by George Elliot Howard entitled "Social Psychology of the Spectator." *Soziologie des Sports* by Heinz Risse was published in Germany in 1921 (Wohl, 1966).

By the middle of the 1930s, play, games, and sport had become sufficiently important to be the subject of comprehensive analysis. In 1938, Jan Huizinga, a Dutch historian, wrote *Homo Ludens*, in which he shows the role of play within nearly every aspect of culture, from war to religion (Huizinga, 1955). His work is now referred to by members of several different disciplines. Roger Caillois, a French sociologist, going beyond Huizinga, in his *Man, Play, and Games* classified games into four major types and endeavored to show the function of each type in society (Caillois 1961). Peter McIntosh, of England, speaking more directly to sport *per se* and from an excellent historical perspective, discussed several dimensions of sport in contemporary society, drawing in part upon both Huizinga and Caillois (McIntosh, 1963). There have been other comprehensive works, including Natan's book, *Sport and Society* (1958), and Magnane's *Sociologie du Sport* (1964).

The study of leisure, an area of increasing interest to sociologists, has resulted in several works that are of interest to the sport sociologist.[3] Larrabee and Meyersohn (1958) make an important contribution by bringing together in one

---

[3] For an early example (1934) see G. Lundberg, *et al.*, "The Amount And Uses of Leisure," in E. Larrabee and R. Meyersohn, *Mass Leisure*, Glencoe, Ill.: Free Press, 1958, and more recently, see S. de Grazia, *Of Time, Work, and Leisure*, Garden City, New York: Doubleday, 1962, and M. Kaplan, *Leisure in America: A Social Inquiry*, New York: Wiley, 1960.

volume both a collection of outstanding readings on the problem of leisure, and a comprehensive bibliography on the subject. Now available in English is *Toward a Civilization of Leisure* by the French sociologist Joffre Dumazedier (1966).

In summary, from an historical perspective the sociology of sport has yet to become a relatively unified discipline. Although workers from many and diverse fields have written on sport or the related phenomena of play and games, few have committed their career to the study of the interrelationships between sport and society.

SPORT SOCIOLOGY IN CONTEMPORARY PERSPECTIVE

It is only recently that several social scientists have committed themselves on a full-time basis to the study of the social significance of sport. Their commitment has resulted in: (1) frequent calls for a sociology of sport, (2) the emergence of national and international organizations dedicated to the field, (3) the appearance in increasing amounts of writing and research, and (4) the instituting of courses of study in various colleges and universities. Suffice it to say that this heightened interest has come not from a single source but from many. It comes from writers representing both physical education and the social sciences. Men in all stages of their career, and from all parts of the world, are becoming interested and are engaged in the sociology of sport. Such activity has culminated in the appearance of a number of pleas urging the formalization of a field of study. For example, Horkheimer, a German sociologist, has said:

> The more light [that] is thrown on the functions and possibilities of life in a sporting community, the more necessary it will become to make sport the subject of very serious theoretical and empirical studies, a subject for scientific research. (1963, p. 26)

In the interest of social planning for leisure, Dumazedier, a French sociologist, has stated:

> For the sociologist, sport is still very young, and we do not know very much about it. It should be added, moreover, that the characteristics of sport, now, are very different from those which de Coubertin saw. His words on amateur sport are attractive; nevertheless, we have to think about the sport of today and tomorrow and evolve a forward looking policy for a mass civilization where leisure predominates. . . . It is certainly an excellent thing to take inspiration from de Coubertin, but it is nonetheless necessary to establish in our industrial society a sociology of sport in order to be able to take appropriate decisions. (1963, p. 55)

Wohl of Poland says:

> The enormous development of the sports movement, its universal character, its growing importance and role in the world of our times, its interrelation with various momentous problems of our epoch, make it necessary to pass

over as far as social problems of sports are concerned from vague argumentation to systematic analyses, based on verified methods and research techniques. (1966, p. 6)

From the Soviet Union, Kukushkin writes:

The study of the sociological regularities of the development of physical culture in the Soviet Union is one of the most important aspects of research work in this field of science. (1966, p. 242)

In the words of Kane and Murray from England:

There is no doubt that as sport becomes more and more an important social and economic element of mass culture, there is a growing need to apply the disciplined regimen of social science in examining the implications of the various forces which have helped to shape its development, structure and organisation. (1966, p. 111)

Thus, there appears to be consensus that the serious study of sport would be a fruitful undertaking. However, there has emerged already some different orientations to the field. The result of the development of distinct viewpoints has been conflicting conceptualizations of what is the proper subject matter of sport sociology, the most appropriate methodology or the best theoretical frames of reference. This apparent confusion is, in one sense, to be expected as a characteristic of any emerging field. In another sense, it reflects relatively widespread activity, and as such augurs well for its growth.

In the first section of readings some of these differing orientations are treated in detail. The present perspective of the sociology of sport goes beyond these simple programmatic statements, however. Most of those cited above have also undertaken research studies in the field. Moreover, in 1967, we saw the beginnings of cooperative efforts among sport sociologists from a variety of countries, which will certainly aid in taking the field beyond its largely conjectural state.[4]

ORGANIZATIONS DEVOTED TO SPORT SOCIOLOGY. As interest develops in any enterprise, it is typical for those involved to come together both informally and formally. A major development in this respect occurred in 1964 when an eleven-member committee on sport sociology, comprised of both physical educators and social scientists, was formed as an outgrowth of the International Council for Sport and Physical Education. Later it also became an affiliate of the International Sociological Association. Both parent bodies are affiliates of UNESCO. The committee has maintained a truly international flavor by basing its membership upon a diversity of national origins.[5] The group has since held several meet-

[4] International Workshop in the Sociology of Sport in its Cross-cultural Aspects, University of Illinois, Champaign, Ill., April 9–15, 1967.

[5] Members of the Committee as of fall, 1968, are as follows: Andrzej Wohl, Poland, President; Günther Lüschen, West Germany, General Secretary; Ralf Albonico, Switzerland; Joffre Dumazedier, France; Günther Erbach, East Germany; Kalevi Heinilä, Finland; Peter McIntosh, England; Aleksander Novikof, Soviet Union; Gregory Stone, United States; Kyuzo Takenoshita, Japan.

ings culminating in its first biennial Congress held in 1966 in Cologne, based upon the theme, "Small Group Research in Sport" (Lüschen, 1966). With a corresponding membership of over ninety, the committee has become a significant force in sport sociology. In addition to publishing the *International Review of Sport Sociology*, it is also coordinating some cross-national research studies concerning sport involvement. Strong national organizations have not yet appeared, nor are they likely to do so within the immediate future, as in any given country there are only a few who are actively engaged in research, teaching, and writing. Typical of what has occurred on a small scale is the formation of a committee on sport sociology as a part of an ongoing project concerned with identifying a body of knowledge for a discipline whose primary focus is sport and physical activity, sponsored by departments of physical education of ten universities of the midwestern United States (Big Ten) (Zeigler and McCristal, 1967).

RESEARCH AND WRITING. The quantity of literature that touches upon sport in society, over and above that of a journalistic nature is astonishingly great. It appears in many forms, from a part of the "community" studies, as, for example, Hollingshead's *Elmtown's Youth* (1949), from a part of the "elite" studies, such as Baltzell's analysis of "an American business aristocracy" (1962), to the reporting of empirical research in social science journals.[6] In addition, much of the work reported in the area of leisure, in some way relates to sport (Larrabee and Meyersohn, 1958). It is true that the quality of writing is uneven, but this is more or less true in any field. With the creation of the *International Review of Sport Sociology*, the quality and quantity should rise, however. The works reprinted in Parts II, III, and IV, together with those listed in the bibliography, provide some indication of the wide variety of theoretical and methodological orientations already existing in this youthful subfield.

COURSES OF STUDY. Another illustration of the extent to which the sociology of sport is becoming organized is seen in the attention paid it by members of the academic community. Up to a decade or so ago, little interest could be found in the form of research or course work. Today however the picture has changed. In the United States over thirty institutions offer a course focusing upon the role of sport in society. Nearly all are offered by departments of physical education. Departments of Sociology offer courses in the problem of leisure but thus far seem to have avoided the term "sport." Unfortunately, not all who are teaching sport sociology today are as well prepared as they might be. Some amelioration of this situation is in sight, however. It is now possible at at least three universities to pursue doctoral study with a specialization in the sociology of sport.[7] These programs entail considerable interdisciplinary study provided by cooperation between departments of physical education and sociology.

In Europe no simple pattern seems to exist. For example, research and doctoral study in the sociology of sport may exist in sociological research insti-

---

[6] In this regard, it is interesting to note that the *American Sociological Review* has yet to include an article on the subject of sport.

[7] The Universities of Illinois and Wisconsin, and Michigan State University.

tutes affiliated with a university such as the Forschungsinstitut für Soziologie of the University of Cologne, or as an integral part of a semi-autonomous institute for physical culture, such as the Deutsche Hochschule für Korperkultur in Leipzig. In both Europe and America it is much too early to say which form of formal study will emerge as the dominant one.

In summary, it can be seen that while interest in sport from a social perspective is not new, it is only recently that several significant steps have been taken to establish a legitimate sociology of sport. We have selected the readings that follow with a view of reflecting both historical antecedents and today's "state of the art." If present indications are correct, the reader can expect, before many years pass, a genuine basis for a new selection of contributors. However, we believe that the work of the authors contributing to this volume will not be forgotten, but rather will be considered as a forerunner to what, hopefully, will be a thriving and sophisticated sociology of sport.

PART TWO

frames of reference

OVERVIEW

THE SOCIOLOGY OF SPORT AS A DISCIPLINE

From our point of view there appears to be emerging within the field of sport sociology two distinct orientations, with a further separation within one of these. Although devotion and seriousness of purpose are shared by most writers and researchers, the distinctions among them would seem to be explained by differences in goals they seek, which in turn are precipitated by their background of training, experience, and environment. We have called the two major approaches *normative* and *nonnormative*.

NORMATIVE ORIENTED SPORT SOCIOLOGY. Those who appear to be subscribing to this approach seem to be assuming that certain social goals are implicitly established and that considerable consensus exists as to their nature. This basic orientation seems to be shared by two groups of writers. First, there are those primarily in the United States, England, and other Western countries, who visualize sport and exercise as vehicles to character formation in the tradition of Christian-Judaic morality—"The battle of Waterloo was won on the playing fields of Eton." Second, there are those, primarily from Eastern European countries and the Soviet Union, who carry on their work in a Marxist-Leninist tradition. Members of the former group seem to be in search of a justification of their goal, that is, "We know that sport contributes to the development of 'desirable' personality traits and thus to 'wholesome' communities, but what we need now is hard evidence so that we can convince others." Daniels, whose major interest lay in the role of sport in culture, appeared to be a member of this group. Despite the fact that he has argued for a rigorous scientific sport sociology, he has said:

> When we are better able to understand the role of sport in society, . . . perhaps the status of sport in the culture will find a level heretofore unachieved by expressions of concern alone. (1966, p. 161)

Moreover, he has raised the question of whether sport can be "wholesome catharsis" and writes about sport as an index of the "quality of a society" (Daniels, 1966). Thus, we present Daniels' paper, "Sport as an Element of Culture," as a conceptual framework we would consider as rising from one form of a normative orientation.

Similarly, those sociologists of sport working within a Marxist context also accept established ends, namely, the shaping of various social institutions, including sport, to facilitate progress toward the ultimate achievement of a Communist society. The question writers in this tradition seem to be posing is, "How can sport be organized and employed most efficiently to meet the goals of a socialist state?" For example, Artemov of the Soviet Union, in his discussion of time budgets, suggests that their use ". . . is one of the most rational methods for the determination of social and particularly economic effectiveness of physical culture" (1966, p. 81). Similarly, Wohl of Poland calls for a sport sociology that would meet the needs of the sport movement or more specifically to ". . . supply data for the establishment of development models for sport" (1966, p. 7). He has outlined what he considers to be four interdependent "functions and spheres" of sport, each of which has deep roots in the ". . . social micro-structures of all the problems of our contemporary life. That is why sport belongs to the vision of the world we want to create" (1966, p. 14). That sport sociology has a mission, that of improving the practice of physical culture for its greater contribution to society in general, is also the position taken by Erbach of the German Democratic Republic (East Germany). That the ultimate ends or goals are clearly established and provide the very justification for research in the sociology of sport can be inferred from his statement that:

> [The development of sport sociology as an independent discipline] is in accordance with the growing process of differentiation and integration in science as a whole and makes it possible for Marxist social sciences to examine the concrete social processes of physical culture in detail, as well as to make sociological generalizations needed for scientifically founded guidance and direction. (p. 66)

Thus, we present Dr. Erbach's article, "The Science of Sport and Sports Sociology," as an example of a second form of normative oriented sociology of sport whose adherents differ from those of the first form in their choice of goals, but agree in the belief that the field should ultimately lead to an improved society.

NONNORMATIVE SPORT SOCIOLOGY. More in the tradition of Western social science (but not Western physical education) are those sociologists of sport who subscribe to the position that the study of society should be as objective as possible, namely, *value-neutral*. The basic question asked by members of this school is, "Since sport is neither *a priori* good nor *a priori* bad—that is, its goals are neither accepted nor rejected—how can we explain the influence of sport as a social system upon other social systems, or conversely, the influence of other social systems upon sport?"

It is to this position that we subscribe, thus we present our own article, "Toward a Sociology of Sport," as the final reading in this section of the text.

POINTS OF CONVERGENCE. In conclusion, it is to be recognized that although we believe the distinctions between normative oriented and nonnormative oriented sport sociology are real, there remains much common ground. Although the two major approaches have different objectives, they do share in the belief that research must employ the best and latest social scientific knowledge and method. Daniels, for example, speaks of "sound scientific inquiry" (1966, p. 161). Wohl states that "journalistic work" alone, while useful and based upon extensive knowledge of a given author, with a bioad world outlook, maturity, and logical judgment,

> . . . can no longer satisfy anybody. And that is so because it does not provide the foundation for looking deeper into the sociological sports problems and turns into a barren field, if it lacks sufficiently exhaustive factual data. Though such a type of reasoning could sometimes yield conclusions and proposals that turn out to be justified and rational and which could help to popularize the idea of sports, this may nevertheless sometimes also be conclusions and proposals which are the outcome of convictions, whose only justification are emotional factors. In the latter case such reasoning could lead to a fixation of myths in which sports abounds and which are of a doubtful value for sports activity (1966, p. 8).

Finally, a not-to-be-overlooked point of convergence between representatives of the two approaches is the enthusiasm and the devotion of all who are presently active in the sociology of sport. Regardless of their orientation, they meet together, plan cooperative research projects together, and generally agree that the sociology of sport, although in its infancy, shows promise of becoming an established subdiscipline of social science.

CONCEPTS, DEFINITIONS AND CLASSIFICATIONS

The development of any new field is characterized by various statements of orientation, as presented above. Such orientations function in several ways, but chiefly to suggest the locus, context, and method of inquiry. That is, they outline a domain, provide a perspective from which to view it, indicate which variables are to be taken into account, and how these should be empirically dealt with.

Closely associated with the appearance of various programmatic statements is what sometimes seems like a preoccupation with concepts, definitions and classifications. Once general orientations indicate which concepts are to be taken into account, the need to clarify these immediately emerges. In addition to enhancing communication, the defining of key concepts helps to delineate those few aspects of reality of crucial concern for a given area of study. When such key concepts are related to one another in an orderly manner we have a taxonomy, which in turn is of considerable value in classifying and describing aspects of the domain of inquiry having research relevance. As noted by Zetterberg, "when faced with any subject of research, the sociologist can immediately identify its crucial aspects or variables by using his taxonomy as a kind of 'shopping list'" (1965, p. 25).

In the second section of readings in this part of the text are presented articles by three writers who have attempted to define and categorize basic concepts related to the sociology of sport. Roger Caillois' paper, "The Structure and Classification of Games," is presented first. In this article Caillois criticizes Huizinga's definition of play as being too broad and ignoring certain forms of games. He then suggests a game typology based on four categories according to whether in the different games, the role of competition, luck, disguise, or pursuit of vertigo "predominates." Caillois labels these categories as *Agôn*, *Alea*, *Mimicry*, and *Ilinx*, respectively.

As Caillois believes that Huizinga fails to adequately treat *games* in his discussion of *play*, we feel that Caillois does not adequately deal with *sport* in his treatment of games. Thus the second article, "The Nature of Sport," represents an attempt by Loy to define the concept *sport* and to develop a taxonomy of sport participants. The concluding article by Kenyon considers the concept *physical activity* in both theoretical and empirical terms; presenting, and testing a conceptual model for its characterization.

the sociology of sport as a discipline

the study of sport as an element of the culture

A. S. DANIELS

Introduction

Scientific inquiry of the sociology of sport is of fairly recent origin. David Riesman [1] has commented on the strangeness of the fact that students of society have missed almost completely the importance of sport in their investigations. He also feels that those who teach and guide sport activities have omitted the relevance of sociology and social psychology. Most international councils and committees primarily concerned with sport and the culture, have had their origin within the last two decades, some of the major ones, within the past decade. The same is true for national and international scientific seminars, congresses, and conferences.

In the literature of cultural and physical anthropology, little is found on the scientific study of sport in society. Cozens and Stumpf [4] believe the difficulty in finding acknowledgement of sport as an important item in cultural history is because sports did not function in many of the fields conventionally credited with making important contributions to history. Although there are some references to sport in most cultures of the past, these are largely of a limited nature.

[1] Unpublished letter to the author.

• From the *International Review of Sport Sociology* 1 (1966), 153–165. © 1966 ARS Polona, Krakowskie Przedmiescie 7, Warsaw, Poland.

Much information regarding the sociology of sport can be found in such histories as those written by Dulles [5], Krout [15], Holliman [8], Manchester [19], and Steiner [25]. This is logical inasmuch as history, in a sense, is sociology in the past tense, a record of social progress.

The term sports sociologist is also of recent origin. The Committee on Sports Sociology of the International Council of Sport and Physical Education was appointed in 1964. The Council, which is sponsored by UNESCO, was formed in 1959.

Much of the significant literature in sports sociology has been published in the past fifteen years. (Huizinga, 1949 [10]; Cozens and Stumpf, 1953 [4]; Riesman, 1954 [23]; Natan, 1958 [22]; Maheu, 1960 [18]; Morton, 1963 [21]; McIntosh, 1963 [20]; Jokl and Simon, 1964 [12]; Jokl, 1965 [11]; Vetö, 1965 [29]).

Graduate courses in Sport and Society or Sports Sociology are being offered in increasing numbers at universities that have graduate departments in health, physical education, and recreation (e.g., Indiana University, Ohio State University, University of California, Iowa State University, Columbia University, and Bridgeport University).

Research emphasis on sport sociology is broadening and deepening. The International Council of Sport and Physical Education has sponsored important conferences and seminars. The published papers from these scientific meetings constitute a large part of the foundation literature in sport sociology. There is a growing spirit of inquiry regarding the role of sport in society in the major countries of the world. Sociologists and scientifically inclined physical educators are making searching studies of sport, often with the encouragement and financial backing of their governments. It is a reasonable assumption that the study of sport within the culture will experience a steady growth now that international and national councils and committees, as well as university departments and individual scholars and scientists, have become alerted to its significance.

This paper is not concerned with a systematic coverage of sports in society, with the elements neatly structured and packaged. The focus of the paper is on the examination of the potential of sport in society as an area of scientific research, on the delineations of some values of the study of sport as one of the indexes to the quality of a society. In this connection, Morton [21] feels, "Analysis of a nation at play reveals the stuff of its social fabric and value system, and tells us much about other facets of political and economic life, particularly in modern industrial society" (p. 13).

Cozens and Stumpf [4] believe, "Sports and games provide a touchstone for understanding how people live, work, and think, and may also serve as a barometer of a nation's progress in civilization" (p. 2).

In the treatment of the subject, some effort will be given to defining the domain of sports sociology. A tentative definition of sports sociology will be offered. My major purpose, however is to suggest guidelines to the study of sport in the culture, emphasizing values, approaches, and selected resource materials.

This presentation was motivated by the knowledge that this infant area of social inquiry is one of tremendous significance to society in general, as well as to students of sport, physical education, and leisure.

The Study of Sport As an Element of the Culture

As acquaintance with the literature of sports sociology grows, the impression is strengthened that this is an area of study of cultural significance. Cozens and Stumpf [4] state, "Sports and physical recreation activities belong with the arts of humanity. Such activities have formed a basic part of all cultures, including all racial groups and all historical ages, because they are as fundamental a form of human expression as music, poetry, and painting" (p. 1).

Despite the significance of sport in society, this field of inquiry is more characterized by neglect than by scholarly and scientific treatment. Students of society will find their efforts fruitful in the study of sport and the culture, within the developing disciplines of physical education and recreation.

Where does the study of sport fit in human knowledge and human experience? The behavior of sports crowds and the motivation of individuals and groups involve the behavioral sciences. A study of the customs, traditions, value systems, and economic aspects of sport points to the social sciences. The physical sciences come into the picture when exercise physiology, biomechanics, and motor learning are considered. And what about sports and the enrichment of life and understanding of the culture? Are we not dealing with the humanities at this point? When the total picture of sport in society is assayed, despite outreaches into several disciplines, the field of study must logically be the social sciences, with sports sociology as the accepted identifying label.

One of the great challenges facing the sports sociologist is the matter of determining the place of sport in the cultural hierarchy. Is the place on the scale of values the same for advanced industrial societies as for the emerging countries? Is there a relationship? And does the status of sports in advanced societies influence the values placed on sports in less advanced societies? Finally, are the purposes and values different and influenced by the gap in cultural progress?

Maheu [18] has expressed concern that sports do not have the same status in the culture as do art, music, and literature. His analysis of the reasons for his belief merits further investigation. McIntosh [20] points out that sport has become a worldwide and international phenomenon with problems and issues involving sport having their counterparts in many countries. The status of sport in the culture was given careful thought at the Helsinki conference on *Sport, Work, Culture* [24]. One of the reasons

advanced for the relatively low status was that too few are trained intellectually for this rather complex subject. Leemans [16], Horkheimer [9], Vlot
[29], and Dumazedier [6] present a sociological analysis of sport in society,
and in the process make notable strides in establishing the sociology of sport
as an academic and scientific function. Their excellent papers are cast in the
framework of sociology, and should be carefully reviewed by all those with
academic aspirations regarding the study of sport in the culture.

Kenyon and Loy [14] make a strong case for a sociology of sport in the
tradition of the social sciences. They make an excellent contribution to the
growing recognition of the need for scientific inquiry of sport in society. Their
treatment of techniques of inquiry is particularly valuable.

In a field as young as sport sociology, there are more problems, issues,
and questions than there are solutions and answers. The framing of intelligent
questions and the design and execution of sound research are necessary before
many answers can be expected.

An effort will be made at this point to identify areas and problems which
merit investigation. What is the place of sport in the cultural hierarchy?
What factors influence the status of sport in society? What effect will world-
wide and strong governmental support have on the status of sport? Will the
current emergence of sport as an international phenomenon, including the
organization of professional and scientific international councils, have a positive effect on the status of sport in the culture?

What is the role of sport in emerging countries? Does it have value in
contributing to unification, identity, recognition, control and or support of
the masses, national security, promotion of the general welfare, and wholesome catharsis?

Are there values in sport as an instrument for social good? For example,
is there a relationship of sport to: development of individual and group value
systems, improvement of race relations, suppression of asocial behavior, provision of educational and economic opportunity, outlets for recreation, recognition, and expression for the less privileged, international understanding and
good will. Can value studies in sport be made without the sports sociologist
preestablishing or implying the values themselves?

Assuredly there is need for greater understanding of the interrelations
of sport with other elements of the culture. In the complex fabric of total
society, sports have influences upon, and in turn are influenced by politics,
social structure, economics, religion, the military, education, technology, music,
art, science, and literature. We need to know a great deal more about these
relationships, particularly the cause and effect aspects.

In the study of human nature and human affairs, much that is of value
can be gained through the study of sport which is part of the quest for meaning and value in life. Sport has roots in the humanities through providing
life enrichment and fulfillment opportunities. It is an important interest of
people throughout the world (Natan [22]).

The study of sport in society is becoming established as scientific inquiry based in the social sciences. As in all study of man, lines go out to other sciences, including the behavioral and physical sciences. Following the lead of Maheu, Riesman, and others, we must also study sport from philosophical and humanities bases as well. Apart from the relationships with other cultural elements, sport must be understood for its meaning to man and the fulfillment of his purposes as an intellectual, social, and physical being.

Tentative Approaches to the Study of Sport in Society

One of the first problems to be considered is the domain of the study of sport in society. Kenyon [13] hypothesized that values held for physical activity have at least six semi-independent dimensions: social experience, health and fitness, pursuit of vertigo, aesthetic experience, catharsis, and ascetic experience. At the Helsinki conference the emphasis was on the cultural, social, artistic, and work implications of sport. It was stated, "Sport is an integral part of modern culture and has important tasks to fulfill in education. Its influence is not limited to sports fields but extends to many realms in the modern, rapidly developing society" (p. 12).

The main theme of the conference, was given by its title—*Sport, Work, Culture.* During the meetings much consideration was also given to the contribution of sport to international understanding.

The domain of sport sociology includes the interrelationships of sport with other elements of the culture. Broadly speaking, and deliberately avoiding a precise definition of sports sociology at this point, it seems that a tentative definition might be somewhat as follows: "Sports sociology is concerned with the study of sport in society as it affects man's development, his forms of expression, his value systems, and the interrelationships of sport with other elements of the culture." A more sophisticated definition may be developed after more research is accomplished.

The Philosophical Bases of Sport in Society

The social significance of play of which sport is a part has interested philosophers, psychologists, psychiatrists, and sociologists since the time of Socrates. The efforts to explain play as a human phenomenon has resulted in the development of theories of play. (Barnes and Ruedi [1]) Spencer held that play was needed to get rid of surplus energy. Tarde pointed out the role of imitation in play. Lazarus felt play was "recreative" and a means of recovering from fatigue. Groos held that play was preparation for adult life. Appleton assigned to play a physical basis and associated it with bodily changes occurring during growth. Hall developed the "Recapitulation Theory" in which play was viewed as a reliving of our savage ancestral activities. Shand saw play as expressing joy. McDougall felt play was motivated by the instinct of rivalry. Adler held play was used to overcome inferiority complexes.

Huizinga, who has given us the most comprehensive analysis of play, claimed his definition embraces all forms of play in animals, children, and adults. Each of the theories makes a contribution to the interpretation of the place and function of play in life.

In reviewing the efforts to define the function of play in human experience, the report of the UNESCO sponsored Helsinki Conference in 1959 must be regarded as a major contribution. The works of Maheu, McIntosh, Natan, Jokl, and historians, Dulles and Krout, must also be acknowledged as fundamental to the study of sport sociology.

Maheu's views on sport and the culture are of special interest. He feels the status of sport in society is not as high as it should be. He expresses concern over the failure of artists and intellectuals to incorporate sport in their work, despite the fact that sport, the arts and intellectual pursuits all spring from the same source—leisure. He believes that the reasons sport has not achieved the cultural acceptance it merits have their bases in the sociology of religious ethics, intellectual literature, the utilitarian ideology of mechanization, and scientific positivism, all of which place a low value on the body. Another deterrent to the cultural elevation of sport, in Maheu's view, is that it is a mass movement which tends to separate it from cultural pursuits. Although this may be true, there are a number of factors that may be regarded as bridging the gap between intellectualism, the arts, and social stratification. Although all positions and analyses must be carefully considered, it is far too early in the development of sports sociology to accept present concepts as anything but tentative. Much research remains to be done in order to gain an understanding of sport in society.

The Interrelationships of Sports with Other Elements of the Culture

In pursuing the major theme of the study of sport in society, we have touched on the purposes and values of such study, and the rational or philosophical bases of sport as social experience. Our third point concerns the interrelationships of sport in the culture.

Cozens and Stumpf saw significance in the manner in which sports related to other phases of living. In developing a framework within which to study sports in the culture with any completeness, they felt it necessary to select those areas of the culture which seemed to have the greatest degree of relationship. When considering other cultural elements and sport, one begins to move in the direction of examining forces and influences which have a bearing on sport and vice versa. The Prime Minister of Finland, in his opening address at the Helsinki Conference [24] said, "We can wonder whether the world of sports until very recently has not been rather closed so that its contacts with other fields of human activity have been scarce? The fact has not been fully appreciated that sports which certainly constitute the biggest popular movement on earth with their huge masses of supporters and participants, are not an isolated and separate field of activity but an essential part of the total picture of our culture. Only recently has there emerged a correct understanding of the individual, social, and even economic significance of sports and physical culture in the changed conditions brought forth by urbanization, industrialization, and automation" (p. 23).

Those who have chronicled life in America have made note of the important place which sport occupies in all classes of society. It can be said that in varying degrees, this same situation holds in most modern cultures. Much attention is currently attached to the development of sports all over the world.

It is clear that we cannot study sport in society without investigating the interrelationships with our major social institutions, including the role of spectator sports, as an integrating social force.

For illustrative purposes some of the cultural elements bearing upon sports will be listed here. It must be kept in mind that these are illustrative rather than all-inclusive. Those which appear most worthy of further investigation are the relationships of sport with: politics and government including nationalism, social classes, economics, religion, education, the military establishment, arts, music, literature, science, mass communication, and medicine. The place of women in sport as well as international comparative studies are also as fruitful fields of study.

A few of the above areas will be briefly developed to indicate the relationship with sport, and hopefully, reveal research possibilities.

The relationship of sport and religion down through the ages shows many fluctuations with respect to acceptance and nonacceptance. In America, the attitude of the church toward sport parallels the general cultural transition from the Puritan ideal of no play, to the permissive and supporting positions noted today.

The extent to which sport and physical education is accepted as an integral part of American education is reflected in the programs one finds in elementary schools, secondary schools, and colleges and universities. The same may be said for the schools and educational systems of most modern countries.

The medical profession has clearly accepted sports, physical education, and recreation for their values in preventive medicine as related to physical and mental health. Sports and recreation are also used in therapeutic and rehabilitative services. Sports medicine, a developing medical speciality, is concerned with the welfare of the athlete.

Sports, in one form or another, have always been related to the politics of a given culture. Perhaps the strongest example of the interrelationship of politics and sport in America concerns the efforts of the late President Kennedy, the late General MacArthur, President Lyndon Johnson, and the United States Congress, to resolve the deep-rooted conflict between the Amateur Athletic Union and the National Collegiate Athletic Association. Another example is found in the report by Hanna, entitled, "The Politics of Sport" [7], which recounts the difficulties of Indonesia as host of the Fourth Asian Games.

Sport and physical education have a long history of relationships with the military establishment and national security. In World War II, sports were used as part of the training experience in preparing personnel for combat and service duty. They were also used for maintaining morale and fitness in rest areas in the theatres of combat. Toward the end of the war, and for some time following, they were included as an integral part of the military medical rehabilitation program. Today, fitness through sports and exercise is considered a primary factor in national security.

Physical recreation (sport) constitutes a major leisure time interest of a large percentage of the population of the world. As we have moved in recent years from the leisure classes to the leisure masses, it is noted that sports activities predominate in the manner in which leisure time is used.

Group Research in Sports

The last point to be discussed in this theme of the study of sport in society, concerns group research. This type of research deals with specific and limited investigations of sports.

The framework for sociological research in sports is well illustrated in the writings of Leemans, Horkheimer, Vlot, and Dumazedier.

Small group research is aimed at discovering more about the experiences of subgroups within the culture. This type of research will be the major focus of an international seminar on sports sociology to be held in Cologne in April 1/66. Examples of studies of this type have been done by Stone [25, 26], Betts [2], Boroff [3], Wenkart [30], Lüschen [17].

Horkheimer has stated that from the point of view of the social sciences we know very little about sports. He feels a great deal of research is needed in sport sociology. Some examples of needed research are listed below:

Crowd behavior in sports situations; the nature of the social and psychological attractions of spectator and participant sports; (sports crowds are consistently the largest crowds in America, and in many other countries as well); the role of sports in influencing individual and group value systems; sports and child growth and development; the influence of sport on family life; the nature of personal and group goals in seeking expression through sports; the social phenomena surrounding sports events (cocktail parties, smokers, brunches, luncheons, picnics, reunions); moral and ethical values in sport; factors motivating participation in competitive sports; the influence of selected factors on sports interests in America (industrialization, urbanization, immigration, leisure, income, commercial promotion, education, governmental support, the military, the church); the social forces which influence choice of spectator and participant sports; and women in sport.

It is recognized that many of the topics listed above are quite broad. Within them as specific investigations, however, reside many studies which would add much to our knowledge of sports in society.

Conclusion

Because of the limited amount of research done in sports sociology to date there are conflicting and sometimes confusing views on purposes, values, status, and the understanding of the total role of sports. Although recognizing the social importance of sport, Leemans regards the sociology of sports as one of the lagging spheres of this science. He feels the absence of a systematic sociological research into sport complicates the task of understanding the role of sport in society. Despite the superficial nature of the examination of sports to date, he feels we are dealing with a complex social phenomenon. A review of the literature supports his contentions.

We do not know why sport occupies such an important place in the leisure pursuits of western society, when the functions served by sports might well be performed to the same extent by other leisure outlets (e.g., music, drama, art). We can offer no scientific explanation why football in some American universities will draw 85,000 spectators into the stadium six times in a span of ten weeks, while no other university program in music, art, or even education and science can approach this. Nor do we know why community interest in the quality of the local high school football or basketball teams elicits inquiries never matched by a concern expressed for the quality of the English or mathematics departments. We do not say these things are good or bad, but we do want to know why.

When we are better able to understand the role of sports in society, basing our interpretations on sound scientific inquiry, perhaps the status of sport in the culture will find a level heretofore unachieved by expressions of concern alone.

Progress to date gives reason to hope that sports sociology will eventually take its place as a legitimate branch of the sciences concerned with the study of man.

REFERENCES

1. Barnes, H., and Ruedi, O. M., *The American Way of Life*, Prentice-Hall, Inc., Englewood Cliffs, N. J., 1950, Chapter XXVIII, p. 741.
2. Betts, J. R., *Organized Sport in Industrial America*, University Microfilms, Ann Arbor, No. 3322.
3. Boroff, D., "A View of Skiers as a Subculture," *Sports Illustrated*, November 23, 1964.
4. Cozens, F. W., and Stumpf, F. S., *Sports in American Life*, University of Chicago Press, Chicago, 1953 (out of print).
5. Dulles, F. R., *America Learns to Play*, Appleton-Century-Crofts Company, New York, 1965.
6. Dumazedier, J., "The Point of View of a Social Scientist." In Jokl, E., and Simon E. (eds.), *International Research in Sport and Physical Education*, Thomas, Springfield, Illinois, 1964, pp. 212–217.

7. Hanna, W. R., *The Politics of Sport*, American Universities Field Staff, New York, 1962.
8. Holliman, J., *American Sport, 1785–1835*, Durham, The Sieman Press, 1931.
9. Horkheimer, M., "New Patterns in Social Relations," Jokl, E. and Simon, E., (eds.), *International Research in Sport and Physical Education*, Thomas, Springfield, Illinois, 1964, pp. 173–185.
10. Huizinga, J., *Homo Ludens: A Study of the Play Element in Culture*, Routledge and Kegan Paul, Ltd., London, 1949.
11. Jokl, E., *Medical Sociology and Cultural Anthropology of Sports and Physical Education*, Thomas, Springfield, Illinois, 1964.
12. Jokl, E., and Simon, E. (eds.), *International Research in Sport and Physical Education*, Thomas, Springfield, Illinois, 1964.
13. Kenyon, G. S., "The Contribution of Physical Activity to Social Development," *Symposium on Integrated Development*, Lafayette, Indiana, 1964, pp. 48–54.
14. Kenyon, G. S., and Loy, J. W., "Toward a Sociology of Sport," *Journal of Health, Physical Education, and Recreation*, 35:5, May, 1965, p. 24.
15. Krout, J. A., Annals of American Sport, Volume 15, *The Pageant of America*, Yale University Press, New Haven, 1929.
16. Leemans, E. J., "A Sociological Approach to Sports," Jokl, E., and Simon, E. (eds.), *International Research in Sport and Physical Education*, Thomas, Springfield, Illinois, 1964, pp. 152–159.
17. Lüschen, G., "Die Funktion des Sports in der modernen Gesellschaft" (The Function of Sport in Modern Society), in *Die Leibeserziehung*, 1963/12, Germany.
18. Maheu, R., "Sport and Culture," *International Journal of Adult and Youth Education*, UNESCO, Volume XIV, No. 4, 1962, p. 169 (Also in JOPHER 34:30–22+, 1963).
19. Manchester, H., *Four Centuries of Sport in America*, Derrydale Press, New York, 1931.
20. McIntosh, P. C., *Sport in Society*, C. A. Watts Company, London, 1963.
21. Morton, H. W., *Soviet Sport*, Collier Books, New York, 1963.
22. Natan, A., *Sport and Society*, Bowes and Bowes, London, 1958.
23. Riesman, D., *Individualism Reconsidered*, Free Press, Glencoe, Illinois, 1954.
24. *Sport, Work, Culture*, Report of International Conference on Contribution of Sports to Improvement of Professional Abilities and Cultural Development, Organized by government of Finland's request and assistance of UNESCO, Helsinki, August, 1959.
25. Steiner, J. P., *Americans at Play*, McGraw and Hill, New York, 1932.
26. Stone, G. P., "American Sports: Play and Dis-Play," *Chicago Review*, University of Chicago Press, Fall 1955.
27. Stone, G. P., "Some Meanings of American Sport," 60th *Annual Proceedings*, D. C., CPEA. Washington 1957, pp. 6–19.
28. Vetö, J., *Sports in Hungary*, Crovina Press, Budapest, 1965.
29. Vlot, N. G., "Sociological Analysis of Sport in the Netherlands." In Jokl E., and Simon, E. (eds.), *International Research in Sport and Physical Education*, Thomas, Springfield, Illinois, 1964, pp. 198–211.
30. Wenkart, S., "The Meaning of Sports for Contemporary Society," *Journal of Existential Psychiatry* 3:397–404, Spring 1963.

the science of sport and sports sociology—questions related to development—problems of structure

GÜNTER ERBACH

Enlargement of the Sphere of Social Influence of Physical Culture

As a result of the deep and most significant socio-economic changes that took place during the course of the past 100 years, physical culture and sport [1] has been transformed from more or less regionally or nationally limited forms to a world-wide phenomenon. The external outlines of this development are thrown into relief by the setting up of national unions and associations, of international sports federations, the organization of national and international championships, by the crowning highlight: the Olympic Games—and the mass aspect of physical culture and sport in the various social systems, together with their economic, political and cultural results. The development of the productive forces, and the socialization of the working and living conditions following in its wake, create for physical culture and sport in our times completely new conditions that change the attitude of the human being towards physical culture, and as a result the entire social relationship towards physical culture and sport appears in a different light. New aims set for physical culture and sport, due to changed production conditions and more leisure time, participation of growing numbers of people in organized sports activity as well as in informal activity, the markedly higher level of achievements in sport, the efficiency of the entire system of sports institutions, the growing public interest and the activity of the mass media of communication in the field of sports propaganda and information—just to quote only

[1] The customarily used combination of the two terms "physical culture and sport" signifies the total aspect of the social achievements and measures connected with the physical perfection of man. Physical culture serves as the main and guiding concept and includes: planned physical education, sport, physical exercises and all forms of active leisure pursuits. Sport is the dominating form of expression of physical culture (that is why it is as a rule used as a synonym for physical culture in general) and signifies the striving to succeed in physical efficiency, on the basis of the norms and rules in contests of all types. One may approach sport as a system of top-class performance in physical culture training based on scientific foundation—(generalizations in the entire social field of physical culture).

• From the *International Review of Sport Sociology* 1 (1966), 59–73. © 1966 ARS Polona, Krakowskie Przedmiescie 7, Warsaw, Poland.

a few of the most striking aspects—point to the whole complex of social problems which are facing us in connection with this. Therefore it is fully justified and of theoretical as well as practical significance, that in recent publications [2] the actual requirements, which are the outcome of the new socio-economic conditions, are being taken into consideration, as they are in a decisive way shaped by the technical and cultural revolution and make it necessary to establish qualitatively new criteria for the further development of the system of physical education. This desire finds its expression in the transferal to a scientifically founded long-term development planning system as an always effective means and principle to bring about a planned development of physical culture. This requires theoretical thinking with foresight and an analytical examination of the state of development [3, 6, 17].[3]

From research and discussions so far, one can draw one important conclusion that our present-day system of physical culture must be substantially perfected, so that it can fully satisfy the growing requirements of citizens for many-sided physical culture and education. Quite new requirements are the result of this process of development addressed to the science of physical culture (science of sport).[4]

In the process of social relations, taking place on various levels, between people, in individual and collective development, in school, in professional work and during leisure time, physical culture and sport are accepted parts of an all-round formation of personality, are more and more highly valued, receive more and more attention, and are practiced by growing numbers of people. The problem of top-class performances in sport is today not only the concern of the active and proper sports institutions and organizations, but of a wide strata of the population and to some extent of the entire society. Should one ask for the reasons of this exceptionally high social and political evaluation of physical culture and sport, which can today be noticed every-

---

[2] See among others such publications as E. Buggel [3, 4], R. Florl [8], F. Gras [9], J. Kukuschkin [18], A. D. Novikov [11], G. Röblitz [12], H. Schwitdmann [16], H. Schnurpel [13], R. Schultz [15], F. Trogsch [21, 22], G. Erbach [6, 7], as well as the contributions published in the special issue *Über philosophische und soziologische Probleme der Köperkultur* (Philosophical and Sociological Problems of Physical Culture of the magazine "Theorie und Praxis der Körperkultur," Berlin, September, 1964.

[3] See also: *Outdoor Recreation for America*, The Report of the Outdoor Recreation Resources Review Commission to the President and to the Congress. Washington, 1962; *Friluftlivet in Sveringe* (Outdoor Recreation in Sweden), Part I and II, Stockholm, 1964; *Sport and Community*, The Report of the Wolfenden Committee for Sport. London, 1960; (*Soovenzioni per lo sport in Europe*. Subvention for Sport in Europe) Traguardi, Roma, 1963, 6.

[4] The conception science of sport is gradually also being accepted in the international field as a main term for the various specialized scientific disciplines which concentrate on the discovery of general and special laws and rules in physical culture and sport as a social phenomenon. We understand this as the combination of all the scientific branches, specializing in lecturing and research on physical culture (institutionally arranged into academic training facilities and research centers) which in this process have developed a relative independence.

where in the international arena, one relatively quickly finds the answer: it is based on the significance of teaching people to live a healthy life, of obtaining high physical efficiency in one's profession as well as in life in general, on the importance of developing valuable traits of character and utilize one's spare time in a sensible way; and finally (one of the most important factors) it gives pleasure and joy and teaches people to adopt an optimistic attitude towards life. All these factors that were mentioned (by no means are these all of them) play their role in social reality, in the social process of development, and the spreading of physical culture and sport. And it is precisely this that gives rise to new problems for the science of sport, especially in the area of research connected with the social conditions, relations, and requirements as a starting point for the establishment of trends of development [6, 16, 17]. For a prognostic determination of the trends of development, as well as for a concrete analysis of the social conditions and circumstances regarding the development of physical culture, it is necessary to establish specialized philosophical and sociological, as well as scientific organizational research in the science of sport (theory of physical culture, sport sociology, the science of organization of physical culture [7]. Thus there has been found a wide field for social research, and the aims and structure of sports science will, due to the establishment of a proper profile of tasks set for the social science branches, gain a more complete aspect.

Sport As a Component of Culture

The basic stimuli for the development of physical culture and sport stem from those spheres of life where true activity and expressions of life of the human being actually take place, such as economy, politics, science and culture. These forms of activity exert their influence in other spheres of life and have already turned into relatively important components of the conscious shaping of the life of the individual as well as society as a whole. This objective connection, which can be understood only from the dialectical point of view, is of basic significance for the determination of the social functions of physical culture and sport and of their scientific reflection. As is generally known, the creative and productive activity of man is a presupposition of culture. Marxist philosophy considers culture to be the material and intellectual result of the creative ability of the human being, a process of physical and intellectual perfection of man, his upbringing and education, the ideological, artistic, and scientific reflection of these processes, as well as the achieved level in cooperation between human activity in practical life and the objective rules of nature and society. In this sense culture is the expression and measure of the humane aspects of life, the mastering of nature and society, order and the conscious shaping of social relations [10]. As social phenomena and as a social process, physical culture and sport are an integral part of culture. They reflect the achievements of physical perfection and the development of the physical prowess of man, which in the practical process of life find their expression in the aspirations to lead a life in which there is place for healthy cultural and sports activity.

Without such an aim, a humanistic culture and physical culture would be unthinkable and always socially determined. As a product of nature and as a social being, man is in this sense the final product of the cultural development and at the same time the most important productive force [22, p. 935 ff.].

The Marxist-Leninist ideology and science considers it one of its most important tasks to bring about an all-round physical and intellectual development and education of man that would reach such a level where he would in a conscious way make use of the laws of nature and society for the benefit of the individual and society as a whole. In the social process of work man changes nature and shapes it according to his requirements. In this process he changes (as was proved by Marx and Engels in a most comprehensive way) his own nature as well, and in the historical course of social development there takes place a steady change of his physical and intellectual forces. This aspect of the psycho-physical unity of man in the process of social development leads us to the question of why physical culture and sport has to be accepted as man's expression of life and as a social phenomenon of a relatively independent character.

The physical qualities of man were in the past, and are to this day, one of the fundamental conditions of material production. However, during the process of the physical and mental interrelations in the field of material production and during the creation of intellectual and cultural values, changes are taking place, in the existing conditions of our times, in other relationships than in the past. The main purpose of physical culture and its specific forms (sport, gymnastic, games, tourism, etc.) is always the perfection of physical efficiency, and in the broadest sense, the preservation and strengthening of health. The great variety of phenomena, experiences, achievements, and skill, which are the outcome of the efforts made to achieve physical health and efficiency within the social development process and which can be approached only in connection with all the forms and results of the intellectual and psychic development, point to the inseparable connection between physical culture and culture. That is why man as the creative producer of material and spiritual values and his all-round physical and intellectual development are the very centre of the science specializing in physical culture (the science of sport).

Sphere of Activity of the Science of Sport and Review of the Structure

The science of sport has already gathered quite a substantial amount of knowledge. But one could not yet state that we already have sufficient experience and can master the laws governing this many-sided social process which is the basis of the appearance of new biological capacities of performance.

Establishment of order as regards knowledge, systematizing of experiences, and determination of the mutual relation between the various branches and of the entire system of the science of sport have therefore become a necessity in order to understand in a scientific way the biological and social function of physical culture and the important role it plays in the cultural life with its complex radiation and influence. In this sense the following explanations are to help to answer these questions. The starting point is the fact that physical culture and sport are a social process, which in a purposeful and systematic way brings about the perfection of the physical qualities and efficiency of people, as an integral part of the rising cultural level of society. Employed in a conscious way they make their contribution to turn man into a creative producer of material and spiritual values. The object on which the science of sport should concentrate could therefore be defined in the following way: The science of sport examines the biological and social laws existing in the sphere of physical perfection of man as a psycho-physical unit in the process of development; it reveals the basic features and causal connections of these processes; it examines them in practical social life and presents them in the form of conceptions, categories, and theories.

"Physical perfection" signifies the process of all social efforts, the purpose of which is achievement of physical perfection. In this connection the term "physical perfection" [11] means a system of experiences of the biological and social development of social norms of health and physical efficiency that are worth aspiring to and in this sense it is a concrete historical category.

The science of sport is a type of science that has many various layers and is of a most complex nature; its [subject] matter makes it necessary to give up the thus far obliging division lines and to adopt the principle of units of science. In such a way it will be possible to provide proof of the independence of the science of sport, as well as of its connections with kindred or principal branches of science.

Already a rough survey of the various branches of science that deal with the social process of physical perfection, reveals their great variety and complexity. This is knowledge gained in the following fields:

Philosophy and philosophical sciences. Dialectical materialism, natural, society, and cognitive theory (Erkenntnistheorie), logics, aesthetics, ethics.
Social sciences. Sociology, history, pedagogics, psychology, political economy, law, culture, art.
Natural sciences. Medicine (including anatomy, physiology, social hygiene), biology (anthropology), physics, chemistry, mathematics.

All these sciences teach the most fundamental knowledge, but often they also provide detailed knowledge regarding the physical efficiency of man. However, this aspect is not the central item of these sciences, though it would certainly be a good thing, and it would be fully justified to pay more attention to this. Putting things together, generalizations, concrete application, and exploring of the general processes of physical perfection exclusively from the point of view of sport is, after all, the task of the science of sport. Research and teaching (on the university level) led to the formation of special scientific branches of the science of sport, which taken all together form the system of the science sport [7, 20].

The process of the differentiation and integration of the sciences, which is still in the stage of formation, will therefore, out of necessity, also in the science of sport lead to new fields of work, to divisions, and the establishment of certain profiles. Therefore, scientific and theoretical dissertations, in the form of a prognosis as well as those related to existing facts, will become more important for the science of sport, in order to be able to recognize in time trends of development and to draw from this the proper structural conclusions, also regarding personnel. One of the branches of science that shows very rapid development recently is Marxist sociology and we should examine what the results of this are.

Sports Sociological Research—a Necessary and Topical Task

As regards works in the field of the history of culture, Wohl and Trogsch [24, 22] deal above all with the development of physical culture and its forms of organization, with respect to the socio-economic class relations. They emphasize the social or rather political aspects regarding the efficacy of and the aims set in the past for the large associations of physical culture and certain individual personalities as well, and in such a way they give a fundamentally new historical and materialistic evaluation of the historical development of physical culture. However, this does not yet cover all the laws of a social nature existing in a concrete historical formation of society. It suffices to point to the fact that side by side with the history of physical culture, inclusive historical research, one needs a discipline which would examine the social problems of physical culture, together with all the interrelations with other social phenomena in the past as well as in our time.

One should consider this as the starting point for research in the field of sports sociology, and such research embraces the historical and logical as well as empirical approach.

The fact that the social sciences develop more and more into sciences directing all social processes and in such a way that the habit of sticking to once accepted laws has been overcome, and the fact that the various parts of the social structure as a whole, as well as the interrelations of the social associations and groups, have to be approached on the basis of the various separate scientific findings—has made it clear, precisely in the field of the science of sport, how important the development of philosophical disciplines is, such as the theory of physical culture and also of the corresponding sociological disciplines, such as sports sociology. This task can be solved only through collective work, because despite all the division lines and differentiation of purposes, there nevertheless exists in the case of the various separate disciplines an overlapping due to the complexity of the social domain.

This becomes already obvious when decisions are made as to the objects to be dealt with and the tasks to be tackled (and all the specialists are unanimous as to that).

Braunreuther was absolutely right when he declared that "the exploration of the problems of the life of society cannot be squeezed into the narrow school frames of traditional disciplines" [1]. The same is true as regards research connected with the social problems of physical culture and shows at the same time how important it is to embark upon the social questions related to physical culture, in order to obtain knowledge and learn about the laws governing this field, which would make it possible to direct this social field in a scientific way and to draw the proper conclusions.

Social Research and the Sociological Aspect

The manifold social processes in the sphere of physical culture are the expression of the efficacy of the general rules of social development as well as of the existence of specific laws. These are above all: the effectiveness of material and ideological factors to convince people to indulge in regular sports activity and the development of an attitude where sports activity is a necessity of life, where it serves to protect health and improve the efficiency of people in all spheres of life, as well as the effectiveness of educational, moral, and aesthetic factors in the many-sided social process of sports and cultural activity.

Regional research, the collection of objective values of the various sides of these complex processes, is the general components of this Marxist social research. F. Trogsch gave in 1962 a most instructive review about their application in the field of physical culture and sport dealing simultaneously also with methodological basic problems [21].

The final results of the social research serve Marxist sociology as the material for generalizations, for the exploration of general and special laws ruling social life. Concrete social research is only in that case of any deeper scientific significance, if it is combined with this sociological aspect, with the sense of possible and necessary generalization. Thus it can, as a branch of science, make its contribution to the discovery of universally valid laws of society, or can provide concrete proof of the efficacy of these laws in that field of social life that is the subject of this branch of science. Several disciplines of the science of sport conduct research whose purpose is the discovery of the special laws of social processes in the field of physical culture. Concrete social research is conducted by teachers and psychologists in the sphere of school, mass, and top-level sports; the entire sport literature is market like with a red thread by philosophical and sociological questions. It is getting evident everywhere that there arise new aspects and connections and that we are witnessing the process of a scientific approach to and penetration of physical culture as a whole, with emphasis on the interrelation of all its various parts. But we should not overlook the danger caused by such a deep penetration, namely that one may forget about the connections with the fundamental and general laws.

And this precisely is the task facing sports sociology, which bases itself on the achievements of general sociology and examines the specific laws governing physical culture as a whole and its relation to other social phenomena. Inside the scientific system of physical culture it develops into an independent discipline, just like the history of physical culture, sports pedagogics, and sports psychology.

This is in accordance with the growing process of differentiation and integration in science as a whole and makes it possible for Marxist social sciences to examine the concrete social processes of physical culture in detail, as well as to make the sociological generalizations needed for a scientifically founded guidance and direction.

The Tasks and Objectives of Sports Sociology

Dependence, relationship, interrelations, and mutual influence of physical culture in regard to other large spheres of society, such as economy, politics, culture, and science, exert a stronger influence than ever before in the practical field of social management. One objective consequence of these problems embracing society as a whole finds its expression in socialist conditions in the purposeful way of shaping the science of sport as a relatively independent system of science. As physical culture and sport, according to their nature, are an expression of human life and in this sense an integral part of the mode of life, they are bound to be also an expression of the entire social cooperation—which, according to Braunreuther and Steiner, should be understood as cooperation and coexistence of a large number of different people with a great variety of presuppositions and functions and which effect all spheres of social life [2]. To the forms of expression of this type belongs the fact that people with different traits and features (age, sex, experience gained in life, professional qualifications, education, family and living conditions, personal interest) unite in sport groups and clubs jointly to practice sport. They meet in their work establishments, the area where they live, in their spare time in the evenings, on Sundays and during their holidays to indulge in sports activity, to participate in contests, to observe rules, and to travel and to establish new relations between people that often are of long duration.

In such a way could be established many most instructive interrelations, which not only exert their influence on the social relations in general, but also exert a quite clearly visible influence on the personal course of life and the attitude of the individual towards society. Inside the organized sports movement there exist attitudes, typical of the various groups, which stem from the aforementioned characteristic features as well as from the character of the specific sports branch. These social processes provide the objective justifications for the necessity of the formation and relative independence of sports sociology as a scientific discipline within the framework of the science of sport.

Characterization of the Objectives of Sports Sociology

We do not consider it useful to continue the controversy conducted inside the bourgeois sociological trends, whether the socalled "Bindestrichsoziologien" (hyphenated sociologies) have any sense or not. The objectively existing social problems of sports have themselves given the answer to it. If one would try not to recognize them or to pay any attention to them, this would mean to close one's eyes to the real processes taking place inside society, processes embracing millions of people today. Knowledge, theories, and laws regarding the function of physical culture in society, its role in personal life and inside groups, clubs, and social units, are not the outcome of the construction and schematic combination of separate facts, but can be obtained only with the help of research of the entire great variety of empirical facts and the reality of social interrelations. One of the tasks of research in the field of sports sociology is to reveal the inner mechanism of the socially determined behavior of people in the process of physical culture (in its various fields). Only in close and direct contact with the requirements of the entire social practice is it possible to examine the concrete processes of physical culture as a social phenomenon and to make the proper generalizations.

The range of social questions that arises is very broad in such a social field as physical culture and sport. It embraces such personally determined motives as proof of efficiency, prestige, and confirmation of one's own value and glory to basic problems of a socio-political nature, such as furtherance of health by means of regular practicing of sport, questions connected with education and upbringing, top-class achievements in sport as the expression of the level of development of the entire society—sport as a political factor in the competition and contest of different social systems. Not all the above-mentioned factors can be directly related to socio-economic foundations, though we actually are aware of the fact that they are the highest authority and the decisive element for the social behavior of society as a whole. A remarkably important role in sport is played by psychological stimuli and experiences. Sports sociology will in such a way with the help of socio-psychological knowledge be able to contribute substantially to the discovery of social laws governing the behavior of individuals, teams, and sports groups of the various branches. Questions from the fields of sports sociology and socio-psychological ones are closely interrelated. Other disciplines of the science of sport, such as sports pedagogics (dealing among others with the specific aspect of training and educating various age-groups of people who practice sport) and the theory of physical education (the pedagogical and methodological process of physical perfection in regard to various age-groups) as well as theory and methodology of sport in various, relatively independent spheres (school, top-class performance in sport, sport for adults), and finally the history of physical culture, the science of organization, and also sports medicine examine certain aspects of the entire social process of physical culture and supply answers to some quite detailed questions. Only the thorough evaluation of such detailed knowledge resulting from large-scale social research conducted in many individual disciplines of the science of sport permits the establishment of general trends and laws governing physical culture as a whole. Generalizations needed to direct the entire process have to be based on social detailed research and also on sociological complex research.

Special social research is to proceed side by side with general and complex sociological fundamental research. This principle should also be binding in connection with the various disciplines of the science of sport that conduct social research and consider sports sociology as a relatively independent discipline of science.

From this point of view and summing up what was said above, we want to add a definition of the subject of sports sociology.

Sports sociology examines the dialectics of general and specific social development in the field of physical culture and sport, the interrelations to other social phenomena, the behavior of people, influenced by physical culture and sport, people who belong to organized sports associations and groups and who individually and regularly indulge in sports activity; it examines the concrete behavior of social groups and units in their attitude towards physical culture and sport, in order to discover in such a way laws which play their role in determining the social general behavior of people under relevant social conditions in the process of their development.

By gathering comprehensive empirical material and with the help of the proper generalizations, conditions are created for the social direction of all the processes of physical culture.

This definition is to make it possible to find the general trend for research work and to select and arrange the proper subject for investigation. Taking into consideration the present stage of development of sports sociology, this can only serve as a means for orientation. However, that has always been the rule in the history of science, because generally accepted definitions of the subject matter of a discipline make their appearance only after all-round research of a most general character has already taken place and even in this case it is constantly necessary to look for the proper profile.

It seems that for our specialized scientific orientations, on the basis of the temporary definition, the aspects for concrete sociological research mentioned by Braunreuther, are most purposeful and significant.

1. Without the need to yield hastily to generalizations, there should, nevertheless, be undertaken any kind of sociological research in practical life and any theoretical discussion in this connection, in order to discover the laws and their effect.

2. Social relations ultimately determined by political and economic factors, have to be examined from the point of view of behavior and the connections of modes of behavior of people.

3. Taken into consideration should be socio-relevant states and modes of behavior, for which categories have to be established in the case of each concrete investigation.

4. Attempts should be made to find the possibilities, implicit in the existing social conditions and modes of behavior, to turn them into explicit ones, and, if possible to develop them in a planned way, sometimes in variants.

5. Existing conditions and behavior are not to be described as something static, but have to be understood in their entire dynamic aspect, taking into consideration the laws determining this dynamic aspect [1].

Mode of Procedure of Sports Sociological Research

The practical application of these aspects requires at the same time the drawing of clear outlines in the organizational scientific manner of carrying out the intention to conduct sociological research. There actually exist two fundamental starting points which have to be taken into consideration, first, the precise theoretical definition of the aim to be pursued (taken from sociological theory), and second, the exact definition of the methodological and technological manner in which it is to be carried out (manner of selection, choice of method, system of evaluation).

On the basis of experiences gained during the carrying out of a representative, complex, territorial survey, conducted in the spring of 1965, according to the sample method, about the role of physical education in connection with leisure pursuits of the citizens of the German Democratic Republic [3, 6], the following methods of work should be observed:

First of all there should be laid down a central, complex, or guiding subject for research stemming from the requirements of social practical life. This is to be succeeded by a clearly defined conception for research and general outlines of the undertaking—taking its starting point from the historical laws and concrete social purposes in the given social field. This includes a concrete determination of the aim of the research, most precise hypotheses and statements in the form of theses, destined for the programming of the general analysis (a program of questions, trends, and types of the elaborations of the subject matter for research).

Though no "encyclopedia-like completeness" is required, because constantly new problems make their appearance and there are enlargements of the problems (greater precision), much depends on the most thorough preparation of the first fundamental conception (scope, media, forces). The latter is also to some extent a measure for the obtained degree of theoretical and ideological clarity in a research collective. Side by side with the conception there must be prepared as well a plan regarding organization and instructions for the practical implementation (training of assistants, sphere of responsibility, system of control, long-term development plan, detailed organizational problems, etc.). This has to be accompanied by the preparation of a bibliographic review (knowledge of the state of development in the international field), decision regarding proceedings according to the sample method, the method (questionnaire, interview, analysis of documents, etc.).

Proceedings according to the sample method and the methods to be adopted for research (starting point and the order in which one proceeds) have to be prepared with special attention, taking into consideration data obtained later and the general evaluation (monographs, individual reviews, and general reviews), because this is of decisive significance for the achievement of the ultimate aim.

Already this short review points to the fact that fundamental and purposeful research in the field of sports sociology can only be a success if one adheres to the principle of collective work and if groups are set up of specialized research workers from the various disciplines, such as representatives of philosophical and theoretical branches, from psychology—if possible social psychology—from the sphere of mathematical statistics, the science of organization, social hygiene and finally the proper specialists, namely, representatives of sports sociology, as far as they have specialized in this field of education or have developed, coming from various disciplines.

REFERENCES

1. Braunreuther, K., *Die marxistische Soziologie und die Pädagogen* (Marxist Sociology and Pedagogues), in "Pädagogik," Berlin, 19 (1964), 2.
2. Braunreuther, K. and Steiner, H., *Soziologische Problem der sozialistischen Wissenschaftsführung* (Sociological Problems of the Socialist Economy), in "Wirtschaftswissenschaft," Berlin (1964), 10.
3. Buggel, E., *Über eine repräsentative komplex-territoriale Stichprobenerhebung in der DDR für den Bereich der Körperkulture* (A Representative, Complex, Territorial Survey on the Basis of the Sample Method in the G.D.R. in the Field of Physical Culture), in "Theorie und Praxis der Körperkultur," Berlin, 14 (1965), 4.
4. Buggel, E. and others, *Sport und Touristik im Urlaub an der Ostsee und im Mittelgebirge—Methoden und Ergebnisse einer Untersuchung im Juli 1963 in Heringsdorf und Friedrichroda* (Sport and Tourism During the Holidays at the Baltic Sea and in the Mountains—Methods and Results of a Survey Conducted in July 1963 in Heringsdorf and Friedrichroda), in "Wiss. Zeitschrift der DHfK," Leipzig, 6 (1964), 2.
5. Erbach, G., *Internationaler Kongress der Sportwissenschaften in Tokio vom 3–8.10.1964.* (International Congress of the Sciences of Sport in Tokyo, Oct. 3–8.10.1964), in "Theorie und Praxis der Körperkultur," Berlin, 14 (1965), 3.
6. Erbach, G., *Über die Bedeutung der wissenschaftlichen Perspektivplanung auf dem Gebiet der Körperkultur, unter Berücksichtigung sportsoziologischer Grundlagenforschung* (The Significance of Long-term Development Planning

in the Field of Physical Culture, from the Point of View of Research on Sports Sociological Foundations), in "Theorie und Praxis der Körperkultur," Berlin, 14 (1965), 4.

7. Erbach, G., *Gedanken zur Einordnung der Theorie der Körperkultur als Lehr- und Forschungsdisziplin in das System der Sportwissenschaft* (Ideas Regarding Inclusion of the Theory of Physical Culture As One of the Branches and Research Fields of the System of the Sceince of Sport), in "Theorie und Praxis der Körperkultur," Berlin, September 1964, Sonderheft: Über philosophische und soziologische Probleme der Körperkultur.

8. Florl, R., *Volkssport im sozialistischen Dorf. Versuch einer komplex-territorialen Analyse als Beitrag zur Leistungstatigkeit sportlicher Führungsorgane, dargestellt am Beispiel einer Untersuchung in der Landgemeinde Kyhma* (Sport in a Socialist Village. Attempt to Give a Complex, Territorial Analysis as a Contribution to the Work of Leading Sports Bodies, Presented With the Help of a Survey Conducted in a Rural Community in Kyhma), Dissertation an der DHfK, Leipzig, 1964.

9. Gras, F., *Die Beziehungen zwischen dem Belastungsverlauf bei landwirtschaftlichen Arbeiten und der Gestaltung einer regelmäBigen sportlich-kulturellen Betätigung für die Beschäftigten in der sozialistischen Landwirtschaft— dargestellt am Beispiel der Gemeinde Machern, Krs. Wurzen* (Interrelations Between the Burden of Agricultural Labour and the Taking Shape of a Regular Sports and Cultural Activity for People Employed in Socialist Agriculture. Example: Community Machern).

10. John, E., *Der wissenschaftliche Kulturbegriff* (The Scientific Conception of Culture), in "Deutsche Zeitschrift für Philosophie," Berlin, 6 (1958), 4.

11. Novikov, A. D., *Über das Probleme der Kategorien der körperlichen Erziehung* —"Körperliche Entwicklung," "Körperliche Erzichung," "Körperliche Vollkommenheit"—und ihre wechselseitige Beziehung (The Problem of Categories of Physical Education—"Physical Development," "Physical Education," "Physical Perfection"—and their Interrelations), in "Theorie und Praxis der Körperkultur," Berlin, Sonderheft, 1964.

12. Röblitz, G., *Freizeitnutzung und sportliche Betätigung der lernenden Jugend. Versuch einer pädagogischen Grundlegung* (Leisure Pursuits and Sports Activity of Studying Youth), Habilschrift an der DHfK, Leipzig, 1964.

13. Schnürpel, H., *Analyse der materiell-technischen Bedingungen für Körperkultur und Sport im Bezirk Leipzig 1962, unter besonderer Berücksichtigung von Problemen der komplex-territorialen Perspektivplanung* (Analysis of the Material and Technical Conditions for Physical Culture and Sport in the Region of Leipzig), Dissertation an der DHfK, Leipzig, 1964.

14. Schnürpel, H., *Zu einigen volkswirtschaftlichen Aspekten der Materielltechnischen Bedingungen für Körperkultur und Sport* (Some Aspects of the Material and Technical Conditions for Physical Culture and Sport from the Point of View of the National Economy), in "Theorie und Praxis der Körperkultur," Berlin, 14 (1965), 4.

15. Schulz, R., *Über Wesen und Methoden wissenschaftlicher Soziologie* (The Nature and Methods of Scientific Sociology), in "Theorie und Praxis der Körperkultur," Berlin, 10 (1961), 2.

16. Schwidtmann, H. and Sieger, W., *Wissenschaftlich-technische Revolution*

und sozialistische Körperkultur (Scientific and Technical Revolution and Socialist Physical Culture), in "Einheit," Berlin, 19 (1964), 12.

17. Sieger, W., *Zur wissenschaftlichen Planung und Leitung im Bereich der Körperkultur* (Scientific Planning and Direction of Physical Culture), in "Theorie und Praxis der Körperkultur," Berlin, 13 (1964), 4.

18. Kukuschkin, J., Sonderheft der Zeitschrift "Theorie und Praxis der Körperkultur," Berlin, September 1964 (hrsg. von G. Erbach). *Über philosophische und soziologische Probleme der Körperkultur* (Philosophical and Sociological Problems of Physical Culture).

19. Stajkov, Z., *Sektion der Sportsoziologie* (Section of Sports Sociology), in "Vupr. fizic. kult," Sofija, 9 (1964), 5.

20. Stranai, K., *Über die Notwendigkeit, die Theorie der Körpererziehung als selbständige wissenschaftliche Fachdisziplin auszubilden* (The Necessity to Shape the Theory of Physical Culture into an Independent Specialized Discipline), in "Theorie und Praxis der Körperkultur," Berlin, 11 (1963), 9.

21. Trogsch, F., *Marxistische Sozialforschung auf dem Gebiet von Körperkultur kultur und Sport* (Marxist Social Research in the Field of Physical Culture and Sport), in "Wissenschaftl, Zeitschrift der DHfK," Leipzig, 4 (1962), 2.

22. Trogsch, F., *Körperübungen als menschliche LebensäuBerung und kultureller Entwicklungsfaktor* (Physical Exercises as an Expression of Life and Factor of Cultural Development), in "Deutsche Zeitschrift für Philosophie," Berlin, 12 1964), 8.

23. Trogsch, F., *Entwicklungsdeterminanten und -tendenzen im Bereich von Körperkultur und Sport* (Determinants and Trends of Development in the field of Physical Culture and Sport), in "Theorie und Praxis der Körperkultur," 14 (1965), 8.

24. Wohl, A., *Die gesellschaftlich-historischen Grundlagen des bürgerlichen Sports* (The Socio-Historical Foundations of Bourgeois Sport), in "Wiss. Zeitschrift der DHfK," 6 (1964), 1.

toward a sociology of sport

GERALD S. KENYON AND
JOHN W. LOY

To declare that sport, during the present century, has become a cultural phenomenon of great magnitude and complexity is an affirmation of the obvious. Sport is fast becoming a social institution, permeating education, economics, art, politics, law, mass communications, and international

• From the *Journal of Health, Physical Education, and Recreation* 36 (1965), 24–25, 68–69. © 1965 American Association for Health, Physical Education and Recreation, Washington, D.C.

diplomacy. Its scope is awesome; nearly everyone has become involved in some way, even if only vicariously. As a business enterprise alone it represents an annual expenditure by the American public of over $20 billion. For the services of a single performer, $400 thousand apparently is not too much to pay. Sport has become a potent social force with a capacity to create needs ranging from seats on the fifty-yard line to stretch pants in pastel colors.

Despite the magnitude of the public's commitment to sport, as a social phenomenon it has received little serious study. The ubiquitous presence of sports has largely been taken for granted by social scientists and physical educators alike. A clear description, let alone explanation of this social force, is largely nonexistent. Many of its manifest and most of its latent functions have been ignored. For the physical educator, sport provides a medium for pursuing educational goals. For almost anyone else it probably serves quite different purposes. In neither case is its social significance understood. Therefore, we urge the development of a "sociology of sport" as a division of an academic discipline such as that recently described by Franklin Henry.[1]

The Nature of Sport Sociology

If sociology is the study of social order—the underlying regularity of human social behavior—including efforts to attain it and departures from it,[2] then the sociology of sport becomes the study of the regularity, and departures from it, of human social behavior in a sports context. As we see the social psychology of sport as having much in common with its sociology, we include the content and method of the former within the realm of our subdiscipline.[3] Thus, if social psychology is "an attempt to understand and explain how the thought, feeling, and behavior of individuals are influenced by the actual, imagined, or implied presence of other human beings," [4] then the social psychology of sport is the study of individuals in social and cultural settings associated with sport. Just as exercise physiology deals with something less than the whole of physiology, the concern of a psychosociological study of sport is with something less than the whole of social psychology or sociology.

A psychosociological inquiry into sport and physical activity requires a concern for such concepts as *basic social units* (including individuals, groups, institutions, societies, and cultures), *primary social psychological attributes*

---

[1] F. M. Henry, "Physical Education: An Academic Discipline," *Journal of Health, Physical Education, Recreation,* September 1964, p. 32.

[2] A. Inkeles, *What is Sociology?* Englewood Cliffs, N. J.: Prentice-Hall, 1964, p. 27.

[3] It is assumed that for most subsequent references to the *sociology* of sport, the *social psychology* of sport is implied also.

[4] Gordon W. Allport, "The Historical Background of Modern Social Psychology," in G. Lindzey (ed.), *Handbook of Social Psychology,* Vol. 1, Reading, Mass.: Addison-Wesley, 1954, p. 5.

(such as interpersonal response traits, motives, attitudes, and values), and *fundamental social processes* (socialization, social control, social conflict, social stratification, and social change).

For an illustration of the significance of this framework, we refer to the work of Roberts and Sutton-Smith,[5] an anthropologist and a psychologist collaborating to study the role of games in various societies. They have shown that the type of games played reflect values inherent in a particular culture and at the same time serve to teach certain cultural values and attitudes. For example, with respect to child rearing practices, obedience training is associated with a culture stressing games of strategy, responsibility training with games of chance, and achievement training with games of physical skill. Thus Roberts and Sutton-Smith argue that individuals in different cultures (basic social units) perceive games differently, depending upon the values and attitudes prevalent within a particular culture (primary social psychological attributes) and that such games serve to relieve social conflict and consequently enhance socialization (fundamental social processes). It follows that such a framework could be useful for the study of the many social facets of sport.

We suggest, therefore, that the observational techniques and the theoretical rationale available to the sport sociologist could provide unique possibilities for viewing the social significance of sport. To illustrate, the classification of activities into such schemes as individual, dual, or team sports so familiar to the physical educator, or into factors such as intensity, frequency, and duration, so familiar to the exercise physiologist, will give way to classifications appropriate for a social context, such as Caillois' conception of games as competition, chance, drama (mimicry) and the pursuit of vertigo.

WHAT THE SOCIOLOGY OF SPORT IS NOT. Having briefly described what the sociology of sport *is*, we turn now to what it is *not*, in an effort to distinguish between the goals of science and those of education or physical education. The sport sociologist does not base his inquiries upon the assumption that "physical activity is good." Sport sociology, as we view it, is a value-free social science. It is not an effort to influence public opinion or behavior, nor is it an attempt to find support for the "social development" objective of physical education, as described in the writings of Hetherington, Williams, Nash, Oberteuffer, and others. The sport sociologist is neither a spreader of gospel nor an evangelist for exercise. His function is not to shape attitudes and values but rather to describe and explain them. By taking such a position, in no way do we suggest that *physical education* ought to be value free; it must have its objectives, certainly. We *do* suggest, however that the choice of both ends and means may be enhanced considerably by drawing from the findings of a well-developed sport sociology.

PREPARING THE SPORT SOCIOLOGIST. To perform the functions of a sport sociologist obviously requires some preparation. Students of sport sociology,

---

[5] See references given at conclusion of article, page 47.

in addition to an interest in an understanding of sport, should have a strong background in the behavioral and social sciences, especially psychology, sociology, social psychology, and cultural anthropology. The exciting developments occurring in both the theoretical and empirical aspects of these fields make it essential that the student pay considerable attention to each. With the degree of mathematical thinking in the social sciences increasing rapidly, adequate preparation in mathematics and statistics is essential to understand certain theoretical models and data analysis procedures.

A Brief Historical Perspective

Although a work entitled *Soziologie des Sports* was published in Germany in 1921, few publications referring directly to sport sociology can be found. Up to the present, much of the writing, varying widely in scope and depth, has been largely descriptive in nature.[6] Nevertheless, these writers have often provided cogent observations, suggesting hypotheses worthy of test. With the exception of some of Cowell's work,[7] serious empirical study of sport sociology *per se* has not been popular. Few investigators from physical education have devoted a substantial period of their career to the subject. The work of others, such as sociologists, usually has been conducted in the broader context of use of leisure.[8] While it would be false to assert that the sociology of sport has acquired a substantial subject matter, some work— both theoretical and empirical—does exist.

THEORETICAL EFFORTS. Theories of sports and games have long been of interest to social scientists. At the beginning of the century G. T. W. Patrick wrote on the "psychology of football." Numerous theories of play as means to certain social ends have been advanced. These theories came to be discarded when found contradictory to evidence provided by empirical psychology. In the 1930s, however, Huizinga argued that play ought to be considered for its own sake, as an end in itself rather than a means to some other end. He showed how play pervades all cultural institutions. Although his work is frequently alluded to, little effort has been made to extend his theory and test the hypotheses it suggests. Another work linking sport and

[6] For example, see F. W. Cozens and F. S. Stumpf, *Sports in American Life*, Chicago: University of Chicago Press, 1953, for a well-documented account of the diversity of sport in the United States with frequent reference to historical developments. For more recent reflections on sport as a social institution, particularly from an international viewpoint, see P. C. McIntosh, *Sport in Society*, London: Watts, 1963 and Natan, *Sport and Society*, London: Bowes & Bowes, 1958.

[7] For example, see Charles C. Cowell, "The Contributions of Physical Activity to Social Development," *Research Quarterly*, May 1960, p. 286, a review of literature which includes five of his own research reports.

[8] For an early example (1934) see G. Lundberg *et al.* "The Amount of Uses of Leisure," in E. Larrabee and R. Meyersohn, *Mass Leisure*, Glencoe, Ill.: Free Press, 1958; more recently, S. de Grazia, *Of Time, Work and Leisure*, Garden City, N. Y.: Doubleday, 1962.

culture is that of Caillois who attempts to demonstrate that the health of a society is reflected in the types of games it encourages.

EMPIRICAL STUDIES. Much of the work cited by Roberts, Sutton-Smith, and coworkers was based upon empirical cross-cultural data. Their hypothesis that games model the major maintenance problems of a given society is illustrated using the highly competitive society of the United States, where sports and games permit youth to rehearse competitive roles without experiencing the adverse anxiety experienced by adults striving for success. Other studies include Weinberg and Arond's discussion of the occupational culture of the boxer; Grusky's treatment of managerial succession and organizational effectiveness in baseball; Riesman's description of the cultural diffusion of football and its bearing on ethnic differentiation and social mobility; and Stone's work, which offers a number of interesting hypotheses about the relationships between sport and socioeconomic status.

EUROPEAN INTEREST. Although workers in this country have been leaders in several aspects of the science of physical activity, it is interesting to note that at present the greatest interest in sport sociology seems to be centered in Europe. In addition to work cited elsewhere in this paper, a number of other essays and research studies have been published during the past few years.[9]

Avenues for Future Inquiry

Sport sociology as an empirical science is in its infancy, but it need not remain this way. The interested researcher soon becomes aware of the numerous possibilities, first, by taking cognizance of the many theoretical models explaining group and individual behavior, and second, by taking advantage of such technical advances as electronic computers and multivariate methods of data reduction and analysis. For fruitful inquiry the relevant developments in other disciplines cannot be ignored any more than the curriculum worker can afford to ignore concept learning, teaching machines, programed learning, and team teaching.

Our consideration of the numerous possibilities for research has been a natural outgrowth of the thought associated with some modest studies under way at the University of Wisconsin. At present, work is in progress in four areas: the diffusion of innovations in American sport; the significance of physical activity for adults as a function of age, sex, education, socioeconomic

---

[9] For example, see R. Helanko, "Sports and Socialization," *Acta Sociologica*, 2 (1957), 229–40; Helge Anderson and others, "Sports and Games in Denmark in the Light of Sociology," *Acta Sociologica*, 2 (1956), 1–28; and Rene Maheu, "Sport and Culture," 9–22; E. J. Leemans, "A Sociological Approach to Sports," 152–59; N. G. Vlot, "A Sociological Analysis of Sport in the Netherlands," 198–211; and Joffre Dumazedier, "The Point of View of a Social Scientist," 212–17 in E. Jokl and E. Simon (eds.), *International Research in Sport and Physical Education*, Springfield, Ill.: Charles C Thomas Publishers, 1964.

status, and national origin; the development of models for the characterization of values held for physical activity; and cross-national studies of attitudes
toward physical activity as a function of certain cultural and educational
factors. It has been our further observation that many promising avenues of
inquiry are opened by becoming familiar with general sociological theory.

THE USE OF SOCIAL THEORY IN EXPLAINING THE ROLE OF SPORT IN SOCIETY.
The role of theory is the same for the sport sociologist as for the scientist in
general. Theory provides a logical foundation for research, that is, it circum-
scribes and characterizes the phenomenon in question; it suggests significant
hypotheses; it relates seemingly discrete findings by summarizing facts into
generalizations and systems of generalizations; and it identifies gaps in knowledge. Perhaps most important, theory "by providing a rationale . . . introduces a *ground for prediction* which is more secure than mere empirical
extrapolation from previously observed trends." [10]

Fortunately for the sport sociologist, several contemporary sociological
theories are relevant for studying the many ramifications of sport in modern
society. Although these may require slight modification by virtue of use in
a sports situation, they should be applicable if there is regularity to human
social behavior. For example, Parson's theoretical scheme differentiating four
levels of structural organization—primary, managerial, institutional, and
societal—permits analysis of any social system in terms of the functional problems such systems must solve in order to survive.[11] He labels these problems
as adaptive, goal-attainment, pattern-maintenance and tension management,
and integrative.

Less general theories applicable to the sport setting include those concerned with collective behavior, such as the recent and rather complete framework of Smelser.[12] Admittedly, a riot such as that which occurred at a
Peruvian soccer match in the spring of 1964 bringing death to several hundred
persons is relatively rare. However, other forms of collective behavior associated with sports are quite common.

POSSIBLE RESEARCH AREAS.   Other approaches which we believe warrant
some investigation include the following:

1. Computer Simulations. The technological advances in computer design and
   application are more rapid than had been anticipated. Recent developments
   in computer simulation techniques [13] could be applied to team dynamics, sport
   development and decline, and spectator behavior.

[10] Robert K. Merton, *Social Theory and Social Structure*, Glencoe, Ill.: Free Press,
1957, p. 98.

[11] Talcott, Parsons, "General Theory in Sociology," in R. K. Merton and others
(eds.), *Sociology Today*, New York: Basic Books, Inc., 1959.

[12] Neil J. Smelser, *Theory of Collective Behavior*, New York: Free Press of Glencoe,
1963.

[13] For example, see A. Newell and H. A. Simon, "Computers in Psychology," in
R. D. Luce, R. R. Bush, and E. Galanter (eds.), *Handbook of Mathematical Psychology*,
Vol. 1, New York: Wiley, 1963.

2. Game Situation Laboratory. The development of a facility capable of simulating the environment surrounding the game would afford a compromise between the uncontrollable actual condition and the artificial conditions of the laboratory.
3. Interdisciplinary Studies. Instead of independent work by exercise physiologists, psychologists, sociologists, and sport sociologists, work in concert would yield knowledge heretofore unknown. As Roger Bannister recently pointed out, "maximum athletic performance cannot be explained by physiology alone." [14]
4. Social Model Development. The construction of models, both static and dynamic, could produce one basis for describing and explaining the significance of sport for individuals and groups. McPhee's "addiction model" represents one approach for predicting the course of "enthusiasms" or "passions" for a given pastime, intellectual or physical. [15]
5. Cross-National and Cross-Cultural Studies. Whatever laws that may be discovered and theories developed, the crucial test lies in their potential for generalizing to other countries and other cultures.
6. Game Theory. The application of the now well-established theory of games apparently has failed, to a large extent, to interest investigators studying sport.
7. The Significance of Sport and Physical Activity as a Leisure Pursuit. During the past few years considerable interest has been shown in the sociology of leisure, both in this country and abroad. [16] Although a leisure use theory depends upon acquiring more data, a number of studies have been completed, and several national and international conferences held.
8. Social Change and Sport. Among the most profound characteristics of contemporary Western civilization is the rapidity of social change, change in the nature of social institutions and social values. What is it about the "Great Society" that explains the Mets outdrawing the Yankees?

This list of potential research areas is not meant to be exhaustive, or to contain mutually exclusive subjects for investigation. Moreover, it will be noted that we are suggesting not only points of departure for future research but also some techniques of inquiry, many of which have only recently become available for practical use.

In summary, we have suggested that the explanation of the contemporary pervasiveness of sport requires a sociology of sport in the tradition of the social sciences. We have attempted to show what the characteristics of such a subdiscipline might be, drawing examples from studies both completed and proposed. With the vastness of sport today, together with its anticipated growth in the future, the potentiality of a sociology of sport becomes apparent. To become firmly established, however, will require well-

[14] "The Meaning of Athletic Performance," paper presented at the International Conference of the International Council for Sport and Physical Education, Paris, October 1963.

[15] W. N. McPhee, *Formal Theories of Mass Behavior*, New York: Free Press of Glencoe, 1963.

[16] For a summary of studies together with an extensive bibliography, see E. Larrabee and R. Meyersohn (eds.), *Mass Leisure*, Glencoe, Ill.: Free Press, 1958.

prepared and dedicated workers using a value free approach to an often value charged subject matter.

REFERENCES

Caillois Roger, *Man, Play and Games*, Glencoe, Ill.: Free Press, 1961.

Grusky, Oscar, "Managerial Succession and Organizational Effectiveness," *American Journal of Sociology*, July 1963, 69, (1), 21–31.

Huizinga, Johan, *Homo Ludens*, Boston: Beacon Press, 1960.

Patrick, G. T. W., "The Psychology of Football," *American Journal of Psychology*, July–October 1903, 14, (3–4), 104–17.

Rapaport, Anatole, *Fights, Games and Debates*, Ann Arbor: University of Michigan Press, 1960.

Riesman, David and Reul, Denny, "Football in America," *American Quarterly*, 1951, 3, 309–19.

Roberts, John M., and others, "Games in Culture," *American Anthropologist*, August 1959, 61, 597–605.

Roberts, John M. and Sutton-Smith, Brian, "Child Training and Game Involvement," *Ethnology*, 1962, 1, 166–85.

Roberts, John M., and others, "Strategy in Games and Folk Tales," *Journal of Social Psychology*, 1963, 61, 185–99.

Stone, Gregory P., "Some Meanings of American Sport," *College Physical Education Association 60th Annual Proceedings*. Washington, D. C.: CPEA, 1957.

Sutton-Smith, Brian, and others, "Game Involvement in Adults," *Journal of Social Psychology*, 1963, 60, 15–30.

Weinberg, S. K., and Arond, H., "The Occupational Culture of the Boxer," *American Journal of Sociology*, March 1952, 57, 460–69.

concepts, definitions, and classifications

the structure and classification of games

ROGER CAILLOIS

In 1933, the rector of the University of Leyden, J. Huizinga, chose as the theme of his solemn speech, "the boundaries of play and of work in culture." He was to take this subject up again and to develop it in a powerful and original work published in 1938, *Homo Ludens*. Most of the statements in this book are debatable. Nonetheless, it opens the way to extremely fertile research and reflection. It is to Huizinga's lasting credit that he masterfully analyzed the fundamental characteristics of play and that he demonstrated the importance of its role in the development of civilization. He wanted on the one hand to find an exact definition of the essential nature of play; on the other hand, he attempted to shed some light on that part of play that haunts or enlivens the principal manifestations of all culture, the arts as well as philosophy, poetry as well as juridical institutions, and even certain aspects of war.

Huizinga achieved brilliantly what he set out to do. However, if he discovered play, whose presence and influence had until then been overlooked, he deliberately neglected to describe and classify the games themselves, as if all play represented an answer to the same need and explained the same psychological attitude. Thus a study of his first formulae helps us to understand the strange lacunae in his inquiry. We recall that he defined play in the following manner:

• From *Diogenes*, 12 (Winter, 1955), pp. 62–75. © 1955 Editions Galbimard, 5 Rue Sibastren-Bottin, Paris 7e, France.

Summing up the formal characteristics of play we might call it a free activity standing quite consciously outside "ordinary" life as being "not serious," but at the same time absorbing the player intensely and utterly. It is an activity connected with no material interest, and no profit can be gained by it. It proceeds within its own proper boundaries of time and space according to fixed rules and in an orderly manner. It promotes the formation of social groupings which tend to surround themselves with secrecy and to stress their difference from the common world by disguise or other means.[1]

Such a definition, though all the words have value and meaning, is both too broad and too narrow. It is meritorious and fruitful to have grasped the affinity between play and secrecy or mystery, but this relationship should not enter into a definition of play, which is almost always ostentatious. Undoubtedly secrecy, mystery, and disguise lend themselves to an activity of play, but it should be immediately added that this activity necessarily takes place at the expense of secrecy and mystery. It exposes, publicizes and in a way expends secrecy, tending, in a word, to deprive it of its very nature.

Then again, that part of Huizinga's definition which alludes to play as an action devoid of any material interest entirely excludes betting and games of chance—that is, gambling houses, casinos, horse races, lotteries which, for good or evil, occupy an important place in the economy and in the daily life of different peoples, under an infinite variety of forms which makes the constancy of the relations between risk and profit all the more impressive. Games of chance, which are also money games, figure almost not at all in Huizinga's work. This deliberate exclusion is not without consequence.

Under these circumstances, it would be better to address ourselves to another formula of Huizinga's, less fruitful than the preceding one, but which, in my opinion at least, does not give rise to any major difficulty:

Play is a voluntary action or occupation executed within certain fixed limits of time and place, according to rules freely accepted but absolutely binding, having its aim in itself and accompanied by a feeling of tension, joy and the consciousness that it is "different" from "ordinary" life.[2]

Although this second definition does not deliberately ignore games of chance, neither does it attribute a sufficient place to them. Moreover, the last part of it not only advantageously replaces the too explicit mention of secret and of mystery, but also gives one to understand that play could consist in the representation of something. Here, it is no longer the world of betting that is taken into consideration, but that of spectacle and interpretation, of dramatic play.

These observations, which extend very markedly the domain explored by Huizinga, still overlook such things as kites, crossword puzzles, and rock-

[1] *Homo Ludens*, London: Routledge & Kegan Paul, 1949, p. 13.
[2] *Ibid.*, p. 28.

ing horses, and to some extent dolls, games of patience, Chinese puzzles, hoops, most toys, and several of the more widespread diversions.

What do we get from these summary observations? First, that play is certainly an activity that is

1. Free: the player cannot be forced to participate without the game immediately changing its very nature.
2. Separate: circumscribed within boundaries of time and space that are precise and fixed in advance.[3]
3. Regulated: subject to conventions which suspend ordinary rules and temporarily establish a new law which alone counts.

However, these three attributes—whose prime importance I in no way challenge—imply, perhaps because of the fact that they do not affect the structure of the data they define, that such data should in turn be made the object of a distribution which attempts, this time, to take into account, not the characteristics which oppose them as a whole to the rest of reality, but those which confer upon them, among other things, their decidedly irreducible originality. In other words, once the *genus proximum* has been determined, it becomes urgent to state precisely the *differentia specifica* of each subsidiary category.

To this end, I suggest a division under three principal headings in accordance with whether, in the different games, the role of competition, luck, or disguise predominates. For all practical purposes only one of these, the first, attracted Huizinga's attention. I shall call them, *agôn, alea* and *mimicry*, respectively. All three definitely belong to the realm of play. One *plays* football or billiards or chess (*agôn*); roulette or the lottery (*alea*); pirates or Nero or Hamlet (*mimicry*). However, these terms do not cover the world of play in its entirety. Perhaps one should also single out the existence of a common principle of diversion, of turbulence, of free improvisation and of insouciant self-expression whereby a certain uncontrolled fantasy, which we shall call *paidia*, manifests itself. It likewise seems necessary to define a complementary tendency that is the inverse of this instinct in certain respects but not in all: the penchant for adapting play to arbitrary, imperative, and deliberately hindering conventions in order to obtain a perfectly useless although strictly determinate result. I shall call this last component *ludus*.

It is not my intention, in employing this foreign nomenclature to establish some sort of pedantic mythology, totally devoid of meaning. But, because I had to assemble disparate manifestations under a single rubric, it seemed to me that the most economical way of so doing was to borrow from this or that language both the most significant and the most comprehensive term

---

[3] As for space: the hopscotch diagram, the checker-board, the chess board, the stadium, the playing field, the track, the ring, the dueling ground, the stage, the arena, etc. . . . As for time: the beginning and the end of a game, the complications of a possible prolongation, the kind of disgrace entailed by a default, which the fact of calling "I give up," represents or by any withdrawal during the course of a game or of a match, unless it is caused by a physical accident.

possible in order to keep each ensemble studied from being uniformly marked by the particular characteristic of one of the elements that compose it; this could not fail to happen if the name of one element was used to designate the entire group. Besides, as I proceed with my attempt to establish the classification which I have fixed upon, everyone will have the opportunity to appreciate for himself the necessity of utilizing a nomenclature that does not refer too directly to concrete experience, which it is partly designed to break down according to a hitherto unstated principle.

Agôn

A whole group of games appears in the form of competition, as a struggle in which equality of chance is artificially created in order to make sure that the antagonists confront each other under ideal circumstances. This will give a precise and incontestable worth to the victor's triumph. Each time, therefore, the contest hinges on a single quality—speed, endurance, vigor, memory, deftness, ingenuity, etc.—operating within defined limits and without any external help. The winner will therefore appear to be the best in a precise category of feats. Such is the rule for athletic contests and the *raison d'être* of their multiple subdivisions, whether two individuals or two teams are competing (polo, tennis, football, boxing, fencing, etc.), or whether an indeterminate number of competitors are participating (races of all kinds, riflery, golf, athletics, etc.). Games in which each contestant begins with the same number of identical elements also belong to this category. Draughts and chess are perfect examples. The quest for equality of chance from the start is so obviously the essential principle of the contest that it is reestablished by assigning a handicap to players of superior ability. In other words, within the equality of chance established from the start, a second inequality, proportional to the supposed relative strength of the participants, is created. It is significant that such a system exists for the muscular type of *agôn* (sports matches) as well as for the most cerebral type of *agôn* (chess, for example, in which the weaker player is given an extra pawn, knight or rook).

For each contestant the mainspring of the game is his desire to excel and win recognition for his ability in a given domain. Furthermore, the practice of *agôn* presupposes concentration, appropriate training, assiduous effort, and the will to win. It implies discipline and perseverance. It makes the champion rely solely on his own resources, encourages him to make the best possible use of them and forces him to utilize them fairly and within fixed limits which, being the same for everyone, result in rendering the superiority of the winner indisputable. The *agôn* appears as the pure form of personal merit and serves to demonstrate it.

Outside often on the periphery of play, one observes the notion of *agôn* in other cultural phenomena that conform to the same code: the duel, the tournament, certain constant and remarkable aspects of what we call polite warfare.

Alea

In Latin this is the word for the game of dice. I use it here to designate all games—in contrast to *agôn*—that are based upon an inequality external to the player, over which he has not the slightest control. Consequently, it is far less a question of triumphing over an adversary than over destiny. To put it more plainly, fate is the sole agent of victory, and where rivalry exists, victory means only that the winner was luckier than the loser. Dice, roulette, heads or tails, baccarat, lotteries, etc. provide unmistakable examples of this category of games. In this case not only is no attempt made to eliminate the injustice of chance, but it is the pure arbitrariness of luck that constitutes the sole mainspring of the game.

Alea signalizes and reveals the boons of fate. The player's role is an entirely passive one. He does not display his abilities or his propensities, the resources of his skill, of his muscles, or of his intelligence. All he does is to wait for the decision of fate. He gambles a stake. Justice forever sought after, but this time differently, and, here again, prone to operate under ideal circumstances—rigorously accurate, the proportionate reward for his gamble. All the efforts referred to above to equalize the contestants' chances are employed in this case to scrupulously balance *alea* and profit.

In contrast to *agôn*, *alea* negates work, patience, skill, qualifications. It eliminates professional endowments, order, and training. In one instant it abolishes accumulated results. It is either total failure or absolute favor. It bestows upon the lucky player infinitely more than a lifetime of work, discipline, and hardship could procure for him. It seems like an insolent and supreme mockery of merit.

Agôn is a vindication of personal responsibility, *alea* a resignation of the will, a surrender to destiny. Certain games like dominoes, and most card games combine *agôn* and *alea*: chance governs the way the "hands" of each player are composed and they then do their best, according to their lights, to exploit the lot that a blind fate has assigned to them. In a game like bridge, science and reason constitute the only means a player has to defend himself, and it is these that permit him to make the very most of the cards dealt to him; in a game like poker the attributes of psychological insight and human understanding are more likely to count.

Generally speaking, the role of money is all the more important, as chance plays a greater part and consequently the player's opportunities to defend himself are less good. The reason for this is very clear: *alea's* function is not to make the most intelligent person win the money, but, on the contrary, to abolish the natural or acquired superiority of individuals in order to place everyone on an absolute and equal footing in the face of luck's blind verdict.

As the result of *agôn* is necessarily uncertain and must, paradoxically, relate to the effect of pure chance, given the fact that the contestants' chances are, in principle, as even as possible, it then follows that any encounter that possesses the characteristics of an ideally regulated competition can be the object of betting, in other words of *aleas*: to wit, horse races, or greyhound races, football or Basque pelota matches, cock-fights. It even happens that the stakes vary constantly during the game, according to the ups and downs of *agôn*.[4]

Agôn and *alea* represent contrasting attitudes, and in some way, symmetrical ones, but they both conform to the same law: the artificial establishment of conditions of absolute equality among the players, which reality denies mankind. For nothing in life is clear unless it is precisely that everything in it, luck as well as merit, is always disorder in the beginning. Play, *agôn* or *alea*, is therefore an attempt to substitute perfect situations for the normal confusion of everyday life. These perfect situations are such that the role of merit or of luck appears clear and unequivocal. They also imply that everyone must enjoy exactly the same possibilities to prove his worth, or, on the other scale, the exact same chance to win. In one way or another one escapes from the world by making *it* other. One can also escape from it by making *oneself* other. This is what we call mimicry.

Mimicry

Every game presupposes the temporary acceptance, if not of an illusion (although this last word means nothing more than entry into play, *inlusio*), at least of a closed, conventional, and, in certain respects, fictitious universe. The play can consist not in the unfolding of an activity or in experiencing one's fate in an imaginary setting, but in becoming an illusory person oneself and in behaving accordingly. One then finds oneself confronted by a diversified series of manifestations whose common characteristic is that they rest on the fact that the subject plays at believing, at pretending to himself, or at making others believe that he is someone other than he is; he temporarily forgets, disguises, strips his own personality in order to be another. I choose to designate these manifestations by the term *mimicry* (which, in English, is the word for the mimetism of insects), in order to emphasize the primitive, elementary and quasi-instinctive nature of the impulse which produces them. They include, first of all, the behavior of a child who pretends he is an airplane (and acts like one by stretching out his arms and imitating the roar of a motor), who plays soldier, pretends he is a musketeer or a gangster, etc. They also embrace any diversion that requires a mask or a costume and consists in the very fact that the player is disguised and in the consequence of this. Finally, it is clear that theatrical representations and dramatic interpretations rightfully belong to this group.

The pleasure resides in being someone else or in making others think

---

[4] For example, in the Balearic Islands at a game of pelota, or in Colombia and the Antilles, at cock-fights.

you are someone else. But as this is play we are discussing, it does not essentially involve fooling the spectator. A child who pretends to be a train will readily refuse his father's kiss, saying that one shouldn't kiss a locomotive. He does not attempt to make his father believe that he is a real locomotive. At a carnival, a masked person does not try to convince others that he is a real marquis, or a real toreador, or a real Indian, any more than an actor tries to make people believe that he "really" is Lear or Charles V.

The spy or the fugitive, however, disguises himself to really fool people because he is not playing a game.

Activity, imagination, interpretation, *mimicry* can scarcely have a relation to *alea*, which imposes upon the player the immobility and the chill of mute expectancy. *Agôn*, however, is not necessarily excluded. At the very moment when an actor plays a part, he tries, more indistinctly but also more profoundly, to be a better actor than the others, or to interpret a role that was created before him better than the others have done. He knows that he is subject to the public's judgment and to criticism. He plays, in the sense that he represents such or such a hero, but he also plays because he expects a prize in a prolix but unceasing competition with living or dead rivals.

Mimicry contains most of the characteristics of play: freedom convention, suspension of the real, circumscribed time and space. But continuous submission to precise and imperious regulations is less obvious here than elsewhere. I know of course that on the stage the actor must adhere to his lines, but one can hardly compare this servitude to the observance of fixed regulations which define the structure of a game. In the latter, it is a matter of a *framework* always necessarily identical with itself; and in the former, a matter of a *content* which may vary in each case, which is not a limitation but rather the substance, the very being of the character to be invoked. The frame work is, in truth, nothing more than the text.

Rules are inseparable from play as soon as it acquires what I shall call an institutional existence. From that moment on, they become a part of its nature, transforming play into a fertile and decisive instrument of culture. But it remains true that a primary freedom, which is the need for relaxation and the whole field of diversion and fantasy, resides at the source of play. This freedom is the indispensable prime mover of play, and remains at the origin of its most complex and rigidly organized forms. Such primary power of improvisation and gaiety, which I call *paidia*, is fused with the taste for gratuitous difficulty, which I propose to call *ludus*, in order to bring about the different games to which, without exaggeration, a civilizing property can be attributed. They illustrate, in fact, the moral and intellectual values of a culture. Moreover, they help to fix and define them.

I chose the term *paidia* because its roots signify the word "child" and because I do not wish to disconcert the reader needlessly by using a term borrowed from an antipodal language. But the Sanskrit word *krēdati* and the Chinese word *wan*, as far as I can judge by the indications that Huizinga provided and reproduced, seem to me both richer and clearer. *Krēdati* denotes the play of adults, of children, and of animals. It applies more specifically to gambols, that is to say, to sudden and capricious movements which a super-abundance of gaiety or vitality engenders. It is also used to signify erotic, illicit relations, the ebb and flow of waves, and all things that undulate to the caprice of the wind. The word *wan* is even more explicit, as much in regard to what it defines as to what it does not: it means essentially childish play, but also all the varieties of carefree and frivolous diversion which, for example, the verbs to frolic, to frisk, to jest,[5] to trifle, etc., evoke. Besides, and this is more revealing, it also means to examine, to manipulate, to fashion into trinkets, which connects it with the modern category of *hobbies*, in other words, the collector's mania. It evokes, as well, the peaceful and soothing softness of moonlight.[6] Finally, *it is not used* to denote either competition, games of skill, dice games, or dramatic interpretation; in other words, it excludes equally all three categories of institutional games: *agôn*, *alea*, and *mimicry*.

In the light of these relationships and of these semantic exclusions, what can be the scope and the significance of the term *paidia*? I, for one, would define it as the word that encompasses the spontaneous manifestations of the instinct of play: the cat entangled in a ball of yarn, the dog licking himself, the infant laughing at his rattle—all these represent the first identifiable examples of this kind of activity. It occurs in all joyous exuberance, the kind that is expressed by an immediate and disordered agitation, by an impulsive, relaxing, and deliberately immoderate pastime, whose impromptu and unruly character remains its essential, if not its sole *raison d'être*. We do not lack perfectly clear illustrations of this kind of sudden movement, of color, or of noise, from pencil marks to daubing with paint, from squabbling to uproar.

Such manifestations generally have no label and cannot have one, precisely because they remain within the bounds of stability of every distinctive sign, of every clearly differentiated existence which would enable our vocabulary to sanction its autonomy by a specific appellation. Besides, soon the conventions, the techniques, the tools appear, and with them the first games: leap-frog, hide and seek, the hoop, blind man's bluff, dolls. Here the contradictory paths of *agôn*, *alea*, and *mimicry* branch off. The pleasure one feels in resolving a difficulty occurs here too; we are speaking of the complication that is deliberately created, arbitrarily defined, so that the fact that one has finally seen it through brings no advantage other than the inner satisfaction of having solved it. This mainspring which is clearly *ludus* also can be observed in the different categories of games, with the exception of those that depend entirely upon a decision of fate. It appears as both complement of an instruc-

---

[5] It goes without saying that this last need is to be understood in its actual sense, because the baguenaude is really an assemblage of things, the manipulation of which is complicated and demands the player's extreme concentration and which, therefore, belongs to the category of *ludus*.

[6] Information which Duyvendak communicated to Huizinga, of *Homo Ludens*, p. 32.

tion for *paidia*, which it disciplines and enriches. It provides the opportunity for training and normally results in the conquest of a determined skill in the acquisition of a particular mastery, in the management of such or such an apparatus, or in the capacity to find a satisfactory answer to problems of a strictly conventional order. It differs from *agôn* in that the player's tension and his talent function without any sense of competition or rivalry: he struggles against the obstacle and not against one or several contestants. Games like *bilboquet* (cup and ball), *diabolo* and yo-yo can be classified as manual skills. These simple instruments readily make use of natural, elementary laws; for example, in regard to the yo-yo, weight and rotation are involved and the skill consists in converting alternate, rectilinear movements into a continuous circular one. Inversely, the hoop rests on the exploitation of a concrete atmospheric condition. One can easily see that the possibilities of play are almost infinite. Games like solitaire or *baguenaude* (ring puzzle) belong to another category of games: they make a constant appeal to the turn for computation and combination. Finally, crossword puzzles, mathematical pastimers, anagrams, logogriphic verse of all sorts, the kind of active detective-story reading that is an attempt to discover the guilty party, chess or bridge problems—all these, devoid of instruments, constitute so many variations of the most widespread and the purest form of *ludus*.

One also observes a situation that in the beginning has a tendency to repeat itself infinitely, but on the basis of which new combinations can develop. They inspire the player to compete with himself and enable him to observe the stages of his progress on which he prides himself vis-à-vis those who share his taste. The relationship of *ludus* with *agôn* is evidenced in this way. Moreover, it is possible that, in the case of chess or bridge problems, the same game may appear sometimes as *agôn* and sometimes as *ludus*.

The combination of *ludus* and *alea* occurs just as frequently; it is particularly evident in games which one plays alone and where the ingenuity of the maneuvers influence the result to some extent, and in which the player can, to a slight degree, calculate how much impetus to give to the ball that marks the points and attempt to direct it. Nonetheless, in both these examples, it is mainly luck that determines the outcome. However, the fact that the player is not entirely helpless and that he knows he must rely on his skill or talent, even though this counts for very little, is enough to combine the character of *ludus* with that of *alea*.

Here, too, the player is competing with himself in a way, because he expects the next effort to succeed where the last failed, or he hopes to accumulate a higher number of points than his last score yielded. It is in this way that the influence of *agôn* is manifest, coloring, in fact, the general atmosphere of *ludus*. And even though both these games are played alone and, in principle, do not call for competition, it is quite simple to start a match at any time, with or without a prize, the kind, for example, that newspapers occasionally organize. Nor is it pure accident that slot machines are to be found in cafés—places where it is the custom for people to gather in groups, thus forming the embryo of a public.

There is one characteristic of *ludus* which, in my opinion, can be explained by the presence of *agôn*, and which is a constant burden: the fact that it depends largely upon fads of the moment. The yo-yo, the *bilboquet*, the *diabolo*, the *baguenaude*, came into being and then disappeared as if by magic. They took advantage of a certain passing fad that was to disappear without a trace and that was quickly replaced by another. Although somewhat more stable, the fad for intellectual pastimes is nonetheless a transitory one: riddles, anagrams, acrostics, charades—all these have had their hour. It is quite probable that crossword puzzles and mystery stories will suffer the same fate. Such a phenomenon would be enigmatic if *ludus* represented as individualistic a pastime as it appears to; in reality, it is steeped in an atmosphere of competition. It can subsist only to the extent that it enjoys public favor, which transforms it into a virtual *agôn*. Lacking this, it is powerless to survive. In truth, it is not sufficiently supported by an organized spirit of competition, which is not essential to its practice, and neither does it provide material for any kind of spectacle capable of attracting the attention of a crowd. It remains uncertain and diffuse. It provides *paidia* with perpetually renewed forms. It invents a thousand opportunities and a thousand structures in which are to be found man's desire to relax and mainly his need, of which he apparently cannot be quit, to utilize the science and concentration, the skill and intelligence he possesses in the cause of pure uselessness.

In this sense, it represents that element in play whose cultural importance and fertility seem to be the most striking. It does not express as decided a psychological attitude as *agôn*, *alea*, or *mimicry*, but in disciplining *paidia*, it works behind the scenes to give to the three fundamental categories their purity and their excellence.

There remains a last species of games which does not seem to belong to those already mentioned and which can be considered the only truly modern innovation in this domain; games which are based upon the pursuit of *vertigo*.

Without question, people have for a long time deliberately sought out the confusion that a slight giddiness provokes, for example, the activities of the whirling derivishes and the Mexican voladores (flying fish). Nor must we overlook, in the realm of the most anodymic play, the merry-go-round and the ancient swing. Every child knows well, how, in turning rapidly around and around, he is able to attain a centrifugal state of flight, and wild prankishness in which his body has difficulty regaining its place and perception its clarity. Unquestionably he does it for fun and delights in it.

I suggest the term *ilinx* to include these different manifestations. It is Greek for whirlpool, from which is derived, precisely, and in the same language, the word *vertigo* (lingos). This designation also includes the *vertigo* to be found in certain animals, particularly in sheep, many of the effects of intoxication, some dances like the waltz, and finally, the giddiness induced by high speed, the kind one experiences on skis, in a motorcycle, or in an open car. Powerful machines are necessary to give these sensations the kind of intensity and brutality that can cause giddiness in adults. It is therefore not astonishing that we had to await the industrial age to see *vertigo* really become a category of play. Actually, it is dispensed to an avid multitude by a thousand implacable machines set up in the market places and in the amusement parks. Here, small wagons run on rails whose outline forms an almost perfect semi-circle, so that the vehicle, before it uprights itself, seems about to fall into space and the passengers, tied to their seats, feel as if they are falling with it. Elsewhere, other enthusiasts are locked in a series of cage-like seats which balance them and keep them upside down at a certain height above the crowd. In a third kind of machine, the sudden release of a giant spring catapults a car, which slowly returns to take up its position in front of the mechanism that will catapult it once again. Everything is calculated to incite visceral sensations of terror and of psychological panic: speed, fall, shocks, accelerated gyration combined with alternating climbs and descents. A final invention makes use of centrifugal force. This force is applied to the wall of a gigantic cylinder of unsupported bodies, immobilized in all kinds of postures, paralyzed, while the floor slips away and descends a few inches. The bodies remain "stuck together like flies," as the establishment's publicity reads.

These machines would obviously have exceeded their purpose if it were merely a question of exacerbating the organs of the middle ear upon which one's sense of balance rests. But the entire body is subjected to the kind of treatment that anyone would fear if he didn't see others falling all over each other in similar fashion. Indeed, it is worth our while to observe people as they leave these machines. They are pale, they stagger, they are on the verge of nausea. They have been shrieking with fear, they have been breathless, and they have had the terrible sensation that all their insides, their very vitals, were afraid, were curling up in an attempt to escape from some horrible attack. Yet, even before they have calmed down, most of them rush off to another ticket-window to purchase the right to suffer once again the same torture from which they expect enjoyment.

I say enjoyment because I hesitate to call such rapture inversion; it is far more akin to a spasm than to a pastime. Thus pleasure and the quest for vertigo exist when the latter is the object of *play*, when, in other words, it occurs under precise and fixed circumstances, isolated from the rest of reality, and when one is free either to accept or refuse it.

It seems legitimate, therefore, to inscribe the term *ilinx* next to *agôn*, *alea*, and *mimicry*, in order to complete the picture of the motives of play. The penchant for vertigo must be added to those that are expressed, first, by an ambition to succeed solely through the meritorious agency of fair competition; second, by a resignation of the will in exchange for an anxious and passive awaiting of the decree of fate; and third, by the illusion of being cloaked in another's personality. In *agôn*, the player relies only on himself

table 1

	AGÔN (COMPETITION)		ALEA (CHANCE)	MIMICRY (PRETENSE)	ILINX (VERTIGO)
PAIDIA	races combats etc.	} not regulated	*comptines* heads or tails	childish imi- tation masks	children's swings merry-go-round
noise agitation	athletics			costumes	teeter-totter waltz

laughter
dance
hoop
solitare
games of
    patience
crossword
    puzzles
	boxing
	fencing
	football
	checkers
	chess
			betting
			routlette
			
			lotteries
			    compounded
			    or parlayed
				theatre	outdoor sports
					skiing
					mountain-
					    climbing

↓ LUDUS					

Note: In each vertical column, the games are classified very approximately in such order that the *paidia* element constantly decreases, while the *ludus* element constantly increases.

and he bends all his efforts to do his best; in *alea*, he relies on everything except himself and he surrenders to forces that elude him; in *mimicry* he imagines that he is other than he really is and invents a fictitious universe; *ilinx*, the fourth fundamental tendency, is an answer to one's need to feel the body's stability and equilibrium momentarily destroyed, to escape the tyranny of perception, and to overcome awareness.

The variety and fertility of the games that tend to satisfy these cardinal temptations attest to their importance and to their permanence. It is certainly not rash to suggest that psychology, along with sociology, will derive useful additions and instructive lessons from a study of games.

the nature of sport:
a definitional effort

JOHN W. LOY, JR.

Sport is a highly ambiguous term having different meanings for various people. Its ambiguity is attested to by the range of topics treated in the sport sections of daily newspapers. Here, one can find accounts of various sport competitions; advertisements for the latest sport fashions, advice on how to improve one's skills in certain games, and essays on the state of given organized sports, including discussions of such matters as recruitment, financial success, and scandal. The broad, yet loose encompass of sport reflected in the mass media suggests that sport can and perhaps should be dealt with on different planes of discourse if a better understanding of its nature is to be acquired. As a step in this direction we discuss sport as a *game occurrence*, as an *institutionalized game*, as a *social institution* and as a *social situation* or social system.

I. Sport As a Game Occurrence

Perhaps most often when we think of the meaning of sport we think of sports. In our perspective sports are considered as a specialized type of game. That is, *a sport* as one of the many "sports" is viewed as an actual game occurrence or event. Thus in succeeding paragraphs we briefly outline what we consider to be the basic characteristics of games in general. In describing these characteristics we continually make reference to sports in particular as a special type of game. A *game* we define as any form of playful competition whose outcome is determined by physical skill, strategy or chance employed singly or in combination.[1]

A. PLAYFUL

By "playful competition" we mean that any given contest has one or more elements of play. We purposely have not considered game as a subclass of play,[2] for if we had done so sport would logically become a subset of play and thus preclude the subsumption of professional forms of sport under our

---

[1] This definition is largely based on the work of Caillois (1961) and Roberts and others (1959). Other definitions and classifications of games having social import are given in Berne (1964) and Piaget (1951).

[2] As have done Huizinga (1955), Stone (1955) and Caillois (1961).

• From *Quest*, Monograph X (May, 1968), pp. 1–15. © 1968 Quest Board (The National Association for Physical Education of College Women, and The National College Physical Education Association for Men), College Park, Maryland.

definition of the term. However, we wish to recognize that one or more aspects of play constitute basic components of games and that even the most highly organized forms of sport are not completely devoid of play characteristics.

The Dutch historian, Johan Huizinga, has probably made the most thorough effort to delineate the fundamental qualities of play. He defines play as follows:

> Summing up the formal characteristics of play we might call it a free activity standing quite consciously outside "ordinary" life as being "not serious," but at the same time absorbing the player intensely and utterly. It is an activity connected with no material interest, and no profit can be gained by it. It proceeds within its own proper boundaries of time and space according to fixed rules and in an orderly manner. It promotes the formation of social groupings which tend to surround themselves with secrecy and to stress their difference from the common world by disguise or other means (Huizinga, 1955, p. 13).

Caillois has subjected Huizinga's definition to critical analysis (Caillois, 1961, pp. 3–10) and has redefined play as an activity which is free, separate, uncertain, unproductive, governed by rules and make-believe (Caillois, 1961, pp. 9–10). We shall briefly discuss these qualities ascribed to play by Huizinga and Caillois and suggest how they relate to games in general and sports in particular.

1. FREE. By free is meant that play is a voluntary activity. That is, no one is ever strictly forced to play, playing is done in one's free time, and playing can be initiated and terminated at will. This characteristic of play is no doubt common to many games, including some forms of amateur sport. It is not, however, a distinguishing feature of all games, especially those classified as professional sport.

2. SEPARATE. By separate Huizinga and Caillois mean that play is spatially and temporally limited. This feature of play is certainly relevant to sports. For many, if not most, forms of sport are conducted in spatially circumscribed environments; examples being the bullring, football stadium, golf course, race track and swimming pool. And with few exceptions every form of sport has rules which precisely determine the duration of a given contest.

3. UNCERTAIN. The course or end result of play cannot be determined beforehand. Similarly a chief characteristic of all games is that they are marked by an uncertain outcome. Perhaps it is this factor more than any other which lends excitement and tension to any contest. Strikingly uneven competition is routine for the contestants and boring for the spectators; hence, efforts to insure a semblance of equality between opposing sides are a notable feature of sport. These efforts typically focus on the matters of size, skill and experience. Examples of attempts to establish equality based on size are the formation of athletic leagues and conferences composed of social organizations of similar size, and the designation of weight classes for boxers and wrestlers. Illustrations of efforts to insure equality among contestants on the basis of

skill and experience are the establishment of handicaps for bowlers and golfers; the designation of various levels of competition within a given organization as evidenced by freshmen, junior varsity and varsity teams in scholastic athletics; and the drafting of players from established teams when adding a new team to a league as done in professional football and basketball.

4. UNPRODUCTIVE. Playing does not in itself result in the creation of new material goods. It is true that in certain games such as poker there may occur an exchange of money or property among players. And it is a truism that in professional sports victory may result in substantial increases of wealth for given individuals. But the case can be made, nevertheless, that a game *per se* is nonutilitarian in nature.[3] For what is produced during any sport competition is a *game*; and the production of the game is generally carried out in a prescribed setting and conducted according to specific rules.

5. GOVERNED BY RULES. All types of games have agree-upon rules, be they formal or informal. It is suggested that sports can be distinguished from games in general by the fact that they usually have a greater variety of norms and a larger absolute number of formal norms (i.e., written prescribed and proscribed norms).[4] Similarly, there is a larger number and more stringent sanctions in sports than games in general. For example, the basketball player must leave the game after he has committed a fixed number of fouls, the hockey player must spend a certain amount of time in the penalty box after committing a foul, and a football player may be asked to leave the game if he shows unsportsmanlike conduct.

With respect to the normative order of games and sports one explicit feature is that they usually have definite criteria for determining the winner. Although it is true that some end in a tie, most contests do not permit such an ambivalent termination by providing a means of breaking a deadlock and ascertaining the "final" victor. The variety of means of determining the winner in sportive endeavors are too numerous to enumerate. But it is relevant to observe that in many sport competitions where "stakes are high" a series of contests are held between opponents in an effort to rule out the element of chance and decide the winner on the basis of merit. A team may be called "lucky" if it beats an opponent once by a narrow margin, but if it does so repeatedly then the appellations of "better" or "superior" are generally applied.

6. MAKE-BELIEVE. By the term make-believe Huizinga and Caillois wish to signify that play stands outside "ordinary" or "real" life and is distinguished by an "only pretending quality." While some would deny this characteristic of play as being applicable to sport, it is interesting to note that Veblen at the turn of the century stated:

    [3] *Cf.* Goffman's discussion of "rules of irrelevance" as applied to games and social encounters in general (1961, pp. 19–26).
    [4] E.g., compare the rules given for games in any edition of Hoyle's *Book of Games* with the NCAA rule books for various collegiate sports.

Sports share this characteristic of make-believe with the games and exploits to which children, especially boys, are habitually inclined. Make-believe does not enter in the same proportion into all sports, but it is present in a very appreciable degree in all. (Veblen, 1934, p. 256)

Huizinga observes that the ". . . 'only pretending' quality of play betrays a consciousness of the inferiority of play compared with 'seriousness' . . ." (1955, p. 8). We note here that occasionally one reads of a retiring professional athlete who remarks that "he is giving up the game to take a real job," [5] and that several writers have commented on the essential shallowness of sport.[6] Roger Kahn, for example, has written that:

The most fascinating and least reported aspect of American sports is the silent and enduring search for a rationale. Stacked against the atomic bomb or even against a patrol in Algeria, the most exciting rally in history may not seem very important, and for the serious and semi-serious people who make their living through sports, triviality is a nagging, damnable thing. Their drive for self-justification has contributed much to the development of sports. (Kahn, 1957, p. 10)

On the other hand, Huizinga is careful to point out that ". . . the consciousness of play being 'only pretend' does not by any means prevent it from proceeding with the utmost seriousness . . ." (Huizinga, 1955, p. 8). As examples, need we mention the seriousness with which duffers treat their game of golf, the seriousness which fans accord discussions of their home team, or the seriousness that national governments give to Olympic Games and university alumni to collegiate football? [7, 8]

Accepting the fact that the make-believe quality of play has some relevance for sport, it nevertheless remains difficult to empirically ground the "not ordinary or real life" characteristic of play. However, the "outside of real life" dimension of a game is perhaps best seen in its "as-if" quality, its artificial obstacles and in its potential resources for actualization or production.

(a) In a game the contestants act as if all are equal and numerous aspects of "external reality" such as race, education, occupation and financial status are excluded as relevant attributes for the duration of a given contest.[9]

[5] There is, of course, the amateur who gives up the "game" to become a professional.

[6] For an early discussion of the problem of legitimation in sport, see Veblen, 1934, pp. 268–270.

[7] An excellent philosophical account of play and seriousness is given by Kurt Riezler (1941, pp. 505–517).

[8] A sociological treatment of how an individual engaged in an activity can become "caught up" in it is given by Goffman in his analysis of the concept of "spontaneous involvement" (1961, pp. 37–45).

[9] For a discussion of how certain aspects of "reality" are excluded from a game situation see Goffman's treatment of "rules of irrelevance." Contrariwise see his treatment of "rules of transformation" for a discussion of how certain aspects of "reality" are permitted to enter a game situation (1961, pp. 29–34).

(b) The obstacles individuals encounter in their daily work-a-day lives are not usually predetermined by them and are "real" in the sense that they must be adequately coped with if certain inherent and socially conditioned needs are to be met; whereas, in games obstacles are artificially created to be overcome. Although these predetermined obstacles set up to be conquered can sometimes attain "life and death" significance as in a difficult Alpine climb they are not usually essentially related to an individual's daily toil for existence.[10]

(c) Similarly, it is observed that in many "real" life situations the structures and processes needed to cope with a given obstacle are often not at hand; whereas, in a play or game situation all of the structures and processes necessary to deal with any deliberately created obstacle and to realize any possible alternative in course of action are potentially available.[11]

In sum, then, games are playful in nature in that they typically have one or more elements of play: freedom, separateness, uncertainty, unproductiveness, order, and make-believe. In addition to having elements of play, games have components of competition.

B. COMPETITION

Competition is defined as a struggle for supremacy between two or more opposing sides. We interpret the phrase "between two or more opposing sides" rather broadly to encompass the competitive relationships between man and other objects of nature both animate and inanimate. Thus competitive relationships include:

1. competition between one individual and another, e.g., a boxing match or 100-yard dash;
2. competition between one team and another, e.g., a hockey game or yacht race;
3. competition between an individual or team and an animate object of nature, e.g., a bullfight or deer hunting party;
4. competition between an individual or team and an inanimate object of nature, e.g., a canoeist running a set of rapids or a mountain climbing expedition; and finally,
5. competition between an individual or team and an "ideal" standard, e.g., an individual attempting to establish a world land speed record on the Bonneville salt flats or a basketball team trying to set an all-time scoring record. Competition against an "ideal" standard might also be conceptualized as man against time or space, or as man against himself.[12]

[10] Professional sports provide an exception, of course, especially such a sport as professional bullfighting.

[11] Our use of the term "structures and processes" at this point is similar to Goffman's concept of "realized resources" (1961, pp. 16–19).

[12] Other possible categories of competition are, of course, animals against animals as seen in a horse race or animals against an artificial animal as seen in dog racing. As noted by Weiss: "When animals or machines race, the speed offers indirect testimony to men's excellence as trainers, coaches, riders, drivers and the like—and thus primarily to an excellence in human leadership, judgment, strategy, and tactics" (1967, p. 22).

The preceding classification has been set forth to illustrate what we understand by the phrase "two or more opposing sides" and is not intended to be a classification of competition *per se*. Although the scheme may have some relevance for such a purpose, its value is limited by the fact that its categories are neither mutually exclusive or inclusive. For instance, an athlete competing in a cross-country race may be competitively involved in all of the following ways: as an individual against another individual; as a team member against members of an opposing team; and as an individual or team member against an "ideal" standard (e.g., an attempt to set an individual and/or team record for the course).[13]

C. PHYSICAL SKILL, STRATEGY AND CHANCE

Roberts and Sutton-Smith suggest that the various games of the world can be classified

> . . . on the basis of outcome attributes: (1) games of *physical skill*, in which the outcome is determined by the players' motor activities; (2) games of *strategy*, in which the outcome is determined by rational choices among possible courses of action; and (3) games of *chance*, in which the outcome is determined by guesses or by some uncontrolled artifact such as a die or wheel. (Roberts and Sutton-Smith, 1962, p. 166)

Examples of relatively pure forms of competitive activities in each of these categories are weight lifting contests, chess matches and crap games, respectively. Many, if not most, games are, however, of a mixed nature. Card and board games, for instance, generally illustrate a combination of strategy and physical skill. Although chance is also associated with sport, its role in determining the outcome of a contest is generally held to a minimum in order that the winning side can attribute its victory to merit rather than to a fluke of nature. Rather interestingly, it appears that a major role of chance in sport is to insure equality. For example, the official's flip of a coin prior to the start of a football game randomly determines what team will receive the kickoff and from what respective side of the field, and similarly, the drawing of numbers by competitors in track and swimming is an attempt to assure them equal opportunity of being assigned a given lane.

D. PHYSICAL PROWESS

Having discussed the characteristics which sports share in common with games in general, let us turn to an account of the major attribute which distinguishes sports in particular from games in general. We observe that sports can be distinguished from games by the fact that they demand the demonstration of physical prowess. By the phrase "the demonstration of physical prowess" we mean the employment of *developed* physical skills and abilities within the context of gross physical activity to conquer an opposing

---

[13] The interested reader can find examples of sport classifications in: Schiffer (1965), McIntosh (1963) and Sapora & Mitchell (1961).

object of nature. Although many games require a minimum of physical skill they do not usually demand the degree of physical skill required by sports. The idea of "developed physical skills" implies much practice and learning and suggests the attainment of a high level of proficiency in one or more general physical abilities relevant to sport competition such as strength, speed, endurance, or accuracy.

Although the concept of physical prowess permit sports to be generally differentiated from games, numerous borderline areas exist. For example, can a dart game among friends, a horseshoe contest between husband and wife, or a fishing contest between father and son be considered sport? One way to arrive at an answer to these questions is to define *a sport* as any highly organized game requiring physical prowess. Thus a dart game with friends, a horseshoe contest between spouses or a fishing contest between a father and son would not be considered sport; but formally sponsored dart, horseshoe or fishing tournaments would be legitimately labeled sport. An alternative approach to answering the aforementioned questions, however, is to define *a sport* as an institutionalized game demanding the demonstration of physical prowess. If one accepts the latter approach, then he will arrive at a different set of answers to the above questions. For this approach views a game as an unique event and sport as an institutional pattern. As Weiss has rather nicely put it:

> A game is an occurrence; a sport is a pattern. The one is in the present, the other primarily past, but instantiated in the present. A sport defines the conditions to which the participants must submit if there is to be a game; a game gives rootage to a set of rules and thereby enables a sport to be exhibited (1967, p. 82).

II. Sport As an Institutionalized Game

To treat sport as an institutionalized game is to consider sport as an abstract entity. For example, the organization of a football team as described in a rule book can be discussed without reference to the members of any particular team; the relationships among team members can be characterized without reference to unique personalities or to particular times and places. In treating sport as an institutionalized game we conceive of it as distinctive, enduring patterns of culture and social structure combined into a single complex; the elements of which include values, norms, sanctions, knowledge and social positions (i.e., roles and statuses).[14] A firm grasp of the meaning of "institutionalization" is necessary for understanding the idea of sport as an institutional pattern, or blueprint if you will, guiding the organization and conduct of given games and sportive endeavors.

The formulation of a set of rules for a game or even their enactment on a particular occasion does not constitute *a sport* as we have conceptualized

[14] This definition is patterned after one given by Smelser, 1963, p. 28.

it here. The institutionalization of a game implies that it has a tradition of past exemplifications and definite guide lines for future realizations. Moreover, in a concrete game situation the form of a particular sport need not reflect all of the characteristics represented in its institutional pattern. The more organized a sport contest in a concrete setting, however, the more likely it will illustrate the institutionalized nature of a given sport. A professional baseball game, for example, is a better illustration of the institutionalized nature of baseball than a sandlot baseball game, but both games are based on the same institutional pattern and thus may both be considered forms of sport. In brief, a sport may be treated analytically in terms of its degree of institutionalization and dealt with empirically in terms of its degree of organization. The latter is an empirical instance of the former.

In order to more adequately illustrate the institutionalized nature of sport we contrast the organizational, technological, symbolic and educational spheres of sports with those of games. In doing so we consider both games and sports in their most formalized and organized state. We are aware that there are institutionalized games other than sports which possess characteristics similar to the ones we ascribe to sports, as for example chess and bridge, but we contend that such games are in the minority and in any case are excluded as sports because they do not demand the demonstration of physical prowess.

A. ORGANIZATIONAL SPHERE

For present purposes we rather arbitrarily discuss the organizational aspects of sports in terms of teams, sponsorship and government.

1. TEAMS. Competing sides for most games are usually selected rather spontaneously and typically disband following a given contest, whereas, in the case of sports, competing groups are generally selected with care and, once membership is established, maintain a stable social organization. Although individual persons may withdraw from such organizations after they are developed, their social positions are taken up by others and the group endures.[15]

Another differentiating feature is that as a rule sports show a greater degree of role differentiation than games. Although games often involve several contestants (e.g., poker), the contestants often perform identical activities and thus may be considered to have the same roles and statuses. However, in sports involving a similar number of participants (e.g., basketball) each individual or combinations of just a few individuals perform specialized activities within the group and may be said to possess different roles. Moreover, to the extent that such specialized and differentiated activities can be ranked in terms of some criteria, they also possess different statuses.

2. SPONSORSHIP. In addition to there being permanent social groups established for purposes of sport competition there is usually found in the

---

[15] Huizinga states that the existence of permanent teams is, in fact, the starting-point of modern sport (1955, p. 196).

sport realm social groups which act as sponsoring bodies for sport teams. These sponsoring bodies may be characterized as being direct or indirect. Direct sponsoring groups include municipalities who sponsor Little League Baseball Teams, universities who support collegiate teams, and business corporations who sponsor AAU teams, whereas indirect sponsoring groups include sport good manufacturers, booster clubs and sport magazines.

3. GOVERNMENT.   Although all types of games have at least a modicum of norms and sanctions associated with them, the various forms of sport are set apart from many games by the fact that they have a larger number, more formal and more institutionalized sets of these cultural elements. In games, rules are often passed down by oral tradition or spontaneously established for a given contest and forgotten afterward, or, even where codified, are simple and few in number. In the case of sports, however, rules are usually many in number and formally codified and typically enforced by a regulatory body. There are international organizations governing most sports, and in America there are relatively large social organizations governing both amateur and professional sports. For example, amateur sports in America are controlled by such groups as the NCAA, AAU, and NAIA, and the major professional sports have national commissioners with enforcing officials to police competition.

B. TECHNOLOGICAL SPHERE

In *a sport* technolgy denotes the material equipment, physical skills and body of knowledge which are necessary for the conduct of competition and potentially available for technical improvements in competition. Although all types of games require a minimum of knowledge and often a minimum of physical skill and material equipment, the various sports are set apart from many games by the fact that they typically require greater knowledge and involve higher levels of physical skill and necessitate more material equipment. The technological aspects of *a sport* may be dichotomized into those which are intrinsic and those which are extrinsic. Intrinsic technological aspects of *a sport* consists of those physical skills, knowledge and equipment which are required for the conduction of a given contest *per se*. For example, the intrinsic technology of football includes: (a) the equipment necessary for the game—field, ball, uniforms, etc.; (b) the repertoire of physical skills necessary for the game—running, passing, kicking, blocking and tackling abilities, etc.; and (c) the knowledge necessary for the game—rules, strategy, etc. Examples of extrinsic technological elements associated with football include: (a) physical equipment such as stadium, press facilities, dressing rooms, etc.; (b) physical skills such as possessed by coaches, cheer leaders and ground crews; and (c) knowledge such as possessed by coaches, team physicians and spectators.

C. SYMBOLIC SPHERE

The symbolic dimension of *a sport* includes elements of secrecy, display and ritual. Huizinga contends that play "promotes the formation of social groupings which tend to surround themselves with secrecy and to stress their difference from the common world by disguise of other means" (1955, p. 13). Caillois criticizes his contention and states to the contrary that ". . . play tends to remove the very nature of the mysterious." He further observes that ". . . when the secret, the mask or the costume fulfills a sacramental function one can be sure that not play, but an institution is involved" (1961, p. 4).

Somewhat ambivalently we agree with both writers. On the one hand, to the extent that Huizinga means by 'secrecy' the act of making distinctions between "play life" and "ordinary life" we accept his proposition that groups engaged in playful competition surround themselves with secrecy. On the other hand, to the extent that he means by "secrecy" something hidden from others we accept Caillois' edict that an institution and not play is involved.

1. The latter type of secrecy might well be called "sanctioned secrecy" in sports. For there is associated with many forms of sport competition rather clear norms regarding approved clandestine behavior. For example, football teams are permitted to set up enclosed practice fields, send out scouts to spy on opposing teams and exchange a limited number of game films revealing the strategies of future opponents. Other kinds of clandestine action such as slush funds established for coaches and gambling on games by players are not always looked upon with such favor.[16]

2. A thorough reading of Huizinga leads one to conclude that what he means by secrecy is best discussed in terms of display and ritual. He points out, for example, that "the 'differentness' and secrecy of play are most vividly expressed in 'dressing up';" and states that the higher forms of play are ". . . a contest *for* something or a representation *of* something"—adding that "representation means display" (1955, p. 13). The "dressing-up" element of play noted by Huizinga is certainly characteristic of most sports. Perhaps it is carried to its greatest height in bullfighting but it is not absent in some of the less overt forms of sport. Veblen writes:

> It is noticeable, for instance, that even very mild-mannered and matter-of-fact men who go out shooting are apt to carry an excess of arms and accoutrements in order to impress upon their own imagination the seriousness of their undertaking. These huntsmen are also prone to a histrionic, prancing gait and to an elaborate exaggeration of the motions, whether of stealth or of onslaught, involved in their deeds of exploits (1934, p. 256).

A more recent account of "dressing-up" and display in sports has been given by Stone (1955) who treats display as spectacle and as a counterforce to play. Stone asserts that the tension between the forces of play and display constitute an essential component of sport. The following quotation gives the essence of his account:

---

[16] Our discussion of "sanctioned secrecy" closely parallels Johnson's discussion of "official secrecy" in bureaucracies (1960, pp. 295, 296).

Play and dis-play are precariously balanced in sport, and, once that balance is upset, the whole character of sport in society may be affected. Furthermore, the spectacular element of sport, may, as in the case of American professional wrestling, destroy the game. The rules cease to apply, and the "cheat" and the "spoilsport" replace the players. . . . The point may be made in another way. The spectacle is predictable and certain; the game, unpredictable and uncertain. Thus spectacular dis-play may be reckoned from the outset of the performance. It is announced by the appearance of the performers—their physiques, costumes, and gestures. On the other hand, the spectacular play is solely a function of the uncertainty of the game (p. 98).

In a somewhat different manner another sociologist, Erving Goffman, has analyzed the factors of the uncertainty of a game and display. Concerning the basis of "fun in games" he states that ". . . mere uncertainty of outcome is not enough to engross the players" (1961, p. 68); and suggests that a successful game must combine "sanctioned display" with problematic outcome. By display Goffman means that ". . . games give the players an opportunity to exhibit attributes valued in the wider social world, such as dexterity, strength, knowledge, intelligence, courage, and self-control" (1961, p. 68). Thus, for Goffman, display represents spectacular play involving externally relevant attributes, while, for Stone, display signifies spectacular exhibition involving externally nonrelevant attributes with respect to the game situation.

3. Another concept related to display and spectacle and relevant to sports is that of ritual. According to Leach, "ritual denotes those aspects of prescribed formal behavior which have no direct technological consequences" (1964, p. 607). Ritual may be distinguished from spectacle by the fact that it generally has a greater element of drama and is less ostentatious and more serious in nature. "Ritual actions are 'symbolic' in that they assert something about the state of affairs, but they are not necessarily purposive, i.e., the performer of ritual does not necessarily seek to alter the state of affairs" (Leach, 1964). Empirically ritual can be distinguished from spectacle by the fact that those engaged in ritual express an attitude of solemnity toward it; an attitude which they do not direct toward spectacle.

Examples of rituals in sport are the shaking of hands between team captains prior to the start of a game, the shaking of hands between coaches after a game, the singing of the national anthem before the beginning of a game, and the singing of the school song at the conclusion of a game.[17]

D. EDUCATIONAL SPHERE

The educational sphere focuses on those activities related to the transmission of skills and knowledge to those who lack them. Many, if not most

[17] For an early sociological treatment of sport, spectacle, exhibition and drama see Sumner (1960, pp. 467–501). We note in passing that some writers consider the totality of sport as a ritual, see especially Fromm (1955, p. 132); and Beisser (1967, pp. 148–151 and pp. 214–225).

people learn to play the majority of socially preferred games in an informal manner, that is, they acquire the required skills and knowledges associated with a given game through casual instruction of friends or immediate associates. In the case of sports, however, skills and knowledge are often obtained by means of formal instruction. In short the educational sphere of sports is institutionalized, whereas in most games it is not. One reason for this situation is the fact that sports require highly developed physical skills which games often do not, and to achieve proficiency requires long hours of practice and qualified instruction, i.e., systematized training. Finally, it should be pointed out that associated with the instructional personnel of sport programs are a number of auxiliary personnel such as managers, physicians and trainers, a situation not commonly found in the case of games.

III. Sport As a Social Institution

Extending our notion of sport as an institutional pattern still further we note that in its broadest sense, the term sport supposes a social institution. Schneider writes that the term *institution:*

> . . . denotes an aspect of social life in which distinctive value-orientations and interests, centering upon large and important social concerns . . . generate or are accompanied by distinctive modes of social interaction. Its use emphasizes 'important' social phenomena; relationships of 'strategic structural significance' (1964, p. 338).

We argue that the magnitude of sport in the Western world justifies its consideration as a social institution. As Boyle succinctly states:

> Sport permeates any number of levels of contemporary society, and it touches upon and deeply influences such disparate elements as status, race relations, business life, automotive design, clothing styles, the concept of the hero, language, and ethical values. For better or worse it gives form and substance to much in American life (1963, pp. 3, 4).

When speaking of sport as a social institution we refer to the *sport order.* The sport order is composed of all social organizations in society which organize, facilitate, and regulate human action in sport situations. Hence, such organizations as sporting goods manufacturers, sport clubs, athletic teams, national governing bodies for amateur and professional sports, publishers of sport magazines, etc., are part of the sport order. For analytical purposes, four levels of social organization within the sport order may be distinguished; namely, the primary, technical, managerial and corporate levels.[18] Organizations at the primary level permit face-to-face relationships among all members and are characterized by the fact that administrative leadership is not formally delegated to one or more persons or positions. An example of a social orga-

---

[18] Our discussion of these four levels is similar to Caplow's treatment of small, medium, large and giant organizations (Caplow, 1964, pp. 26, 27).

nization associated with sport at the primary level is an informally organized sport team as evidenced in a sandlot baseball game.

Organizations at the technical level are too large to permit simultaneous face-to-face relationships among its members but small enough so that each member knows of every other member. Moreover, unlike organizations at the primary level, organizations at the technical level officially designate administrative leadership positions and allocate individuals to them. Most scholastic and collegiate athletic teams, for example, would be classified as technical organizations with coaches and athletic directors functioning as administrative leaders.

At the managerial level organizations are too large for each member to know every other member but small enough so that all members know one or more of the administrative leaders of the organization. Some of the larger professional ball clubs represent social organizations related to sport at the managerial level.

Organizations at the corporate level are characterized by being bureaucratic in nature with centralized authority, a hierarchy of personnel, protocol, and procedural emphases, and stress on rationalization of operations and impersonal relationships. A number of the major governing bodies of amateur and professional sport at the national and international level illustrate sport organizations of the corporate type.

In summary, the sport order is composed of the congeries of primary, technical, managerial, and corporate social organizations that arrange, facilitate, and regulate human action in sport situations. The value of the concept lies in its use in macro-analyses of the social significance of sport. We can make reference to the sport order in an historical and/or comparative perspective. For example, we can speak of the sport order of nineteenth-century America or contrast the sport order of Russia with that of England.

IV. Sport As a Social Situation

As was just noted, the sport order is composed of all social organizations in society which organize, facilitate and regulate human action in sport situations. Human "action consists of the structures and processes by which human beings form meaningful intentions and, more or less successfully, implement them in concrete situations" (Parsons, 1966, p. 5). A sport situation consists of any social context wherein individuals are involved with sport. And the term *situation* denotes ". . . the total set of objects, whether persons, collectivities, culture objects, or himself to which an actor responds" (Friedsam, 1964, p. 667). The set of objects related to a specific sport situation may be quite diverse, ranging from the elements of the social and physical environments of a football game to those associated with two sportniks [19] in a neighborhood bar arguing the pros and cons of the manager of their local baseball team.

Although there are many kinds of sport situations most if not all may

[19] The term sportnik refers to an avid fan or sport addict.

be conceptualized as social systems. A social system may be simply defined as ". . . a set of persons with an identifying characteristic plus a set of relationships established among these persons by interaction" (Caplow, 1964, p. 1). Thus the situations represented by two teams contesting within the confines of a football field, a father and son fishing from a boat, and a golf pro giving a lesson to a novice each constitute a social system.

Social systems of prime concern to the sport sociologist are those which directly or indirectly relate to a game occurrence. That is, a sport sociologist is often concerned with why man gets involved in sport and what effect his involvement has on other aspects of his social environment. Involvement in a social system related to a game occurrence can be analyzed in terms of degree and kind of involvement.

Degree of involvement can be assessed in terms of frequency, duration and intensity of involvement. The combination of frequency and duration of involvement may be taken as an index of an individual's "investment" in a sport situation, and intensity of involvement may be considered an index of an individual's "personal commitment" to a given sport situation.[20]

Kind of involvement can be assessed in terms of an individual's relationship to the "means of production" of a game. Those having direct or indirect access to the means of production are considered "actually involved" and are categorized as "producers," and those individuals lacking access to the means of production are considered "vicariously involved" and are categorized as "consumers." We have tentatively identified three categories of producers and three classes of consumers.

Producers may be characterized as being primary, secondary or tertiary with respect to the production of a game. (1) "Primary Producers" are the contestants who play the primary role in the production of a game, not unlike the role of actors in the production of a film or play. (2) "Secondary Producers" consist of those individuals, who while not actually competing in a sport contest, perform tasks which have direct technological consequences for the outcome of a game. Secondary producers include club owners, coaches, officials, trainers and the like. It may be possible to categorize secondary producers as entrepreneurs, managers and technicians. (3) "Tertiary Producers" consist of those persons who are actively involved in a sport situation but whose activities have no direct technological consequences for the outcome of a game. Examples of tertiary producers are cheerleaders, band members, and concession workers. Tertiary producers may be classified as service personnel.

Consumers like producers are designated as being primary, secondary, or tertiary. (1) "Primary Consumers" are those individuals who become vicariously involved in a sport through "live" attendance at a sport competition. Primary consumers may be thought of as "active spectators." (2) "Secondary Consumers" consist of those persons who vicariously involve themselves in a sport as a spectator via some form of the mass media such

---

[20] *Cf.* McCall and Simmons, 1966, pp. 171, 172.

as radio or television. Secondary consumers may be thought of as "passive spectators." (3) "Tertiary Consumers" are those individuals who become vicariously involved with sport other than as a spectator. Thus an individual who engages in conversation related to sport or a person who reads the sport's section of the newspaper would be classified as a tertiary consumer.

In concluding our discussion of the nature of sport we note that a special type of consumer is the *fan*. A fan is defined as an individual who has both a high personal investment in and a high personal commitment to a given sport.

REFERENCES

Berne, Eric, *Games People Play*, New York: Grove Press, 1964.

Beisser, Arnold R., *The Madness in Sports*, New York: Appleton-Century-Crofts, 1967.

Boyle, Robert H., *Sport—Mirror of American Life*, Boston: Little, Brown, 1963.

Caillois, Roger, *Man, Play and Games*, (translated by Meyer Barash) New York: Free Press, 1961.

Caplow, Theodore, *Principles of Organization*, New York: Harcourt, Brace & World, 1964.

Friedsom, H. J., "Social Situation," in Julius Gould and William L. Kolb, eds., *A Dictionary of the Social Sciences*, New York: Free Press, 1964.

Fromm, Eric, *The Sane Society*, New York: Fawcett, 1965.

Goffman, Erving, *Encounters*, Indianapolis: Bobbs-Merrill, 1961.

Huizinga, Johan, *Homo Ludens—A Study of the Play-Element in Culture*, Boston: Beacon Press, 1955.

Johnson, Harry M., *Sociology: A Systematic Introduction*, New York: Harcourt, Brace & Co., 1960.

Kahn, Roger, "Money, Muscles—and Myths," *Nation*, 185, 9–11 (July 6, 1957).

Leach, E. R., "Ritual," in Julius Gould and William L. Kolb (eds.), *A Dictionary of the Social Sciences*, New York: Free Press, 1964.

Lüschen, Günther, "The Interdependence of Sport and Culture," (a paper presented at the National Convention of the American Association for Health, Physical Education and Recreation, Las Vegas, 1967.

McCall, George J. and J. L. Simmons, *Identities and Interactions*, New York: Free Press, 1966.

McIntosh, Peter C., *Sport in Society*, London: C. A. Watts, 1963.

Parsons, Talcott, *Societies—Evolutionary and Comparative Perspectives*, Englewood Cliffs, N.J.: Prentice-Hall, 1966.

Piaget, Jean, *Play, Dreams and Imitation in Childhood* (translated by C. Gattegno and F. M. Hodgson), New York: W. W. Norton, 1951.

Riezler, Kurt, "Play and Seriousness," *The Journal of Philosophy*, 38, 505–517 (1941).

Roberts, John M. and others, "Games in Culture," *American Anthropologist* 61, 597–605 (1959)

Roberts, John M. and Brian Sutton-Smith, "Child Training and Game Involvement," *Ethnology*, 1, 166–185 (1962).

Sapora, Allen V. and Elmer D. Mitchell, *The Theory of Play and Recreation* (3rd ed.), New York: Ronald Press, 1961.

Schiffer, Donald, "Sports," *Colliers Encyclopedia* (1965) 21:449–460.

Schneider, Louis, "Institution," p. 338 in Julius Gould and William L. Kolb (eds.), *A Dictionary of the Social Sciences*, New York: Free Press, 1964.

Smelser, Neil J., *The Sociology of Economic Life*, Englewood Cliffs, New Jersey: Prentice-Hall, 1963.

Stone, Gregory P., "American Sports: Play and Display," *Chicago Review* 9, 83–100 (Fall 1955).

Sumner, William Graham, *Folkways*, New York: Mentor, 1960.

Torkildsen, George E., "Sport and Culture," M.S. Thesis, University of Wisconsin, 1967.

Veblen, Thorstein, *The Theory of the Leisure Class*, New York: The Modern Library, 1934.

Weiss, Paul, *Sport: A Philosophic Study*, unpublished manuscript, 1967.

a conceptual model for characterizing physical activity

GERALD S. KENYON

The study of gross motor behavior frequently requires dealing with such concepts as *play, game, physical activity, sport*, and other similar terms. Yet the meaning of any one of these is complex; a fact that quickly becomes apparent upon even the most superficial analysis. Is adult play the same as child play, or football the same as craps? Is everything that appears on the sports page sport? Although difficulties seldom arise in their informal use, serious inquiry demands explicit definitions of all essential terms.

REVIEW OF LITERATURE. Some writers have been satisfied with somewhat general definitions such as the meaning Huizinga (14) attaches to the concept *play*. Others have seen the utility in reducing a term to more fundamental components, such as the classifications of games by Caillois (4), Roberts and Sutton-Smith (25), and McIntosh (22).

When a conceptual domain is reduced to a logical system of subdomains

• From *The Research Quarterly*, 39, 1 (March, 1968), pp. 96–105. Copyright © 1968, by the American Association for Health, Physical Education, and Recreation, National Education Association. The writer is indebted to Jacqueline Damgaard, John W. Loy, Jr., Robert Pruzek, and Albert Solomon, for their assistance with one or more phases of the research; to Professors Owen Bergsrud, State University of Wisconsin, River Falls, and Phillis Roney, State University of Wisconsin, Oshkosh, and their colleagues for providing subjects; and to Professor Frances Z. Cumbee of the University of Wisconsin, for reading the manuscript. The research upon which this paper is based has been supported by National Institute of Mental Health Grants, MH 08214-01 and MH 11038-01, and University of Wisconsin Graduate School Research Committee Grant, 63-851.

the nature of the resulting components depends upon the use to which the classification is to be put. For example, the term *physical activity*, when used in an instructional setting, such as in physical education, is often reduced to such heuristic categories as "individual and dual activities," "team games," "rhythmics," "aquatics," and "dance." However, a structure based solely upon pedagogical considerations may be of limited use in another context. Wrestling and tennis are "dual" activities, but beyond this fact they may have little else in common.

PURPOSE.   It is the purpose of this paper to report efforts to construct a model characterizing physical activity as a sociopsychological phenomenon. The work was based upon the assumptions that physical activity can be reduced to more specific components; i.e., a set of all physical activities can be reduced to logical subsets, and that a meaningful basis for such a procedure is the instrumental value physical activity is perceived to have for the individual. That is, it was postulated that different classes of physical activities are perceived to provide different sources of satisfaction—a "perceived instrumentality" (27).

DEFINITIONS.   For this study *physical activity* denotes organized, (structured), nonutilitarian (in an occupational or maintenance sense), gross human movement, usually manifested in active games, sports, calisthenics, and dance. Although the term *model* [1] has come to have a variety of meanings, for the work described herein, it is a system of representation for a phenomenon (in this case, physical activity) which furnishes new ways of regarding or thinking about empirical objects and events (17: 78–80).

Procedure

The work reported herein was precipitated by a need for a more adequately defined "psychological object" about which one has positive or negative feelings (attitude). In developing a scale for assessing attitude toward physical activity, the question faced immediately was, "What does one mean by physical activity?" In an attempt to answer this question a combination of formal, empirical, and (admittedly) intuitive methods were employed.

RATIONALE

As the object was to determine whether the domain *physical activity* can be reduced to several independent or quasi-independent subdomains, the first

[1] Although not without difficulties, the term *model* was felt to be more suitable than *frame of reference, analogy,* or *paradigm*. It would be greatly premature to employ the term *theory*, even in a limited sense. Although a model is often regarded as a "separate system" the structure described in this paper was formulated in conjunction with the development of scales to measure attitude toward physical activity. The latter work is described in a companion paper written by the author, "Six scales for assessing attitude toward physical activity," *Research Quarterly*, 39:3 (October, 1968), pp. 566–574.

step was to formulate structural models, the components of which were to represent various hypothesized instrumental values of physical activity, manifest or latent. Such multidimensional models would be tested empirically by acquiring responses to verbal stimuli thought to represent each of the dimensions. If subdomains were independent of each other, responses should correlate within dimensions (internal consistency) but not between.

In all, three hypothetical models were postulated, the first two of which are described only briefly. The initial attempt consisted of six subdomains. These were: *physical health, mind-body dichotomy, cooperation-competition, mental health, social intercourse*, and *patriotism*. The basis for these was a combination of intuitive and traditional conceptions of the dimensions of physical activity. Statements thought to represent each of the subdomains were incorporated in an inventory which was administered to a randomly selected sample of 756 adults [2] and to a convenient group of approximately 100 college students. Intercorrelations and factor analysis of each set of data provided little evidence of a meaningful structure. Reflection upon this failure suggested several explanations for this result, including the use of too few stimuli, the possibility that subdomains were in themselves multidimensional, or the possibility that the deduced subdomains were not all on the same level of discourse.

Based in part upon an analysis of the results of the first attempt, and in part upon further reflection upon the instrumental value of physical activity, a second structure was formulated, also consisting of six subdomains: physical activity as a *social experience*, for *health and fitness*, as *the pursuit of vertigo*, as an *aesthetic experience*, as a *recreational experience*, and as a *competitive experience*. To test the integrity of this configuration, the universe of content was more systematically defined for each subdomain. Seventy-three Likert-type attitude statements were evaluated by judges, revised, incorporated into an inventory, and administered to 176 college men and women. A factor analysis of the item intercorrelation matrix yielded a solution that warranted the assumption of multidimensionality. For two of the subdomains—physical activity as a recreational experience and as a competitive experience—the results were still unsatisfactory, in that collecting the items thought to represent each did not account for any sizable amount of the common factor variance, again suggesting imprecision in the original definitions. The revision of the conceptual basis for these subdomains together with the apparent efficacy of the other four, was the basis of a third model (Figure 1) the nature and integrity of which will be described in some detail.

Although not all of equal logical rigor, the rationales underlying each of the six subdomains thought to represent the perceived instrumental value of physical activity were as follows:

  1. PHYSICAL ACTIVITY AS A SOCIAL EXPERIENCE. Claims that participa-

---

[2] As part of a survey of adult opinion based upon Project 120 of Wisconsin Survey Research Center. Population: all noninstitutionalized, nonmilitary adults over the age of 21 in the state of Wisconsin.

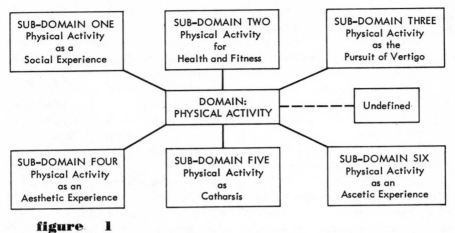

figure 1
Structure of Model for the Characterization of Physical Activity.

tion in physical activity can meet certain social needs of individuals have long emanated from professional sources (13, 24, 29). For this study it was postulated that lay opinion would be similar, that is, physical activity engaged in by groups of two or more is perceived by many as having some social value. To the extent that physical activity is play, Huizinga writes that such experiences provide opportunities for "sharing something important" (14:12). Thus physical activity as a social experience was characterized by those physical activities *whose primary purpose is to provide a medium for social intercourse, i.e., to meet new people and to perpetuate existing relationships.* Although such events as school or college dances and bowling immediately come to mind, almost any physical activity can serve such a purpose, either incidently or by design.[3]

2. PHYSICAL ACTIVITY FOR HEALTH AND FITNESS. That a sizable proportion of contemporary Western people, whether active themselves or not, believe that physical activity has the capacity to enhance personal health probably needs little documentation. The formation of the President's Council on Physical Fitness, the widely prevalent health studio, the writings of physical educators (6), and the statements of the medical profession (1), all serve to suggest that it is plausible to believe that many consider health through physical activity as both possible and desirable. Therefore, it was posited that some physical activity can be characterized primarily by its *contribution to the improvement of one's health and fitness.* Obviously, calisthenics and other conditioning exercises are for such a purpose, but conceivably, many activities could be similarly oriented.

[3] See companion paper for examples of verbal stimuli used to represent each subdomain.

3. PHYSICAL ACTIVITY AS THE PURSUIT OF VERTIGO. The suggestion that certain physical activities can provide a medium for pursuing vertigo comes from Caillois (4). Games based on the pursuit of vertigo

> . . . consist of an attempt to momentarily destroy the stability of perception and inflict a kind of voluptuous panic upon an otherwise lucid mind. In all cases, it is a question of surrendering to a kind of spasm, seizure, or shock which destroys reality with sovereign brusqueness. . . .
>
> Various physical activities . . . provoke these sensations, such as the tight rope, falling or being projected into space, rapid rotations, sliding, speeding, and acceleration of vertilinear movements separately or in combination with gyrating movement.
>
> . . . men surrender to the intoxication of many kinds of dance, from the common but insidious giddiness of the waltz to the many mad, tremendous [sic] and convulsive movements of dances. They derive the same kind of pleasure from the intoxication stimulated by high speed on skis, motor cycles, or in driving sport cars (4: 23–25).

McIntosh (22), has criticized Caillois' concept of games for the pursuit of vertigo pointing out that the sensation one receives on an amusement park device (classified by Caillois as vertiginous) is not the same as an activity over which the participant has some control.

> Caillois' category of vertigo is thus seen not to be fundamental but to subdivide within his classification of competition and chance depending on whether resourcefulness or resignation is the dominant factor (22: 126).

Despite such criticism, physical activity as the pursuit of vertigo has been retained as a category in the present model, since early empirical evidence showed it to have considerable promise. However, the chance element has been attenuated so that physical activity as the pursuit of vertigo is considered to be *those physical experiences providing, at some risk to the participant, an element of thrill through the medium of speed, acceleration, sudden change of direction, or exposure to dangerous situations, with the participant usually remaining in control.* In that he usually approaches vertigo without actually achieving it, the experience becomes the *pursuit* of vertigo. It is possible that the instrumental value here is latent. The participant may not recognize vertigo as the common element, but rather views sports such as skiing, diving from a high platform, heavy weather sailing, mountain climbing, sky diving, etc., as apparently unrelated.

4. PHYSICAL ACTIVITY AS AN AESTHETIC EXPERIENCE. The proposition is advanced here that many people believe that at least some forms of physical activity are generally pleasing to the eye, and have a capacity for satisfying aesthetic tastes (7, 18). Although some may consider skilled movement as beautiful in a broad perspective from ballet to Olympic gymnastics, others would insist on a much narrower range of physical activities—perhaps restricted to the creative and expressive movements primarily found in the

dance. The important point is that physical activity is often perceived of as having *aesthetic value for the individual—that is activities are conceived of as possessing beauty or certain artistic qualities.*

5. PHYSICAL ACTIVITY AS CATHARSIS. Upon analysis of the results of using "recreational activities" as a category of physical activity, it became apparent that the concept was too nebulous to be useful, and that it did not sufficiently characterize the function of a certain kind of activity for the individual. It seemed that both these difficulties might be overcome by narrowing the conception to *physical activity perceived as providing a release of tension precipitated by frustration through some vicarious means.* The notion that a reduction in tension is achieved by expressing hostility and aggression, either directly, by attacking the instigator of the frustration, or more commonly, through venting one's hostilities through some equivalent form of aggressive behavior, is the "catharsis hypothesis" (3). The use of catharsis in this sense, however, departs somewhat from the meaning the term has in the context of Greek drama. Nevertheless, writers from philosophers to psychiatrists, have, for some time, been employing *catharsis* in a more general sense, often with respect to physical activity and sport. Nietzsche wrote of ". . . simple outlets for getting rid of sudden congestion by a violent muscular exertion . . ." (23:291). Menninger (20:343) claimed that ". . . competitive games provide an unusually satisfactory social outlet for the instinctive aggressive drive. . . ." Wenkert (28:403) alluded to catharsis through sport spectatorship. Despite the frequently made claims for catharsis through substitute aggression, including the use of play and sport (8, 9, 15, 19), the findings of Berkowitz (3) cast doubt upon the existence of the phenomenon. Again, however, what is important is whether or not physical activity is *perceived* as having a cathartic function, that is, the belief that physical activity can provide a release from frustration and so called pent-up emotions created by pressures of modern living.

6. PHYSICAL ACTIVITY AS AN ASCETIC EXPERIENCE. An attempt to conceive of certain forms of physical activity as providing a "competitive" experience did not prove successful. Either the choice of stimuli was poor, or the concept *competition* is not a unitary phenomenon. The latter position is supported in part by McIntosh (22). In his analysis of Caillois' category "competition," he discusses four subcategories of competitive games, all of which provide a means for expressing the "desire for superiority." It was reasoned that if sport provides a medium for the expression of superiority as McIntosh suggests, then those who aspire to high levels of achievement, regardless of the sport, recognize the need to delay gratification and to be able to endure long and strenuous periods of training.[4] The associated punishment of the body (although seldom inflicting permanent damage) is seen by some to be somewhat akin to religious asceticism (19).

[4] Caillois himself alludes to this element of competition, but he does not see the need for a separate category (4:16).

. . . by detaching the senses [from objects of enjoyment] . . . and by rigorously practicing austerities [men] gain that state [even] in this [world]. —The Laws of Manu (26:183).

It would seem that contemporary sport provides an analogy. Championship performance today require athletes to undergo a kind of "ascetic" experience whereby physical activity for him involves long strenuous, and often painful training and stiff competition demanding a deferment of many gratifications.[5]

EVALUATING THE INTEGRITY OF THE STRUCTURE

If the conceptual structure proposed above is to have merit as a model serving to represent the sociopsychological charcteristics of physical activity, two conditions need to be met: (a) each subdomain must be univocal, i.e., internally consistent, and (b) the various subdomains must be relatively independent of one another. In essence, this approach represents the testing of the model for construct validity (5). To accomplish this objective, data were acquired from college freshmen (353 men, 215 women) consisting of responses to Likert-type attitude statements thought to be representative of each of the subdomains of the hypothesized model. Many of these stimuli were revisions of statements used to test previous forms of the model. Separate inventories for men and women were used, using sex-appropriate statements where necessary. Response styles were evaluated, and item analyses performed [6] providing criteria for selecting the best statements for subsequent analyses. The degree of internal consistency of each subdomain was determined using Hoyt's analysis of variance approach. Coefficients were maximized by rescaling the *a priori* weights of the best items using a reciprocal averages procedure (2). The structural integrity of the model was tested using an incomplete image analysis (10, 11) followed by an oblique rotation (12) of the first six factors.[7]

Results

INTERNAL CONSISTENCY

The degree of internal consistency for each of the six subdomains is given in Table 1. For each form maximized Hoyt *r*'s were determined both for the original 84 items and for the "best items" based upon item analysis. For both men and women, *r*'s for the "social experience" dimension were lowest, while those for "pursuit of vertigo" were highest.

[5] No claim is made that physical activity as an ascetic experience represents all elements of competition.

[6] Details are given in the companion paper.

[7] For exploratory purposes, a second approach was attempted. A multidimensional scaling analysis of the first four subdomains was carried out based upon dissimilarity data acquired from inventories developed especially for this purpose.

table 1

HOYT RELIABILITIES FOR EACH OF SIX SCALES BASED ON
SAMPLES OF 353 MEN AND 215 WOMEN

SCALE	ORIGINAL ITEMS (FORM C)		BEST ITEMS (FORM D)	
	N_I [a]	HOYT r	N_I	HOYT r
1. Social experience				
Men	14	0.70–0.72 [b]	10	0.70–0.72
Women	14	0.70–0.74	8	0.68–0.72
2. Health and fitness				
Men	14	0.74–0.77	10	0.79
Women	14	0.79–0.82	11	0.83
3. Pursuit and vertigo				
Men	14	0.88–0.89	10	0.88–0.89
Women	14	0.83–0.84	9	0.86
4. Aesthetic experience				
Men	14	0.80–0.82	10	0.82
Women	14	0.83–0.85	9	0.87
5. Catharsis				
Men	14	0.69–0.78	9	0.77
Women	14	0.72–0.80	9	0.79
6. Ascetic experience				
Men	14	0.82–0.82	10	0.81
Women	14	0.74–0.79	8	0.74–0.78

[a] Number of items used to represent each scale.

[b] The first coefficient is based upon *a priori* weights, the second, based upon weights rescaled to optimize reliability. Where rescaling did not increase *r*, only the original coefficient is given, i.e., based upon the *a priori* weights 1 through 7.

INDEPENDENCE OF SUBDOMAINS

Although item reliabilities are generally low [8] and thus precipitate a large error variance (21), an oblique rotation of the first six factors following an incomplete image analysis yielded clusters of items clearly corresponding to each of the six postulated subdomains. Table 2 presents for each factor the number of items with loadings of 0.30 or higher compared to the number of items predicted to represent each subdomain.[9] The greatest consistency was with the *pursuit of vertigo* scale. Although the six domains appeared to be relatively independent some of the factors were correlated, as seen in Table 3. The stronger relationships appeared to be among the *catharsis, health and fitness* and *ascetic* dimensions. However, no two factors shared more than 32

---

[8] For this study squared multiple correlations based upon loadings for as many as twenty factors seldom exceeded 0.50 for a given item. Thus common factor variances were expectedly small—between 40 and 50 percent, depending upon the number of factors considered.

[9] Pattern matrices are available upon request.

table 2

NUMBER OF ITEMS LOADING ON EACH FACTOR CONTRASTED WITH NUMBER PREDICTED TO REPRESENT EACH SUBDOMAIN (FORMS CM AND CW)

SUBDOMAIN	NUMBER OF ITEMS PREDICTED	NUMBER OF ITEMS WITH LOADINGS OF .30 OR BETTER ON FIRST SIX FACTORS					
		1	2	3	4	5	6
1. Social experience							
Men	10	3	0	0	1	0	6
Women	9	3	0	0	0	0	7
2. Health and fitness							
Men	10	3	0	0	1	6	0
Women	11	3	0	1	9	0	0
3. Pursuit of vertigo							
Men	10	0	10	0	1	0	0
Women	9	1	0	9	0	0	0
4. Aesthetic experience							
Men	10	0	0	9	0	0	0
Women	9	0	9	0	0	0	0
5. Catharsis							
Men	9	9	0	0	0	0	0
Women	9	4	0	0	0	5	1
6. Ascetic experience							
Men	10	0	0	0	10	0	0
Women	8	8	0	1	0	1	0

table 3

FACTOR INTERCORRELATIONS RESULTING FROM OBLIQUE ROTATION OF SIX INCOMPLETE IMAGE FACTORS—INDEPENDENT CLUSTER SOLUTION (FORMS CM AND CW)

MEN	1	2	3	4	5	6
1. Catharsis	1.00	0.18	0.14	0.45	0.52	0.18
2. Vertigo		1.00	0.07	0.17	0.15	0.16
3. Aesthetic			1.00	0.04	0.22	0.39
4. Ascetic				1.00	0.44	0.01
5. H and F					1.00	0.03
6. Social						1.00

WOMEN	1	2	3	4	5	6
1. Ascetic	1.00	0.20	0.45	0.57	0.57	0.44
2. Aesthetic		1.00	0.02	0.11	0.08	0.18
3. Vertigo			1.00	0.28	0.29	0.16
4. H and F				1.00	0.38	0.12
5. Catharsis					1.00	0.36
6. Social						1.00

percent of the variance—usually much less. The "social" and "aesthetic" dimensions showed the greatest independence.[10]

Discussion

Although some success was met in developing a model for characterizing physical activity as a sociopsychological phenomenon, the work described herein represents only a crude beginning. First, no claim is made that the entire domain of physical activity has been exhausted. The model presented here may represent only a few of the actual dimensions. Second, the test of a model lies in its application. Although attitude scales have been developed based upon the characterization of physical activity as described in this paper, it is not known whether the model would have other uses, such as the classification of interests. Thus considerable caution is in order.

Summary

An attempt was made to develop a multidimensional conceptual model for characterizing physical activity from the standpoint of its perceived instrumental value for individuals. The two necessary conditions for testing the worth of the hypothesized structure, namely, internal consistency and subdomain independence, were sufficiently met to warrant the conclusion that the conceptual model postulated herein has some validity. This does not imply that all the dimensions of physical activity have been accounted for, nor does it suggest that this is the only approach to characterizing physical activity.

REFERENCES

1. AMERICAN MEDICAL ASSOCIATION. Resolutions on health and fitness. Passed by house of delegates, June 1960.
2. BAKER, F. B. Univac Scientific Computer Program for Scaling of Psychological Inventories by the Method of Reciprocal Averages. *Behav. Sci.*, 5:268–69, 1960.
3. BERKOWITZ, L., *Aggression: a Social Psychological Analysis*, New York: McGraw-Hill, 1962.
4. CAILLOIS, R., *Man, Play, and Games*, New York: The Free Press of Glencoe, 1961.
5. CRONBACH, L., and MEEHL, P. E., Construct Validity in Psychological Tests, *Psychol. Bull.*, 52:281–302, 1955.
6. CURETON, T. K., *Physical Fitness and Dynamic Health*, New York: Dial Press, 1961.
7. H'DOUBLER, M., *Dance, A Creative Art Experience*, Madison: University of Wisconsin Press, 1962.

[10] When the multidimensional scaling approach was used a meaningful solution was obtained, although the level of "stress" was only "fair to good."

8. GARDNER, G. E., Recreation's Part in Mental Health, *Recreation*, 45:446–48, 1952.

9. GERSTL, J. E., Leisure, Taste, and Occupational Milieu, in E. O. SMIGEL (ed.), *Work and Leisure*, New Haven, Conn.: College and University Press, 1963.

10. GUTTMAN, L., Image Theory for the Structure of Quantitative Variates, *Psychometrika*, 18:277–96, 1953.

11. HARRIS, C. W., Some Rao-Guttman Relationships, *Psychometrika*, 27:247–63, 1962.

12. HARRIS, C. W., and KAISER, H. F., Oblique Factor Analytic Solution by Orthogonal Transformations, *Psychometrika*, 29:347–62, 1964.

13. HETHERINGTON, C. W., *School Program in Physical Education*, Yonkers on Hudson, New York: World Book Co., 1922.

14. HUIZINGA, J., *Homo Ludens*, Boston: Beacon Press, 1950.

15. HUSMAN, B. F., Aggression in Boxers and Wrestlers as Measured by Projective Techniques, *Res. Quart.*, 26:421–25, 1955.

16. KENYON, G. S., A Multidimensional Scaling Approach to Validating an *a priori* Model for Characterizing Values Held for Physical Activity. Paper presented at national convention, AAHPER, Dallas, Texas, March 20, 1965. Mimeographed.

17. LACHMAN, R., The Model in Theory Construction, in M. H. MARX (ed.), *Theories in Contemporary Psychology*, New York: Macmillan Co., 1963.

18. LANGER, S. K., *Philosophy in a New Key*, New York: Mentor, 1942.

19. MAHEU, R., Sport and Culture, *J. Hlth. Phys. Educ., Rec.*, 34:30–32, Oct. 1963.

20. MENNINGER, W. C., Recreation and Mental Health, *Recreation*, 42:340–46, 1948.

21. MESSICK, S., and Ross, J. (eds.), *Measurement in Personality and Cognition*, New York: Wiley, 1962.

22. McINTOSH, P. C., *Sport in Society*, London: Watts, 1963.

23. NIETZSCHE, F., *The Dawn of Day* (1881), in D. LEVY (ed.), *The Complete Works of Friedrich Nietzsche*, Edinburgh: Foulis, 1909–1913.

24. OBERTEUFFER, D., and ULRICH, C., *Physical Education*. New York: Harper and Row, 1962.

25. ROBERTS, J., and SUTTON-SMITH, B., Child Training and Game Involvement, *Ethnology*, 1:166–85, 1962.

26. RADHAKRISHNAN, S., and MOORE, C. A. (eds.), *A Source Book in Indian Philosophy*, Princeton: Princeton University Press, 1957.

27. ROSENBERG, M., and others, *Attitude Organization and Change*, New Haven: Yale University Press, 1960.

28. WENKERT, S., The Meaning of Sports for Contemporary Man. *J. Exist. Psychiat.*, 3:397–404, 1963.

29. WILLIAMS, J. F., *The Principles of Physical Education*, Philadelphia: Saunders,, 1964.

PART THREE

sport and social organization

OVERVIEW

The sociology of sport in its broadest sense is concerned with the description and explanation of the interrelationships between sport and various levels of society. More specifically, sport sociology is the study of primary units of social life, basic social institutions, and fundamental social processes influencing, and affected by human behavior in sport situations. The distinguishing feature of a *sociological* approach to the analysis of sport in contrast to other approaches long employed is its focus upon *social organization*. As succinctly stated by Blau and Scott,

"Social organization" refers to the ways in which human conduct becomes socially organized, that is, to the observed regularities in the behavior of people that are due to the social conditions in which they find themselves rather than to their physiological or psychological characteristics as individuals. The many social conditions that influence the conduct of people can be divided into two main types, which constitute the two basic aspects of social organizations: (1) the structure of social relations in a group or larger collectivity of people, and (2) the shared beliefs and orientations that unite the members of the collectivity and guide their conduct.[1]
These two dimensions of social organization—the network of social relations and the shared orientations—are often referred to as the social structure and culture respectively. Every society has a complex social structure and a complex culture, and every community within a society can be characterized by these two dimensions of social organization, and so can every group within a community (except that the specific term "culture" is reserved for the largest social systems).[2]

[1] Blau, Peter M. and W. Richard Scott, *Formal Organizations*, San Francisco: Chandler, 1962, p. 2.
[2] *Ibid.*, p. 4.

Accordingly, the focus on social organization underscores most of the sociological analyses of sport contained in the readings of Part Three. Moreover, the selected readings in combination illustrate well the relationships between: (1) sport and a variety of primary social units, including groups, communities, associations and total societies; (2) sport and basic social institutions such as the polity and economy; and (3) sport and fundamental social processes including stratification, socialization, social change and mass communication. Thus the articles in this Part are grouped into four categories: Sport in Ethnic Cultures; Sport in Comparative Perspective; Sport and Social Institutions; and Sport and Social Processes.

SPORT IN ETHNIC CULTURES

This section contains four articles showing the relationship between sport and the cultural dimension of social organization within macro-social systems. Frederickson in the introductory article makes a cogent case for the study of sports in the cultures of man, and illustrates the complexity of the role of sports in culture with special reference to spectator behavior and the ritual function of sport. Dunlap in the second article draws upon historical documents to portray the relationship between sport and several institutional sectors of Samoan society in the early nineteenth century. In addition, she discusses some effects of foreign cultural contact upon changes in the functions of sport in Samoan culture during the late nineteenth and early twentieth century. In the third article Roberts and Sutton-Smith show how games play a dual role in social life: providing for the expression of individual needs and providing cultural models of requisite socialization patterns for given cultures. The final article by Fox concerning the introduction of a competitive sport in a noncompetitive culture demonstrates how social conflicts are engendered when there are changes in the social structure without corresponding changes in the cultural structure of a social system.

SPORT IN COMPARATIVE PERSPECTIVE

In this section three readings are presented emphasizing the relationship between sport and the structural aspect of social organization within large social systems. Betts, in the first reading, accounts for the rise of sport in America during the latter half of the nineteenth century in terms of social factors associated with and arising from the Industrial Revolution. In the second article, Andersen and others draw upon three surveys in presenting the status of sport in Denmark. They give figures demonstrating the degree of both active and passive involvement in sport, describe the relation between sports and other interests, and discuss what motivates individuals to become involved in sport. Morton, in his article on "Soviet Sport in the 1960's," describes the scope of the Soviet sport program and discusses its relationship to the Communist Party and the Russian people.

SPORT AND SOCIAL INSTITUTIONS

This section consists of four articles stressing the relationship between sport and certain basic social institutions. The first, an outspoken article by Alex Natan, treats the relation between sport and politics at both the national and international level. Emphasis is placed on the problem of amateurism and the contrasting control of sport in communist and noncommunist countries. In the second reading Neale describes the unique relationship of professional sports to the economic sector of society. Robinson in the third article, reveals the relationship between sport and legal institutions of American society in examining the rather ambivalent position of sport with respect to antitrust laws. Finally, Jackson portrays the relationship between sport and educational institutions in his analysis of the commercial aspects of collegiate football.

SPORT AND SOCIAL PROCESSES

The final section of Part Three is composed of eight references, each pertaining to the relationship between sport and certain fundamental social processes. The first three articles by Sutton-Smith and associates, Lüschen, and Eggleston, deal with the association between sport involvement and social stratification in the United States, Germany, and England, respectively. Turning to the phenomenon of sport and socialization, Coleman shows how outstanding high school athletes and scholars act as success models in adolescent culture. Next are two papers treating the topic of sports and social change. In the first article Riesman and Denney describe the cultural diffusion of football from England to America and account for the radical modifications of the sport in our culture, whereas in the second reading, Loy discusses technological change in sport as a function of the differential adoption of innovations by sportsmen. Concluding Part Three are two articles illustrating the association between sport and mass communication. In one reading, Tannenbaum and Noah analyze sports page communication; in the other Denney discusses at length the ethos of the American spectator.

In brief, then, the readings selected for inclusion in Part Three cover a variety of sport forms related to a number of social products and processes in different parts of the world. Although many of the articles represent a low order of theoretical analysis and reflect little methodological sophistication, they nevertheless suggest fruitful frameworks for further inquiry and provide a number of hypotheses for empirical test.

It is suggested, for instance, that the substance of several of the readings can be encompassed in a functional analysis of sport in society using a Parsonian framework. According to Parsons every social system is confronted with the functional problems of: (1) adapting to its external environment, (2) attaining collective goals, (3) assuring continuity of shared beliefs and orientations, and recruitment, retention and training of group members, and (4) integrating and coordinating the many actions of its individual members. The patterned mechanisms for solving these problems at the societal level are typically assigned to selected subsystems of society. For example, the economy is chiefly concerned with the adaptive problem, the polity is related primarily to the goal attainment problem, educational institutions deal with the pattern maintenance problem, and various kinship and communal institutions cope with the integrative problem.[3] The above overview of readings makes it clear that sport is related to each of these societal subsystems. Thus it follows that the social significance of sport might be profitably analyzed in terms of its contribution to the functional problems of society, especially to the problem of pattern-maintenance and tension management.

[3] For light introductions into the work of Parsons the reader is referred to: Talcott Parsons, "General Theory in Sociology," Chapter 1, pp. 3–38, in Robert K. Merton *et al.* (eds.), *Sociology Today*, New York: Basic Books, 1959; and William C. Mitchell, *Sociological Analysis and Politics*, Englewood Cliffs, N.J.: Prentice-Hall, 1967.

sport in ethnic cultures

sports and the cultures of man

FLORENCE STUMPF FREDERICKSON

Summary

In this discussion emphasis is placed upon the importance of the study of sports in the cultures of man, for the following reasons: (1) to broaden the perspective of the common ethnocentric attitude, (2) to fill a gap in the kinds of research being undertaken, (3) to promote a deeper understanding of variations in cultural definitions of work and play, and (4) to seek an understanding of causes, effects and social controls in the sports scene.

Illustrations are given from the literature of cultural and social anthropology. For example, the ancient sport of wrestling is shown to have performed important social functions—such as serving as: (1) a legal and judicial mechanism for settling the boundaries of rice fields; (2) a part of initiation and puberty rites, (3) a means of selecting a mate, (4) a demonstration of prestige and power, and (5) a means of insuring a successful harvest.

In order to lend perspective to an examination of the meaning of sports in our own culture, spectator behavior in other cultures is considered; and the ritualistic function of sports is taken into account as a cultural phenomenon.

Although the literature dealing with the relationship of sports and culture is limited, there is a growing awareness of the importance of this subject; and it provides a rich field for research by properly qualified persons.

In all human societies, rituals, festivals, dances, music, pictorial art, sports and games, not only give pleasure but in addition provide outlets for

---

• From *Science, and Medicine of Exercise and Sports*, edited by Warren R. Johnson, pp. 633–646. © 1960 Harper & Bros., New York.

creativity and reinforce the group identity and solidarity. Such activities also tie closely into social, religious, economic, and other phases of life (28). The preceding statements have been amply documented by the research and writings of anthropologists, ethnologists, sociologists, historians, travelers, missionaries, and others. Yet only a small part of this wealth of material has been subjected to study, analysis, and synthesis by research workers.

Important as all the basic questions are which remain to be solved through the scientific work yet to be done in physiology, anatomy, kinesiology, psychology, and related fields, their importance in no way overshadows the value of the understandings to be sought in cultural research. In fact the multiplicity of public and practical problems into which culture enters as a consideration, and to which our past culture makes us heir, are obviously at least as important and as pressing as the problems that are touched by our biological physiques, natures and evolutionary rooting (30).

Whether or not the cultural approach properly belongs in the category of "science" is still being debated in many quarters. For example, one expert has expressed the opinion that the "science of man viewed naturally and culturally, individually and collectively, biogenetically and historically, is an incoherent conglomerate of mutually incompatible theories" (51), whereas another expert has argued that "behind the apparent lawlessness of social phenomena there is a regularity of configuration and tendency which is just as real as the regularity of physical processes in a mechanical world, though it is a regularity of infinitely less apparent rigidity and of another mode of apprehension on our part" (44). Nevertheless, the pursuit of knowledge which leads to greater understanding is undeniably worthwhile and rewarding, whether or not the particular methods or results qualify under a rigid definition of science.

A panorama of the ever changing, and yet recurringly familiar pattern of man's participation in sports presents a fascinating field for cultural research. There is no society known to man which does not have games of the sort in which individuals set up purely artificial obstacles and get satisfaction from overcoming them (32). We wish to differentiate at this point between sports as a cultural pattern [1] and the spontaneous activities and random interests of the young child at play—whether running about, jumping, building huts, or throwing objects. Both sorts of activities may originate from the same impulse to play. This is something about which there is little genuine understanding, in spite of the many explanations and interpretations which are offered (5).

To say that the impulse to play is an "instinct," a "need," or a "drive" explains very little. Man also has an impulse and a need to exercise his sexual

---

[1] One explanation of the scarcity of research literature in the cultural aspects of sport lies in the fact that the eyes of the profession have been so intently focused on the epiphenomenon of sports as a part of the school curriculum rather than sports as a cultural pattern in society as a whole.

powers and to eat. The bald statement tells nothing of the elaborate structure of courting, mating, marriage, procreation, divorce, and perversions that have eventuated from the sex "drive" in man. The stark statement that man must eat reveals nothing of the cultural patterns of food gathering, growing, distribution, and consumption that stem from this simple fact. The same thing is true of the play impulse and its failure to explain in itself the manifold forms of games, sports, and contests, and their attendant cultural paraphernalia.

Whether at any given time in history man plays for fun and self-expression, for prestige, power, and glory, for financial gain or political advantage, his motivations are to a large degree culturally determined. Whether or not sports hold a place of esteem as an expression of national pride and strength, as a respected instrumentality for propitiating the deities or upholding the honor of the tribe or the nation, or as an accepted means of educating the youth—these things are culturally determined. Whether participation brings respect and reward, or disdain and disagree, depends on the cultural climate in which it takes place.

The cultural role of sports in our present day society is little understood. Over the period of the major part of our existence as a nation, recreation for its own sake has not been a value widely held in American culture; the emphasis has always been on work. There were always play and recreations, of course, even in our early history. But often these were rationalized in work terms—the barn-raisings, the house-warmings, the corn-husking contests. Even the pleasures of hunting and fishing were rationalized as contributing to the food supply.[2]

Rather overwhelming evidence exists of a profound cultural change with regard to the role of sports and physical recreation in present day American culture. There are only a few localities remaining in which it is not possible or entirely acceptable for adult men and women to go forth with golf clubs, tennis rackets, fishing reels, skis, or what-have-you and have no other reason than the pursuit of pleasure (14).

This trend in our culture seems to be the result of more than a lessening of puritanical objections to pleasure for pleasure's sake. Rather it is, according to many students of our society, a shift in fundamental objectives and goals. From an era when character was largely formed for work and at work, we have shifted to an era where character is increasingly formed for leisure and during leisure (43). Research in communication and public opinion supplies further evidence of this changing cultural pattern. In the realm of popular biography there has been a marked shift from reading about the "idols of production" to the "idols of consumption" (33).

An understanding of the current cultural definitions of work and play in

[2] In this connection, see the discussion of Maslow's theory of motivation as applied to play and sports in the chapter, "Personality Dynamics in Relation to Exercise and Sports," by Cofer and Johnson.

American culture would seem to be a basic requirement for all those concerned with the administration of sports and physical education, as a prerequisite to policy-making, programming, and action.

Expansion in cultural research will mean that the profession and its students will no longer limit their study and investigations almost exclusively to the past or present achievements of their own country and Western European society, but bring an enlarged vision and a widened tolerance of societies modeled on plans entirely different from their own, motivated by ideals that are never without justification no matter how crude or extraordinary they may seem (6). A significant trend in current history is the acceleration of culture contact and culture change which is going on all over the globe. No nation plays a more central role in the process than the United States. One item in this total picture of culture change and culture contact is sports and the attendant complex of ideas concerned with physical fitness.

One of the prime values of science has always been acknowledged to be in its predictive function. Prediction in the matter of human behavior could not proceed along very successful lines so long as it was based on the naive assumption of a homogeneous "human nature." The assumption within this framework was that all human thinking proceeds from the same premises; that all human beings are motivated by the same needs and goals. As Murphy puts it (40), it was the repudiation of the concept of "human nature everywhere the same" which led to the riches of cultural anthropology. In the cultural framework the thought processes are understood to emerge from radically different premises, especially unconscious or unstated premises. Utilizing the concept of culture the research worker will attempt to look beneath the surface and bring the culturally determined premises into the light (31).

Sport is primarily a cultural product and must be understood as such, even though its incidence and formal development rest on considerations of a biological and psychological nature. Research is thus concerned with the problem of seeing sports and sports history in the larger framework of human behavior in the individual and in society.

Why Cultural Research?

The most cogent explanation of the need for a cultural study of sports lies in the fact that there is no relation of simple function between specific organic needs rooted in the body and mind of man, or in his environment, and his cultural activities. Although organic factors are always present and operative, another set of factors intervenes between the impulse and the act. These are the factors represented in the ideas, beliefs, and practices of the particular culture of which the individual is a part (30). Cultural research in sports is pointed toward a clearer understanding of the degree to which cultural living has blocked, modified, encouraged, or redirected the energies that are operative primarily at an animal level (40).

One of the chief attractions of this field of research lies in the fact that most of the work is yet to be done and most of the questions remain to be answered. To recognize and describe classes of phenomena is a legitimate aim of scientific inquiry. Yet as Staley has pointed out, this has not been done for sports within our own culture, let alone the cultures of others, past and present. Although the American people are currently participating in more than 250 sports, there is available in the literature historical accounts for something less than 50 of the lot, and as Staley has further pointed out, most of those are out-of-date, and/or unreliable, and/or sketchy in character (46).

Lacking classification, data are merely gathered facts. They must be organized according to some scheme or they are not susceptible of systematic treatment. Therefore schemes of classification vary in accordance with the problem that is being analyzed, and classification thus becomes an essential first step toward analysis (20).

At this point we take the liberty of paraphrasing the words of Herskovits (24) in his discussion of classification and process in the study of culture. Categories of classification of sport with which we are familiar (competitive, noncompetitive, individual, utilitarian, nonutilitarian, team, recreational, developmental) are valid in that they designate certain types of activity and the behaviors and outcomes ordinarily associated with them. However, if the problems we seek to understand and to solve in this aspect of culture concern the nature of the experience, the way in which its many manifestations are interrelated, its function in the total life of a people, then such categories are too simple. These are dynamic problems that go beyond mere classification, and here as in all phases of the study of culture, it is in dynamics, not descriptions, that the key to understanding is to be sought.

If we wish to understand the role of sports in the Fascist and Nazi cultures of pre-World War II it is not particularly important to know which sports were so vigorously promoted but why, how, and for what purpose.

Cultural research has shown that there are certain "common denominators," in all cultures, and has accented the ways in which people are alike rather than those ways in which people differ (39). It has also shown that it is in the leisure and play aspects of human culture that the hard crust of conservatism that divides one people from another is at its weakest (27). It has demonstrated that the ways of satisfying the needs of a people grow out of the culture of that people, and any culture functions best when it comes nearest to achieving a balance between the needs of a people and the resources and institutions existing to meet these needs. Such research has shed new light on many old problems (4): the adolescents' struggle for adjustment and acceptance (37), the culturally derived processes of competition and cooperation as they function in certain societies (36), and the all-powerful "success" drive in American culture with some of its resultant implications (35,21).

The Complexity of the Role of
Sports in Culture

Research has shown that sports always play a complex role in cultures, from the simplest to the most highly developed. Underlying their obvious identification as amusements and pleasurable tests of physical supremacy, are often unstated but implicit functions in the culture. As old as the history of sport itself is the story of the use of sport as an instrumentality for accomplishing something else.

Using as an example one of the most ancient of all sports, wrestling, it can be shown in its various historical roles as: (1) a legal and judicial mechanism for settling the boundaries of rice fields in the Philippines and villages in Pukapuka, (2) a part of initiation and puberty rites, (3) a means of selecting a mate, (4) a demonstration of the prestige and power of a tribal chief, and (5) as a means of insuring a successful harvest.

Trial by wrestling was used throughout Ifugao, preëminently to settle cases of disputed rice-field boundaries. Since a rice terrace maintained by a stone wall was a decided rarity in the Ifugao country of the Philippines, boundaries were subjected to the inevitable processes of nature. Erosion by rainfall in wet weather, caking and crumbling in dry weather, meant a boundary not well marked and disputes were sure to follow. These were settled by wrestling matches. The reasoning behind this practice was that the ancestral spirits of the contestants knew which party was in the right, just where the true boundary was, and would see to it that he who was right would win. In spite of this expressed faith in supernatural intervention, the Ifugao were sufficiently practical to insist that the wrestlers be approximately evenly matched. Owners of adjacent fields could do the actual wrestling, or might choose champions to represent them. Disputes between kinsmen resulted in matches usually friendly, but between those not related there was often a great deal of very unfriendly feeling.

On the day selected for the match the two parties met at the disputed boundary, and took up a position at opposite ends of the disputed land. Midway between the contestants stood a party of the kinsmen of each man, along with the family priest. After lengthy prayers by the priest, each of the adversaries was led by one of his own kinsmen to the spot where the first wrestling was to occur. This was very ceremoniously done, and suggested the heralding of the champions as in feudal days.

The contestants often worked themselves down half-thigh deep in the mud, water, and slime of the rice field. Finally, amid the shouts and loudly chanted prayers of the spectators the wrestling began. Each man attempted to push his opponent into the territory that the opponent was defending, and to down him there. If A threw B into B's field, say 10 feet from the line on which they were wrestling, A won 10 feet of the rice field at that point. Eventually there was a fall that capsized one or both of them in the black mud, and one point in the boundary was thus determined. At intervals of 15 to 20 feet along the disputed boundary a rematch was held. The new boundary was then established at a line running through every point at which there had been a fall (3).

On Pukapuka, an atoll in the Northern Cook Island Group, anthropologists learned how the boundaries of the villages had been settled more than 300 years before their arrival. A form of stick wrestling called *tutuki* was the means employed. In this technique a stick of *wetau* wood, four to six feet long was grasped by two men facing each other, with each trying to push his opponent backward. The position of the weapon dictated the advance or retreat of the boundary. Pairs of opponents stationed along a provisional boundary began the struggle at a given signal. It was permissible to insult, grimace at, or threaten one's opponent, but each contestant was honor bound to stop wrestling when his opponent relaxed, thus giving him time to recover his breath. Also permitted were attempts to edge the opponent's hands off the end of the stick, to twist the weapon from his hands, or to throw him off balance by wrenching or twisting the stick or by grasping him around the waist. The wrestling continued for seven days and when finally stopped the line drawn from one weapon to the next was accepted as the final boundary between the villages (7).

Another example of how skill in wrestling was interwoven in Pukapukan life was its use in the rite by which the adolescent boy assumed adult status. When the parents decided that their adolescent child had reached maturity, a formal report was made at the village meeting. The decision usually involved all members of a particular birth class, that is, all girls and boys in the village born in the same six-months' period were also declared to be mature. Proclamation was made in the villages of the names of the children graduating, and the rite was usually held during the first new moon of each six-months' period.

For the boys this meant a trip to the reserves to gather nuts on each of two days. After the boys had filled the big canoes with nuts, and been allowed to stuff themselves with birds, talo, crabs, and other food, they sailed in the evening back to their island. Upon approaching the beach the champion wrestler of the group stood in the bow of the foremost canoe and challenged the champion of the young men's group awaiting them on the beach. As the canoes beached, the challenger leaped to the shore and engaged his opponent before the assembled people. Often there were several bouts between the graduates and the young men's group. If a graduate champion defeated the champion of the young men's group, he gained great renown and the right to call himself champion of the island. This wrestling event on the evening of the second day ended the rite of adulthood and the boys were now considered young men (7).

Among the Dukawa of Nigeria it was the accepted custom for girls to select their husbands at wrestling matches. Girls in search of a husband attended the public exhibitions of athletic skill armed with a small bag of flour. The choice was signified by the girls sprinkling the flour on the head of her chosen one, whereupon the athlete's father immediately entered into negotiations with the parents of the girl (48).

Ancient Hawaiian chiefs customarily kept a stable of good wrestlers in their retinue. When a chief was expected, in whose train were any distinguished wrestlers, it was customary to send a challenge previous to his arrival to permit his host to prepare as best he could for the contests to follow. Ellis, writing more than 150 years ago, evokes a vivid picture:

> It is not easy to imagine the scenes that must often have been presented at one of their *taupitis*, or great wrestling matches, when not less than four or five thousand persons dressed in their best apparel, and exhibiting every variety of costume and brilliancy of colour, were under the influence of excitement. One party were drumming, dancing, and singing, in the pride of victory, and the menace of definance; while, to increase the din and confusion, the other party were equally vociferous in reciting the achievements of the vanquished, or predicting the shortness of his rival's triumph (18).

Stories of the ancient Japanese Empire are dotted with incidents related to wrestling. In the eighth century it is reported that the Emperor instituted wrestling as a part of the ceremonies of the autumn festival of the Five Grains. Since the year proved a fruitful one, the custom was continued. To avoid disputes a judge of wrestling matches was appointed, complete with proper badge of office (a fan upon which were written the words "Prince of Lions"). All throws not specified in the 48 fixed as fair were considered foul. Fair throws consisted of 12 lifts, 12 twists, 12 throws, and 12 throws over the back. The wrestling ring was constructed of 16 rice-bales in the shape of 1 large bale, supported by 4 pillars at the 4 points of the compass (15).

Spectator Behavior

A recent study of Kistler (29) is concerned with an attempt to explore certain factors of current behavior in sports participants and spectators. Cultural research reveals that the vagaries of spectator behavior probably began with the first sports contest ever staged and have continued in various forms since that time. It also suggests that an understanding of the behavior of spectators might more profitably be sought in the realm of custom, convention, and cultural pattern than in the realm of ethics and morality. Two examples from cultures of widely differing levels of development will serve to illustrate. Bryson (11) reports that in the conduct of dueling contests in 16th century Italy the spectators were such a problem that among the circumstances under which a duel might be postponed was included "if there was interference by disorderly spectators." It was customary before the combat for a herald to make a proclamation to the spectators warning them that the penalty for such offenses as being present with weapons, or entering the dueling field were punishable by confiscation of property and corporal punishment (such as the amputation of a hand!). Spectators were also warned to refrain from speaking loudly, coughing or spitting, or doing anything which would attract the attention of the duelists.

Among many Polynesians the prelude to a wrestling match was the concerted chanting by spectator partisans of one party of the most derisive and insulting remarks they could fashion to the spectator partisans of the opponent. Once the match was finished bedlam ensued: "The vanquished was scarcely stretched on the sand, when a shout of exultation burst from the victor's friends. Their drums struck up; the women rose, and danced in triumph over the fallen wrestler, and sung in defiance to the opposite party" (18).

The Ritual Function of Sports

The most cursory acquaintance with sports in the cultures of man will reveal their importance as ritual. Yet one must be wary of the blanket assigment of a strictly religious motif to all games and contests of all eras but our own. This is a circumstance in which perspective is improved by the intervening lapse of time. Although frequently held in conjunction with a religious ceremony and inseparably intertwined with religious ritual, it might be as erroneous as it undoubtedly would be to attribute some intensely nationalistic portent to the singing of the Star-Spangled Banner which currently precedes a college football game or a professional boxing match in the United States.

There seems to be a widespread failure (or refusal) to appreciate how much the element of ritual enters into our own publicly staged sports contests. The skeptics (and those not imbued with the cultural point of view) immediately decry this with the "facts"—that such contests are business enterprises, staged for profit, and far removed from any comparison with ancient or archaic times. Yet college sports have taken on a meaning far beyond the actual "game," a fact which those controlling (or attempting to control) such activities sometimes fail to realize.

Culturally—realistically—such sports contests often form a link between the old grad and his school. Sometimes this is the only link that is warm and alive to him. It provides a vicarious but highly prized contact for many noncollege men with *their* school. It being their school not by virtue of actual attendance but strictly by adoption, and valued sometimes as is the adopted child by the childless.

In these days of rising land values and growing pressures for space to expand the colleges and universities, why are the football stadiums not demolished to make room for laboratories of science and research, and for conventional classrooms? From the cultural point of view one answer might be that a stadium (so far—in our culture) is something infinitely more than a huge construction of wood, steel, and concrete. Each one has a personal history, and although each means many different things to different people, a stadium always stands as a symbol of man's love of a contest, spectacularly staged. They are monuments to the pride of individuals, institutions, and nations in the skill and prowess of their youth. They are an affirmation of a philosophy of life that insist man's life is better and fuller for having such moments of excitement and splendor, and that fitting homage should be paid the heroes who bring such color and emotion into the life of the average citizen.

Some Hints to the Interested Investigator

One of the first things the student must do is to learn to disregard the sweeping statements made by some well-intentioned writers on the history of sports and games. For example: "Primitive man likewise was too busy to feel any need of games. It was only when civilization brought periods of peace and security to certain nations that games were invented . . ." (10). Compare this statement with the description of William Ellis, that intrepid missionary to the Society and Sandwich Islands: "Freed, in a great degree, so far as the means of subsistence were concerned, from anxiety and labour, the islanders were greatly devoted to amusements: war, pagan worship, and pleasure, appear to have engaged their attention, and occupied the principal portion of their time. Their games were numerous and diversified, and were often affairs of national importance" (18). Or consider the New Zealand Maoris who worked hard during the periods of crop-planting and harvesting, but once the crops were gathered and stored gave themselves wholeheartedly to the "Arts of Pleasure and of Joyfulness."

The picture of nonliterate man which emerges from the research of the cultural anthropologist and the ethnologist is not of the overworked beast, automaton and infantile, driven eternally in a constant search for food and shelter. This is not true of the African continent, of the American Indian as he was before culture contact had so greatly modified his way of life, and it was certainly not true of the Polynesians, who had what is probably the highest standard of leisure the world has ever known (27).

A prime requisite of the student interested in cultural research is the capacity to achieve a high degree of objectivity in examining the sports of other cultures. If such data are to be judged against a value scale of present-day western civilization their contribution may eventuate in nothing more than amusement or astonishment at the "strangeness" that emerges and the enhancing of self-satisfaction with the way things are currently done in his own culture.

Conversely the studying of the role of sports in other cultures throws an interesting light on the role of sports in our own culture, and the discovery of unexpected similarities may prove a delight to the investigator. For example, the Maoris contrived water-wings for their children in teaching them how to swim. Taking two dried-out gourds and tying them together with a piece of flax, so that one could be fitted under each arm of the learner, and flaring out to their job of keeping the child buoyant, they have an extraordinary resemblance to modern inflated bits of rubber which we use for the same purpose (8).

Knowing how the peculiar and particular language of sports has infiltrated the English tongue, it is exciting to discover that this is also true of other languages. Disc-pitching was a favorite indoor game in Samoa. A community set of discs, owned by the young men of the village, were kept in a large coconut shell cup. We find a Samoan saying denoting *finality* is translated as "The discs are all in the container" (12). Few modern golfers take more pride in their favorite driver than the Fijian did in his favorite *tinqua*. This was a game played by throwing from the forefinger a reed of three or four feet long, armed with a six-inch oval point of heavy wood. While the reed shafts might be cut from the brush as needed, good players regarded their ironwood heads with great pride (49).

The Status Quo, with Promise for Improvement

Within the confines of professional publications in the United States the quantity of reported research in sports and physical education utilizing the cultural approach is not extensive. The pages of the *Research Quarterly* of the American Association for Health, Physical Education and Recreation reveal few studies that could be classified in this area. Stumpf and Cozens (47), and Dunlap (17), demonstrated in studies on the Maoris, the Fijians, and the Samoans that an understandable and fairly comprehensive picture may emerge when thorough investigation is applied to tracing the interrelationships of sports to other elements of the culture within the microscopic world of modern primitive societies. An attempt at utilization of the cultural approach is also to be found in one book published in 1953 (14) and another in 1956 (26).

If this were the total story it would seem a tale hardly worth the telling, but it is not. The growth of awareness of the importance of such investigation is manifest in many ways that have so far not produced much actual research, but which promise well for the future.

In 1951 the American Academy of Physical Education invited Margaret Mead to give the R. Tait Memorial Lecture, in which she discussed the changing role of physical education in our culture. The initial publication of the Academy contained an excellent section devoted to the implications of research in cultural anthropology for physical education (1). Some of the newer textbooks in the field are accenting the importance of this concept, (13) and others are at least acknowledging its existence.

The list of microcard publications in health, physical education, recreation, and allied areas contains a few titles which indicate that here and there the interest in such research is germinating and sometimes bearing fruit (20,2,34).

The untimely death of Frederick W. Cozens in 1954 interrupted a promising program of cultural research which had resulted in half a dozen master's theses and stimulated the interest of many students in research of this type (17,45,42,19,9,22).

The February, 1955, issue of *The Journal of Educational Sociology* contains several articles which not only utilize the cultural approach, but also illustrate the importance of the use of such an approach in interpreting the field of sports to students and scholars in another discipline (38,50).

A recent UNESCO publication, *The Place of Sport in Education* is indicative of an expanding interest. This comparative study was conceived with the idea of provoking discussion and giving rise to further studies (41). Two books are particularly noteworthy in this regard. One is written by the Dutch historian Huizinga, titled *Homo Ludens* (25), and is indispensable reading for any student interested in the role of sports in the cultures of man. Another, of much less ambitious scope, is presented in the study of the origins of ball games, *Ball, Bat and Bishop*, by Robert Henderson (23).

Culture, representing the widest context of human behavior, is as vital an area of study for physical educators and other students of sports as it is for psychologists, historians, linguists, philosophers, theologians, and anthropologists. We need an understanding of the processes and products of culture, and its relation to basic facts of human psychology and the organic processes of the human body. By what other means can we hope to understand the relationship of our specific activities to humanity and society as a whole?

There is perhaps no better way to bring this discussion to a close than with a quotation from a recent volume of the College Physical Education Association *Proceedings*: "As we look around us and see the deep roots and great influences which sports exert as an element of our culture, what do we know about causes, effects and social controls needed in the great American scene?" (16).

REFERENCES

1. American Academy of Physical Education, *Profess. Contr.*, 1951, 1, 51–72.
2. Ashton, D., An Ethnologic Approach to Regional Dance, unpublished doctoral dissertation, State Univ. of Iowa, 1951. Microcards.
3. Barton, R. F., Ifugao Law, *Univ. Calif. Publ. Am. Archaeol. & Ethnol.*, 1919, 15, 11–105.
4. Bateson, G., Experiments in Thinking about Observed Ethnological Material, *Phil. Sci.*, 1941, VIII, 53–68.
5. Beach, F. A., The Play of Animals, *Encyclopaedia Britannica*.
6. Beaglehole, E., New Zealand Anthropology Today, *J. Polynes. Soc.*, 1937, 6, 154–172.
7. Beaglehole, E., & Beaglehole, Pearl, Ethnology of Pukapuka, *Bernice P. Bishop Mus. Bull.*, No. 150, Honolulu: 1938.
8. Best, E., Games and Pastimes of the Maori, *Dominion Mus. Bull.*, No. 8, Wellington: 1925.

9. Bonnickson, J. M., A Study of Highly Organized Sports Programs for Boys, unpublished M.A. thesis, Univ. of Calif., 1954.
10. Brill, A. A., The Why of the Fan, *North Amer. Rev.*, 1929, 228, 427–434.
11. Bryson, F. R., *The Sixteenth-Century Italian Duel*, Chicago: Univ. of Chicago Press, 1938.
12. Buck, P., Samoan Material Culture, *Bishop Mus. Bull. No. 75*, Honolulu: 1930.
13. Cowell, C. C., *Scientific Foundations of Physical Education*, New York: Harper, 1953.
14. Cozens, F. W., and Stumpf, Florence, *Sports in American Life*, Chicago: Univ. of Chicago Press, 1953.
15. Culin, S., *Korean Games with Notes on Corresponding Games of China and Japan*, Philadelphia: Univ. of Pennsylvania, 1895.
16. Daniels, A. S., *Coll. Phys. Educ. Assoc. Proc.*, 1955, 28.
17. Dunlap, Helen Louise, Games, Sports, Dancing and Other Vigorous Recreational Activities and their Function in Samoan Culture, *Res. Quart.*, 1951, 22, 298–311.
18. Ellis, W., *Polynesian Researches, No. 1*, London: Fisher, Son, and Jackson, 1829.
19. Ervin, R. W., Views of Some American Catholic Leaders in Regard to Sports and Physical Recreation, unpublished M.A. thesis, Univ. of California, 1956.
20. Eyler, M. H., Origins of Some Modern Sports, unpublished doctoral dissertation, Univ. of Illinois, 1956, Microcards.
21. Gorer, G., *The American People*, New York: Norton, 1942.
22. Gregg, G. W., A study of certain factors influencing participation in sports, unpublished M.A. thesis, Univ. of California, 1950.
23. Henderson, R., *Ball, Bat and Bishop*, New York: Rockport Press, 1947.
24. Herskovits, M. J., *Man and His Works*, New York: Knopf, 1948, pp. 595–607.
25. Huizinga, J., *Homo Ludens: A Study of the Play-Element in Culture*, London: Routledge & Kegan Paul, 1949.
26. Jokl, E, *et al.*, *Sports in the Cultural Pattern of the World*, Helsinki: Institute of Occupational Health, 1956.
27. Keesing, F. M., *Education in Pacific Countries*, Shanghai: Kelly and Walsh, 1937.
28. Kessing, F. M., *The South Seas in the Modern World*, New York: John Day, 1941.
29. Kistler, Joy W., Attitudes Expressed about Behavior Demonstrated in Certain Specific Situations Occurring in Sports, Louisiana State Univ., 1956, unpublished.
30. Kroeber, A. L., *Anthropology*, New York: Harcourt, Brace, 1948, p. 841.
31. Linton, R. (ed.), *The Science of Man in the World Crisis*, New York: Columbia Univ. Press, 1945, p. 103.
32. Linton, R., in R. F. Spencer (ed.), *Method and Perspective in Anthropology*, Minneapolis: Univ. of Minnesota Press, 1954, p. 165.
33. Lowenthal, L., Biographies in popular magazines, in Lazarsfeld and Stanton (ed.), *Radio Research, 1942–43*, New York: Duell, Sloan & Pearce, 1944.
34. McCann, June W., A Study of Factors Affecting the Values of Coeducational Physical Education and Corecreational in the Public High Schools of Cali-

fornia, unpublished doctoral dissertation, Univ. of Southern California, 1954, Microcards.

35. Mead, Margaret, *Coming of Age in Samoa*, New York: Morrow, 1928.
36. Mead, Margaret, *Coöperation and Competition among Primitive Peoples*, New York: McGraw-Hill, 1937.
37. Mead, Margaret, *And Keep Your Powder Dry*, New York: Morrow, 1942.
38. Metheny, Eleanor, Relative Value in Athletics for Girls, *J. Educ. Sociol.*, 1955, **28**, 265–270.
39. Murdock, G. P., Common Denominators of Culture, in R. Linton (ed.), *Science of Man in the World Crisis*, New York: Columbia Univ. Press, 1945.
40. Murphy, G., *Personality, a Biosocial Approach to Origins and Structure*, New York: Harper, 1947.
41. *The Place of Sport in Education: A Comparative Study*, Educational Stud. and Doc., No. 21, Paris: UNESCO, 1956.
42. Riemcke, C. A., The Role of Spectator Sports in American Culture During the Nineteen-Twenties, unpublished M.A. thesis, Univ. of California, 1954.
43. Riesman, D., Glazer, N., and Denney, R., *The Lonely Crowd*, New Haven: Yale Univ. Press, 1950.
44. Sapir, E., The Status of Linguistics as a Science, *Language*, 1929, **5**, 207–214. (See also reprint in D. G. Mandelbaum (ed.), *Selected Writings of Edward Sapir in Language, Culture, and Personality*, Berkeley: Univ. of California Press, 1951, p. 166.)
45. Slusser, J. H., The Sports Page in American Life in the Nineteen-Twenties, unpublished M.A. thesis, Univ. of California, 1954.
46. Staley, S. C., Next Steps in College Physical Education, President's Address, in *Coll. Phys. Educ. Assoc. Proc.*, 1956.
47. Stumpf, Florence, and Cozens, F. W., Some aspects of the role of games, sports, and recreational activities in the culture of modern primitive peoples, *Res. Quart.*, 1947, **18**, 198–218; *Res. Quart.*, 1949, **20**, 2–20.
48. Temple, O., Notes on the Tribes, Provinces, Emirales and States of the Northern Provinces of Nigeria, cited by R. Briffault, *The Mothers*, New York: Macmillan Company, 1927, p. 97.
49. Thomson, B., *The Fijians, A Study of the Decay of Custom*, London: Heinemann, 1908.
50. Woody, T., School Athletics and Social Good, *J. Educ. Sociol.*, 1955, **28**, 243–248.
51. Znaniecki, F., *Cultural Sciences*. Urbana: Univ. of Illinois Press, 1952, p. 110.

games, sports, dancing, and other vigorous recreational activities and their function in Samoan culture

HELEN L. DUNLAP

The original interest in making this study came from reading an article entitled: "Hidden Possibilities for Research in Physical Education and Recreation (24)."

Purpose of the Study

The article brought out the fact that the literature in the field of physical education and recreation is primarily concerned with the use of this "educational tool" in the countries of our "Western civilization." In contrast to this, it pointed out that the writings of anthropologists, ethnologists, and others contain an abundance of information on the amusements and play life of all people, everywhere; and suggested that a diligent investigation of these materials would provide a better understanding of the inter-relationships of physical education and recreation with other major aspects of living and a fuller picture of the contributions which they have made in enriching the daily living of the diverse peoples of the world.

The culture element of games, sports, and dancing has been classified by an eminent anthropologist as one of the "common denominators" of all human cultures (16). The task of investigation and analysis of the particular role of this culture element in the total culture of any given people remains to be done.

It is hoped that this study will be a contribution to such an understanding. The purpose of the study is two-fold: (1) to determine the manner in which games, sports, dancing and other vigorous recreational activities entered into the total culture of the Samoan people of the early nineteenth century; and (2) to discover the changes which were brought about in Samoan vigorous recreational activities through culture contact.

Two factors were primarily influential in the selection of the Samoans for investigation. First, they were in a relatively primitive and "untouched" state at the time contacts were made with the white man; and secondly, the explorers, missionaries and others, who made some of the contacts left a wealth of written material as a result of their first-hand observations.

• From *The Research Quarterly* 22 (1951), pp. 298–311. Copyright © 1951 by the American Association for Health, Physical Education, and Recreation, National Education Association.

Since 1947, when the possibility for this type of historical research in physical education was pointed out, two parts of one such investigation have been published. The study which is in progress is entitled: "Some Aspects of the Role of Games, Sports, and Recreational Activities in the Culture of Modern Primitive Peoples (25)."

The purposes of the total investigation are:

(1) to show that sports, games, and recreational activities form a universal and fundamental element of human culture; and
(2) to illustrate how immensely more complex than is often supposed are the forces that produce the activities commonly described as recreational (25, p. 198).

Method of Procedure

As the data for this study were collected from the literature on Samoa, a critical review was made of this material. Answers were sought for the following questions: what games, sports, dances and other vigorous recreational activities were engaged in by these people when they were first discovered by European explorers; how did this phase of living fit into their total culture, i.e., how was it integrated with the other major aspects of living, such as religion, government and education; and what effect did the cultural changes, brought about as a result of the discovery of the islands, by foreign powers, have on these activities?

In order to obtain as complete a picture as possible of the Samoan vigorous recreational activities, the physical recreation patterns of the islanders were traced from the early nineteenth century to the 1930s. In addition, such major aspects of their early culture as their social, religious, economic, warfare and educational systems were carefully examined in order to form a basis for the understanding of the interrelationships existing between them and the phase of culture being investigated.

Geographical Setting—1930, and
Brief History of Early Samoa

The inhabitants of Samoa are members of the Polynesian Race. They live on 14 islands, with a total land area of some 1,700 square miles, located in the southwestern Pacific in the large ocean area of isolated island groups known as Polynesia.

The existence of these inhabited islands was not known to the so-called "Civilized World" until 1722 when they were briefly sighted by a Dutch explorer named Roggenween. After that event, several other exploring ships and whaling vessels made brief contacts with the islands. But, it was 1830 before anyone remained in Samoa long enough to gain an understanding of the Samoan way of life.

At that time, John Williams of the London Missionary Society established a Christian Mission there (28). That event provided for the settlement of several missionaries. It also provided an opening for the entrance of traders, planters and official representatives of foreign nations interested in the area.

Recreational Life Involving Vigorous Physical Activities— Early Nineteenth Century

In Samoa, during the early nineteenth century, a considerable amount of time was spent by individuals of all ages and ranks in a variety of games, sports and dances. These, they appeared to enjoy exceedingly (28). So much so, in fact, that one foreign observer was moved to report that:

Life has no engagement so important that the islander will not cancel it at once on the plea of sport (6, pp. 562, 563).

Many of their activities took place in the ocean and along the shore. There the natives spent hours enjoying swimming (2), diving (15), canoeing (2), sailing (21), surf-riding (5), turtle riding (1), sliding (5), and fishing (26).

The activities played on land ranged from simply organized games to highly organized sports. They included such things as hide and seek (2), pulling or tug of war (21), racing (26), juggling (5), tobogganing (5), spear parrying (26), boxing (21), wrestling (21), kicking matches (21), club fighting (19), dart throwing for distance (5), pigeon hunting (20), and dancing (21).

Participants in these physical recreational activities ranged from a few members of one village playing in an informal manner to the mustered forces of villages or districts competing in a formal manner for a championship in one or more events.

Their sports meetings always started with a great deal of ceremony. There was presentation of food and gifts, drinking of kava, and the delivery of speeches by all parties, in which each extolled the greatness of their opponents and their own humbleness (6).

At such gatherings the traditional rules for all activities were strictly adhered to, as a serious breach was likely to be considered an insult to be wiped out by war. Each activity always had prescribed judges and other officials who were responsible for seeing that it was properly conducted.

Victory was highly regarded and was everywhere recorded in legend and song. Defeat was a stain which the vanquished hoped to remove later.

The Inter-relationship of Sports, Games, Dancing, and Other Recreational Activities with the Major Aspects of Samoan Culture—Early Nineteenth Century

Although neolithic in material culture, the early Samoans had a highly organized social order. They were a very ceremonious people, with practically every phase of their life regulated by elaborate codes of behavior.

SOCIAL ORGANIZATION

> . . . social organization is the principal preoccupation in Samoa. . . . The Samoans regard the social structure, a hierarchy of titles carrying with them specific privileges, as of paramount importance (18, p. 481).[1]

This observation although made of the people of the 1920s was equally true of those living in 1830.

The Samoans spent a great deal of time visiting one another for religious, governmental, economical, ceremonial, and recreational purposes. At every one of their major meetings some vigorous physical activities were enjoyed.

Some meetings were especially planned to determine championships in certain games. In considering the benefits derived from participation in these activities one authority (5, pp. 573–74) reported the following:

> The social value of the community games was important. The smaller competitions in the same village brought the young people and adults together and gave them some relaxation from the perpetual quest for food on land and sea. The competitions between different sections of a village or different villages brought together a larger group of people on terms of social intercourse. The local people had to provide food for the visitors, spectators as well as competitors, and the occasions were social events in which all feasted as the foundation of enjoyment. Singing and dancing added to the festive nature of such occasions.

In this atmosphere of friendly social intercourse group unity was welded. Everyone had some role to play and in so doing felt himself a necessary part of the gathering. This element of unity was all important in Samoa in view of the fact that political power rested with the group which had the strength to overcome all others in warfare. Strength then as now was greatly dependent upon unity.

Competitive games also gave the people an outlet for the intense spirit of rivalry which they had. Families, villages, and districts were continually striving to gain prestige in all things deemed worthwhile, and victory in any sport was a distinction coveted by all.

In these intercommunity activities, prestige was sought for the village, not the individual (6) and all members of the winning group, whether or not they actually played, gloried in the victory.

Certain activities, such as pigeon netting, bonito fishing, and some types of dancing, were reserved for those of high rank. Such events served to point out the importance of these individuals in Samoan society. The best was set aside for them.

A wide variety of games, sports, and dances played an important part in the ceremonies marking the life crises of birth, puberty, marriage, and death. Although not mentioned in any of the source material, it would seem that

[1] Reprinted by permission of the Royal Anthropological Institute.

these diversions were partially influential in alleviating the emotions such crises aroused in the people. At death, for example, when they were filled with great sorrow and fear, they played all kinds of games. Perhaps, by participating in activities which caused some amusement at a time when life was otherwise mournful and solemn, the people were sooner able to adjust to the situation which had developed.

RELIGION

The gods of the Samoans were legion. To them the islanders ascribed human feelings and actions, and believed that they derived great enjoyment from human diversions.

> When there were funerary festivals, first fruits rites, and on all such cere-monial occasions of the first order of importance, the gods concerned were not regarded as far off somewhere in the sky looking on, but were believed to be present with their worshippers, enjoying with them the exhilarating effects of the feasting, dancing, singing, and social emulation (11, p. 88).

Their deities were ever present and ever worshipped as it was from them that the natives thought that they and all of nature received power, or mana, to accomplish desired results. In addition to daily worship they were accorded special festivals. There were annual rites for propitiating the more important ones. At those events, club fights were engaged in by all participants until the blood flowed. The blood was an offering which was thought to cause the gods:

> . . . to be all the more pleased with their devotedness, and answer prayer for health, good crops and success in battle (26, p. 57).

Dancing, especially of the erotic type, was also a part of these services. Handy (11, p. 210) wrote the following concerning the purpose it served:

> The dancing at the religious festivals was closely related to the offerings and feasts in honor of the gods: they were believed to entertain the gods, and at the same time to rouse and stimulate them. Mana in one funda-mental sense, meant procreative power. The erotic dancing of the tropical islands of Polynesia, which was at its origin a form of worship, was designed to stimulate and to bring into action the mana of the gods who were be-lieved to be animated by the same emotions as men and on whose procrea-tive activities the fecundity of human beings, the earth, and sea depended.

At all ceremonies for whatever purpose some part was devoted to wor-ship. In considering the possible religious implications of their birth celebra-tions, one authority (11, pp. 220–21) reported:

> Soon after a child's birth, the Samoans celebrated a great feast with games and dances. There was another such celebration when the child could sit up, and still others when the child could crawl, stand upright and walk. . . . Although in Samoa these functions may have been mainly social, for here the social aspect rather than the religious always assumes the place of

larger importance in festivities, there was undoubtedly present the thought that the feasting, sham-fighting and night dancing . . . had the effect of empowering the child through rapport, of stimulating its growth, and endowing its spirit with those qualities that were being exhibited about it, which would enable it to take its place when grown as a distinguished leader in festivities, in social and political life, and among the communities fighters.

In thus providing opportunity for men and gods to mingle in activities enjoyed by both, at times when the influence of the gods was desired, amusements of a vigorous physical nature held an important place in Samoan religious life.

WARFARE

Warfare held quite a prominent place in Samoan life; everywhere men talked of the glory and honor to be gained on the field of battle.

Many of the games and sports of the islanders involved the same skills which were used in war, namely, those concerned with the handling of spears, clubs and slings. Specific amusements in which these were perfected were disc and stick throwing for distance, spear throwing for accuracy, spear parrying and club fighting.

Although wars were frequent, the Samoans had no particular group of men who were especially trained for that purpose. All served as warriors and their principal form of training was participation in contests involving the above mentioned activities (2). Such contests were included in all of their social gatherings.

In their battles, strength and endurance were factors to success. These elements were also important in victory at such sports as boxing, wrestling, kicking matches and club fighting. In fact, the natives preferred games involving great physical exercise and good wrestlers and club fighters were always praised (2). Games, by thus promoting the development of attributes essential in warfare, were of vital importance to it.

Some early writers even said that war, as practiced by the natives, was a form of sport. One observer (29, p. 66) wrote:

The tribal wars have really been athletic sports.

ECONOMIC SYSTEM

Obtaining a livelihood was a co-operative enterprise, with the participants giving labor and receiving the fruits of labor according to their position of importance in Samoan society.

Activities involved in obtaining some of the economic necessities of life were highly recreational in nature.

Fishing was a sport as well as a food procuring activity. Some of the community methods were occasions of fun and excitement and corresponded to a combined picnic and sports gathering that took place in the most important Polynesian playground, the lagoon (5, p. 517).

Pigeon netting, another means of getting food, was a highly developed sport restricted to those of rank.

Food was also obtained as a result of victory in games. Turner (26), Brown (2), and Stair (21), all report that the defeated party usually gave the winning group some kind of food.

These inter-village competitions were of importance to the economic system in that they provided the incentive for host groups to produce goods to share with their visitors. Prestige came from sharing and giving, and each community strove to outgive all others when its turn came to sponsor a meeting.

EDUCATION

. . . boys and girls as pupils and servants of their elders learned the roles they were to play in adult life, while environmental conditions, fears, admonitions, and the urge to emulate and excel in forms of activity valued by the group all combined to harden the plastic material of their biological heritage along "Samoan" lines (14, p. 414).[2]

At an early stage Samoan children started learning the games and dances of their people. They learned a great deal through observation and imitation, some through special instruction from slightly older children, with whom they played, and some through instruction from interested adults.

Except at informal village dances where they performed for the entertainment of all, children were not admitted as participants in adult amusements. They were, however, allowed to be present as spectators. Like children of today, most of their play was carried on with others of their own age.

The informal village dance had a special part to play in the education of the child. According to Mead [3] (17, pp. 117–118):

The significance of the dance in the education and socialisation of Samoan children is two-fold. In the first place it effectively offsets the rigorous subordination in which children are habitually kept. Here the admonitions of the elders change from "Sit down and keep still!" to "Stand up and dance!" The children are actually the centre of the group instead of its barely tolerated fringes. . . . Each child is a person with a definite contribution to make regardless of sex and age. . . . The second influence of the dance is its reduction of the threshold of shyness.[4]

Samoan children seem not to have learned to work through learning to play as most primitive children did (17). They learned both to play and to work; each was important in itself. Any labor that they were capable of doing and which others did not desire to perform was given to them. Their play was like that of their parents in kind and interest (17).

[2] Reprinted by permission of George Allen & Unwin, Ltd.
[3] Although this study was made in the 1920s it is believed that the information on the role of the dance and the place of play in the lives of the people applies equally as well to the 1830s.
[4] Reprinted by permission of William Morrow & Co., Inc.

Vigorous physical amusements also played a part in the education of the child in the ethics of his countrymen. Many of the Samoan proverbs, phrases and similes which served in this sort of training had their origin in specific sports (3). Pigeon netting seems to have produced more such sayings than any other activity (5).

Some Effects of Culture Contact

When the eighteenth century European explorers discovered the islands, the natives had a chance to observe people whose patterns of living differed from theirs. All of the newcomers who arrived, after the discovery, had some effect upon the lives of the Samoans. However, missionaries and government officials appear to have been more influential than the rest in instigating the culture changes which evolved.

CHANGES WROUGHT BY THE MISSIONARIES

When the first missionaries arrived in 1830, they found a people who were eager to learn about the new religion. Williams, the earliest missionary to arrive, had with him a converted Samoan of high rank who was extremely helpful in promoting Christianity in his native country. That Williams appreciated his ability is clearly shown in his missionary records; there (28, p. 332) he wrote:

> In all our conversations with that individual, we were impressed with his intelligence, shrewdness, and good sense, but never more so than on the morning we arrived at the place of our destination, when he led us to a private part of the vessel, and requested us to desire the teachers not to commence their labours among his countrymen by condemning their canoe races, their dances and other amusements, to which they were much attached, lest in the very onset, they should conceive a dislike to the religion which imposed such restraints.

However, as the missionaries sincerely believed that some of these activities were detrimental to Christian living, they soon started encouraging the natives to renounce them. This was especially true of dancing, partly because some of it was of an erotic nature and partly because the early missionaries had a tendency to regard all dancing as immoral. They also frowned upon bathing and swimming on Sunday because these activities took too much time away from religious duties (27). Pigeon hunting expeditions, too, were discouraged, as they were believed to lead to immoral practices.

Many Samoans accepted and worshipped the Christian God. However, in accepting the faith of the newcomers the islanders did not find it necessary to adopt other aspects of foreign culture (13).

With the discarding of the old system of worship some of the taboos which had restricted specific amusements to those of rank gradually lost their power. For example, natives of lower groups began to participate in pigeon netting, and bonito fishing. But, occasions at which individuals of rank engaged in these and other activities continued to be of prime importance.

With the acceptance of Christianity the religious festivals previously mentioned were discontinued. The vigorous physical amusements which had been a part of these events lost their religious significance. In spite of this they continued to be an important element in Samoan culture.

It is true that bans were placed on certain amusements (particularly dancing) and were effective in some places in eliminating these activities for a time; but, they were not permanently effective as the Samoans would not, or perhaps could not, without losing all zest for living, relinquish them.

That Christianized natives tried to follow these prohibitions is definitely stated in writings left by early island visitors. Perhaps the best way to show the actual results of these restrictions is to quote some of the pertinent observations made by such writers. Wilkes, who was in the islands in 1839 noticed that:

> Their dances and other amusements are in a great degree abolished, but they are still practiced in the heathen villages, and even the Christian women may still be induced to exhibit the former, which they call the siva (27, p. 141).

From this report it can be seen that the bans were being followed to some extent.

In the 1860s Hood, who was traveling through Samoa, reported that:

> In the evening we went to the dance. I believe all are not conducted so decorously as this was; were they so, it would be much better that the national amusement should not be discontinued, seeing that we give the light-hearted people no substitute in the way of pleasure (12, p. 48).

This observation, in addition to showing that dancing although prohibited had not entirely died out, brought out a fact expressed by others of that day; the fact that the missionaries offered no adequate substitute for the element of life which they sought to prohibit.

About 1890 the religious leaders also began to realize this truth. Robert Louis Stevenson, who lived in Samoa at that time wrote:

> The native pastors (to everyone's surprise) have moved of themselves in the matter of native dances, desiring the restrictions to be removed, or rather to be made dependent on the character of the dance (22, p. 24).[5]

Thus, after years of religious opposition, dancing again became an accepted activity. However, during the struggle it had changed to some extent. The more erotic type of dancing which had been such an important part of the old dances had gradually disappeared.

CHANGES INSTIGATED BY OFFICIALS OF FOREIGN GOVERNMENTS

Foreign governments became involved in island affairs because their citizens settled there, and because of values which they expected to derive from the area. The British were the first to make official alliances with some

---

[5] Reprinted by permission of Charles Scribner's Sons.

of the Samoan leaders. They were followed by the Americans and Germans and finally by the New Zealanders.

These governments were able to carry out certain of their political edicts because they could exert superior physical force if necessary. The islanders were aware of this fact, and acquiesced when it was impossible to do anything else.

In considering the changes which were made in vigorous physical amusements because of the actions of these powers, it appears that many were the result of their economic interests. For instance, when the traders first arrived they gave the islanders guns in exchange for native products. Before long the gun had taken the place of native arms in warfare. When these implements lost their place in war they started losing their place in the amusements of the people; kicking matches, club fighting, spear parrying, and disc throwing which had been important, gradually became events of the past (8). Spear throwing remained, perhaps because it was still essential in fishing and pig hunting.

Also, with the substitution of guns for native arms, fighting lost some of its attraction. Pritchard (20, p. 60), in speaking of a plan to end a particular war aptly demonstrated this fact. He reported:

> The proposition was readily entered into by the Savaii people, as the opportunity to escape from a war in which, as they naively said, the victory was not won by the strongest arm in wielding the club or parrying the spear, for a youth only just tattooed could with a musket shoot the strongest and most daring warrior. This was the secret of the unpopularity of the war.

Eventually warfare was eliminated altogether, partly because it had lost some of its attraction, but primarily because the foreign governments became strong enough to put a stop to an activity which they considered extremely wasteful to economic effort.

As the powers gained influence, they all, at one time or another, placed some restrictions on travel for ceremony or sport. This was not done because the officials objected to the amusements of the Samoans, but rather because of the time which such visits consumed. They thought that if they could get the islanders to stay at home more often they might be induced to develop more systematic methods of agriculture.

These bans did not bring the desired results. The Samoans would work only so long as it took to obtain the things they wanted for immediate use. They continued to spend much of their time participating in vigorous recreational activities. In American Samoa, for instance, where inter-village cricket matches were forbidden except by special permit from May until February, the courts were filled with cases concerning the playing of cricket without permission (23).

The same foreign leaders who attempted to regulate sports meetings were responsible for giving the natives new games. In some of their moments of relaxation, they, too enjoyed play. At such times they and their countrymen usually participated in games of their own native lands. The islanders observed those activities and adopted the ones which appealed to them.

From the British they learned the sport of cricket. That game, in a modified form, soon became *the* sport of the Samoans. They had men's, women's and children's teams. All of the people of a village would accompany the men's team as it toured the islands to engage in contests with other villages. While away, such groups were freely housed and fed by their hosts. In these events all of the able-bodied men of both villages participated. Sometimes there were as many as two hundred on a team (7). A game consisted of a single inning and was finished when every player had had a chance to bat. This took anywhere from four to twelve days (9).

Cricket finally began to take so much of the natives' time and wealth that all of the foreign powers made some regulations limiting its play.

Other major sports enthusiastically accepted by the natives were rugby and baseball. In these games, as in cricket, changes were instituted in order to make the games more compatible with Samoan play customs.

Thus, it can be seen that although foreign influence brought about several changes in the element of vigorous physical amusements, this element remained an important part of Samoan culture.

Samoa in 1930

In 1930, after one hundred years of foreign influence, Samoan culture was not greatly changed from what it had been when the missionaries first arrived. Keesing (14, p. 477) attributed this to:

> Samoa's smallness, isolation, and tropical climate, together with the political rivalry of the powers and the elements of disunity inherent in native polity. . . .[6]

Buck (5, p. 5), in attempting to account for this phenomenon wrote:

> The pleasure derived from the exercise of native institutions is perhaps the most important factor that has led to the persistence of Samoan customs and helped to resist the disintegration that has taken place in other parts of Polynesia.

Undoubtedly it was the combination of these reasons which enabled native life to stand fairly firm.

It is true that many changes were made in their material culture and in those aspects of their social culture concerned with religion, warfare, education and government. Such changes, however, were gradual and were fitted into native living in a manner which enabled it to remain distinctively Samoan (4).

Amusements of a vigorous physical nature remained highly important. The natives still devoted so much time to them that American and New Zealand officials, who were then in control, saw fit to continue regulating intervillage meetings for ceremony and sport (14). In spite of this, traveling for ceremony and sport appears to have been the rule of the day (10).

[6] Reprinted by permission of George Allen & Unwin, Ltd.

Except for the changes pointed out in the section of this paper entitled "Some Effects of Culture Contact," the integration of Samoan recreational life with such major aspects of Samoan culture as their social, economic and educational systems remained much as it had been in 1830.

Summary and Conclusions

In an endeavor to add to the understanding of the contributions which the element of games, sports, dancing and other vigorous recreational activities has made in enriching the daily living of the diverse peoples of the world, the place of this element in Samoan culture was studied. Because Samoa was a fairly isolated area until a little over one hundred years ago, when it came in contact with Western culture, it was possible to discover pertinent information concerning the role of vigorous physical amusements in Samoan life before and after that event.

Before the advent of the Western powers a great deal of time was spent by individuals of all ages and ranks in a great variety of games, sports, and dances. Participation in these activities ranged from a few members of one village playing in an informal manner to the mustered forces of villages or districts competing in a formal manner for a championship in one or more events.

A critical examination of Samoan culture indicates the close interrelationship of the social organization, religion, warfare, economic pursuits, and education with the recreational life involving vigorous physical activities.

1. In their social life the element of games, sports and dancing fulfilled the following needs:

a. Provided social intercourse of a- friendly and enjoyable nature through which group unity was promoted.
b. Afford socially approved outlets for feelings of rivalry.
c. Provided for situations in which the leaders of the people were allowed to participate in select activities.
d. Afford the opportunity for groups of individuals to gain prestige and honor through victory in events highly approved by all.
e. Provided an outlet for excessive emotions connected with the life crises of birth, marriage and death.

2. In their religious life vigorous physical amusements were important in that the natives believed that their gods derived great enjoyment from such diversions. For this reason, when they desired the influence of their deities they engaged in elaborate religious rites in which various sports and dances held a prominent part. Particular amusements practiced at these events appear to have been of religious significance in the following ways:

a. Club fights which were so fierce as to cause the blood to flow served to demonstrate their devotion to their gods. It was thought that for such devotion the deities answered prayers.

b. Dancing of an erotic nature was believed to stimulate the gods and to cause them to bring about fertility in all of nature.

3. Warfare in Samoan society was interrelated with the element of games and sports in that:

a. The skills of war were perfected through the specific amusements of disc and stick throwing for distance, spear throwing for accuracy, spear parrying and club fighting. These events were favored by the Samoans and had a place in all of their social gatherings.
b. The factors of physical strength and endurance which were essential for success in their games were also essential for success in their wars.

4. Some of their economic pursuits were highly recreational in nature. Fishing and pigeon netting were organized sports as well as food procuring activities.

5. In Samoan education, training the youth in the amusements of the people was considered essential in preparing them to take their place in adult society where such activities were highly significant. Training in dancing appears to have had a special place in their education. In this diversion they were given an opportunity to contribute something to the social life of their community without being reproved for presuming above their age. Such participation served also to help them overcome their feelings of shyness.

THE EFFECTS OF CULTURE CONTACT

The literature reveals that two major agencies of culture contact effected changes; the missionaries and official and unofficial representatives of foreign governments.

1. The missionaries who strenuously objected to Samoan amusements because they considered some of them as immoral and all of them as detrimental to true Christian living were influential in bringing about the following changes:

a. Vigorous physical amusements lost their religious significance.
b. Bonito fishing and pigeon netting which men of rank had been able to restrict to themselves because of their sacredness became sports of all.
c. Dancing of an erotic nature was discontinued.

Even though the natives accepted Christianity; games, sports, and dancing continued to be highly important in their culture. As the years passed the missionaries became more broadminded and eventually realized the importance of such activities in promoting wholesome living.

2. Officials from foreign governments, traders and others whom they represented were instrumental in instigating the following changes:

a. Guns which they introduced changed the methods of warfare and led to the elimination of those amusements which had served in preparing warriors to use the native arms of the spear, club, and sling.
b. Travel for ceremony and sport was restricted.

c. Games which were played by the foreign element were adopted by the natives. Cricket, baseball, and rugby, all modified to meet Samoan play-methods became particularly important.

Except for the above changes, the interrelationships existing between the element of games, sports and dancing and the other major elements of Samoan life remained essentially the same as they had been in 1830. Despite the force of culture contact to which the Samoans were subjected, the native culture including the vigorous recreational life remained fairly stable and integrated.

SELECTED REFERENCES

1. BOYNTON, S. S., "Life in Samoa," *Overland Monthly*, N. S. 13: (May, 1889), 533–540.
2. BROWN, GEORGE, *Melanesians and Polynesians*, London: MacMillan and Co., 1910.
3. ——, "Proverbs, Phrases and Similes of the Samoans," *Australian Association for the Advancement of Science*, 14: (1913), 401–433.
4. BUCK, P. H. (Te Rangi Hiroa), "Samoan Education," *The Friend*, (March, 1932), 101–102, (May, 1932), 346–348x.
5. ——, "Samoan Material Culture," *Bernice P. Bishop Museum Bulletin*, 75 (1930).
6. CHURCHILL, LLEWELLA PIERCE, "Sports of the Samoans," *Outing*, 33: (March, 1899), 562–568.
7. CHURCHILL, WILLIAM, *My Consulate in Samoa*, London: Richard Bentley and Sons, 1887.
8. COFFEE, FRANK, *Forty Years in the Pacific* (pp. 136–160; 184–188), New York and Sydney, Australia: Oceanic Publishing Co., 1920.
9. FREEMAN, LEWIS R., *In the Track of the Trades* (pp. 212–282), New York: Dodd Mead and Co., 1920.
10. GREEN, WILLIAM M., "Social Traits of Samoans," *Journal of Applied Sociology*, 9: (November–December, 1924), 129–135.
11. HANDY, E. S. CRAIGHILL, "Polynesian Religion," *Bernice P. Bishop Museum Bulletin*, 34 (1927).
12. HOOD, T. H. COCKBURN, *Notes on a Cruise of H.M.S. Fawn in the Western Pacific in the Year 1862* (pp. 28–145), Edinburgh: Edmonston and Douglas, 1863.
13. HUMPHREY, SETH K., *Loafing Through the Pacific* (pp. 26–74), Garden City, New York: Doubleday Page and Co., 1927.
14. KEESING, FELIX M., *Modern Samoa*, London: George Allen and Unwin Ltd., 1934.
15. KOTZEBUE, OTTO VON, *A New Voyage Round the World in the Years 1823, 1824, 1825, and 1826* (pp. 251–289), London: Henry Colburn and Richard Bentley, 1830.
16. LINTON, RALPH, *The Science of Man in the World Crisis*, New York: Columbia University Press, 1945.

17. MEAD, MARGARET, *Coming of Age in Samoa*, New York: William Morrow and Co., 1928.

18. ——, "Role of the Individual in Samoan Culture," *Journal of the Royal Anthropological Institute*, **58**: (1928), 481–495.

19. NIGHTINGALE, THOMAS, *Oceanic Sketches* (pp. 72–93), London: James Cochrane and Co., 1835.

20. PRITCHARD, W. T., *Polynesian Reminiscences or Life in the South Pacific* (pp. 50–208), London: Chapman and Hall, 1866.

21. STAIR, JOHN B., *Old Samoa or Flotsam and Jetsam from the Pacific Ocean*, London: Religious Tract Society, 1897.

22. STEVENSON, ROBERT LOUIS, *Vailima Letters (Vol. 17) Works of Robert Louis Stevenson*, New York: Charles Scribners Sons, 1896.

23. STONACH, ALEXANDER, "The White Judge in Tutuila," *Asia*, **21**: (April, 1921), 357–361.

24. STUMPF, FLORENCE AND FREDERICK W. COZENS, "Hidden Possibilities for Research in Physical Education and Recreation," *Research Quarterly*, **18**: (May, 1947), 104–108.

25. ——, "Some Aspects of the Role of Games, Sports, and Recreational Activities in the Culture of Modern Primitive Peoples" (in 2 parts), Part I: "The New Zealand Maoris"; Part II: "The Fijians," *Research Quarterly*, **18**: (October, 1947, 198–218; **20**: (March, 1949), 2–20.

26. TURNER, GEORGE, *Samoa a Hundred Years Ago and Long Before*, London: MacMillan and Co., 1884.

27. WILKES, CHARLES, *Narrative of the United States Exploring Expedition During the Years 1838, 1839, 1840, 1841 and 1842* (5 Vols.), Philadelphia: C. Sherman Co., 1844.

28. WILLIAMS, JOHN, *A Narrative of Missionary Enterprise in the South Sea Islands*, (pp. 326–358, 410–468, 480–502 and 531–549), London: J. Snow Co., 1838.

29. WOOLEY, MARY V. AND JOHN B. WOOLEY, *South Sea Letters* (pp. 33–100), Chicago: The New Voice Press, 1906.

child training and
game involvement

JOHN M. ROBERTS
BRIAN SUTTON-SMITH

Games are systemic culture patterns which are distinctive, ancient, and widespread among the cultures of the world. Although games and gamesters have long claimed the scholarly interest of anthropologists and psychologists, no general consideration of the phenomenon of involvement in games has yet been given from both cross-cultural and intracultural points of view. The evidence presented herein shows that variations in the distributions of games among cultures throughout the world, and in the game playing of American children and adults, are related to variations in child training. It is held that these relationships can be viewed in terms of psychological conflicts that lead people to become involved in games and other models. In the main, this discussion is limited to game involvement, but it must be recognized that there are other important aspects to game playing. Additional features will be treated in subsequent reports.

In an earlier publication (Roberts, Arth, and Bush, 1959, p. 597), games were defined as recreational activities characterized by organized play, competition, two or more sides, criteria for determining the winner, and agreed-upon rules. Many of the activities described as "games" in the ethnographic literature, however, do not satisfy the above requirements. Instead they are amusements: group pastimes such as the ritual game of dialogue, "Mother, Mother, the Pot Boils Over"; stunts such as diving and juggling; model play as with dolls, pets, and toy trains; and various other noncompetitive recreational activities. Although this article is focused on games, there is evidence that child-training variables are systematically related to classes of amusements as well.

Games may be grouped into three classes on the basis of outcome attributes: (1) games of *physical skill,* in which the outcome is determined by the players' motor activities; (2) games of *strategy,* in which the outcome is

• From *Ethnology,* 1 (1962), pp. 166–185. © 1962 University of Pittsburgh, Pittsburgh, Pennsylvania. This investigation was supported in part by a PHS research grant, M-4161, from the National Institute of Mental Health, Public Health Service. In the earlier stages of the project, the junior author received special assistance from the Penrose Fund of the American Philosophical Society. Acknowledgment is made to William Lambert for generous theoretical and practical aid. The authors also appreciate the help received from Irving Child, whose provision of the Bacon, Barry, and Child ratings made this article possible.

determined by rational choices among possible courses of action; and (3) games of *chance*, in which the outcome is determined by guesses or by some uncontrolled artifact such as a die or a wheel. On the basis of the presence or absence of the attributes of strategy or chance, games of physical skill can be further subdivided into (a) games of pure physical skill where only the defining attribute of physical skill is present, as in weight lifting, racing, or bowling; (b) games of physical skill and strategy, such as fencing, baseball, or football, where rational decisions also influence outcomes; (c) games of physical skill and chance, such as tipcat, musical chairs, or grab, where chance is a factor as well as physical skill; and (d) games of physical skill, strategy, and chance, such as Queenie or steal the bacon (Sutton-Smith, 1959), where all three defining attributes are present. Games of strategy (which must lack the attribute of physical skill) are subdivided into (a) games of pure strategy, such as chess, checkers, or go, where the attribute of chance is absent, and (b) games of strategy and chance, such as bridge, poker, or cribbage, where both attributes are present. The category of games of chance is not subdivided, as by definition this class must lack the attributes of physical skill and strategy. It includes such games as roulette, bingo, dice, and coin matching. The fundamental character of a game appears to be related to the principal defining attribute, whether it be physical skill, strategy, or chance; the attribute distributions within the subdivided classes of physical skill and strategy serve only to add secondary characteristics.

Although play is a cultural universal, games, as defined above, are not. True, games are found in most tribal and national cultures, but in some interesting cultures they are either absent or very restricted in kind and number. Among the game-playing societies throughout the world the variations in games and game playing are extraordinarily great. All such societies have games of physical skill. Fewer have, in addition, games of strategy, or of chance, or of both. Among societies with identical games there can still be variation in gamesters. Although participation in the local array of games can be very broad in some societies, every group restricts the playing of games, in greater or lesser degree, on the basis of age, sex, health, intelligence, social status, and a variety of cultural factors. Finally, within a single society the involvement of individual gamesters is never constant throughout the life cycle, and it can differ greatly from individual to individual. There is even a class of nonplayers—individuals who, though qualified for participation in games, either do not play them at all or play them only involuntarily. These cross-cultural, intracultural, and individual differences in game involvement require explanation.

Like other systemic patterns, games are especially amenable to historical and distributional treatment, but the culture history of games must be conjoined with functional analysis if the invention, diffusion, persistence, embellishment, and extinction of games are to be understood. As games appear to be projective or expressive behaviors, it is reasonable to consider them in relation to learning or, more specifically, to child training. If specific game types can be associated with specific child-training variables, a step toward the functional understanding of game involvement will have been made.

The present inquiry is based on an earlier cross-cultural study of games (Roberts, Arth, and Bush, 1959) in which games were viewed as expressive models. Games of strategy were related to cultural complexity; games of chance to the benevolence or coercibility of supernatural being; and games of physical skill to the environmental setting. These relationships, together with some association with child-training variables, suggested that all games are exercises in mastery, with games of strategy, chance, and physical skill being related, respectively, to the mastery of the social system, the supernatural, and the nexus of the self with the environment. The present study builds on this analysis, but it goes beyond the notion of mastery to offer a conflict interpretation of game involvement.

Method

We have utilized a list of child-training ratings for 111 societies prepared by Bacon, Barry, and Child (1952). The authors rated the relative indulgence or severity of child training in the initial infant period, the degree of transition anxiety from infancy to childhood, and the amount of over-all childhood indulgence. Boys and girls were rated separately for child-training procedures with respect to responsibility, obedience, self-reliance, achievement, nurturance, and independence. For each of these latter variables the ratings provide information on the degree of rewards received for behaving in a particular way, e.g., being self-reliant, the amount of anxiety about not performing the behavior (punishments inflicted for not showing the behavior), the frequency of the behavior, and the amount of conflict over it. It is thus possible to judge whether a child-training procedure is mainly a positive one involving simply rewards and frequent performance, or mainly a negative one involving anxiety and conflict. As Bacon, Barry, and Child were unable to provide ratings on all their categories for all of their 111 societies, there are differences in the number of tribes listed in the tables which follow.

A pilot study made use of a more comprehensive set of ratings, including information on such primary socialization variables as weaning and toilet training. Although these ratings were not available for the larger sample covered in the present study, results of the pilot study are coordinated with the present findings where they provide amplification and illumination.

In 1959 the Cross-Cultural Survey Files and Human Relations Area Files at Yale University were searched for information on games and game playing for those tribes on which there were child-training ratings. The files on 27 tribes contained moderately complete descriptions of games, and those on an additional 29 societies provided descriptions which were usable though incomplete. Confidence in the descriptions varied with the degree of attention paid to detail and with the presence or absence of explicit statements about the adequacy of coverage. Negative instances presented a problem, as a type of game may have been present but unobserved by the ethnographer, or the ethnographer may not have been interested in the subject of games. The uneven quality of the descriptions resulted in such anomalies as that a particular tribe could sometimes be used for certain comparisons but not for others. It was frequently possible, for example, to ascertain that particular cultures clearly possessed games of chance or of strategy even though little was specifically reported about the games themselves.

Although the importance of acculturation in the study of games was recognized, recently introduced games were excluded from consideration. Games were scored without regard to the age or sex of the players, as the ethnographic evidence did not always provide such information (probably, however, boys and/or men played most of the games noted). For this reason it is uncertain what value should be placed on the distinction between male and female child-training ratings. According to Bacon, Barry, and Child, females tended to receive only positive ratings (reward and frequency), whereas males received both positive and negative ratings; the ratings on infants grouped both sexes together. It was therefore decided to consider the ratings on both boys and girls as presenting a general picture of childhood in a particular society rather than to view them as independent accounts.

Our cross-cultural analysis deals with only four classes of games: (1) those of physical skill, (2) those of physical skill and strategy, (3) those of strategy, and (4) those of chance. No games of physical skill, strategy, and chance were encountered among the tribes used in our survey. The class of physical skill and chance and that of strategy and chance occurred too infrequently in the sample to permit separate discrimination; games of the former class were consequently grouped with those of physical skill, and those of the latter class with games of strategy. The distribution of the four classes of games among the 56 societies of our samples is as follows:

1. Games of physical skill, of physical skill and strategy, of strategy, and of chance. Complete information: Chagga, Chewa, Hopi, Thonga, Zuni. Incomplete information: Azande, Dahomeans, Papago, Venda. Total: 9 societies.
2. Games of physical skill, of physical skill and strategy, and of strategy. Complete information: Ganda, Lamba. Incomplete information: Ashanti, Gikuyu, Lakher, Masai, Mbundu, Tanala, Tiv. Total: 9 societies.
3. Games of physical skill, of physical skill and strategy, and of chance. Complete information: Comanche, Crow, Kwakiutl, Nauruans, Navaho, Muria, Ojibwa, Omaha, Samoans, Trukese. Incomplete information: Aleut, Araucanians, Aymara, Baiga, Chukchee, Kaska, Konde, Mandan, Tallensi. Total: 19 societies.
4. Games of physical skill and of physical skill and strategy. Complete information: Andamanese, Bena, Koryak, Kurtatchi, Maori, Pukapukans. Incomplete information: Ainu, Alorese, Aranda, Marquesans, Timbira, Trobrianders, Wogeo, Woleaians. Total: 14 societies.

5. Games of physical skill only. Complete information: Lepcha, Lesu, Siriono. Incomplete information: Balinese. Total: 4 societies.
6. No games. Complete information: Murngin. Total: 1 society.

As a world sample of cultural variation the foregoing list of tribes is at best only partially defensible in conventional ethnographic terms. Witness, for example, the preponderance of African tribes among those groups possessing games of strategy. Enlargement of the sample, however, would involve finding additional tribes with adequate data on both child training and games as well as making new ratings with new judges—a procedure which at this state in the general inquiry would be prohibitively expensive. We have therefore sought an alternative means of strengthening confidence in the findings.

Cultural variation occurs within as well as between social groups. Under favorable circumstances, therefore, it is possible to study the relationships among variables at two levels of generality, e.g., in a world sample of societies and in subcultures within a single national culture. If generalizations established on the basis of cross-cultural study are found to have predictive power within particular cultures, confidence in the cross-cultural generalizations is increased. This technique of validation through subsystem replication is used in the present study.

The United States is one in a set of societies in the world, and is also one in which there is great cultural variation within the national culture. Among such cultural differences are those between sex categories, i.e., between boys and girls, men and women. Since differences also occur in the socialization of males and females, and since the expression of game preferences is relatively free in the United States, the relationships between child training and game preferences by sex categories should be those predicted by the cross-cultural analysis.

Through analysis of children's responses to an 180-item play scale, previously collected for another purpose, Sutton-Smith and Rosenberg (1959) have used the cross-culturally derived generalizations to predict the game preferences of 1,900 children in the third, fourth, fifth, and sixth grades in twelve midwestern American townships. Adult preferences have not been tested in as thorough a fashion, but preliminary work with survey data on file at Williams College supports the general conclusions.

Results

The important findings of the cross-cultural investigation are presented in Table 1. Here ordinary tests of significance are given on the assumption that tribes are defensible as independent cultural units. In a sense, both this assumption and the use of a small, unevenly distributed sample are limitations of the study.

GAMES OF STRATEGY

As a relationship has been demonstrated (Roberts, Arth, and Bush 1959) between social complexity (as measured by the degree of political

table 1

CROSS-CULTURAL RELATIONSHIPS BETWEEN GAMES AND
CHILD-TRAINING VARIABLES

GAME CLASSES		CHILD TRAINING VARIABLES	MALE FEMALE INFANT	CONTIN-GENCY TABLE CELLS a b c d				LEVEL OF SIGNIFI-CANCE [a]
Strategy	1	Reward for Obedience	M	12	5	7	26	0.01
	2	Reward for Obedience	F	12	3	9	22	0.01
	3	Frequency of Obedience	M	10	7	5	25	0.01
	4	Frequency of Obedience	F	12	3	11	23	0.01
	5	Anxiety over Nonperformance of Obedience	M	11	6	4	25	0.01
	6	Amount of Childhood Indulgence	I	9	6	6	22	0.05
	7 [b]	Relative Importance of Love-Oriented Techniques of Punishment by Parents	I	5	1	2	8	0.05
	8 [b]	Defecation Permissiveness (less)	I	7	0	3	8	0.005
	9 [b]	Rank of Severity of Weaning (higher)	I	6	2	3	9	0.05
	10 [b]	Rank of Severity of Independence Training (higher)	I	6	2	1	10	0.01
Chance	11	Reward for Responsibility	M	18	9	8	18	0.05
	12	Reward for Responsibility	F	16	11	6	17	0.10
	13	Anxiety over Performance of Achievement	M	15	11	6	13	0.20
	14 [b]	Severity of Sex Training	I	9	1	4	8	0.025
	15 [b]	Rank of Severity of Sex Training	I	7	2	3	9	0.05
Physical Skill	16	Reward for Achievement	M	14	7	4	19	0.01
	17	Reward for Achievement	F	13	4	4	11	0.02
	18	Frequency of Achievement	M	15	8	4	17	0.01
	19	Frequency of Achievement	F	12	6	4	12	0.05
P. S. & Strat.	20	Anxiety over Nonperformance of Achievement	M	12	6	4	21	0.02
All 4 vs. 2	21	Anxiety over Performance of Achievement	M	8	1	1	11	0.005
	22	Conflict over Achievement	M	7	2	3	9	0.05

[a] Levels of significance were ascertained by chi squares or Fisher's exact probability test, whichever was appropriate according to the size of the N. All game classes were tested against all ratings. All other associations were non-significant.
[b] From the smaller Cornell sample.

integration and the amount of social stratification) and the presence of games of strategy, it is not surprising that games of strategy are linked either directly with obedience training or with variables which have some bearing on obedience. Indeed, it is virtually certain that every complex social system makes certain demands on obedience (with a corresponding emphasis on commanding or managing). Although the present ratings are concerned only with obedience, it is highly probable that obedience training is only one part of a larger system of giving and taking orders which is involved in the functioning of any complex society. Tribes possessing games of strategy were found more likely to have high ratings on child-training procedures which involved rewarding children for being obedient (see Table 2), punishing for being

table 2

REWARD FOR OBEDIENCE AND PRESENCE OF GAMES OF STRATEGY

	ABOVE MEDIAN	BELOW MEDIAN
Strategy Present	Ganda (14), Venda (14) Ashanti (13), Chagga (13), Gikuyu (13), Hopi (13), Tanala (13), Azande (12), Lamba (12), Masai (12), Papago (12), Mbundu (11)	Thonga (10), Tiv (10), Zuni (9), Chewa (7), Lakher (7)
Strategy Absent	Ainu (13), Aymara (13), Chukchee (12), Tallensi (12) Nauruans (12), Lesu (11), Konde (11)	Crow (10), Kwakiutl (10), Mandan (10), Muria (10), Omaha (10), Navaho (10), Ojibwa (10), Samoans (10), Alorese (9), Balinese (9), Lepcha (9), Pukapukans (9), Murngin (9), Aleut (9), Woleaians (9), Aranda (8), Araucanians (8), Kaska (8), Trukese (8), Wogeo (7), Kurtatchi (6), Comanche (5), Maori (5), Siriono (5), Trobrianders (5), Marquesans (4)

Median = 10
$p = 0.01$

disobedient, anxiety about nonperformance of obedience, conflict over obedience, and high frequency of obedient behaviors. In addition, they were, in general, less indulgent in their child-training procedures. The smaller sample showed relationships between games of strategy and higher ratings on love-oriented disciplinary techniques, greater severity of independence training, and less defecation permissiveness. There is in these relationships evidence of a pervasive form of child-training and recreational preferences (cf. Kardiner, 1949, p. 43).

It may be noted that the presence of severity and love-oriented disciplines in association with games of strategy provides a possible parallel to Miller's finding that, in the United States, there is a greater tendency in middle-class (than in lower-class) child training for reasonable requests for obedience to be associated with severe toilet training and severe weaning, together with the use of psychological controls and symbolic rewards. Middle-class families, he found (Miller and Swanson, 1959), also show a preference for conceptual rather than physical recreations.

Although nine of the eleven tribes with games of strategy and above median reward for obedience listed in Table 2 are African, it must be remembered that modern nations with their games of strategy were not included in the list of 11 societies for which data were gathered. The geographical distribution, though restricted, is compatible with the association between games of strategy and systems of authority.

GAMES OF CHANCE

When tribes with games of chance were compared with those lacking such games, relationships were noted with reward for responsibility, frequency of responsibility, and anxiety about the performance of achievement. The smaller sample added several indices of severity of sex training. From Table 3 it will be noted that seven of the nine exceptional societies with games of

table 3

REWARD FOR RESPONSIBILITY AND GAMES OF CHANCE

	ABOVE MEDIAN	BELOW MEDIAN
Chance Present	Araucanians (13), Muria (13), Dahomeans (12), Aymara (11), Baiga (11), Venda (11), Chagga (11), Hopi (11), Konde (11), Navaho (11), Chukchee (11), Ojibwa (11), Papago (11), Tallensi (10), Mandan (10), Chewa (9), Samoans (9), Thonga (9)	Aleut (8), Zuni (8), Kaska (7), Kwakiutl (7), Omaha (7), Comanche (6), Crow (5), Nauruans (5), Trukese (4)
Chance Absent	Masai (13), Kurtatchi (11) Ainu (10), Gikuyu (10), Ashanti (9), Ganda (9), Murngin (9), Balinese (9)	Alorese (8), Trobrianders (8) Koryak (8), Lamba (8), Lesu (8), Mbundu (8), Wogeo (8), Woleaians (8), Aranda (7), Bena (7), Lepcha (7), Maori (7), Timbira (7), Tanala (7), Tiv (7), Pukapukans (5), Siriono (4), Marquesans (2)

Median = 8
$p = 0.05$

chance but low scores on reward for responsibility are North American Indian tribes. Although this distribution affects the generality of the present thesis, it suggests that the intensity of the game outcome may be important, for in some contexts games of chance are games of courage.

The association between games of chance and training for responsibility is more puzzling than the linkage between games of strategy and obedience. There is, however, an economic theme in these relationships, for many of the responsibilities figuring in the ratings are for the performance of routine chores of an economic nature, while gambling (which is often associated with chance) is likely to entail the transfer of property. Perhaps the association is that of chance and low-status drudgery.

GAMES OF PHYSICAL SKILL

Games of physical skill, whether considered separately as pure physical skill or as physical skill and strategy jointly, show significant relationships with reward for achievement and frequency of achievement. In addition, however, the subclass of physical skill and strategy demonstrates a relationship with anxiety about the nonperformance of achievement. These particular games—the most complex of those involving physical skill—are therefore more highly associated with punishment for not achieving. Tables 4 and 5 provide some sample distributions.

table 4

REWARD FOR ACHIEVEMENT AND NUMBER OF GAMES OF PHYSICAL SKILL, INCLUDING GAMES OF PHYSICAL SKILL AND STRATEGY

	ABOVE MEDIAN	BELOW MEDIAN
9 or more games	Crow (15), Chagga (14), Comanche (14), Kwakiutl (14), Ojibwa (14), Aranda (13, Maori (13), Papago (13), Aleut (12), Gikuyu (12), Omaha (12), Pukapukans (12), Thonga (12), Chukchee (12)	Nauruans (11), Hopi (10), Samoans (10), Koryak (9), Zuni (8), Kaska (6), Trukese (6)
8 or fewer games	Araucanians (13), Mandan (13), Ganda (12), Bena (12)	Venda (11), Konde (11), Masai (11), Muria (11), Navaho (11), Chewa (10), Balinese (10), Siriono (10), Tallensi (10), Tanala (9), Murngin (9), Woleaians (8), Ainu (7), Azande (7), Mbundu (7), Aymara (6), Wogeo (6), Lepcha (5), Lesu (5)

Median number of games = 8
Median rating = 11
$p = 0.01$

GAMING

The foregoing relationships show fairly specifically that strategy is associated with obedience and not with responsibility or achievement, chance

table 5

ANXIETY ABOUT NONPERFORMANCE OF ACHIEVEMENT AND
NUMBER OF GAMES OF PHYSICAL SKILL AND STRATEGY

	ABOVE MEDIAN	BELOW MEDIAN
4 or more games	Chagga (13), Ojibwa (13), Crow (12), Kwakiutl (12), Aranda (11), Comanche (10), Hopi (10), Maori (10), Thonga (10), Venda (9), Chukchee (9), Samoans (9)	Araucanians (8), Mandan (8), Omaha (8), Pukapukans (8), Nauruans (6), Timbira (5)
3 or fewer games	Konde (11), Aleut (10), Ganda (9), Bena (9)	Gikuyu (8), Masai (8), Navaho (8), Papago (8), Chewa (7), Balinese (7), Muria (7), Zuni (7), Aymara (6), Koryak (6), Murngin (6), Siriono (6), Ainu (5), Mbundu (5), Tanala (5), Azande (4), Kaska (4), Tallensi (4), Lepcha (3), Wogeo (3), Lesu (2)

Median number of games = 3
Median rating = 8
$p = 0.02$

with responsibility and not with obedience, and physical skill with achievement and not with obedience and responsibility. There is, however, one additional general finding, namely, that those societies possessing games of strategy, chance, or both, as well as games of physical skill, show anxiety over the performance of achievement (see Table 6). In other words, persons in gaming cultures, particularly those with games of both strategy and chance, are more likely to be directly disapproved, ridiculed, and punished for showing achievement, or to suffer because of the time and effort they must devote to such achievement. Similar relationships emerged between the presence of games of chance and strategy and of conflict over achievement. As games of chance and strategy are symbolic forms of competition, a relationship is established between anxiety over achievement and symbolic forms of competition.

In sum, three of the six major child-training variables (achievement, obedience, and responsibility) used in this study appear to be associated with ludic expressions in the form of true games. Preliminary work indicates that the remaining three variables (independence, nurturance, and self-reliance) may be associated with ludic expressions other than games. Thus, for example, there seems to be a relationship between independence training and certain

table 6

ANXIETY OVER THE PERFORMANCE OF ACHIEVEMENT AND
NUMBER OF GAME CLASSES

	ABOVE MEDIAN	BELOW MEDIAN
4—PS, PS + S, S, C	Thonga (10), Zuni (10), Azande (9), Papago (9), Chewa (8) Chagga (8), Hopi (8), Venda (7)	Dahomeans (4)
3—PS, PS + S	Mbundu (12), Ganda (9), Tiv (7)	Tanala (6), Ashanti (6), Masai (6), Gikuyu (6)
3—PS, PS + S, C	Ojibwa (11), Samoans (11) Crow (10), Araucanians (9), Kwakiutl (9), Navaho (8), Aleut (8), Mandan (8), Omaha (7)	Aymara (6), Nauruans (6), Konde (6), Trukese (5), Tallensi (5), Comanche (4), Kaska (4)
2—PS, PS + S	Aranda (9)	Maori (6), Bena (6), Korayk, (5), Timbira (5), Pukapukans (4), Ainu (4), Wogeo (4)
1—PS		Lesu (4), Lepcha (4), Balinese (4)
0—No games		Murngin (5)

group pastimes. Nurturance may be associated with certain types of model play, and stunts with self-reliance. Research in progress is dealing with these forms of ludic expression.

SUBSYSTEM VALIDATION

Barry, Bacon, and Child (1957) have shown, in a cross-cultural study based on the same ratings as those used here, that there are consistent differences cross-culturally in the training of boys and girls. Boys, for example, are given higher achievement training, while girls are given more consistent obedience and responsibility training. These differences in socialization correspond to the general differences between adult male and female roles over the world. A number of investigations have indicated that, in the United States, achievement is stressed more often in the child training of boys (see Sears, Maccoby, and Levin, 1957, p. 404). There is support, too, for the view that girls receive higher obedience training. Sears, Maccoby, and Levin (1957, p. 407) report that those mothers who made the greatest sex-role differentiation imposed higher demands on girls for instant obedience. With regard to responsibility training, the same investigators (1957, p. 404) state:

In the overall amount of help and chores assigned, there was no sex differences, but there was clear evidence of sex typing in the nature of the chores assigned.

Doing the dishes, making beds, and setting tables were more often girls' work, while the boys more frequently emptied trash, ash cans, and wastebaskets. It will be noted that the girls' tasks are regular daily chores, whereas those of the boys are more intermittent and nonroutine in nature. Miller and Swanson (1958, p. 106) mention routine responsibilities only in relation to girls. It would appear, therefore, that American boys receive more achievement training and less obedience and responsibility training than do American girls. In these respects the differences between boys and girls in the United States are analogous to the differences observed in societies throughout the world. If a universal association exists between child-training variables and ludic preferences and expressions, it would be possible to predict the game preferences of American boys and girls. With such a congruence, the following relationships would be expected to hold:

1. Girls with their higher training in obedience should show a greater preference for games of strategy than boys.
2. Girls with their higher training in responsibility should show a greater preference for games of chance than boys.
3. Boys with their higher training in achievement should show a greater preference for games of physical skill than girls.
4. The difference between boys and girls should be less in regard to games of pure physical skill than in the case of games of physical skill and strategy, since the former are less strongly related to achievement anxiety.

In order to test these hypotheses the responses of 1,900 school children to a list of games were submitted to a chi-square analysis for sex differences. As indicated in Table 7, all the results are in the direction predicted. A difference is assumed when an item differentiates between the sexes at the 5 percent level of significance or better in at least one of the grades (third to sixth) used in the study.

A full report on adult male and female game preferences will be forthcoming. Preliminary analyses of survey data, however, have confirmed the preference of women for games of strategy and of chance and the preference of men for games of physical skill. Moreover, persons with semi-skilled occupations (emphasizing responsibility) have been found to exhibit a greater preference for games of chance when compared with people in the professions (emphasizing achievement and obedience), who show a greater preference for games of physical skill and games of strategy. These are the findings which would have been expected in the light of the implications of the foregoing cross-cultural and intracultural analyses.

Although the above subsystem validation may not be fully convincing, it is promising enough to warrant further inquiry. It certainly suggests that

table 7

NUMBER OF GAMES DIFFERENTIATING BETWEEN THE
SEXES AT $p = 0.05$ OR BETTER

GAMES CLASSES	NONSIGNIFICANT	FAVORING GIRLS	FAVORING BOYS
Strategy	Beast, Birds & Fish, Dominoes, Chess, Parcheesi, Scrabble, Tic Tac Toe, Clue, Monopoly (8)	I've Got a Secret, Name That Tune, Checkers, Twenty Questions, I Spy (5)	(0)
Chance	Coin-Matching, Forfeits, Cards, Seven-Up (4)	Bingo, Spin the Bottle, Post Office, Musical Chairs, Letters, Colors, Initials (7)	Dice (1)
Pure Physical Skill	Quoits (1)	Hopsotch, Jump Rope, Jacks, Tiddleywinks (4)	Bowling, Horseshoe, Racing, Tug of War, Darts, Shuffleboard, Bows & Arrows, Throwing Snowballs, Shooting (9)
Physical Skill and Strategy	Handball, Tennis, Volleyball, Prisoner's Base, Fox & Hounds, Ping Pong (5)	Pick up Sticks (1)	Marbles, Wrestling, Boxing, Basketball, Football, Capture the Flag, Punt Back, Pool, Billiards, Baseball, Soccer (11)

cross-cultural findings may be used to predict intracultural variation. At the same time it enhances the confidence with which cross-cultural generalizations may be accepted.

Discussion

The foregoing results detail a relationship between child-training variables and games which must be explained. Although the results permit the formulation of a conflict interpretation of game involvement, it must be recognized that this interpretation is as yet unconfirmed. Studies now in progress are being directed toward this task.

Any theory of free game participation must account for the players' voluntary entry into games. The conflict hypothesis of game involvement holds that players become initially curious about games, learn them, and ultimately acquire high involvement in them because of specific psychological conflicts, and that the eventual decrease in involvement is related, apart from biological changes, to learning or enculturation. Addicted players, it is assumed, remain in a high state of inner psychological conflict, which is not resolved through physical development or learning. But to postulate such a relationship with conflict is to entertain an association which is much more complex than it is novel (*cf.* Freud, 1924). It seems necessary first to assay its credibility.

The research by Child, Storn, and Veroff (1958) on the child-training variables of conflict, reward, frequency, and anxiety suggests that there is substantial correlation among them, so that whenever a rating is received on any one, a certain amount of positive variance in the others can also be assumed. For example, where there is reward there is usually some conflict, and where there is anxiety there is usually some reward. In addition, it is not unusual to regard anxiety as a conflict-producing drive (see Wurtz, 1960). When a child is punished for, let us say, achievement, he gradually learns to anticipate punishment whenever he is stimulated to achieve, so that anxiety becomes a drive state in conflict with achievement. The anxiety-instigated responses conflict with those induced by the child's need to achieve. While the present study cannot fully clarify the differential effects of the variety of conflicts noted in the data—those involving anxiety about performance (Table 1, Nos. 13 and 21), anxiety about nonperformance (Table 1, Nos. 5 and 20), and interactions between these two (Table 1, No. 22)—the occurrence of definite associations does suggest the credibility of a conflict formulation of games.

Current play therapy, which sees children's spontaneous play as a projective system (see Erikson, 1943), implies that games are symbolic substitutes for responses which are incompatible with the normal behavior of the child. Games of strategy, for example, would reflect an association with anxiety about nonperformance of obedience. Presumably there is here a conflict between being obedient and being anxious about nonperformance of obedience or, to put it more simply, a conflict between obedience and disobedience. When it is remembered that the pattern of child training associated with games of strategy involves much severity (Table 1, Nos. 6, 8, 9, and 10) and therefore much implicit frustration and provocation to aggression, but that it is, at the same time, a pattern in which obedience is strongly rewarded and in which the parents do not practice aggression, the need for a displaced and considerably attenuated form of aggression becomes evident. The players are presumably those who remain obedient to the social system but who relieve their ambivalence about it by displaced attack in the miniature social worlds of the strategy games. Indeed, Menninger (1942, p. 175) has explicitly taken this last position, saying of a game of strategy: "It enables us to express aggression without reality consequences; we can hurt people without really hurting them; we can even kill them without really killing them." Such a line of argument, however, goes beyond the data provided in the child-training ratings used in this paper.

The explanation of the relationship between conflict and games of chance would also need to invoke variables not provided in the material of this paper. These games are in fact the most enigmatic of all those considered in this research. Yet the cross-cultural relationships between games of chance and responsibility training and the intra-cultural relationship between these phenomena and female preferences, while surprising, do not seem fortuitous. Other papers have also established an overlapping cluster of relationships between chance, the benevolence of divine beings (Roberts, Arth, and Bush, 1959), and responsibility (Lambert, 1959). Responsibility training is the inculcation of a necessary routine which allows little scope for personal initiative or autonomy. That chores and economic tasks must be done is self-evident, and punishment for not doing them is apparently unnecessary (see Table 1, Nos. 11 and 12), since chance playing is not coupled with anxiety about nonperformance of responsibility (which means punishment for not being responsible) as strategy playing is coupled with punishment for not being obedient (Table 1, No. 5). But although chance players are not punished as part of their responsibility training, they do receive punishment in other related aspects of training, namely, for showing initiative (Table 1, No. 13) or interest in sex (Table 1, Nos. 14 and 15). It would seem reasonable that punishment for not showing initiative would be likely to force a child into a reliance upon the most elementary of stratagems, a trust in the omnipotence of his own thought processes. And this elementary trust is, according to some (Bergler, 1957), the source of all wishful thinking, gambling, and chance-taking activity. According to this interpretation, a game of chance is a response to the passivity of the player's normal life role and an expression of incompatible responses toward irresponsibility which are in conflict with the diligent role of the responsible provider. Benevolent fate, if not fantasy, may lift the routine worker out of his or her present life tasks with magical efficacy.

Games of physical skill appear to be a direct and microcosmic representation of achievement. Indeed they are often used on the tribal level as training procedures for hunting (archery or hoop-and-pole) and in the psychological laboratory, in the form of ring toss and darts, for the measurement of level of aspiration and achievement motivation (McClelland, 1955). Nevertheless, although the only obvious relationships we have demonstrated for games of pure physical skill are with reward for achievement and frequency of achievement (Table 1, Nos. 16, 17, 18, and 19), it seems reasonable to assume that there should also be some association with anxiety and conflict. This is definitely the case with games of physical skill and strategy (Table 1, No. 20). Perhaps persons who play these games are in conflict about real achievement and use the simulated achievement of games to assuage their anxiety. It may be concluded for these and other games, as Kagan (1960) has concluded about apperceptive techniques, that they are a better index of preferred modes of defense than they are of motive strength.

It might be noted parenthetically that, if this conception of games of physical skill is correct, it is injudicious to use such games in laboratory experiments as supposedly "neutral" measures of need achievement. The cross-cultural evidence at this point amplifies doubts recently expressed about such usage by Broverman, Jordan, and Phillips (1960).

It is clear from the foregoing formulations that while games of strategy, chance, and physical skill may be played by persons who are in conflict about obedience, responsibility, or achievement, respectively, there are important differences in the relationships between the types of conflict and the nature of the games. Games of strategy and chance express the child-training variables of obedience and responsibility only indirectly, while games of physical skill give direct expression to achievement training. It may be that the differences between the "general expression" theory of fantasy (McClelland, 1955) and the "alternative-channels" theory (Lazarus, et al., 1957) may be resolved by a theory which postulates that different types of variables lead to different types of expression in fantasy. In any case, there are similarities between these game-type differences and those which have been found in clinical work with children's fantasy within our own culture. It is true that fantasy expression is not the same as game expression, but any formulation that promises an understanding of both is worthy of consideration. It would, in addition, provide a further indication that a relationship which has been found to apply cross-culturally can have value for the understanding of intra-cultural variation.

The present game data permit the formulation of the proposition that there is an inverse relationship between the degree of conflict induced by the learning processes (child-training ratings) and the complexity and symbolism of the games (or, as it will be termed later, their scale of participation). It is noteworthy that games of pure physical skill, which are the least complex and most motor of games, have the fewest obvious associations with indices of conflict; that games of physical skill and strategy, with their higher degree of symbolism and complexity, have an added association with anxiety; and that games of chance and of strategy have many such associations. This statement closely parallels a recent formulation of the relationship between individual conflict and individual fantasy responses to apperceptive stimuli. Kagan (1960) has found that an individual's fantasy is a function of his degree of conflict and of the ambiguity of the stimulus presented to him. In games, the ambiguity of the stimulus and the character of the response are prescribed by the rules. In the clinical situation the investigator manipulates the stimuli and judges from the individual's responses the nature and degree of his conflict. In the game situation, the stimuli and responses are patterned, and individuals who have the necessary conflicts opt their way in. Perhaps even more important than the establishment of this parallel is the fact that it becomes possible to subsume these two quite distinct types of fantasy behavior—cross-cultural ludic models and private individual fantasies—within the confines of Miller's (1959) statement of learning theory, which says, in effect, that the greater the degree of conflict the greater will be the displacement of affect. The existence of such cross-cultural and intra-cultural regularities makes a propitious background for the "scale of participation" to be introduced below.

A question not discussed above is that of the difference between conflict which leads simply to exploratory activity, such as that described by Berlyne (1960) and termed "ludic" by him, and conflict of the sorts which lead to the repetitive substitutive sorts of behaviors with which we are here concerned. It has been customary to reserve the term "ludic" for these latter manifestations alone (Huizinga, 1949). The important question, however, is whether the difference between exploratory activity and repetitive ludic behavior is simply one of degree or whether there is some ascertainable hiatus between them. Piaget (1957), who speaks of normal and "distorting" assimilations, apparently assumes the difference to be a matter of degree.

The arguments presented here affirm the credibility of a relationship between psychological conflict and the playing of games, and suggest that the principles governing such a relationship may transcend games and be applicable to intra-cultural variation in fantasy. Thus far, only the motivation which brings the player to the point of game involvement has been discussed. It is suggested that, being in conflict, he becomes interested in the game because it provides a means of assuaging conflict. Attention will now be directed to other features of ludic models yet to be investigated in future papers.

Implications

The joint consideration of anthropological, clinical, and experimental concepts of fantasy adds weight to the view that games are just one part of a cultural participation scale that varies from dreams at one end to full-scale cultural behavior at the other. At the beginning of childhood there are presumably individual dreams and solitary play. As the child develops, these find a matching in such cultural models as songs, dances, folktales, poems, programs, riddles, rhymes, and games. There are arrays of models available at any age level, and within any type a series ranging from lesser to greater complexity. Across all models there is a broader path leading toward greater cultural participation or away from such participation. As models approach full-scale cultural participation they increase in scale, becoming nearer in nature to the reality they copy. As they proceed in the other direction, the scale is reduced and the participation is often vicarious. It is also true that models, regardless of scale of participation, can differ along a scale of similitude, with exact copies marking one end and distorted representations the other.

This discussion can be illustrated by considering specific models. Games, for example, are expressive models of a particular sort. Like the cultural activities which they model, e.g., dueling, war, court trials, or market transactions, they involve behavior in interactive situations, but, unlike their analogies in full-scale cultural life, they involve participation which is usually defined as being recreational or nonsignificant (or, alternatively, smaller in scale). Admittedly, there are times when game activities become salient in a culture, as with professional baseball during a World Series, but even here there is recognition that baseball is recreational and expressive. On the other hand, games also have their analogues in folktales. Cinderella, for example, was clearly a "winner," and the wicked stepsisters were "losers." Many tales, stories, or plays, of course, do not resemble games so much as they resemble other noncompetitive ludic expressions such as pastimes or model play, but many tales can be scored in terms of outcome just as if they were games. In a preliminary study it has been demonstrated that there is a relationship between the presence of games of strategy in a society and the importance of strategic determinations of outcomes in folktales from the same society. Those societies which have an outcome in one ludic model tend to have it in the other. This indicates that games, as part of the participation scale, have their analogs both in full-scale social behaviors and in smaller-scale folktales. A schematic relationship between models and behaviors may be suggested as follows:

SCALE OF PREPARATION

OUTCOME DETERMINATION	FULL-SCALE (ACTIVITY)	SMALL-SCALE (MODELS)	
		BEHAVIORAL (GAMES)	VICARIOUS (TALES)
Physical Skill	Herding on Foot	Footrace	Tortoise and Hare
Strategy	Market Activities	Monopoly, Poker	The Fisherman and His Wife
Chance	Striking It Rich in a Gold Field	Roulette	Cinderella

These dimensions of scale and similitude are only two of those involved in the conceptualization of a cultural participation scale. The authors are turning their attention to such dimensions, but as yet the studies have not been completed.

It remains to identify the enculturative effects that games may be supposed to have. The presentation of the participation scale, of course, implies that there is some normal procedure whereby individuals work their way through parts of the scale, presumably as the result of maturation and learning. In general, it is suggested that each game is a microcosmic social structure in which the polarities of winning and losing are variously represented. The individual in conflict is attracted to a model because he can find in it a codification of the emotional and cognitive aspects of his conflict, which is unavailable to him, at his level of maturity, in full-scale cultural participation. In a game of strategy, for example, he can practice deception against his powerful opponent, and can even "kill" him, but in addition he can also command his own forces (as he is commanded by those whom he normally obeys). Because the codification is so adequate to his needs and level of maturity, he is implicitly taught a characteristic success style. Each type of game in unique fashion contributes information as to the relative values and nature of different types of chance, skill, and strategy in assuaging conflict and in learning how to handle social competition. Between the ages of seven and twelve years the child learns, in simple direct form, how to take a chance, how to show skill, and how to deceive. Increasingly, in complex games, he learns the reversibility of these styles—when to rely on one type of success gambit rather than another, how to combine them, etc. What he learns from the games are the cognitive operations involved in competitive success. These cannot be learned by young children in full-scale cultural participation. They can be learned only through models, whether games or models of other types. Unlike the judgments of weight or volume dealt with by Piaget, they are intellectual operations of multi-dimensional complexity, incapable of being represented by simple codifications.

In earlier sections we presented evidence and interpretation in support of the view that psychological conflict leads to game involvement. In considering the implications of our research we have gone further and have advanced (more speculatively) a theory of games which seeks to reconcile the classic theories of play as exercise (Groos, 1919) and play as conflict (Freud, 1924). This theory asserts that both psychological conflict and cognitive structures must be taken into account in understanding the cultural function of games as part of ludic models in general. The theory implies (1) that there is an over-all process of cultural patterning whereby society induces conflict in children through its child-training processes; (2) that society seeks through appropriate arrays and varieties of ludic models to provide an assuagement of these conflicts by an adequate representation of their emotional and cognitive polarities in ludic structure; and (3) that through these models society tries to provide a form of buffered learning through which the child can make enculturative step-by-step progress toward adult behavior.

It must be stressed that the research results presented in this paper do not substantiate a conflict-enculturation interpretation. Rather, the results lead to various tentative formulations which represent the first step in the development of an explicit set of hypotheses to be tested in future research. Exploratory research with undergraduate game players at Cornell University, for example, indicates that addicted players of games of strategy are in conflict about their positions in social system. Earlier studies by Sutton-Smith (1951, 1959) of relationships between Maori and European games suggest that field studies of game acculturation are likely to be illuminating. It is reasonable to presume that culture contact develops both psychological conflicts and needs for cognitive restructuring which lead to a readiness for new games and to the rejection of old ones. In fact, the historical changes in games in the culture of the United States should be symptomatic of changes in basic child-training procedures (Sutton-Smith and Rosenberg, 1961). Clearly, there is need for additional research in the complex area of games and gamesters.

REFERENCES

Bacon, M., H. Barry III, and I. L. Child, 1952. "Raters' Instructions for Analysis of Socialization Practices with Respect to Dependence and Independence." Mimeographed.

————, 1955. "Cross-Cultural Ratings of Certain Socialization Practices." Mimeographed.

Barry, H., M. K. Bacon, and I. L. Child, 1957. "A Cross-Cultural Survey of Some Sex Differences in Socialization," *Journal of Abnormal and Social Psychology*, 55:327–332.

Bergler, E., 1957. *The Psychology of Gambling*, New York.

Berlyne, D. E., 1960. "Conflict Arousal and Curiosity," New York.

Broverman, D. M., E. J. Jordan, Jr., and L. Phillips, 1960. "Achievement Motivation in Fantasy Behavior," *Journal of Abnormal and Social Psychology*, 60:374–378.

Child, I. L., T. Storn, and J. Veroff, 1958. "Achievement Themes in Folk Tales Related to Socialization Practice," *Motives in Fantasy, Action, and Society*, ed. J. W. Atkinson, pp. 479–492, New York.

Erikson, E. H., 1943. "Clinical Studies in Children's Play," *Child Behavior and Development*, ed. R. G. Barker *et al.*, pp. 411–428, New York.

Freud, S., 1924. *Beyond the Pleasure Principle*, New York.

Groos, K., 1919. *The Play of Man*, New York and London.

Huizinga, J., 1949. *Homo Ludens*, London.

Kagan, J., 1960. "Thematic Apperceptive Techniques with Children," *Projective Techniques with Children*, ed. A. I. Rabin and M. R. Haworth, pp. 105–129, New York and London.

Kardiner, A., 1939. *The Individual and His Society*, New York.

Lambert, W. W., L. M. Triandis, and M. Wolf, 1959. "Some Correlates of Beliefs in the Malevolence and Benevolence of Supernatural Beings: A Cross-Cultural Study," *Journal of Abnormal and Social Psychology*, 58:162–169.

Lazarus, R. S., R. W. Baker, and D. M. Broverman, 1957. "Personality and Psychological Stress," *Journal of Personality*, 25:559–577.

Menninger, K., 1942. *Love Against Hate*, New York.

McClelland, D. C., 1955. "Measuring Motivation in Phantasy: The Achievement Motive," *Studies in Motivation*, ed. D. C. McClelland, pp. 401–413. New York.

Miller, D. R., and G. E. Swanson, 1958. *The Changing American Parent*, New York.

————, 1959. *Inner Conflict and Defense*, New York.

Miller, N. E., 1959. "Liberalization of Basic S-R Concepts: Extension to Conflict Behavior, Motivation, and Social Learning," *Psychology: A Study of Science*, ed. S. Koch, 2:196–292.

Piaget, J., 1957. *Logic and Psychology*, New York.

Roberts, J. M., M. J. Arth, and R. R. Bush, 1959. "Games in Culture," *American Anthropologist*, 61:597–605.

Sears, R. R., E. E. Maccoby, and H. Levin, 1957. *Patterns of Child Rearing*, Evanston.

Sutton-Smith, B., 1951. "The Meeting of Maori and European Culture and Its Effects upon the Unorganized Games of Maori Children," *Journal of the Polynesian Society*, 60:93–107.

————, 1959. *The Games of New Zealand Children*, Berkeley.

Sutton-Smith, B., and B. G. Rosenberg, 1960. *Play and Game List* (I. B. M. Form I. T. S. 100 A 6058), New York.

————, 1961. "Sixty Years of Historical Change in Game Preferences of American Children," *Journal of American Folklore*, 74:17–46.

Sutton-Smith, B., B. G. Rosenberg, and E. Morgan, Jr., 1961. "Sex Differences in Role Preferences for Play Activities and Games," paper Presented to the Society for Research in Child Development.

Wurtz, K. P., 1960. "Some Theory and Data Concerning the Attenutation of Aggression," *Journal of Abnormal and Social Psychology*, 60:134–136.

Pueblo baseball:
a new use for old witchcraft

J . R . F O X

The ideals of harmony and cooperation and the outlawing of competition among the Pueblo Indians have become an anthropological commonplace over the last few decades.[1] Benedict's confusion of institutions with personality traits which led her to believe that the Puebloans were "harmonious" people has since been corrected. Such books as *Sun Chief* [2] have shown vividly the amount of hate, aggression, and suspicion that lies behind the conscious harmony of Pueblo social life. If one could characterize the content of interpersonal relations in the Pueblos with one word, I think "cautious" would be that word. One has to be careful in dealing with others for fear of "what people will say." The power of public opinion in these crowded little communities is the strongest force for social conformity, and manifests itself in the extreme fear of witchcraft accusations. Indeed, the fear of being accused is greater than the fear of actual witchcraft. Informants are vague about the

[1] The research on which this paper is based was made possible by the Social Science Research Council and the Laboratory of Social Relations, Harvard University. It was carried out largely in the Pueblo of Cochiti, New Mexico (approximate population in 1959: 500, of which 300 were actually resident in the Pueblo).

[2] *Sun Chief: The Autobiography of a Hopi Indian*, ed. Lee W. Simmons, New Haven: Yale University Press, 1942.

• From the *Journal of American Folklore*, 9–16, Vol. 74 (1961). Copyright © by the American Folklore Society.

powers and practices of witches and often complain that they have forgotten what witches are supposed to do—"only the old people remember what the *kanatya* do." [3] But everyone is agreed that the most terrible thing that one can say of another is "everyone knows he (or she) is a witch." Thus, while the cultural trappings and elaborations surrounding witch behavior have largely been forgotten, the motivational basis for this projective system remains strong. It exists, as it were, in the raw.

Everyone is suspect. The Sun Chief of Oriabi even suspected his own mother on her deathbed of being a "two-heart." All interpersonal relations are fraught with danger and there are few people one can wholly trust. In particular women do not trust each other. The Don Juanism of the males and the relative promiscuity of the women means that no woman can be really sure that any other is not her husband's lover, or has not been at some time. A woman can trust her sisters, more or less, and of course her mother, primarily because it would be difficult for members of the same household group to carry on affairs under each other's noses.[4] Affines are very much mistrusted and often with good cause.

What is involved is not so much sexual jealousy as, again, the fear of "talk." This also is not just fear of gossip. Words have power and are not to be used lightly. "Bad thoughts" have tremendous repercussions and are believed to have effects in the real world. Bad words, as the manifestations of bad thoughts, "poison the air of the Pueblo." [5] The real repercussions of accusation and insults are in fact disturbing to Pueblo peace. In societies based on extended kin groupings one cannot insult one person at a time. Thus any accusations may lead to a widespread split-up of the village, and this fear of internal dissension provides strong motivation for not making open accusations, or at least for toning them down. In the case of a philandering husband caught *in flagrante delicto*, relatives on both sides will try to patch the matter up or at least persuade the pair to part quietly and without fuss. In "the old days" a woman could be rid of her husband fairly easily by ordering him out of her house. This is becoming more impossible today as men are now more likely than women to be housewives. In the Eastern Pueblos the Catholic Church complicates matters by forbidding divorce and remarriage. A wronged woman will often go to live with her sister or mother, taking her children, but life becomes hard because she cannot remarry and she risks priestly censure if she takes another mate.

[3] Full descriptions of witch beliefs in Cochiti are to be found in Noël Dumarest, *Notes on Conchiti, New Mexico, Memoirs of the American Anthropological Association,* VI, No. 3, 1919, and E. S. Goldfrank, *The Social and Ceremonial Organization of Cochiti, Memoirs of the American Anthropological Association,* No. 33, 1927.

[4] The number of actual matrilocal households is declining in Cochiti, but as Fred Eggan says of the Hopi, ". . . the *conceptual* unity of the household group still remains," *The Social Organization of the Western Pueblos,* Chicago, 1950, p. 30.

[5] "Breathing" and "blowing" are two common ritual gestures and there is a whole system of beliefs concerning the taking in and giving out of power by breathing. Thus the importance of "the air" of the village.

The frustrations consequent upon these limitations to direct action cause much bitterness between women, and witchcraft accusations are more likely to be female affairs than male. In the old days the War Captains, ceremonial police of the Pueblos, would have dealt with the witches once sufficient proof had been gathered of their activities. Death or banishment would have been the punishment. Today, however, and often in the past, nothing would be done about it. "People just got mad and didn't speak to each other or they left the village." Today also the relatively sophisticated Cochiti realize that white people think these beliefs silly, and tend to shrug off or deny them. Some members of the ultra-Catholic progressive faction share the white man's contempt for these beliefs. But beneath this air of careless disbelief and denial there lies the motivational and social basis for the interpersonal fear that has not changed.

Formal Pueblo institutions, then, as a counter to, rather than an acting out of, personality forces, stress harmony and cooperation. People must dance together, work together, play together. They are enjoined to think good harmonious thoughts so as not to spoil the air of the Pueblo. Bad thoughts are as dangerous as bad deeds and conscious effort should be made to eradicate them. Drunkenness is feared, as it lets loose all the aggressive impulses which one must constantly work to damp down. All forms of overt hostility are taboo.

In Cochiti, the intricate criss-crossing of clans, societies, Kivas (dual ceremonial organizations), extended families, church and other groups helps to ensure that no permanent oppositions and cleavages can occur which would channel hostilities into armed camps. The factional split (conservatives and progressives) came nearest to open war, but the cross-cutting of these divisions by others (particularly extended families) saved the village from complete disintegration. As long as any two groups continue to exchange women in Cochiti, it is difficult for them to remain in hostile opposition. All formal divisions within the village have been divisions of labor and not enmity or opposition. The cooperation of the two Kivas is essential to the proper performance of public ceremonies and they in no way compete with each other. All medicine societies complement each other's work—there are never two societies for one cure. A careful political balance is struck so that every group is evenly represented on the council. As the village is small, the result is a series of overlapping roles with a consequent impossibility of permanent conflict, despite the fact of continually recurring conflicts.

The old competitive games of the Pueblo followed this principle and were never played between any two formal groups. For races and shinny games the categories of "married" versus "unmarried" were employed, or teams were picked from the young men on a count-out method. There was never a competitive alignment in terms of the existing social groupings and teams were not permanent affairs. Since the advent of baseball in Cochiti, however, and particularly within the last decade, a new and unique situation has arisen. Cochiti now has two baseball teams playing in the same league

(Inter-Pueblo Baseball League) [6] and in open competition with each other. The original team, now called the Redskins, was formed many years ago and old photographs testify to the long-standing interest in baseball in the Pueblo. Support comes from all sections of the population including the old medicine men and the ceremonial heads of the Kivas. Baseball is not thought of as alien. Most men now playing grew up in a society which was already enthusiastic about the sport. The present *cacique*, the religious leader of the tribe, was for a long time a pitcher for the second team. On his assuming office the medicine men forbade him to continue, as playing ball was not consonant with the dignity of his office—but he is the sole exception. The original team, first known as the Eagles, was the sole focus of interest for many years, but with the return of servicemen to Cochiti after the Second World War, interest grew and a second team, the Silversmiths, was formed. This team, now known as the Braves, claimed independent status, built its own ball park and entered the league in competition with the Redskins. They were immediately successful and won the championship three years in succession. Thus a new and potentially dangerous situation occurred—these two teams had to meet each other in the village and fight it out twice a year. The situation was wildly at variance with the whole Pueblo ethos.

What happened was interesting. The first game was played and while all went reasonably well on the field there were fights on the sidelines and these between the *mothers* of the players. As the momentum of the game increased these ladies began to abuse each other, to brawl, and finally to do open battle. The horrified Pueblo council immediately banned all future games between the teams in the Pueblo.

An examination of the original membership in the two teams shows that, because of the voluntary nature of their recruitment, they were a perfect breeding ground for factions. One was not constrained by kinship ties, initiation, or any other automatic factor to join either team, but could choose. The Braves, when they broke away from the Redskins, broke away by family groups, i.e., several families of players left the one and formed the other. Thus the choice was made, not by individuals, but by families. It seems from the statements of informants that there have always been, within living memory, two ill-defined groups of extended families which formed opposing "blocks" on the basis of quarrels now forgotten. Previously these two blocks had never had occasion or excuse to come out in opposition to each other, as there had been no basis for such an oppositional grouping, and the two groups even cut across the conservative-progressive factional boundaries—but in the baseball split there was a unique opportunity for the old latent hostilities to come to the surface. Allegiance to the team is patrilineal as with the Kivas, but the two teams are by no means coterminous with the Kivas. Thus the two teams represent a dual alignment of families for purely competitive purposes. Fam-

[6] The teams are: Cochiti (2), Santa Ana, San Felipe, Santa Clara (2), San Juan, San Ildefonso, Tesuque, Santa Fe Jays (based at the Santa Fe Indian School).

ilies which mistrusted or disliked each other could readily line up on opposite sides of the fence and even to uncommitted families the infection spread. The crosscutting tendency in Pueblo institutions of course works to mitigate this as it did with the factions, but here the essential factor of the exchange of women has not had time to work itself out. What is more, the away games of the teams have increased the chances of young men to meet girls from outside the village and hence increased the number of outmarriages. The wives of these marriages, having no female relatives in Cochiti, tend to become assimilated into the husband's mother's extended family and this increases the gap between the two sides. Out of eight marriages in one year, three were to San Juan girls—results of the popular away games at that Pueblo. It is not the young wives, however, but rather the older women who are the "trouble-makers." These women who would formerly have had little chance to attack other women they disliked without invoking the frightening subject of witchcraft, now have excuse and opportunity to do battle royal over the bodies of their sons and grandsons. The epithet *cheater* has become a virtual synonym for witch.[7]

The council ban was effective in preventing open war in the village for a time, but it only served to drive the feelings underground. Suspicion and hostility grew until this year (1959), when they broke out again into the open. By this time the antagonism had spread to the players. Previously the teams had made strenuous efforts to be fair and play the game, but the noise from the sidelines had made this difficult. This year the Braves had indulged in a series of rulebreaking episodes which flared into open quarrels. These were accentuated by the fact that after a trial game last year which rumbled but went off without incident, the council had reluctantly decided that the annual games could be played again. Significantly the games were placed at the beginning of the week during which the annual corn dance was to take place, on the feast day of the village saint (St. Bonaventure). Thus they should come at a time when "all hearts are in harmony" and everyone is bending his efforts towards the success of the great commutal dance for rain, good harvest and long life.

The Braves, according to their opponents, had not been in with the spirit of the thing. A Redskin commented, "Rules don't mean nothing to them; they don't care." It seems that the Braves had gone to town with the rule book. They had: (1) played people in the finals who had not played five consecutive games; (2) failed to turn up for games but refused to forfeit the points for them; (3) played men who had previously played for other sides and refused to relinquish them even after threats of suspension; (4) cheated in the games; (5) threatened umpires (unspecified); (6) attempted to maim

---

[7] There was a chance that the "Little League" team, formed in 1958, would pull the two teams together by drawing on children of both parties. This failed to happen and such was the bickering and dispute over the children's team that this year it was discontinued. No one wanted the responsibility for it, as there was too much fighting between the mothers.

opponents. A rule which was not in the official book but which, I was told, the Braves and their female supporters broke most often was to influence the course of the game by occult means—witchcraft. Particularly, it seems, they attempted to cause "accidents," to make the ball hit a runner, etc. To any enquiries as to why they hadn't been suspended or denied the replays, I was told, "they get their own way because the other teams are scared of them." San Juan had a good claim to two forfeited games but gave in because "they were scared." The manager of the Braves is a feared man in being the *Kwirena Nawa*, head of the powerful *Kwirena* society, one of the "managing societies" in Pueblo ceremonial. He is also head of the Pumpkin Kiva. Some of the Redskins spoke out against the Braves' conduct at meetings of the league, and in a confused bit of political maneuvering the Braves were alternately suspended, reinstated, quit the league, and rejoined. By the time of the Cochiti games they were in again but had lost points for two games the league decided they must forfeit.

The Cochiti games, set on Sunday, were to have made up a double-header—the first game in the morning after Mass and the second in the afternoon prior to the Kiva practice for the corn dance. For some reason I was never able to fathom, the Braves failed to show up for the morning game. The Redskins, in an attempt to be friendly and keep things on an even keel, agreed to play the lost game on the following Saturday. Several female relatives of the Redskins muttered that the game should have been claimed; "the men are too soft." But the men were making a conscious if nervous effort to keep things going smoothly. Several men said they would not watch the game: "they'll only fight, those ladies; they'll just yell and shout and upset everybody; people don't forget easily." "They don't care about the game, they just want to fight and upset other people." Sometimes, "they don't speak to each other for a year or more." Other times, "they are just mad in the season, they forget it in the winter," The Redskins' supporters could name only one Braves family which was consistently friendly with any Redskin family. Asked why this antagonism didn't exist between Kivas, they told me, "Why should it? They don't have nothing to fight about." But no one could explain why the antagonism was there in the first place, or rather no one was willing to risk the analysis for fear of reaching conclusions too unpleasant to bear about his beloved village. All the men agreed that it was the fault of "them old ladies. I guess they just like fighting."

The afternoon game was played in a fit of nerves and deliberate efforts were made to keep things calm. To lend weight to the authority of the council, both the Governor and the Lieutenant Governor came and sat together, and the War Captain and his assistant were present, strategically placed between the supporters of the two sides. The men of the village deliberately chose a neutral spot behind the wire and huddled there while the women of the teams stood around their respective dugouts.

The game progressed in a lively fashion and the women gathered force as it went on. The comments, at first mild—"Get him glasses, he can't see,"

"He can't hit what he can't see; he's blind"—became bitter, personal and obscene.[8] The men meanwhile made polite comments and factual observations and differences of opinion were glossed over. At one point the comments of the women became so noisy that the Redskins' manager, at his team's request, hurried over to the female supporters and gave them a lecture. This had no noticeable effect. However, the game passed off without any really unruly incident, although the nervousness of the players led to a phenomenal number of errors. Two factors led to a relaxation of tension: there was a neutral umpire (a colored boy from Virginia), and the game was never in doubt. The Redskins went into an early lead and finally won eighteen to eight. Everyone left the ball ground quickly and irate old ladies were hustled away by sons and grandsons.

During the following week tension mounted towards the second game. Many people declared they would stay away, and others were equally sure they wouldn't miss it for anything. The latter were usually women. "There's going to be a lot of accidents," I was told by a Redskin mother, " 'cause them Braves is sure mad they lost last Sunday." The corn dance served to lessen the tension somewhat in midweek, and opposing families had to dance together in the communal prayer for harmony and happiness. But by the Saturday morning the tension was high again. The intention to stay away was carried out by many people. Those that came, perhaps lacking the feeling of safety in numbers, stayed mostly in their pick-ups and cars and watched from inside. The Lieutenant Governor, himself not a regular fan, placed himself between the two blocks of women and invited me to join him. Some Redskins had been to the local Spanish-American town of Pena Blanca and returned drunk and excited. Twice in the previous week I had been cautioned to "watch out for their (the Braves') magic."

I did not have long to wait. After the game had been tied up at one-one for four innings and the tension was increasing, the skies suddenly darkened. Lightning flashed and thunder rolled, but no rain fell. A huge pre-storm wind swept across the valley and lifted clouds of sand many feet into the air. The field was obliterated and players crouched down to avoid being blinded by the stinging dirt. I took refuge in a Redskin car, where it was pointed out to me that had the other ground been used (the Redskins') this would not have happened as there was less lose dirt there. But the Braves had insisted on using their own inferior ground, "so that they could work more of their magic." How this complete stoppage of play was to the Braves' advantage, I failed to see.

The game should have been halted until the sand cleared but the Braves insisted on continuing to play. So play went on sporadically between sharp bursts of wind, swirling sand-storms and the crashing of thunder. And still no rain fell. Sun Chief describes how if, instead of rain, at the end of a

---

[8] "Baseball talk" is all in English. See my "Note on Cochiti Linguistics," in Charles H. Lange, *Cochiti: A New Mexico Pueblo, Past and Present*, Austin: University of Texas Press, 1959.

Katsina dance only a strong wind blew spreading sand, then this showed that those who sent for the Katsinas had bad hearts and had done evil. This feeling was present at the Cochiti game. Thunder, lightning and storm clouds which bring only the dead dust and no life-giving rain are the worst of portents. One Redskin going out to bat fell on his knees, crossed himself, and muttered a prayer.

Things were complicated by the presence of a nonneutral umpire. He was in fact of the Redskin faction, but was courting the daughter of a prominent Braves family (Q*). The only reason he was made umpire was that he was on leave from the Navy and hence would be returning taking any bad feelings with him. He gave a faulty seeming decision which cost the Redskins a base. Immediately insults were flung at him by the Redskin women. Out loud they called, "Some of the Q* dirt has rubbed off on you!" and "She's got you under her skin, that Q* girl." Amongst themselves they used other epithets than girl, and muttered about "influences." Complications were added by the fact that the umpire was the son of the Lieutenant Governor, and no one wished to offend the much liked and respected official. This served in some ways to prevent more trouble.

In between the sand-storms the game continued and the score leveled to two-two at the bottom of the eighth inning. In the final innings the Redskins seemed to go to pieces as the sand lashed their faces, while the Braves hit two runs to win the game four to two. The players ran to shake hands, although some refused—an unheard-of thing in previous games. The male participants by and large tried to keep things calm. The Braves women were screaming with delight at the success of their side, and the Redskin women went away tight-lipped and furious, convinced of dirty work. That dirty work was involved was obvious to these women. The storm, the influenced umpire, the unaccountable reversal of the Redskins (an admittedly superior team under "normal" conditions), all added up—to witchcraft.

In the weeks following the games, tension remained high, with rival families not speaking. About three weeks after, however, an incident occurred which brought the whole thing out again. The Redskins had just lost a game and were returning home disconsolate, when a Braves mother accosted one of them as he entered his house. The burden of her remarks seemed to be that he had lost the game because his love life was sapping his strength. All this was said in the presence of the Redskin's wife, who was furious but mute. The Redskin hurled a few replies and went indoors. The Braves mother had not finished however; she stood on her own roof top and hurled insults across at her neighbor. The Redskin took his whole family to the Governor's house and asked for the council's protection against these onslaughts. That evening a council meeting was called, and in typical Pueblo fashion the combatants were told to shake hands and apologize to each other. An announcement was made to the Pueblo to the effect that this baseball antagonism must cease or the sport would be stopped. This was a desperate measure and a test of the council's authority that may only serve to weaken it, as the council has precious few sanctions left at its disposal. The young people are not at all likely to give up baseball whatever the council may say, and the antagonism is likely to continue. However, as harvest and winter approach and the baseball season draws to a close, hard feelings tend to soften and some wounds to heal. This factor obviously helps to preserve harmony, as there is time during winter to forget the summer's quarrels.

Competitive Western games that have been introduced into primitive societies have usually been substituted for some more violent forms of competition. For example, football in New Guinea replaced intervillage spear fighting. Baseball in the Pueblos is a competitive intrusion into essentially noncompetitive social systems. Although competition is between villages, no untoward events occur, as this is in line with tradition, but within villages, it is, as we have seen, potentially destructive. Pueblo institutions act as a counter to aggressive tendencies in the Puebloans and are so constructed as to eliminate and nullify aggressive conflict between people by placing them in automatically determined overlapping role situations. The baseball teams, based on voluntary recruitment and stressing competition, allow for the acting out of aggressive and competitive tendencies. Various steps are taken by the Pueblo to neutralize this effect, but the participants seem bewildered in the face of the turn of events. Resort to naked authority in the settlement of interfamilial disputes is a new thing to Cochiti and in a way a confession of weakness in the social system, previously so ingeniously adequate to deal with conflict. It looks for the moment in Cochiti as if the male forces of authority and order may be able to keep the peace for the time being. But the women especially have married the old witch fears to the new sport and thus directed a whole body of deep-rooted motivations into new and pertinent channels. When the tension is high and feelings rise, the old cries of "witch" fly from the women and the suppressed rages are given full vent. It may even prove therapeutic.

SECTION TWO

sport in comparative perspective

the technological revolution and the rise of sport, 1850–1900

JOHN RICKARDS BETTS

The roots of our sporting heritage lie in the horse racing and fox hunting of the colonial era, but the main features of modern sport appeared only in the middle years of the nineteenth century.[1] Organization, journalistic exploitation, commercialization, intercommunity competition, and sundry other developments increased rapidly after 1850 as the agrarian nature of sport gave way gradually to the influences of urbanization and industrialization. Just as the Industrial Revolution was to alter the interests, habits, and pursuits of all classes of society, it was to leave a distinct impress on the development of sport.

Many other factors were responsible for the directions taken by sport in the half century from 1850 to 1900. Continuing rural influences, the decline

[1] Among the most useful works to be consulted on early American sport are John A. Krout, *Annals of American Sport* (New Haven, 1929); Jennie Holliman, *American Sports, 1785–1835* (Durham, 1931); Foster R. Dulles, *America Learns To Play: A History of Popular Recreation, 1607–1940* (New York, 1940); Robert B. Weaver, *Amusements and Sports in American Life* (Chicago, 1939); and Herbert Manchester, *Four Centuries of Sport in America, 1490–1890* (New York, 1931). For certain aspects of ante-bellum sport, see Arthur M. Schlesinger and Dixon R. Fox (eds.), *A History of American Life*, 13 vols. (New York, 1927–1948).

• From the *Mississippi Valley Historical Review*, XL, 231–256 (1953). Copyright © 1953 by the Organization of American Historians.

of Puritan orthodoxy, the English athletic movement, the immigrant, frontier traditions of manliness and strength, and the contributions of energetic sportsmen were to have a significant effect on the sporting scene. Industrialization and urbanization, however, were more fundamentally responsible for the changes and developments in sport during the next generation than any other cause. Manufacturers, seeking cheap labor, encouraged immigration; factories were most efficiently run in larger towns and cities; urban masses, missing the rustic pleasures of hunting and fishing, were won to the support of commercialized entertainment and spectator sports; the emergence of a commercial aristocracy and a laboring class resulted in distinctions every bit as strong in sport as in other social matters; and the urgency of physical exercise as life became more sedentary was readily recognized.

The revolution in manufacturing methods, which had such profound social consequences for the American way of life, derived from a powerful inventive spirit which flourished throughout the nineteenth century. From England and western Europe we borrowed many mechanical innovations and most of our scientific theory, but Americans demonstrated a native ability soon recognized everywhere as "Yankee ingenuity." These inventions were to revolutionize transportation, communication, manufacturing, finance, and all the many facets of economic life. Although the tendency in narrating the history of sport has been to emphasize the role of individuals, the changing social scene was of equal importance in directing sport into the channels it eventually took in modern society. The impact of invention had a decisive influence on the rise of sport in the latter half of the century. By 1900 sport had attained an unprecedented prominence in the daily lives of millions of Americans, and this remarkable development had been achieved in great part through the steamboat, the railroad, the telegraph, the penny press, the electric light, the streetcar, the camera, the bicycle, the automobile, and the mass production of sporting goods.

The transformation of the United States from a rural-agrarian to an urban-industrial society, of course, affected the development of sport in other ways. Urbanization brought forth the need for commercialized spectator sports, while industrialization gradually provided the standard of living and leisure time so vital to the support of all forms of recreation. But it is the relationship of invention to sport, and that alone, which constitutes the theme of this study.

Early American interest in outdoor exercise was largely confined to hunting, fishing, horse racing, field sports, and the informal games of the local schoolyard. As the nation became more commercially minded in the decades after the War of 1812, many of those who lived in rapidly growing cities became concerned over the sedentary habits of clerks, office workers, and businessmen. In the years before 1850 there emerged a limited interest in rowing, running, prize fighting, cricket, fencing, and similar activities, but the only organized sport which excited the minds of most Americans was the turf. A more general interest in horse racing appeared in the 1820s and 1830s, and many jockey clubs held meetings attended by throngs of spectators in their carriages and barouches.[2]

From the early years of the century steamboat captains engaged in racing on the Hudson, Ohio, Mississippi, and other rivers, and the steamboat served as a common carrier of sports crowds. By the 1850s it became an indispensable means of transport to the races along the eastern seaboard and in the Mississippi Valley. As one of the first products of the age of steam it played a significant role in the rise of the turf and outdoor games.[3]

In the years preceding the Civil War the turf was also encouraged by the development of a railroad network. As early as 1838 Wade Hampton was transporting race horses to Charleston by rail; [4] in 1839 the Nashville Railroad was carrying New Orleans crowds to the Metairie Course; [5] in 1842 the Long Island Railroad was already suffering the abuse of irate passengers swarming to the races; and three years later it carried some 30,000 passengers to the Fashion-Peytona race at more than fifty cents each.[6] Kentucky became the leading breeding center for thoroughbreds and Louisville could announce in 1851: "Lexington, Georgetown, Frankfort, Paris and other towns in this State, are now but a short ride from our city by railroad conveyance. Horses can come from Lexington here in five hours." [7] The famous trotter Flora Temple began barnstorming tours; racing and trotting benefited from the cooperation of railroad lines; and "speed trials" at agricultural fairs during the 1850s were attended by excursionists.[8] Other outdoor sports also profited

---

[2] See the New York *American*, May 27, 1823; New Orleans *Daily Picayune*, March 27, 1839; New York *Weekly Herald*, May 17, 1845, July 11, 1849; and accounts of many races in the *Spirit of the Times* (New York) for prewar years. In an era when bridges were more the exception than the rule the ferry was an indispensable means of transportation. See, for example, Kenneth Roberts and Anna M. Roberts (eds.), *Moreau de St. Méry's American Journey, 1793–1798* (Garden City, 1947), 173; New York *American*, May 27, 1823.

[3] For examples of the steamboat in early sport, see the New York *Herald*, June 17, 1849; *Wilkes' Spirit of the Times* (New York), XII (August 5, 1865), 380; New Orleans *Daily Picayune*, December 1, 1855, December 10, 1859; *Spirit of the Times*, XX (June 19, 1869), 276; New York *World*, June 19, 1869. When the passenger lines began converting to steam in the Civil War era, the development of international sport was facilitated to a considerable degree. In the latter decades of the century the steam yacht became the vogue among American millionaires.

[4] John Hervey, *Racing in America, 1665–1865*, 2 vols. (New York, 1944), II, 101.

[5] New Orleans *Daily Picayune*, March 27, 1839.

[6] *American Turf Register and Sporting Magazine* (Baltimore), XIII (July, 1843), 367; New York *Daily Tribune*, May 14, 1845.

[7] *Spirit of the Times*, XXI (July 12, 1851), 246.

[8] Albert L. Demaree, *The American Agricultural Press, 1819–1860* (New York, 1941), 203–204. Specific instances of such aid can be found in the *Cultivator* (Albany), IX (March, 1842), 50; *American Agriculturist* (New York), II (October 16, 1843), 258; New York *Daily Tribune*, September 18, 1851; *Transactions of the Illinois State Agricultural Society* (Springfield), I, 1853–54 (1855), 6; II, 1856–57 (1857), 24–32; *Report and Proceedings of the Iowa State Agricultural Society . . . October, 1855* (Fairfield, 1856), 24; *Fifth Report of the Indiana State Board of Agriculture . . . For the Year 1856*

from the interest shown by certain lines. When excitement over rowing began to catch on in the late 1830s the first boat shipped west of the Appalachians went by way of the Erie Canal.[9] It was a railroad, however, which encouraged the holding of the first intercollegiate rowing race between Harvard and Yale in 1852.[10] Baseball clubs were organized throughout the East and Midwest during the decade and the National Association of Base Ball Players was formed in 1857, soon after both sections had been connected by rail. Chicago had its first baseball team in 1856, two years after it was linked by rail to Baltimore, Maryland, and Portland, Maine. In 1860 the Excelsior Club of Brooklyn made a tour of upper New York state. Most of the early prize fights were held along the rivers served by steamboats; the Harlem Railroad carried fight crowds in the early 1850s to the Awful Gardiner-William Hastings (*alias* Dublin Tricks) match sixty miles north of New York City and to a highly publicized championship fight at Boston Four Corners, New York,[11] and the John Morrissey-John Heanan match on the Canadian shore near Niagara Falls in 1858 was advertised by the Erie Railroad.[12]

The Civil War failed to halt turf meetings and outdoor recreation in the North. It was, however, only with the return of peace that the nation felt a new sporting impulse and began to give enthusiastic support to the turf, the diamond, the ring, and other outdoor activities. The game of baseball, spreading from cities to towns and villages, became a national fad, and matches were scheduled with distant communities. A tournament at Rockford, Illinois, in 1866 was attended by teams from Detroit, Milwaukee, Dubuque, and Chicago.[13] In 1869 Harry Wright's Cincinnati Red Stockings were able to make a memorable transcontinental tour from Maine to California; a New Orleans club visited Memphis, St. Louis, and Cincinnati; and eastern teams condescended to travel as far west as the Queen City. The Erie line offered to convey a New Orleans club, then visiting Cincinnati, to New York and return at half-fare rates. When the Cincinnati Red Stockings made their tour by

---

(Indianapolis, 1858), 34, 482–83; *Kentucky Farmer* (Frankfort), I, (July, 1858), 12; *Wisconsin Farmer and North-Western Cultivator* (Madison), IX (October, 1857), 873; XI (October, 1859), 386–87; Springfield *Weekly Illinois State Journal*, September 5, 19, 1860. The "ploughing matches" of the ante-bellum era attracted large crowds seeking both entertainment and the latest improvements in agricultural implements.

[9] Samuel Crowther and Arthur Ruhl, *Rowing and Track Athletics* (New York, 1905), 11.

[10] James N. Elkins, superintendent of the Boston, Concord and Montreal Railroad, agreed to pay all transportation costs for the crews and their equipment to the New Hampshire lake where the race was to be held. Robert F. Kelley, *American Rowing: Its Background and Traditions* (New York, 1932), 100–101.

[11] New York *Daily Times*, October 13, 1853; Boston *Advertiser*, October 14, 1853.

[12] New York *Herald*, October 23, 1858.

[13] *Wilkes' Spirit of the Times*, XIV (July 7, 1866), 294. More rural areas felt the impact somewhat later, Warrenton, Mississippi, holding a tourney in 1885 to which special trains were sent. New Orleans *Daily Picayune*, July 19, 1885.

boat, local lines, and the Union Pacific in 1869 it was reported: "The boys have received every attention from the officers of the different roads. . . . At all the stations groups stare us almost out of countenance, having heard of the successful exploits of the Club through telegrams of the Western Associated Press." [14]

Baseball clubs made use of the rapidly expanding network of the 1870s, and the organization of the National League in 1876 was only possible with the continued development of connecting lines. In the 1886 edition of *Spalding's Official Base Ball Guide* the Michigan Central advertised: "The cities that have representative clubs contesting for the championship pennant this year are—Chicago, Boston, New York, Washington, Kansas City, Detroit, St. Louis and Philadelphia. All of these cities are joined together by the MICHIGAN CENTRAL Railroad. This road has enjoyed almost a monopoly of Base Ball travel in former years." Throughout the 1870s and 1880s the expanding railroad network played an indispensable role in the popularization of the "national game." [15]

A widespread interest in thoroughbred and trotting races also was in great part sustained by railroad expansion. In 1866 the Harlem, Rensselaer and Saratoga Railroad Company, realizing the advantage of encouraging the racing public, arranged to convey race horses at cost by express train from New York to Saratoga. *Turf, Field and Farm* pointed to the need for better transportation arrangements and predicted, "The completion of the Pacific Railroad will not be without effect upon the blood stock interests of the great West." [16] Jerome Park, Long Branch, and Gravesend catered to New York crowds, Baltimore attracted huge throngs of sportsmen, and in California racing was encouraged by the building of lines into the interior of the state. In the 1870s western turfmen began sending their horses by rail to eastern tracks, the Grand Circuit linked Hartford, Springfield, Poughkeepsie, and Utica with Rochester, Buffalo, and Cleveland, and racing associations formed in virtually every section. When Mollie McCarthy and Ten Broeck raced at Louisville in 1877, "Masses of strangers arrived by train, extra trains and steamboats." People from "all over the land" attended the Kentucky Derby in 1885, the City

[14] New York *World*, August 21, 1869; Cincinnati *Commercial*, September 22, 1869; San Francisco *Evening Bulletin*, October 5, 1869. Their use of Pullman cars set a precedent in sports circles. Advertising by local lines for an approaching game appeared in the Cincinnati *Commercial*, August 24, 1869.

[15] See *Spalding's Official Base Ball Guide* (New York, 1886), appendix. The Memphis Reds Base Ball Association sent a printed circular to Harry Wright of the Boston team in 1877 in which it stressed the reduced rates to any club visiting St. Louis or Louisville. Harry Wright Correspondence, 7 vols., I (1865–1877), 40, Spalding Baseball Collection (New York Public Library). In the 1880s enthusiastic crowds turned out to the railroad station to welcome home the victorious nines. *Frank Leslie's Boys' and Girls' Weekly* (New York), XXXV (October 6, 1883), 174; New York *Sun*, September 7, 1886.

[16] *Turf, Field and Farm* (New York), I (September 2, 1865), 69; VIII (May 28, 1869), 344.

Council declared a holiday, and sixteen carloads of horses were sent from Nashville to Louisville.[17] Agricultural fairs, with the cooperation of numerous companies, drew thousands to their fairground tracks, and the railroads encouraged intersectional meetings by introducing special horse cars in the middle eighties.[18]

In the decades after the Civil War an apologetic but curious public acquired a "deplorable" interest in prize fighting, and railroad officials were not slow to capitalize on the crowd appeal of pugilism despite its illegality. When Mike McCoole met Aaron Jones in 1867 at Busenbark Station, Ohio, "Tickets were openly sold for excursion trains to the bout" and sporting men from the East were in attendance, while another McCoole fight in 1869 encouraged the lines to run specials from Cincinnati and other nearby cities.[19] After 1881 John L. Sullivan, the notorious "Boston Strong Boy," went on grand tours of the athletic clubs, opera houses, and theaters of the country, his fights in the New Orleans area with Paddy Ryan, Jake Kilrain, and James J. Corbett luring fans who jammed the passenger coaches. When the Great John L. met Kilrain near Richburg, Mississippi, in 1889, the Northeastern Railroad carried a tumultuous crowd from New Orleans to the site, even though Governor Robert Lowry of Mississippi issued a proclamation against the affair and called out armed guards to prevent any invasion of the state. After the brawl the Governor requested the attorney general "to begin proceedings to forfeit the charter of the Northeastern railroad." [20] Railroad companies expressed only a minor concern for such sporadic events, it is true, but the prize ring was greatly aided by their cooperation.[21]

Poor connections, uncomfortable cars, and the absence of lines in rural sections remained a problem for some years.[22] Many of the difficulties and inconveniences of travel remained throughout these expansive years of railroading, but all sports were encouraged by the improved transportation of the post-bellum era. Immediately after the war a New York crew visited Pitts-

[17] *Wilkes' Spirit of the Times*, XIV (May 19, 1866), 185; San Francisco *Evening Bulletin*, October 15, 1869; Baltimore *American and Commercial Advertiser*, October 25, 1877; New Orleans *Daily Picayune*, April 20, 1884, May 9, 15, 1885; Charles E. Trevathan, *The American Thoroughbred* (New York, 1905), 371.

[18] New York *World*, April 29, 1884.

[19] Alexander Johnston, *Ten—And Out! The Complete Story of the Prize Ring in America* (New York, 1947), 42–43.

[20] Dunbar Rowland (ed.), *Encyclopedia of Misisssippi History*, 2 vols. (Madison, 1907), II, 142; St. Paul and Minneapolis *Pioneer Press*, February 8, 1882; New Orleans *Daily Picayune*, August 6, 1885; New York *Sun*, May 12, 1886.

[21] Railroad interest in sport was illustrated by the *New York Railroad Gazette*: "Horse-racing tracks of the violest [sic] character are encouraged (indirectly, it may be) in more than one case by railroads normally law-abiding. Sunday excursions patronized chiefly by roughs who conduct baseball games of a character condemned by all decent people are morally the same as prize fights in kind though not in degree." Quoted in the New Orleans *Daily Picayune*, August 6, 1885.

[22] For illustrations of the difficulties of railroad travel, see the Walter Camp Correspondence, Box 64 (Yale University Library, New Haven).

burgh to participate in a regatta held on the Monongahela River.[23] The first intercollegiate football game between Rutgers and Princeton was attended by a group of students riding the train pulled by "the jerky little engine that steamed out of Princeton on the memorable morning of November 6, 1869." [24] Intercollegiate athletics depended on railroad service for carrying teams and supporters to football, baseball, and rowing, as well as track and field contests.

Harvard's crack baseball team made the first grand tour in 1870, "the most brilliant in the history of college baseball," according to Henry Chadwick almost two decades later. Playing both amateur and professional clubs, Harvard won a majority of the games played in New Haven, Troy, Utica, Syracuse, Oswego (Canada), Buffalo, Cleveland, Cincinnati, Louisville, Chicago, Milwaukee, Indianapolis, Washington, Baltimore, Philadelphia, New York, and Brooklyn.[25] Amateur and professional cycling races were held throughout the country,[26] while rod and gun enthusiasts relied on branch lines into rural preserves.[27] By the closing years of the century virtually every realm of sport had shared in the powerful impact of the railroad on American life.

Almost contemporaneous with the development of a continental railroad system came the diffusion of telegraph lines throughout the nation. From its invention in 1844 the electric telegraph rapidly assumed a significant role in the dissemination of news.[28] When the Magnetic Telegraph Company's line reached New York, James Gordon Bennett's *Herald* and Horace Greeley's *Tribune* installed apparatus in 1846. Direct contact was made between the East and New Orleans two years later, largely to meet the urgent demand for quicker news from the Mexican War front. By 1861 San Francisco was connected by wire with the Atlantic coast, and throughout the war years use of the telegraph was extended in military operations.

During the pioneer years telegraphic messages were both costly and brief, and sports events were reported on a limited scale. One of the first reports by wire was that of the Tom Hyer-Yankee Sullivan brawl at Rock Point,

[23] *Wilkes' Spirit of the Times*, XIII (October 14, 1865), 102.

[24] Parke H. Davis, *Football, The American Intercollegiate Game* (New York, 1911), 45.

[25] *Outing* (New York), XII (August, 1888), 407–408.

[26] By the 1890s many railroads carried bicycles as free freight and professional cyclists could tour their National Circuit in luxury cars. New York *Journal*, September 18, 1897.

[27] Scores of railroads in every section of the country served those seeking to hunt or fish in the rustic countryside. See, particularly, Charles Hallock (ed.), *The Sportsman's Gazetteer and General Guide* (New York, 1877), Pt. II, 1–182. See also the Chicago and Northwestern Railway advertisement in the *Spirit of the Times*, XCII (August 19, 1876), 53.

[28] For the early development of the telegraph, see James D. Reid, *The Telegraph in America and Morse Memorial* (New York, 1887); Waldemar Kaempffert (ed.), *A Popular History of American Invention*, 2 vols. (New York, 1924); and Robert L. Thompson, *Wiring a Continent: The History of the Telegraph Industry in the United States, 1832–1866* (Princeton, 1947).

Maryland, in 1849. A New York dispatch read, "We hope never to have to record a similar case of brutality in this country," and even Greeley, an inveterate foe of the prize ring, permitted the printing of dispatches of this brutal encounter. Interest was not confined to Baltimore, Philadelphia, and New York, for some newspapers in the West noticed it. In the next decade several fights were widely reported by telegraph. When Morrissey and Heanan fought for the American championship in Canada in 1858, anxious crowds waited at Western Union offices for the news; when Heanan met Tom Sayers in England two years later the news was spread by wire after it was brought to America by the *Vanderbilt*.[29] Horse racing and yachting news was less novel and less sensational, but Lady Suffolk's appearance on the course at the Rochester, New York, fair in 1851, the victory of Commodore John Cox Stevens' yacht *America* at Cowes in the same year, and the exciting trotting races of the decade were given extensive wire coverage.[30] When Lexington met Lecomte at New Orleans in 1855, however, there seems to have been little reporting of the race in the North. Newspapers of that section were primarily concerned in that year with the trouble in Kansas, the rise of the Republican party, the heat of the abolitionist crusade, and the public furor over the murder of pugilist William Poole.

The expansion of sporting news in ensuing years was directly related to the more general usage of telegraphy, which made possible instantaneous reporting of ball games, horse races, prize fights, yachting regattas, and other events. Box scores, betting odds, and all kinds of messages were relayed from one city to another, and by 1870 daily reports were published in many metropolitan papers. In that year the steamboat race of the *Natchez* and the *Robert E. Lee* was reported throughout the country in one of the most extensive telegraphic accounts of any nonpolitical event prior to that time.[31] Not only did the newspapers make a practice of publishing daily messages from all corners of the sporting world, but crowds formed around Western Union offices during any important contest.[32] When the Associated Press sent its representatives in 1889 to the Sullivan-Kilrain fight in New Orleans, reporters appeared from "every prominent journal in the Union," and Western Union was said to have employed 50 operators to handle 208,000 words of specials following the fight. Poolrooms and saloons were often equipped with receiving sets to keep customers and bettors posted on baseball scores and track results, while newspapers set up bulletin boards for the crowds to

---

[29] Boston *Daily Journal*, February 7, 8, 9, 1849; New York *Daily Tribune*, February 8, 9, 1849; Milwaukee *Sentinel and Gazette*, February 10, 1849; Boston *Daily Courier*, October 21, 1858; New York *Times*, October 21, 1858; New Orleans *Daily Picayune*, May 6, 7, June 29, 1860; Nashville *Daily News*, April 29, 1860.

[30] New York *Daily Tribune*, September 19, 1851; Natchez *Courier*, September 19, 1851.

[31] New Orleans *Daily Picayune*, July 6, 1870.

[32] *Ibid*. See also New York *Times*, October 21, 1858; *Harper's Weekly* (New York), XXVII (October 13, 1883), 654.

linger around.[33] And the business transactions of sporting clubs and associations were often carried on by wire.

Sport had emerged into such a popular topic of conversation that newspapers rapidly expanded their coverage in the 1880s and 1890s, relying in great part on messages sent over the lines from distant points. Among the leaders in this field during these formative years of "yellow journalism" were such New York papers as Bennett's *Herald*, Charles Dana's *Sun*, and Joseph Pulitzer's *World*. The sports page was not solely the result of improvements in telegraphy, however, for popular interest had encouraged the employment of specialists who were extremely quick, as were the publishers, to capitalize on the news value of sporting events. Chicago produced the pioneers in baseball writing in such masters of breezy slang and grotesque humor as Leonard Washburne, Charles Seymour, and Finley Peter Dunne. Cincinnati newspapers, staffed by experts like Harry Weldon, O. P. Caylor, and Byron (Ban) Johnson, were among the most authoritative journals in the diamond world. In 1895, when William Randolph Hearst invaded the New York field and bought the *Journal*, he immediately brought in western writers and, within a few years, developed the first sports section.[34] The telegraph retained its functional importance in recording daily box scores and racing statistics, but it was no longer the one indispensable factor it had been in earlier decades.

The Atlantic cable, successfully laid in 1866 by Cyrus Field, had overcome the mid-century handicap of reporting two- or three-weeks-old English sporting news. At the end of that year James Gordon Bennett, Jr., with the aid of the Associated Press, featured cable dispatches of the great ocean race. When the Harvard crew rowed against Oxford in a highly publicized race in

[33] Oliver Gramling, *AP; The Story of News* (New York, 1940), 232; New Orleans *Daily Picayune*, July 10, 1889. For poolrooms, saloons, and bulletin boards, see the New York *Sun*, October 6, 1878; New York *Herald*, February 7, 1882; New Orleans *Daily Picayune*, May 17, 1884, July 6, 1885; New York *World*, September 8, 1892. Also see *Harper's Weekly*, XXVII (October 13, 1883), 654; XXXVI (April 2, December 17, 1892), 319, 324, 1210. Henry L. Mencken, in *Happy Days, 1880–1892* (New York, 1940), 225, nostalgically recalled how, since there were few sporting "extras" in Baltimore in the 1880s, "the high-toned saloons of the town catered to the [baseball] fans by putting in telegraph operators who wrote the scores on blackboards."

[34] The New York *Transcript* and the *Sun* sensationalized the news as early as the 1830's and began reporting prize fights. James Gordon Bennett's *Herald* exploited sporting interest in pre-Civil War years and his son continued to do so in the period following the war. Magazines which capitalized on sport included the *American Turf Register and Sporting Magazine*, the *Spirit of the Times*, the *New York Clipper*, and the *National Police Gazette* (New York), as well as a host of fishing and hunting journals. Through the 1880s and 1890s the New York *Sun* and the *World* competed for the sporting public, only to be outdone by the *Journal* at the end of the century. Among the prominent writers of the era were Henry Chadwick, Timothy Murnane, Harry Weldon, Harry C. Palmer, Al Spink, Sam Crane, Walter Camp, Caspar Whitney, and Charles Dryden. See William H. Nugent, "The Sports Section," *American Mercury* (New York), XVI (February, 1929), 329–38; and Hugh Fullerton, "The Fellows Who Made the Game," *Saturday Evening Post* (Philadelphia), CC (April 21, 1928), 18 ff.

1869, "the result was flashed through the Atlantic cable as to reach New York about a quarter past one, while the news reached the Pacific Coast about nine o'clock, enabling many of the San Franciscans to discuss the subject at their breakfast-tables, and swallow the defeat with their coffee!" [35] The combination of cable and telegraph aroused a deeper interest in international sport. Nor must we ignore that forerunner of the modern radio, the wireless which was demonstrated publicly in America for the first time in the yacht races of 1899. From Samuel F. B. Morse to Guglielmo Marconi the revolution in communication had encouraged the rise of sport.

Public interest in sport was also aroused by the enlarged format and greater circulation achieved by numerous inventions which revolutionized the printing process. By 1830 the Napier double-cylinder press was imported from England and developed by R. Hoe and Company, printing those cheap and sensational papers which were the first to feature horse races, prize fights, and foot races—the New York *Sun*, the New York *Transcript*, and the Philadelphia *Public Ledger*.[36] James Gordon Bennett, Sr., recognized the value of catering to the whims of the masses and occasionally featured turf reporting in the *Herald* of the 1840s.[37] In 1846 the Hoe type-revolving cylinder press was introduced by the *Public Ledger*, enabling newspaper publishers, after improvements were made in the machine, to print 20,000 sheets an hour.[38] Other inventions facilitated the mass publication of the daily paper, making possible the sensationalized editions of Bennett, Pulitzer, and Hearst.[39] With the arrival of the new journalism of the 1880s, sporting news rapidly became a featured part of the metropolitan press.[40]

Publishers also aided in the popularization of outdoor sport throughout this whole era. From the 1830s onward sporting books appeared, the most famous of prewar authors being Henry William Herbert, whose illustrious pseudonym was Frank Forester. After the Civil War cheap methods of publication gave a great stimulus to the dime novel and the athletic almanac. While the vast majority of the thrillers and shockers concerned the Wild

[35] New York *Herald*, December 30, 31, 1866; Cincinnati *Commercial*, August 24, 28, 1869; *Frank Leslie's Illustrated Newspaper* (New York), XXIX (September 28, 1869), 2.

[36] The origins of the penny press are ably discussed in Willard G. Bleyer, *Main Currents in the History of American Journalism* (Boston, 1927), 154–84; and in Frank L. Mott, *American Journalism, A History* (New York, 1941), 228–52.

[37] Bleyer, *History of American Journalism*, 197, 209; Alfred M. Lee, *The Daily Newspaper in America* (New York, 1937), 611; New York *Weekly Herald*, May 15, 17, 1845, and *Herald* files for the 1840s.

[38] Bleyer, *History of American Journalism*, 394.

[39] *Ibid.*, 394–98.

[40] Joseph Pulitzer's New York *World* began an intensive exploitation of sport as a front-page attraction almost immediately after its purchase in 1883, and by the following year first-page accounts of pedestrian matches, dog shows, and similar topics became regular features.

West or city crime, athletic stories and manuals were put out by Beadle & Adams, the leading publisher of the paper-backed dime novel.[41] After the establishment of A. G. Spalding & Brothers the *Spalding Guide* developed into the leading authority on rules of play, and all sorts of handbooks were included in the *Spalding Library of Athletic Sports*. The *New York Clipper* began publishing a theatrical and sporting *Clipper Almanac* in the 1870s, and newspapers like the New York *World*, the New York *Tribune*, the Chicago *Daily News*, the Washington *Post*, and the Brooklyn *Daily Eagle* issued almanacs listing athletic and racing records and sporting news. Richard Kyle Fox of the *National Police Gazette* published *Fox's Athletic Library* and sporting annuals. By the end of the century book publication had grown to astronomic proportions when compared to the Civil War era, and the Outing Publishing Company issued more than a hundred titles on angling, canoeing, yachting, mountain climbing, hunting, shooting, trapping, camping, cycling, and athletics.

A few dime novels had taken up the athletic theme in the 1870s, but more mature stories like Mark Sibley Severance's *Hammersmith: His Harvard Days* (1878), Noah Brooks's *Our Baseball Club* (1884), and, of course, Thomas Hughes's English classics, *Tom Brown at Rugby* and *Tom Brown at Oxford*, were responsible for the rising desire for sports fiction. By the 1890s a demand for boys' athletic stories was met in the voluminous outpouring of the heroic sporting achievements of Gilbert Patten's "Frank Merriwell." [42] Along with the newspaper and the sporting journal the field of publishing, with its improved techniques and expanded output, did much to attract attention to athletics at the turn of the century.

Much of the angling and hunting equipment and horseman's supplies came from England in the colonial era, but in the years before and after the American Revolution several dealers in sporting wares appeared in Philadelphia, New York, and Boston. From the early years of the nineteenth century merchants and gunsmiths in Kentucky supplied the settlers west of the Appalachian range.[43] Field sports were still enjoyed mainly by schoolboys and sportsmen with their simple rods in the 1840s and 1850s, but from the 1830s onward fishing and hunting purely for recreation developed into a sporting fad, the end of which is not in sight. Charles Hallock, noted sportsman, conservationist, and journalist of the post-Civil War era recalled how the rural folk of Hampshire County, Massachusetts, responded to a visiting sportsman of the 1840s who brought with him a set of highly finished rods, reels, and fly-fishing equipment.

---

[41] Albert Johannsen, *The House of Beadle and Adams and its Dime and Nickel Novel: The Story of a Vanished Literature*, 2 vols. (Norman, 1950), I, 260, 377–79.

[42] John L. Cutler, *Gilbert Patten and His Frank Merriwell Saga*, University of Main Studies (Orono), Ser. II, No. 31 (1934).

[43] Charles E. Godspeed, *Angling in America: Its Early History and Literature* (Boston, 1939), 285 ff.

Ah! those were halcyon days. No railroads disturbed the quiet seclusion of that mountain nook. . . . Twice a week an oldfashioned coach dragged heavily up the hill into the hamlet and halted in front of the house which was at once post-office, tavern, and miscellaneous store. . . . One day it brought a passenger. . . . He carried a leather hand-bag and a handful of rods in a case. The village *quidnuncs* said he was a surveyor. He allowed he was from Troy and had "come to go a-fishing." From that stranger I took my first lesson in fly-fishing.[44]

By the 1850s the manufacture of cricket bats and stumps, billiard tables, archery equipment, guns, fishing tackle, and other sporting accessories was carried on by a host of individual craftsmen and by such concerns as J. W. Brunswick & Brothers of Cincinnati, Bassler of Boston, Conroy's of New York, and John Krider's "Sportsmen's Depot" in Philadelphia.

Mass-production methods of manufacture were still in their infancy in post-Civil War decades, but the factory system became ever more deeply entrenched. While the sporting goods business never attained any great economic importance in the nineteenth century,[45] much of the popularity for athletic games and outdoor recreation was due to standardized manufacturing of baseball equipment, bicycles, billiard tables, sporting rifles, fishing rods, and various other items.[46] Although most American youths played with restitched balls and a minimum of paraphernalia, college athletes, cycling enthusiasts, and professional ballplayers popularized the products of George B. Ellard of Cincinnati, Peck & Snyder of New York, and other concerns.[47]

By the end of the century A. G. Spalding & Brothers was the nationally recognized leader in this field. As a renowned pitcher for the Boston and Chicago clubs and then as the promoter of the latter, Albert Spalding had

[44] Charles Hallock, *The Fishing Tourist: Angler's Guide and Reference Book* (New York, 1873), 18.

[45] In 1900 the value of sporting goods manufactured was only $3,628,496. United States Bureau of the Census, *Statistical Abstract of the United States* (Washington, 1909), 188.

[46] See the *Spirit of the Times*, XX (May 4, 1850), 130; Natchez *Courier*, November 26, 1850; Madison *Daily State Journal*, March 26, 1855; New Orleans *Daily Picayune*, April 4, 1856. As midwestern merchants began to purchase large stocks from the East, John Krider advertised widely. Madison *Daily State Journal*, April 13, 1855. Michael Phelan, who in 1854 developed an indiarubber cushion permitting sharp edges on billiard tables, joined with Hugh W. Collender in forming Phelan and Collender, the leading billiards manufacturer until the organization of the Brunswick-Balke-Collender Company in 1884. Gymnastic apparatus, created by Dudley A. Sargent and other physical educators, was featured by many dealers, while the readers of *American Angler* (New York), *Forest and Stream* (New York), and other sporting journals were kept informed of the latest models of rifles, shotguns, and fishing rods and reels.

[47] George B. Ellard, who sponsored the Red Stockings, advertised his store as "Base Ball Headquarters" and "Base Ball Depot," with the "Best Stock in the West." Cincinnati *Commercial*, August 24, 1869. Other merchandisers included Horsman's Base Ball and Croquet Emporium in New York and John H. Mann of the same city. Peck & Snyder began dealing in baseball equipment in 1865 and by the 1880s claimed to be the largest seller of sporting goods.

turned to the merchandising of athletic goods in 1876.[48] One of the most avid sponsors of the national game, he branched out into varied sports in the 1880s, and acquired a virtual monopoly over athletic goods by absorbing A. J. Reach Company in 1885, Wright & Ditson in 1892, as well as Peck & Snyder and other firms. By 1887 the Spalding "Official League" baseball had been adopted by, the National League, the Western League, the New England League, the International League, and various college conferences, and balls were offered to the public ranging in price from 5 cents to $1.50. To gain an even greater ascendancy over his rivals A. G. Spalding published a wide range of guides in *Spalding's Library of Athletic Sports*, in which his wares were not only advertised but those of rivals were derided as inferior.

The sewing machine was one of many inventions which made possible the more uniform equipment of the last decades of the century when local leagues and national associations took shape throughout the United States. Canoeing and camping were other diversions which gave rise to the manufacture of sporting goods on an ever larger scale. In the latter years of the century the mail-order house and the department store began to feature sporting goods. Macy's of New York began with ice skates, velocipedes, bathing suits, and beach equipment in 1872, although all sporting goods were sold by the toy department. By 1902, with the addition of numerous other items, a separate department was established. Sears, Roebuck and Company, meanwhile, devoted more than eighty pages of its 1895 catalog to weapons and fishing equipment, and within a decade not only hunting and fishing equipment but also bicycles, boxing gloves, baseball paraphernalia, and sleds were featured.[49]

When Thomas A. Edison developed the incandescent bulb in 1879 he inaugurated a new era in the social life of our cities. Although the first dynamo was built within two years, gas lighting did not give way immediately, and the crowds which jammed the old Madison Square Garden in New York in 1883 to see John L. Sullivan fight Herbert Slade still had to cope not only with the smoke-filled air but also with the blue gas fumes. The Garden had already

---

[48] Moses King (ed.), *King's Handbook of the United States* (Buffalo, 1891), 232; Arthur Bartlett, *Baseball and Mr. Spalding: The History and Romance of Baseball* (New York, 1951), *passim; Fortune* (New York), II (August, 1930), 62 ff.; Arthur Bartlett, "They're Just Wild About Sports," *Saturday Evening Post*, CCXXII (December 24, 1949), 31 ff.; *Spalding's Official Base Ball Guide for 1887* (New York and Chicago, 1887), *passim.*

[49] It was on mass manufacture of baseballs and uniforms that Spalding gained such a leading position in the sporting goods field. Since the business was restricted in these early years certain difficulties had to be overcome. To make the most out of manufacturing bats Spalding bought his own lumber mill in Michigan, while Albert Pope received little sympathy from the rolling mills in his first years of manufacturing bicycles. *Wheelman* (Boston), I (October, 1882), 71. For department and mail-order stores, see Ralph M. Hower, *History of Macy's of New York, 1858–1919* (Cambridge, 1946), 103, 162, 234–35, 239; Boris Emmet and John C. Jeuck, *Catalogues and Counters: A History of Sears, Roebuck and Company* (Chicago, 1950), 38; David L. Cohn, *The Good Old Days* (New York, 1940), 443–60.

installed some electric lights, however. At a six-day professional walking match in 1882 the cloud of tobacco smoke was so thick that "even the electric lights" had "a hard struggle to assert their superior brilliancy" over the gas jets. Even "the noisy yell of programme, candy, fruit and peanut venders who filled the air with the vilest discord" failed to discourage the crowd, according to a philosophically minded reporter who wondered what Herbert Spencer would think of "the peculiar phase of idiocy in the American character" which drew thousands of men and women to midnight pedestrian contests.[50]

Within a few years electric lighting and more comfortable accommodations helped lure players and spectators alike to Y.M.C.A.'s, athletic clubs, regimental armories, school and college gymnasiums, as well as sports arenas. In 1885, at the third annual Horse Show in Madison Square Garden, handsomely dressed sportswomen reveled in the arena, "gaudy with festoons of racing flags and brilliant streamers, lighted at night by hundreds of electric lights," while visitors to the brilliantly lighted New York Athletic Club agreed that "fine surroundings will not do an athlete any harm." [51] The indoor prize fight, walking contest, wrestling match, and horse show were a far cry from the crude atmosphere of early indoor sport. In 1890 carnivals were held at the Massachusetts Mechanics' Association by the Boston Athletic Association and at the new Madison Square Garden in New York by the Staten Island Athletic Club; the horse show attracted fashionable New Yorkers to the Garden; and indoor baseball, already popular in Chicago, was taken up in New York's regimental armories.[52] A decade of electrification, paralleling improvements in transportation and communications, had elevated and purified the atmosphere of sport. The saloon brawls of pugilists in the 1850s and 1860s were gradually abandoned for the organized matches of the 1880s and 1890s. At the time of the Sullivan-Corbett fight in the New Orleans Olympic Club in 1892, an observer wrote in the Chicago *Daily Tribune*, September 8, 1892: "Now men travel to great boxing contests in vestibule limited trains; they sleep at the best hotels . . . and when the time for the contest arrives they find themselves in a grand, brilliantly lighted arena."

Basketball and volleyball, originating in the Y.M.C.A. in 1892 and 1895, were both developed to meet the need for indoor sport on winter evenings. The rapid construction of college gymnasiums and the building of more luxurious clubhouses after the middle eighties stemmed in great part from the

---

[50] New York *Herald*, October 23, 1882; New York *Sun*, August 7, 1883. The introduction of electric lighting in theaters was discussed, while the opposition of gas companies was recognized. *Scientific American*, Supplement (New York), XVI (November 10, 1883), 6535–36.

[51] *Harper's Weekly*, XXIX (February 14, November 14, 1885), 109, 743.

[52] See *ibid.*, XXXIV (March 1, 8, 1890), 169, 171, 179. A new Madison Square Garden with the most modern facilities was built in the years 1887–1890; the California Athletic Club in San Francisco featured a "powerful electric arc light" over its ring; and electric lights in the Manhattan Athletic Club's new gymnasium in 1890 "shed a dazzling whiteness." *Ibid.*, XXXIV (April 5, 1890), 263–64; New York *Daily Tribune*, November 2, 30, 1890.

superior appointments and more brilliant lighting available for athletic games, and much of the urban appeal of indoor sport was directly attributable to the revolution which electric lighting made in the night life of the metropolis.

Electrification, which transformed everything from home gadgets and domestic lighting to power machinery and launches, exerted an influence on the course of sport through the development of rapid transit systems in cities from coast to coast. Horse-drawn cars had carried the burden of traffic since the 1850s, but the electric streetcar assumed an entirely new role in opening up suburban areas and the countryside to the pent-up city populace. Soon after the Richmond, Virginia, experiment of 1888, the streetcar began to acquaint large numbers of city dwellers with the race track and the ball diamond.[53] Experimental lines had been laid even earlier in the decade, and Chicago crowds going to the races at Washington Park in 1887 were jammed on "the grip," one reporter noting the "perpetual stream of track slang," the prodding and pushing, and the annoying delay when it was announced that "the cable has busted." [54] Trolley parks, many of which included baseball diamonds, were promoted by the transit companies; ball teams were encouraged by these same concerns through gifts of land or grandstands; and the crowds flocked to week-end games on the cars.[55] At the turn of the century the popular interest in athletic games in thousands of towns and cities was stimulated to a high degree by the extension of rapid transit systems, a development which may possibly have been as significant in the growth of local sport as the automobile was to be in the development of intercommunity rivalries.

Numerous inventions and improvements applied to sport were of varying importance: the stop watch, the percussion cap, the streamlined sulky, barbed wire, the safety cycle, ball bearings, and artificial ice for skating rinks, among others. Improved implements often popularized and revolutionized the style of a sport, as in the invention of the sliding seat of the rowing shell, the introduction of the rubber-wound gutta-percha ball which necessitated the lengthening of golf courses, and the universal acceptance of the catcher's mask.

Vulcanization of rubber by Charles Goodyear in the 1830s led to the development of elastic and resilient rubber balls in the following decade, and eventually influenced the development of golf and tennis balls as well as other sporting apparel and equipment. The pneumatic tire, developed by Dr. John

[53] After the completion of the Richmond line rapid transit spread throughout the country. Although in 1890 there were only 144 electric railways in a national total of 789 street lines, by 1899 there were 50,600 electric cars in operation as compared to only 1,500 horse cars. Gilson Willets et al., Workers of the Nation, 2 vols. (New York, 1903), I, 498. For the suburban influence, see the Street Railway Journal (New York), XVIII (November 23, 1901), 760–61.

[54] Chicago Tribune, July 5, 1887.

[55] Street Railway Journal, XI (April, 1895), 232; XII (May, November, 1896), 317, 319, 708; Cosmopolitan (New York), XXXIII (July, 1902), 266; Collier's (New York), CXXV (May, 1950), 85; Oscar Handlin, This Was America (Cambridge, 1949), 374; New Orleans Daily Picayune, February 27, 1899.

Boyd Dunlop of Belfast, Ireland, in 1888, revolutionized cycling and harness racing in the next decade. Equipped with pneumatic tires, the sulky abandoned its old highwheeler style, and the trotter and pacer found it made for smoother movement on the track. Sulky drivers reduced the mile record of 2:08¾ by Maud S. with an old highwheeler to 1:58½ by Lou Dillon in 1903 with a "bicycle sulky." According to W. H. Gocher, a racing authority, the innovation of pneumatic tires and the streamlining of the sulky cut five to seven seconds from former records, which was "more than the breeding had done in a dozen years." [56] The pneumatic tire, introduced by racing cyclists and sulky drivers, went on to play a much more vital role in the rise of the automobile industry and the spectacular appeal of auto racing.

The camera also came to the aid of sport in the decades following the Civil War. Professional photography had developed rapidly in the middle period of the century, but nature lovers became devotees of the camera only when its bulkiness and weight were eliminated in the closing years of the century. Development of the Eastman Kodak after 1888 found a mass market as thousands of Americans put it to personal and commercial use. Pictorial and sporting magazines which had been printing woodcuts since the prewar era began to introduce many pictures taken from photographs, and in the late 1880s and early 1890s actual photographic prints of athletes and outdoor sportsmen came into common usage. *Harper's Weekly, Leslie's Illustrated Weekly, Illustrated American,* and the *National Police Gazette* featured photography, and by the end of the century the vast majority of their pictures were camera studies.[57] Newspapers recognized the circulation value of half-tone prints, but because of paper and technical problems they were used sparsely until the New York *Times* published an illustrated Sunday supplement in 1896, soon to be imitated by the New York *Tribune* and the Chicago *Tribune.* The year 1897 saw the half-tone illustration become a regular feature of metropolitan newspapers, rapidly eliminating the age-old reliance on woodcuts. At the turn of the century sport was available in visual form to millions who heretofore had little knowledge of athletics and outdoor games.[58]

It was in 1872 that Eadweard Muybridge made the first successful attempt "to secure an illusion of motion by photography." With the help of

[56] W. H. Gocher, *Trotalong* (Hartford, 1928), 190.

[57] Robert Taft, *Photography and the American Scene: A Social History, 1839–1889* (New York, 1910), II, 534–35.

[58] Photography developed throughout the nineteenth century as an adjunct of the science of chemistry. Chemical and mechanical innovations were also responsible for the improvements of prints and all kinds of reproductions. Woodcuts were featured in the press, engravings were sold widely, and lithographs were found in the most rural home. Nathaniel Currier (later Currier & Ives) published hunting, fishing, pugilistic, baseball, rowing, yachting, sleighing, skating, trotting, and racing scenes for more than half a century. Cheap prints, calendars, and varied reproductions of sporting secnes did much to popularize the famous turf champions and sporting heroes of the era. See Harry T. Peters, *Currier & Ives: Printmakers to the American People* (Garden City, 1942).

Leland Stanford, already a noted turfman, he set out to prove whether "a trotting horse at one point in its gait left·the ground entirely." [59] By establishing a battery of cameras the movements of the horse were successively photographed, and Muybridge later turned his technique to "the gallop of dogs, the flight of birds, and the performances of athletes." In his monumental study entitled *Animal Locomotion* (1887) he included thousands of pictures of horses, athletes, and other living subjects, demonstrating "the work and play of men, women and children of all ages; how pitchers throw the baseball, how batters hit it, and how athletes move their bodies in record-breaking contests." [60] Muybridge is considered only one among a number of the pioneers of the motion picture, but his pictures had presented possibly the best illusion of motion prior to the development of flexible celluloid film. A host of experimenters gradually evolved principles and techniques in the late 1880s which gave birth to the true motion picture. Woodville Latham and his two sons made a four-minute film of the prize fight between Young Griffo and Battling Barnett in 1895, showing it on a large screen for an audience, an event which has been called "the first flickering, commercial motion picture." [61] When Bob Fitzsimmons won the heavyweight championship from James J. Corbett at Carson City, Nevada, in 1897, the fight was photographed for public distribution. With the increasing popularity in succeeding years of the newsreel, the short subject, and an occasional feature film, the motion picture came to rival the photograph in spreading the gospel of sport.[62]

When sport began to mature into a business of some importance and thousands of organizations throughout the country joined leagues, associations, racing circuits, and national administrative bodies, it became necessary to utilize on a large scale the telephone, the typewriter, and all the other instruments so vital to the commercial world. Even the phonograph, at first considered a business device but soon devoted to popular music, came to have an indirect influence, recording for public entertainment such songs as "Daisy Bell," "Casey at the Bat," "Slide, Kelly, Slide," and, early in the present century, the theme song of the national pastime, "Take Me Out to the Ball Game." All of these instruments created a great revolution in communication, and they contributed significantly to the expansion of sport on a national scale.

The bicycle, still an important means of transport in Europe but something of a casualty of the machine age in the United States, also had an im-

[59] Frank L. Dyer and Thomas C. Martin, *Edison: His Life and Inventions*, 2 vols. (New York, 1910), II, 534–35.

[60] Kaempffert, *Popular History of American Inventions*, I, 425.

[61] Lloyd Morris, *Not So Long Ago* (New York, 1949), 24.

[62] The pioneer years of the motion picture industry are described by numerous other works, among them Deems Taylor, *A Pictorial History of the Movies* (New York, 1943), 1–6; Leslie Wood, *The Miracle of the Movies* (London, 1947), 66 ff.; George S. Bryan, *Edison: The Man and His Work* (Garden City, 1926), 184–94; Josef M. Eder, *History of Photography*, trans. by Edward Epstean (New York, 1945), 495 ff.; Taft, *Photography and the American Scene*, 405–12; Morris, *Not So Long Ago*, 1–35.

portant role. After its demonstration at the Philadelphia Centennial, an interest was ignited which grew rapidly in the 1880s and flamed into an obsession in the 1890s.[63] Clubs, cycling associations, and racing meets were sponsored everywhere in these years, and the League of American Wheelmen served as a spearhead for many of the reforms in fashions, good roads, and outdoor exercise. Albert H. Pope was merely the foremost among many manufacturers of the "velocipede" which became so popular among women's clubs, temperance groups, professional men, and, at the turn of the century, in the business world and among the trades. Contemporary observers speculated on the social benefits to be derived from the cycle, especially in enticing women to the pleasures of outdoor exercise. Bicycling was discussed by ministers and physicians, it was considered as a weapon in future wars, police squads in some cities were mounted on wheels, mail carriers utilized it, and many thought it would revolutionize society.[64]

As a branch of American industry the bicycle was reputed to have developed into a $100,000,000 business in the 1890s. Mass-production techniques were introduced, Iver Johnson's Arms and Cycle Works advertising "Every part interchangeable and exact." The Indiana Bicycle Company, home of the Waverley cycle, maintained a huge factory in Indianapolis and claimed to be the most perfect and complete plant in the world: "We employ the highest mechanical skill and the best labor-saving machinery that ample capital can provide. Our methods of construction are along the latest and most approved lines of mechanical work." [65]

Much of the publicity given to competing manufacturers centered around the mechanical improvements and the speed records of their products.

[63] There was a brief craze in 1869, during which year, according to Albert H. Pope, "more than a thousand inventions were patented for the perfection and improvement of the velocipede." *Wheelman*, I (October, 1882), 70. Interest declined, however, until the Philadelphia celebration of 1876. Although race meetings and cycling clubs were widely reported in the 1880s, there were only 83 repair establishments in 1890 and the value of products in bicycle and tricycle repairs was only about $300,000. By 1900 there were 6,378 repair shops and the value in repairs exceeded $13,000,000. United States Bureau of the Census, *Statistical Abstract of the United States* (Washington, 1904), 516.

[64] For summaries of the impact of the bicycle, see E. Benjamin Andrews, *History of the Last Quarter-Century in the United States, 1870–1895*, 2 vols. (New York, 1896), II, 289–90; Arthur M. Schlesinger, *The Rise of the City 1878–1898* (New York, 1933), 312–14; Roger Burlingame, *Engines of Democracy: Inventions and Society in Mature America* (New York, 1940), 369–74.

[65] *Harper's Weekly*, XL (April 11, 1896), 365. It is interesting that the "father of scientific management," Frederick W. Taylor, a tennis champion and golf devotee, was said to have learned through sport "the value of the minute analysis of motions, the importance of methodical selection and training, the worth of time study and of standards based on rigorously exact observation." Charles De Fréminville, "How Taylor Introduced the Scientific Method Into Management of the Shop," *Critical Essays on Scientific Management*, Taylor Society *Bulletin* (New York), X (February, 1925), Pt. II, 32. Mass-production techniques, however, were only partially responsible for the outpouring of athletic goods which began to win wider markets at the turn of the century. The manufacture of baseball bats remained a highly specialized trade, while Scotch artisans who came to the United States maintained the personalized nature of their craft as makers of golf clubs. Despite the

Between 1878 and 1896 the mile record was lowered from 3:57 to 1:55⅕. While recognizing the effect of better riding styles, methodical training, improved tracks, and the art of pacemaking, one critic contended, "The prime factor . . . is the improvement in the vehicle itself. The racing machine of 1878 was a heavy, crude, cumbersome affair, while the modern bicycle, less than one-sixth its weight, equipped with scientifically calculated gearing, pneumatic tires, and friction annihilators, represents much of the difference." [66] Roger Burlingame has pointed out the impact of the bicycle on the health, recreation, business, and the social life of the American people, and on the manufacture of the cycle he claimed that "it introduced certain technical principles which were carried on into the motor car, notably ball bearings, hub-breaking and the tangential spoke." [67] Little did cycling enthusiasts realize that in these same years a much more revolutionary vehicle, destined to transform our way of life, was about to make its dramatic appearance on the national scene.

One of the last inventions which the nineteenth century brought forth for the conquest of time and distance was the automobile. During the 1890s the Haynes, Duryea, Ford, Stanley Steamer, Packard, and Locomobile came out in quick succession, and the Pierce Arrow, Cadillac, and Buick were to follow in the next several years.[68] Manufacturers of bicycles had already turned to the construction of the motor car in a number of instances. As early as 1895 Herman H. Kohlsaat, publisher of the Chicago *Times-Herald*, sponsored the first automobile race on American soil. One of the features of this contest, run through a snowstorm and won by Charles Duryea, was the enhanced reputation achieved for the gasoline motor, which had not yet been recognized as the proper source of motor power. A number of European races inspired American drivers to take to the racecourse, and the experimental value of endurance or speed contests was immediately recognized by pioneer manufacturers. Nor were they slow to see the publicity value of races featured by the newspapers.[69]

Henry Ford "was bewitched by Duryea's feat," and he "devoured reports

---

great improvements in gun manufacture, Elisha J. Lewis asserted in 1871 that there were thousands of miserable guns on the market: "The reason of this is that our mechanics have so many tastes and fancies to please, owing principally to the ignorance of those who order fowling-pieces, that they have adopted no generally-acknowledged standard of style to guide them in the getting up of guns suitable for certain kinds of sport." Elisha J. Lewis, *The American Sportsman* (Philadelphia, 1871), 435. Although numerous industries had taken up the principle of interchangeable parts, mass-production techniques were to come to the fore only with the assembly lines of Henry Ford and the automobile industry in the years before World War I.

[66] *Harper's Weekly*, XL (April 11, 1896), 366.
[67] Burlingame, *Engines of Democracy: Inventions and Society in Mature America*, 3.
[68] Herbert O. Duncan, *World on Wheels*, 2 vols. (Paris, 1927), II, 919 ff.
[69] Lawrence H. Seltzer, *A Financial History of the American Automobile Industry* (Boston, 1928), 91; Pierre Sauvestre, *Histoire de L'Automobile* (Paris, 1907), *passim;* Ralph C. Epstein, *The Automobile Industry, Its Economic and Commercial Development* (Chicago, 1928), 154; Reginald M. Cleveland and S. T. Williamson, *The Road Is Yours* (New York, 1951), 175–76, 194–97.

on the subject which appeared in the newspapers and magazines of the day."
When other leading carbuilders sought financial backing for their racers, Ford
determined to win supremacy on the track. After defeating Alexander Winton
in a race at Detroit in 1902, "Ford's prowess as a 'speed demon' began to appear in the columns of the widely circulated trade journal *Horseless Age*." [70]
In later years he was to contend, "I never thought anything of racing, but the
public refused to consider the automobile in any light other than as a fast
toy. Therefore later we had to race. The industry was held back by this
initial racing slant, for the attention of the makers was diverted to making
fast rather than good cars." The victory over Winton was his first race, "and
it brought advertising of the only kind that people cared to read." Bowing to
public opinion, he was determined "to make an automobile that would be
known wherever speed was known," and he set to work installing four cylin-
ders in his famous "999." Developing 80 horse power, this machine was so
frightening, even to its builders, that the fearless Barney Oldfield was hired
for the race. Oldfield had only a tiller with which to drive, since there were
no steering wheels, but this professional cyclist who had never driven a car
established a new record and helped put Ford back on his feet. The financial
support of Alex Y. Malcomson, an admirer of "999," gave him a new start:
"A week after the race I formed the Ford Motor Company." [71]

The next few years witnessed the establishment of Automobile Club of
America races, sport clubs in the American Automobile Association, the Vanderbilt Cup, and the Glidden Tour. Reporting on the third annual Glidden
Tour in 1906, *Scientific American* defended American cars, heretofore considered inferior to European models: "Above all else, the tour has demonstrated that American machines will stand fast driving on rough forest roads
without serious damage to the cars or their mechanism. Engine and gear
troubles have practically disappeared, and the only things that are to be
feared are the breakage of springs and axles and the giving out of tires.
Numerous shock-absorbers were tried out and found wanting in this test; and
were it not for the pneumatic tires, which have been greatly improved during
the past two years, such a tour would be impossible of accomplishment." [72]

The Newport social season featured racing, Daytona Beach soon became
a center for speed trials, and tracks were built in various parts of the nation,
the first of which may have been at Narragansett Park in 1896.[73] Not until
the years just prior to World War I did auto racing attain a truly national
popularity with the establishment of the Indianapolis Speedway, but the emphasis on speed and endurance in these early years spurred manufacturers to
build ever faster models and advertisers to feature the record performances

---

[70] Keith Sward, *The Legend of Henry Ford* (New York, 1948), 14.

[71] Henry Ford and Samuel Crowther, *My Life and Work* (Garden City, 1927),
36–37, 50–51.

[72] *Scientific American*, XCV (August 11, 1906), 95.

[73] G. F. Baright, "Automobiles and Automobile Races at Newport," *Independent*
(New York), LIV (June 5, 1902), 1368.

of each car. Henry Ford had long since lost interest, while the Buick racing team was discontinued in 1915. By then mass production had turned the emphasis toward design, comfort, and economy. Racing was not abandoned and manufacturers still featured endurance tests in later years, but the heated rivalry between pioneer builders had become a thing of the past.[74]

Technological developments in the latter half of the nineteenth century transformed the social habits of the Western World, and sport was but one of many institutions which felt their full impact. Fashions, foods, journalism, home appliances, commercialized entertainment, architecture, and city planning were only a few of the facets of life which underwent rapid change as transportation and communication were revolutionized and as new materials were made available. There are those who stress the thesis that sport is a direct reaction against the mechanization, the division of labor, and the standardization of life in a machine civilization,[75] and this may in part be true, but sport in nineteenth-century America was as much a product of industrialization as it was an antidote to it. While athletics and outdoor recreation were sought as a release from the confinements of city life, industrialization and the urban movement were the basic causes for the rise of organized sport. And the urban movement was, of course, greatly enhanced by the revolutionary transformation in communication, transportation, agriculture, and industrialization.[76]

[74] In these years the motorcycle and the motorboat also created interest, Sir Alfred Harmsworth (later Lord Northcliffe) establishing the Harmsworth Trophy for international competition in 1903. Air races also won widespread publicity in the press from 1910 onward. Glenn H. Curtiss achieved an enviable reputation as an aviator, newspapers sponsored air meets, and considerable attention was given to the "new sport of the air." *Ibid.*, LXIX (November 3, 1910), 999.

[75] Lewis Mumford, *Technics and Civilization* (New York, 1934), 303–305; Arnold J. Toynbee, *A Study of History*, 6 vols. (London, 1934–1939), IV, 242–43.

[76] Technological developments throughout the business world transformed the pattern of city life. The electric elevator and improvements in the manufacture of steel made possible the skyscrapers of Chicago and New York in the late 1880s. Concentration of the business community in the central part of the city was increased also by the telephone switchboard and other instruments of communication. Less and less open land remained for the youth living in the heart of the metropolis, and it was to meet this challenge that the Y.M.C.A., the settlement house, the institutional church, the boys' club, and other agencies expanded their athletic facilities. The playground movement and the public park grew out of the necessity for recreational areas for city dwellers, and public authorities early in the twentieth century began to rope off streets for children at play. The subway, the streetcar, and the automobile made possible the accelerated trend toward suburban development, where the open lot or planned play area offered better opportunities to participate in sport. The more general implications of the impact of the technological revolution on society, already considered by several outstanding scholars, are not discussed here, the principal aim of this study being to describe the interrelationship of sport and invention in the latter half of the nineteenth century. Although the account of the auto slightly transgressed the limits of this study, it was felt necessary to give it an abbreviated treatment. The twentieth century, and the role of improved sporting equipment, racing and training devices, the radio, television, improved highways, and bus and air transport, would require an equally extensive study.

The first symptoms of the impact of invention on nineteenth-century sports are to be found in the steamboat of the ante-bellum era. An intensification of interest in horse racing during the 1820s and 1830s was only a prelude to the sporting excitement over yachting, prize fighting, rowing, running, cricket, and baseball of the 1840s and 1850s. By this time the railroad was opening up new opportunities for hunters, anglers, and athletic teams, and it was the railroad, of all the inventions of the century, which gave the greatest impetus to the intercommunity rivalries in sport. The telegraph and the penny press opened the gates to a rising tide of sporting journalism; the sewing machine and the factory system revolutionized the manufacturing of sporting goods; the electric light and rapid transit further demonstrated the impact of electrification; inventions like the Kodak camera, the motion picture, and the pneumatic tire stimulated various fields of sport; and the bicycle and automobile gave additional evidence to the effect of the transportation revolution on the sporting impulse of the latter half of the century. Toward the end of the century the rapidity with which one invention followed another demonstrated the increasingly close relationship of technology and social change. No one can deny the significance of sportsmen, athletes, journalists, and pioneers in many organizations, and no one can disregard the multiple forces transforming the social scene. The technological revolution is not the sole determining factor in the rise of sport, but to ignore its influence would result only in a more or less superficial understanding of the history of one of the prominent social institutions of modern America.

sports and games in Denmark in the light of sociology

HELGE ANDERSEN, AAGE BO-JENSEN,
N. ELKAER-HANSEN AND A. SONNE

1. Problem and Material

The present examination throws light on a number of interesting problems concerning Danish sports, games, and athletics from a sociological point of view. The words, sport, games, and athletics, are used here in such a way as to comprise purely sports activities only. In the first place such a delimitation of the words implies concentrating on a group of actions demanding

• From Acta Sociologica, 2 (1956), Fasc. 1, pp. 1–28. Copyright © 1956 by Acta Sociologica, Copenhagen, Denmark.

physical training and efforts. In the second place such actions must bear the stamp of play and competition, and the essential interest for the participant should not be financial advantage.

The material for the examination derives partly from the sports statistics prepared by the Department of Statistics since 1938 at intervals of five years, which will be referred to as "the Sports Count," and partly from three inquiries on the basis of interviews, in the following pages termed "the National Survey," "the Odense Survey," and "the International Match Survey."

Primarily we have endeavored to shed light on the interest taken in sports and games, and, unlike previous investigations, it has been considered important to analyse the active athlete's as well as the spectator's interest in sports.

The interest in sports finds expression in active participation, in passive membership of sports clubs, in people's attending sports matches, and in their reading the sports accounts and comments of the dailies and the sports papers. Concurrently with the sports accounts in the press we may mention listening to sports broadcasts.

The extent of the interest in sports is first and foremost reflected by the number of active athletes, and in this respect the most copious data are found in the Sports Count. In order to supplement the official statistics we have tried in the National Survey to obtain information concerning active athletes. A few questions put in the other survey based on interviews also yield a certain amount of information on the active exercise of sports and games.

As for passive membership of sports clubs, information may be collected from the Sports Count, and as in the case of active participation this information has been supplemented by means of the interview inquiries.

There are no statistics available as regards people's attending sports matches. The only piece of information provided by the Sports Count on this point is an estimate of the total amount of gate-money derived from sports meetings. The data concerning the number of spectators which the athletic organizations are in possession of hardly convey the correct idea of the population's interest in attending sports matches as spectators. Hence it was decided to try to shed light on the spectators' interest by means of the three surveys.

The interest in sports which is manifested in the press and radio can be directly gauged by computing the amount of column millimetres occupied by the sports accounts in the dailies and weeklies, and by calculating the number of sports broadcasts. However, this gives no indication of the intensity of the spectators' sports interest, and consequently we have endeavoured by means of interviews to collect information on the extent to which the spectators follow the sports accounts in the dailies, the sporting papers, and over the radio. These matters are discussed in Section 3.

After this attempt at elucidating the extent of the interest taken in sports and games, the next question in the approach to the problem was to examine the motives underlying the interest in sports. On this point there is no clue in the official statistics. To a certain extent it was, however, possible to utilize articles and interviews in the dailies, sports papers, and perodicals. A systematic investigation into the motives for the interest in sports was attempted by interviewing active athletes as well as spectators, and in all the three inquiries based on interviews information is furnished concerning these matters. It may be expedient to emphasize at this stage that an examination on the basis of interviews limits the possibilities for collecting data concerning the motives. In answering the questions the subjects will often place the easiest answer first, and a detailed account of the reasons why people should prefer, e.g., playing football to spending their spare time on other occupations is seldom elicited in the course of the individual interview. By combining various questions we have, however, tried to restrict the possibilities of reply, and we have endeavoured to throw light on the strength of certain essentially different motives.

An investigation into the motives underlying the interest taken in sports, whether this finds expression in active participation or in passive attendance at sports matches, in itself lays claim to a certain interest. The investigation, however, had an ulterior object, as we have endeavoured, with the extent and motives of sports and games as a point of departure, to clarify the relationship between the interest in sports and other interests. As an important factor we may mention the difference between the active athletes' and the passive spectators' participation in other kinds of club life. Further we have analysed the interest taken in reading and films on the part of the active and the passive group. The importance of comradeship in sports and games makes itself felt partly in the clubs, and partly by the fact that to a certain extent people accompany each other to sports matches where they see and discuss the performances together. The rôle of sports and games as a contact factor also manifests itself in relations between family members, and here both a positive and a negative effect may be imagined. The positive effect occurs if the members of a family take the same interest in sports, while the negative effect is seen where the members of a family hold widely divergent views. In the Odense Survey it was specially endeavoured to ascertain the kind of influence that resulted in a person joining the sports organization in question.

Relations between the management and the private members of an association are of particular interest. The immediate motive for membership of a sports club must be interest and a desire to participate in sports and games actively. The members' opinion of their club partly depends on a judgment of whether the individuals in question have their demand for direct participation in sports and games satisfied with a sufficient amount of expediency, and partly on a judgment of whether the number of members joining the club is satisfactory—in other words whether sufficient attractions are offered to outsiders, for instance friends, to make it possible to induce new and desirable individuals to join the club. A detailed examination of the extent to which the various interests and needs of club members are satisfied will easily lead to a fruitless consideration of "club politics." Hence we have confined ourselves to seeking information as to whether members have other interests which they find it desirable that their club should attend to. Thus, in the Odense Survey the active participants in the sports meetings were asked whether they would like their club to attend also to general cultural tasks such as arranging talks, study circles, etc. They were also asked whether they were interested in the club arranging dances and other festivities.

Since the two large sports organizations represented in the Odense Survey hold different views on whether the organization should participate in national defence, it was natural to ask the private members, i.e., the active members, if, in their opinion, the athletic organization should in addition to purely sports interests also participate in national defence. In that connexion we endeavored to collect information on the attitude of the members towards politico-military questions concerning co-operation under the Atlantic Pact and their membership of the Home Guard and Women's Voluntary Services.

In the International Match Survey the main object was to ascertain the composition of the spectators attending an international match and to find out the extent to which the same individuals attend other sports events.

THE NATIONAL SURVEY

Instead of carrying out the first survey as a nation-wide inquiry it was decided to make six uniform local inquiries; for this purpose three local areas were chosen in Jutland, one in Funen, and two in Zealand, viz. the towns of Silkeborg, Odense, and Frederikssund and the following rural districts: the neighborhood of Ribe, Djursland, and an area in South Zealand between Slagelse and Næstved. The same number of interviews was made in each place. The Capital was left out in this survey, because the opinions of its inhabitants do not reflect accurately the whole nation's attitude towards and opinions on sports and games. Within the areas mentioned the interviews were distributed according to the quota method: 53 percent of those interviewed are men and 47 percent are women, this division corresponding to the distribution of the two sexes in the parts of the country examined. In preparing the survey we decided to divide the interviews between three social groups: (1) The workers, by which term are meant individuals receiving weekly wages and individuals of the same social standing, and inferior public servants and similar categories. Two thirds of the interviews were made among workers. (2) The middle classes, comprising independent tradesmen with the exception of managers, manufacturers, and other large-scale business men who cannot be considered as belonging to the middle classes. The majority of public servants and employees in responsible positions were included in this group. Approximately one fourth of the interviews fell in this group. (3) Finally, the third social group comprises the well-to-do, who are defined as that 10 per cent of the population who are financially best situated, including managers, manufacturers, large independent business men, people in easy circumstances in the liberal professions, etc. As appears from the definition itself, 10 percent of the interviews fell into this group. As regards the distribution of the interviews over age groups, an equal number of interviews were made in the age groups 15–25 years, 25–35 years, 35–50 years, and over 50 years.

As the particular importance of this very classification was realized beforehand, it was held inadvisable to weaken the scant material by employing an age distribution corresponding to that of the population. This would have involved an excessive representation of the older strata of the population and hence would have particularly impaired the prominence of those age groups which are active in sports and games. Consequently it was decided to collect an identical number of interviews in each of the four age groups mentioned; this means that in a comparison between the groups the greatest statistical reliability is obtained in a given number of interviews.

The collection, which comprises 1013 interviews, was made in April, 1953, by trained interviewers who were specially briefed with a view to the present investigation. The questionnaire used had been tested beforehand through a trial inquiry.

THE ODENSE SURVEY

In July, 1954, the Danish Gymnastic Clubs and the Danish Rifle, Gymnastic, and Athletic Clubs held a national meeting in Odense. The meeting lasted from 22 to 25 July.

The interviews were collected by trained interviewers. Two questionnaires were used, one for active members and one for spectators. As far as the active members were concerned, the collection took place in the very sports grounds after the events, whereas the spectators were interviewed in the enclosure for spectators. In this survey it was impossible to make any allocation of quotas, except for the fact that a collection of interviews was arranged in the shooting-ranges in such a way that gymnasts and riflemen were interviewed in approximate accordance with their proportionate representation at the meeting. Altogether 762 interviews were made among active members and 401 interviews among spectators.

THE INTERNATIONAL MATCH SURVEY

This was carried out in connection with the Danish-Swedish football match in the Copenhagen Sports Grounds on June 21, 1953.

In this survey trained interviewers were also employed, but since the aim was to ascertain the composition of the spectators, it was impossible to instruct interviewers in advance as to which individuals were to be questioned. Interviewers were placed at the various entrances to the Sports Grounds and interviewed people both in the queues at the entrances and later in the spectators' enclosure itself. The interviewers were distributed in proportion to the number of spectators in the various parts of the enclosure. The interviewers only included Danish-speaking individuals, and possible visitors from Sweden were excluded. Interviewers were instructed, when interviewing people in the queues, to proceed systematically by selecting every third, fifth, or seventh person in the queue. Altogether 77 interviews were made.

It is a characteristic of all the three surveys based on interviews that the interviewers were everywhere well received. The population was most willing to answer questions. In reply to inquiries the interviewers stated that the intention of the survey was to map out the population's opinions on and participation in sports events.

THE SPORTS COUNT

This comprises statistical inquiries into the extent and conditions determining the exercise of sports and games. As mentioned, this materal was prepared by the Department of Statistics, which both issued questionnaires to the individual athletic clubs and collected data in the individual municipalities. These sports statistics are available for the years 1938, 1943, 1949, and 1953.[1] It should be emphasized that the sports statistics do not include school sports or sports and games outside the organizations.

2. The Sports Count

PRINCIPAL SPORTS ORGANIZATIONS

The largest of the principal sports organizations, *the Danish Sports Federation* (D. I. F.), which was founded in 1896, has as its aim to further Danish amateur sports and games. Danish amateur sports organizations (special associations) may be admitted as members.

Of the tasks attended to by D. I. F. may be mentioned: (1) The establishment of common amateur rules, uniform rules for the use of various gymnastic appliances, and uniform rules for competition; (2) Provision of medical facilities (D. I. F. has established a number of medical consultation rooms where athletes may receive free examination and advice); (3) Organization of teaching, instruction, etc.; (4) D. I. F. decides what contests for Danish championships are to be held; (5) D. I. F. has established a sports library; (6) During the unemployment period in the "thirties" D. I. F. undertook the task of trying to induce unemployed individuals to go in for sports; (7) D. I. F. takes up a neutral attitude towards political, religious, and other opinions, but cooperates in solving Danish common national problems. As instances of this we may mention the support given in order to further sports and games in North Slesvig after the reunion in 1920 and the support granted during recent years to further sports in the Faroe Islands and in Greenland, and Danish athletics in South Slesvig. Besides, D. I. F. represents its members in govern-

---

[1] Published in Statistical News (Statistiske Efterretninger), the latest issue dating from August 7, 1954.

ment institutions and main sports organizations abroad, and issues a monthly publication: Sports Life (Idrætsliv).

Thirty-two special associations, with a total of 4736 clubs having 472,030 active and 359,942 passive members, are attached to the Danish Sports Federation.

The Danish Rifle, Gymnastic, and Athletic Clubs (D.D.S.G. & I.) was founded in 1861. During the first years this organization exclusively went in for rifle-shooting and drill, its objects clause bearing a strong national and military stamp. In 1870 the members of the organization began going in for gymnastics. In 1930 a considerable proportion of the gymnasts resigned their membership and formed the Danish Gymnastic Clubs (D.D.G.). Simultaneously the name of the association was changed to the present one, thus signifying that athletics were to have an equal status with shooting and gymnastics in the organization. Later (at the Gråsten meeting, June 7, 1941) the objects clause was formulated as follows: "The object of the association is to create a vigilant and healthy Danish youth with a view to strengthening the love of our country and the cause of national defence."

The organization is divided into a rifle group, a gymnastics group, and an athletics group. It has a total of 38 county clubs, each consisting of parochial or municipal circles totaling approximately 1700. D.D.S.G. & I. issues the paper Danish Sports (Dansk Idræt).

The number of members of D.D.S.G. & I. amounts to approximately 185,000 [2] active and approximately 90,000 passive members.

As mentioned above, the *Danish Gymnastic Clubs* was founded in 1930. The aim of the organization is "to create a physically and intellectually healthy Danish youth by means of gymnastics and other educational work among young people." Apart from gymnastics, members go in for folk-dancing, ball games, swimming, and athletics.

The Danish Gymnastic Clubs publishes the paper Youth and Sports (Ungdom og Idræt). In D.D.G. there are 156,000 [3] active and approximately 100,000 passive members.

The Sports Association of Danish Firms (Dansk Firmaidræts Forbund), founded January 20, 1946, is a collective organization of clubs consisting of workers and employees in various business enterprises. The main object of the organization is to induce those who would otherwise probably keep away to go in actively for sports and games, and the association organizes its own meetings and tournaments. The association numbers approximately 50,000 members, 25,000 of whom are active.

NUMBER OF ACTIVE ATHLETES

There is no available calculation of the total number of active athletes. The official statistics deal with those athletes who are organized in the clubs,

[2] Including approximately 47,000 children below the age of 14.
[3] Including approximately 56,000 children below the age of 14.

and thus we have no data on sports and physical training as exercised outside the clubs. As the data concerning the number of active athletes are based on reports from the sports organizations, one is liable to commit the error of reckoning with double calculations in adding the members of the clubs, since an athlete who goes in for several forms of sports is as a rule a member of several clubs. Double calculations may also occur in the case of those clubs covering several sports branches, whose members may possibly go in for various sports within the same club. The Department of Statistics has, however, estimated that in this country there are a maximum of 700,000 active athletes, corresponding to approximately 45 percent of the population in the age groups from 15 to 40 years.

In the following account we have confined ourselves to dealing with the nine largest sports branches and the groups of boxing, wrestling, and weight-lifting.

Another manner of measuring the extent of active sports and games than by considering the number of active athletes may be by comparing the number of active athletes with the size of the population. Such a computation has been made by the Department of Statistics, calculating with the age groups from 15 to 40 years as an expression of the population. From Table 1 it appears in the case of 11 sports branches how great a percentage of the population is active in the Capital, in other parts of the islands, and in Jutland, respectively.

table 1

TOTAL NUMBER OF ATHLETES AND THEIR PERCENTAGES
OF THE POPULATION AGED 15 TO 40 YEARS

	NUMBER WHOLE COUNTRY	PERCENTAGES OF THE POPULATION AGED 15 TO 40 YEARS			
		CAPITAL	OTHER PARTS OF ISLANDS	JUTLAND	WHOLE COUNTRY
1. Football	199,079	11.9	11.6	14.6	13.0
2. Gymnastics	184,687	6.2	15.4	12.6	12.1
3. Handball	119,983	4.6	9.7	8.2	7.8
4. Shooting	47,994	2.6	4.1	2.7	3.1
5. Swimming	31,273	3.4	1.5	1.7	2.0
6. Athletics	30,651	2.3	2.4	1.5	2.0
7. Badminton	30,327	2.1	2.5	1.5	2.0
8. Tennis	20,524	2.1	1.4	0.9	1.3
9. Rowing	14,259	1.4	0.8	0.8	0.9
10. Boxing	5,728	0.7	0.2	0.3	0.4
11. Wrestling, weight-lifting	6,347	0.7	0.4	0.3	0.4

It will be seen that 13 percent of the population (aged 15 to 40 years) play football, and as only men go in for football, this really means that approximately one fourth of all men aged 15 to 40 years are active football players. To this calculation, as well as to all those mentioned in what follows, the general remark should be added that the material of the Department is based on reports from the clubs, and in collecting the data it was not critically examined whether the members who figure as active members in the clubs are really active, or whether they are active athletes to a limited extent only.

Besides, it will appear from the table that the number of active gymnasts and handball players is relatively smaller in the Capital than in the country taken as a whole, whereas the groups of swimming, tennis, rowing, boxing, wrestling, and weight-lifting have relatively more active members in the Capital than in the other parts of the country.

There are a number of sports which women seldom or never go in for. This is for instance true of football, boxing, wrestling, weight-lifting, and cycling. On the other hand there do not occur sports (at least not in the surveys issued by the Department of Statistics) which women but not men go in for. In a few groups, however, women are more numerously represented than men, which fact will appear from Table 2.

table 2

NUMBER OF MEN AND WOMEN IN A FEW
SPORTS BRANCHES IN PERCENTAGES OF THE
POPULATION AGED 15 TO 40 YEARS

	MEN P. C.	WOMEN P. C.
Gymnastics	9.6	14.6
Handball	7.6	8.1
Swimming	1.6	2.4

DEVELOPMENT OF SPORTS AND GAMES

No general historical account of the development of sports and games in Denmark will be presented, but as the number of individuals joining athletic organizations has been very strongly on the increase during the last ten years or so, it was thought natural to describe the development during this period.

In the period 1938–1953 the number of active athletes in some of the principal sports rose as shown in Table 3.

The average increase for these groups of athletes can be calculated to be 109 percent, if the 1938 number of active athletes is made the basis of the calculation of the average.

This very heavy rise in the number of athletes from 1938 to 1953 cannot be explained as resulting from changes in the population structure, since the age groups from 15 to 40 years only rose by approximately 2½ percent during this period. As far as the age groups from 10 to 40 years are concerned, the increase is even slighter. The age groups from 15 to 30 years which must be assumed to account for the largest number of active athletes even fell from approximately 970,000 to approximately 885,000 during the period 1938–1953.

table 3

INCREASE OF THE NUMBER OF ACTIVE
ATHLETICS FROM 1938 TO 1953

	INCREASE
Football	165 p. c.
Gymnastics	45 —
Handball	327 —
Shooting	245 —
Swimming	1 —
Athletics	140 —
Badminton	104 —
Tennis	79 —
Rowing	78 —
Boxing	5 —
Wrestling and weight-lifting	146 —

The increase in the number of athletes varies greatly in the individual sports, thus resulting in a violent dislocation among the groups. If the increase in the individual groups is compared with the calculated average increase for all the 11 groups, a very considerable progress will be noticeable in the groups of handball and shooting, whereas the groups of swimming, gymnastics, and boxing show a relative decline. The development in the groups of badminton, tennis, and rowing during the 1938–1953 period does not essentially deviate from the average dislocation in all the 11 groups.

PASSIVE MEMBERS OF THE SPORTS ORGANIZATIONS

The largest number of passive club members is found in football, gymnastic, shooting, and handball clubs. The number of passive members in percentages of active athletes appears from Table 4:

table 4

NUMBER OF PASSIVE MEMBERS IN PERCENTAGES
OF THE NUMBER OF ACTIVE ATHLETES

1. Football	129 p. c.
2. Gymnastics	50 —
3. Handball	47 —
4. Shooting	170 —
5. Swimming	21 —
6. Athletics	78 —
7. Badminton	35 —
8. Tennis	22 —
9. Rowing	80 —
10. Boxing	214 —
11. Wrestling and weight-lifting	129 —

EXPENSES IN CONNEXION WITH SPORTS AND GAMES

The expenses incurred in connexion with sports and games are met by the athletes themselves, through the gate-money paid at sports meetings, through the distribution of the surplus derived from the football pool, and through grants from the public funds.

No exact calculation of the total expenses has been made. The Department of Statistics in its investigation has collected data from all sports associations concerning the total amount received through subscriptions, and even though these data are not complete, the Department has been able to estimate that the total subscriptions amount to something between 8 and 9 million kroner, which equals rather more than 10 kroner per athlete.[4]

Apart from subscriptions the athletes have expenses for accessories and clothes. It has not been ascertained how much these items amount to. In the National Survey it was asked what sports and games cost active athletes. An estimate based on the answers offered gives as a main result an annual expense amounting for men to about 80–85 kroner, for women to about 40–45 kroner.

The gate-money at the sports meetings has been estimated at approximately 5 million kroner annually by the Department of Statistics on the basis of data concerning the number of spectators.

The total public grants including the amount from the football pool can be estimated at about 13 million kroner (about 9 million kroner from the municipalities, about 3 million kroner from the football pool, about 1 million kroner from the employment acts), to which should be added that the municipalities place grounds, gymnasiums, etc., at the free disposal of the clubs. After the amendment to the football pool act in March, 1956, the grant from the football pool is expected to rise considerably.

3. The National Survey

EXTENT OF THE INTEREST IN SPORTS

The considerable extent of the interest in sports and games appears immediately from the comprehensive sports items in the press and the radio. Hence the widespread interest in sports should both be reflected in people's reading the sports pages in the press and in their listening to the various sports broadcasts. It has been endeavored to throw light on these matters by means of interviews.

Thus 62 percent of the persons interviewed state that they are regular readers of *the sports pages in the papers*, whereas 35 percent do not read them.

[4] D. I. F. for its organizations has estimated the annual subscription at approximately 24 kroner per active member, and D. D. S. G. & I. has estimated the following subscription amounts for active adults: Riflemen 10–24 kroner, gymnasts, 12 kroner, and various sports 30–40 kroner.

The remaining 3 percent read the accounts occasionally only. A distribution of the subjects by sexes reveals that men read the sports pages more often than women—viz. 69 percent of the men interviewed as against 53 percent of the women interviewed.

Moreover, there is a considerable difference between the reader percentages of the various age groups, with the largest percentages for the youngest groups. The figures appear from the following tabulation:

	READ	DO NOT READ	READ OCCASIONALLY
15–25 years	71 p.c.	26 p.c.	3 p.c.
25–35 years	66 —	32 —	2 —
35–50 years	59 —	38 —	3 —
over 50 years	50 —	47 —	3 —

As was to be expected, it is a larger percentage of the active athletes than of the passive spectators that read the sports pages of the dailies, viz. 76 percent of the former as against 55 percent of the latter. It was found that special sports papers are read by about 20 percent of those interviewed, viz. 27 percent of the men and 11 percent of the women. Of the active athletes, 33 percent read such papers, as against 13 percent of the passive group.

The interest in *the sporting reports on the radio* seems to be as widespread as the interest in the sports pages of the dailies, 64 percent of those interviewed stating that they listen regularly to the Sunday sports broadcast in connexion with the news. Three percent are occasional listeners, and 33 percent state that they never listen to these broadcasts. A division of those interviewed into sexes and into active and passive subjects reveals deviations from the average similar to those obtaining as regards the reading of the sports pages in the press.

The long Sunday broadcast of 25 minutes is not quite so much listened to, only 38 percent of those interviewed listening in to this broadcast (viz. 47 percent of the men and 26 percent of the women). The comparatively greatest interest in this broadcast is observable among the active athletes, 52 percent of whom state that they listened regularly to it.

A very considerable number of people listen to the running commentaries on the various international football matches. Thus 80 percent of the subjects interviewed stated that they listened regularly to those broadcasts, while four percent were only occasional listeners. Here, too, a greater interest is noticeable among men than among women, and those most interested are the active athletes.

It is especially among older people that there are many nonlisteners. Thus the percentage of nonlisteners is as follows:

AGE GROUP	DO NOT LISTEN TO RUNNING COMMENTARIES ON SPORTING EVENTS
15–25 years	12 p. c.
25–35 years	15 —
35–50 years	16 —
over 50 years	23 —

Whereas the sports interest that finds expression in the reading of the press and listening to the radio must be characterized as passive, *membership of the clubs* reflects a more active interest in sports and games.

Of the total number of persons interviewed approximately 38 percent are members of a sports club. By way of comparison it may be mentioned that approximately 31 percent of those interviewed are active athletes.

A not inconsiderable proportion of the subjects interviewed (roughly 13 percent) prove to belong to the category of "passive club members." This category is particularly large among the men. Conversely it appears that on an average about six percent of the interviewed active individuals were not attached to any sports club, and this category of individuals interested in sports and games is more numerous among women than among men. Thus among active as well as among passive individuals membership of a club is most frequent in the case of the men.

The trend of the members' interest in club life will appear from the following facts: It has been ascertained that at some time or other an average of 60 percent of the club members have attended the general meeting of their club. In this respect there is the greatest interest among male members, viz. 66 percent, as against 49 percent of the female club members. Interest in the less businesslike aspects of club life seems to be much greater. Thus an average of 75 percent of the club members state that they attend the nonathletic arrangements of the club (77 percent of the men and 70 percent of the women).

To take a particular example, there is a considerable interest in dances and social gatherings.

Next, it is intended to go one step farther and ascertain how many of the total number of subjects interviewed have attended a sports match. In illustration of this, Table 5 records the answers given by the total number of individuals interviewed to the question: "When did you last attend a sports match?"

It being taken for granted that those not interested in sports are primarily to be found among the persons who do not attend sports matches, one notices that an average of 12 percent of the subjects interviewed have never attended a sports match, viz. nine percent of the men and 15 percent of the women.

table 5

WHEN DID YOU LAST ATTEND A SPORTS MATCH?

	TOTAL P. C.	MEN P. C.	WOMEN P. C.	15–25 YEARS P. C.	25–35 YEARS P. C.	35–50 YEARS P. C.	OVER 50 YEARS P. C.
1953	45	54	37	58	47	46	28
1952	24	22	25	30	23	21	21
1951 or earlier	10	8	13	3	14	11	14
A long time ago	7	6	8	2	6	6	14
Never	12	9	15	6	9	14	21
Do not know	2	1	2	1	1	2	2
Total	100	100	100	100	100	100	100

The division into age groups shows that approximately one-fifth of those over 50 have never attended a sports match. As the figures for the younger age groups are essentially lower, the table is seen to reflect a very heavy increase of the interest in sports in the course of the last generation.

ACTIVE ATHLETES

Of the 1013 subjects interviewed, 311 or 31 percent state that they are active, and 702 or 69 percent state that they are passive. Activeness is most common among the men. Thus a distribution by sexes shows that 34 percent of the men interviewed are active as against only 27 percent of the women interviewed. The decrease of activeness with increasing years will appear from the following tabulation:

	ACTIVE P. C.	PASSIVE P. C.
15–25 years	61	39
25–35 years	30	70
35–50 years	20	80
over 50 years	9	91

The activeness reaches its maximum somewhere in the age interval of 15–25 years and then decreases, at first heavily, later at a more moderate rate, and again heavily in the older age groups.

As a consequence of the age distribution of the selected material mentioned in Section 1, the very high average activeness of the age group from 15 to 25 years and the slight average activeness of the age group comprising those over 50 have the effect that the total percentage of activeness arrived at (31 percent) becomes too large in comparison with the actual average activeness of the adult population.

From a division into social groups of those interviewed it appears that among workers 33 percent were active, in the middle classes 26 percent, and finally among the well-to-do 23 percent.

If we consider the age groups 15–25 years and 25–35 years, which are numerically equal in the material, it would seem possible to reach the conclusion that approximately 45 percent of the population between 15 and 35 years of age are active athletes. This tallies fairly well with the conclusions that may be drawn from the Sports Count, cf. Section 2.

In order to throw light on people's *motives* for going in for sports four different reasons were selected, which may be assumed to cover all the primary single motives. The active athletes were asked which of these four reasons they consider the most important, cf. Table 6. In practice this was done by handing the interviewed person a card with four motives for going in for sports. In several cases there are double answers, especially among the men interviewed, but in the percentual distribution of the answers a correction was made, in that the number of answers was made equal to 100 percent.

table 6

WHICH OF THE REASONS STATED BELOW IS, IN YOUR
OPINION, THE MOST IMPORTANT?
(100 PER CENT: ALL ANSWERS)

	TOTAL P. C.	MEN P. C.	WOMEN P. C.
Health	47	43	60
Comradeship	38	38	39
Recreation	10	12	1
Competition	5	7	0
Total	100	100	100

It is noteworthy that the competitive factor takes up a modest position— and is without any significance to women.

The amount of *time* spent on sports and games may be realized from Table 7.

From this it appears that athletes spend an appreciable amount of time on sports. Thus 70 percent of the active athletes practise twice a week or more, and 8 percent of those interviewed even state that they spend all their spare time on sports. Thus it may be concluded from the table that a considerable portion of the athletes' leisure is spent on the sports grounds. A distribution by sexes reveals that the men spend far more time on sports and games than do the women.

In assessing the division into age groups in this table it must be borne in mind that it only comprises active athletes and hence there are a comparatively greater number in the youngest groups than in the oldest. Among

table 7

HOW MUCH TIME DO YOU SPEND ON SPORTS AND GAMES?

PER WEEK	TOTAL P. C.	MEN P. C.	WOMEN P. C.	15–25 YEARS P. C.	25–35 YEARS P. C.	35–50 YEARS P. C.	OVER 50 YEARS P. C.
Less than once	3	3	2	3	—	2	14
Once	9	6	13	8	8	11	14
Twice	26	21	32	30	22	17	24
3 times	14	16	12	17	14	11	5
4 times or more	30	33	26	26	38	36	24
Whole leisure	8	10	5	8	8	8	5
Season	4	6	2	3	4	8	5
Do not know	6	5	8	5	6	7	9
Total	100	100	100	100	100	100	100

the older athletes there is a pronounced tendency towards spending less time on sports, but the differences are so slight that there is basis for concluding that whereas age has a strong influence on the percentage of athletes, it has less influence on the amount of time spent on sports by the active athletes.

Most athletes—viz. two-thirds of those interviewed—are of opinion that somehow sports and games are *of importance to their work*. On the other hand only a minority—26 percent of the active athletes—think that their employer is positively interested in their going in actively for sports. On this point there is no essential difference between men's opinion and that of women.

It is difficult to decide in what way the employer's interest manifests itself, as over two-thirds of the individuals answering the question as to their employer's interest in the affirmative are unable to offer any comments on this point. It is quite remarkable that it should have been found that no more than 8 percent of the active athletes are able to mention concrete forms of support to the athlete on the part of the employer.

By way of illustrating *the importance of the competitive factor* the active athletes were asked whether or not they go in for competitive sports, *cf.* Table 8.

table 8

DO YOU PARTICIPATE IN SPORTS CONTESTS?
(100 PER CENT: ALL ACTIVE ATHLETES)

	TOTAL P. C.	MEN P. C.	WOMEN P. C.
Yes	45	55	29
No	55	45	71
Total	100	100	100

The competitive sports will be seen to be most widespread among the men.

A division into age groups reveals that the two younger age groups lie abreast, one-half of the active members of these groups participating in competitions, whereas barely one-third of the active athletes over 35 take part in contests.

In order to illustrate *the duration of sports activities* the previously active athletes were asked how many years they were active, *cf.* Table 9.

table 9

FOR HOW MANY YEARS WERE YOU ACTIVE?
(100 PER CENT: THOSE PREVIOUSLY ACTIVE)

	TOTAL P. C.	MEN P. C.	WOMEN P. C.
0– 1 years	6	4	9
2– 4 years	27	26	28
5– 9 years	27	28	28
10–15 years	18	20	15
15 years and more	15	19	11
Do not know	7	3	9
Total	100	100	100

On the basis of the table the average period of activeness can be estimated to be approximately 11 years. The men's period of activeness is slightly longer than that of the women (12 and 9 years, respectively).

RELATIONS BETWEEN SPORTS AND OTHER INTERESTS

In order to illustrate the relationship between *sports and club life* all the subjects included in the survey were requested to state whether they are members of other than athletic clubs, and if so, of what kind the other clubs are.

The answers are distributed as shown in Table 10.

From this it would seem to appear that on the whole the interest in clubs is greater among the active than among the passive. This especially applies to social clubs, whereas on the other hand the interest in political and professional clubs is greatest among the passive.

It will be seen that interest in other clubs is greatest in the oldest age groups and least in the age groups covering 25–35 years. The interest in political clubs is intensified with increasing years, while the converse is the case as regards social clubs. Professional clubs have the largest number of members from the age group covering 25–35 years.

Relations between *the interest in sports and the home may inter alia* be demonstrated through the question below. The individuals attending sports matches were asked how their family reacts when they attend matches. The

table 10

WHAT CLUBS, APART FROM ATHLETIC CLUBS,
ARE YOU A MEMBER OF?

	TOTAL P. C.	MEN P. C.	WOMEN P. C.	ACTIVE P. C.	PASSIVE P. C.
No membership of other clubs	35	26	48	30	40
Membership of other clubs	65	74	52	70	60
Total	100	100	100	100	100
Distribution of membership:					
Political clubs	20	20	19	15	22
Professional clubs	36	41	27	35	38
Social clubs	19	18	20	25	16
Other clubs	25	21	34	25	24
Total	100	100	100	100	100

table 11

WHAT CLUBS, APART FROM ATHLETIC CLUBS,
ARE YOU A MEMBER OF?

	15–25 YEARS P. C.	25–35 YEARS P. C.	35–50 YEARS P. C.	OVER 50 YEARS P. C.
No membership of other clubs	41	53	27	33
Membership of others clubs	59	57	73	67
Total	100	100	100	100
Distribution of membership:				
Political clubs	12	17	23	24
Professional clubs	29	43	37	37
Social clubs	26	17	19	14
Other clubs	33	23	21	25
Total	100	100	100	100

subjects were distributed by sexes and by active and passive individuals, *cf.* Table. 12.

These figures reflect the fact that when a person attends sports matches, this is apparently resented by the family in a slight degree only.

This assumption is corroborated by the fact that 48 percent of the total number of subjects interviewed state that other members of the household also attend sports events, 41 percent state that the other members of the household do not attend matches, while the remaining 11 percent comprise

table 12
WHAT DOES YOUR FAMILY SAY TO YOUR
ATTENDING SPORTS MATCHES?

	TOTAL P. C.	MEN P. C.	WOMEN P. C.	ACTIVE P. C.	PASSIVE P. C.
Nothing	58	59	57	61	54
Joins me	8	6	10	4	10
Does not like it	3	4	1	3	2
Content	16	18	13	24	12
Do not know	15	13	19	8	22
Total	100	100	100	100	100

those interviewed with no household or who do not hazard an opinion on this subject. It is especially the interviewed women and active athletes who state that other members of the household attend sports matches. This may be accounted for by the fact that a woman's household very frequently contains men, and that these take the comparatively greatest interest in sports and games, just as the active athlete's family must be expected to attend sports events to a larger extent when the athlete himself takes part in them.

It appears from Table 13 what members of the household are particularly interested in attending sports matches (double answers occur).

table 13
WHAT OTHER MEMBERS OF THE HOUSEHOLD
ALSO ATTEND SPORTS MATCHES?

	TOTAL P. C.	MEN P. C.	WOMEN P. C.	ACTIVE P. C.	PASSIVE P. C.
The partner	40	30	61	26	47
Sisters and brothers	23	21	29	42	13
Parents	11	13	10	18	7
Children	33	39	32	19	39
Others	6	8	3	6	5
Whole family	7	5	11	6	7
Total	120	116	146	117	118

As a rule the spectators—apart from the interviewed person himself— are either the partner, sisters and brothers, or children. The different distribution of the answers according to the sexes is presumably ascribable to the fact that men attend sports matches to a greater extent than do women. Thus 61 percent of the women interviewed state that their partner (the husband) also attends sports events, whereas only 30 percent of the men interviewed are able to state as much about their wives.

The different age distribution affects the structure of the household in the active and the passive category. Thus comparatively more households in the passive group will consist of the partner and children, whereas in the active group sisters and brothers and parents are more numerously represented.

It appears from Table 14 that approximately one-half of those interviewed attend sports matches by themselves, and that men go by themselves more often than women. The answers contain double answers which cannot occur among those who go by themselves. Besides it will be seen that most frequently the active accompany friends, while the passive accompany their partners, other family members and friends at about the same rate of frequency.

table 14
WITH WHOM DO YOU GO TO SPORTS MATCHES?
(IN PERCENTAGES OF THOSE WHO ATTEND SPORTS MATCHES)

	TOTAL P. C.	MEN P. C.	WOMEN P. C.	ACTIVE P. C.	PASSIVE P. C.
By myself	47	53	36	38	51
Together with:					
My partner	18	11	27	13	20
Other family members	16	14	20	15	17
Friends	26	28	25	41	19
Others	3	3	3	3	2
Various people	4	6	2	3	5
Total	114	115	113	113	114

The literary interest of athletes may be realized from Table 15, where the interviewed men and women and the active and passive groups are divided into two categories according as they state reading books or not.

table 15
DO YOU READ BOOKS?

	TOTAL P. C.	MEN P. C.	WOMEN P. C.	ACTIVE P. C.	PASSIVE P. C.
Yes	71	70	71	79	67
No	29	30	29	21	33
Total	100	100	100	100	100

The subjects interviewed were similarly classified according as they stated borrowing books from public libraries or not. At the same time the material was distributed by age groups, *cf.* Table 16.

The tabulation shows that active participation in sports and games does not—as might perhaps be expected—involve any restrictions in the zest for reading. On the contrary active athletes seem to take a greater interest in reading than the passive group.

This finding cannot have been influenced by the fact that there is a different age distribution in the active and passive groups. The older age groups are more frequent borrowers at the libraries than the younger (see Table 16),

table 16

TO WHAT EXTENT DO ACTIVE AND PASSIVE MEMBERS
BORROW BOOKS FROM PUBLIC LIBRARIES?

	BORROW P. C.	DO NOT BORROW P. C.	TOTAL P. C.
Active men	35	65	100
Active women	34	66	100
Total	35	65	100
Passive men	33	67	100
Passive women	30	70	100
Total	32	68	100
15–25 years	32	68	100
25–35 years	28	72	100
35–50 years	34	66	100
Over 50 years	36	64	100
Total	33	67	100

and the active count most heavily in the youngest age groups. Hence the interest in borrowing must actually be assumed to be greater in the active than in the passive category.

The interest in films was examined by asking those interviewed how often go to the cinema. On the basis of the answers the average number of annual visits to the cinema was calculated, *cf.* Table 17.

table 17

AVERAGE ANNUAL NUMBER OF
VISITS TO THE CINEMA

	ACTIVE	PASSIVE
All	25	15
15–25 years	32	30
25–35 years	24	20
35–50 years	16	12
Over 50 years	9	8

SPORTS AND GAMES AS ENTERTAINMENT AND AMUSEMENT

The sports movement is supported not only by interest in direct participation, but just as much by the interest in attending and enjoying the various sports achievements.

By way of illustrating the rôle played by this entertainment and amusement factor all the subjects were asked when they last attended a sports match.

It appears that 69 percent of the subjects interviewed had attended a sports match at least within the previous 18 months. A sorting out by sexes revealed that the men were more frequent spectators than the women and that young people were more frequent spectators than old.

The various motives underlying the spectators' desire to attend sports and games are illustrated in Table 18, in which the subjects are divided into sexes and into an active and a passive category.

In conformity with the inquiries made to throw light on the active athletes' motives for going in for sports and games, five different reasons were selected, and the spectators were asked to which of these they attach the greatest importance, cf. Table 18. The answers were sorted out by sexes and by active and passive subjects. Double answers occur in numerous cases, especially in the active category, but on this point a correction was made in the percentual distribution.

table 18

WHY DO YOU ATTEND SPORTS MATCHES?
(THE NUMBER OF ANSWERS EQUALS 100 PERCENT)

	TOTAL P. C.	MEN P. C.	WOMEN P. C.	ACTIVE P. C.	PASSIVE P. C.
To see good sport	50	50	49	52	48
For the sake of entertainment and excitement	32	36	27	31	33
To bet in the totalisator	1	1	—	1	1
Because my friends and family go there	7	5	11	7	7
Because I know one of the entrants	10	8	13	9	11
Total	100	100	100	100	100

It appears that the spectators—and especially the active athletes among them—prefer the fine sports performance to the purely entertaining and exciting factor in sports matches. The most remarkable thing, however, is that presumably 32 percent openly admit that they attend sports matches for the sake of entertainment and excitement.

The three kinds of sports most popular with the public are football, gymnastics, and handball, these taken together being preferred by approximately 70 percent of those interviewed.

The most popular sport with men is football, and with women gymnastics.

To shed further light on the interest in football those who attend sports matches were asked when they last attended a football match.

It appears that only eight percent of the men, as against 30 percent of the women, had never attended a football match. Sixty-seven percent of the men and 46 percent of the women had attended one at least within the previous 12 months. The interest in football matches seems to be comparatively greater among the active athletes.

Concerning the spectators' views on sports it may be stated that nearly all—*viz.* 96 percent of the subjects interviewed—are of the opinion that it is wholesome to go in for sports. In the opinion of the majority (86 percent) the wholesomeness is primarily justified from sanitary considerations, whereas eight percent emphasize comradeship. Men and women and active and passive individuals offered essentially identical answers.

Opinions vary with regard to *public support of sports and games.* Thus altogether 35 percent of those interviewed consider the support sufficient, and 34 percent hold the opposite view. The remaining one-third are at a loss how to answer this question.

Finally we may mention the views of the public on *professional sport.* The subjects interviewed were asked whether they are opposed to professional sport, and it appears that the opponents of professional sport form a minority both among men and among women. The case is different, however, as far as opinions on the individual sports branches are concerned; thus there is absolute opposition to Danish football becoming professional.

Definite standpoints are especially found among the men, whereas the women tend to be indifferent.

4. The Odense Survey

In Denmark, sports in the country are mainly exercised in clubs attached to either the Danish Rifle, Gymnastic, and Athletic Clubs (D.D.S.G. & I.) or the Danish Gymnastic Clubs (D.D.G.). These two organizations, which are of about equal size, officially voice fairly different views on the further aim of sports and games. Whereas D.D.S.G. & I. emphasizes questions of national defence, D.D.G. sets itself the task of creating a physically and intellectually healthy Danish youth through gymnastics and other educational work among young people. Furthermore it should be mentioned that D.D.S.G. & I. receives grants from the football pool, whereas D.D.G. is on principle opposed to such grants. (Instead, the latter organization receives a roughly corresponding grant from the ordinary funds of the Treasury.) The meeting in Odense was a common meeting, both the two main organizations participating, and a number of questions in the interview inquiry were intended to clarify the views of the participants—those of active athletes as well as those of spectators—on the two organizations and their different objects.

By way of introduction it should be mentioned that over half the number of active athletes when questioned stated that only one organization was represented in their native place, so that these members had had no opportunity of choosing between the two organizations. Besides, seven percent of the active athletes had changed from one organization to the other, as a rule because of change of address, and as much to one organization as to the other.

Of the 762 active athletes interviewed 311 had had an opportunity of choosing between the two organizations. The men had chosen one organization as often as the other, whereas the women had more often than not preferred D.D.G. to D.D.S.G. & I.

Besides, it is remarkable that about 90 percent had become members before they were 18, 70 percent of the women before they were 14, and a total of 88 percent stated that they had been members ever since their school-days.

On this basis it was particularly interesting to ascertain who had influenced the individual subjects to join the club in question. A large number (approximately one-third) stated that their friends had been most influential in their decision. It is characteristic that according to the statements offered the influence of parents had had a heavier weight with women than with men.

Taking the early and perhaps somewhat casual choice of organization into consideration, it is presumably not so surprising that 80 percent of the participants in the meeting should not have been conscious of any difference between the two main organizations and that the ideological differences between the organizations should only have been mentioned by two percent of the participants.

From the answers given it must at any rate be permissible to conclude that the different objects of the two organizations, emphasized by their managements, have no essential significance for the majority of the members.

On the whole the participants in the meeting expressed satisfaction at having joined their respective athletic organizations, and the fifth who were dissatisfied were unable to state very exact reasons for this.

Of the participants of the two organizations only one-third held that their athletic clubs should also attend to questions of national defence—and there was a remarkably slight difference in the answers made by the members of the two organizations (34 percent from D.D.S.G. & I. and 29 percent from D.D.G.). On the other hand there was a significant difference between the attitudes of the male and female participants (40 percent of the men and 20 per cent of the women took up a sympathetic attitude towards the organizations attending to questions of national defence).

Over three-fourths of the participants thought that their athletic clubs should also attend to "cultural tasks" (talks and other educational work), and over 90 percent held that the clubs ought to arrange dances and festivities.

Ninety percent of those participating in the meeting stated that they were not members of other athletic clubs than the one they represented at the meeting. On this point there was no difference between the two organizations, and an appreciably greater number of men than of women were members of several athletic clubs (12 percent and three percent, respectively). More than half the number of participants had not previously gone in for other sports.

Judging from the interviews, gymnastics are practiced once or twice a week—seldom more frequently. Of the other sports, participants took the greatest interest in swimming and the least in boxing.

About 20 percent of the participants were directly opposed to professional sport, and approximately two-thirds stated that they were not against professionalism. Finally, 13 percent were indifferent.

In the opinion of the majority, the most important advantage derived from being an athlete was comradeship itself. Exercise and health were considered to be of secondary importance.

Over half the participants in the meeting when questioned stated that they attended football and handball matches as spectators, whereas one-third seldom or never attended other sporting events.

By way of illustrating the contacts created and kept up through sports and games it may be mentioned that almost 60 percent of the participants in the meeting had all their five nearest friends in the same sports club and less than 10 percent stated that they had none of their closest friends in the club. The athletic club must, therefore, be considered a contact possibility of the greatest importance to the overwhelming majority of the members.

As far as the family's views on sports and games are concerned, it should be mentioned that 70 percent, viz. 60 percent of the men and 85 percent of the women, stated that their families prompted them to go in for sports.

As mentioned above, the two main organizations hold divergent views as to football betting. Hence it is remarkable that among the members of both organizations there should have been no appreciable difference between the percentages of non-bettors in the two organizations. Of the men there were approximately 40 percent and of the women about 75 percent who did not bet.

As mentioned above, there is an essential difference between the attitudes of the two principal organizations towards questions of national defence. Judging from the survey, this difference does not manifest itself in any difference as regards membership of the Home Guard and Women's Voluntary Services on the part of the two participating groups. On an average it proved that 10 percent were attached to these organizations. Of the riflemen proper 25 percent, however, were members of the Home Guard.

There were slightly more adherents of the Atlantic Pact among the participants from D.D.S.G. & I. than among those from D.D.G., but in both groups the indifferent and the opponents were the majority. Forty-four percent of the riflemen proper were adherents of cooperation under the Atlantic Pact.

Of the male participants who had been through their military service one-third were members of a soldiers' club. Over half the riflemen proper were members of such a club.

A special interview inquiry was made among the spectators at the Odense meeting. From this it appeared that about one-half of the spectators were members of one of the two organizations arranging the meeting—and the overwhelming majority of these were active athletes themselves. Of the total number of spectators approximately one-fourth were women.

Most of the spectators had come to the meeting accompanied by others —primarily family members—and only about one-fourth came by themselves.

Only very few were accompanied by their fellow workers. Forty percent of the spectators had previously attended a similar meeting (which is held every seventh year).

Most spectators (two-thirds) stated that they came to see good sportsmanship, whereas only about 10 percent emphasized the entertainment factor.

Ten percent of the spectators stated as their reasons for attending that they knew one of the entrants. Of the athletic branches represented at the meeting gymnastics would seem to have aroused the greatest interest.

Although, as mentioned, more than half the spectators were members of one of the two main organizations, only one-fourth voiced particular interest in any of the two organizations.

Many more men (about 30 percent) than women (about 20 percent) expressed such a positive interest in one of the organizations. Whereas the men's interest was equally divided between the two organizations, all the women who were positively interested mentioned D.D.G. Unfortunately it was not possible to ascertain the reason for this preference—which corresponds to the result of the inquiry made among the active athletes.

Over 70 per cent of the spectators had themselves gone in for sports and games, mostly gymnastics, but in the case of the men also to a large extent football and handball, especially among the younger people.

More than 70 percent of the spectators stated that they attended other athletic meetings as well; this applied more largely to men than to women and more to the younger than to the older age groups. Of the other sports, football was most popular with the men, handball with the women.

5. The 1953 International Match Survey

On the basis of 777 interviews at the Danish-Swedish football match in the Copenhagen Sports Grounds on June 21, 1953, it was found that about one-fourth of the spectators were women, that almost one-half of the spectators belonged to the working class, and that rather more than one-third were between the ages of 25 and 35.

As their reason for attending the international match, 85 percent of the men stated that they came to see good sport, and the women to a higher degree attached importance to the entertainment element. Twelve percent of the women stated as the reason for their presence that they were accompanied by others, whereas only one percent of the men alleged this motive.

One-fourth of the spectators came by themselves, especially men in the higher age groups. Over three-fourths of the female spectators stated that they had come together with their family, whereas only 30 percent of the men stated this. Barely one-fourth stated that they attended the match with their fellow workers.

Eighty-five percent of the spectators had previously attended an international match (90 percent of the men and 67 percent of the women).

Of the subjects interviewed 7 percent stated that they only attended international football matches. This particularly applied to the women and the older spectators. The majority of the spectators, *viz.* between 80 and 90 percent, also attended divisional matches and other football matches.

Most spectators stated that they also attended other kinds of sports contests, whereas 25 percent stated that they only attended football matches. Among the other sports and games handball would seem to be the one most popular, next follow bicycle races, gymnastics, and swimming.

It was characteristic that there were more of the older spectators than of the younger who only attended football matches, and that there were comparatively more of the old than of the young spectators who attended horse-racing. There seemed to be the difference between the various social groups that the members of the working classes attended bicycle races more often than the higher income brackets, and that conversely the highest income group attended horse-racing comparatively more frequently.

Finally it should be mentioned that 30 percent of the male spectators stated that they played football themselves, 55 percent had previously done so, and 16 per cent had never played.

Soviet sport in the 1960's

HENRY W. MORTON

Nikita S. Khrushchev some years ago confessed to being an ardent soccer fan (soccer is Russia's most popular spectator sport). "Whenever a player kicks the ball," he said, "it is Khrushchev who kicks it, and whenever a player gets kicked in the shins, it is Khrushchev who gets kicked." [1] The First Secretary's reaction to sport is not atypical. Russians are sport enthusiasts, and their natural love for athletics, fostered by the Communist Party, has now been whipped into a tremendous national pastime. In a society that does not provide a great variety of recreational facilities sport is truly all-pervasive.

Only fifteen years ago Soviet athletes were an unknown quantity. Today they rule the international sport scene, having outdistanced the world's leading competitors in the last two Olympic Games (1956 and 1960) and having scored innumerable triumphs in international sport competitions. To understand the phenomenon of Russia's success it is necessary to examine the role

[1] *New York Times*, October 28, 1957.

• From Morton, Henry W., *Soviet Sport*, New York: Collier Books, © 1963, pp. 17–33.

of sport as part of the total Soviet environment and the impact it has made on Soviet society as well as on the outside world.

Party slogans since the 1930s have demanded of Soviet athletes that they beat bourgeois sport records. It was a Central Committee resolution of December 1948, however, which launched the Soviet sport offensive of the 1950s. After many years of preparation the Soviet sport machine was confidently ready to challenge the world's top athletes. Subsequent sport triumphs have given the Soviet Union much favorable publicity and have inflated Soviet prestige abroad. By systematically organizing sport exchanges with nations from all over the world the USSR has won valuable beachheads of influence which have been exploited to create a positive image of the Soviet Union and to induce foreigners to see advantages in the Soviet system. Here is a further example to underdeveloped countries of how to move quickly from backwardness to excellence, in sport as in industry. As Soviet technicians are welcome in various parts of the world, so are Soviet coaches.[2]

Soviet sport successes gained abroad are even more important for domestic considerations. Sport excites strong feelings. It arouses sentiments of national pride and a keen sense of satisfaction. In this area Russia no longer has to take second place to the West. The Soviet citizen is encouraged to identify team loyalty with state loyalty, and sport acts as a legitimizing force of the Soviet system in the eyes of the citizen. Soviet athletes are portrayed as active champions of peace and friendship, generously received by people of foreign nations as they spread good will and strengthen cultural ties. Every victory, athletic achievement, and new world record is cited in support of the contention that "the triumph of our athletes . . . is proof of the superiority of the Soviet socialist culture over the rottenness of the culture of capitalist countries." [3]

Sport devotees in the West have been increasingly concerned with the changing trend in world sport. But (quite naturally) they are asking the most immediate questions: "How can we beat the Russians?" "Are Soviet athletes professionals and do they thus have an unfair advantage?" "How is the Soviet Union using sport to help it win the cold war?" Questions of this nature can only be answered by an examination of the dynamics of Soviet sport.

Scope of the Program

The Soviet sport program is of heroic proportions, patterned on (though the Soviets will never say so) the calisthenics of Germany and the Scandi-

[2] *Soviet Weekly,* January 18, 1962. "Soviet sports organizations," writes *Soviet Weekly,* "readily meet the many requests from foreign countries for coaching or assistance and many more Soviet sport experts will be visiting such countries this year." Soviet coaches have been sent to Burma, Brazil, Cuba, and India.

[3] S. L. Akselrod, *Fizicheskaia Kultura i Sport v SSSR* (Moscow: Fizkultura i Sport, 1954), p. 52.

navian countries and the sport-games of England and the United States, and including certain indigenous sports. National championships are held in more than forty-six different sports, and leagues graded according to caliber of play determine division championships in soccer, hockey, basketball, volleyball, and water polo. The soccer season, similar to the American baseball season, stretches from April to November and is avidly followed by millions. Gymnastics are popular in sport groups, and mass gymnastic demonstrations are spectacular events.

There are approximately 186,000 *kollektivy* (sport groups) with a membership of *thirty million* (as of 1961, ten million more than in 1959) [4] in factories, offices, and collective and state farms, as well as in schools, labor reserve units, the armed forces, and the security police. These groups are set up under specific rules of the sport administration and are affiliated either with trade union or non-trade union sport societies. Individuals are constantly urged to join sport groups and to engage in physical exercise. Sport facilities are made available at a nominal membership fee. A spectacular feature of the Soviet sport program are the *spartakiady* (sport festivals) [5] of the "Peoples of the USSR," of trade unions, armed forces, school children, etc., which periodically enlist literally tens of millions in sports. Competitions are scheduled in a great variety of sports on an elimination basis as the best teams from district, province, republic, and federal levels meet to contest for the championship of their level.

There are approximately 25,000 soccer fields, 200,000 basketball and volleyball courts (but few tennis courts and no golf links), 7,000 gyms, and 2,200 ski centers in the Soviet Union.[6] As a further stimulus in winter, which is usually severe and lasts from six to eight months, skating surfaces in cities are flooded to provide frozen pathways in parks and near large stadiums. In Moscow and Leningrad people troop about happily on skis, although much of the park area is flat,[7] and impromptu hockey matches are staged by youngsters in the shadow of the Kremlin. In summer group hiking is encouraged, and hundreds of touring centers and camps are now being built. Periodically, important roadways are blocked off to stage mass relays, bicycle and motorcycle races, and other sporting events. Throughout the year the broadcasting day begins with the announcer cheerily calling out morning exercises. And a unique program, on-the-job calisthenics, is a device, typical of the Party's utilitarian attitude, to improve labor productivity. Ten million workers in

---

[4] *Sovetskii Sport*, August 4, 1961. The Soviet Union is fascinated by statistics in every area of her development. This holds true for sport statistics, which tend to be inflated and seldom feature breakdowns of figures. The uses of Soviet sport statistics and their reliability are discussed later in the book (pp. 149–50).

[5] *Spartakiady* is the plural, *spartakiada* the singular.

[6] *Pravda*, August 13, 1960.

[7] All school children, particularly in rural areas, must learn to ski. In winter their transportation may depend upon it.

28,000 plants engage in periodic exercises during working hours to stimulate tired muscles.[8]

Sport pavilions and pictorial displays are commonplace; so are sport reels shown in movie theaters, and sport attractions over television. *Sovetskii Sport*, the central sport paper, is very popular because of its readability and content; it appears six times a week, but it is only one of eighteen sport periodicals published in the USSR. The sport administration has its own state publishing house (*Fizkultura i Sport*), which in 1957 published 811 books and pamphlets with a total printing of 9,631,000 copies.[9]

Obviously, the Soviet sport program did not spring full-blown into Russian life in the 1950s when Soviet sport successes attracted the attention of the world. Neither was the program originally developed because of strong popular demand. The *deus ex machina* for sport, as for everything else, was the Party. Soviet sport is an integrated part of the Soviet millieu, a microcosm of Soviet life in which all basic characteristics of Soviet society are operative to a much larger extent than is appreciated by the outside world, which shows interest only in Soviet performances at international competitions.

The Soviet sport program dates back to the early years of the Revolution. Its character has been determined by four important resolutions issued by the Central Committee of the Communist Party, the first in 1925, the latest in 1959. Until 1959 sport was conducted by an All-Union (federal) Committee of Physical Culture and Sport (AUC) attached to the USSR Council of Ministers. The Committee was in fact a complex ministry responsible for the over-all direction, planning, and financing of sport. In 1959 that Committee was dissolved on Party orders, only to be transformed (with some minor changes) into the USSR Union of Sport Societies and Organizations (USSO), ostensibly with a democratically elected leadership. The change has not in the least affected Party control over sport nor significantly altered the mode of administration, but it was an outcome of Khrushchev's statement at the 21st Party Congress in January 1959 (which points up the close ties between sport and politics) that in certain areas the state might begin to *wither away*. Sport was to be the first state agency (so far it is the only one) to be replaced by public organization as the USSR entered the phase of "constructing communism." [10]

Sport in the Soviet Union is subject to detailed planning. The present Seven Year Plan calls for *fifty million sportsmen* by 1965, 24,000 Masters of Sport (there were 13,529 as of January 1, 1959), and fourteen million athletes

[8] *Sovetskii Sport*, August 12, 1961. This is a practice which the Party decried as exploitive—that is, making the worker produce more for the same wages—when applied in non-Communist countries.

[9] Boris I. Gorokhoff, *Publishing in the U.S.S.R.* (Bloomington: Indiana University Press, 1959), Supplement No. 2.

[10] See Chapter 6.

who will have achieved one of the six sport categories below the master level. Republics, provinces, districts, and cities have to meet specific membership and proficiency goals. An active recruitment drive, which has as its minimal goal the Seven Year Plan objective of fifty million, is in progress. If it succeeds (and all indications point to it), almost *one quarter* of the people in the USSR, the most vital and youthful sector of the society, will be enrolled members in sport groups—a staggering total.[11]

The Program and the Party

Why this overwhelming concern with physical activity? The reasons for conducting sport on a mass scale are many and go far beyond the traditional uses of sport to which we in the West are accustomed. The Soviet sport program has always had specific political tasks assigned to it. These were stated as early as 1925 in a Party resolution:

> Physical culture must be considered not only from the point of view of physical training and health but should also be utilized as a means to rally the broad working masses around various Party, Government and trade union organizations through which the masses of workers and peasants are drawn into social and political life. . . . Physical culture must play an integral part in the general political and cultural training and education of the masses.[12]

Sport is used by the Party as a lever of social control, offering the Soviet regime a wonderful opportunity to exploit genuine enthusiasm and at the same time channel leisure-time activity toward Party-inspired goals. Sport societies, through which most athletic activity is conducted, can be and have been abolished or restructured to serve Party purposes. For example, when Khrushchev reorganized Soviet industry in 1957, trade union sport societies were reorganized to conform to the new territorial principle now in vogue.

Spontaneous organization of sport groups without Party permission is impossible—*and not necessarily desired by a society which traditionally worshipped state power and naturally accepts the idea that the state should take charge of all important functions.* Sport societies and groups are formed according to prescribed "model statutes," and training and selection of sport cadres is supervised.

Party leaders realize that with more leisure time available and with the planned radical reduction of working hours (the Seven Year Plan calls for a 30- to 35-hour week by 1965), it will be more difficult to control and channel

---

[11] The drive's slogan, "One Plus Two," signifies that every physical culturist is expected to enlist at least two persons in the sport movement. One word of caution regarding the fifty-million target figure: Even if the total is achieved it will be difficult to evaluate what percentage of the membership will be frequent, active participants.

[12] Resolution of the Central Committee of the Russian Communist Party (b), July 13, 1925. Reprinted in *Kalendar Spravochnik Fizkulturnika na 1939 God* (Moscow: Fizkultura i Sport, 1939), pp. 5–7.

the activities of millions. They have given much more thought to the "leisure problem" than we in the West, who do not generally view it as a problem for government but believe leisure-time activity still to be an individual's private pursuit. According to the Soviet world view, man's activity at work or play must be directed to a purposeful end. This view is positively stated again in the new *Party Program* of 1961, the Soviet blueprint for the next twenty years:

> People will increasingly devote their leisure to public pursuits, cultural intercourse, intellectual and physical development and artistic endeavor. Physical training and sport will become part and parcel of the everyday life of people.[13]

The nature of leisure time is often "discussed" at meetings held in factories, offices, farms, schools, sport centers, and so forth.[14] In a discussion at the Dinamo electrical engineering works in Moscow on the "Communist future," the speaker, a philosophy professor, declared that "the nearer to communism, the more leisure we shall have. We should direct the attention of our people to the need to use their free time for study, for rational cultural pastimes, for sporting activities."

"But what about people who aren't interested in self-improvement?" he was asked. "Many people prefer to spend their free time in dancing, playing cards, and drinking!"

It was "the duty of everyone to help re-educate such people," said the professor.[15]

Here is the reason behind the most recent drive to enroll so many workers in sport societies, where, along with benefitting from physical exercise, they are under Party supervision. In recent years the Party inaugurated a drive to enlist people over forty in physical-culture groups. As of 1961 four million members in that age group were engaged in sport. Moscow's Central Stadium has 100 groups of women, each numbering thirty housewives, workers, and pensioners between the ages of 45 and 70, who meet twice weekly, under guided supervision, for gymnastics, swimming, and other sports.[16]

Development of physical culture has also figured prominently in two major concerns of the Party: heightening *labor productivity* and *military preparedness* (the latter a traditional function of sport in the modern state system). That "athletes are obliged to raise the productivity of labor by all means at their disposal to perform exemplary work at their jobs, and at the same time help their friends achieve victories of production" is a common theme in the Soviet sport press.[17]

Not only is sport considered essential for the physical fitness and mental

[13] *Program of the Communist Party of the Soviet Union* (Draft) (New York: Cross Currents Press, 1961), p. 110.

[14] These meetings are held periodically and are an important instrument through which the Party exercises supervision and control.

[15] *Soviet Weekly*, January 25, 1962.

[16] *Ibid.*, December 7, 1961.

[17] *Sovetskii Sport*, March 25, 1951.

alertness of the worker, but it should also inculcate "in young people a love of labor." [18] Physical fitness has become the patriotic obligation of every citizen; it should help him perform his job with joy and greater efficiency and thus become an "active builder of communism." Toward this end, too, on-the-job calisthenics is greatly encouraged by the Party. *Kommunist* (the leading Party organ) recently prodded factory managers with the criticism that "unfortunately there are still many factories and plants where the introduction of calisthenics is proceeding at a snail's pace" and that many republics "still continue to underestimate the importance of calisthenics as a means of improving health and raising labor productivity." [19]

Secondly, physical culture is an essential factor in paramilitary training. All must learn to bear arms in case "reactionary forces" will not permit the transition to communism to take place peacefully. Soviet sport has a long history as a subsidiary arm of the military. Since 1931 the basic aims of higher labor productivity and military preparedness have been combined in a mass physical fitness program appropriately called "Ready for Labor and Defense" (*Gotov k Trudu i Oborone*, usually abbreviated as GTO). Since its inception, more than seventy million persons have successfully mastered the GTO requirements. In addition to providing a mass physical culture base, one of the primary purposes of the GTO system is to attract those who are physically able to participate in a program designed to provide Soviet leadership with soldier-workers, militarily trained and in glowing health. The GTO system contains such test categories (for all divisions and both sexes) as grenade throwing for distance, rifle shooting for accuracy, cross-country skiing, and the scaling of physical obstacles. Gliding, parachute jumping, and other "sports" having military value are greatly encouraged.

In 1958, to help celebrate the fortieth anniversary of the *Komsomol* (the Young Communist League), a nationwide sport festival in applied military sports was held. Supervised by the Voluntary Society for Assistance to the Army, Air Force and Navy (DOSAAF) in close cooperation with the sport administration, it received broad coverage in the *Komsomol* press, which stresseed the importance of military preparedness of youth. Despite reduction in the Soviet armed forces and a spate of Soviet disarmament proposals, there has been no indication that the emphasis on the military application of sport is being reduced or that it will be reduced in the immediate future.

The Program and the People

Though the Party views sport as a transmission belt to further nonsport objectives, sport as a medium has inherent qualities which engender voluntary mass enthusiasm while safely permitting emotional release. It develops a spontaneity which, along with serving as a safety valve for the release of emotions, also carries an innate apolitical quality which is inviolable. Although

[18] *Pravda*, July 9, 1954, p. 1.
[19] *Kommunist*, No. 13, September 1959.

art, music, and literature have become increasingly popular mass art forms as the literacy rate has shot up sharply in Soviet society, sport is the medium most fully comprehended and enjoyed by the great multitude.

Mass sport and organized athletic competition in clubs, societies, leagues are an important by-product of modern industrial society. Urbanization, increase in population, technological advancement, leisure time; modern transportation, making inter-area and international competition possible; modern communications, television, the sport page; improved equipment and sport structures—all have contributed toward focusing millions of eyes upon sport arenas large and small.

Sport is a drama. Its great attraction lies in the vicarious experience it imparts to the spectator. It is truly heroic—at once glorious and tragic. Sport telescopes the human struggle for power, offering a spectacle which plays upon the emotions but rarely leaves lasting effects. Prestige for past victories counts for naught; the need for proving oneself is ever demanded anew. The attractiveness of sport lies in its genuine element of suspense, which can be capitalized on but not twisted out of shape by political demands.

In the Soviet system, however, where everything is political to a greater or lesser degree, sport (like science) offers one of the greatest possible avenues of retreat.[20] Athletes are subjected to constant political supervision in their sport group by Party or *Komsomol* activists, as are all groups. If they openly flout political protocol, star athletes suffer Party reprimands, loss of future career opportunities, or even imprisonment in extreme cases. On the other hand, those engaged in full-time athletics do not have to spend their lives dodging Party doctrine. Here there is no quarrel about content, and their intellect remains relatively unscarred by the demands of Party "truth."

Although framed in ideology, the playing field itself is not a canvas for socialist realism (the optimistic and idealistic portrayal of Soviet society), as are literature and art. Neither is the Soviet athlete alienated by the system, hiding his talents in Aesopian language, writing for the drawer (that is, not for publication but only for trusted friends), or painting what he does not feel. He can exhibit his talents proudly for the world to see with full approval of the Party.

It is not surprising, then, that sport is an essential and popular leisure (or full) time pursuit. Soviet leisure time, incidentally, should not be viewed in an American or Western context. The Russian urbanite, today 50 percent of the population, lives in overcrowded quarters (there is, in fact, no word for "privacy" in Russian), often three and four to a room, and has little incentive to stay indoors. His leisure is basically oriented outside his home. This is particularly true of the younger family member who wants to get away from the numerous occupants of the household.

It is in the street, so often filled with hurrying throngs; at places of

---

[20] See George Sherman, "Soviet Youth: Myth and Reality," *Daedalus*, Vol. XCI, No. 1 (Winter 1961), p. 225.

public entertainment—sport events, movies, theaters, concert halls, museums; at the many exhibitions, grandiose and complex and filled with industrial wonders which hold such attraction for the mechanically interested Russian; and at public parks—aptly called "for rest and culture," as they provide music (via public loudspeaker systems), cafes, and chess boards—that he will find his home away from home, queuing up, indefatigably, as one of the great entertainment-hungry crowd.

I still vividly recall a memorable Sunday in the summer of 1959 spent in one of the most magnificent sport complexes in the world, built in the Luzhniki section of Moscow. It is situated along the Moscow River and was completed in 1956. It has many sports buildings. The Lenin Central Stadium (where Khrushchev often speaks after returning from abroad), a massive rotund structure, one of the largest in Europe, is the most impressive. Smaller in scale, but as neatly structured, are many arenas and practice fields, including a court for hockey seating 12,000 spectators, two giant swimming pools surrounded by concrete stands, a children's stadium, and basketball and volleyball courts.

It was a beautiful day. A huge crowd had gathered early, choking the major and minor arteries leading from the Metro station to the Central Stadium (no cars, *ergo* no parking problem), hustling and bustling in characteristic Moscow fashion. A trade fair (state-owned) had set up its numerous booths for the season. Along the pathways and girding the major and minor stadia were hundreds of stalls selling a great variety of goods: clothing, glassware, scarves, shoes, electrical appliances, books (the bookstall had the slogan "Everyone should have his own library"). Many were drawn to Luzhniki to shop and browse, and the familiar queues formed, particularly in front of the food counters which dished out large quantities of red caviar and sliced sausages on open bread with beer and fruit soda.

Sport, however, is the main attraction at Luzhniki, which because of its varied facilities is able to present a sport carnival practically every Sunday. The day's program began in the morning with an international tennis match, held in the small arena, with players (but no big names) from Denmark, France, Great Britain, Hungary, Poland, and the USSR participating. The feature event of the day was reserved for the spacious Central Stadium, and tickets from three to ten rubles [21] were sold at a brisk pace as the crowd, quite frolicsome on ticket lines, good-humoredly shouted and shoved.

The program was divided into two parts. At three o'clock there was a dual track meet which matched Soviet athletes against those of East Germany. The latter trailed their Soviet counterparts, in true satellite fashion, across the finish line to the quiet and polite approval of the spectators. The second feature event was a championship soccer match which pitted *Spartak* of Moscow against *Zenit* of Leningrad. It was early evening by then, 6:30 to be

---

[21] "Old rubles." In 1961 "new rubles" with a monetary value ten times higher were issued.

exact, and the stands were packed to capacity (not so for the track meet). The summer sky was still fairly bright and blue, but the lights came on for the second half. The tense excitement of the crowd overflowed, whenever a goal was scored, in the joyful release of many colored balloons bought for the purpose. The balloons drifted serenely skyward while the fierce competition continued below. (The Soviet sport crowd is generally well behaved though vocal in its partisanship.) An inevitable part of the setting, surely more striking to the foreigner, was the solitary, gigantic banner, white on red, which covered an entire side of the stadium and proclaimed: GLORY TO THE COMMUNIST PARTY OF THE USSR. The Central Stadium contrasts two modern electric scoreboards and amazingly perfect acoustics for the loud-speaking system (no echo) with kerchiefed women groundskeepers tidying up the turf between events.

At the end of the contest, which, to almost everyone's satisfaction, was won by the local *Spartak* team, the huge crowd swarmed out of the stadium and down the walks to the Metro. It soon was flanked by a cordon of militia (police) and soldiers, some on horseback, who were there to direct the tens of thousands to the station in an orderly line. Once below, however, a peculiar characteristic of Russian crowds manifested itself. With trains hurtling into the station at intervals of less than a minute apart, all semblance of order ceased, the column of a moment ago forgotten. When the train doors (three to a coach) were opened, everyone rushed to enter, immediately jamming up the doorways; if they had entered two or three abreast, all would have been quickly absorbed, but this apparently would have taken the fun out of it. Finally one would be catapulted forward, with the rest tumbling after him in great disorder. The animated pushing and crushing lasted over three quarters of an hour. It was done in the highest good spirits, and only a few timid souls (I was one) stood back aghast at the spectacle before them. Of course, anyone attempting to leave the train at that station was in sorry straits. Wright Miller, in his fine book *Russians as People*, reports that he lost his temper in one such avalanche and lashed out at all sides to get some breathing space, provoking the Russians to remark indignantly, "to have to travel with such people!" [22]

Highly disciplined in some ways, the Russians are happily unperturbed by regulations in others. Over the loudspeaker at the Hippodrome, the Moscow race track, a visitor was surprised to hear a voice urging, "Citizens, stop crossing the track. The race has begun, comrades." [23]

Limitations

Before Luzhniki was built, major sport competitions took place, as some still do, at the Dinamo Stadium of Moscow which seats more than seventy

[22] New York: E. P. Dutton & Co., 1961, p. 68.
[23] Ronald Hingley, *Under Soviet Skins* (London: Hamish Hamilton, 1961), p. 63.

thousand people. On the same Sunday described above, a soccer match was also in progress there, as were soccer matches in six additional stadia in various parts of Moscow. In fact, throughout the USSR a varied sport program is maintained, and every large city has its own sport structures. The largest of these have become tourist sights (in addition to the Central and Dinamo stadiums in Moscow, there are Kirov Stadium in Leningrad and Khrushchev Stadium in Kiev), and are shown with a great sense of pride and achievement.

Some visitors to the Soviet Union, awed by *sputniki* and space flights, have an exaggerated preconception of the general level of Soviet development. They are soon enlightened. Similarly, all sport facilities are not to be judged by the description of Lenin Central Stadium. The USSR is still a land of marked contrasts. Russian towns are far from having such high schools equipped with gymnasiums and swimming pools as we are accustomed to in America. Actually there are less than seventy-five indoor swimming pools in the entire Soviet Union. Playing areas and equipment are likewise in insufficient supply, but steadily increasing (before the Revolution sport facilities were almost nonexistent).

The two major physical culture institutes in the country, in Moscow and in Leningrad, are both housed in old pre-revolutionary buildings. Having toured the Moscow Institute (named after Stalin in 1935, which appellation has now presumably been dropped), I was surprised at the poor condition of the playing field and disappointed by the gymnasium. I did not see a swimming pool, but the classrooms were excellently kept with elaborate pictorial displays of Soviet and prerevolutionary sport history and decorated with busts of Lenin. F. I. Samoukov, the assistant director of the Moscow Institute, hoped that at the end of the Seven Year Plan the Institute would be housed in a new building and that it would have a stadium seating fifty thousand (at the time the stands could at best accommodate five hundred).

The USSR has demonstrated that even with limited physical plants she can achieve tremendous results. The strenuous life which Russians lead may in fact prepare them better for the rigors of sport competition. They do not have a chance of getting "soft"; most of them do not ride in automobiles, they walk. With much of life in Russia still based on human energy rather than on push-button appliances, durability is a necessity. Soviet women skiers at an Alpine meet in Switzerland some years ago went so far as to scorn the use of the ski lift, claiming it to be just another symbol of bourgeois softness. However, at the first Western-style skiing resort currently being built at Bakuriani, high in the Transcaucasian mountains of the Georgian Republic, it is understood that ski lifts will be provided.[24]

[24] *New York Times*, January 21, 1962.

sport and social institutions

sport and politics

ALEX NATAN

Never has a state risen so swiftly to world power as has sport. It has within sixty years hurried through a development for which empires have needed five centuries. At the same time no other world power has ever shown such considerable symptoms of decay in so short a span as has the sporting movement. The anachronistic nature of the modern concept of the amateur has involved a set of social morals which would elsewhere have been opposed as being extremely immoral. In an age which has seen the rise and fall of totalitarian régimes, sport has long since become a means of propaganda and has therefore assumed a continually increasing political significance. International competitive sport, in which the political elements are most clearly revealed is, to be sure, not a political force of importance in itself, because the majority of its administrators seem to be of only moderate intelligence. But today it has become everywhere—whether openly or secretly—a propaganda weapon in world affairs which through the incitement of inherent nationalist instincts points way and means to new methods of psychological warfare.

Competition on the international level is a sop thrown to the warmonger in man. It has evolved into a ritualistic struggle of one national community against the others. Olympic athletes have become soldiers of sport who are indoctrinated with grotesque conceptions of national prestige. The ideals that sixty years ago moved Baron de Coubertin to give modern international sport new life have been debased by the hypocrisy and veiled political intentions of his successors to such an extent that its present adherents put one in the mind of the loose women of Eastern temples who prostitute themselves in the shadow of the sacred idols. It is significant that throughout the world the only people to deny the political nature of competitive sport are those whose liveli-hood depends on such lies, who are more interested in holding their positions in international sports organizations.

The Melbourne Olympic Games have provided proof enough of the extent to which a sports meeting can be contaminated by political feeling and of the impossibility of sport staying in its ivory tower. You had only to glance at the Press in those November days of 1956 to see how much space sports news claimed on the political pages of the newspapers. Even the conservative *Times* succumbed to this tendency, although not without protests from some of its readers, who thought they saw in the accumulation of sports reports an inducement to an outbreak of undesirable nationalism. Who reading of the preparations which were under way in Melbourne for a record entry for the Games would have thought that the world was on the brink of fateful de-velopments? At that moment these events came to a head on the Nile and the Danube. I do not know whether the youth of the world sitting in Melbourne gave any thought to the victims in Hungary, Egypt, and Israel. But in any case a positive orgy of sports reporting broke out which in no way differen-tiated between the battle spots of Port Said and Budapest, and Melbourne. Whilst there was a "police action" in the Suez region with far from friendly arms, in the Australian arena there was a "war with friendly arms," as the Nazi General von Reichenau once defined sport.

When, under the pressure of the November disturbances six nations withdrew from the Games, Mr. Brundage, President of the International Olympic Committee, said: "By their decisions these countries show that they are unaware of one of our most important principles, namely that sport is completely free of politics." This was certainly not the first time that this remarkable American had shown his colossal ignorance of the interrelationship between sport and politics. The German weekly *Der Spiegel* of December 9, 1956, not only spoke of the "politically soured atmosphere" inside the com-bined German team but also published a string of details which furnished proof that the presumed unity of the German team existed only in the imagi-nation of those sports leaders who were interested in a deceptive make-believe. Over fifty Hungarians took advantage of the Olympic Games politically by seeking asylum in the West. Some other members of Slav countries took the same steps. In the water polo match between Russia and Hungary the game was fought in such a "sporting spirit" that the face of one of the Hungarian players was "completely covered with blood." During the diving events the public demonstrated against a Russian woman judge who had deliberately "awarded points according to political convictions." In the *Manchester Guardian* one learnt that "the last twenty minutes of the football final between Russia and Yugoslavia resembled a wrestling match in which no holds were barred."

This is only a small selection of examples to give us proof that those leaders responsible who sat in their boxes of honor and partook of sumptuous banquets must have been suffering from some sort of sporting euphoria which deceived them into thinking that sport and politics were peace-loving brothers-in-arms. Although Mr. Brundage asserts that sport has nothing to do with politics, his own past pronouncements prove the contrary and only stress the fact that so many millions had been invested in Melbourne that any cancellation of the Games would have entailed still more irreparable financial losses than were actually incurred. It was purely these economic grounds and not respect for the dead of Port Said and Budapest that led Mr. Brundage to carry on with the Games and announce them as a great success. In classical Hellas arms would have been laid aside as the times for the contest approached. Today one may be sure that the Olympic Games would have to be carried through for commercial reasons even if the world stood in flames. The Basle *Nationalzeitung* drew the following conclusions from the unrealistic attitude of Mr. Brundage and his International Olympic Committee. "At the Press conference given at the end of the competitions at Melbourne, he reached an all-time high in the over-estimation of his own importance and of his Olympic office when, in a glow of triumph at the glorious completion of the Games in spite of the drawn-out, brutal and bloody rape of Hungary by Russia, he made the arrogant claim that the Olympic Committee fully deserved the award of the Nobel Peace Prize for this their service towards the friendship of peoples. This is such an incredible display of impudency that a plain gold medal cannot be considered worthy enough for its commemoration; recourse must be made to more precious metals such as plutonium or uranium. For it is impossible to push the overrating of one's own services and the blind misuse of the true feeling for peace to more absurd and bull-headed lengths."

This disease of preserving national prestige is running amok. Emotional incitement and unsparing mercilessness ensure the revival of the atmosphere of the gladiator fights in the Circus Maximus. Nationalism is sport's deadliest enemy. It has given sport a political character and at the same time imposed on it a taste which is in direct contradiction to its original meaning of being a natural game for relaxation after the day's toil. Fritz Erb, the distinguished chief editor of the Swiss newspaper *Sport*, has sarcastically pointed out in an essay in which he significantly calls "Peace on Earth—War in Sport" how modern competitive sport, which has almost nothing to do with the individual's enjoyment of sport, has created an international jargon which can be understood by every general staff, though it would be unintelligible to any genuine sportsman. UNESCO in its recent study *The Place of Sport in Education* also drew attention to the increasing dangers that the indoctrination of sport with politics entails: "The Olympic Games are now regarded by many as merely a testing ground for two great political units."

It is significant that the individual competitor who enters his own name for an international competition and pays his expenses out of his own pocket has long gone out of fashion. There are not any amateurs any more; all that is left is hypocrisy. In fact national sports organizations now pay for expenses at the Olympic Games, and they are for the most part financed by their Governments. Great Britain is an exception. But she received more than £100,000 through private subscription and did not need a penny's support from the State, whereas the expedition of the Federal German Republic in 1952 to Helsinki swallowed up three times as much as the British expedition because the Bonn Government came to its financial aid, as it realized the prestige value of the reappearance of a German Olympic team in the international arena.

With this method of financing, political pressure is directly or indirectly applied. The national sports federations have only one right left to them and that is sending in the entries. There are plenty of examples to show how an increasingly powerful political influence has infiltrated into the spheres of sport in general. In South Africa no colored man has the remotest chance of entering even the trial contests for the national team selection, which is solely picked from the white population. On the other hand Ghana and Nigeria will hardly allow any white man in their teams. Israel and the Arab States show similar mutual intolerance. In South America barbed-wire fences must be put up for the protection of visiting foreign players from the wrath of infuriated nationalism. American universities give athletes full scholarships as long as they are likely to do credit to American prestige and are able to show a leg. The terrible accidents at the Le Mans twenty-four hours motor-car race and at the "Mille Miglia" at Brescia did not prevent any competitor from completing the course, because the rivalry of car industries was at stake. In the Communist countries the Commissar for Sport has full control and may encourage the making of records even under the threat of reprisal.

International competitive sport has become an arena for ideologies, mirroring the same tensions as are seen throughout the world on the purely political plane. There has never been any proof of sport contributing to peace anywhere in the world; it has merely incited previously latent chauvinistic impulses. It is not denied that the young people themselves behave "fairly" in such international meetings and are generally only interested in seeing who is best. But the results have news value, which is commented upon. Talks are given that often produce radical political provocation of such a nature that such indiscretions are immediately cut off by the broadcasting stations, as happened in 1954 when the president of the German Football Association boasted about the victory of the German team in the world championship in such a way that the tenor of his speech was thought to endanger Germany's political relations with foreign countries. The essence of competitions may be harmless enough. It is its political consequence which has now made it into a dangerous power factor in any assessment of this world.

And yet the international high priests of sport still celebrate their *Missa Quasi Solemnis*. "Market or Temple! Sportsmen, you must choose!" so they shout. We are assured that the Olympic spirit is an eternal message of optimistic youth and lasting peace among nations. But youth does not have any choice. Today it is involved by the political strategists in sport in a contest which is handled for political or economic ends. It is ridiculous to say that from the Olympic arena "a Gothic cathedral will arise for the celebration of divine service by all mankind." What are given in these gigantic arenas are spectacles for which the public pays money and which are only made possible by the obols given by the people. Whether one Olympic spirit or another is the driving force is all one to the public. It wants its emotions stirred. It directly or indirectly affects the majority of mankind. Every weekend millions who burn their incense in de Coubertin's tabernacle of sport have indeed no choice between market and temple. They have become chattels who are used either to make money by entertaining the public or for political propaganda.

Baron de Coubertin was a child of his age, that *fin de siècle* whose symbol was boundless imperialism and whose pioneers, bred and nurtured on Nietzsche, wanted to enforce eternal peace from the heights of physical strength. The French nobleman who with the revival of the Olympic Games wanted to create a peace festival of universal significance could have had no idea that the struggle of political ideologies would water down the meaning of his intended project, if it did not completely falsify it. Whoever concerns himself with the life and work of Baron de Coubertin will notice a strange contradiction in the man and in many of his ideas. The man who had summoned the world's youth to peaceful play was basically a convinced militarist, who, as a teacher, refused to talk youth over to peace because "the joy of fighting was fixed in its nature." What a grotesque aberration! De Coubertin could never have comprehended the meaning of a democratic State because he was and remained a reactionary and an aristocrat of the *ancien régime*. Without wanting it, he made essential contributions towards turning sport on the international level into a political force. As a political thinker he must be considered a forerunner of totalitarianism. This is indeed probably the real reason why the Nobel Peace Prize of 1935 was awarded not to him but to Carl von Ossietzky, who was tortured in a Nazi concentration camp. De Coubertin was a *philosophe manqué* like so many others among the sublime optimists at the turn of the century. As a propagandist, as an organizer, as a wizard in a land of make-believe his name will be remembered as long as the Olympic Games are carried on, although their pedagogic value promises to become more and more problematical. De Coubertin may have been an idealistic dreamer, though I doubt it very much, Anyway, he left behind many penetrating remarks which go to show why competitive sport has today become a means of attracting young and old.

In this century sport has become an integral part of civilization which wants to taste blood, literally or metaphorically. And those innocent acolytes of people visit innumerable sports fields and stadia to watch the *élite* of the timistic youth and lasting peace among nations. But youth does not have such that 100,000 players play a game in front of 22 spectators but that 22 players put on a sporting entertainment for 100,000 spectators, who pay a sum of money and in return claim the right to place an ideological evaluation on the game, particularly if it has an international flavor. Although the sports movement in the Western hemisphere denies that it has ideological motives and repeatedly emphasizes its unpolitical nature, Communist sport unhesitatingly acknowledges its political character.

The German weekly *Das Parlament* has devoted a detailed investigation into "Sport Behind the Iron Curtain" (April 11, 1956), from which it is clearly seen that international sporting relations are used as a try-out for purely political events, and that in the Communist countries their policy and execution are centrally controlled. Because the unpolitical nature of sport received repeated official affirmation in non-Communist countries, it has become the official Communist policy in sport to buttonhole the "unpolitical" sportsman of the West on the sports fields and cleverly arouse his interest in events in the East. Since the end of the war, the Soviet Union has taken part in sports events which have increased in frequency and provide an even more effective means for broadcasting the great successes which Russia and her satellites aim for. It is no secret that the Soviet Union will try all she can to use her successes in the Olympic Games as a propaganda weapon in the Communist sport ideology. States such as Hungary, Poland, and Czechoslovakia have also announced similar intentions.

In the Eastern *bloc* the participation in international events is exclusively a matter for the Governments. "They are political operations with political motives and for that reason they cannot be left to the initiative of individual sportsmen or clubs. The Government not only plans the sports tours abroad but also ensures that the teams in question are fully prepared for the carrying out of the missions." To the forefront of every participation in a meeting comes national prestige, and the chief concern of the Communist States is the victory of their teams. To lose is practically high treason. An ideological set-up like this necessitates a highly organized system of team selection. At regular intervals official commissions decide which players and sportsmen can be considered of the first class, so that there is always a proved pool from which teams can be selected.

This method of selection is very carefully worked out and goes to prove that sport and play in the Eastern *bloc* do not represent any voluntary and personal activity but rather a form of conscription for the sporting front line. The numerous training camps financed by the Government have produced that "State amateur," for whom political schooling before each event plays an important part. Anyone interested in such matters will find ample material in the memoirs of the ex-Czech tennis star Drobny, who like many other sportsmen from the East saw fit to emigrate to the West. For this reason all Communist touring teams are closely watched by political observers. Such teams always travel abroad on a collective pass, and their members must give up all their personal papers before departure. According to a Reuter report in June 1955 the Communist representatives on the International Olympic Committee were said to have demanded that the Russian "bodyguards" at the Melbourne Games should be allowed to carry weapons. Apart from the ideological schooling which is a compulsory duty for everyone who plays sport behind the Iron Curtain, there is another aim behind sport for the masses in the Communist States. The idea of carrying out military training under the cloak of "sport" is the basic principle of organizations which have been founded in all the nations of the Eastern *bloc*. Military sport is a form of propaganda which refers directly back to German experiments prior to and during the Hitler régime.

Sport in the West has never been immune from the infiltration of political elements. In the Weimar Republic it was deliberately used to weaken the respect of the youth for the democratic régime. In contrast to the German political "Workers' Sport Movement," so-called bourgeois sport declared itself to be "politically neutral," which merely meant that it did not commit itself to any party line. The chauvinism of the German gymnasts belongs to one of the most interesting chapters of modern German history and must be held responsible for the violently anti-German and chauvinistic "Sokol" movement among the suppressed minority races of the former Habsburg dual monarchy. When, after 1918, the "Schwarze Reichswehr" (an illegal army organization) was founded, a special "Olympia Sports Club" was formed as a blind and devoted itself to the practice of the then forbidden practice of small-bore rifle shooting and hand-grenade throwing, which was also pursued quite openly at the universities. One of these dangerous sport-ideologists was the late Nazi General von Reichenau, who openly stated that sport was a substitute for national service. One of the most notable pioneers of sport in Germany was able to say, "War is the noblest sport of all," and thereby opened the door to military sport and advanced still further the ideological seduction of German youth. It is not surprising that Goebbels's weekly *Das Reich* could boast in 1940 that it had been the declared aim of German sports education to prepare its youth for "Der Tag," those months of *revanche* for the humiliating Treaty of Versailles. And so it is no wonder that most of the German sports leaders of the Weimar Republic were acceptable to Hitler and his Nazi régime, because they had already joined his ranks. Nor should it be overlooked that the blame for this development lay partly in Minister Stresemann's problematical declaration that it was not the task of the Weimar Government to bring up an "aristocracy of biceps." By such statements the sporting youth was time and again driven into the clutches of those men who made unscrupulous use of them.

These examples from a democratic country suffice to show that sport can be used as a powerful political factor even in a democracy. That this can happen even more easily in an autocratic State is shown by the story of sport under Hitler. The Third Reich successfully attempted to relegate all sport to the aim of creating an army of strong young men. Participation in sport and play became a duty towards the State. The organization and development of the Olympic Games in Berlin, 1936, became a political triumph for the Third Reich. The film producer Leni Riefenstahl showed in the first part of her monumental Olympia film the way in which Hitler and Goebbels were able to use games for political propaganda. Because Jesse Owens was a Negro, the Führer refused to receive this "subhuman man" to congratulate him on his quadruple victory.

Today the nations of the world rank differently according to the amount of interest their Governments take in the organization of sport. On the one side, are those States whose sport is fully integrated in the political system and thus becomes an important instrument in Government policies. At the other end of the scale are found those countries in which sport is organized by independent bodies and is itself free of any political organization save when it involves international competition. The difference lies not in the organization and the nature of the aim but above all in the ideological attitude. There can be no doubt that in most Western countries genuine efforts have been made to exclude politics from sport. But I am still convinced that such an unpolitical organization of sport is today apparent rather than real. There are political implications in modern sport which are unavoidable. Not even is England free of them, as is shown by the cricket controversy between Britain and Australia in 1932. Thirty years ago Nurmi and Suzanne Lenglen were sent to America by their countries to run and play for the sake of political help. When Dr. Roger Bannister became the first man to break the mile barrier, the Foreign Office sent him on a goodwill visit to the United States. The British Government paid all expenses. The Russian sports tours in Asia and Europe seek similar results. Whoever has read grossly exaggerated reports such as have appeared in German newspapers about the visit of German athletes to Japan will understand why some reporters are able to speak of a "brilliant political success" and of "mutual national interests."

All this merely goes to show that the claim of Western sport not to pursue political aims is to be taken *cum grano salis*. In a world where every success in sport and play is considered as a measure of national vitality and national prestige, one must be reconciled to the fact that sport has become the tool of politics. Ultimately it is a very significant social phenomenon. The world-wide enthusiasm for sports events brings to mind the decadence of the Roman Empire when similar physical exercises formed a circus spectacle which whipped up the tired nerves of paying spectators. The colours which the gladiators wore for show in the ancient Colosseum are the same as those borne by the soldiers of political sport today. And yet one must not condemn modern sport out of hand. We ought no longer to be subjected to the blandishments of the magic of sport, but we should as realistically as possible attempt to a revaluation of the role that sport plays in society. This role has become one of eminent political importance, though least of all in Britain where politics still is a profession and sport a leisurely vocation.

the peculiar economics of
professional sports

WALTER C. NEALE

Professional sport promoters and owners of professional teams have long claimed a special position in respect to the monopoly laws and the constitutional prohibition against slave labor, and recently they have been deservedly successful in appeals to Congress. This paper presents the results of serious thought about the problem, serious thought engaged in *after* choosing sides on the issue. I submit that the "firm" in professional sports is indeed in a peculiar position vis-à-vis our accepted way of looking at the firm in a competitive market. The basic proposition can be called the

Louis-Schmelling Paradox

If we ignore for the moment the legal reasons in the United States for avoiding a monopoly position, it is clear that the ideal market position of a firm is that of monopoly, whether to maximize profits or to maximize the comfort of life. If we consider the monopoly laws, the ideal position is as close to monopoly as the antitrust division will permit without prosecution. In brief, a firm is better off the smaller or less important the competition, and it will try to attain a situation in which it is the sole supplier.

But now consider the position of the heavyweight champion of the world. He wants to earn more money, to maximize his profits. What does he need in order to do so? Obviously, a contender, and the stronger the contender the larger the profits from fighting him. And, since doubt about the competition is what arouses interest, the demonstration effect will increase the incomes of lesser fighters (lower on the rating scale or lighter on the weighing scales). Pure monopoly is disaster: Joe Louis would have had no one to fight and therefore no income.

The boxing champion is the striking case, but the problem is equally great for any professional team. Suppose the Yankees used their wealth to buy up not only all the good players but also all of the teams in the American League: no games, no gate receipts, no Yankees. When, for a brief period in the late fifties, the Yankees lost the championship and opened the possibility of a non-Yankee World Series they found themselves—anomalously—facing sporting disgrace and bigger crowds.[1] If the Yankees, then, do not wish to

---

[1] When the San Diego Chargers of the American Football League ran roughshod over their competitors in the fall of 1961 the fans began to stay away.

• From *The Quarterly Journal of Economics*, **LXXVIII**, No. 1 (February 1964) pp. 1–14.

monopolize their own league, why don't they buy out the National League? The answer is, of course, all those World Series receipts. "Oh Lord, make us good, but not that good," must be their prayer.

Now we must face the question of whether it is possible that there is a business which, contrary to all we have learned about the business world, finds monopoly unprofitable. The answer, economists will be pleased to learn, is no—that a business monopoly is profitable in the sporting business as well as in the business of life. The first peculiarity of the economics of professional sports is that receipts depend upon competition among the sportors or the teams, not upon business competition among the firms running the contenders, for the greater the economic collusion and the more the sporting competition the greater the profits. The paradox appears because the firm in law, as organized in the sporting world, is not the firm of economic analysis; and the item sold by the sporting firm is not the product of these firms, or not entirely. We have, in fact, the phenomenon of

The Inverted Joint Product or the Product Joint [2]

We have long been used to the idea of a firm producing several products from an indivisible process. The sporting firms produce an indivisible product from the separate processes of two or more firms (in law). But the product itself is a peculiar mixture: it comes divisible into parts, each of which can be and is sold separately, but it is also a joint and multiple yet indivisible product.

To be specific, professional baseball teams produce a complex product; or in common parlance several interrelated streams of utility. There is first the saleable unit of the seat in the ball park during the game, the service sold by each firm (Yankees, Senators, and intermediaries) and generally regarded as the business of and the utility produced by the sporting firm. Then there is that strange sale of the utility of TV viewing where we the people enjoy the utility while nonsporting businesses pay the bill for us.[3] However, there are two other streams of utilities. There is the pennant race enjoyed by all and paid for by none. This we call the

League Standing Effect

Of itself there is excitement in the daily changes in the standings or the daily changes in possibilities of changes in standings. The closer the standings, and within any range of standings the more frequently the standings change,

[2] As a joint product refers to two products technologically resulting from a single process, we need another term for a single product resulting from discrete technological processes, and following the profession's tradition of jumbling words (value of marginal product, marginal value product) we here invert the words to symbolize single product of two processes.

[3] Which raises an interesting question about whose marginal rates of substitution on what indifference map.

the larger will be the gate receipts. Thus the free provision of the *race utility* has a favorable feed-back effect upon gate receipts, and we may treat this effect as a kind of advertising. Note that this advertising is also free to the advertising sporting firms—it has no opportunity cost—and that it too illustrates the Louis-Schmelling Paradox in that the more successful in sporting competition the firm is, the less effective is the advertising feed-back or race utility. The "league standing effect" is not limited to the consumer utility stream and the advertising feed-back because it is also a marketable commodity, but not for the producers. This quirk we may call the

Fourth Estate Benefit

Newspapers report the play, the outcomes, and the resulting "league standings" of games, and these reports are a major cause of sales and therefore of direct and advertising revenues to newspapers (and of course to sports magazines): in fact, a case of economies external to the industry. Two separate sets of activities are needed to produce the game write-up—the game and the reporter-newspaper-printer-distributor complex. The former could occur without the latter, but the latter cannot occur without the former; yet the latter is the financial beneficiary of his product joint from two different economic spheres (although we must allow for the advertising feed-back to gate receipts from press stories).

So far as the argument has carried us we may conclude that the product of professional sporting activity is not merely (1) the match, but also (2) the "league standings" (or championship), the progress towards a championship or changes in the standings, topics of conversation, and press reports. Furthermore, (3) a business firm—Joe Louis or the New York Yankees—cannot produce any of these streams of utilities alone. It must have the cooperation of a second business firm even to produce the game; to produce the other utilities it must have the cooperation of several business firms.[4]

The conclusion, then, is that the business firm as understood in law (and therefore in common discussion)—Louis or the Yankees—is not the firm as understood in economic theory. Rather, the firm is the league, or all professional heavyweights. Once this point is realized, the theoretical conclusion is clear: each professional sport is a natural monopoly. The several joint products which are products joint of legally separate business firms are really the complex joint products of one firm, and this firm is necessarily an all-embracing firm or natural monopoly.

A natural monopoly as commonly understood is an industry in which a single firm can satisfy the market in the declining portion of its long-run average total cost curve. If defined as one in which a single firm can satisfy

---

[4] It might be argued that any firm buying inputs from another firm requires the cooperation of the second firm, but this is stretching the meaning. The cooperating firms in sports are not willing buyers and sellers from and to each other but together (and with the press) sell to third parties.

demand at a lower long-run average total cost than can be achieved if two or more supply the industry's product, it would be possible to have a natural monopoly where long-run costs are constant, if their level varies with the number of firms, or where average costs are rising if the minimum and rising portions are so low that any division of the market between two firms results in higher costs for both on the declining portion of the cost curve because of diseconomies external to the firm although internal to the industry.

In law a firm is regarded as a person, persons, or organization having the right to own property and to contract. In economics a firm may be defined as a "decision-making unit whose major objective is profit" (however Harry Wismer may define the term), but this definition assumes that the "decision-making" and the "profit-taking" units are identical, whereas in professional sports, while the legal firm takes the profits, the league makes the decisions. Professor Robert Dorfman suggests parallels to the league in trade associations, the Eastern Railway Conference, the combination of various firms for construction jobs, and the joint ventures of Gimbel's and Macy's in the United Parcel Service and the bridge connecting the stores, holding that in none of these cases have the business firms merged. But each of these organizations is a firm by the definition, "a decision-making unit whose major objective is profit." The railways make decisions jointly about through-routing and rates, to maximize their profits, and so small a cooperative effort as common billing by a trade association is a joint decision made to reduce costs (i.e., increase profits). In short, although legally separate, in substance the associations and conferences act as would the management of a trust or holding company insofar as they reach joint decisions on marketing and pricing, and therefore can be regarded as merged.

If department stores were to withdraw from all business except the joint ownership of a delivery firm, or if railway companies were to restrict their activities to the joint management of a terminus, one would think of them as merged for any questions of economic substance. Operations such as the cooperative selling to each other and to other buyers by plumbers, carpenters, and builders in the construction industry do parallel sporting firms in that both are

Multiform Plants

Familiarity with the concept of a multiplant firm should not blind us to an occasional reversal of form created largely by the peculiarities of our law of property. The "plant" of the construction trades is the building site. At a minimum one might say that the "plant" of the sporting firms is the playing field, but without the league the playing field is incapable of producing the championship product, so the concept of "plant" must be enlarged to encompass the league. Furthermore, the parallel between the building industry and the sporting firms is not complete, for the sporting firms sell an indivisible product (once divided it is no product at all) to the consumer and *contribute exactly the same inputs.* The parallel should be with two or more plumbing companies joining together to sell their services as a single source of supply. Where there is joint decision-making because it is cheaper to do so, the resulting arrangement may be more easily seen as a monopoly if a (partial) cartel may be considered, as I would, a firm.

As for Gimbel's and Macy's, my mother-in-law assures me that "everyone knows they are in each other's pockets." [5]

An objection may be raised that one can have several leagues, and that these leagues are, or should be, competing firms. As one surveys the history and present state of the sporting trades one must admit the possibility, but one must also recognize that as a matter of observation there appears to be a strong tendency toward a single league, and this for one good reason: only a single league can produce that most useful of all products joint, the World Champion. Analytically we must regard the National League and the American League as one, for they come together each autumn to produce the World Series. Despite the differences in form, the substance of this World Series product is identical with the single league championship in the National Football League arrived at by business collusion in cooperative sporting competition between an "eastern division" and a "western division" team. Hereafter we should therefore refer to the two major leagues in baseball as "divisions" within the larger league-firm.

At the present time the trade of professional football is divided in two in the United States, with a competitor in Canada. There is no meeting on the field of play between the National and the American Football Leagues. The result is an absence of sporting competition, but very strong interfirm competition between the old and new leagues. Do we therefore have oligopoly? Yet, in the short run, in the same way that some American railroads have tried to compete; but in the long run, No, because this is inherently a temporary state of affairs. We witnessed a similar situation just after World War II when the All-America Conference challenged the National Professional Football League. The result in that instance was the demise of the Conference with the older League absorbing some of the teams of the bankrupt Conference. Logically we may distinguish four cases or four possible histories of interleague business competition:

1. The Major League Baseball solution: the joining of economically competing oligopolistic firms into sportingly competitive natural monopolies.
2. The professional football solution of the forties: bankruptcy for one or the other of the economically competing firms.
3. The survival of two or more leagues because they are not economically competitive. This case occurs when the leagues are operating in different geographical areas or are inherently noncompetitive in both the sporting and economic sense, as in the case of boxers of different weights, or, a few years ago, baseball players of different colors.

[5] Mrs. Paul B. Sheldon, New York City, oral communication, March 23, 1963.

4. The survival of two or more leagues which are economically competitive and which could be sportingly competitive.

The first two cases have been historically the common ones. The third is actually rarer than one might expect. Of course, when it is patently ridiculous to compete in sport—to match a heavyweight with a flyweight—two leagues or championships co-exist, but where sporting competition is prevented by geographical difference the tendency is to enlarge the area of sporting competition until in fact there is only one league. Thus we find that Australian, West Indian, Pakistani, and English cricket, separated about as much as is possible (or was possible before Gagarin) merge in that great international cartel, the Test Matches. Again, soccer (mistakenly called football by literally minded foreigners), which is formally organized in teams merged in national leagues, has become a cartel of international matches. As cartelization is necessary not only to maximization of profits but also, even especially, to maximization of output, the geographical division of the market is an inherently unstable situation usually replaced by a naturally monopolistic firm whose market region is everywhere that the sport is played.[6]

Whether or not two leagues can survive within the market area—our fourth logically possible case—depends on the facts of the matter, or, put more realistically, on the relative shapes and positions of the demand and cost functions. From the sports pages it is difficult to glean solid data to which to fit functions, but one does form the impression from the history of sports that such survival is unlikely. In effect, the argument here depends upon the acceptance of premises for which direct evidence is thin on the grounds that the conclusion reached from the premises is consistent with observation.

The long-run cost curve of seats-at-games for the league-firm is probably flat or almost flat. As one expands the firm the quality of the product is affected by two contrary tendencies. The first is because the quality of raw materials declines as less efficient inputs are drawn into the sport. One may treat this as producing an inferior product for which there is another, lower demand function for lower quality "game seats" (which means a reduction in revenue per game seat).[7] Alternatively one may regard the diminishing quality returns as an increase in the cost of producing the same quality of game seat. In either case there is a limit to the size of the most efficient (least minimum average cost per constant quality game seat) league-firm, given by the cost

[6] The apparent exceptions of United States and Japanese baseball and of the sportingly independent United States and Canadian football leagues partly reflect difficulties of amalgamation across national boundaries, but more important, both Japanese and Americans agree that the Japanese teams could not win an international World Series and it is thus unnecessary to prove by formal competition that the American winner is the champion. But even here when exhibition games begin to show the American superiority at its own sport is questionable, one should expect cartelization into an international league. Perhaps, too, the pressure for Canadian-United States competition is low because it is not widely believed that the Canadians might win.

[7] However, we know by introspection that the reduction will be small as the appeal of the seat depends mostly on the uncertainty of the outcome and on the weather.

function. The limit on size applies no matter how few or many leagues there are, so that one large league can provide any quantity of product as cheaply as two or more smaller firms. Thus there is no efficiency argument against monopoly, and there is a likelihood that the first league in the sport—like the first utility in a city—will become a monopoly. But any upward shifts in costs (or downward shift of quality and therefore the substitution of a new demand curve) are counteracted by the

Input-Enthusiasm Effect

Whereas one finds that human abilities in various directions are randomly distributed in any population, one also finds that skillabilities in sports are concentrated regionally. How else can we explain the disproportionate number of first-class tennis players and cricket batsmen from Australia, or runners from Australia, England and Scandinavia, or of passing quarterbacks from Texas, other than by reference to the public attention and private concentration put into the development of these particular skills? And this input into the inputs is a result of the enthusiasm for the sport in the area, which in turn is both a consequence and a cause of the scale of operations of the sport in the area. In other words, the larger the scale of operations, the higher the quality of inputs and of products, or the lower the cost of a constant quality game seat.

When one shifts one's focus from the use of resources or the quality of product to the money costs it is reasonable to suppose that less perfect inputs (producing lower quality games) will earn a lower return, so that the cost per quality unit will not change as much as the quality changes. Both the "enthusiasm effect" and the lower salaries of lower quality sportsmen will flatten any rising tendency in money costs consequent upon diminishing returns. Enthusiasm simultaneously increases (1) the demand for game admissions and therefore the derived demand for skilled players and hence their salaries, so that the monetary cost of each unit of the larger supply of higher quality players rises; and increases (2) the supply of skilled players. The net effect of the increase in demand on gate receipts and on derived demand will merely tend to shift the curves northeastward without a "squeeze" on profits, while the underlying "enthusiasm effect" will lower the supply schedule of inputs. Larger scale, therefore, does not necessarily increase costs more than revenue.

All this, of course, is in conformity with our economic expectations, but the supply mechanism is not market pricing. The supply of skilled inputs is developed in the sphere of amateur activity—specifically in the schools—so that the equilibrating mechanism works not through price response but through enthusiastic response and the human desire to conform to standards of group approval.

The net effect of diminishing returns, of the tendency toward constant money costs in quality units of input, and of the "enthusiasm effect" may

be constant costs, increasing costs, or decreasing costs. In the absence of information, I guess that the long-run supply curve of the league-firm is roughly
constant for output units of games by pairs of teams.

One usually expects a constant cost industry to be competitive, *ceteris
paribus;* but *cetera non sunt paria.* Even if professional sports are constant
cost industries the "World Champion utility" can only be created by cceteliza-
tion. Furthermore, there is interdependence between demand and supply.
The total size of the industry (in game-seats) is determined by the intersection
of demand with supply, and if the long-run supply curve is horizontal, one
might say that it is strategically determined by demand. But demand itself is
in large part a reaction to the sporting importance of the events, the sporting
importance depends upon the "fourth estate effect" and the "public conversation effect," and since these effects in turn depend upon the scale and uni-
versality of the championship at stake, the function will move up to the right
for a more conclusive championship, and down to the left if the leagues decided to avoid meeting in a play-off. Thus demand and supply tend to intersect
at the point of a single, monopoly championship wherever that intersection
may be (the You Don't Say Law).

On the supply side the long-run cost curve is horizontal, but the height
of the curve above zero depends on the costs to the business or league-firms.
These costs consist mostly of two elements: (1) fixed costs of interest or rent
on the stadium capital and the cost of equipment and transportation for the
firm, and (2) quasi-rents for the players. The price of any player is partly a
function of his willingness to play, for the athlete need not enter the players'
market as he has alternative opportunities, but once his minimum supply
price is met the team firm is paying for an unreproducible talent, or a quasi-
rent. If there are two firms bidding for his talents the quasi-rent will probably
be higher than if there is only one bidder who is engaged with the player in
bilateral bargaining. As league firms typically prohibit multiple bidding by
their team component firms counterbidding arises only when there are two independent leagues.[8] The existence of economically but not sportingly competing leagues thus raises the money costs to both leagues and so endangers
profits. Although in logic there is no reason why both leagues cannot continue
to enjoy profits, or at least no losses, they are unlikely to do so. The salary of a
player has much in common with ground rents, but the analogy must be understood to apply by lot, and is not complete. As in the result only one store
actually uses one lot, so only one league employs one player. But whereas

---

[8] A variety of liberties and restraints characterize the quasi-rent bargaining process in
professional sports. In American football the "player draft" eliminates within-league counterbidding; in baseball the teams must bid against each other to contract with a new player but
once the contract is signed the other teams cannot make counteroffers during the following
years. Similar arrangements exist in other team sports, but in the sports of individual competition, e.g., boxing, the player and the business firm merge so that the quasi-rent payment
to the competitor merges with his windfall profits and his income is undifferentiated.

several stores can compete in a shopping area when they sell the same products because nonrental costs of and demand for the products of each store are the same, two or more leagues probably will not enjoy identical nonrental costs and demand. Transport to and from Kansas City from other points will not be the same as to and from Houston, while the urge to go to a ball game will differ from city to city (or from the Bronx to Brooklyn). Only in the unlikely event that both leagues field teams in exactly the same cities (and with exactly the same appeal to historic loyalties) will there be a no-profit-no-loss Chamberlinian equilibrium. One therefore expects competitive bidding eventually to raise quasi-rents for one league or the other above the spread between its other costs and its receipts, at which point the fourth solution becomes the second.[9]

Competition exists not between teams or leagues but between sports. Paying fans and newspaper readers prefer one or another sport—I suspect largely because Dad preferred it—but shifts in taste do occur and the leagues, or even the component teams acting independently, can encourage such shifts. Between the wars the New York (football) Giants built a loyal following by selling tickets extremely cheaply to children. Colorful people, youth leaders, immoral people, all can be used to attract attention to a sport. Ice hockey undoubtedly has increased its popularity over what it would otherwise have been by the public notice of brawls during games.

Definite divisions of the sports market seem to be characteristic. First there are the national divisions, marking off American baseball from Commonwealth cricket, American football from international soccer. Second, there are the seasonal divisions, leaving baseball dominant in the spring and summer, football in the autumn, and basketball in the winter. Third, there are divisions among social classes: cricket is upper-class and soccer working-class in England; baseball was the sport of the small town in America, whereas professional football grew up in the industrial cities. Although these divisions may not be immutable they are certainly hard to change. Professional football

---

[9] Professor Benjamin Higgins pointed out that some other trades require competition to succeed. One is law, a single firm needing others to fight in court; another is fashion, the interest arising from the differences between two designers. There are perhaps more for there is no reason to believe that a "peculiar economics" is confined to professional sports alone. However, the two examples, while requiring competition for profits, are not cases on all fours with professional sports. Fashion requires separate, economically as well as aesthetically, competing units and so does not tend to coalesce into a monopoly. Furthermore, the supply of fashionable goods is the product of many factories and stores all over the world, not of the designers themselves. They are more like leading architects than leading coaches. The practice of law also does not tend toward monopolization of the business firms; and unlike both sports and fashion its practice cannot be called inconsequential. The need for competition within the courts stems not from the economics of business, as it does in professional sports, but rather from the adversary structure of our system of justice. Whereas sports require sporting competition and business monopoly, fashion and law require both interfirm business as well as aesthetic and legal competition.

has crept back into the late baseball season and forward into the basketball-hockey season, but efforts to establish an American soccer league in monopolistic competition with baseball (during June, July, and August) have met with little favor.

Within the general framework of a whole-sport monopoly there are some additional peculiarities. We are familiar with the cobweb theorem, which depends upon next period's supply responding to this period's demand. But in professional sports we have the

Roger Maris Cobweb

The demand for Roger Maris' services for next year depends upon his performance this year. The cobweb has been inverted with demand reacting after a delay to supply; and the 1962 quasi-rent depended upon how ruthlessly Maris pursued the home-run mantle [sic] in 1961. Note that to introduce the concept of expectations does not alter the point, for the famous hog cycle —in which the sex urge of pigs responds to slaughtering prices in Chicago—is also one of expectations. Here one might note that an explosive cobweb is unlikely since the supply curve of talent in the quasi-rent range must be vertical and the height above the minimum price which Mr. Maris will accept and the depth below the maximum which the Yankees will offer Mr. Maris depends upon bargaining technique. Below the minimum which Mr. Maris will take we have a horizontal supply curve and Mr. Maris leaves the market.

Whether marginal analysis of input pricing will work at all is doubtful. Whereas one can speak of the marginal steel worker without naming him it seems a little foolish to speak of the marginal quarterback of the Steelers. Marginalism seems to break upon the

Bobby Layne Rigidity

There are possibilities of substitution of an indirect sort. Clearly one cannot field more than eleven laborers in a football game, "nor can one use two poor quarterbacks instead of one good one"; but one can use a better line to give a weaker passer more time or a faster fullback to make up for the absence of two first-class halfbacks. Such considerations obviously weigh with teams in their drafting and trading operations since Baltimore let Mr. Lipscombe go and the Giants put more effort into finding defensive personnel than into finding new offensive backs. But here one fails to see just how the Colts and the Giants compute the marginal returns of tackles, of pass receivers, and so forth. In baseball batting averages and earned-run ratings provide a better guide to marginal productivity computations, but in both sports the value of the marginal product is only indirectly and roughly related to these sporting measures, as it is the effect upon the gate reecipts which counts and gate receipts have no stable functional relationship with the sporting measures. In boxing the idea breaks down completely, as the entire labor input is one and always tries to be its best. Thus the ultimate of the Bobby Layne Rigidity is the

Archie Moore Indivisibility

Having discussed the demand and cost structure of the professional sports industry certain parallels with other industries will be apparent. The firm of economic theory is the league, and the league is a natural monopoly with demand and cost and profit adjustments always tending toward unification of all league-firms into a single *firma-firmorum*.

The plant of economic theory is the game, which requires three factors of production: namely, land, labor, and labor [sic]. In different sports each of the factors has a critical minimum beyond which additions to output fall off rapidly; but the law of variable proportions is here invariable as two of the factors can be used simultaneously only in specified quantities and in some sports all three are subject to this limitation and the additional inputs logically come under the classification "repair and renewal." At this point one can also see the importance of institutionalism for the limits on the employment of labor trace back to ancient and irrational traditions of sportsmanlike behavior, and to break them by, say, fielding a fifth back armed with switch blade would be impermissible to members of the tribal society despite the fact that any United Nations expert could point out the obvious technical advantages. To my knowledge only the Canadians have adopted the fifth back, and there is no evidence in published reports that even the Canadians have equipped this man properly. On the other hand, economic sophistication of a high order is shown by the larger end zone and the elimination of the fourth down in a country with large unused areas of land and a small population.

We often think that if plant costs are constant (but here remember that the team or business firm does not constitute a plan) there can be no advantages of scale except as monopsonistic power is exerted; but we have already established those internal and external economies of scale called "league standing" and "fourth estate effect." Thus we justify horizontal integration in a natural monopoly.

Vertical integration takes different forms in different sports. We would have to stretch meanings to visualize vertical integration in boxing, but we are all familiar with the phenomenon in baseball. Here one familiar with the problems of underdeveloped countries and the earlier stages of industrialization will recognize the characteristic need to recruit and commit the labor force. It is also the arena of free contract negotiation and is finally analogous to the tomato farms held by Heinz.

In American football there is still another organization often referred to as the university. The idea is to develop commitment before recruitment largely on the grounds that it is cheaper—or rather, on the grounds that the social costs of selection and training are shifted onto the community of academics, alumni, and taxpayers. But here we can go no further since this information is as well hidden as are the accounts of peasants.[1]

Variety of organization is found in the organization of recruitment more than in any other facet of the economy of professional sports. One can mention, in addition to the two forms already discussed, the feudal organization of village and county cricket, the climatic-linguistic character of ice-hockey recruitment, and less recently the religious qualifications for animal wrestling in the Roman arena. Here alone I feel economists should support the remaining elements of freedom, conflict, and competition in the business organization of professional sports.

Otherwise it is clear that professional sports are a natural monopoly, marked by definite peculiarities both in the structure and in the functioning of their markets. Consequently professional leagues have every economic ground to appeal to legislatures, to courts, and to the public on the ground that

> We fall if you divide us;
> We stand if Johnny Unitas.

[1] The university farm team also appears to be the last stronghold of the third kind of intergation problem. Most economists oppose integration of business firms either horizontally or vertically, but somehow manage at the same time to favor racial integration. This paradox is explained by the economic inefficiency of racial segregation, and the uneconomic character is perhaps sufficiently illustrated by an old lament of the Southwest which my daddy used to sing:

> There was a blackguard from the South
> For our sisters he was born too uncouth;
> He couldn't play Royal's
> Or even Frank Broyles',
> So Syracuse hired the youth.

professional sports and the antitrust laws

W. CLYDE ROBINSON

"If the law supposes that," said Mr. Bumble, ". . . the law is a ass, a idiot."—CHARLES DICKENS, *Oliver Twist*

Until recent years antitrust activity in the field of professional sports was virtually unknown. Sports were generally considered distinct from the normal run of business activities, and little attention was paid to their internal affairs. This situation changed rapidly with the boom in sports which followed the Second World War. The introduction of television and the multimillion-dollar scope of professional sports raised problems concerning the economic nature of such enterprises. Questions were raised about restrictive practices which limited competition within the various types of professional sports. Lawsuits were initiated by aggrieved individuals and by the federal antitrust agencies alleging that certain professional sports enterprises were violating the Sherman Antitrust Act. In the ensuing controversy, the lack of coordination among Congress, the courts, and the antitrust authorities that plagues the effective formulation of antitrust policy has been brought sharply into focus. The importance of judicial review as a factor in antitrust enforcement has been demonstrated by the decisions of the United States Supreme Court in cases concerning the position of professional baseball, football, and boxing under the monopoly laws.

The crux of the problem lies in the definition of "interstate commerce" as the term is interpreted by the courts. Unless professional sports are engaged in interstate commerce, the legality of any of their monopolistic arrangements cannot be questioned under the federal antitrust laws. Assuming that sports are included in the realm of interstate commerce, the further problem remains of evaluating restraints of trade by their effect on the public interest. To date, the Supreme Court has shown little consistency in its approach to these problems.

Baseball Is Not a Business

The question of the inclusion of professional sports enterprises under the antitrust laws was first decided by the Supreme Court in the Federal

• From the *Southwestern Social Science Quarterly*. 38 (1957), pp. 133–141. © Southwestern Social Science Association.

League case of 1922, which involved organized baseball.[1] The Federal League was a "wildcat" one that attempted to enter into competition with the established major-league clubs in the American and National Leagues. In the ensuing struggle the Federal League lost all its member clubs except the one in Baltimore. The Baltimore club brought suit, alleging that the major leagues conspired to monopolize the baseball business by buying up some of the clubs in the Federal League and by various means inducing the others to leave. The whole structure of rules and regulations that bound together the clubs in organized baseball was cited as an unreasonable restraint of trade. It was contended that players in organized baseball were reluctant to accept offers from the Federal League clubs because of coercive regulations that threatened black-listing and banishment from the organized segment of baseball. Its inability to procure trained players, plus the loss of member clubs that provided playing opposition, spelled destruction for the Federal League.

In a lower court the Baltimore club was awarded treble damages totaling $240,000 under the Sherman Act, but the ruling was reversed on appeal to the Supreme Court. The Court declared that organized baseball was not a subject of commerce within the scope of the federal antitrust laws. The Court went even further and stated that organized baseball was not commerce at all.[2]

This position went unchallenged until the Gardella case of 1949.[3] Gardella was one of a number of major-league players who left organized baseball in 1946 to play in the newly formed Mexican League, an association not affiliated with organized baseball. In order to halt the exodus of playing talent, Baseball Commissioner A. B. Chandler announced that any player who quit a major-league club to play in the Mexican League would be banned from organized baseball for a period of five years. Gardella returned to the United States before the expiration of the ban and sought reinstatement in the ranks of organized baseball. When his application was refused, he contended that organized baseball was an illegal monopoly depriving him of a livelihood. The monopoly allegation was given legal support by a federal court, which felt that the 1922 decision was no longer a controlling factor because of changed conditions in the baseball business.[4]

The Gardella case was later settled out of court, but repercussions from the opinions expressed in the case were eventually felt in the halls of Congress. Owing to the doubt over the antitrust status of baseball created by the Gardella opinion, new litigation was instituted in 1951 by other baseball figures. Several interested congressmen, including Senator E. C. Johnson, of Colorado, and Representative A. S. Herlong, of Florida, hastened to defend baseball from adverse judicial decisions by sponsoring bills designed to grant a complete exemption from the antitrust laws to all organized professional

---

[1] *Federal Baseball Club of Baltimore, Inc. v. National League of Professional Baseball Clubs et al.*, 259 U.S. 200 (1922).

[2] *Ibid.*

[3] *Gardella v. Chandler*, 172 F 2d 402 (1949).

[4] *Ibid.*

sports enterprises. The interest of Johnson and Herlong stemmed from their association with organized baseball as president of the Western League and former president of the Florida State League, respectively.[5]

The bills were referred to the Celler Subcommittee of the House Committee on the Judiciary, which was then engaged in a long-range examination of the impact of the antitrust laws on various segments of the economy. After a series of hearings [6] the Subcommittee published a report in 1952 in which no legislative action was recommended in view of the fact that several baseball cases were pending before the Supreme Court. The report made it clear that Congress was looking to the Supreme Court for a current evaluation of professional sports. The Subcommittee deemed it "unwise to attempt to anticipate judicial action with legislation." [7] As a result the exemption bills never reached the floor of Congress.

The litigation involving the monopoly position of organized baseball culminated in 1953 with the decision in the Toolson case.[8] Toolson was under contract to the New York Yankees, who assigned him to one of their minor-league affiliates at Binghamton, New York. When he refused to report, he was barred from further participation in organized baseball. Toolson claimed that this arbitrary assignment and subsequent black-listing constituted an unreasonable restraint of trade in violation of the Sherman Act. "Without re-examination of the underlying issues," [9] the Supreme Court applied the 1922 decision to the 1953 situation. The wording of the Toolson opinion indicated that the Court refused to assume any responsibility for evaluating the status of baseball under the antitrust laws in the light of changed conditions in the thirty-one-year interval. The Court sidestepped the issue by upholding the Federal League decision "so far as that decision determines that Congress had no intention of including the business of baseball within the scope of the antitrust laws." [10]

The intent of Congress is expressed plainly in the Sherman Antitrust Act of 1890: it declares every contract, combination, or conspiracy in restraint of trade involving interstate commerce illegal. Congress has never exempted any professional sports enterprise from the antitrust laws. The attempts to pass exemption bills in the Eighty-second Congress indicate that baseball was believed to be within the scope of the law. The only stumbling block to a new evaluation of the antitrust status of baseball was the judicial exemption from the monopoly laws conferred by the Court in 1922.

[5] *Organized Baseball: Report of the Subcommittee on Study of Monopoly Power of the Committee on the Judiciary, Pursuant to H. Res. 95, House of Representatives*, 82d Cong., 2d sess. (1952), pp. 1–2, hereafter referred to as *Report*.

[6] *Hearings before the Subcommittee on Study of Monopoly Power of the Committee on the Judiciary of the House of Representatives (Organized Baseball)*, 82d Cong., 1st sess. (1952). Serial No. 1, Part 6, hereafter referred to as *Hearings*.

[7] *Report*, p. 232.

[8] *Toolson v. New York Yankees, Inc.*, 346 U.S. 356 (1953).

[9] *Ibid.*

[10] *Ibid.*

In refusing to reexamine the underlying issues of professional baseball in 1953, the Court was saying, in effect, that nothing had changed since 1922. The Court shifted its burden of enforcing the laws to the shoulders of Congress when it declared that ". . . if there are evils in the field [organized baseball] which now warrant application to it of the antitrust laws it should be by legislation." [11] The legislation was provided in 1890. The missing element was a realistic appraisement of professional baseball as it existed in 1953, not in 1922.

Part of Football Is a Business

Organized baseball greeted the Toolson decision with a sigh of relief, but agitation over the antitrust position of professional sports was still evident. Three days after the Toolson decision a federal district court delivered an opinion in a case brought by the National Football League.[12] The government sought to enjoin certain practices of the league which restricted the broadcasting and telecasting of professional football games. The rules of the league gave each club exclusive jurisdiction over radio and television accounts of professional football games within a seventy-five-mile radius of the home city. No outside club could broadcast or telecast games into the territory of another league city without the permission of the home club. The effect of these rules was to preserve a geographic monopoly over all aspects of professional football for each club in its home territory.

The league asked for a dismissal of the charges on the grounds that football is not trade or commerce. The court refused to apply the decision handed down in the baseball cases, however, by holding that "it is immaterial whether professional football by itself is commerce or interstate commerce." [13] The court distinguished between the antitrust position of the football business itself as opposed to the broadcasting and telecasting of football games by holding that "radio and television clearly are in interstate commerce." [14]

The court then proceeded to evaluate the restrictive practices in the light of their effects on competition among the football clubs. The prohibition against televising outside games into the home territory of a club when that club was playing in its stadium was upheld as a reasonable restraint of trade. The presentation of televised games was found to cut down on attendance at the stadium, and, consequently, to alter the competitive position of the clubs in the league. An injunction was allowed against all other restrictions found to be unreasonable for the maintenance of effective competition in the football business.

The remedy applied in the football case had the effect of classifying pro-

[11] Ibid.
[12] United States v. National Football League, 116 Supp. 319 (1953).
[13] Ibid.
[14] Ibid.

fessional football as a business engaged in interstate commerce, though the court did not state this specifically. A somewhat tenuous distinction was drawn between the radio and television activities of professional football and the business of exhibiting football games. Perhaps the court reasoned that the broadcasting phase of professional football was not an integral part of the business. The division of football into two neat categories, however, relieved the court from being bound by the precedent established in the baseball cases. Part of professional football had violated the Sherman Antitrust Act. The legal status of the football business itself was still in doubt.

A Sports-Minded Congress

The antitrust status of professional sports received further attention from Congress in 1954, when a move developed in the Senate to force baseball to sever all ties with business concerns that were subject to the antitrust laws.[15] The event precipitating the move was the purchase of the St. Louis Cardinals by A. A. Busch, Jr., owner of the Anheuser-Busch Brewery. The baseball club was set up as a wholly owned subsidiary of the brewery, and it was claimed that the Cardinals were being used as an advertising vehicle for Budweiser beer. Senator E. C. Johnson sponsored a bill to make baseball clubs owned by beer or liquor interests subject to the antitrust laws because of such ownership. The Senator pointed out that it was not unusual for other business interests to acquire baseball clubs but that in the past the baseball clubs had been set up as separate and distinct corporations. In referring to other business interests in baseball, Johnson stated that P. K. Wrigley, owner of the Chicago Cubs, kept his baseball club completely separate from his chewing-gum business. The same separation had been made by the late Colonel Jake Ruppert in his ownership of the New York Yankees and the Ruppert Brewery.

Apparently, Johnson felt that baseball's judicial exemption from the law was based upon its classification as a sport rather than as commerce in the Federal League case. Unless baseball was free from the taint of commerce, its implied exemption might be threatened. When the Justice Department opposed his bill on the grounds that it discriminated against beer and liquor interests, Johnson indicated that he was willing to broaden the bill to include all businesses under the monopoly laws. To complicate matters further, Stanley N. Barnes, then head of the Antitrust Division, made a counter-proposal. Judge Barnes wanted to make all of organized baseball, not just those clubs owned by businesses, subject to the antitrust laws.[16] The controversy was little more than a tempest in a teapot, however, since none of the proposals were ever enacted into legislation.

[15] *The New York Times*, February 21, 1954, p. 1.
[16] *Ibid.*, March 19, 1954, p. 26.

Boxing Is a Business

Confusion was compounded in 1955 when the Supreme Court was asked to rule on the status of professional boxing. The Antitrust Division contended that the International Boxing Club of New York had conspired to monopolize the promotion and exhibition of championship boxing bouts.[17] Between June, 1949, and March, 1952, the International Boxing Club promoted all but two of the twenty-one championship fights held in the United States. In addition, it controlled the broadcasting, telecasting, and film rights of these contests.

It was alleged that the conspiracy began in 1949 with an agreement between the club and heavyweight champion Joe Louis. By the terms of the agreement, the club acquired the exclusive right to negotiate contracts with contenders for Louis' title. In addition, it gained exclusive rights to broadcast, televise, and film these championship bouts. Any boxer desiring an opportunity to fight for the title had no alternative but to negotiate with the International Boxing Club. Control over each championship match since 1949 had been maintained by requiring each contender, as a condition to a title match, to assign to the club those exclusive rights surrounding the exhibition of championship fights. Later it extended its control over championship matches to other weight-divisions.

The International Boxing Club contended that boxing was a sport, not commerce, and rested its case on its similarity to baseball. The Court pointed out that the Toolson decision, exempting baseball, did not apply to all athletic enterprises. No court had ever held that the business of boxing was exempt from the antitrust laws. Therefore, the present issue was not the continuance of a previously granted exemption but whether exemption should be granted. The Court declined to grant boxing an exemption because "that issue is for Congress to resolve, not this Court." [18]

Apparently, the Supreme Court did not recognize its contradictory position inherent in its boxing decision: Boxing was not granted an exemption by the Court because only Congress had this power; yet the only exemption ever granted baseball was conferred by the Supreme Court in 1922 and confirmed in 1953. The distinction drawn by the Court was that baseball was not engaged in interstate commerce. Boxing, on the other hand, derived approximately 25 per cent of its revenue from radio and television activities. This figure was high enough to cast doubt upon boxing's status as a sport. The Court neglected to mention that it did not take into consideration the amount of revenue derived by professional baseball from radio and television activities in 1953.

In contrast to the district court decision in the case of professional foot-

[17] *United States v. International Boxing Club of New York, Inc.*, 348 U.S. 236 (1955).

[18] *Ibid.*

ball, the Supreme Court did not consider the radio and television activities of boxing separately from the exhibition of boxing bouts. The boxing business in its entirety was held to be subject to federal antitrust laws.

All of Football Is a Business

In February, 1957, the Supreme Court declared that the business of professional football is subject to the antitrust laws.[19] The decision was delivered in a damage suit brought by William Radovich, a former professional football player, charging the National Football League with monopolizing the football business. The case was similar to the Gardella and Toolson cases in that Radovich complained of coercive restrictions and black-listing by the league which prevented competition by the various clubs for his services as a player. The decision did not carry with it a conviction. As in the case of boxing, the football ruling merely admitted that the business is engaged in interstate commerce, and as such it is subject to the law.

By this time the Supreme Court was hard put to rationalize the baseball decision. Boxing and football it admitted are interstate businesses. Baseball, alone, remains in a pristine state, removed from any tawdry aspects of commerce. The Court admitted, however, that if it were considering "baseball for the first time upon a clean slate" [20] there would be no doubt that it, too, is subject to the antitrust laws. So far as the Court is concerned, baseball will remain outside the antitrust law until Congress passes specific legislation placing baseball in the same category as football and boxing. The decisions of 1922 and 1953 will stand despite any evidence to the contrary. Evidently, the Court refuses to face the economic facts.

Economic Aspects of Baseball

In describing the baseball business in 1922, Justice Oliver Wendell Holmes was of the opinion that it could hardly be "called trade or commerce in the commonly accepted use of those words." [21] The definition of "commerce" has undergone an interesting metamorphosis in the hands of the Court. At one time the Court removed manufacturing from the scope of the antitrust laws by declaring that "commerce succeeds to manufacture and is not a part of it." [22] Labor unions, though not mentioned specifically in the Sherman Act, were brought under the law by judicial interpretation.[23] The records are replete with cases where the courts have seized upon the slightest bit of evidence in order to classify a business as interstate commerce. The attitude of the Supreme Court toward the New Deal legislation of the 1930's

---

[19] *Wall Street Journal*, February 26, 1957, p. 3.
[20] *Ibid.*
[21] 259 U.S. 200 (1922).
[22] *United States v. E. C. Knight Co.*, 156 U.S. 1 (1895).
[23] *Loewe v. Lawlor*, 208 U.S. 274 (1908).

demonstrates forcefully the tractability of the concept of interstate commerce.

That baseball is a business is a fact hardly subject to debate. Baseball clubs are enterprises actively engaged in profit-seeking ventures. The business produces an exhibition of skill for which an admission price is charged, similar to other forms of entertainment. Baseball is not only business, but "it is Big Business—a $100,000,000 industry." [24]

Justice Holmes held the opinion that baseball games are purely local affairs, and the mere fact that state lines are crossed in the transportation of players and equipment does not transform these exhibitions into commerce among the states. It is still true in 1957 that baseball games are local exhibitions, but a vast industrial structure, undreamed of in 1922, has been built up around these games. Baseball today has not only an interstate but an international scope as well. The term "organized baseball" refers to the sixteen major-league clubs and their minor-league subsidiaries and affiliates throughout the United States, Canada, Mexico, and Cuba. These modern baseball clubs exhibit many economic characteristics interstate in nature.

All major-league clubs are engaged in intercorporate ownership through their affiliation with "farm" clubs, which are teams operating in the smaller towns and cities. The farm clubs are a part of the minor leagues that are used to supply trained players for the "big" leagues. The stock or assets of these minor-league business corporations may be owned in whole or in part by the major-league clubs. Another form of intercorporate activity is the "working agreement" whereby the parent baseball club, though not necessarily owning any share of the minor-league clubs, agrees to assume some portion of its financial liability. The agreement usually covers players' salaries and training expenses. In return for its financial aid, the parent club may receive a first option on the contracts of promising players performing for the minor-league club. [25]

In 1951 there were 364 minor-league clubs in operation in organized baseball. Of these, 75 were owned outright by major-league clubs, 120 were controlled by working agreements, and 169 were independent operators. The typical major-league club is, in fact, a holding company possessed of diverse geographic holdings. For example, in 1951 the Washington (D.C.) club of the American League owned clubs in Chattanooga, Tennessee; Charlotte, North Carolina; Havana, Cuba; and Orlando, Florida. Controlled by working agreements were clubs in Fulton, Kentucky; Erie, Pennsylvania; and Big Spring, Texas. [26]

In 1922 interstate telegraphic reports of games were considered so incidental to the main business they were dismissed from consideration. Since

[24] *Hearings*, p. 474.

[25] For an excellent discussion of the inner workings of organized baseball, see Simon Rottenberg, "The Baseball Players' Labor Market," *Journal of Political Economy*, June, 1956, pp. 242–58.

[26] *Hearings*, pp. 765–66.

then, radio and television have become an integral part of professional sports. This fact was recognized by the Supreme Court in the case of football and boxing. The Court did not acknowledge that radio and television contributed more than $4 million to organized baseball in 1951. This figure comprised more than 10 per cent of total income from all sources for the sixteen major-league clubs.[27] Recent contracts negotiated in the field of radio and television indicate that income from this source has probably risen both absolutely and proportionately.

Although baseball games are played within the boundaries of a single state, the revenue from admissions to these contests is shared by each of the participating clubs. Part of the receipts from the sale of tickets to certain seats in the stadium is paid to the visiting club for its contribution in attracting spectators. In 1950, 14 per cent of all major-league income was derived from games played away from the home stadium.[28]

Conclusion

If there is any discernible difference among the sports enterprises considered by the Court, it is in the type of uniform worn by the participants. All are engaged in interstate commerce and all should be subject to federal antitrust laws. It is difficult to understand the action of the Supreme Court in applying the 1922 decision to the present situation. Certainly it is not the result of any judicial awe for precedent. In 1954 this same Court saw fit in the segregation decision to overrule the "separate but equal" doctrine which had stood for over half a century. More likely the baseball decision is due to the degree of selectivity which the Court exercises in considering cases for review. The result has been to make even more difficult the formulation of a consistent antitrust policy.

[27] *Report*, p. 86.
[28] *Ibid.*, p. 106.

college football has become a
losing business

MYLES JACKSON

In fiscal 1961–62, U.S. college football grossed an estimated $65 million, and the game continues to be the most entertaining and spectacular business enterprise associated with American higher learning. But during the past ten years the economics of college football have become progressively less entertaining to such spectators as university regents and trustees: costs have been going up rapidly and, like other businesses in these times, football is finding out what a profit squeeze feels like. In some cases the squeeze has resulted in outright strangulation.

If football were no more costly than soccer or lacrosse, the prospect of its losing money would be of no great concern: some expenditures on athletics is essential in a balanced university curriculum. As of last season, however, the cost of fielding a three-platoon football team was as high as $760,000 (FORTUNE's estimate) for schools that operated at big-time levels of competition; the cost was not much less than half that for numerous lesser schools that played football of marketable quality. When sums of this magnitude are involved—they are about double what they were ten years ago—there has to be a proportionate increase in concern about the possibility of going into the red.

During college football's lusher years, when profits were relatively easy to come by, the argument was sometimes whether amateur college football should be *allowed* to make all the money it did. Nowadays the basic question is whether or not football should be allowed to do what has to be done in order to keep from *losing* all that money. The question is as new as the profit strangle, and in order to answer it, trustees and regents must soon make new and realistic estimates of the real nature of football's contribution to academic life.

They have several options. They may decide to push football even harder as a business. But when operating costs are high, a business has to be run in a businesslike manner, in which case the game should be officially recognized as a business and the players paid like professionals. Developments along this line have already taken place. Another option is to pay the price for a top-ranking team out of the general fund, which is money designed primarily for higher education and which is taxpayers' money in state-supported schools. The college trustees or administrators could also decide that the whole thing is more trouble than it is worth, not to say irrelevant,

---

• From *Fortune* magazine, December, 1962, pp. 119–121, ff. © Time-Life Inc., 1962.

and drop football altogether. This has happened in the case of eighty-six colleges and universities, mostly small schools, since 1951. The much hashed-over question of football ethics, then, has been superseded by some more pragmatic questions.

There is no doubt that for the majority of colleges there will be a market for college football for some time to come. National Collegiate Athletic Association commercials during televised games this season reported: "Almost 21 million fans set an all-time collegiate record last year, as total attendance increased for the eighth straight season." College-football attendance has in fact increased 18 percent over 1951. Generally, gross football income has increased along with attendance, rising to last year's $65 million from a national total of about $45 million in 1951. The network-television portion of the total has gone up from $700,000 to $4 million. (The networks, of course, get more than their money's worth out of college football.) New stadiums, and seats added to old ones, have increased capacity by at least 10 percent; and a growing number of colleges are boosting income by moving from a nine to a ten-game schedule.

Outside the big-city areas, professional football has not really turned out to be the serious competition that many colleges feared. The majority of college games are played in relatively small towns and cities, and this can constitute an economic advantage. In some areas there just isn't much else to do besides go to a football game on a Saturday afternoon; this factor is of more significance to the gate than competition from distant professional teams. For example, at Columbus, around noon on a football Saturday, 12,-000 automobiles from out of town begin to stream toward the Ohio State University stadium along streets temporarily turned one-way, as a traffic-control helicopter swings overhead. Even without O.S.U.'s enviable win record, activity of this kind creates an enjoyable presentment of marvelous events to come. In the small and rather drab prairie town of Norman, Oklahoma (it has one main-street movie theatre), the same effect is generated late Saturday morning as 150 to 200 private airplanes, carrying football customers, begin to land on the grass of the nearby university airport.

But it is apparent that the market will not, in most cases, be large enough to offset increased costs. The 18 percent rise in college-football attendance need only be compared with an 84 percent national increase in student enrollment to indicate a decrease in student interest. The University of Southern California is an example (although not necessarily typical) of how student enthusiasm for the game has flagged. In 1948, 83 percent of the undergraduates attended U.S.C. home games; last season, student attendance was 51 percent. The University of Colorado has an undergraduate enrollment of 12,000; for the past few years the student newspaper, presumably representing a cross section of student opinion, has opposed the big-time brand of football Colorado plays. Colorado won the Big Eight championship in 1961. This year there were some 6,600 students who were not enough interested in big-time football to pay $6 for a season ticket book. Because of student pressure at Colorado, football tickets have been separated from the incidental fees that all students pay at registration.

Even though absolute attendance figures are up, the generally acknowledged doubling of costs in a single decade has more than eaten up the additional revenue. In fact, costs may be something more than double if one judges by the comment of Michigan's athletic director, Fritz Crisler, on the occasion of the Big Ten universities' raising allowable ticket prices to a $5 top in 1961. "If ticket prices had increased in proportion to costs, we would have to sell them for $10 to $15."

The net result, according to estimates by N.C.A.A. officials, various athletic administrators, and conference officers, is drenched in red ink. Of the 200-odd schools that were playing anything like marketable football last year, and whose athletic departments had any aspirations of at least breaking even, only thirty to forty were definitely in the black. Of these, the majority were operating on a progressively diminishing margin of profit—or as nonprofit institutions prefer to phrase it, "excess of income over expenditure." At Oklahoma—which during the past few years has not been the power it was when it won twelve conference championships in a row but is still pretty mighty—athletic-department excess of income over expenditure in 1960 (excluding cash reserves) was $3,000. Last year Oklahoma's "excess" was down to $300.

The Big Time Price

Once a college administration or board of trustees has taken the decision to preserve intercollegiate football in the teeth of rising costs, the next question is whether the school should remain at its current competitive level: the cost factors of marketable college football are closely related to the competitive level at which a school chooses to play. The levels are roughly three: the Big Time, the Middle Time, and the Small Time. The Big Time consists of some eighty-odd teams across the nation that carry the regional stature and the national standing of the Midwest's Big Ten—although, as we shall see, almost any college can qualify for the Big Time if it is willing to pay the Big Time price. The Middle Time numbers more than 130 schools, typified by such conferences as the Mid-American Conference (Miami of Ohio, Bowling Green, Kent State, etc.), and the Southern Conference (Citadel, Furman, William and Mary, etc.). It includes in its numbers many of the marginal producers for which the moment of decision looms closest. The Small Time—300-odd schools—finds its market at the bottom of the pileup. It has already cut its costs and its pride to fits its revenues, or it has reconciled itself to viewing intercollegiate football as just another expense. Austin College of Sherman, Texas (enrollment 700), was trying to play lower Middle Time ball as a member of the Texas Conference (Abilene Christian, Texas A. & I., etc.) and Austin's 1953 football deficit was more than $33,000. The following year Austin dropped out of the Texas Conference and now plays such Small

Time schools as Sewanee and Ouachita Arkadelphia, Arkansas, at a yearly cost of approximately $14,000.

The alternatives before a college in search of its level are not unfamiliar to business: the school can retreat strategically to the smaller time or it can make the old college try and fight it out in the Big Time market. The later course involves redoubled efforts—probably hiring a new coach, investing in increased stadium capacity, intensifying recruiting of players, etc. There are still sizable incentives. The successful Big Time school can run its revenues as high as Ohio State's $1,372,000 or Army's $825,675 in 1961. (Total Army football gross from 1952 to 1961 inclusive: $7,546,000.) As it builds its name and record it has a chance at the big intersectional and post-season bowl games, and at the fees for national telecasting. Fees for national TV run about $135,800 per team per game, and are usually divided among conference members.

The move upward is not to be taken lightly, however. By FORTUNE's calculations the rock-bottom cost of fielding a team somewhere in the Big Time is $400,000 a year.

The Mystery of the Costs

The figure itself will come as a surprise to many colleges that are paying it. In gathering material for this article FORTUNE canvassed more than a dozen colleges, including Yale, Brown, Cornell, West Point, Ohio State, Illinois, Northwestern, Oklahoma, Colorado State, Austin College, the University of Southern California, Clemson, Centre College in Kentucky, West Virginia Wesleyan, and Bowling Green, Ohio. Some colleges gilded facts, some distorted them, some did their level best to clarify them, but it is FORTUNE's conviction that not one really knew how much football was costing.

Football income was recorded to the penny, but expenditures were a blur. Primary football expenses were usually lumped with total athletic-department expenditures. Yale stood almost alone in knowing how much its stadium was costing in yearly operating expense and maintenance; at most of the other schools there was a single entry for athletic plant maintenance, which included the field house, hockey rink, and other buildings as well as the stadium. Ohio State listed nineteen items under "football expenditures"—uniforms, travel, movies, officials, etc.—and the total came to $174,083.63. This did not include football coaches' salaries, or a number of overhead items. In cooperation with FORTUNE, Ohio State athletic-department officials worked out estimated percentages of other costs, including any expenditure that would not exist if there were no football, and such items as the publicity-bureau, ticket-office, and general-administration expenditures directly applicable to football, as well as an estimate of the stadium's yearly operating and maintenance costs. Total football expenditures then turned out to be $760,000. This is something like what it costs to field a team in the very top

of the Big Time but well above average for the general Big Time category.
The $400,000 figure was arrived at by averaging similar detailed cost estimates
from other schools.

One reason for the blur in football bookkeeping is that football is
traditionally supposed to bear the expense of all of its poor-relation intercollegiate sports, and there is no pressure on the athletic department to
isolate its football expenditures. Football is generally regarded as losing
money if the total intercollegiate athletic program runs in the red, and the
idea of using taxpayers' money to make up athletic-department deficits is considered sinful. "Not a single penny of taxpayers' money is used to support
intercollegiate athletics at this institution" is a phrase often repeated at
West Point and other state-supported schools. The system requires football to
make more money than it needs to make to be strictly self-supporting; it adds
to the compulsiveness of schools that fight for the Big Time football dollar.
Football's financial responsibility for intercollege sports is the price it pays
for being acceptable to the academic community. It is a symbol of a delicate
and nervous relationship that has influenced the development of the game
from its earliest days and still clouds a realistic outlook on football's role in
college affairs.

From Hacking and Throttling to Finesse

Historians have not recorded the name of the incipient athletic director
who first turned away from watching the players on the field and counted
the spectators. The first intercollegiate football game (soccer) was played in
relative innocence, between Princeton and Rutgers, in 1869. But by the
late 1870s someone had discovered that as many as 4,000 spectators were
willing to pay 50 cents a head to watch Yale play Princeton, and subsequent
changes in the rules of the game were made with some reference to what
they might like. There was a slightly increased emphasis upon finesse and
tactics, rather than brute force. In the late 1870s and early 1880s, Rule 28
of the Intercollegiate Football Association of America forbade "hacking,
throttling, butting, tripping up . . . or striking with closed fist" and Rule 19
enjoined the referee to ". . . disqualify any player whom he has warned
twice for intentional violation of Rule 28." Later the rules also banned Pudge
Heffelfinger's trick of stopping the lead man in a flying wedge by jumping into
his chest feet first. After eighteen players were killed in the 1905 season, the
tedious and destructive mass-wedge plays were ruled out at the instigation
of President Theodore Roosevelt. The forward pass was ruled in. Paid coaches
appeared: Yale spent $4,300 on this item in 1911, up from $700 in 1909.
Rigorous, scheduled training and training tables had come into being: Yale's
training-table expense doubled in two years, to $3,000 in 1911. Players were
recruited and subsidized, and magazine articles bemoaned this fact. In 1911
Yale's football expenditures included $4,000 for "Merchandise and Sporting
Goods" and $1,500 for "Carriages and Streetcar Fares." Total expenditures

amounted to $54,000. Income was $80,000. As of fiscal 1910–11 there was also an accumulated reserve-fund account of $165,000. Comparable sums were being piled up by other schools, thus providing the base for the first American era of college-bowl building. The Yale field by this time had wooden stands that could seat 20,000, but the supply of seats was far short of demand; the 70,000-seat Yale Bowl was built in 1914 at a cost of $700,000.

Athletic Associations and Good Works

Someone had to manage all this financing, and since the universities themselves didn't care to get mixed up with football, the job was done by athletic associations, which were in effect private corporations. University administrations exercised little more than nominal control over them. As football profits and investment multiplied during the Twenties, so did the criticism from those who thought the game should be strictly an amateur sport. The only way the athletic departments could defend themeslves against such criticism—short of giving up the business they had started from scratch, which they weren't about to do—was to step up their financing of deficit sports. They could finance the construction of golf courses and gymnasiums, to be used by ordinary students as well as varsity teams. This would help to create a favorable image for profit-making football; it would help to elevate the athletic associations and departments in the esteem of their academic communities.

In this way total athletic-department expense came to be considered the same as football expense. The burden football was expected to bear increased as athletic-department operations grew in size. By the late Thirties at least a score of football schools had athletic departments with assets totaling well over $5 million and yearly departmental expenditures rapidly approaching $1 million. The latter was football's burden—at a time when the game was approaching the era of the profit squeeze.

The point at which present-day football began to groan under its traditional financial burdens can be dated to within a year or two—around 1946. In 1946 football coaches had a chance to make a dramatic and inexpensive improvement in the quality of their product. The athletes among returning war veterans constituted an overabundant supply of experienced talent. G.I. Bill veterans demanded little in the way of financial aid. The result was the introduction of the two-platoon system, in which specialized offensive and defensive players did their jobs with precision. Frequent rest periods made it possible to entertain customers with full-speed play throughout the entire game. Football was booming all over the country during the late Forties, and profits were high, largely because players were abundant, skilled, and cheap.

Then the veterans graduated. The standards of football quality had to be maintained, and this could be done only through increased effort in recruiting the best of high-school talent. Athletic departments were still striving to promote an image that would satisfy the academic community, and this had the effect of keeping them from giving open and aboveboard financial assistance to players (except in the South, where schools have been giving athletic scholarships, as such, since the Thirties). One way or another, above-board, below board, or sideways, every single school in the country that had a football team of any standing was engaged in buying high-school foot-ball players. These activities received publicity, and as one florid exposé followed another, the athletic departments ran up against a fully matured Big Time dilemma. If they continued doing what had to be done in order to produce quality football, they would have to give up all pretense of being practical amateur sportsmen. But if they gave up trying to produce quality football they would lose money and would not be able to finance deficit sports with football profits—thus robbing the game of a primary justification for its existence. It was a time when all the old ethical questions relating to foot-ball had to be answered once and for all.

The Ivy League Pays the Big Time Price

The resolution found by the Ivy League universities, and others oper-ating on the same principles, is one that will allow relatively high-pressure football to survive among schools that can afford substantial yearly losses. The Ivy League approach had its origin during the depression era. Athletic associations at some of the smaller eastern schools found themselves no longer able to meet expenses—mainly because of diminished football income, not increase in costs—and the schools had to decide whether or not football was worth continuing. They decided it was. This meant that deficits had to be made up with money from the general fund, and executive power over athletics passed to the body that supplied the money. By 1941 the athletic association at some universities, like Brown, had become a regular university department. It was made directly responsible to the president. At least tech-nically, it was no longer an outside business enterprise.

As equivalent changes were wrought at other schools, university admin-istrators and academicians, in turn, accepted the idea that intercollegiate sports were worthwhile, provided they could be kept in their proper place. That meant a reduction of practice time for football players and required that teams compete only against schools that held similar views. It was as a result of such developments that the Ivy League came into being in 1954.

The word "de-emphasis" has often been associated with Ivy League athletics, football in particular, and it is misleading. Ivy League football is still Big Time. A school that can afford to lose a lot of money on athletics has to be considered just as Big Time as a school that makes a lot of money. Last year Cornell, which supports twenty-one intercollegiate sports, had an athletic-department deficit of $313,000 (including plant maintenance), which is a Big Time expenditure. Brown had a deficit of $204,000 (excluding plant maintenance). The Yale athletic-department expenditure last year was $1,-

049,000, with income of $755,000. These sums are not considered deficits, but merely athletic expenses. Yale's athletic-department appropriation (deficit) of $294,000 was only 0.7 percent of total university operating expenses of $44,460,000, not an unreasonable sum to spend on intercollegiate athletics, if you have Yale's endowment.

"De-emphasis" is misleading too in the sensitive area of recruiting. Louisiana State can dazzle a certain type of player with its $944,500 air-conditioned athletic dormitory, which has stereo and color television in the rec hall and a telephone in each two-man room. Ivy League schools can impress another kind of player by letting him take a look at a genuine ivy-covered wall and the broad vistas of social and economic prestige attached thereto. The geographical spread of Ivy League alumni recruiters is far greater than that of any average Big Time state university. And while Ivy League schools do not offer athletic scholarships as such, good football players with acceptable grades happily fall within the admissions director's charter to favor the "well-rounded" candidate.

The Ivy League solution to the football dilemma, then, differs from that of other Big Time schools principally because Ivy schools can *afford* to differ. They can afford, both economically and politically, to have athletic departments that operate at a deficit.

Squeeze in the Middle Time

Most other colleges must face up to the discipline of the profit-and-loss statement, a procedure best illustrated in the Middle Time school that is determined to make its own way in football. Such a school must begin by competing with the Big Time for a share of the best high-school talent. Tuition, room and board, books and fees cost about the same at a Middle Time as at a comparable Big Time school, so grants-in-aid must be roughly the same. In some cases the upper Middle Time school must spend more on player recruitment than Big Time schools spend. The Middle Time school does not have as many helpful alumni. Its name does not have the Big Time aura—frequently brightened by TV games—that is in itself attractive to high-school players. Many basic expenses—coaches, promotion, entertainment, football uniforms, training-room facilities, laundry, etc.—are roughly comparable to Big Time expenses. And thanks to TV, the Middle Time school is often obliged to compete with Big Time schools for customers. Last October, for instance, potential spectators in the vicinity of Abilene, Texas, who might otherwise have bought a ticket to a Middle Time game between Hardin-Simmons and Trinity University, instead stayed home and watched the regionally televised game at Dallas between Rice and S.M.U.

The Middle Time school has learned that if it wants to go on making money it has no choice but to try for the Big Time income. Once the decision is taken, the school's first move will be to get out of a Middle Time conference and into a bigger one. Athletic conferences, however, are run by hard-headed sportsmen, and a school that wants to join must demonstrate that it will be an asset, not a liability. Sometimes there are no openings available, and then a new conference must be formed, made up of schools that are Big Time bound. Just this sort of impulse led to the formation, this summer, of the new Western Athletic Conference, which, according to its information brochure, is made up of six universities "from the most progressive and rapidly growing area in America": Arizona, Arizona State, Brigham Young, New Mexico, Utah, and Wyoming. These are the strongest schools, in terms of all-round economic potential, from two older conferences, the Border and the Mountain States—both of which were obliged to disband when the new conference was formed.

The Western Conference schools have a lot going for them, and some stand a fair chance of breaking even in the Big Time. Arizona State, for example, is at Tempe, another medium-sized town where college football is a major diversion. All games are played at night. The air is dry and balmy. Under the dark sky the lights on the bright green grass make a kind of enclosed theatre of the stadium, and a game takes on the mood of a social event: downtown restaurants provide game buses for their dinner guests; ladies in the stands wear cocktail dresses and high heels. Good tickets have become prime status symbols in the town, and this year the Sun Devils were to play eight night games at home in their lower Big Time, 33,500-seat stadium. The University of New Mexico has a sympathetic state legislature on its side: in 1960–61 New Mexico's total athletic-department expenditure, most of it for football, came to about $505,000; income, mostly from football, was $350,000. The deficit was covered by a specific legislative appropriation of $110,700. This left the athletic department only a few thousand dollars in the red for the year. New Mexico has a two-year-old stadium of 30,000 capacity.

Fighting Up From the Bottom

As for the schools that were elbowed out when the new Western Athletic Conference was formed, some will be forced to retreat into the Small Time, but at least one—Colorado State University—intends to fight. Colorado State has a stadium that holds 13,000 and is rarely filled. The nearby town of Fort Collins has a population of only 26,000. Denver is an accessible sixty miles away, but that market is pretty much the property of the Air Force Academy and the University of Colorado—which itself was once a member of the Mountain States Conference but moved up to the Big Eight in 1948. But C.S.U. has not said die. President William E. Morgan says there is "no foreseeable means of financing a new stadium," and he is heavily engaged in finding the money to build $4 million worth of new non-athletic buildings—a library, humanities building, faculty-classroom building, and miscellaneous research facilities. Nevertheless, space has been allowed for a new stadium in long-range campus planning. Interested local parties continue to exert pressure in favor of a bigger football effort, and this year

C.S.U. hired a new football coach. He is Gray Flannel. The school has increased the number of full-ride grants-in-aid for football players from forty-four in 1956 to seventy-five for 1962–63. This season the C.S.U. football team, playing over its head with U.C.L.A. on its schedule, lost its first six games by an average of twenty-six points each, and may end up in the red, as it did last year. The Big Time is still some distance away for C.S.U.

How Costs Run

A Middle Time school scouting Big Time possibilities will do well to keep in mind that officially recorded costs are conservative more often than not. The largest single item of football expenditure is the full-ride grant-in-aid, now an accepted fixture at schools that hope to play profitable football. At Ohio State the price for 108 players, including freshmen, amounts to $111,000, which compares with a Big Ten average of about $118,000. (Ohio's all-sports grant total was $219,000, paid for out of athletic-department profits —some of which come from basketball.) The University of Colorado spent over $100,000 on football grants. Oklahoma and U.S.C. together, including some partial grants, averaged over $90,000. If we average all of these and take off about 15 percent for the sake of being very conservative, we will have a minimum Big Time grant-in-aid estimate of about $90,000.

Sooner or later the ambitious Middle Time school will find itself adding capacity to its stadium. Construction costs vary enormously with stadium design: during the past few years Clemson has increased its stadium capacity from about 25,000 to 45,000 at a cost of $450,000. Indiana recently built a new 48,000-seat stadium that cost $6,600,000. It is difficult to make anything but a rough estimate of what average costs would amount to in yearly debt-service payments, but the yearly sum being paid by Colorado, which nearly doubled capacity to 41,000 a few years ago, would probably be close to what a new arrival in the Big Time might expect to pay: about $20,000 a year.

The basic construction costs of the older and larger stadiums—like the $2,279,000 Ohio Stadium—were paid off long ago, and the main yearly expenses is in operating and maintenance costs. Yale's uniquely detailed records of its bowl maintenance expenses show 1961–62 operating and maintenance expense at $70,000 (excluding property taxes). Illinois spent about $84,000. Ohio State's stadium expense (including $4,000 a year for wooden-seat replacements, and other sums for painting, concrete and plumbing repair, playing field surface maintenance, plus game-day expenses such as wages for ticket takers, car parkers, physicians, post-game cleanup) was an estimated $67,500 for five home games. Oklahoma's estimate of $22,000 is probably conservative. Although the variation in these sums is considerable, they average out to $60,000, and this is a fairly sound minimum estimate of Big Time stadium operating and maintenance costs alone. If we reduce this sum by a conservative factor of about 15 percent, to $50,000, and add to it a typical stadium debt-service payment such as Colorado's $20,000, we have at least a working conception of the minimum yearly sum required to operate a recently enlarged stadium in the Big Time: $70,000.

The most elusive cost is player recruiting. A self-study conducted by the Big Ten in 1956 reported that about 95 percent of all football lettermen in the Big Ten had been "actively recruited." By now the percentage applies to all schools from the Middle Time up. Oklahoma's total recruiting-cost estimate is $14,000. U.S.C.'s is $11,500. Ohio State has an item called "Entertainment," which is connected with recruiting, and is the only listing in that area: $2,200. This is not so conservative as it might seem, considering the renowned vigor of the Ohio alumni. One of the more accurate estimates is the Colorado item listed under "Recruiting": $23,488. Adding together everything a school might spend in "actively recruiting" 95 percent of its varsity football players, we can't go wrong in assigning this item the rock-bottom sum of $15,000.

A number of operating expenses are more or less constant across the country: uniforms and equipment cost about $22,000 at Cornell, $21,700 at Oklahoma, $24,000 at West Point. Training-table cost was $18,000 at U.S.C., $17,500 at Colorado. Ohio State spent $20,600 on motion pictures—there is a camera going at almost every practice session—but this was only Parkinson's Law in action at a rich football school, as photography expenses rose to meet available income. (The Cleveland Browns got along with $15,000 worth of movies.) Motion-picture expense did not often rise above $6,000 at other big schools. Team travel averages $25,000 with one intersectional trip. The average of these sums, plus another $50,000 for training-room supplies and salaries, equipment manager's salary, insurance, extra medical expense, and laundry adds up to what can be termed minimum team operating expenses: $120,000. Add another $3,000 for the marching band. (High-stepping Ohio State spends $19,000 on uniforms and two trips for the 120-piece band—which has ten E-flat cornets, ten tenor horns, ten flügelhorns, and no trombones at all.)

Coaching is the last major item. The minimum range for a Big Time coach is $15,000 to $17,000, but the school probably will have to offer him perquisites equal in value to at least the amount of his salary—e.g., a rent-free house (renovated before he moves in), and perhaps a new car. He will need five to ten assistants at $6,000 to $10,000 each. The total football coaches' salary item at Ohio State was $98,000 last year, $70,000 at Yale; but for a minimum we can drop it to $65,000.

Add to this some $40,000 worth of overhead usually covered in the college administrative budget (news bureau, telephones, office supplies, etc.) and we get our $400,000 as a rock-bottom estimate of how much it costs to play nine or ten football games in the lower fringes of the Big Time.

It is a figure of this magnitude that hangs over the heads of trustees, regents, overseers, and even taxpayers as they ponder the decision of what to do about college football. If a school seems to be in a position to earn $400,-

000 or more it can go on with the Big Time game. If it can afford to play at this level because deficits are made up out of the general fund—by alumni, endowments, or legislative appropriation—it can also go on. In some cases trustees and administrators who wanted to keep a $400,000 football team operating in the black would need only to take traditional nonfootball athletic-department expenses off football's back. This course has a certain virtue because it leaves marketable college football where it ought to be— recognized as an out-and-out business proposition, not a benevolent service to other sports.

If all these "ifs" add up to a negative decision, the future need not be so bleak as alumni might think. Colleges playing below the $400,000 level will find themselves in the pleasurable company of other institutions of higher learning that are moving back to amateur football—Small Time, no grants, no worry, no guilt complex, little profit, little loss, and after all is said and done still a fairly rousing game.

sport and social processes

game involvement in adults

BRIAN SUTTON-SMITH,
JOHN M. ROBERTS, AND
ROBERT M. KOZELKA

A. Introduction

The most common explanation for individual differences in recreative interest is that they are the outcome of such nonpsychological factors as differences in wealth, group membership or ecologic opportunity (2, 18). It is held here, however, that persistence in recreations of various sorts is linked with the expression of characteristic motives. Earlier papers (10, 11, 12, 15), have shown that when games of the three major classes of strategy, chance, and physical skill are examined cross-culturally they are systematically related to specific variables both in the sphere of child training and elsewhere in the general culture. Thus, games of strategy are related to obedience training and to cultural complexity, games of chance are associated with high responsibility training and a belief in the benevolence of the gods, and games of physical skill are related to an emphasis on achievement.

These relationships suggested a *conflict-enculturation* hypothesis of model involvement which stated (11,12,15) that conflicts induced by social learning in childhood and later (such as those related to obedience, achievement, and responsibility) lead to involvement in expressive models, such as

• From *The Journal of Social Psychology*, **60** (1963), 15–30. © 1963 by Journal Press, 2 Commercial Street, Provincetown, Mass. Received in the Editorial Office on November 26, 1962, and published immediately in accordance with our policy of special consideration for cross-cultural research. This investigation was supported by Public Health Research Grant, MH 04161-03, from the National Institute of Mental Health, Public Health Service.

games, through which these conflicts are assuaged and as a result of which a process of buffered learning occurs which has enculturative value for the competences required in the culture (such as acquiring the competitive styles of strategy, physical skill or chance). The same *conflict-enculturation* hypothesis will be cited in the discussion of game involvement in American adults.

In an earlier publication (11), the game relationships were based on cross-cultural comparisons and the findings from this source were then strengthened by using them as a basis for predictions within the United States (a technique termed subsystem replication). Thus it was held that girls who have higher obedience and responsibility training than boys would play more games of strategy and games of chance, whereas boys who have higher achievement training than girls would play more games of physical skill. These predictions were confirmed in the case of a sample of 1,900 Ohio school children. In an attempt to strengthen these findings even further, the present paper extends this subsystem replication to cover sex, economic, and occupational differences in the recreational involvements of national samples of adults.

The predictions for adult game preferences in the United States which have been derived from earlier studies are the following:

1. Because games of strategy are associated cross-culturally with severe primary socialization, psychological discipline, high obedience training and complex cultures, they will be preferred in this culture by the persons who have had greater experience of such a child training pattern, that is, the higher status groups as compared with the lower, and women as compared with men.

2. Because games of chance are associated cross-culturally with high routine responsibility training, punishment for the display of initiative, and a belief in the benevolence of the gods, they will be preferred in this culture by members of the lower status groups as compared with the higher and by women as compared with men.

3. Because games of physical skill are associated cross-culturally with high achievement training, they will be preferred in this culture by the upper as compared with the lower status groups and by men as compared with women.

With respect to the third prediction the state of the literature does not permit the definite statement that the relationship between need achievement and status is a linear one (3). There are some indications that upper middle groups may have as high an achievement motivation as the upper groups. Two cautionary points are necessary with respect to these predictions. First, there is no implication in this account that those adults who are highly involved in games need have any awareness of the motivations associated with their preferred games. Phenomenologically they may enjoy playing and they like to win. Secondly, it is not claimed that all differences between status groups in game preferences can be explained in terms of the present categories of psychological motivation. Other variables of an historical and social psychological sort are certainly involved in recreational choice as a considerable literature attests (4). The purpose here is to show, rather, that if the present psychological considerations are taken into account they can predict to major effects for which other more satisfactory general theoretical formulations do not exist.

B. Method

Three survey polls made in 1940 and 1948 were used in this study.[1] All polls provided tests for some or all of the above hypotheses. The polls are described briefly below:

1. THE AMERICAN INSTITUTE OF PUBLIC OPINION (Gallup) Poll of 1940 (U.S.A.—A.I.P.O., No. 187) in which 3,242 subjects were asked, amongst various questions of a political and recreative sort: "Which of the following games have you played in the last year?" The list included tennis and golf; bridge and checkers; bingo, craps, and dice. Tennis and golf are games of physical skill; bridge and checkers taken together constitute a combination category of chance and strategy; and bingo, craps, and dice are games of pure chance. Responses classified by sex and occupation were used in this study.

2. THE MINNESOTA POLL, NO. 53, 1948 in which 598 respondents were asked: "These are some questions dealing with recreation, that is, the things people do in their spare time for their own enjoyment. Which of these things do you like to do most in your spare time?" Responses to the items "doing miscellaneous sports" (which included fishing, hunting, bowling, football and baseball, golf, skating, and swimming) and "watching sports contests" were analyzed by sex and level of education. While some of the above items are not games, it is assumed that dominance of physical skill games in this category is the major determinant of responses.

3. THE ROPER-FORTUNE SURVEY, NO. 73 OF 1948 was a survey devoted completely to recreation. The responses of 3,008 subjects were classified in terms of sex, income, education and occupation. Subjects were asked which of several activities they most enjoyed doing in their spare time. The responses most relevant to this inquiry were those having to do with sports. These have been arranged in terms of activities involving direct participation (doing outdoor sports, going out for sports and other participant sports) and vicarious participation (watching sports, attending sports and listening to sports on radio). The very different levels of response in Table 3 are due to the fact that items No. 1 and 4 were provided by the questionnaire while items No. 2, 3, 5, and 6 were written in by the respondents.

The use of the poll data to test the predictions was quite straightforward. The actual techniques used can be plainly inferred from the results presented below.

[1] All data were available through the facilities of the Roper Public Opinion Center at Williams College, Williamstown, Massachusetts.

C. Results

All the results from the first poll were in the predicted direction, which means that the findings from the cross-cultural study have now been replicated both with children and adults within the United States. As Table 1 indicates the males who are assumed to have had higher achievement training than the females played more games of physical skill (tennis and golf)

table 1

A.I.P.O. POLL NO. 187. SEX AND OCCUPATIONAL RESPONSES TO GAMES

RESPONDENT GROUP	N	PERCENTAGE OF RESPONSE		
		GOLF TENNIS	BRIDGE CHECKERS	DICE, CRAPS BINGO
Males	2163	21	58	1.10
Females	1079	17	62	2.22
Professionals	289	49	74	0.34
Proprietors	497	36	66	1.00
Clerks	539	35	72	0.73
Skilled workers	254	21	54	0.78
Servants	99	15	63	2.10
Semiskilled workers	377	14	52	3.40
Other unskilled	218	9	43	1.80
Farmers	652	7	53	1.60
Farm laborers	26	7	42	0.00

($t = 2.78$, $p = <0.01$).[2] The females who have had more obedience and responsibility training played more games of strategy and chance (checkers and bridge) ($t = 2.19$, $p = <0.05$) and more games of chance (bingo, craps and dice) ($t = 2.23$, $p = <0.05$) than the males.

The occupational differences are also in general accord with the predictions. The professional classes, who it is assumed have had the highest achievement and obedience training, showed a greater interest in physical skill and strategy games than any of the other classes. For games of physical skill all differences are significant at $p = <0.01$. For games of strategy, the differences between the professional classes and some of the intermediate groups (viz. clerks) were reduced, but the former still displayed a significantly greater preference for such games than all the worker groups (servants, skilled, unskilled and semiskilled) ($p = <0.05$). Again, as predicted, most of the worker categories in which responsibility and routine occupations were held to be characteristic showed a greater interest in games of chance than the professional group, although only the difference between the semiskilled worker group and the professional group was significant ($p = <0.01$).

[2] All tests are t-tests and are based on the significance of the difference between the percentage of responses.

The second poll (No. 53) provided a more fitting test of the hypothesis concerning achievement and sports because the recreations mentioned are more general, and not necessarily those which would be associated in common expectation with higher status groups (as are golf and tennis). The sex difference is stronger in this case being significant both for doing sports ($t = 5.38$, $p = <0.01$) and watching sports ($t = 6.36$, $p = <0.01$). The tendency in the results was for the college educated to show more interest than the high school educated, who showed more interest than the grade

table 2

MINNESOTA POLL NO. 53, 1948. SEX AND EDUCATIONAL
RESPONSES TO SPORTS ITEMS

| | | PERCENTAGE OF RESPONSE | |
| | | MISCELLANEOUS, SPORTS, FISHING, HUNTING, BOWLING, FOOTBALL, BASEBALL, GOLF, | WATCHING SPORTS |
RESPONDENTS	N	SKATING, SWIMMING	CONTESTS
Male	296	28	33
Female	302	11	12
College graduate	66	23	28
College (incomplete)	64	28	36
High school graduate	163	24	25
High school (incomplete)	106	15	23
Grade school	192	16	14

school educated. None of these differences for engaging in sports were significant though they were all directional. Thus for the college incomplete group compared with the grade school group, $t = 1.93$ and for the combined college group compared with the grade school group, $t = 1.95$. All differences were greater for watching sports. Both combined college ($t = 3.75$, $p = <0.01$) and combined high school groups ($t = 2.77$, $p = <0.01$) manifested a significantly higher level of preference than the grade school group.

Table 3 indicates that as in Tables 1 and 2 there was a tendency for higher status groups (education and income) to display a greater participant and vicarious interest in sports. The educational status index followed the predicted pattern most consistently with the college groups showing higher percentages than the grade school groups on all comparisons. Five out of six of the differences were significant at $p = <0.05$ (Nos. 1, 2, 3, 4, 6), the other was directional (No. 5). The highest economic status group (A) had significantly higher percentages than the lowest economic status group (D) on two out of the six possible comparisons (Nos. 1 and 4). Two were directional (Nos. 2 and 3). The occupational extremes (professional vs. factory wages) did not show any significant difference in favor of the professionals; in fact, factory wage workers evinced a significantly greater preference for

table 3

ROPER FORTUNE SURVEY NO. 73. RESPONSES TO RECREATIONAL ITEMS BY SEX, ECONOMIC STATUS, EDUCATIONAL STATUS, AND OCCUPATIONAL STATUS

RESPONDENTS	N	DIRECT PARTICIPATION			VICARIOUS PARTICIPATION		
		1 DOING OUTDOOR SPORTS	2 GO OUT FOR SPORTS	3 OTHER PARTIC. SPORTS	4 WATCHING SPORTS	5 ATTEND SPORTS	6 LISTEN TO SPORTS ON RADIO
Sex							
Male	1502	21	2.0	6.0	26	4.4	3.0
Female	1506	6	0.8	2.0	5	0.8	0.5
Economic							
Class A	185	18	1.1	4.8	19	1.1	2.1
B	702	13	1.7	7.7	19	4.4	1.8
C	1354	15	1.7	4.0	16	2.4	1.3
D	767	12	0.5	2.3	11	1.8	2.3
Educational							
College	684	17	1.7	6.1	20	3.6	2.3
High school	1378	15	1.8	5.2	17	2.2	1.9
Grade 1–8	873	9	0.4	1.7	11	2.6	1.0
Occupational							
A Professional	133	15	0.7	10.6	20	4.5	5.2
B Proprietor	239	21	1.5	7.6	25	4.5	2.0
C Salary exec.	101	27	—	10.0	34	5.0	3.0
D Salary minor	285	17	4.2	5.5	23	2.4	1.0
E Factory wgs.	326	23	2.1	5.3	27	3.6	3.0
F Other wages	365	14	1.9	4.9	20	3.2	2.0
G Farm propr.	207	19	1.5	2.5	15	3.3	0.9
H Farm wages	92	21	1.0	4.4	17	3.3	3.0
I Housekeeper	1048	7	0.6	1.8	4	0.6	0.3
J Student	66	25	6.0	10.6	33	9.0	0.0

attending sports (No. 4; $p = <0.05$). Salary executives did show stronger directional preferences than factory wage workers on most of the items, though none of the differences were significant.

In sum, of the 18 comparisons between the extremes in each status category (college vs. grade school; economic A vs. economic D; professional vs. factory wage workers), seven favored the hypothesis, 10 were nonsignificant and one was in a contrary direction.

D. Discussion

The major predictions of this study have been confirmed. Both the cross-cultural findings and the smaller scale regional subsystem findings with children have now been replicated on these three national adult samples. Additional support for some of these empirical findings may be found in the studies reported by Caillois (1), Clarke (2), de Grazia (5) and White (18), where they overlap with this inquiry. In the present study, games of strategy have been shown to be associated with women and higher status, games of chance with women and lower status, and games of physical skill with men and higher status. It will be recalled that these predictions have a basis in the hypothesized intervening psychological variables of obedience, responsibility and achievement training which we found to be related to games in the cross-cultural study. Thus in earlier studies, conflict over obedience induced by child training procedures were shown to be related to the presence of games of strategy on one level and cultural complexity on another (10,11). The same relationships were discovered to hold for the relative importance of strategic outcomes in tales (12). Responsibility training was shown to be related to games of chance and a belief in the benevolence of the gods. Games of physical skill were related to achievement training. The fact that, cross-culturally, women generally have higher obedience and responsibility training led to the present predictions that in this culture also they would show more preference for games of strategy and chance than men. In addition because men have higher achievement training it was predicted that they would prefer more games of physical skill than do women. The association of games of strategy with cultural complexity and of obedience training with higher social status led to the prediction that these games would be associated in this culture with higher social status. The association of games of chance with responsibility training, which involves menial and low level drudgery and routine activities, led to the prediction that these games would be preferred by persons of lower social status. Again the association of achievement with higher social status led to the prediction that persons of higher status would play more games of physical skill. All of the various findings support the *conflict-enculturation* hypothesis stated in the introduction.

Although the results of this study have followed the predictions with considerable consistency there has been one important exception. The professional occupational group (Table 3), failed to show a high percentage of response to interest in physical game activities. The other high status group (the salary executives) and a low status group (the factory wage workers), both showed significantly higher percentages of interest. One interpretation of this result is that the occupational status index is not as adequate an index of need achievement as are the economic and educational indices in which no such reversal of expectation occurred. Kaltenbach and McClelland (7), using a sociometrically based criterion of perceived success, placed the occupational index as the least adequate criterion. In an earlier paper, however, the present investigators have taken another position which would seem to handle this exception more comprehensively. Thus in the earlier cross-cultural work it was discovered that the number of types of games in a culture is positively associated with achievement training (11). It seemed reasonable then to view games as various types of achievement models. From which it was postulated that those who practice persistently at a particular game type should be rehearsing the success style that is involved in that model. Those persisting with games of strategy would be practicing a style in which success is contingent upon clever decision making (a strategic success style); those practicing games of physical skill would be practicing a style in which success is contingent upon a display of power, motor skill or courage (Potency); those playing games of chance would be practicing a style in which success is contingent upon the omnipotence of the player's luck (Fortunism). In a study with children (15), in which a sociometric instrument based on these stylistic characteristics was used to predict intelligence, socioeconomic status, personality attributes and game preferences, it was found that those to whom a fortunist style was attributed by their peers tended to be more often seen as failures both by children and by teachers, and to be of lower intelligence and socioeconomic status; that those to whom a potent style was attributed were of high group status, were perceived of as good at sport, showed a higher preference for games of physical skill, but were of low intelligence; that those who were seen as strategists were also of high group status, were seen as not good at physical sports, preferred games of strategy, and were of high intelligence. These findings permit the formulation that achievement by high status persons may be differentiated into at least two types: that with a basis in power, and that with a basis in strategy.

In the high economic and educational status groups of Table 3, these two achievement styles are presumably mixed together. In the occupational section, however, it seems a differentiation has occurred by occupational group. Salary executives who show greater preference for physical skill games than professionals may be said to show a higher preference also for a power style than the professionals do, that is, if the earlier finding with children with regard to competitive styles and game choices can be safely extrapolated to this present data. The higher choice that professionals have for games of strategy (Table 1) is consistent with this interpretation. Further support for the formulation comes from a study by Veroff, Atkinson, Feld, and Gurin (17), in which a T.A.T. measure of power and achievement was used in a nationwide sample. Analysis of the relationships between occupational groups and power (p. 23) shows a ranking somewhat similar to that shown above for the interest in physical sports (Table 3). Salary Executives and Factory Workers have a higher ranking than professionals on both power and physical sports interest. Conversely, the Veroff rankings on achievement are similar to those in Table 1 for strategy. None of these parallels can be regarded as finally convincing, but the suggestion certainly follows that the present relationships might be further explicated in future research by the measurement of achievement which is differentiated in terms of strategy and power.

Although the *conflict-enculturation* hypothesis has been described in other publications (11,12,15), it is relevant here to explicate the hypothesis in terms of its relationships to achievement motivation since this particular motivation has been given most attention in this paper. Discussion of the hypothesis in relation to obedience and responsibility, as well as to achievement, will be found elsewhere (11,12,15) and a much more elaborate treatment of the hypothesis will be forthcoming.

It will be recalled that games of all types have been shown to have some relationship to achievement training and that all games can be viewed as achievement models, particularly those which model achievement through power and skill. Games of pure physical skill (weight lifting, bowling) model only these last characteristics, but games of physical skill and strategy (boxing, football) model in addition the attributes of strategy.

The *conflict-enculturation* hypothesis involves a number of propositions, each of which will be stated abstractly below and then followed by the relevant details. The first two propositions have to do with *conflict* and include the concepts of conflict arousal, curiosity, and model involvement. The second two propositions are concerned with *enculturation* and include the concepts of social learning and personality adjustment.

> 1. (a) Conflict induced in children or adults by achievement training arouses in them curiosity about those expressive models that contain a representation of winning and losing as a result of the application of power and skill.

The hypothesis holds that learning can produce conflicts (a balance of approach and avoidance tendencies), which heighten an individual's interest in the variables which are involved in his conflict. This is the familiar concept of conflict-induced drive (19). The positive and negative discipline which might be expected to underly such approach-avoidance tendencies have been established in earlier research (11). Thus playing games of physical skill was found in tribal cultures with a high frequency of achievement training, a high reward for achievement, but at the same time high punishment for nonperformance of achievement. It would seem that children, seriously limited in size, skill and power, yet motivated to achieve and anxious about being able to do so, can seldom find in full scale cultural participation sufficient behavioral opportunities to match adequately both their desire and their anxious incompetence. It is believed that in childhood this achievement anxiety expresses itself most frequently as a fear of failure. The contemporary psychological definition of achievement drive as competition against a standard of excellence, tends to underplay the extent to which in childhood such an achievement standard is usually part of an interpersonal relationship, so that to achieve the subject must face some other person's expectations, or alternatively must face the rivalry of another competitor, usually a sibling, peer or parent. Anxiety about achievement in childhood is primarily anxiety acquired in such interpersonal situations. This leaves children with an interest in winning, particularly if there is the possibility of doing so in some way that will reduce their fear of failure and provide appropriate "matching" for their limited talents. Their "curiosity" about achievement models has this origin.

> 1. (b) Persons who are made curious about achievement by their conflict over it readily become involved in achievement as represented in expressive models.

Desiring to beat opponents but frightened to lose, the child is motivated to explore and to be curious about opportunities to deal with his conflict in a more manageable fashion. He is attracted to a variety of culturally provided expressive models. Some of these may be vicarious as in folktales, comics, and television and may suggest that the small participant can win (Jack and the Giant Killer, Mighty Mouse), or that the central figure may have powers to overcome insuperable odds (Superman). Or the expressive models may be of the participant variety like physical skill games in which the consequences of winning and losing are drastically reduced. Noticeably, in the earliest forms of physical skill and strategy games such as tagging and hide-and-seek, both winning and losing are episodic and their intensity is decreased by the instability of the sides. There is, in addition, no final explicit outcome so that there is a lack of clarity about which players have actually won or lost. This reduction in the objective clarity of winning and losing, however, permits rather than prevents subjective estimates of success to assume relatively egocentric proportions. Thus Piaget has shown very young children all imagine they have won in the games that they play (9). And Maccoby has demonstrated that six-year-olds anticipate success with their peers in a way far exceeding the limits of possibility (8). With the passage of chronological age there is a developmental change in the models in which children can find a statement for their problems of winning and losing. The diffuse skill models of the earlier years give way to games in which the requirements for winning are more rigorous and the penalties for losing more obvious (marbles, football) (14). Children of different maturity levels, therefore, can find a matching for the maturity of their achievement conflicts somewhere in each of the many series to be found in the cultural model array of tales and games, etc.

The second part of the present theory is that once the child becomes *involved* in games a further series of circumstances occur to which the broad

term *enculturation* has been given. At the present time in the development of
this theory, the term *enculturation* is being used to apply to two distinct
processes, the first of which can be called "social learning" and the second
"personality adjustment." Both seem necessary to explain the players' continued involvement and the cultural significance of expressive models.

> 2. (a) In the case of children, and to a lesser extent adults, participation
> in achievement games contributes to physical, intellectual, and social learn-
> ing, each of which in due course may contribute to the participant's ability
> to survive in the full scale success systems of the larger culture.

It has been assumed traditionally that various physical, intellectual and,
particularly moral, characteristics have been learned as a result of participation
in games, more especially team games. Whether or not these traditional assumptions are well founded, it is contended here that in achievement games
there is learned a capacity to master the contingencies of winning and losing
in interpersonal competition, and that the development of this capacity is
fostered by the game-contained demands. There is some, if partial, evidence
for this latter claim (6). The argument is, that because games reduce the
scale on which the competition occurs, then winning and losing as complex
interpersonal events become more readily assimilable by the child. Even loss
is more acceptable when it is known that victory may occur in a second
episode. The dangers and threats associated with both winning and losing are
thus much reduced, while the gratification in winning is not. Furthermore,
losers are defended by the play convention that the game is only for "fun"
anyway. Privately, at least, a victor may think what he likes about winning.
The view that expressive models make social and behavioral complexities more
assimilable (both cognitively and emotionally) to the participants is a part
of a more general argument of the present investigators that expressive models
exist for the very reason that they can convey to participants information
which cannot be assimilated more simply nor without overwhelming anxiety
in large-scale cultural participation.

In sum, the final reason for a player's involvement in any particular
model is that the model has scaled down the dimensions of his conflict to a
point where it is intellectually and emotionally comprehensible. In turn, the
player's involvement in the clarity and safety of the model's presentation,
facilitates learning.

> 2. (b) Expressive models contribute to a player's adjustment to the cultural
> pressures which have given rise to his conflict (child training pressures for
> children, current success pressures for adults), because they are exercises in
> mastery.

By scaling down the conflict dimensions the games give their participants
the confidence that winning and losing as complex interpersonal processes
and anxiety inducing ones can be mastered. It is in this sense that the game
is a mechanism of personality adjustment. It is legitimate to call this an

enculturative function, however, because the adjustment involved means that the underlying process of achievement training adopted by the parents has greater assurance of success, and that the pressures put upon children to achieve and be concerned about achievement will not lead to overwhelming despair and inferiority. Likewise with adults, contemporary pressures towards success may be similarly reduced to assimilable proportions. If this theoretical position be correct, then the various achievement models which have survived in our culture do so because they continue to have this culturally adaptive significance. It has, for example, always been something of a puzzle to explain the persistence of some of the most elementary of expressive models such as tagging (16). We now consider that it is their function to preserve within the player the confidence that some of the incompatible pressures which afflict him are manageable and that he may continue to survive successfully in the cultural system that engenders his conflicts. This increased confidence in himself would be a second reason for the player's involvement in the expressive models.

An alternative conceptualization of this "adjustment" process would be to say that the game "involves" the player because it "resolves his conflict." The difficulty with this formulation in the present case, however, is that the player's original conflict is not resolved. It continues and it must continue if the child training system or the adult cultural system is to be preserved, and to be successful. Perhaps a tension-reduction conceptual paradigm is not the most appropriate one. A level of aspiration paradigm might be more appropriate. The fantasied success and reduced loss would in these terms, not change the large scale world directly, but by increasing the confidence of the players in analogous competitive processes, may elevate their general level of aspiration with respect to these same processes in the large-scale world. In this case the "fun" of the game derives from an exercise in competence rather than an exercise in tension assuagement. There is some supportive if not definitive evidence for this view in the earlier work of these investigators showing that those who prefer games of particular types (physical skill, or strategy) seem to be successful in the same ways (power or strategy) with their peers (15).

Much of the preceding discussion necessarily deals with child training, but this paper is concerned with adults. In the various researches on achievement training in this culture there is suggestion of both reward and anxiety in the training of child achievers, though the various investigations are by no means consistent on this point (3). What is neglected in most research on achievement training is the investigation of the achievement motivation of the parents. As adults are themselves the mediators of the general pressures at work in the larger community, we might expect that the parents who induce high achievement training conflict in children will also be in similar conflict about achievement in adult concerns. The conflict-enculturation theory implies that the child training relationship to expressive models is but a part of a larger system which has in its total nature been adaptive in culture. Thus we would speculate that the adults most concerned to induce achievement in their children would themselves have high achievement aspirations in terms of the various status indices by which persons in this culture "score" their achievement—roles, houses, annual income, possessions, and the likes. The fact that high status adults will continue to play games of physical skill is supportive of this latter interpretation. The enculturative function, for the adults as compared with the children, however, is presumed to be dominantly adjustive. The game enables these adults to continue to be achievement motivated without succumbing to the pressures that this motivation entails. The game playing ensures periodic innoculations of manageable success and manageable failure, reassuring the participant that he is indeed one who can tolerate such pressures in his own psychic economy. To be sure, some game-related physical skills are learned even by adults, but it is doubtful that much important and progressive social learning takes place through games after biological and cultural maturity has been attained.

These statements do not preclude the possibility that even in adulthood, changes in life circumstances may induce achievement conflicts which will in turn lead to game playing.

In sum, the conflict-enculturation hypothesis says that child training induces conflict which leads to curiosity about representations (as in expressive models) of the dimensions of this conflict. Involvement in models follows because their microcosmic representation reduces the conflict's complexities to cognitive and emotional comprehensibility and because of the successes a player may gain while in the model. This involvement in turn has enculturative value because the participant can learn about the cognitive and emotional aspects of winning in a model in a way that he cannot do outside of it, and because his successes give him increased confidence that he can manage the achievement pressures in full-scale cultural participation. The models thus have the general cultural function that they contribute to the learning and adjustment of persons who must maintain a high level of achievement motivation if the general cultural norms are to be sustained.

This paper has presented the results of a subsystem replication among American adults which when conjoined with the earlier cross-cultural study and subsystem replication among Ohio school children supports a *conflict-enculturation* hypothesis of game involvement. Certainly, this hypothesis will require further study before it is proved, but the results thus far obtained are encouraging. At the very least, this study represents the first large-scale empirical substantiation of the view that psychological factors are of major importance in game preferences.

E. Summary

In previous cross-cultural research, relationships were established between child training variables, game playing, and general cultural variables. Using three national surveys with adults the following hypotheses derived from the cross-cultural study were confirmed within this culture:

1. Because games of strategy are associated cross-culturally with severe primary socialization, psychological discipline, high obedience training, and complex cultures, they will be preferred in this culture by the persons who have had greater experience of such a child training pattern, that is by the higher status groups as compared with the lower and by women as compared with men.
2. Because games of chance are associated cross-culturally with high routine-responsibility training, punishment for the display of initiative, and a belief in the benevolence of the gods, they will be preferred in this culture by members of the lower status groups as compared with the higher and by women as compared with men.
3. Because games of physical skill are associated cross-culturally with high achievement training, they will be preferred in this culture by the upper as compared with the lower status groups and by men as compared with women.

The results were conceptualized in terms of a *conflict-enculturation* theory of games.

REFERENCES

1. CAILLOIS, R., *Man, Play and Games*, Glencoe: Free Press, 1961.
2. CLARKE, A. C., Leisure and Occupational Prestige, *Am. Sociol. Rev.*, 1956, 21, 301–307.
3. CRANDALL, V. J., Achievement, in H. W. Stevenson (Ed.), *National Society for the Study of Education: Yearbook*, 1963, pp. 416–459.
4. DENNEY, R., & MEYERSOHN, M. L., A Preliminary Bibliography on Leisure, *Am. J. Sociol.*, 1957, 62, 602–615.
5. GRAZIA, S. DE, *Of Time, Work and Leisure*, New York: Twentieth Century Fund, 1962.
6. GUMP, P. V., & SUTTON-SMITH, B., The "It" Role in Children's Games, *The Group*, 1955, 17, 3–8.
7. KALTENBACH, J. E., and McCLELLAND, D. C., Achievement and Social Status in Three Small Communities, in D. C. McClelland *et al.* (Eds.), *Talent and Society*, New York: Van Nostrand, 1958.
8. MACCOBY, M., The Game Attitude, Ph.D. thesis, Lab. of Soc. Relations, Harvard University, 1960.
9. PIAGET, J., *The Moral Judgment of the Child*, Glencoe, Ill.: Free Press, 1948.
10. ROBERTS, J. M., ARTH, J., and BUSH, R. R., Games in Culture, *Amer. Anthrop.*, 1959, 61, 597–605.
11. ROBERTS, J. M., & SUTTON-SMITH, B., Child Training and Game Involvement, *Ethnology*, 1962, 1, 166–185.
12. ROBERTS, J. M., SUTTON-SMITH, B., & KENDON, A., Strategy in Games and Folktales, *J. Soc. Psychol.*, 61 (1963), 185–199.
13. SUTTON-SMITH, B., A Formal Analysis of Game Meaning, *Western Folklore*, 1959, 18, 13–24.
14. ———, *The Games of New Zealand Children*, Berkeley: Univ. of California Press, 1959.
15. SUTTON-SMITH, B., & ROBERTS, J. M., Rubrics of Competitive Behavior, *J. Genet. Psychol.*, 105 (1959), 13–37.
16. SUTTON-SMITH, B., & ROSENBERG, B. G., Sixty Years of Historical Change in

the Game Preferences of American Children, *J. Am. Folklore*, 1961, 74, 17–46.

17. VEROFF, J., ATKINSON, J. W., FELD, S. C., and GURIN, G., The Use of Thematic Apperception to Assess Motivation in a Nation-Wide Interview Study, *Psychol. Monog.*, 1960, 74 (Whole No. 499), 1–32.

18. WHITE, C. R., Social Class Differences in the Use of Leisure, *Am. J. Sociol.*, 1955, 61, 145–150.

19. WHITING, J. W. M., and CHILD, I. L, *Child Training and Personality*, New Haven: Yale Univ. Press, 1953.

social stratification and social mobility among young sportsmen

GÜNTHER LÜSCHEN

Social stratification and mobility have formed a popular field of research in German sociology over the past ten years. However, problems concerned with occupations, occupational groups, and religious affiliations were placed in the forefront, whereas the topic of social class as related to use of leisure time has been discussed relatively seldom. This is very surprising, since leisure time, together with the family and youth, was the most prominent field of interest in post-war German sociology.

Studies of leisure time sociology have been generally restricted to a descriptive presentation of various activities with departures from expected behavior being interpreted as questions of basically pedagogic interest. Generally, whether there is a relationship between social status and leisure time has not been discussed. If occasionally this question was considered, then it was often argued that leisure time was definitely not characterized by structures related to distinct social classes. Instead, in this age of mass produced goods, conspicuous consumption during leisure periods has become the predominant pattern of behavior. This was stated most clearly by Helmut Schelsky after David Riesman: In a manner typical for the way in which facts were presented for the "unstratified middle class society," the former said: "it appears as if the position of the consumer, instead of class status, is becoming the central determinant in all forms of behavior, whether it be in the rearing of children, in politics, or in cultural domains, so that the negative process of leveling of social classes should be determined positively as the evolution of

• From Lüschen, Günther, "Soziale Schichtung und Soziale Mobilität Bei Jungen Sportlern," *Kölner Zeitschrift für Soziologie und Sozialpsychologie*, 15 (1963), 74–93. © Translated by John M. Harkin, with comments by Günther Lüschen.

a highly industrialized leisure and consumer society." [1] The theory of conspicuous consumption, which conveniently supported the reasoning of cultural critics, was after the appearance of Schelsky's work adopted by H. J. Knebel in his publication on modern tourism.[2] On the other hand since the publication by George Lundberg, Mirra Komarkowsky and Mary A. McInery on *Leisure: A Suburban Study,*[3] or the studies by the W. Lloyd Warner School, there have been specific investigations on the relationship between social class and leisure time in American sociology. The scientific validity of the findings concerning this relationship, for example, in the studies of August B. Hollingshead,[4] or Leonard Riesman,[5] was certainly as high, based on the discriminating analysis of empirical material, as that of the followers of Thorstein Veblen. However, in Germany these remained unnoticed for a long time; the only corresponding work in reliable scientific publications is found in the study of Renate Mayntz [6] concerning participation in leisure time organizations. Even Ralf Dahrendorf, under the influence of the theory of conspicuous consumption, and while speaking about the "entertainment industry," talks about the "typical leisure time occupation of people of all classes." [7] Sport is also regarded in close connection with the entertainment industry and like no other leisure time occupation, is always an object of controversial discussion. At least as the subject of personal and mass communication, it has become the most important aspect of leisure time. The consumption theory has also been applied to sport; and Hans-Joachim Knebel, who defines it as "the intrinsic touristic behavior," [8] states in this connection that it is characterized by "consumption of means in the form of equipment, facilities, and clothes." [9] In the sense presented by Dahrendorf, sport, like movies and television, is a typical leisure time occupation of people of all classes. The statistics presented by Karl-Gustav Specht and the tentative conclusions he draws from them seem to suggest this strongly.[10] If one can believe the cultural critics, then sport is the most striking characteristic of a general massifi-

---

[1] Helmut Schelsky, "Social Change." *Offene Welt*, 1956/41.

[2] Hans-Joachim Knebel, *Sociological Structure Changes in Modern Tourism.* Stuttgart, 1960.

[3] George A. Lundberg, Mirra Komarowsky, and Mary Alice McInery, *Leisure: A Suburban Study*, New York, 1934.

[4] A. B. Hollingshead, *Elmtown's Youth.* New York, 1949.

[5] Leonard Riesman, "Class, Leisure, and Participation." *American Sociological Review*, 1954/1, Vol. 19.

[6] Renate Mayntz, *Social Stratification and Social Change in an Industrial Region.* Stuttgart, 1958, page 241. An unpublished diploma thesis that could be cited is H. Meier, "Leisure Time and Social Status." Köln, 1957.

[7] Ralf Dahrendorf, *Social Classes and Class Conflict in Industrial Society.* Stuttgart, 1957, page 69.

[8] Hans-Joachim Knebel, *loc. cit.*, page 163.

[9] *Loc. cit.*, page 160.

[10] Karl G. Specht, "Sport From the Sociological Standpoint." *Studium Generale*, 1960/I.

cation in culture and therefore should be expected to be associated with the lower classes of society.[11]

Preliminary Methodological Remarks

First, for sport, a clear distinction must be drawn between active and passive participation. Here we find different attitudes and behavioral patterns according to class, as is confirmed by the investigation of Gregory P. Stone in Minneapolis, U.S.A.[12] In the following the discussion will be restricted to active sportsmen, their social class and social mobility. Here it should be pointed out that all the individuals examined by us were youths between the ages of 15 and 25 organized in sports clubs.[13] It should also be mentioned that the study, carried out in 1958, was referring to youth studies of that time, and from the beginning was intended to be directed primarily toward leisure time activities of sportsmen. It included characteristics of social class only as routine data—certainly not for theoretical objectives. Consequently only objective criteria could be used for assessing social class. In future, however, self-rating methods and attitudes toward social stratification and toward the behavioral patterns specific to social classes should be investigated with particular reference to sport.

For the objective criteria, data on the occupation, occupational status, and education of the youth, and that of their fathers and mothers, were available. The income of the fathers was not requested, since the income of the father was often not known, particularly among the younger age groups. The increasing importance of occupation emphasized by Hans-Jürgen Daheim [14] cannot be regarded too highly for the evaluation of social status in Western society since according to Talcott Parsons [15] it is a manifestation of personal achievement and its evaluation and reward by the social environment. Consequently, in systems that are oriented toward achievement, where only achieved status is recognized, occupation is almost the sole criterion that could be accepted for determining social classes. However, at the age of the youths investigated by us the final occupational role has not yet been reached by most of the youths. In many cases it cannot even be guessed at. Their

[11] The numerous prejudices against sport, which are directed mainly against spectators, records, and the appearance of sport in mass media, have been discussed by the author in: "An Introduction to Sociology of Sport." *Kölner Zeitschrift für Soziologie und Sozialpsychologie*, 1960/3.

[12] Gregory P. Stone, "Some Meanings of American Sport." *Proceedings*, College Physical Education Association, 60th Annual Meeting, Columbus, Ohio, 1957, p. 66.

[13] Two-stage random sample, representative of 15 to 25 year old members of sports clubs in Federal German Republic and West Berlin. The sampling was taken according to the size of the club, the proportion of individual sports types, sex, and federal state, and encompassed 1880 cases from 121 clubs; the results of the investigation will be published soon by J. A. Barth, Publishers, Munich.

[14] Hans-Jürgen Daheim, "Conceptions of the Middle Class." *Kölner Zeitschrift für Soziologie und Sozialpsychologie*, 1960/2.

[15] Talcott Parsons, "An Analytical Approach to the Theory of Social Stratification." *Essays in Sociological Theory*, Glencoe, Ill., 1958, p. 69.

education is therefore an additional criterion that must be used to assign youths into social classes. Of course, in questionable cases, the data for the father might be taken. However, the social mobility that can be observed for many of the youths following their education relative to their fathers' status could not then be evaluated. In the case of the investigated group it cannot be denied that the evaluation of social class creates a number of serious problems. Indeed, social status in our society can really only be determined with finality after the age of 30. For the sake of reliability in the results, in doubtful cases the subjects were classified in the lower of the two plausible categories.[16]

Social Stratification Among Young Sportsmen

For the population investigated (sportsmen between the ages of 15 and 25 organized in clubs) the following distribution among social classes was found using the characteristics already mentioned, using a method based largely on the work of Morris Janowitz: [17]

	IN PERCENT
lower class	32.5
lower middle class	35.0
middle middle class	21.0
upper middle class	11.0
non-classifiable	0.5
n = 1880	100.0

[16] Factors considered included:
1. Occupation and occupational position of the youth, provided that the role in their occupation was already established and the future position could clearly be discerned.
2. Education of the youth.
3. Occupation and occupational position of the father. This was used primarily with students or in such cases in which the occupation and occupational status could not be clearly discerned.
4. Education of the father.
5. Occupation and occupational status of the mother, if she was the main provider.

Lower class and middle class were divided according to manual and non-manual occupations, non-self-employed craftsmen being allocated to the lower middle class.
Examples for class assignments:
Upper Middle Class (including Middle Upper Class)—self-employed professionals, higher civil servants, higher ranked office workers, higher ranked self-employed.
Intermediate Middle Class—intermediate and average level civil servants, qualified office workers, intermediate self-employed.
Lower Middle Class—lower civil servants, ordinary office workers, lower self-employed, non-self-employed craftsmen, farmers.
Lower Class—skilled laborers, partially, and unskilled laborers, farm hands.
[17] Morris Janowitz, "Social Stratification and Mobility in West Germany." *Kölner Zeitschrift für Soziologie und Sozialpsychologie*, 1958/1.

Since in many cases it could not be decided definitely from the information given by the youths whether the father was a skilled or unskilled worker, no further differentiation was made among the lower class. At a rough guess, the lower lower class among sporting youths appears to be very poorly represented with a proportion of about 5 percent.

If we wish to compare the social stratification among young sportsmen with the distribution found by Janowitz for the total population, it must be taken into account that he assigned employed master craftsmen, who are represented to the extent of 3 percent of the sample, to the lower class. In addition, it follows from our investigation that sportsmen from the lower class have fewer, while those from the upper middle class have more multiple memberships in sports clubs than average. Owing to the method of sampling, the upper middle class is therefore over-represented by 1 percent, and the lower class is under-represented by 1 percent. Therefore, the corrected values for sporting youth in comparison with the general social stratification of the Federal German Republic is as follows: [18]

	SPORTSMEN [a] IN PERCENT	GERMAN FEDERAL REPUBLIC [b] IN PERCENT
lower class	36.5	51.9
lower middle class	53.0	38.6
upper middle class	10.0	4.6
non-classifiable	0.5	4.9
	[a] n = 1880	[b] n = 3385

According to these figures, a progressive increase in the number of young sportsmen by higher social class can be seen. In view of the small proportion of youths from the lower lower class, and of the high proportion of the lower middle class, which we have differentiated further into middle and lower middle class for the purposes of our analysis, sport on the whole *cannot* be regarded as a leisure time occupation of *all social classes*. And in regard to its critics it proves to be primarily *an activity of those social classes to which these critics in general themselves belong*. To exclude a one-sided interpretation, it should be acknowledged that sport nonetheless is distributed over all classes and is certainly not the means of enjoyment solely of a leisure class, as it was regarded by Thorstein Veblen.[19] It is apparent that a high proportion of skilled workers, who, with regard to their sporting interests, behave as the middle class.

It is still very questionable whether in the future an approximation toward the general social stratification is to be expected; this cannot be in-

[18] Morris Janowitz, *loc. cit.*, page 10. Farmers were allocated by us to the lower middle class. For comparison, the lower middle class, which was sub-divided into a lower and intermediate middle class, was reunified.

[19] T. Veblen, *Theory of the Leisure Class*. In German: *Theorie der Feinen Leute*, Köln, 1957.

ferred from our data. However, it is clear that in the parent generation sport probably was placed in a higher social position. Since the extent to which parents contributed to socialization into sport was only six percent in the lower class, and in contrast; twelve, seventeen, and fifteen percent in the three middle classes, it can be assumed that the parent generation in the lower classes had a weaker attachment to sport than that of the middle class. The objection that the relationship between youths and parents might be worse in the lower class does not hold. On the contrary, it can be seen from the strong relationships with the parents, and from the small number of family conflicts, that the family conditions improve with decreasing status among sporting youths, whereas the numbers determined by EMNID for youths in general show an opposite tendency.[20] With all due skepticism towards this comparison it can still be assumed that of those youths from the lower class who are accepted into organized sport the preference goes to those from favorable family backgrounds. Consequently, the constantly emphasized function of sport as a substitute for social rehabilitation can hardly be considered correct.

The stratification relative to the two sexes is also very informative.

	SPORTSMEN	
	MALE IN PERCENT	FEMALE IN PERCENT
lower class	37.5	15.5
lower middle class	33.5	39.5
middle middle class	18.0	32.0
upper middle class	10.5	13.5
non-classifiable	0.5	0.5
	n = 1474	n = 405

There appears still to be a rather strong social barrier for girls from the lower class. This is an indication that there is hardly any emancipation of the woman's role in the lower class. This points as well to an abundance of prejudices, particularly in orthodox religious circles.

[20] Question: "Where can you discuss quite openly anything that is troubling you?" (Sporting youth).
  "Do you have someone with whom you can discuss your worries and needs?" (EMNID, Youth between 15 and 23, Bielefeld, 1955, page 149).

		FATHER OR MOTHER NAMED (OR BOTH NAMED)	
		YOUTH IN GENERAL ACCORDING TO	
SPORTING YOUTH	IN PERCENT	OCCUPATION OF FATHER	IN PERCENT
Lower Class	97	Laborers	49
Lower Middle Class	89	Office Workers	60
Middle Middle Class	90	Civil Servants	59
Upper Middle Class	81	Self-employed	55
		Farmers	52

With regard to change in the stratification according to age groups, there appears to be no significant difference, although there is probably a change specifically related to social class with increasing age.[21]

It might be suspected that the sole reason for the somewhat higher social position of the young sportsmen lies in the fact that here a leisure time activity is linked to an organization. The privileged social position in sport would then merely represent a particular case of the long recognized fact that the number of memberships in voluntary organizations is higher among the middle and upper classes than in the lower class.[22] Undoubtedly the organization of German sport could produce a trend of this kind. There certainly is such an influence, as is to be expected, after the results of Erich Reigrotzki.[23] However, from investigations of the DIVO in 1960, it can be assumed that sport represents a leisure activity with stronger participation from the middle and upper classes even independent of organization into clubs.[24] The increasingly positive correlations between the participation in sport, both informally and formally, and education and income indicates an equally strong correlation with class, such as follows from our figures for the social stratification among organized sportsmen. In addition, the connection between high achievement motivation and class [25] strongly suggests that a system which is so strongly determined by achievement as sport involves a corresponding connection with social class; this is indeed the case according to our figures, which show a progressive increase with a rise in social class. In absolute figures the main accent is on the already achievement motivated "middle mass" (skilled laborers and lower middle class).

Social Stratification According to Kinds of Sport

Although sport in general can be defined, on the one hand, as a leisure occupation of the middle class and those skilled laborers for which the middle class is also the reference group, it can be recognized, on the other hand, that despite this relatively close knit relationship, with regard to particular types of sport, there is a strong differentiation according to social class. The youths investigated were therefore asked their "favorite kind of sport." This question naturally gave an opportunity to reveal any possible relationship between the types of sport and social class. The following classification resulted for the various sports:

[21] According to the education of the father there is a smaller proportion of youth of higher class with increasing age. However, this is not reflected significantly in the stratification, because of proportion of self-employed fathers is slightly higher.

[22] See Riesman, loc. cit. and Murray Hausknecht, The Joiners, New York, 1962, page 15.

[23] Erich Reigrotzki, Social Interconnections in the Federal German Republic. Tübingen, 1956, page 173.

[24] DIVO, Press release, May, 1960/II.

[25] David C. McClelland, The Achieving Society. New York, London, 1961, page 324.

IN PERCENT	LOWER CLASS	LOWER MIDDLE CLASS	MIDDLE MIDDLE CLASS	UPPER MIDDLE CLASS
Soccer (470) [a]	53 [b]	29	12	5
Wrestling, Wt. Lifting (35)	51	26	14	9
Field Handball (158)	43	31	19	6
Badminton (33)	27	46	24	3
Gymnastics (with apparatus) (279)	31	39	23	7
Table Tennis (73)	23	44	24	8
Canoeing (34)	21	41	38	
Gymnastics (44)	16	43	41	
Riding (33)	18	49	15	18
Swimming (143)	17	41	31	11
Track and Field (231)	19	40	24	17
Rowing (57)	12	47	26	14
Skiing (72)	11	33	20	36
Field Hockey (34)	3	26	53	18
Tennis (101)	2	27	28	42

[a] number of cases.
[b] in percent.

The "hierarchy within the various types of sport" claimed by Carl Diem and Gerda Engelhard [26] is plainly recognizable, judging from the stratification we found. In order to investigate this hierarchy more closely, a numerical index of social status was worked out for each sport by considering the proportion of participants in each stratum.[27] According to this procedure there are four groups into which the individual types of sport can be classified:

		INDEX NUMBER
I.	tennis	209
	field hockey	186
	skiing	181
II.	rowing	141
	athletics	139
	swimming	136
	riding	133
III.	gymnastics	125
	canoeing	117
	table tennis	116
	apparatus gymnastics	106
	badminton	103

[26] Carl Diem and Gerda Engelhard, "Sport," in W. Bernsdorf and F. Bülow (editors), Dictionary of Sociology, Stuttgart, 1955, page 513.

[27] The index number was derived by allocating a zero to the lower class, a one to the lower middle class, a two to the middle middle class, and a three to the upper middle class.

	INDEX NUMBER
IV. field handball	87
field athletics	81
association football	68

According to data of Janowitz [28] the index number for the total population lies around 70. Consequently, football lies closest to the index for the general population, as far as its relationship to patterns of social stratification is concerned. Much of the popularity for this kind of sport can certainly be explained by this fact. Since Group IV corresponds largely to the general social stratification in the Federal German Republic, we could designate it as "sport of the common man."

Group III corresponds to the average index for young sportsmen, which lies at 110. This group can therefore be termed "middle class sports." Group II should therefore be called "the upper middle, and Group I the "elite" sports.

This assignment of the particular types of sports certainly contains one or two surprises. According to Diem and Engelhard,[29] one would certainly have expected to find riding at the head of the list, for they speak of it as an "artistocratic" kind of sport. However, the number of aristocratic riders is small in comparison to the large number of rural riders, who are mainly independent land-owners that should be assigned to the lower middle class, and in addition have some skilled laborers or farm laborers among them. In addition, a sub-division in the social stratification in riding would have to be made according to rural and urban population, for the social stratification has different characteristics in rural and urban communities.[30] The relatively low number of cases does not permit such a sub-division. Therefore, some reservations should be maintained with regard to the allocation of riders into the higher social group.

All of the types of sport that are not mentioned in the presentation had less than 30 cases in the sample. It appears that a fifth social group ought to be added to which boxing and cycling would belong. An interesting point is the high average social status of the basketball players investigated, for in the country of origin of this sport, namely the U.S.A., the class to which the players belong does not have that correspondingly high position. At this point we can establish our first thesis concerning the difference in stratification among the particular types of sport. *The newer a sport, the higher its social position; thus, fashionable trends in sport can clearly be seen.*[31] These developments help to explain at least in part the strikingly decreased social status of soccer or even of gymnastics since the turn of the century. Thus, even in

[28] An approximate calculation by us.

[29] Carl Diem and Gerda Engelhard, *loc. cit.*

[30] See Karl Martin Bolte, *Social Advancement and Regression*, Stuttgart, 1959, page 49.

[31] See in this connection René König, "Fashion in Human Society," in René König and Peter Schupisser (editors), *Fashion in Human Society*, Zürich, 1957, page 3.

some fields of sport the theory of Naumann concerning "sunken cultural traits," though a subject of great controversy in cultural sciences, can be applied. In order to explain the differential patterns of stratification in sport, a second thesis can be proposed, namely *that with increasing importance of individual achievement, the social status of a sport becomes higher.* This thesis can also be applied to the diminished status of non-competitive football and gymnastics, where less emphasis is placed upon achievement, since individual achievement has become evaluated more highly socially since the turn of the century. The third thesis is the following: *the higher the social status of a sport, as determined by the class to which its participants belong, the more it is dependent upon organization into clubs.*

The division of sports into four social categories as in our investigation is only provisional, particularly as a classification scheme for the overall population. However, such social categories have a definite relevance for the behavior of youths. Sportsmen in Social Group I did not select even a single sport in Social Group IV as their second most favorite sport, and vice versa, no one from the latter group quoted tennis, for example, alongside football as his favorite sport. When, however, sports were included in which youths participated in addition to their favorite sport (secondary sports) it was found that the social stratification determined on the basis of the favorite sport became somewhat erratic.

Sports that are played informally (that is, outside of clubs) or in schools show great divergence and thus equalize social classes. For example, badminton, table tennis, track and field, swimming, and skiing are practiced by sportsmen from the lower class as well as by those from the upper middle class frequently as the second or third favorite sport. However, they are selected relatively infrequently as favorite sports unless they are typical for that particular class of person. This is a clear confirmation of the relationship of class of particular sports, which is valid not only for Germany,[32] but according to the data of Roland von Euler also for Sweden.[33] The connection between social class and sport and individual types of sport is also evident for the U.S.A., although here detailed investigation must still be carried out.[34]

According to these results, for club-organized youths between 15 and 25 who represent more than a third of the total active and passive members

[32] A corresponding stratification can also be seen in an East German town following the not highly differentiated analysis by H. Perleberg, "The Social Stratification of Sports Participants in Individual Kinds of Sport," Thesis, Griefswald, 1955.

[33] Roland von Euler, "Work and Social Group," in Sten Svenson (editor), *Svensk Idrott,* Malmö, 1953, page 212.

[34] American sport is clearly stratified socially from the beginning by the fact that higher class people participate in sport in colleges, and lower non-academic classes in recreation. On the other hand the number of sports clubs is small. It is only the religious youth groups that correspond in their number of some degree with German club situation and thus give some indication of a similar stratification. See the passive interests and attitudes toward individual kinds of sports depending upon education and socio-economic level in Stone, *loc. cit.*

of German sports clubs, participation in sport is a rather general characteristic of those with a high social status in our society, and participation in certain kinds of sport, particularly those of the "common man" and "upper social group" serve largely as a criterion for membership in a certain social class. Thus differentiations can be seen in sport which are at least as strong as stratifications seen in the general population. Thus, for example, although according to objective criteria no great difference in social standing can be shown between football and gymnastics; yet in both sports the participants feel themselves to be clearly separated socially. On the basis of this fact, and in consideration of the results concerning the stratification in the particular sports, the question arises for sociology whether the class models given so far reflect such differentiations sufficiently or whether there are not barriers here at certain positions in the social rank order which would still not be adequately described by a six- or seven-strata model—set-up on the basis of objective characteristics that are not behavior specific—such as suggested in the work of Werner S. Landeckers on "Class Boundaries" in the U.S.A.[35]

Following this result it might be stated further that the selection of a sport is to be explained not only psychologically—as previously has almost invariably been the case in physical education—but sociologically—as based on class factors—as well. In some sports such as tennis or boxing, for example, they are of primary importance. Two main consequences follow from this connection between sport or particular types of sport and social class for the youths within the age groups in this study:

1. Participation in sports through clubs effects social integration in general, for the young sportsman encounters individuals belonging to the same class and experiences a system of norms and values that conform to the class his club represents. Sport is therefore an important factor in socialization within specific classes. The importance of sport for socialization to the general norms and values of a culture have been discussed elsewhere using the example of competitive sports.[36] The significance of sports for the socialization to the basic rules of social behavior in a group has been discussed by Rafael Helanko.[37] It follows from his figures that the influence of sport is dominant for a longer period than that of any other youth group activity.[38]

Thus, youth sport must not be regarded as an inconsequent leisure time activity, but be recognized even by the youths themselves (even if subconsciously) to be of importance for social integration in the broadest sense. This follows from the frequent appearance of sports in investigations of leisure time, where sport was found to be the "hardest" leisure time occupa-

[35] Werner S. Landecker, "Class Boundaries," *American Sociological Review*, Vol. 25, 1960/6.

[36] Günther Lüschen, "Active Sport and Its Dependence upon the Socio-Cultural System," *Zentralblatt für Arbeitswissenschaft*, 1962/12.

[37] Rafael Helanko, "Sports and Socialization," *Acta Sociologica*, Vol. 2, 1957, page 229.

[38] Rafael Helanko, *loc. cit.*, page 232.

tion alongside reading.[39] However, if the method of time-budgeting had been applied during the investigations, it would probably have been found that active participation in sport would certainly not have taken such a top place.

2. A second consequence of the relationship between social status and sport follows from its importance for social integration: sport can be a lever for socially mobile persons. The extent to which this is the case is discussed in the following section.

Social Mobility Among Young Sportsmen

Two-thirds of the youths interrogated stated that they were attempting to obtain a "better position" than their parents. However, only 35 percent feel certain that they will improve, whereas 29 percent state that they would "possibly" attain a better position than their parents. Distinct variations are found depending upon the social class.

EXPECTED SOCIAL MOBILITY COMPARED WITH
PARENTS ACCORDING TO CLASS
(Question: Do you believe that you will attain this position?)

IN PERCENT	LOWER CLASS	LOWER MIDDLE	MIDDLE MIDDLE	UPPER MIDDLE
Yes	32	43	38	30
Possibly	41	28	27	17
Do Not Expect Improvement	27	27	39	53
n =	613	655	394	208

A feeling of self-improvement is encountered most frequently among track and field athletes (47 percent) and among top level performers in general (44 percent). It is interesting in connection with the possible influence of an achievement oriented system towards level of personal achievement motivation, that a higher expectation of definite improvement is encountered among Catholics—39 percent—than among Protestants—33 percent ($p < 0.10$).

Naturally it is not possible to draw a final conclusion concerning the extent of inter-generational mobility, that is the increase or decrease from one class to another, for sporting youths in comparison to the extent of general mobility, for the final social position of such young people is not yet established.[40]

An aspect of final mobility that is relatively certain, concerns the differences between manual and non-manual occupations of male youth. Practically all manual occupations are represented within the age range of those investi-

---

[39] See Viggo Graf Blücher, *Leisure Time in Industrial Society*, Stuttgart, 1956.

[40] Comparability of the numbers of socially mobile is necessarily restricted, for this depends upon the empirical number of classes selected.

gated (15.7–25.7 yrs., mean = 20.0). The few who may fail middle-school (weiterführende Schulen) and become workers, are statistically trivial. Youth who have reached at least the middle-school mid-point cannot be expected to enter a manual occupation. Therefore, a declaration concerning the mobility of manual and non-manual workers is already possible, with the only important source of uncertainty being those manually working youth who later become self-employed, or through technical high schools get into leading positions.

MOBILITY BETWEEN MANUAL AND NON-MANUAL
FATHER-SON-OCCUPATIONS

| | OCCUPATION OF FATHER | |
| | NON-MANUAL IN % | MANUAL IN % |
OCCUPATION OF SON [a]		
Non-Manual	76.0	33.5
Manual	23.0	64.5
Unclassified	1.0	2.0
N	901	496

[a] Pupils of middle-school are classified as non-manual

In comparison with the Lipset and Bendix [41] data on mobility between manual and non-manual occupations from three German investigations, wherein very different results were found regarding downward mobility (between 20 and 38%), sporting youth, judging by the above figures, apparently exhibit a lesser downward mobility from non-manual to manual occupations. With further development of their careers this is certainly to be expected, for, on the one hand, the above-mentioned tendency to rise to self-employed positions or to an engineer or architect, and on the other hand, a generally stronger intra-generational mobility towards non-manual occupations, are likely. In consideration of these factors, the definitely significant differences in the number of mobile persons from manual occupations in the parent generation to non-manual occupations of the sons is certainly higher among sporting youth than in the overall population, for whom Lipset and Bendix give an average value of 29 percent.[42] This difference is admittedly not very large according to the mobility that can be recognized at present, and for an improved final appraisal subjects for comparable age groups would need to be examined. However, data of this kind are not available.

Renate Mayntz claims that over a quarter of skilled laborers' sons enter non-manual occupations,[43] thus confirming the slightly positive tendency among sporting youths.

[41] Seymour M. Lipset and Reinhard Bendix, Social Mobility in Industrial Society. Second edition, Berkeley and Los Angeles, 1960, page 17.

[42] Lipset and Bendix, loc. cit., page 25.

[43] R. Mayntz, loc. cit., page 164.

For a large number of the youths investigated, mobility from one social class to another can already be recognized. With due consideration to their education, and the occupation and occupational status of the youths and their fathers the numbers that can be considered to be inter-generationally mobile are as follows:

Upwardly mobile	14%
Downwardly mobile	7%

n = 1880

Since here again very sharp discriminations were made, borderline cases are not contained in the socially improving group, whereas, a number of controversial cases were considered to be downwardly mobile. In view of this, the ratio of upward to downward mobility should be described as favorable, for both Janowitz [44] and also the data of Lipset and Bendix [45] indicate a slightly higher value for downward inter-generational mobility in the Federal German Republic. Regardless of the intra-generational mobility for the group of persons investigated, which cannot yet be evaluated, the observed positive relationship is of considerable significance, because sporting youth has on account of its higher social status, a greater chance of regression than the average for the overall population. The mobility within the lower class, which on account of the small proportion of unskilled and partially skilled laborers among the youths studied can almost invariably lead only to a rise in social status, is not considered in the figures of 14 and 7 percent for the reasons already given.

Upward and Downwardly Mobile Sportsmen

The two groups of upward and downwardly mobile young sportsmen were examined more closely with respect to their attitudes and behavioral patterns because conclusions can be drawn from these two dichotomous groups concerning the general social function of sport, a subject which has always been of great controversy. Both friends and critics of sport were able to illustrate their arguments with examples, but seldom were in the position to determine the significance of these examples and to present proof of the extent to which sport was in fact "a cultural parasite phenomenon" [46] or "the great hope of the future." [47]

The first question discussed at this point will concern the correlation between high achievement in sport and social mobility. The criterion for high achievement chosen by us was second place or better in local championships in individual sports, and the regional championship in team sports. Thus, the

[44] M. Janowitz, loc. cit., page 12.
[45] Lipset and Bendix, loc. cit., page 25.
[46] Alfred Peters, Psychology of Sport, Leipzig, 1927, page 58.
[47] Heinz Risse, Sociology of Sport, Berlin, 1921, page 5.

number of sportsmen with high achievement among the total numbers for
our groups were:

	IN PERCENT	TOTAL N
Upwardly mobile	25	263
Downwardly mobile	7	133
Stationary	15	1484
Average	16	1880

On the basis of these results it can be stated with a high degree of certainty that in the age group of those studied sport compensates for poor performance in occupation or school to only a small degree. That it does indeed
fulfill this function for a small group is shown by the seven percent of the
sportsmen with respectable performances who were included in the downwardly mobile group. However, based on the total number examined, this
represents only 0.5 percent. Much more important is the group of upwardly
mobile sportsmen with championship class performance who represent a
sizable proportion of 3.5 percent of the total and represent a strongly influential reference group. About half of them occupy leadership positions, while
not a single important office (club officer, training leader, youth counselor)
was occupied by the downwardly mobile individuals.

The factors considered to be "the most important characteristics of
a gymnast or sportsman" by the upwardly mobile group in contrast to the
downwardly mobile group seemed to be important for an appreciation of the
values and norms recognized among sporting youth. Two groups of tendencies in these values can be recognized:

1. A personal partnership attitude (comradeship, fairness, honesty, team
   spirit, self-control)
2. An impersonal sporting attitude (stamina, performance, physique,
   training effort, love of sport)

The distribution of values and norms among upwardly mobile and downwardly mobile sportsmen was as follows:

	MOBILITY	
	UPWARD IN PERCENT	DOWNWARD IN PERCENT
Personal partnership attitude	67	47
Impersonal sporting attitude	26	47
Other	7	6
	n = 263	133

More replies were given to this question by upwardly mobile individuals.
In order to make a comparison, the total number of replies was expressed in
percentages. This shows that with a high degree of confidence ($\chi^2 = 25.6$, 2
degrees of freedom, $p < 0.001$) that upwardly mobile sportsmen are oriented

more strongly towards personal partnership relationships than downwardly mobile individuals. This may be very significant in view of the general correlation between n-achievement and n-affiliation which is found by McClelland not to be clear cut, and sometimes even negative, since the personal partnership values and norms of sporting youths could be considered as being related to the syndrome of "affiliation." [48] The entire system of norms and values of sporting youths also exhibits this general tendency, according to our findings, so that an influence of sport on the struggle for achievement in society with the involvement of personal partnership values and norms, is to be expected. Consequently, dangers attributed to the system of sport on account of its orientation towards high performance which might lead to a one-sided socialization of dubious value from the partnership point of view, should be considered to be small, since the value system of sportsmen themselves exerts a regulatory effect.

Compared with the total number investigated and the downwardly mobile group, the upwardly mobile sportsmen exhibit in many areas the same capacity for achievement as revealed in their sport. Thus, this group has a stronger than average interest in politics. In their replies to the question of what concerned them most in politics most were able to provide intelligent comments on the East-West conflict, as well as on domestic and party politics, whereas half of the downwardly mobile sportsmen had no interest whatsoever in politics. It is interesting that with regard to their attitudes toward work, no great deviations were found between upwardly and downwardly mobile groups. The number of people satisfied with their position is admittedly significantly higher among the upwardly mobile, but the difference between 66 and 50 percent for complete and 29 and 23 percent for tentative satisfaction, does reveal a smaller difference than might have been expected. The slight tendency to substitute sport for "social function" should also be considered in this light. It is significant that the personal relationships at the work place for the downwardly mobile youths are just as good as those of the total sample, who in contrast to youth in general, have a very well balanced relationship with their colleagues at work.[49]

Although we have established the influence of sport on the relationship between performance and personal partnership values and norms, in view of the correlation between sporting achievement and upward social mobility, it might in addition be suspected that sport is, in fact, a stimulating element for social improvement. However, a detailed analysis of this question would be essential, and cannot be deduced from the material available at the moment. The extent to which the various sports correlate with mobility is shown in the table below for the favorite sports indulged in by upwardly and downwardly mobile youths.

[48] See D. C. McClelland, *loc. cit.*, page 159.

[49] See EMNID, *loc. cit.*, page 236. Here too the question examined is somewhat different, so that the actually favorable values found for sporting youth must remain hypothetical.

According to this summary we find individuals more frequently choosing team sports. Moreover, downwardly mobile sportsmen are only seldom encountered in those individual sports in which the principle of effort and achievement is of relatively great importance (track and field, skiing, tennis, and even rowing). On the other hand, downwardly mobile sportsmen are found more frequently in individual sports that place less emphasis on performance (gymnastics, "Turnen," badminton). The difference for male gymnasts (11 percent of the upwardly, and 16 percent of the downwardly mobile) is even more significant. Competitive swimming is oriented towards performance, but not pleasure swimming, which was included in the category of

	MOBILITY		DIRECTION	SIGNIFICANCE
	UPWARD	DOWNWARD	OF DIFFERENCE	OF DIFFERENCE
Football	18	25	negative	$p < 0.10$
"Turnen"	15	16	negative	none
Gymnastics	8	9	negative	none
Track and Field	19	11	positive	$p < 0.05$
Swimming	4	11	negative	$p < 0.01$
European Handball	8	9	negative	none
Tennis	6	4	positive	none
Table Tennis	6	3	positive	$(p < 0.2)$
Skiing	5	3	positive	none
Badminton	2	4	negative	none
Hockey	1	5	negative	$p < 0.01$
Rowing	4	—	positive	$p < 0.05$
Boxing	—	4	negative	$p < 0.01$
Riding	0.5	5	negative	$p < 0.01$
Cycling	1	3	negative	none
Other	15	13	positive	none

n = 263   133

(replicate sampling)

swimming. The fact that downwardly mobile individuals are frequently encountered in boxing and cycling is probably due to the low social status of these sports. In addition, participation in boxing could be explained by the frustration-aggression hypothesis (destructive character of aggression), which might be used more often as an explanation for social recession. With regard to riding, again attention should be called to the different conditions prevalent in rural areas. Two-thirds of the non-inheriting sons of self-employed farmers are downwardly mobile according to the results of Janowitz; [50] while only 4 percent are upwardly mobile. The fact that such downwardly mobile farmers' sons are able to participate in riding in their youth without much effort explains this connection satisfactorily.

It is not surprising that upwardly mobile individuals prefer to participate in the sports that are typical of their reference group. It is, however, somewhat

[50] M. Janowitz, loc. cit., page 15.

surprising that downwardly mobile sportsmen also have their "reference group" but tend to turn more strongly towards the sports of the "common man," although one would expect them to prefer the reference groups associated with Sport Groups I and II, on the basis of their parental status. However, the chances of attaining social improvement from this group is not great so that this relationship is only logical. Both trends substantiate the importance of sport for socialization into the class of which one is already a member.

In conclusion, a comparison between the education of the fathers and that of the youth is made from which it follows that the membership in sporting clubs lasts longer among those youths who are more definitely upwardly mobile. The number of youths grouped according to age attending schools leading to higher education was:

	AGE		
	15–18	19–21	22–25
Fathers	44.5	32	31
Youths	50.5	51	45
	n = 787	554	539

The proportion of youths attending high schools or universities whose fathers had only grade school education is highest in the age group 19–21 and lowest in the age group 15–18. Obviously sport and the club give these youths that self-confidence and behavior which they do not find in their family in the struggle for social improvement. Such a function of sport is indeed probably most important in the age group 19–21, for these are the years in which the transfer to universities occurs, and this is the most important period in which the mobile youth from the lower class needs support in his ambition to improve his social status. The clear disparity with the first age group confirms the extent to which sport is of importance for socialization into the values of a higher class.

Summary

On the basis of an investigation among club-organized sportsmen between the ages of 15 and 25 it was established that sport as a whole is preferentially a leisure-time activity of the middle class and of skilled laborers oriented towards the middle class. Nevertheless, even within sport a general stratification was found according to types of sport, which is at least as well differentiated as social classes otherwise recognizable in the general population. With the aid of a simple status index, four groups of sport were formed whose relevancy to the behavior of sporting youth could be established and which could also be used as secondary indices of social status. The interrelationship between sport and social status has consequences for socialization and the establishment of norms and values conforming to each social class.

On the other hand, this relationship to class can also be used as a lever for upward social mobility. A relatively large number of upwardly mobile young persons are found among sporting youth, with their sports and clubs providing important support in their mobility efforts. The system of norms and values maintained by sporting youth have a positive influence on the attitude found in modern society of respect for one's neighbor while still emphasizing the principle of achievement. This follows from the correlation found between the fundamental importance of the principle of achievement in sport, and the norms and values oriented towards comradeship and partnership. Although one or two of the conclusions are still somewhat hypothetical, active participation in sport during youth can definitely be said to make a positive contribution to the "structural problems in mass society" [51] (in direct contrast to the accusation of cultural destruction mostly made against it). Although a tendency towards conspicious consumption can be detected in some fields of sport, this cannot be considered as dominating to the extent that was to be expected from the views expressed at the beginning. Physiologically and psychologically—since it is manifestly considered by the sportsmen to be a release from tension—and to a certain extent even sociologically, sport may have compensatory functions. However, it is primarily characterized by its functioning for the security and advancement of social life. Thus, work and sport, for example, are not at contrasting poles but exhibit a close relationship.[52] This conclusion may be valid only for this particular leisure activity. However, it is probable that similar structures can also be detected in other leisure pursuits.[53] Certainly, in a society which is divided more and more into classes based upon personal achievement, sport (particularly in its active form) is acquiring an increased importance.

[51] René König, "Problems of Form in Mass Society," in Franz Greib and Fritz Meyer (editors), Economy, Society and Culture. Jubilee Volume for Alfred Müller-Armack, Berlin, 1961, page 559. See also René König, "Leisure Time as a Problem for Modern Man," Universitas, 1961/5.

[52] On the basis of a preliminary count carried out by hand we found in the investigation on "occupation and leisure time" we are carrying out at the moment that sportsmen in Nordrhein-Westfallen participate principally in the kinds of sport that correspond to their occupation.

[53] Compare with the fundamental basic questions here the article by Harold L. Wilensky, "Work, Careers, and Social Integration," Leisure and Society, Special issue of the International Social Science Journal, October, 1960. See also Max Kaplan, Leisure in America, New York, 1960, page 21.

secondary schools and
oxbridge blues

JOHN EGGLESTON

A number of studies have been undertaken to examine the relationship between pre-university schooling and achievement at the university.[1] Almost without exception, however, these studies have been concerned with academic achievement in the undergraduate or post-graduate course and, especially, achievement in final first degree examinations. This is curious in view of the widely held beliefs in the social and other nonacademic advantages to be gained from university life. Indeed concentration on a narrow range of largely examination-based criteria of achievement is something of an ideational and methodological problem in the sociology of education. There are some obvious reasons for this, notably the problems and hazards of measurement of achievement in student societies, extracurricula activities and the other intangibles of student life.[2]

An area where such problems may be overcome is that of athletic performance, where identifiable and measurable marks of achievement exist. Notable amongst these are the "colours" which are awarded in most universities by the student body, for membership of a representative team or club. Of particular interest in Britain are the colours of Oxford and Cambridge, known as "Blues." They are of interest not only for their indication of student achievement but also for their elitist associations within the university and their repute as counters in the subsequent occupational and social status of their holders. University lore is rich in tales which equate the value of an Oxbridge blue with that of a "First" and the reputed composition of the

[1] For example W. D. Furneaux, *The Chosen Few*, 1961; J. G. H. Newfield, "The Academic Performance of British University Students" in *Sociological Studies in British University Education*, Sociological Review Monograph No. 7, University of Keele, 1964; G. D. N. Worswick, "Anatomy of Oxbridge," *Times Educational Supplement*, 3.5.57, pp. 596–7.

[2] Such problems have of course been overcome by some workers in this field, for example J. Coleman, *The Adolescent Society*, 1961.

• From the *British Journal of Sociology* 16, No. 3 (1965), 232–242. Published by the proprietors of Routledge and Kegan Paul, Ltd., Broadway House, 68–74 Carter Lane, London, E.C.4 for the London School of Economics and Political Science. The writer wishes to acknowledge his gratitude to Paul Gaskin, physical education master at Great Barr Comprehensive School, Birmingham, for collecting much of the data used in the survey, also to the following persons for their helpful criticism and advice: Miss F. Conway, Dept. of Economics, University of Leicester; E. Dunning, Dept. of Sociology, University of Leicester; J. S. Hardie, Principal, Loughborough Training College; G. Murray, Marlborough College; C. S. Sayer, Head of Physical Education Dept., Loughborough Training College; R. Wight, School of Education, University of Leicester.

upper echelons of some occupational groups, notably the Church of England ministry, suggests that this may not be entirely without foundation.[3] Certainly the situation is of considerable interest as a model of nonexpanding status availability in conditions of expanding demand which has many parallels in education.

Several studies exist which list the scores of blues obtained by ex-pupils of the various schools in the major university sports.[4] Such studies, though indicating a lengthening of the list of schools from which blues emerge, none the less reveal the persistence of a striking concentration of blue awards to the ex-pupils of some of the major public schools. Blues from ex-pupils of the local education authority schools, though increasing in number are rarely concentrated in a small range of schools, rather they tend to be widely spread and non-recurring.

This study involves examination of the evidence in a different way, to discover if the well-established differential in chance of admission to Oxbridge between the public school and local education authority grammar school population [5] is matched by similar differences in chance of award of a blue.

Investigation of schools of origin of blues presents no major research problem, membership of university teams on qualifying for the award of blues is recorded, with the names of the members school in parenthesis, in the national press and the appropriate sporting almanacs.[6] Using these sources an investigation of the schools of origin of Oxford and Cambridge blues over a ten-year period—1953–54 to 1962–63—was undertaken. To facilitate subsequent comparison the schools of origin were classified in the manner used by

[3] It is hoped to undertake subsequent work in this field.

[4] For example "Schools Behind the Boat Race," *Times Educational Supplement*, 27.3.64, p. 798, and R. McKelvie, "Blues and the Schools," *The Field*, 2.4.64, pp. 625–6. The article lists the top ten "blues producing" schools in five sports for the years 1946–63 as follows:

  Cricket: Dulwich 18; Charterhouse 15; Winchester 15; Repton 12; Eton 9; Radley 8; Rugby 8; Harrow 7; Manchester G.S. 7; Sherborne 7.

  Athletics: Eton 17; Manchester G.S. 16; Epsom 13; Oundle 13; Kingswood 12; Marlborough 12; Wellington 12; Sherborne 11; Malvern 10; Dulwich 10.

  Rowing: Eton 51; Shrewsbury 35; Radley 23; Winchester 17; Oundle 14; Bedford 13; St. Paul's 13; St. Edward's 11; Bryanston 9; Monkton Coombe 9.

  Association Football: Repton 21; Shrewsbury 15; Manchester G.S. 14; Malvern 13; Royal Liberty, Romford 13; Barnsley G.S. 12; Brentwood 11; Charterhouse 9; Winchester 8; Alleyn's 8; Forest 8; St. Clement Danes 8.

  Rugby: Oundle 28; Fettes 15; Sedborgh 14; Marling 13; Clifton 10; Rugby 9; Bristol G.S. 8; Blundell's 8; Tonbridge 7; Stonyhurst 7; Birkenhead 7.

[5] R. K. Kelsall, *Report on an enquiry into applications for admission to Universities Association of Universities of the British Commonwealth*, 1957; Robbins Report. *Higher Education*, Appendix 2B, "Students and their education," H.M.S.O., 1964.

[6] For this study the sources used were the annual issues of Wisden *Cricketers' Almanack* and Playfair *Rugby Annual* and the issues of *The Times* appearing on days following the annual University Association Football match.

Kelsall in the study of admissions to universities in 1955.[7] This classification contained four categories of home schools:

1. Independent schools in membership of the Headmasters' Conference. Schools in membership of the Conference but which were aided by direct grant from the Ministry of Education or fully maintained by Local Education Authorities were not included in this category. Schools in this category are predominantly public schools and will be described by this name (PUBLIC).
2. Direct grant schools. As all direct grant schools featuring in the ten-year survey were, interestingly, in membership of the H.M.C. these schools will be referred to as H.M.C. DIRECT GRANT.
3. Secondary grammer schools maintained by local education authorities. Schools described as 'transitionally assisted,' 'voluntarily controlled' and 'voluntarily aided' were included in this category (MAINTAINED GRAMMAR SCHOOLS).
4. Other schools, most of the schools included in this category are the independent schools not in membership of the H.M.C. (PRIVATE).

So that the larger variables in sporting tradition and facilities between the different categories of schools could be minimized the survey was confined to three major sports: association football, rugby football, and cricket, the most generally available sports in home schools providing full-time education for boys prior to university entrance. Cricket is common to all but a tiny handful of such schools and rugby became increasingly so as many maintained grammar schools adopted this code during the survey period. Association football is the least general of the three; it is played by only 13 of the 80 independent boarding schools in Category 1 and by decreasing numbers of Category 3 schools. It is included because of its complementary relationship to rugby football. No school plays neither code and it is possible for rugby schools to produce soccer blues (there is no record of the converse). The inclusion of association football also offered an opportunity to ascertain if categories of schools under-represented in rugby blues had compensating over-representation in association blues.

This selection of sports has involved the elimination of a number of notable university sports, including rowing, where there is still widely differing opportunity for participation between different categories of schools and where "blue opportunity" is still strikingly concentrated on the ex-pupils of a small group of public schools.[8] Athletics was also eliminated as the wide range of track and field events involves a wide range of facilities making useful comparison of the kind envisaged difficult.

The results of the survey are set in Table 1 and summarized in Table 2. The numbers are numbers of blues not numbers of individuals as it is possible

[7] R. H. Kelsall, *op. cit.*, pp. 7–8.

[8] The concentration of schools producing rowing blues is discussed in "Schools Behind the Boat Race," *Times Educational Supplement*, 27.3.64, p. 798. It is reported that of the 180 rowing blues awarded between 1955 and 1964, 120 went to ex-pupils of 10 public schools.

for one individual to be capped for two, three, or even four years in succession, competing anew each year. Award of blues in more than one sport is possible. A notable case in recent years is that of an ex-pupil of Tadcaster Grammar School, M. Ralph, who won six blues—three for association football, three for athletics.

table 1

(a) SCHOOLS OF ORIGIN OF OXFORD AND CAMBRIDGE BLUES IN ASSOCIATION FOOTBALL, 1953/4–1962/3 SEASONS

YEAR	OXFORD						CAMBRIDGE					
	1	2	3	4	OVER-SEAS	ALL	1	2	3	4	OVER-SEAS	ALL
53/4	3	—	8	—	—	11	3	1	6	1	—	11
54/5	3	—	8	—	—	11	4	2	5	—	—	11
55/6	3	—	8	—	—	11	4	3	5	—	—	12
56/7	3	1	7	—	—	11	3	2	6	—	—	11
57/8	5	1	5	—	—	11	—	2	9	—	—	11
58/9	5	2	4	—	—	11	—	4	7	—	—	11
59/60	3	2	6	—	—	11	1	4	6	—	—	11
60/1	5	1	5	—	—	11	2	3	6	—	—	11
61/2	7	—	4	—	—	11	2	1	7	1	—	11
62/3	2	1	8	—	—	11	2	—	8	1	—	11
Totals	39	8	63	—	—	110	21	22	65	3	—	111
%	35.5	7.3	57.2	—	—	100	18.9	19.8	58.6	2.7	—	100

(b) SCHOOLS OF ORIGIN OF OXFORD AND CAMBRIDGE BLUES IN RUGBY FOOTBALL, 1953/4–1962/3 SEASONS

YEAR	OXFORD						CAMBRIDGE					
	1	2	3	4	OVER-SEAS	ALL	1	2	3	4	OVER-SEAS	ALL
53/4	4	—	1	1	9	15	13	1	—	1	—	15
54/5	5	2	1	1	6	15	10	1	—	2	2	15
55/6	6	1	2	5	3	17	8	—	2	5	—	15
56/7	7	3	2	—	3	15	9	1	1	3	1	15
57/8	6	3	5	—	1	15	9	—	2	3	1	15
58/9	3	3	6	—	3	15	9	—	3	3	—	15
59/60	6	1	7	—	1	15	8	2	2	3	—	15
60/1	8	—	5	—	2	15	4	2	6	3	—	15
61/2	11	—	1	2	1	15	8	—	6	1	—	15
62/3	9	—	1	2	3	15	10	1	4	—	—	15
Totals	65	13	31	11	32	152	88	8	26	24	4	150
%	42.7	8.6	20.4	7.2	21.1	100	58.7	5.3	17.3	16.0	2.7	100

(c) SCHOOLS OF ORIGIN OF OXFORD AND CAMBRIDGE BLUES IN CRICKET, 1953/4–1962/3 SEASONS

	OXFORD						CAMBRIDGE					
YEAR	1	2	3	4	OVER-SEAS	ALL	1	2	3	4	OVER-SEAS	ALL
53/4	6	1	—	—	4	11	7	—	—	—	4	11
54/5	7	—	—	—	3	10	6	2	—	—	3	11
55/6	8	1	—	—	2	11	6	2	—	—	3	11
56/7	7	2	—	—	1	10	4	2	—	1	2	9
57/8	7	3	—	—	1	11	3	2	1	1	4	11
58/9	3	5	1	—	2	11	6	1	1	—	2	10
59/60	3	5	—	—	3	11	7	1	1	1	1	11
60/1	5	3	—	—	3	11	6	—	2	1	2	11
61/2	7	1	—	—	3	11	5	2	2	1	1	11
62/3	8	—	—	—	3	11	7	1	2	—	1	11
Totals	61	21	1	—	25	108	57	13	9	5	23	107
%	56.5	19.4	0.9	—	23.2	100	53.3	12.1	8.4	4.7	21.5	100

The tables indicate interesting variations in the membership of the teams in each sport and between the universities. In both universities for all the survey years public schools predominate in cricket and rugby, in both sports the representation of the maintained grammar schools is small, 20.4 percent and 17.3 percent respectively in rugby and only 0.93 percent and 8.4 percent respectively in cricket. The small showing of the maintained grammar school in cricket is particularly notable in view of the widespread availability of this sport in the schools, their score during the survey period amounted to nine Cambridge cricket blues and only one Oxford blue, in neither university had there ever been more than one ex-maintained grammar school boy in any team. Only in association football does the maintained grammar school pupil appear in large numbers, in almost all the teams in this sport he has comprised the largest group, often holding an absolute majority of places over players from all other types of school.

It is noticeable that only in rugby has Oxford offered a greater number of blues to the maintained grammar school pupils than has Cambridge. In association football Cambridge has offered slightly more, in cricket nine times as many. At both universities the H.M.C. direct grant schools are well represented, notably in cricket, where, despite a substantially smaller number of undergraduates, their score of blues exceeds that of the maintained grammar schools, strikingly so at Oxford. Table 1 indicates however that the strength of the H.M.C. direct grant schools may be declining; this is discussed later. The private schools play little part as a source of blues with the exception of the rugby XVs at Cambridge—an exception largely accounted for by the notable ex-pupils of Marling school.

table 2

SUMMARY OF SCHOOLS OF ORIGIN OF OXFORD AND CAMBRIDGE BLUES IN ASSOCIATION FOOTBALL, RUGBY FOOTBALL AND CRICKET, 1953/4–1962/3 SEASONS

OXFORD

SCHOOL OF ORIGIN	1		2		3		4		OVERSEAS		SURVEY NOS. (= 100%)
	N	%	N	%	N	%	N	%	N	%	
Assn. Football	39	35.4	8	7.3	63	57.2	—	—	—	—	110
Rugby Football	65	42.7	13	8.6	31	20.4	11	7.2	32	21.1	152
All Football	104	39.7	21	8.0	94	35.9	11	4.2	32	12.2	262
Cricket	61	56.5	21	19.4	1	0.9	—	—	25	23.2	108
All blues in these sports	165	44.6	42	11.4	95	25.7	11	2.9	57	15.4	370

CAMBRIDGE

SCHOOL OF ORIGIN	1		2		3		4		OVERSEAS		SURVEY NOS. (= 100%)
	N	%	N	%	N	%	N	%	N	%	
Assn. Football	21	18.9	22	19.8	65	58.6	3	2.7	—	—	111
Rugby Football	88	58.7	8	5.3	26	17.3	24	16.0	4	2.7	150
All Football	109	41.2	30	11.5	91	34.9	27	10.3	4	1.5	261
Cricket	57	53.3	13	12.1	9	8.4	5	4.7	23	21.5	107
All blues in these sports	166	45.1	43	11.7	100	27.2	32	8.7	27	7.3	368

It is possible to compare the survey figures with the contribution of the various categories of schools to the total male undergraduate population of Oxford and Cambridge on two occasions during the period under consideration and calculate the relative chances of achieving a blue for students from different schools of origin. The first of these is in the mid-1950s. For the year 1955–56 Kelsall provides a breakdown of the total first-year undergraduate population by schools of origin. To achieve a basis of calculation it has been assumed that these figures are representative of the total undergraduate population of the year following 1956–57, that is of the total entry for the years 1954, 1955, and 1956. Recent evidence [9] of the slow change of the relative distribution of the schools of origin of Oxford and Cambridge undergraduates suggests that the error involved in this assumption is likely to be more an absolute one than a relative one. Accordingly the numbers of 1955–56 first-year students have been increased threefold to form a basis for calculating the rates shown in Table 3(a). (This is still not an entirely adequate base as the period eligibility for a blue can extend to a fourth undergraduate or post-graduate year. It has proved impossible to achieve any adequate basis for calculating this small additional population and it has therefore been ignored. There is some suggestion, however, that it offers a relatively greater "blue advantage" to the fee-paying student—most generally of independent or overseas school origin.)

For the year 1961–62 details of the schools of origin of the total undergraduate population are available from the Robbins Report.[10] The figures quoted in the Report are based on a sampling fraction of 1 in 22 and to provide a basis of calculation the figures are therefore multiplied by 22. The assumption this time may be justified by the very close reported correspondence of the achieved sample to the sample population envisaged.[11] The rates thereby calculated are shown in Table 3(b). The qualification concerning fourth-year eligibility applied to Table 3(a) also applies here.

Table 3(a) and (b) indicates interesting variations in the chance of achieving a blue for boys from different categories of school. Perhaps the most striking result, however, is the decline in the chances of the H.M.C. direct grant pupils—from a dominance in all sports in 1956–57 to an inferior chance in football to all other schools and a much reduced chance in cricket in 1962–63. Though the small numbers of pupils from these schools accentuate the apparent significance of small fluctuations, inspection of Table 1 suggests that these are not a-typical years and that the position of these schools had declined since the late 1950s.

Major interest centers on the relative chances of the public and the maintained grammar school boy. In both years the public school boys in close association with the small number of private school boys had a greater

[9] Robbins Report, *Higher Education*, Appendix 2B, "Students and their education," H.M.S.O., 1964, p. 12.
[10] *Ibid.*, p. 9.
[11] *Ibid.*, p. 553.

table 3

OXFORD AND CAMBRIDGE BLUES PER 1,000 UNDERGRADUATE POPULATION
ORIGINATING FROM THE HOME SCHOOL CATEGORIES

(a)

SCHOOL OF ORIGIN	NUMBER OF MEN PER 1,000 [a] IN EACH SCHOOL CATEGORY ACHIEVING BLUES IN				
	SOCCER	RUGBY	ALL FOOTBALL	CRICKET	ALL 3 SPORTS
1	1.1	3	4.1	2.1	6.2
2	2.5	3.3	5.8	3.3	9.1
3	3.9	0.9	4.8	0.0	4.8
4	0.0	4.7	4.7	1.5	6.3
All	2.1	2.5	4.6	1.5	6.1

(b)

SCHOOL OF ORIGIN	NUMBER OF MEN PER 1,000 [a] IN EACH SCHOOL CATEGORY ACHIEVING BLUES IN				
	SOCCER	RUGBY	ALL FOOTBALL	CRICKET	ALL 3 SPORTS
1 and 4	1.5	3.4	4.9	2.0	6.9
2	0.5	0.0	0.5	1.7	2.2
3	3.2	2.0	5.2	0.6	5.8
All	1.9	2.4	4.3	1.5	5.9

[a] See comment on basis of calculation in text.

chance of winning a blue once at Oxbridge. If his considerably greater chance
of entry to Oxbridge is taken into account along with this his far greater
opportunity of winning a blue, with its short term and long term rewards,
becomes clearly evident. Within the university the absolute chance of the
independent school pupil is greater in 1961–62 than in 1956–57. His relative
chance compared with the maintained grammar school boy is however slightly
diminished; indeed the chance of the maintained grammar school boys shows
a modest absolute and relative improvement, both categories benefiting from
the decline of the H.M.C. direct grant schools performance. But the maintained grammar school boys' main source of blue opportunity is concentrated
in both years in the lower-status sport of association football. This has indeed
compensated for their lower chance in rugby and has given them a higher
over-all chance of football blues than the independent schools. As the maintained grammar schools adopt rugby there is some evidence of improvement
in the chance of their pupils in this sport. It is in cricket, the sport common
to all the schools, that the disadvantage of the maintained grammar school

boy is most marked. Indeed the chance of a cricket blue can hardly be said to exist for the maintained grammar school boy—inspection of Table 1 indicates that the situation in the years under discussion is representative of the total survey period. This inferior chance of a blue in cricket seems the major factor in the over-all inferior chance of boys from the maintained grammar schools within the universities.[12]

The study indicates that type of school attended is identified as being associated with differential chances of blues and that these chances are further differentiated as between different sports of different status. The full extent of these differences is, of course, only incompletely brought out in this study because of the incomplete range of sports considered, and particularly by the elimination of rowing where the chance of achieving a blue is still strikingly associated with having been a pupil at one of a limited number of public schools.

It must be emphasized that there is no evidence of any kind of overt bias in the selection procedures of any university teams. (This might be tested by examining the number of blues achieving "caps.") Indeed the selection procedure is usually carried out in a highly public manner in the various trial games and seems to embody a genuine attempt to ensure objective assessment of the candidates' prowess.

It is suggested that the disadvantages of the maintained grammar school pupil in rugby and cricket springs from differences in social experience rather than sporting ability. The nuances of team play at university, communication between players, rhythm and pattern of play may be familiar to the boy from the independent school but subtly different from those to which the boy from the maintained grammar school is accustomed. These differences may be reinforced by the coaching techniques and even the coaching language employed. There is also the problem of "outside" feeling by the grammar school boy in a group largely comprising of and often led by boys from a different educational and social background, backgrounds which are often shared in view of the tight concentration of "blue producing" schools in Category 1 in each sport—often with interlocking and exclusive fixture lists. This is in marked contrast with the diffusion of maintained grammar schools producing blues, where a potential blue may have never encountered a blue, and may never consider the possibility of aspiring to be one or even to go to Oxbridge.[13]

[12] Further analysis, suggested during the survey, indicates:

(a) In rugby, position of play may possibly be related to school of origin, forwards coming mainly from the public schools.

(b) Some Oxbridge colleges may offer the grammar school boy a more favorable chance of a blue—notably St. Edmund's Hall.

[13] An interesting parallel with the conditions of student entry to Oxbridge is described in a recent article by Michael Brook:

"Suppose two boys of comparable ability, both fit to be commoners at Oxford, one at a famous public school, the other at a two-stream maintained school. The first headmaster has candidates for Oxford every year and is known in several colleges. He is an

Even in association football where the maintained grammar school boys predominate the largest single group of old blues and aspirant blues may well be the ex-pupils of one of the public schools which specialize in this sport.

There are also differences in the sporting opportunities of boys from the different educational backgrounds, even though cricket and one of the football codes are common to all. The boy from the public school is far more likely to have been under the influence of a former blue as a consequence of the staffing policy of these schools which leads to the appointment of old blues and international players as games specialists. The maintained grammar school however tends to favour the college-trained physical education teacher and may even regard some old blues as unqualified teachers. Furthermore the boy from the independent school is likely to have spent considerably more time on sport—if only because he is more likely to have been a boarder with consequent advantages in experience and physique. Moreover he is also likely to have attended a boys' preparatory school giving a degree of attention to games—and especially cricket—which is seldom matched in the state system. Conversely the maintained grammar school boy destined for Oxbridge is even less likely to spend a considerable time on sport than his own peers in view of his commitment to the time-consuming competition for Oxbridge places. Certainly, he is unlikely to be a boy for whom sporting achievement is of equal importance to academic achievement or who sees sporting opportunity as a main attraction of university life. Indeed, in many maintained grammar schools, an academically able boy whose life is focused on sporting achievement is far more likely to be deflected to a college for teachers of physical education than receive encouragement to apply for a university place, particularly if, as is probable, he heeds the advice of his physical education trained games master. Expenditure on games also distinguishes the schools, notably in cricket where the condition of "the square" in most public and preparatory schools is incomparably better than the average state school. At university the ex-maintained grammar school boy, more frequently depending for his continued financial support on satisfactory reports on his academic performance, tends to be less willing to renounce maximum academic achievement in order to devote substantial time to sport, and this constitutes a particular barrier in cricket where major participation is called for in examination terms. The

---

expert on which college to approach and on how to play his cards. Spurred on by parents who will consider no university except Oxford or Cambridge he makes persistent efforts to place his boy, and at last finds a college to take him.

"The second headmaster has not had a candidate for several years and has no Oxford contacts. He puts the boy in for Oxford once, and when this fails settles for a modern university. Indeed, to say that the "selection" system favors the first headmaster is to put the case too narrowly. The second one may not give the system a chance: he may never enter his boy at all. He has no difficulty in spotting a potential Oxford scholar among his pupils; but he may have a good deal in spotting the potential commoner, and the boy's parents are unlikely to demand a shot at Oxford." M. Brook, "Are Oxbridge Selections Biased?" *The Guardian*, 2.6.62.

immediate economic obligations of. university team membership, both in actual expenses and forfeited vacation work earnings, also tend to constitute a greater problem to the pupil from the maintained grammar school.

It is finally suggested that in the present intensified competition for Oxbridge places the conditions of academic competition for pupils of the direct grants schools are becoming similar to those of the maintained schools involving a diminution of the chances of entry for the outstanding sportsman whose prowess in sport is not matched by academic excellence.

Conclusion

This study of the awards of Oxford and Cambridge University blues in three major sports indicates that the ex-pupils of the maintained grammar schools are at a disadvantage to ex-pupils from the public schools in cricket and rugby, both absolutely and relative to their total representation in the university population.

It has been suggested that causal factors include covert disadvantages in selection situations, differentials in sporting opportunity at school and differentials in the evaluation of sport made by the pupils and by the school —differentials probably reinforced by economic differences.

Type of school attended thus becomes associated with differences in a further area of performance at university—an area which seems to be of considerable importance in view of its likely association with social opportunities in university life and social and occupational prospects in later life.

sports and studies as paths to success

JAMES S. COLEMAN

Introduction

In any social system, status by its very definition is in scarce supply. This is as true in a high school as in society at large. The fundamental competition in a high school is neither for grades, nor for athletic achievements, nor any other such activity. It is a competition for recognition and respect—the elements of which status is composed—in the eyes of one's fellows and the opposite sex. Competition for scholastic or athletic honors, as well as competition in other activities, is important to the competitors, not on its own account, but because it helps win status in the eyes of other teen-agers. To be sure, winning recognition and respect in the eyes of parents is important, too, to most teen-agers; but preceding chapters have indicated its decreasing importance, and its increasing replacement, in the adolescent's scheme of things, by recognition and respect from his peers.

Status is partly gained from activities carried on within a social system, and partly ascribed from without. If status were completely ascribed in a high school, then a girl's or boy's position in the teen-age culture would derive completely from his parents' position in the community. As shown in a previous chapter (III) this external ascription of status occurs to varying extents in these schools, and it occurs more for girls than for boys.

But status in these systems is far from completely determined by the social position of an adolescent's family. Other matters, some of them correlated with family position, but some not, are far more important. These include athletic achievement, good looks and dressing well, doing well in school, maintaining a good reputation while still being willing to have fun, having a car but not being a fanatic about cars, knowing popular songs without being addicted to popular music, and having other less important attributes. Some of these are simply styles of behavior that distinguish the elites from the student body; others are attributes of *achievement*, something a boy or girl can *do* to gain recognition, respect, and attention from his peers. Most important to examine for boys are athletic achievement and scholastic achievement: athletic achievement because it is so pervasive in gaining status for boys in high schools; scholastic achievement because it has an ambiguous position in the status structure, and because it is *the* activity for which schools were created.

Because of the importance of athletic and scholastic achievement, it is useful to examine extensively those boys who were seen by their fellows to be the best students in their grade and those who were seen to be the best athletes. How much status is conferred upon these athletes and scholars? We will consider those boys mentioned two or more times by their classmates in answer to the questions: "Of all the boys in your grade, which boy is the best athlete? . . . the best student?"

Whether these boys are in fact the best athletes and best scholars is irrelevant here, for these are the boys *seen by their contemporaries* to be the best athletes and the best scholars. We want to investigate how such a reputation affects a boy's status in the system—how it affects the tendency of other boys to want to be like him or to be friends with him, how it affects his chances to be in the leading crowd, how it affects the number of friends he has—in other words, how it affects his membership in the various elites.

THE EXEMPLARS

Each of the elites in these schools is important for somewhat different reasons. Other boys' wanting to be friends with a boy or wanting to be like him indicates who the "models" in the system are—who are the exemplars or popular heroes whose success leads other boys to work and strive in the same direction. They indicate, in a sense, the direction in which the *energy* of the system is flowing.

In any society in which achievement in some fields yields recognition and respect, the important question is, *what* fields? In 1942, a revealing study was made of popular biographies in mass-circulation magazines at two time periods, 1901–14 and 1940–41. The object of the study was to examine the characteristics of the "popular heroes" who were the subjects of biographies at these two periods.[1] In 1901–14, the popular heroes were predominantly "heroes of production," that is, men who were leaders in industry, men who were the industrial giants of the period. In 1940–41, the popular heroes were "heroes of consumption," primarily men whose success was achieved in the entertainment world, in the movies, radio, and other media. This result suggested that different "models for success" were dominant in the two periods.

Just as the adult society has models of success, so does the adolescent culture, perhaps to an even greater extent, as the adolescent culture is in greater flux. Its models of immediate success are other boys within the culture, and may include boys who have achieved success in various fields. This, then, is the importance of examining athletes and scholars. It indicates the models for the less successful, and the directions in which energy will be exerted by the not-yet-successful freshmen and sophomores.

THE LEADING CROWD

Membership in the "leading crowd" shows somewhat different aspects of the system. Insofar as the leading crowd has gained its position by achievement, thus being open to all who can achieve in the right directions, it stands as a concrete reward for such achievement: In exactly the same way, a man's membership in the local Kiwanis Club or the town's most exclusive country club stands as a reward for achievement in directions approved by the adult community. Just as the values of the community determine the efficacy of various kinds of achievement in gaining a man entry into the country club, the values placed upon athletic and scholastic achievement determine their efficacy in gaining a boy entry into the leading crowd in the school.

Sometimes, however, a school's leading crowd is partly determined according to parents' position in the community. Previous chapters (III and IV) have shown that this occurs in quite varying degrees in the different schools.

---

[1] Leo Lowenthal, "Biographies in Popular Magazines," P. F. Lazarsfeld and Frank Stanton (eds.), in *Radio Research*, 1942–43, New York: Duell, Sloan and Pierce, 1944, pp. 507–48.

Parents' position is particularly important in Marketville, Maple Grove, Midcity, and Executive Heights. The first three of these are stable communities composed of all social strata, but fairly well dominated by middle-class or upper-class members. Parents' position is least important, in fact almost negligible, in St. John's and Newlawn.

Because of such ascriptive criteria, membership in the leading crowd is only in part an indicator of rewards for achievement. Thus, the athlete's or scholar's being in the leading crowd may be due to his parental background rather than his achievements. This is particularly likely to happen for those named as best scholars, for they often come from higher social strata.

The leading crowd differs further from those whom others want to be like or be friends with, as an indicator of the direction a system's energy takes. Because the leading crowd is in fact a crowd that behaves in a particular way and because it is exclusive, negative as well as positive attitudes develop toward it. In all schools as a whole, 19.8 per cent of the boys and 28.9 per cent of the girls said they did not want to be a member of the leading crowd (spring questionnaire). Consequently, the leading crowd represents an effective reward, and thus a measure of how the energy of the system is being channeled, *only* insofar as it is not purely ascribed and insofar as its behavior leads many people to want to be members.

THE LOCAL LEADERS

The final elite, the "local leaders" who are often named as friends, is important as a different sort of indicator. By looking at the number of boys who name a boy as someone they go around with, we see the degree to which the system centers around him socially—or, in contrast, isolates him. As long as a boy or girl has his own circle of friends, he is not totally deprived of recognition and respect from his peers. To be sure, not many may look up to him or emulate him, but at least he is secure in his own group of friends. But if he is devoid of even this, his problem is more serious; the system not only fails to reward him with status and membership in the elite as a result of his achievement, it even deprives him of a circle of friends from which he can gain his rewards. These different adolescent systems vary considerably in the degree to which they do or do not surround a best athlete or best scholar with friends.

Social Rewards for Athletes and Scholars

The athletes and scholars, defined as such by the nominations of their peers, fared as indicated in Table 1. This table lists the *average member of times* the "best scholar" and "best athlete" and the student body as a whole was mentioned on each of the elite criteria above. Also included in this chart is the average number of times each was mentioned as someone the girls "go for most."

There is no ambiguity about these results. The athlete in every case

table 1

AVERAGE NUMBER OF CHOICES RECEIVED BY ATHLETES, SCHOLARS,
AND ALL BOYS, AS MEMBERS OF THE VARIOUS ELITES

	BE FRIENDS WITH AND BE LIKE	LEADING CROWD	NUMBER OF FRIENDS	POPULAR WITH GIRLS	NUMBER OF CASES
Athletes	5.6	7.8	6.1	3.0	(272)
Scholars	3.4	4.9	5.0	1.3	(278)
All boys	0.8	1.4	3.2	0.4	(4,094)

outdistances the scholar, as the scholar outdistances the student body as a whole. But there are differences between the different criteria. The athletes most outdistance the others in being named as most popular with girls. They do so least in the number of friends they have—a matter which reaches practical upper limits, since it implies some degree of association. Overall, it appears that athletic stardom stands highest as a symbol of success, as an achievement to channel the energies of the naïve freshman, as a means of entry into the leading crowd, as a way to gain popularity with girls, and as the man with the most friends. Being the best scholar also apparently stands somewhat as a desired achievement, for the scholar is above average on all criteria. Most important for the psychological equilibrium of the boys so named, he apparently has a full share of friends, although fewer than does the athlete.

ATHLETES, SCHOLARS, AND ATHLETE-SCHOLARS

Some good students are also good athletes. These achievements are not mutually exclusive; in some high schools they show a high coincidence. Consequently, to learn the effect of athletics and scholarship in bringing a boy recognition and respect from his peers, the two achievements must be separated. The question becomes, not "What is the relative status of athletes and scholars?" but, rather, "What is the relative status of the boy who is *only* an athlete, the one who is *only* a scholar, and the one who is *both?*"

Some schools, and some educational philosophies, emphasize the "well-rounded" boy. Does the adolescent status system concur in this, giving such a boy even greater status than those who are only scholars or only athletes? If so, what about the residual status of the boy who is only one or the other? For example, is the status of the scholars largely due to those among them who are also athletes, or is it independently gained, as a consequence of their being scholars? What about those who are neither scholars nor athletes? How likely are their classmates to want to be like them, to be friends with them, and how likely are they to be considered most popular with girls?

First of all, it is useful to see just how much overlap there is between athletes and scholars. In the small schools, 98 out of 1,032 boys, or 9.5 per cent, were named as athletes; 91, or 8.8 per cent were named as scholars. Of these, 21 boys were named as *both*. This constitutes 21 per cent of the athletes and 23 per cent of the scholars, or 2 per cent of the total students.

In the large schools, there is somewhat more centralization: 175 athletes and 187 scholars were named out of a total of 3,062 boys, constituting 5.7 per cent and 6.1 per cent of the student body, respectively. Of these, 34 were named as both athlete *and* scholar, constituting 19 per cent and 18 per cent of the total of athletes and scholars, respectively, or 1.1 per cent of the total students.

Thus, in the large schools, those boys thought of as both athlete and scholar were a smaller segment of the student body—as one might expect, since each grade is larger in the large schools, and thus any given boy has a smaller chance of being the "best athlete" or "best scholar" in his grade.

There are striking differences in the recognition and respect given these athletes, scholars, and athlete-scholars by their peers. The average number of choices received on each criterion by the athlete-scholar, the athlete-only, the scholar-only, and the neither-athlete-nor-scholar are given in Table 2.

table 2

AVERAGE NUMBER OF CHOICES RECEIVED BY ATHLETES, SCHOLARS, ATHLETE-SCHOLARS, AND OTHER BOYS, IN THE VARIOUS ELITES

	BE FRIENDS WITH AND BE LIKE	LEADING CROWD	NUMBER OF FRIENDS	TOTAL	POPULAR WITH GIRLS	NUMBER OF CASES
Athlete-scholar	9.9	12.5	7.1	29.5	4.9	(54)
Athlete	4.6	6.6	5.9	17.1	2.5	(218)
Scholar	1.9	3.1	4.4	9.4	0.5	(224)
All other boys	0.4	0.8	2.9	4.1	0.2	(3,598)

The athlete-scholar far outdistances all the others. In total choices as a friend, as someone to be friends with or be like, and as a member of the leading crowd, the average athlete-scholar receives over three times as many choices as the average scholar who is not an athlete, and over one and one-half times as many as the average athlete who is not scholar. The boy who is neither athlete nor scholar receives little recognition and respect, an average of only one-seventh the number of choices received by the athlete-scholar.

Thus, there is special attention to the "all-round" boy who is both athlete and scholar. He receives more social rewards from his peers than the boy who achieves in only one area. The athlete-scholars tend to be the focus of attention of the adolescent system. Although they constitute only 1.3 per cent of the total student body, they pre-empt 16.9 per cent of all the "be friends with" and "be like" choices, and 11.7 per cent of all the leading crowd choices (see Table 3). In number of persons who name them as friends they associate with, they stand out least. Yet even here, they stand above the others.

However, there are only a few athlete-scholars, and some attention goes elsewhere. What about the boy who is only an athlete or only a scholar, who does not try to excel in everything? Table 2 showed that the pure scholar fares far worse than does the pure athlete. He is mentioned as someone to be friends with or to be like only about a third as often as is the athlete, and he is mentioned less than half often as a member of the leading crowd. He is seen as popular with the girls only about one-fifth as often as is the star athlete. In short, he fares far worse than he appeared to before the athlete-scholar was considered separately. Scholarship alone receives, in these schools, less than half the recognition and respect from peers than does athletic achievement alone.

From the point of view of the distribution of elites in the system, matters are as follows for the pure athlete and the pure scholar: The pure athlete constitutes 5.3 per cent of the boys' student body, but gets 30.5 per cent of the be-friends-with and be-like choices, and 24.8 per cent of the leading-crowd choices. The pure scholar constitutes 5.5 per cent of the student body, receives 12.7 per cent of the be-friends-with and be-like choices, and 11.9 per cent of the leading-crowd choices. These figures, together with those for the athlete-scholar and the boy who is neither, are shown in Table 3.

table 3

DISTRIBUTION OF ELITE CHOICES AMONG ATHLETE-SCHOLARS,
ATHLETES, SCHOLARS, AND OTHER BOYS

	PART OF TOTAL POPULATION	BE FRIENDS WITH AND BE LIKE	LEADING CROWD	FRIENDS
Athlete-scholar	1.3%	16.9%	11.7%	2.9%
Athlete	5.3	30.5	24.8	9.8
Scholar	5.5	12.7	11.9	7.5
All others	87.9	40.1	51.6	79.7
Total	100.0	100.2	100.0	99.9
Number of cases (or choices)	(4,094)	(3,257)	(5,778)	(13,155)

The concentration of choices upon the athlete-scholars and the athletes is quite high; even the scholars get more than their share of the choices. Taking athletes and athlete-scholars together, 6.6 per cent of the population receives almost half the be-friends-with and be-like choices, and 37 per cent of the leading-crowd choices. Including the pure scholars, 12 per cent of the population preempts 60 per cent of the be-friends-with and be-like choices, and 48 per cent of the leading-crowd choices. The "left-overs," boys who are neither athletes nor scholars, constituting 88 per cent of the population, receive only 40 per cent of the be-friends-with and be-like choices, and only 52 per cent of the leading-crowd choices.

These results show in a striking fashion the large proportion of elite status that goes to the athlete-scholars and athletes, and the small amount left over for the boy who is neither athlete nor scholar. The pure scholars account for somewhat more recognition and respect than their numbers in the population, but they are completely outdistanced by the athlete or the all-around boy who is both athlete and scholar.

These results differ, of course, from school to school, as subsequent sections will indicate, but there are almost no differences due to size of student body, nor to small-town vs. city or suburb. When the five small schools are compared with the five large ones, only a few differences emerge. The differences *within* these groups are far more striking.

ATHLETE, SCHOLAR, AND LADIES' MAN

Before examining the structure of elites in the separate schools, another type of achievement warrants examination—being named by other boys as most popular with the girls, a "ladies' man." We have so far looked at such popularity as a *dependent* phenomenon, a possible consequence of achieving highly in athletic or in studies. So it appears to be, at least for the best athletes, but it is also in part independent. It is an attribute that, however acquired, in turn may give him entry into the leading crowd, and make others want to be friends with him, or to be like him.

Table 4 shows the average number of choices received by the boy who is neither athlete nor scholar, but is most popular with the girls. The pure athlete and pure scholar are repeated for comparison. In every criterion the ladies' man stands between the pure athlete and the pure scholar. He has more friends than the scholar, is more often in the school's leading crowd, and others would more often like to be like him or to be friends with him. He surpasses the scholar most in membership in the leading crowd, least as a person to be friends with or to be like. This reflects the fact that the leading crowd is a crowd of boys *and* girls, an actual crowd that goes around together.

table 4

AVERAGE NUMBER OF CHOICES RECEIVED BY PURE ATHLETE, SCHOLAR, AND LADIES' MAN, AS MEMBERS OF THE VARIOUS ELITES

	BE FRIENDS WITH AND BE LIKE	LEADING CROWD	NUMBER OF FRIENDS	TOTAL	NUMBER OF CASES
Athlete (but not scholar)	4.6	6.6	5.9	17.1	(218)
Scholar (but not athlete)	1.9	3.1	4.4	9.4	(224)
Ladies' man (but neither athlete nor scholar)	2.4	6.4	5.8	14.6	(138)

A boy who is popular with the opposite sex seems to gain recognition and respect among his fellows, not as much as an outstanding athlete, but considerably more than an outstanding scholar. An alternative interpretation, however, is equally reasonable: that the same elements that bring a boy popularity with the opposite sex bring him popularity among other boys. This is undoubtedly true and must account for a part of the status shown by these boys. How much a part is a difficult question, which cannot be answered satisfactorily by these data. However, even this tells us something, for it indicates that a boys status among other boys is dependent on many of the same criteria that make him popular with girls—a strong suggestion that the boy-girl relationship is important in shaping the status system among the boys.

Athletes, Scholars, and Ladies' Men in Each School

There are, of course, differences in the distribution of social rewards in the different schools. A formidable problem arises in comparing the distribution, due to small sample sizes. The athlete-scholars, particularly, are few in number. In Farmdale, there is only one. Maple Grove has the largest number among the small schools, but even here there are only seven. There are more pure athletes and pure scholars (never less than ten), but the numbers are still small. Consequently, the problem of just what differences in social rewards should be taken seriously is a difficult one. This is a sampling problem of a peculiar sort. Each class in school is a sample of children from the community, and in a small school, this sample may be quite unlike the one before it or the next. The class comes to be seen as a particularly athletic class or as a particularly studious one, or a nondescript one, because it is a small sample, different from others. This was evident at one point in a previous chapter (III) of the book, where the importance of "good grades" was examined for each year in each school separately.

The data to be presented shortly on number of choices received by each group may be seen in two ways: first, as purely descriptive of the school in the fall of 1957, in which case all differences should be considered as true differences, their importance in proportion to their size; or second, as descriptive of the school in a more abstract sense, that is, the school apart from the attributes of the particular teen-agers who made it up in the fall of 1957.

Both interpretations are of interest. The purely descriptive one is important because we are interested in examining the consequences of these status systems for the teen-agers within them. The second, more general, interpretation is of interest because we are concerned with the attributes of the school and community that may have helped produce these status systems. In the second case, it is important to know whether the differences found are a stable characteristic of the school, or would likely disappear when another sample of teen-agers from the same community moves into the school a few years hence. For example, in Maple Grove, pure athletes have an average of 6.9 friends, while pure scholars have an average of only 3.7. Is it generally the case that pure athletes in this school have more friends than pure scholars, or is the difference between 6.9 friends for the athletes and 3.7 for the scholars due only to the particular student body in 1957–58?

To answer such a question, a statistical test of the difference is a useful guide. For all these schools, a boy's average number of friends is something between 3 and 4, and the standard deviation is around 2.45.[2] While the distribution of choices is not normal, the distribution of their average for subgroups such as those shown here will tend to be, so that one can use the normal distribution as a rough rule of thumb for comparing two groups. Using this, the standard deviation of a sample of 10 is about 0.8, so that if one is familiar with thinking in terms of "standard error," the number 3.7 would be "3.7 ± 0.8."

A standard error is surpassed only about three times in ten; this would mean that only in about three out of ten "samples of this school" taken in different years would we find that the ten boys named most often as scholars would receive an average of more than 4.5 choices (3.7 + 0.8) or less than 2.9 choices (3.7 − 0.8). (This assumes, of course, that nothing changes about the administration of the school, the teachers, or the community.) Thus, a difference of 6.9 − 3.7 = 3.2 would be hardly likely to occur by chance when the sample sizes are 15 and 10 respectively. In fact, we find it would occur only about two times in a thousand such "samples of this school."

It is well to keep in mind that the data, interpreted directly, measure what *these* particular teen-agers are like in the school. The only differences from school to school for which an explanation should be sought in the community or school are those, like the example above, likely to recur when a new crop of teen-agers comes into the school.

The standard errors for the average number of friends have been calculated, and are nearly the same from school to school. They are approximately as indicated in footnote 3. Data in the tables below will include, however, not only number of friends, but number of times mentioned as a member of the leading crowd, and number of times chosen as someone to be friends with or be like. For this composite result, standard errors are unknown, and some caution should be used in attaching significance to differ-

[2] It would be preferable to compute the standard deviation for each subgroup separately, but the labor involved in this task would outweigh its contribution. The standard deviations in each school as a whole were computed, and are all very close to 2.45.

[3] Standard errors for number of friends:

Sample size 5 ± 1.1	Sample size 20 ± 0.55
Sample size 10 ± 0.8	Sample size 30 ± 0.45
Sample size 15 ± 0.6	Sample size 40 ± 0.40

Roughly, then, differences similar to that between the seven athlete-scholars and the fifteen athletes in Maple Grove (6.6 ± 1.0 and 6.9 ± 0.6) do not warrant seeking an explanation in the school or community, while differences between either of these groups and the scholars (3.7 ± 0.8) do. (The data for this example are taken from the tabulations on which Table 5 is based.)

ences. Only the large differences that are consistent from one criterion of choice to another will be considered in the discussion below.

SOCIAL REWARDS IN THE FIVE SMALL SCHOOLS

The social rewards received by athletes, scholars, and ladies' men differed somewhat among the small schools. In considering the differences, all elite criteria are shown together, for simplicity—leading crowd, someone to be friends with, someone to be like, and number of friends. Table 5 gives the average number of choices received on *all* these criteria taken together. The most reliable comparisons are among the pure athletes and pure scholars, for the numbers of cases are largest in these groups.

table 5

AVERAGE NUMBER OF CHOICES RECEIVED ON ALL ELITE CRITERIA BY
ATHLETE-SCHOLARS, ATHLETES, SCHOLARS, LADIES' MEN, AND
ALL BOYS, IN THE FIVE SMALL SCHOOLS [a]

	FARMDALE	MARKETVILLE	ELMTOWN	MAPLE GROVE	GREEN JUNCTION
Athlete-scholar	18.0	17.0	27.5	28.1	33.6
	(1)	(3)	(4)	(7)	(5)
Athlete	12.3	22.1	18.2	18.7	23.3
	(13)	(15)	(18)	(15)	(16)
Scholar	7.5	14.1	8.7	9.0	8.9
	(10)	(11)	(17)	(10)	(22)
Ladies' man	13.2	17.8	9.1	16.2	16.6
	(5)	(5)	(7)	(5)	(13)
All boys	7.5	6.4	6.2	6.4	6.6
	(70)	(198)	(266)	(217)	(281)

[a] The number of cases is given in parentheses below each category.

For the scholars, Marketville stands out sharply above the others. The social rewards received by a Marketville scholar are far above those in other schools: they are almost twice those received by a Farmdale scholar, and considerably higher than in Elmtown, Maple Grove, and Green Junction. This confirms the differences shown previously (Chapter III), where Marketville boys most often saw "good grades" or "being on the honor roll" as an aid to membership in the leading crowd or to being popular. Just as the boys in this school stood out over the other small schools in the frequency with which they mentioned academic achievement, they stand out here, in the social rewards they actually give to the good student.

Elmtown, Maple Grove, and Green Junction seem to be quite similar in the rewards they give to the pure scholar; Farmdale is somewhat lower. This is not fully consistent with the findings reported in a previous chapter (III), where the boys of Green Junction gave "good grades" no higher a position than did Farmdale boys in the status system. The discrepancy would be somewhat reduced if the various elite criteria were shown separately. It is only his number of friends that brings the Green Junction scholar up to the position shown in Table 5. As someone to be like, or to be friends with, or in the leading crowd, he receives only 4.7 choices, less than in Elmtown (5.1) or Maple Grove (5.3), despite the fact that more choices were *given* on these criteria in Green Junction than in either of these schools (an average of 3.2 per person, compared to 2.8 and 2.9 in Elmtown and Maple Grove).

In general, then, the status of the pure scholar shows Marketville in front, Elmtown and Maple Grove in the middle, and Green Junction and Farmdale at the bottom. Thus, the rewards these scholars actually receive, in the form of recognition and respect from their peers, are consistent with the picture of the value climates seen in Chapter III.

The pure athlete receives most rewards in Green Junction and least in Farmdale. This again is consistent with the value climate expressed in Chapter III, where Green Junction was at the top, and Farmdale at the bottom in the importance of athletics. The other schools give less consistent results: Marketville and Elmtown were in the "intermediate-low" group in the importance attached to athletic success, and Maple Grove was in the "low" group. Yet, there is little difference between the social rewards received by Elmtown athletes and those received by Maple Grove athletes, while Marketville's pure athletes approach those of Green Junction in the rewards they receive.

These discrepancies notwithstanding, the general pattern is roughly consistent with the data of Chapter III, where Green Junction stood out— with St. John's—above the rest. Here it does as well, particularly when the athlete-scholars are included—for the athlete-scholars receive higher social rewards in Green Junction than anywhere else.

STRUCTURAL VARIATIONS IN THE SMALL SCHOOLS

In Elmtown, Maple Grove, and Green Junction, the "all-around boy," the athlete-scholar, receives special recognition and respect—far more than in Farmdale and Marketville. This is easily seen in Table 5—although the numbers of cases are small enough to make inferences only tentative. In Marketville, the athlete and scholar *separately* receive social rewards—with the athlete, as usual, receiving more—but the athlete-scholar receives no extra rewards, and in fact is less rewarded than the athlete. In Farmdale, the pattern is similar, except that the pure scholar gets few rewards—no more than the average boy with 7.5 choices. Here, too, the athlete-scholar receives fewer social rewards than in Elmtown, Maple Grove, and Green Junction.

In other words, the social systems in Elmtown, Maple Grove, and Green Junction seem to encourage athletic success and scholastic success, not as *alternative* paths to prestige, but as simultaneous paths. In Marketville, athletic success and scholastic success seem to be separately rewarded, with no special rewards for the "all-around boy" who is both an outstanding athlete and an outstanding scholar. In Farmdale as well, there are no special rewards for the "all-around boy," but none for the scholar either.

If there is this difference in the reward systems of these schools, then we would expect it to produce another result: in Marketville, boys would not attempt to be both athlete and scholar, but would "specialize," so to speak; whereas in Elmtown, Maple Grove, and Green Junction, many boys would strive for success in both fields. As a consequence, in these latter schools, many boys would be named as *both* athlete and scholar.

This is in fact the case, with great differences between the schools. Table 6 shows the average number of choices as scholar received by the athletes, plus the average number of choices as athlete received by the scholars, divided by the total number of athletes and scholars. The numbers in Table 6 are, therefore, crude measurements of the covariation of athletic achievement and scholastic achievement in each school. The differences are striking and generally accord with the results of Table 5.

table 6

AVERAGE NUMBER OF CHOICES RECEIVED BY SCHOLARS AS ATHLETES
AND ATHLETES AS SCHOLARS IN FIVE SMALL SCHOOLS

	FARMDALE	MARKETVILLE	ELMTOWN	MAPLE GROVE	GREEN JUNCTION
Average number of choices	0.59	0.78	2.32	3.13	1.50
Total athletes and scholars	(27)	(32)	(44)	(39)	(48)

Farmdale and Marketville are at one extreme, with very little overlap between the athletes and scholars. At the other is Maple Grove, followed by Elmtown and then Green Junction.

This difference in structure is not necessarily related to the *amount* of social rewards received by athletes and students in the school. It is quite evident from other data in the study, such as that presented in Chapter III, that scholars are most strongly rewarded in Marketville, followed at some distance by Elmtown and Maple Grove, then by Green Junction, and finally by Farmdale; and that athletes are most highly rewarded in Green Junction, followed at a distance by Marketville and Elmtown, then Maple Grove, and finally Farmdale. There is no relation—or very little—between these *amounts* of reward and the *structure* of reward, overlapping at the one extreme, virtually exclusive at the other.

What accounts for this difference in structure of rewards? There are several alternative explanations:

1. In some schools, like Elmtown, Maple Grove, and Green Junction, the determination of the scholar is not at all clear, so that the outstanding athletes who are reasonably good in their schoolwork are also seen as best scholars.

2. There is an actual norm in some schools, like Maple Grove and Elmtown, to be an "all-around" boy, not to be outstanding as *only* an athlete or *only* a student.

3. In schools like Marketville, there are two distinct systems of evaluation, that of the teachers, which strongly encourages and rewards scholastic success, and that of the students, which encourages and rewards athletic success. Different students are responsive to one or the other of these systems of evaluation, and thus achieve in one or the other area, but not both. In other schools, like Maple Grove, Elmtown, and Green Junction, these systems of evaluation are merged, with the teachers and students holding similar criteria. These criteria include *both* athletic success *and* scholastic success, combining the dimensions that are distinct in Marketville.

4. The difference is not due to a real structural difference in the school, but to the presence of particular boys in some schools, who happen to combine athletic ability and scholastic ability. A few years hence, when different boys are in schools, they might reverse positions.

We will defer the question of which of these possible explanations accounts for the difference, until after examining the large schools in the same fashion as the small ones.

SOCIAL REWARDS IN THE FIVE LARGE SCHOOLS

Just as the patterns of social rewards differ among the small schools, they differ among the large ones. Because the number of cases is larger here, the over-all pattern in each school, including the athlete-scholar, may be examined with some confidence. Table 7 shows these patterns.

table 7

AVERAGE NUMBER OF CHOICES RECEIVED ON ALL ELITE CRITERIA BY
ATHLETE-SCHOLARS, ATHLETES, SCHOLARS, LADIES' MEN, AND
ALL BOYS, IN THE FIVE LARGE SCHOOLS [a]

	ST. JOHN'S	NEWLAWN	MILLBURG	MIDCITY	EXECUTIVE HEIGHTS
Athlete-scholar	32.7	20.2	22.2	33.5	44.5
	(14)	(7)	(9)	(8)	(10)
Athlete	15.1	16.2	17.2	15.5	15.2
	(37)	(29)	(26)	(45)	(41)
Scholar	7.4	6.9	10.2	11.3	7.5
	(29)	(23)	(27)	(53)	(51)
Ladies' man	12.3	11.1	11.0	12.9	21.7
	(21)	(15)	(25)	(41)	(21)
All boys	4.8	4.5	4.9	5.2	5.4
	(732)	(513)	(603)	(954)	(930)

[a] The number of cases is given in parentheses below each relevant category.

Executive Heights shows the greatest range of social rewards for the different kinds of achievement. The athlete-scholar is the object of the greatest amount of attention by far, pre-empting over twice as much as the next highest—which is, surprisingly enough, the boy who is neither athlete nor scholar, but ladies' man. The pure athlete fares more poorly, while the pure scholar gets just about a *sixth* as many choices as does the athlete-scholar, about a *third* as many as does the ladies' man, and is only slightly above the average for all boys.

The pattern in this school, then, seems to be one of the "all-around" boy receiving most attention, and the "social lion," the boy whose claim to status is his ability to get along with the opposite sex, following next. These two types are not seen as distinct and different types in the culture of this school, but both seem set apart from the pure athlete and the pure scholar. This is evidenced by the fact that the average athlete-scholar in Executive Heights received 10.3 mentions as the boy that girls go for most, while the pure athletes received less than one-fifth as many, 2.0, and the pure scholars received only *one thirty-eighth* as many, 0.27, an average only slightly higher than the boys who were named neither as best scholar nor as best athlete.

Thus, in Executive Heights, the athlete-scholar-ladies' man receives an extremely large amount of adulation. The pure scholar, on the other hand, receives very little recognition and respect from his peers. Nearly all the fathers in this community are engaged in pursuits where their primary tool is a trained mind—lawyers, doctors, business executives. In the high school, however, the boy who devotes his attention to scholarship alone is given few social rewards for his achievements, both in relation to others in his own school and in relation to the pure scholar in other schools. Meanwhile, this school literally falls at the feet of the all-around boy, the boy who is an athletic star, gets good grades, and romances the girls.

The pattern is similar—but far more pronounced—to that in Maple Grove, also a school heavily weighted with upper-middle-class, white-collar backgrounds. In that school as well, the athlete-scholar received far more choices as the boy girls go for most (an average of 6.0) than did the athlete-scholar in any other small school, more than the pure athletes in the same school received (an average of 3.1) and far more than the pure scholars in the same school (an average of 0.5).

Looking at a second large school in Table 7, Midcity, the pattern is quite different. Attention is distributed much more among the different groups, concentrated less on the athlete-scholars. In addition, it is distributed considerably more in the direction of the pure scholar. The pure scholar in Midcity receives more recognition from his peers—as measured by the total number of choices he received—than in any other of the large schools, and more than in any small school except Marketville. Midcity and Marketville have been consistently at the top in the evaluation of academic success in their boys' culture. It is worth noting that Midcity had among the seniors the closest thing found to an intellectual subgroup with high status in school. This was a group of boys and girls centered around the debate team, a group which "likes to discuss politics and such things," as one girl put it.

In Midcity there is some tendency for the athlete-scholar-ladies' man syndrome to emerge (athlete-scholars receive an average of 6.8 mentions as the boy most attractive to girls, while the pure athletes receive 2.0, and the pure scholars only 0.53), but the tendency is not nearly so pronounced as in Executive Heights. Furthermore, the pure athlete has higher over-all recognition than the pure ladies' man (15.5 vs. 12.9).

Millburg and Newlawn show little of this special attention for the athlete-scholar. The rewards for the athlete-scholar are much more nearly approached by those of the pure athlete than in Executive Heights. In Millburg, the boys give more attention to the pure scholar, close to that he receives in Midcity. In Newlawn, by contrast, the scholar's social rewards are very meager. In absolute quantity, his prestige is lower than in any other school; but relative to the average number of choices received by all boys, i.e., the average number of choices given, it is about at the level of St. John's and Executive Heights. The low position of the scholar in Newlawn coincides with the general picture of the values of this adolescent subculture, discussed in Chapter III.

The pure athlete in Newlawn and Millburg is not extremely highly rewarded in absolute numbers of choices received, but relative to the average number of choices in these schools (bottom row of Table 7), there is more focus on the pure athlete in these two schools than in any of the other large schools, equalled only by Green Junction among the small ones.

To summarize for Millburg and Newlawn: both give high rewards to the pure athlete, and neither heaps much extra attention on the athlete-scholar. The ladies' man receives some attention, but nothing comparable to what he receives in Executive Heights. In Newlawn, the pure scholar receives few rewards; in Millburg, he receives considerably more, approaching the rewards his counterpart in Midcity receives.

In St. John's, the athlete-scholar is especially prominent, as in Executive Heights, and, to a lesser extent, Midcity. The pure athlete gets more recognition than does the ladies' man, and both get more recognition than the pure scholar. The pattern is much like that in Midcity, with one exception—the pure scholar gets few rewards in St. John's. The position of the pure scholar in this school is similar to that in Newlawn and Executive Heights—quite low.

Considering the five schools together, the rewards show some consistency with the climates, as seen by the boys themselves, but not perfect consistency. The analysis in Chapter III indicated that Midcity and St. John's were high in rewards for scholarship; Millburg, in the middle; and Newlawn and Executive Heights, low. The one school in which the social rewards are inconsistent with this is St. John's. According to the data just examined, St. John's falls at the bottom, alongside Newlawn and Executive Heights.

What is the source of this sharp discrepancy between what the boys at St. John's *report* about the status of "good grades," and the *actual rewards* they give to those who are scholars? It may be a structural matter: more boys are *both* athlete and scholar here than in any other large school, and these athlete-scholars receive high rewards. Perhaps there is a strong constraint on the scholars to become all-around boys, by going out for athletics. Observation in the school in part confirms this. It appears that the sharp distinction among boys in this school is between those who are interested in school, both its athletics and its scholastics, and those whose interests lie wholly outside school. Although such a pattern exists among boys in all the schools (far more than among the girls, for example), it seems most pronounced at St. John's. The school has less to capture the attention of its teen-agers than do most of the others, making the gap greater between those interested in it, on the one hand, and those not interested, on the other.

The rewards given to athletes in the large schools show little variation. The pure athlete gets slightly higher rewards in Newlawn and Millburg, but in these two schools, the athlete-scholar receives fewer. In Chapter III, the schools were grouped closely together in the status they accorded athletics, and this clustering is evident here as well. Despite the clustering, it was possible to classify St. John's high, Midcity low, and the other three large schools medium high. No such pattern appears here in the data of Table 7; little can be said beyond the fact that the schools seem very much alike in the degree of recognition they provide for athletic achievement. In all the schools, athletic achievement, relative to other achievement, maintains the high position it has exhibited in earlier chapters.

One striking addition to the earlier pictures of the large schools in Chapter III is the recognition accorded the ladies' man in Executive Heights. When combined with the athlete-scholar, he forms the complete all-round boy in the eyes of these teen-agers, the boy on whom they heap attention. Even without the added attractions of athletic or scholastic achievement, he is a boy much admired by his fellows, with plenty of friends, and solidly in the leading crowd—more solidly than the pure athlete, and beyond comparison with the pure scholar.

STRUCTURAL VARIATIONS IN THE LARGE SCHOOLS

The large schools exhibit structural variations in the way in which they provide rewards, as was the case for the small schools. At the opposite extremes are Executive Heights and Millburg. In Executive Heights, the pure athlete and pure scholar receive only 22.7 choices combined, just *half* of what the average athlete-scholar receives. In Millburg, the pure athlete and pure scholar receive 27.4 choices combined, *more* than does the athlete-scholar. The other schools also show variations. St. John's shows high rewards for the athlete-scholar, and so does Midcity. Newlawn, on the other hand, is much like Millburg in not giving special rewards to the athlete-scholar.

Does this mean that in St. John's, Midcity, and especially Executive Heights, there is strong pressure to be *both* athlete and scholar, to be an all-around boy? If so, in these three schools—with Executive Heights in the lead —many boys should achieve in both areas, in contrast to Newlawn and Millburg. Thus, the first three schools should be like Maple Grove, with choices overlapping between athlete and scholar. The latter two should be like Marketville and Farmdale, with little overlap.

The data shown in Table 8 show no such result. There is far less variation in overlap than existed in the small schools—Maple Grove showed *more* overlap than any of the large schools, whereas Marketville and Farmdale showed *less*. Millburg, which provides few social rewards for the athlete-scholar, shows as much overlap as does Executive Heights; Midcity, where the athlete-scholar does receive extra rewards, shows least overlap of roles.

table 8

AVERAGE NUMBER OF CHOICES RECEIVED BY SCHOLARS AS ATHLETES
AND ATHLETES AS SCHOLARS IN FIVE LARGE SCHOOLS

	ST. JOHN'S	NEWLAWN	MILLBURG	MIDCITY	EXECUTIVE HEIGHTS
Average number of choices	2.37	1.83	2.10	1.28	2.05
Total athletes and scholars	(94)	(66)	(71)	(114)	(112)

Evidently other factors are operative here to affect the amount of overlap. The composition of the school, for example, must have an important effect in these large schools whose student bodies differ so radically. In Millburg, for example, the *average* boy has a background similar to the Newlawn boy, but the *distribution* is far broader than in this school.

Thus the amount of role overlap does not follow the special rewards given to athlete-scholars in these schools. Despite this, the differences in rewards shown in Table 8 indicates that there are definite differences in the degree to which the roles of athlete and scholar are encouraged separately by the adolescent culture, or combined into a single all-around boy. In Executive Heights and, to a lesser extent, Midcity and St. John's, there are rewards for the combined achievements (although the Midcity culture gives more rewards to the pure scholar than in any other large school); in Millburg and Newlawn, there are no special rewards for the combined achievements (although these schools differ in that the pure scholar is rewarded more in the Millburg culture than in the Newlawn culture).

Sources of the Structural Differences

In examining the small schools, we suggested several possible sources of the role-specialization in Marketville and the combination in Elmtown and Maple Grove. Some of these may be disposed of briefly; the final question of what *is* the source of the differences will remain unanswered.

First, it is evident that the difference is not due to particular persons or one particular class in school. In every class, freshman, sophomore, junior, and senior, in Maple Grove, there is more overlap between athlete and scholar than in Marketville; the high overlap in Elmtown also is distributed over the four classes.

A second possible explanation suggested earlier is that in a school like Marketville, there are two distinct systems of evaluation, provided by teachers, on the one hand, and other boys, on the other. Some boys respond to the first and strive for high scholarships; others respond to the second, thus acquiring athletic prowess. This explanation, however, is not consistent with the facts. The teachers were asked, in a questionnaire, what kind of boy they would like to see as class president: brilliant student, athletic star, or activities leader. The Marketville teachers mention "brilliant student" no more often than do the teachers in the other small schools. The boys themselves were asked, both in fall and spring, to choose how they would like to be remembered. There was just as much shifting from fall to spring between "brilliant student" and "athletic star" in Marketville as in Maple Grove—indicating that there are no more boys in Marketville than in Maple Grove who have fixed permanently on the image of brilliant student or athletic star. There is just as much fluctuating between these images in Marketville as in Maple Grove.

Thus, the source of these structural differences lies neither in genetic chance nor in two separate systems of evaluation. It seems likely that the difference has to do with the *independent* status that scholastic achievement has in a school. Boys in some high schools—including some of the boys in this study—feel that good grades and doing well in school helps gain recognition and respect from others, but *only* if he is also good in other things. If he is also an athlete and a good social companion, then good grades help his cause. If not, then he's a grind, and his good grades merely confirm that he works too hard. In such a school, scholastic achievement has no independent status at all—and in such a school social rewards accrue to the scholar only if he is an all-around boy.

Maple Grove, the most middle-class of the small-town schools, and Executive Heights, the most upper-middle-class of the large schools, are at the extremes in the social rewards they provide for the all-around boy. At the same time, the pure scholar who is not an athlete receives few rewards in Maple Grove, and even fewer in Executive Heights. It may be that in a middle-class community, where most of the adolescents are college-bound, giving rewards to the all-around boy for his good grades together with his other activities is the adolescent culture's compromise with reality—the reality that parents want to see good grades, and the reality that good grades will be important for college. This kind of recognition is very different from the status accorded scholastic achievement in Marketville or Midcity or, to a lesser extent, Millburg, where the pure scholar receives social rewards on his own, *as* a scholar.

football in America: a study
in culture diffusion

DAVID RIESMAN AND REUEL DENNEY

I

On October 9, 1951, Assistant Attorney General Graham Morrison instituted an anti-trust action against a number of universities on account of their efforts to limit TV broadcasts of their games—efforts dictated by the terrible burdens of what we might speak of as "industrialized football." This action occurred only a few weeks after the scandal of the West Point student firings, which, along with the William and Mary palace revolution, indicated that football was indeed reaching another crisis in its adaptation to the ever-changing American environment. Small colleges such as Milligan—a church-supported school in the mountains of Eastern Tennessee—were discovering that football was now so mechanized that they could no longer afford the necessary entry fee for machinery and personnel. Last year, Milligan spent $17,000, or two-thirds of its whole athletic budget—and did not get it all back in the box-office net. Football had come to resemble other industries or mechanized farms, into which a new firm could not move by relying on an institutional lifetime of patient saving and plowing back of profits, but only by large corporate investment. The production of a team involves the heavy overhead and staff personnel characteristic of high-capital, functionally rationalized industries, as the result of successive changes in the game since its post-Civil-War diffusion from England.[1]

It would be wrong, however, to assert that football has become an impersonal market phenomenon. Rather, its rationalization as a sport and as a spectacle has served to bring out more openly the part it plays in the ethnic, class, and characterological struggles of our time—meaning, by "characterological struggle," the conflict between different styles of life. The ethnic significance of football is immediately suggested by the shift in the typical origins of player-names on the All-American Football Teams since 1889. In 1889, all

[1] The growing scale of college football is indicated by its dollar place in the American leisure economy. In 1929, out of $4.3 billion in recreation expenditures by Americans, the college football gate accounted for $22 million. In 1950, out of $11.2 billion in such expenditures, it accounted for $103 million. While something less than 1 per cent of the total United States recreation account, college football had ten times the gross income of professional football. The 1950 gate of $103 million suggests that a total capital of at least $2 billion is invested in the college football industry. The revenue figures, above, of course, do not include the invisible subsidization of football, nor do they hint the place that football pools occupy in the American betting economy.

• From *American Quarterly* 3 (1951), pp. 309–325. © Trustees of the University of Pennsylvania, Philadelphia, Pa.

but one of the names (Heffelfinger) suggested Anglo-Saxon origins. The first name after that of Heffelfinger to suggest non-Anglo-Saxon recruitment was that of Murphy, at Yale, in 1895. After 1895, it was a rare All-American team that did not include at least one Irishman (Daly, Hogan, Rafferty, Shevlin); and the years before the turn of the century saw entrance of the Jew. On the 1904 team appeared Pierkarski of Pennsylvania. By 1927, names like Casey, Kipke, Oosterbaan, Koppisch, Garbisch, and Friedman were appearing on the All-American list with as much frequency as names like Channing, Adams, and Ames in the 1890s.

Although such a tally does little more than document a shift that most observers have already recognized in American football, it raises questions that are probably not answerable merely in terms of ethnic origins of players. There is an element of class identification running through American football since its earliest days, and the ethnic origins of players contain ample invitations to the making of theory about the class dimensions of football. Most observers would be inclined to agree that the arrival of names like Kelley and Kipke on the annual All-American list was taken by the Flanagans and the Webers as the achievement of a lower-class aspiration to be among the best at an upper-class sport. The question remains: What did the achievement mean? What did it mean at different stages in the development of the game? Hasn't the meaning worn off in the fifty-odd years, the roughly two generations since Heffelfinger and Murphy made the grade?

There are many ways to begin an answer to such questions, and here we can open only a few lines of investigation. Our method is to study the interrelations between changes in the rules of the game (since the first intercollegiate contest: Rutgers, 6 goals—Princeton, 4 goals, in 1869) and to analyze the parallel changes in football strategy and ethos. All these developments are to be seen as part of a configuration that includes changes in coaching, in the training of players, and in the no less essential training of the mass audience.

As football is a cultural inheritance from England, such an analysis may be made in the perspective of other studies in cultural diffusion and variation. Just as the French have transformed American telephone etiquette while retaining some of its recognizable physical features, so Americans have transformed the games of Europe even when, as in track or tennis, the formalities appear to be unaltered. Even within the Western industrial culture, there are great varieties, on a class and national basis, in the games, rules, strategy, etiquette, and audience structures of sport. In the case of college football—we shall leave aside the symbolically less important professional game—the documentation of sportswriters (themselves a potent factor in change) allows us to trace the stages of development.

II

A study of Anatolian peasants now under way at the Bureau of Applied Social Research indicates that these highly tradition-bound people cannot grasp the abstractness of modern sports. They lack the enterprise, in their fatalistic village cultures, to see why people want to knock themselves out for sportsmanship's remote ideals; they cannot link such rituals, even by remote analogy, with their own. These peasants are similarly unable to be caught up in modern politics, or to find anything meaningful in the Voice of America. Nevertheless, football itself, like so many other games with balls and goals, originated in a peasant culture.

Football, in its earliest English form, was called the Dane's Head and it was played in the tenth and eleventh centuries as a contest in kicking a ball between towns. The legend is that the first ball was a skull, and only later a cow's bladder. In some cases, the goals were the towns themselves, so that a team entering a village might have pushed the ball several miles en route. King Henry II (1154–89) proscribed the game, on the ground that it interfered with archery practice. Played in Dublin even after the ban, football did not become respectable or legal until an edict of James I reinstated it. The reason was perhaps less ideological than practical: firearms had obsoleted the art of bowmanship.

During the following century, football as played by British schoolboys became formalized, but did not change its fundamental pattern of forceful kicking. In 1823, Ellis of Rugby made the mistake of picking up the ball and running with it toward the goal. All concerned thought it a mistake: Ellis was sheepish; his captain, apologetic. The mistake turned into innovation when it was decided that a running rule might make for an interesting game. The localism, pluralism, and studied casualness of English sports made it possible to try it out without securing universal assent—three or four purely local variants of football, football-hazing and "wall games" are still played in various English schools. Rugby adopted "Rugby" in 1841, several years after Cambridge had helped to popularize it.[2]

This establishment of the running or Rugby game, as contrasted with the earlier, kicking game, had several important results. One was that the old-style players banded themselves together for the defense of their game, and formed the London Football Association (1863). This name, abbreviated to "Assoc," appears to have been the starting point of the neologism, "Soccer," the name that the kicking game now goes by in many parts of the English-speaking world. A second result was that the English, having found a new game, continued to play it without tight rules until the Rugby

[2] A commemorative stone at Rugby reads as follows:
THIS STONE
COMMEMORATES THE EXPLOIT OF
WILLIAM WEBB ELLIS
WHO WITH A FINE DISREGARD FOR THE RULES OF
FOOTBALL, AS PLAYED IN HIS TIME,
FIRST TOOK THE BALL IN HIS ARMS AND RAN WITH IT,
THUS ORIGINATING THE DISTINCTIVE FEATURE OF
THE RUGBY GAME
A. D. 1823

Union of 1871. As we shall see, this had its effects on the American game. The third and most important result of Ellis' "mistake," of course, was that he laid the foundations for everything fundamental about the American game between about 1869 and the introduction of the forward pass. (The forward pass is still illegal in Rugby and closely related football games.)

III

In the Colonial period and right down to the Civil War, Americans played variants on the kicking football game on their town greens and schoolyards. After the war, Yale and Harvard served as the culturally receptive importers of the English game. Harvard, meeting McGill in a game of Rugby football in 1874, brought the sport to the attention of collegiate circles and the press—two identifications important for the whole future development of the game. But if Harvard was an opinion leader, Yale was a technological one. A Yale student who had studied at Rugby was instrumental in persuading Yale men to play the Rugby game and was, therefore, responsible for some of Yale's early leadership in the sport.

It happened in the following way, according to Walter Camp and Lorin F. Deland.[3] The faculty in 1860, for reasons unknown, put a stop to interclass matches for the pre-Rugby variety. "During the following years, until 1870, football was practically dead at Yale. The class of '72, however, was very fond of athletic sports, and participated especially in long hare and hound runs. The revival of football was due in a large measure to Mr. D. S. Schaft, formerly of Rugby School, who entered the class of '73 and succeeded in making the sport popular among his classmates, and eventually formed an association which sent challenges to the other classes."

Soon after the period described by Camp, it became clear that American players, having tasted the "running" game, were willing to give up the soccer form. It became equally clear that they either did not want to, or could not, play Rugby according to the British rules. "The American players found in this code [English Rugby Rules] many uncertain and knotty points which caused much trouble in their game, especially as they had no traditions, or older and more experienced players, to whom they could turn for the necessary explanations," says Camp. An example of such a problem was English rule number nine:

"A touchdown is when a player, putting his hand on the ball in touch or in goal, stops it so that it remains dead, or fairly so."

The ambiguity of the phrase "fairly so" was increased by the statement in rule number eight that the ball is dead "when it rests absolutely motionless on the ground."

Camp's description of these early difficulties is intensely interesting to the student's of cultural diffusion not only because of what Camp observed

[3] Walter Camp and Lorin F. Deland, *Football*, Boston: Houghton Mifflin Co., 1896.

about the situation, but also because of what he neglected to observe. Consider the fact that the development of Rugby rules in England was accomplished by admitting into the rules something that we would call a legal fiction. Although an offensive runner was permitted to carry the ball, the condition of his doing so was that he should *happen* to be standing behind the swaying "scrum" (the tangled players) at the moment the ball popped back out to him. An intentional "heel out" of the ball was not permitted; and the British rules of the mid-nineteenth century appear to take it for granted that the difference between an intentional and an unintentional heel-out would be clear to everyone. Ellis' mistake became institutionalized—but still as a mistake. This aspect of Rugby rule-making had important implications for the American game.

British players, according to tradition as well as according to rules, could be expected to tolerate such ambiguity as that of the heel-out rule just as they tolerated the ambiguity of the "dead" ball. They could be expected to tolerate it not only because of their personal part in developing new rules but also (a point we shall return to) because they had an audience with specific knowledge of the traditions to assist them. In America it was quite another matter to solve such problems. No Muzafer Sherif was present [4] to solidify the perceptions of "nearly so," and the emotional tone for resolving such question without recurrent dispute could not be improvised. Rather, however, than dropping the Rugby game at that point, because of intolerance for the ambiguities involved, an effort was undertaken, at once systematic and gradual, to fill in by formal procedures the vacuum of etiquette and, in general, to adapt the game to its new cultural home.

The upshot of American procedure was to assign players to the legalized task of picking up and tossing the ball back out of scrimmage. This in turn created the rôle of the center, and the centering operation. This in turn led to a variety of problems in defining the situation as one of "scrimmage" or "nonscrimmage," and the whole question of the legality of passing the ball back to intended runners. American football never really solved these problems until it turned its attention, in 1880, to a definition of the scrimmage itself. The unpredictable English "scrum" or scramble for a free ball was abandoned, and a crude line of scrimmage was constructed across the field. Play was set in motion by snapping the ball. Meanwhile Americans became impatient with long retention of the ball by one side. It was possible for a team that was ahead in score to adopt tactics that would insure its retention of the ball until the end of the period. By the introduction of a minimum yardage-gain rule in 1882, the rulemakers assured the frequent interchange of the ball between sides.

The effect of this change was to dramatize the offensive-defensive sym-

---

[4] *Cf.*, his *An Outline of Social Psychology*, New York: Harper & Brothers, 1948, pp. 93–182.

metry of the scrimmage line, to locate it sharply in time ("downs"), and to focus attention not only on the snapping of the ball, but also on the problem of "offside" players. In the English game, with no spatially and temporally delimited "line of scrimmage," the offside player was penalized only by making him neutral in action until he could move to a position back of the position of the ball. In the American game, the new focus on centering, on a scrimmage line, and on yardage and downs, created the need for a better offside rule. From that need developed offside rules that even in the early years resembled the rules of today. American rulemakers were logically extending a native development when they decided to draw an imaginary line through the ball before it had been centered, to call this the "line of scrimmage," and to make this line, rather than the moving ball itself, the offside limit in the goalward motion of offensive players. At first, lined-up players of the two sides were allowed to stand and wrestle with each other while waiting for the ball to be centered; only later was a neutral zone introduced between the opposing lines.

Even with such a brief summary of the rule changes, we are in a position to see the operation of certain recurrent modes or patterns of adaptation. The adaptation begins with the acceptance of a single pivotal innovation (running with the ball). The problems of adaptation begin with the realization that this single innovation has been uprooted from a rich context of meaningful rules and traditions, and does not work well in their absence. Still more complex problems of adaption develop when it is realized that the incompleteness of the adaption will not be solved by a reference to the pristine rules. In the first place, the rules are not pristine (the English rules were in the process of development themselves). In the second place, the tradition of interpreting them is not present in experienced players. In the third place, even if it were, it might not be adaptable to the social character and mood of the adapters.

Let us put it this way. The Americans, in order to solve the heel-out problem, set in motion a redesign of the game that led ultimately to timed centering from a temporarily fixed line of scrimmage. Emphasis completely shifted from the kicking game; it also shifted away from the combined kicking and running possible under Rugby rules; it shifted almost entirely in the direction of an emphasis on ball-carrying. Meanwhile, to achieve this emphasis, the game made itself vulnerable to slowdowns caused by one team's retention of the ball. It not only lost the fluidity of the original game, but ran up against a pronounced American taste for action in sports, visible action. There is evidence that even if players had not objected to such slowdowns, the spectators would have raised a shout. The yardage rule was the way this crisis was met. This, in turn, led to an emphasis on mass play, and helped to create the early twentieth-century problems of football. But before we consider this step in the game's development we must turn to examine certain factors in the sport's audience reception.

IV

A problem posed for the student of cultural diffusion at this point can be stated as follows: What factor or factors appear to have been most influential in creating an American game possessing not only nationally distinct rules, but also rules having a specific flavor of intense legality about many a point of procedure left more or less up in the air by the British game?

We can now go beyond the rule-making aspect of the game and assert that the chief factor was the importance of the need to standardize rules to supply an ever-widening collegiate field of competition, along with the audience this implied. The English rule-makers, it appears, dealt with a situation in which amateur play was restricted to a fairly limited number of collegians and institutions. The power of localism was such that many an informality was tolerated, and intended to be tolerated, in the rules and their interpretation. American football appeared on the American campus at the beginning of a long period in which intercollegiate and interclass sportsmanship was a problem of ever-widening social participation and concern. Football etiquette itself was in the making. Thus, it appears that when early American teams met, differences of opinion could not be resolved between captains in rapid-fire agreement or penny-tossing as was the case in Britain. American teams did not delegate to their captains the rôle of powerful comrade-in-antagonism with opposing captains, or, if they did, they felt that such responsibilities were too grave.[5]

Into just such situations football players thrust all of the force of their democratic social ideologies, all their prejudice in favor of equalitarian and codified inter-player attitudes. Undoubtedly, similar considerations also influenced the audience. Mark Benney, a British sociologist who is familiar with the games played on both sides of the Atlantic, points out that, whereas the American game was developed in and for a student group, the English game was played before quite large crowds who, from a class standpoint, were less homogeneous than the players themselves, though they were as well informed as the latter in the "law" of the game. Rugby football was seldom played by the proletariat; it was simply enjoyed as a spectacle.

Held by the critical fascination the British upper strata had for the lower strata, the audience was often hardly more interested in the result of the game than in judging the players as "gentlemen in action." "The players," Mr. Benney writes, "had to demonstrate that they were sportsmen, that they could 'take it'; and above all they had to inculcate the (politically important) ideology that legality was more important than power." The audience was,

---

[5] "Fifty years ago arguments followed almost every decision the referee made. The whole team took part, so that half the time the officials scarcely knew who was captain. The player who was a good linguist was always a priceless asset." John W. Heisman, who played for both Brown and Penn in the 1890s, quoted in Frank G. Menke, *Encyclopedia of Sports*, New York: A. S. Barnes and Co., 1944, p. 293.

then, analogous to the skilled English jury at law, ready to be impressed by obedience to traditional legal ritual and form, and intolerant of "bad form" in their "betters." The early Yale games, played before a tiny, nonpaying audience, lacked any equivalent incentive to agree on a class-based ritual of "good form," and when the audiences came later on, their attitude towards upper-class sportsmanship was much more ambivalent—they had played the game too, and they were unwilling to subordinate themselves to a collegiate aristocracy who would thereby have been held to norms of correctness. The apparent legalism of many American arguments over the rules would strike British observers as simply a verbal power-play.

Such differences in the relation of the game to the audience, on this side of the Atlantic, undoubtedly speeded the development of the specifically American variant. Native, too, are the visual and temporal properties of the game as it developed even before 1900: its choreography could be enjoyed, if not always understood, by nonexperts, and its atomistic pattern in time and space could seem natural to audiences accustomed to such patterns in other foci of the national life. The mid-field dramatization of line against line, the recurrent starting and stopping of field action around the timed snapping of a ball, the trend to a formalized division of labor between backfield and line, above all, perhaps, the increasingly precise synchronization of men in motion —these developments make it seem plausible to suggest that the whole procedural rationalization of the game which we have described was not unwelcome to Americans, and that it fitted in with other aspects of their industrial folkways.

Spurred by interest in the analysis of the athletic motions of men and animals, Eadweard Muybridge was setting out his motive-like action shorts of the body motion (more preoccupied even than Vesalius or da Vinci with the detailed anatomy of movement) [6] at about the same time that Coach Woodruff at Pennsylvania (1894) was exploring the possibilities for momentum play: linemen swinging into motion before the ball is snapped, with the offensive team, forming a wedge, charging toward an opposition held waiting by the offside rule. In Philadelphia, the painter Eakins, self-consciously following the tenets of Naturalism and his own literal American tradition, was painting the oarsmen of the Schuylkill. Nearby, at the Midvale plant of the American Steel Company, efficiency expert Frederick Winslow Taylor was experimenting with motion study and incentive pay geared to small measurable changes in output—pay that would spur but never soften the workman.[7]

As we do not believe in historical inevitability, nor in the necessary

[6] Sigfried Giedion, *Mechanization Takes Command*, New York: Oxford University Press, 1948, pp. 21–27.

[7] In view of the prejudice against "Taylorism" today, shared by men and management as well as intellectuals, let us record our admiration for Taylor's achievement, our belief that he was less insensitive to psychological factors than is often claimed, and more "humane" in many ways than his no less manipulative, self-consciously psychological successors.

homogeneity of a culture, we do not suggest that the American game of football developed as it did out of cultural compulsion and could not have gone off in quite different directions. Indeed, the very effectiveness of momentum play, as a mode of bulldozing the defense, led eventually to the rule that the line must refrain from motion before the ball is snapped. For the bulldozing led, or was thought to lead, to a great increase in injuries. And while these were first coped with by Walter Camp's training table (his men had their choice of beefsteak or mutton for dinner, to be washed down with milk, ale, or sherry), the public outcry soon forced further rule changes, designed to soften the game. After a particularly bloody battle between Pennsylvania and Swarthmore in 1905, President Roosevelt himself took a hand and insisted on reform.[8]

Camp's colleague at Yale, William Graham Sumner, may well have smiled wryly at this. Sumner was exhorting his students to "get capital," and cautioning them against the vices of sympathy and reformism—a theme which has given innumerable American academies a good living since—while Camp was exhorting his to harden themselves, to be stern and unafraid. In spite of them both, the reformers won out; but the end of momentum play was not the end of momentum. Rather, with an ingenuity that still dazzles, the game was gentled and at the same time speeded by a new rule favoring the forward pass. But before going on to see what changes this introduced, let us note the differences between the subjects of Sumner's and Camp's exhortations on the one hand, and Taylor's on the other.

Frederick Taylor, as his writings show, was already coming up against a work force increasingly drawn from non-Protestant lands, and seeking to engender in them a YMCA-morality, whereas Camp was inculcating the same morality into young men of undiluted Anglo-Saxon stock and middle- to upper-class origins. Not for another fifty years would the sons of Midvale prove harder, though fed on kale or spaghetti, and only intermittently, than the sons of Yale. Meanwhile, the sons of Yale had learned to spend summers as tracklayers or wheat harvesters in an effort to enlarge their stamina, moral toughness, and cross-class adventures.

[8] "In a 1905 game between Pennsylvania and Swarthmore, the Pennsy slogan was 'Stop Bob Maxwell,' one of the greatest linesmen of all time. He was a mighty man, with amazing ability to roll back enemy plunges. The Penn players, realizing that Maxwell was a menace to their chances for victory, took 'dead aim' at him throughout the furious play.

"Maxwell stuck it out, but when he tottered off the field, his face was a bloody wreck. Some photographer snapped him, and the photo of the mangled Maxwell, appearing in a newspaper, caught the attention of the then President Roosevelt. It so angered him, that he issued an ultimatum that if rough play in football was not immediately ruled out, he would abolish it by executive edict." Frank G. Menke, *Encyclopedia of Sports.*

Notice here the influence of two historical factors on football development: one, the occupancy of the White House in 1905 by the first President of the United States who was a self-conscious patron of youth, sport, and the arts; two, the relative newness in 1905 of photographic sports coverage. Widespread increased photographic coverage of popular culture was the direct result of the newspaper policies of William Randolph Hearst, beginning about 1895.

Nevertheless, certain basic resemblances between the purposes of Taylor and those of Sumner and Camp are clearly present. By contrast with the British, the Americans demonstrated a high degree of interest in winning games and winning one's way to high production goals. The Americans, as in so many other matters, were clearly concerned with the competitive spirit that new rules might provoke and control. (British sports, like British industry, seemed to take it more for granted that competition will exist even if one does not set up ideology for it.) Much of this seems to rest in the paradoxical belief of Americans that competition is natural—but only if it is constantly recreated by artificial systems of social rules that direct energies into it.

Back of the attitudes expressed in Taylor, Sumner, and Camp we can feel the pressure not only of a theory of competition, but also a theory of the emotional tones that ought to go along with competition. It is apparent from the brutality scandals of 1905 that President Roosevelt reacted against roughhouse not so much because it was physical violence, but for two related reasons. The first and openly implied reason was that it was connected with an unsportsmanlike attitude. The second, unacknowledged, reason was that Americans fear and enjoy their aggression at the same time, and thus have difficulty in pinning down the inner meanings of external violence. The game of Rugby as now played in England is probably as physically injurious as American football was at the turn of the century. By contrast, American attitudes toward football demonstrate a forceful need to define, limit, and conventionalize the symbolism of violence in sports.

If we look back now at England, we see a game in which shouted signals and silent counting of timed movements are unknown—a game that seems to Americans to wander in an amorphous disorderly roughhouse. Rugby, in the very home of the industrial revolution, seems pre-industrial, seems like one of the many feudal survivals that urbanization and industrialization have altered but not destroyed. The English game, moreover, seems not to have developed anyone like Camp, the Judge Gary of football (as Rockne was to be its Henry Ford): Camp was a sparkplug in efforts to codify inter-collegiate rules; he was often the head of the important committees. His training table, furthermore, was one of the signs of the slow rise in "overhead" expense—a rise which, rather like the water in United States Steel Stock, assumed that abundance was forthcoming and bailing out probable, as against the British need for parsimony. But at the same time the rise in costs undoubtedly made American football more vulnerable than ever to public-relations considerations: the "gate" could not be damned.

V

This public relations issue in the game first appears in the actions of the rules committee of 1906—the introduction of the legalized forward pass in order to open up the game and reduce brutal power play. Between 1906 and 1913 the issue was generally treated as a problem centered about players and their coaches, and thus took the form of an appeal to principles rather than to audiences. However, the development of the high audience appeal that we shall show unfolding after 1913 was not autonomous and unheralded. If public relations became a dominant factor by 1915, when the University of Pittsburgh introduced numbers for players in order to spur the sale of programs, it had its roots in the 1905–13 period. The rules committee of 1906, by its defensive action on roughhouse rules, had already implicitly acknowledged a broad public vested interest in the ethos of the game. Let us turn to look at the speed with which football was soon permeated by broad social meanings unanticipated by the founders of the sport.

By 1913, the eve of the First World War, innovation in American industry had ceased to be the prerogative of Baptist, Calvinist, and North of Ireland tycoons. Giannini was starting his Bank of America; the Jews were entering the movies and the garment hegemonies. Yet these were exceptions, and the second generation of immigrants, taught in America to be dissatisfied with the manual work their fathers did, were seldom finding the easy paths of ascent promised in success literature. Where, for one thing, were they to go to college? If they sought to enter the older eastern institutions, would they face a social struggle? Such anxieties probably contributed to the fact that the game of boyish and spirited brawn played at the eastern centers of intellect and cultivation was to be overthrown by the new game of craft and field maneuver that got its first rehearsal at the hands of two second-generation poor boys attending little-known Notre Dame.

The more significant of the two boys, Knute Rockne, was, to be sure, of Danish Protestant descent and only later became a Catholic.[9] During their summer vacations jobs as lifeguards on Lake Michigan, Rockne and Gus Dorais decided to work as a passing team. Playing West Point early in the season of 1913, they put on the first demonstration of the spiral pass that makes scientific use of the difference in shape between the round ball used in the kicking game and the oval that gradually replaced it when ball-carrying began. As the first players to exploit the legal pass, they rolled up a surprise victory over Army. One of the effects of the national change in rules was to bring the second-generation boys of the early twentieth century to the front, with a craft innovation that added new elements of surprise, "system" and skull-session to a game that had once revolved about an ethos of brawn plus character-building.

With the ethnic shift, appears to have come a shift in type of hero. The work-minded glamor of an all-'round craftsman like Jim Thorpe gave way to the people-minded glamor of backfield generals organizing deceptive forays into enemy territory—of course, the older martial virtues are not so much ruled out as partially incorporated in the new image. In saying this, it must not be forgotten, as sports columnist Red Smith has pointed out, that the fictional Yale hero, Dick Merriwell, is openly and shamelessly repre-

---

[9] "After the church, football is the best thing we have," Rockne.

sented as a dirty player in the first chapters of his career. But the difference is that his deviation from standard sportsmanship consisted largely of slugging, not of premeditated wiliness. In fact, the Yale era, even into Camp's reign, was characterized by a game played youthfully, with little attention to the players' prestige outside college circles. Again, the second-generationers mark a change. A variety of sources, including letters to the sports page, indicate that a Notre Dame victory became representational in a way a Yale or Harvard victory never was, and no Irish or Polish boy on the team could escape the symbolism. And by the self-confirming process, the Yale or Harvard showing became symbolic in turn, and the game could never be returned, short of intramuralization, to the players themselves and their earlier age of innocent dirtiness.[10] The heterogeneity of America which had made it impossible to play the Rugby game at Yale had finally had its effect in transforming the meaning of the game to a point where Arnold of Rugby might have difficulty in drawing the right moral or any moral from it. Its "ideal types" had undergone a deep and widespread characterological change.

For the second-generation boy, with his father's muscles but not his father's motives, football soon became a means to career ascent. So was racketeering, but football gave acceptance, too—acceptance into the democratic fraternity of the entertainment world where performance counts and ethnic origin is hardly a handicap. Moreover, Americans as onlookers welcomed the anti-traditional innovations of a Rockne, and admired the trick that worked, whatever the opposing team and alumni may have thought about the effort involved. One wonders whether Rockne and Dorais may not have gotten a particular pleasure from their craftiness by thinking of it as a counter-image to the stereotype of muscle-men applied to their fathers.

It was in 1915, at about the same time that the newcomers perfected their passing game, that the recruitment of players began in earnest. Without such recruitment, the game could not have served as a career route for many of the second generation who would not have had the cash or impetus to make the class jump that college involved.[11]

The development of the open and rationalized game has led step by

---

[10] One of us, while a Harvard undergraduate, sought with several friends to heal the breach between Harvard and Princeton—a breach whose bitterness could hardly be credited today. The Harvards believed Princeton played dirty—it certainly won handily in those years of the 20s—while Princetonians believed themselves snubbed by Harvards as crude parvenus trying to make a trio out of the Harvard-Yale duo. The diplomatic problems involved in seeking to repair these status slights and scars were a microcosm of the Congress of Westphalia or Vienna—whether the Harvard or Princeton athletic directors should enter the room first was an issue. A leak to the Hearst press destroyed our efforts, as alumni pressure forced denials of any attempt to resume relations, but the compromise formulas worked out were eventually accepted, about the time that the University of Chicago "solved" the problem of the intellectual school by withdrawing from the game altogether.

[11] See George Saxon, "Immigrant Culture in a Stratified Society," *Modern Review*, II, No. 2, February 1948.

step not only to the T-formation, but also to the two-platoon system. These innovations call for a very different relationship among the players than was the case under the older star system. For the game is now a coöperative enterprise in which mistakes are too costly—to the head coach, the budget, even the college itself—to be left to individual initiative. At least at one institution, an anthropologist has been called in to study the morale problems of the home team, and to help in the scouting of opposing teams. To the learning of Taylor, there has been added that of Mayo, and coaches are conscious of the need to be group-dynamics leaders rather than old-line straw bosses.

Today, the semiprofessionalized player, fully conscious of how many peoples' living depends on him, cannot be exhorted by Frank Merriwell appeals, but needs to be "handled." And the signals are no longer the barks of the first Camp-trained quarterback—hardly more differentiated than a folkdance caller—but are cues of great subtlety and mathematical precision for situations planned in advance with camera shots and character fill-ins of the opposing team. James Worthy and other advocates of a span of control beyond the usual half-dozen of the older military and executive manuals might find support for their views in the way an eleven is managed. Industrial, military, and football teamwork have all a common cultural frame.

Yet it would be too simple to say that football has ceased to be a game for its players, and has become an industry, or a training for industry. In the American culture as a whole, no sharp line exists between work and play, and in some respects the more work-like an activity becomes, the more it can successfully conceal elements of playfulness.[12] Just because the sophisticated "amateur" of today does *not* have his manhood at stake in the antique do-or-die fashion (though his manhood may be involved, in very ambivalent ways, in his more generalized role as athlete and teammate), there can be a relaxation of certain older demands and a more detached enjoyment of perfection of play irrespective of partisanship.

The role of football tutor to the audience has been pushed heavily onto radio and TV announcers (some of whom will doubtless be mobile into the higher-status role of commentators on politics or symphony broadcasts). The managerial coalescence of local betting pools into several big oceans has also contributed to the audience stake in the game. Yet all that has so far been said does not wholly explain alumnus and subway-alumnus loyalties. It may be that we have to read into this interest of the older age groups a much more general aspect of American behavior: the pious and near-compulsory devotion of the older folks to whatever the younger folks are alleged to find important. The tension between the generations doubtless contributes to the hysterical note of solemnity in the efforts of some older age groups to control the ethics of the game, partly perhaps as a displacement of their Kinsey-belabored efforts to control youthful sexuality.

[12] See David Riesman (with the collaboration of Reuel Denney and Nathan Glazer), *The Lonely Crowd*, New Haven: Yale University Press, 1950, Chapters 15 and 17.

And this problem in turn leads to questions about the high percentage of women in the American football audience, compared with that of any other country, and the high salience of women in football as compared with baseball imagery (in recent American football films, girls have been singled out as the most influential section of the spectators). The presence of these women heightens the sexual impact of everything in and around the game, from shoulder pads to the star system, as the popular folklore of the game recognizes. Although women are not expected to attend baseball games, when they do attend they are expected to understand them and to acquire, if not a "male" attitude, at least something approaching companionship on a basis of equality with their male escorts.[13]

For all its involvement with such elemental themes in American life, it may be that football has reached the apex of its audience appeal. With bigness comes vulnerability: "inter-industry" competition is invited, and so are rising costs—the players, though not yet unionized, learn early in high school of their market value and, like Jim in Huckleberry Finn, take pride in it.[14] The educators' counter-reformation cannot be laughed off. With the lack of ethnic worlds to conquer, we may soon find the now-decorous Irish of the Midwest embarrassed by Notre Dame's unbroken victories. Perhaps the period of innovation which began in 1823 at Rugby has about come to an end in the United States, with large changes likely to result only if the game is used as a device for acculturation to America, not by the vanishing stream of immigrants to that country, but by the rest of the world that will seek the secret of American victories on the playing fields of South Bend.

[13] Anthropologist Ray Birdwhistell convincingly argues that football players play with an eye to their prestige among teammates, other football players, and other men.

[14] Their pride varies to some extent with their place on the team. Linemen, with the exception of ends, have lower status than backfield men. Many players believe that backfields are consciously and unconsciously recruited from higher social strata than linemen.

socio-psychological attributes associated with the early adoption of a sport innovation

JOHN W. LOY, JR.

A. Introduction

As Katz and others have noted, "It is hardly news that the diffusion of innovations is one of the major mechanisms of social and technical change" (10, p. 237). Similarly, it seems apparent that the diffusion of an innovation within a social system results from the acceptance of a new idea or practice by members of the social system at different points along a time continuum. There is a paucity of empirical generalizations concerning what personality factors may predispose certain persons to adopt innovations earlier than others (11, pp. 631, 632; 12, p. 178; 14, p. 293).

Moreover, although the importance and evidence of social and technical change are quite apparent in nearly every area of modern life, developments in a number of areas have not received serious study. An example of such an area is sport. It has been observed that the "spread of sport through the world and changes in its nature are major phenomena of the twentieth century" (2, p. 360; 13, p. 438). Sportsmen have acknowledged the changes that innovations such as new methods of athletic training, new ways of performing sport skills, and new types of athletic equipment have wrought in sport. Little theoretical or empirical work has been done regarding these changes.

1. PURPOSE

The theoretical purpose of the investigation was to study technological change within a social system associated with a sport by determining the significance of socio-psychological attributes of sportsmen hypothesized to be related to their differential adoption of a new technology. Operationally stated, the objective of the study was to examine an aspect of change in "competitive swimming," as evidenced in England by determining both *the degree* and *the nature* of the relationship between certain personal attributes of British swimming coaches and their date of adoption of the "con-

• From *The Journal of Psychology*, 70 (November, 1968), 141–147. © Journal Press, Provincetown, Mass. This research study was a part of a doctoral dissertation completed at the University of Wisconsin, June 1967. Partial support for the investigation was provided by funds from the NDEA Title IV Supplementary Fund for the General Improvement of Graduate Education. Appreciation is accorded to Joseph W. Elder and A. Eugene Havens, Department of Sociology, and Gerald S. Kenyon, Department of Physical Education, University of Wisconsin, for guidance in the investigation.

trolled interval method" (CIM) of training which was introduced in 1957–58.

2. HYPOTHESES

Socio-psychological variables considered in the investigation were largely selected on the basis of the theoretical frameworks given by Rogers (12) and Hagen (8). Drawing upon a review of over 500 research studies related to the diffusion and adoption of innovations, Rogers cites evidence which indicates that the earliest adopters of innovations have more education, greater financial resources, and are more professional and cosmopolite than later adopters. Furthermore, in discussing as an ideal-type the earliest adopter, which he calls the innovator, Rogers states that: "The major value of the innovator is venturesomeness. He must desire the hazardous, the rash, the daring, and the risking" (12, p. 169). Rather interestingly, Rogers fails to cite one study which directly tests by means of an objective personality inventory whether, in fact, early adopters are more venturesome than later adopters.

Hagen argues in his work, *On the Theory of Social Change*, that "technological progress results from the actions of men characterized by varying degrees of creativity" and that the attribute of creativity is not limited to the ". . . case of genius but to the quality of creativity in general, in whatever degree it may be found in a given individual" (8, p. 88). A hypothesis logically deduced from these statements is that the early adoption of innovations is positively related to creativity. But the investigator knows of no study where such an hypothesis has been submitted to empirical test.

In view of the theoretical frameworks provided by Rogers and Hagen, it was hypothesized that the early adoption of a sport innovation would be positively related to educational status, occupational status, professional status, cosmopoliteness, venturesomeness and creativity.

B. Procedures

1. SUBJECTS

Data were collected from 89 male and 17 female English swimming coaches by means of personal interviews (35 cases) and mailed questionnaires (71 cases) in the spring of 1966. Analyses of data were confined to two samples of Ss taken from the total group of respondents. Sample A consisted of 42 men and 6 women drawn from a population of chief (including three co-chief) swimming coaches, with a minimum of eight years coaching experience, associated with competitive clubs affiliated to the Amateur Swimming Association of England (ASA).

Sample A was limited to chief coaches because assistant coaches often lacked the authority to make the decision to adopt the innovation considered. Secondly, since the innovation was first introduced in 1957–58 only those subjects who had coached at least eight years, and thus had nearly equal opportunity of being an early adopter were considered for data analysis. Finally, data analysis was limited to coaches associated with competitive clubs as the innovation was not relevant for noncompetitive clubs. A competitive club was defined as one which had one or more swimmers place at least third in one or more events at its district championship in 1964. The proportion of clubs represented in Sample A according to districts within the ASA is as follows: North-Eastern District = 11/12, Northern District = 7/17, Midland District = 13/32, Western District = 6/12, and Southern District = 8/15. In sum, the subjects in Sample A represent approximately 50 percent of the coaches associated with competitive clubs affiliated to the ASA.

Sample B consisted of six female coaches included in Sample A and nine additional female coaches drawn from a somewhat broader population (i.e., one including assistant coaches).

2. INSTRUMENTS

Measures of the socio-psychological variables contained in the aforementioned hypotheses were obtained by using two questionnaires developed by the investigator and Form A of Cattell's Sixteen Personality Factor Questionnaire (16PF) (3,4,5). The latter instrument was selected for use in the investigation because: (1) the factors it purports to measure are relevant to the assessment of venturesomeness and creativity; (2) in general, it possesses relatively good evidence of reliability and validity; (3) it may be self-administered and is suitable for an investigation using mailed questionnaires; and (4) it appeared appropriate for the population concerned as it had previously been used for research purposes in England and is designed for adult populations.

3. MEASURES

An operational indicator was developed for each concept given in the previously stated hypotheses.

A.   The concept of "early adoption" was taken as the dependent variable and operationalized as "time of adoption of CIM recorded to the nearest year." The CIM is a sophisticated form of interval training wherein pulse rate is used as a means of determining the intensity of a training bout as well as the length of recovery period between bouts; and as a motivation device and an indicator of a swimmer's level of cardiovascular fitness (cf. 1). The CIM was selected for consideration in the investigation because: (1) having potential for bringing about change in competitive swimming via better performance records, it appeared to be a profound sport innovation; (2) it was distinctive—there are no other methods of training quite like it; (3) it did not have major economic constraints attached to it; (4) it had a pattern of diffusion which could be accurately traced; and (6) it was officially recommended but not required for adoption by the national athletic organization governing swimming in England.

B.   A subject's "educational status" was ascertained by his response to questions regarding years of schooling, types of schools attended, and diplomas and degrees earned.

C.   A subject's "occupational status" was determined by coding his reply to the following question: "What is your main occupation (fulltime job)? Please give a brief description of your job as I am unfamiliar with many kinds of vocational employment in England." By means of criteria given by the General Register's Office *Classification of Occupations 1966*, each subject was classified according to socio-economic group and assigned a respective numeric value.

D.   "Professional Status" was operationalized by determining the degree to which a subject's ability to teach and coach swimming was recognized by the ASA. The governing body for amateur swimming in England has established committees which annually appoint a national panel of examiners who administer tests, both theoretical and practical, at three levels of proficiency. Subjects were ranked in terms of professional competence and assigned a numeric value according to the award received.

E.   "Cosmopoliteness," or the degree to which an individual's orientation is external to the local situation in which he generally operates, was empirically measured by determining a subject's degree of personal communication with nationally and internationally known coaches in the year prior to the investigation.

F.   A subject's degree of "Venturesomeness" was assessed in terms of his score on Factor H of the 16PF test.

G.   "Creativity" was operationally measured by a weighting of sten scores on ten factors of the 16PF (A,B,E,F,H,I,M,N,Q1, and Q2) (9).

4. TREATMENT

A.   In order to determine *the degree of relationship* between the early adoption of an innovation and selected socio-psychological characteristics, each general hypothesis (e.g., the early adoption of an innovation is positively related to creativity) was stated operationally (e.g., time of adoption of CIM is positively related to a subject's creativity score on the 16PF). Each operational hypothesis in turn was restated in the form of a statistical hypothesis. Pearson product-moment correlation coefficients were computed; the 0.05 level of significance (using a one-tailed test) was selected as being sufficient to warrant the rejection of each statistical hypothesis.

B.   In the second stage of the treatment of the data, attention was given to determining *the nature of the relationship* between the dependent variable and the independent variables considered collectively. By means of multiple correlation analysis, an effort was made to explain the greatest amount of variance possible in the dependent variable by using a small number of independent variables which in combination had relatively high partial correlations with the dependent variable.

C. Results

1. DEGREE OF RELATIONSHIP

Results of the investigation show that for Sample A, date of adoption of CIM is positively and significantly related to professional status ($r = 0.56$), cosmopoliteness ($r = 0.51$), occupational status ($r = 0.41$), creativity ($r = 0.30$), and educational status ($r = 0.29$); but not significantly related to venturesomeness ($r = 0.23$).

2. NATURE OF RELATIONSHIP

A. SAMPLE A. A multiple correlation of 0.72 was obtained (after correction of inflated R due to small sample size) between the dependent variable and three independent variables. The independent variables considered with their partial correlation coefficient with the dependent variables were: professional status (0.61), cosmopoliteness (0.44), and creativity (0.39).

As Cattell's composite index of creativity is based on American samples of artists and scientists, it was thought that perhaps not all factors considered or the relative weightings given would be entirely applicable to the sample of English coaches studied. Hence, a selected number of the factors included in the creativity index was examined collectively and unweighted. Ten independent variables in combination produced a multiple correlation of 0.80 with the dependent variable. The ten factors considered and their partial correlation with time of adoption of the CIM included: professional status (0.54), cosmopoliteness (0.48), venturesomeness (H) (0.44), sociability (A) (—0.43), occupational status (0.41), dominance (E) (—0.39), sensitivity (I) (—0.33), imaginativeness (M) (0.33), shrewdness (N) (—0.33), and experimentiveness (Q1) (0.33).

B. SAMPLE B. A multiple correlation of 0.93 was found between the dependent variables for the sample of female Ss. The independent variables taken into account and their partial correlation coefficients with the dependent variable were: perseverance (G) (0.91), dominance (E) (0.89), self-sufficiently (Q2) (—0.83), venturesomeness (H) (0.81), intelligence (B) (0.79), and sociability (A) (—0.47).

D. Discussion

1. DEGREE OF RELATIONSHIP

The values of correlation coefficients between date of adoption of CIM and educational status ($r = 0.29$) and creativity ($r = 0.30$) may be considered low, but they indicate definitely some relationship between variables. In contrast, the correlation coefficients between the dependent and independent variables of occupational status ($r = 0.41$), cosmopoliteness ($r = 0.51$), and professional status ($r = 0.56$) may be viewed as moderate correlations suggesting a substantial relationship between variables (7).

Although the above correlation coefficients are not very high, they are of approximately the same magnitude as those obtained in earlier work related to the adoption of innovations (12). It may not be reasonable to expect any one independent variable to be highly related to adoption behavior, nor to assume that the socio-psychological attributes considered in the investigation are independently related to the adoption of an innovation. In short, not only the degree of relationship between the time of adoption and personal attributes, but also the nature of the relationship among variables must be taken into account.

2. NATURE OF THE RELATIONSHIP

Multiple correlation analyses based on data gathered from English swimming coaches demonstrate that a substantial proportion of the variance associated with the time of adoption of a new technology could be explained by small clusters of socio-psychological attributes.

Notwithstanding the possibility that the very high multiple correlation ($r = 0.93$) obtained for Sample B may result from sampling error associated with a small sample, it is interesting to observe that innovative female coaches have typically masculine characteristics. In addition the personality factors found to be associated with the early adoption of a sport innovation are similar to those found to be related to the prediction of creativity. Notable exceptions to the latter observation, however, are the negative correlations between date of adoption of CIM with dominance ($r - 0.39$) for Sample A, and with self-sufficiency ($r - 0.83$) for Sample B. Venturesomeness, while not significantly related to time of adoption when considered singly, is substantially related to the early adoption of an innovation when considered in combination with other variables.

E. Summary

An investigation was made to determine the degree and nature of the relationship between certain personal attributes of British swimming coaches and their date of adoption of a new training method. Data were collected from 106 coaches by means of personal interviews and mailed questionnaires. Regarding the degree of relationship, results showed that the differential adoption of a sport innovation was significantly ($p \leq 0.05$) and positively related to educational status, occupational status, professional status, cosmopoliteness, and creativity. Concerning the nature of relationship, findings showed that a substantial proportion of adoption variance (52 to 86 percent) could be accounted for in terms of ten or fewer socio-psychological variables.

REFERENCES

1. Amateur Swimming Association of England, *Competitive Swimming*, London: Educational Productions, Ltd., 1962.

2. Baltzell, E. D., *Philadelphia Gentleman*, New York: Free Press, 1958.
3. Cattell, R. B. and Eber, H. W., *Handbook for the Sixteen Personality Factor Questionnaire*, Champaign, Illinois: Institute for Personality and Testing, 1957.
4. ————, *Manual for Forms A and B of the Sixteen Personality Factor Questionnaire*, Champaign, Illinois: Institute for Personality and Ability Testing, 1962.
5. ————, *Supplement of Norms for Forms A and B of the Sixteen Personality Factor Questionnaire*, Champaign, Illinois: Institute for Personality and Ability Testing, 1962.
6. General Register Office, *Classification of Occupations 1966*, London: Her Majesty's Stationery Office, 1966.
7. Guilford, J. P., *Fundamental Statistics in Psychology and Education* (3rd ed.), New York: McGraw-Hill, 1956.
8. Hagen, E. E., *On the Theory of Social Change*, Homewood, Illinois: Dorsey Press, 1962.
9. Institute for Personality and Ability Testing, *Data for Psychologists Selecting Students for Creativity and Research Potential*, Champaign, Illinois: Institute for Personality and Ability Testing, Information Bulletin #10, 1963.
10. Katz, E. and Others, "Traditions of Research on the Diffusion of Innovations," *American Sociological Review*, **28**, 237–252, (1963).
11. Miles, M. B. (ed.), *Innovation in Education*, New York: Bureau of Publications, Teachers College, Columbia University, 1964.
12. Rogers, E. M., *Diffusion of Innovations*, New York: Free Press, 1962.
13. Smithells, P. A. and Cameron, P. E., *Principles of Evaluation in Physical Education*, New York: Harper & Brothers, 1962.
14. Straus, M. A., "Personality Testing the Farm Population," *Rural Sociology*, **21**, 293, 294 (1956).

sportugese: a study of
sports page communication

PERCY H. TANNENBAUM AND
JAMES E. NOAH

It was the age of jazz and the Charleston, of the flapper and raccoon coats, of speakeasies and bathtub gin. But among members of the sporting fraternity, the Roaring Twenties had another claim to fame: it was "the golden age of sports," when the American populace, flush with post-war prosperity, flocked to the arenas and stadia. Not only was this the hey-day of the more conventional sports (boxing, baseball, football) but of the "fringe" sports (e.g., jai-alai and six-day bike racing) as well.

Whether partially responsible for this upsurge in sports interest, or a result of it, or merely coincidental with it, there also arose a new brand of sports writing and reporting during the Twenties. The change-over was almost as dramatic as the difference between a present-day account of a cricket match in a staid British daily and a Big Ten college paper's eulogy of last Saturday's football upset. Informality of style, originality of composition and a new jargon blossomed on the sports pages—but accompanied by a tendency towards verbosity, triteness, and shopworn clichés, synonymns and analogies.[1] The golden age of sports was matched by a slightly tarnished silver age of sports writing.

This situation has undoubtedly been altered somewhat in the past few decades, possibly for the better. Among others, Stanley Woodward, sports editor of the New York *Herald Tribune*, claims sports pages have abandoned most of their "unholy jargon," and are "written as well as the rest (of the paper)." [2] The effect of the Twenties, however, is still evident on today's sports pages. The sports writer still has a greater freedom of expression than most of his newspaperman colleagues, and even Woodward admits that this

---

[1] A fairly thorough and critical analysis of sports writing in the Twenties is to be found in: Robert F. Moscowitz, "Professional Sports Journalism in the 1920's as Recorded in Six Metropolitan Dailies" (M.A. thesis, University of Missouri, 1955).

• From the *Journalism Quarterly*, 36 (1959), 163–170. Copyright © 1959 by the *Journalism Quarterly* and reprinted with the permission of Prof. Percy H. Tannenbaum, Univeristy of Pennsylvania. This study was initiated as a term project by Mr. Noah in a research methods course conducted by Dr. Tannenbaum at the University of Illinois. The senior author expanded the initial study into its present form, and accepts the main responsibility for this report. At the time of publication, Dr. Tanenbaum was director of the Center for the Study of Mass Communications at the University of Wisconsin; Mr. Noah was an instructor in English at Northern Illinois University.

[2] Stanley Woodward, *Sports Page*, New York: Simon and Schuster, 1949, p. ix.

freedom often results in "a conglomeration of heroics, bathos and mixed figures of speech . . . and extremes of word-painting." [3]

Our purpose here is not to evaluate or to pass judgment on contemporary sports language. Good, bad, or otherwise, such a language has evolved. It was spawned on the sports pages of the Twenties, and nurtured by such reporters as Damon Runyon, Heywood Broun, Ring Lardner and Grantland Rice [4]—great writers all, most of whom went on to bigger and better things in journalism after their sports writing performances.

By now, this *patois*—"Sportugese," we might call it—has developed to the stage where it is an intergral part of the sports writer's kit-bag, his stock-in-trade. Faced with the need to reproduce the content and the emotion, the denotation and the connotation, of the event he is reporting, the sports writer is apt to release a barrage of "exact adjectives" ranging from *aghast* to *zany*, and of "action verbs" from *annihilate* to *zoom*.

It is particularly with the verbs of Sportugese that we will be concerned in this study. Commenting on this aspect of the language of the sports page, one observer has been led to note:

> No one wins a game today. Teams rock, sock, roll, romp, stagger, swamp, rout, decision, down, drop, eke out, topple, top, scalp, and trounce opponents, but no one wins a game.[5]

Similarly, a recent issue of the *New Yorker* carried a delightful take-off piece offering some advice—ostensibly for the benefit of the then-uninitiated San Francisco papers covering the newly-arrived Giants—on "the science and art of baseball-headline verbs." This, says the *New Yorker*, has evolved from "a simple matter of 'win' or 'lose' into a structure of periphrasis as complex as heraldry in feudalism's decadence." [6] This build-up leads to an explicit set of rules governing baseball verbs: *edge* for a 2-1 game; *shade* for a 3-2 game; *whip* for a 3-1 game. A 4-2 score ("Uniquely character-less, known professionally as 'the golden mean' or 'absolute zero'") calls for the "bland" terms *beats* or *defeat*, but a 4-1 game gets the "coveted" *vanquish*. This, in turn, leads to a general rule, as rigorous as one could ever hope for:

---

[3] *Ibid.*, p. x.

[4] Rice's famous "Four Horsemen" lead in his account of the 1924 Notre Dame-Army game (*New York Herald Tribune*, Oct. 19, 1924) is often cited as a journalistic classic, and not only of sports writing: "Outlined against a blue-gray October sky, the Four Horsemen rode again. In dramatic lore, they are known as Famine, Pestilence, Destruction and Death. These are only aliases. Their real names are Stuhldreher, Miller, Crowley and Layden. . . ."

[5] Actually composed by one of the authors (Noah, in his term paper report of the pilot study), but it does look much more elegant as an attributed quote. Besides, such a statement—or words to that effect—must have been made. See e.g., *Coronet*, Nov. 1954, p. 121.

[6] *New Yorker*, June 21, 1958, p. 21.

Any three-run margin, provided the winning total does not exceed ten, may be described as a vanquishing. If, however, the margin is a mere two runs and the losing total is five or more, "outslug" is considered very tasty. You will notice . . . the trend called Mounting Polysyllabism, which culminates, at the altitude of double digits, in that trio of Latin-root rhymers, "annihilate," "obliterate" and "humiliate."

Kidding aside—the New Yorker probably wasn't really kidding—there is as much method as mirth in all this. The point is, of course, that in the lexicon of the sports writer different verbs may refer to different point-spreads —all this possibly quite apart from any conscious effort on the part of writer, in the same sense that much of everyday speech, for example, requires little conscious effort to encode. At any rate, this is a working assumption of the present study, and raises a legitimate question for research: Do these different verbs actually denote different point-spreads, not only for the sports writer who encodes them but also for the sports reader who decodes them?

As such, this type of research problem is unique to the sports page. In a sense, we are asking a fundamental question applying to all newspaper communication, indeed to all deliberate communication: Is the intent of the communicator "getting across" to the receiver? The verbs of Sportugese— at least that aspect we have chosen to investigate here—were selected as a focus for the present study partly because of individual preference, but more because the apparent intent is more readily identifiable and can be determined quite objectively. These reasons will probably become more apparent as the study unfolds.[7]

General Procedure and Definitions

The units for investigation in the present study were the verbs used in the reporting of high school basketball games in a sample of Illinois and Missouri dailies [8] and the respective points-spreads of each game. Why basketball games? One reason was the relatively high frequency of such games —in "hoop-mad" Illinois alone, more than 300 high school basketball games are played every Friday during the season. A second reason was that compared with many other sports, the range of point-spreads is much greater in basketball, and hence more susceptible to diversified verb treatment. The third and

[7] At the time of preparation of this report, a similar study is being conducted by one of the authors (Tannenbaum) and largely for these very same reasons. This latter study will deal with the language of political election reporting as a function of the vote spread.

[8] The sample consisted of newspaper accounts of high school basketball games during the 1957–58 season, as reported in the following papers: Bloomington Daily Pantagraph, Champaign-Urbana Courier, Champaign-Urbana News-Gazette, Chicago Daily News, Chicago Tribune, Joliet Herald-News, Moline Daily Dispatch, Peoria Journal, St. Louis Globe-Democrat, St. Louis Post-Dispatch, Springfield Journal.

main reason was that the verbs used in the leads of basketball games reports are more apt to refer to the score as such, and are relatively less "contaminated" by other considerations.[9]

Not all verbs used in an individual story were selected. Rather, only one verb was selected for each story, provided that (a) it referred directly to the score of the game (not, for example, to an individual player's performance), and (b) it appeared in the first two paragraphs of the story, or, in some cases, in the headlines. If a story failed to meet these criteria, it was not included in the sample. The point-spread variable was obviously much simpler to obtain—this is merely the difference between the scores of the winning and losing teams, and as no ties are possible, it can range from one point to practically any number (an 81-point spread was the largest recorded in our sample).

Such data—the actual verb and the point-spread—were recorded for 928 separate game reports, which, because of some over-lap in the games covered by different papers, probably represented a somewhat lesser number of games. A total of 84 *different* verbs was extracted from the 928 stories, and the 928 point-spreads were recorded in units ranging from 1 to 39 points, with one category consisting of 40-or-more points. These formed the raw data for the study.

The 84 different verbs were first examined in terms of their use as judged against their dictionary definition (Phase I). They were then used as stimulus materials in an investigation of the point-spreads they connote among samples of sports writers, regular sports readers and non-readers of sports pages (Phase II). Lastly, the verbs and their respective point-spreads were analyzed in terms of the degree of diversification on verb usage for different point-spread frequencies (Phase III). A more specific presentation of the methodologies employed in each of these phases of the study will be presented below along with their respective findings.

The Three Phases: Results

It is obvious from the above, that the three phases of this study were related to one another. However, it is also apparent that each had a separate purpose and procedure of inquiry. Accordingly, it will be more meaningful to discuss each of these phases independently.

PHASE I: VERB DESCRIPTION

The first approach to this problem of basketball verb usage was to subject the 84 isolated verbs to scrutiny in terms of their dictionary definition —i.e., whether each appeared in a standard dictionary, and secondly, whether

---

[9] In football, for example, the lead verbs are apt to refer to the instrument of victory —e.g., "Ohio State *ground* their way to . . ."; "Illinois *soared* to . . .", apparently referring to a passing attack. Basketball reporting has some of this element also, but apparently less than other sports.

their use on the sports page corresponded with the dictionary definition. No major claims—substantive or methodological—are made for this type of analysis, other than it appeared to be a reasonable first step to take in such an evaluation.

Accordingly, each of the 84 verbs was checked against a standard dictionary source.[10] After preliminary analysis, four categories of correspondence were used: Those verbs whose general sports page usage corresponded, however roughly, to dictionary definition were classified as "acceptable." Some verbs were found in the dictionary but their usage was at considerable variance with that in the dictionary, and these were classed as having "specialized meaning." Other verbs were used in a manner that corresponded, at best to a "strictly slang" usage. And several verbs did not appear in the dictionary at all. Table 1 presents the results of this rather crude analysis, and indicates

table 1

ANALYSIS OF VERBS IN TERMS OF
DICTIONARY CORRESPONDENCE

	N	%
Acceptable Usage	38	45.2
Specialized Meaning	26	31.0
Strictly Slang	12	14.3
Do Not Appear	8	9.5
Totals	84	100.0

a considerable lack of correspondence between the sports verbs and their dictionary definitions.

As one might expect, the most common verbs used are the "generic" ones—*defeated* (59 appearances) and *won* (57). Not far behind were two other stand-by sports verbs—*took* (41) and *whipped* (35). A wide number of verbs occurred with varying frequencies somewhat below the above-mentioned, with the following choices being some that appeared but once each in this sample of 928 verbs: *gouged, humiliated, triggered, squeaked* and *whumped*.[11] Also of interest in the single-frequency category, and demonstrating a marked sensitivity to—if not an overdrawn capitalization on—recent worldly concerns were the following: *H-bombed, atomized* and *orbited*.

Not the least to be noticed, of course, was the tendency toward punning, also observed by the *New Yorker*. All teams with names like "Indians," "Braves," etc., invariably *scalp* their opponents sometime during the season; those endowed with bird names ("Eagles," "Hawks," etc.) *soar* to victory,

[10] *Webster's Standard College Dictionary*, 1954 ed.

[11] Whether *whumped* was a typographical error (for *whomped*) or whether it was some cub reporter's over-zealous combination of *whipped* and *thumped* was not clear.

while "Lions" and "Tigers" *claw* out wins. One team named "Rough Riders" *lassoed, roped, stampeded* and *galloped* to victories.

PHASE II: COMMUNICATION EFFICIENCY OF SPORTS VERBS

In a sense, all of the above is beside the point. Sports verbs may or may not appear in the dictionary; they may or may not be slang, and they may or may not be cases of cliché-ridden analogy. The important question is whether or not they communicate what they intend to communicate. In the present study, the intended bit of information (not to be confused with the "Information Theory" unit of the same name, although somewhat related to it) was assumed to be the point-spread measure.

To assess the communication effectiveness of these verbs, three samples of subjects were used. One consisted of 18 sports writers, all of whom had written or edited basketball copy; a second consisted of 68 college students, mostly males, who classified themselves as "regular readers of the sports page," and a third group of 28 undergraduates, mostly female, who classified themselves as *not* being sports followers or readers of newspaper sports sections.

The procedure here was quite simple. Each group of subjects was presented with the list of 84 verbs, arranged in alphabetical order, and was asked to indicate what they "would estimate the point-spread to be in a basketball game described by each verb." All three groups had the same task. Moreover, for each group we had the same standard for measurement—the actual means of the point-spreads for each verb in the sample of games covered. The basic criterion for each group, then, was the degree of correspondence between the means of estimated point-spreads for each of the 84 verbs and their respective actual mean point-spreads. Such a correspondence, or lack of it, is best measured by a correlation coefficient (r)—a positive high r indicates a high degree of correspondence between estimated and obtained scores, and hence a greater degree of communication efficiency of the verbs used.

The results obtained on such analysis were quite striking. Table 2 gives

table 2
CORRELATIONS BETWEEN ANTICIPATED
AND OBTAINED POINT-SPREADS

GROUP	r
Sports Writers	.81
Regular Sports Readers	.86
Nonsports Readers	.33

the respective r's for each of the three test groups, and demonstrates a remarkable communication efficiency for these basketball verbs—at least among the regular consumers of sports news. If different point-spreads are what such verbs are supposed to communicate, then these verbs do so with a high degree of accuracy.[12] This is particularly true for the encoders of such verbs themselves (our sports writer sample [13]) and for the intended audience (the regular sports readers). However, for the person who does not read or follow sports, these verbs fail in communicating their message. In the present case, at least, this may be as much a function of complete ignorance of the sport itself as well as a lack of familiarity with the verbal terminology. It should be noted that while the difference between the r's for the sports writers and regular readers may be surprising and amusing in terms of its direction, it is not significant in terms of magnitude.

PHASE III: VERB USAGE AS RELATED TO FREQUENCY OF EVENT

These data on verb usage were subjected to an additional analysis that is not only of some significance in itself but which may be of considerable interest to students of language and linguistics. This analysis dealt with the relative diversity or heterogeneity of verb usage as a function of different frequencies of occurrence of the events to which they refer.

It is a fairly common assumption among linguists and anthropologists that the more frequent an event in a given linguistic culture—or, at least, the more important that event is within that culture—the greater the number and diversity of words associated with that event. The notion here is simply that the language vocabulary mirrors the interests of the people who speak that language. Klineberg,[14] in his discussion of this phenomenon, cites some instances: The exceptional significance of the camel in Arab culture is reflected in some 6,000 different "words derived from the camel and attributes associated with it"; the Eskimos are said to have several dozen words to discriminate between different aspects of snow, what for most of us is a single phenomenon; the Chuckchee of Northeasten Siberia designate different aspects of the reindeer by a wide variety of distinctive terms, and so on.

The above examples, and the many more usually cited, refer to the variety of *nouns* associated with different events of the environment. Sapir [15] also mentions similar evidence for other grammatical classes, including some intriguing variations in verb usage between different language groups. In any event, it was thought that a similar analysis in terms of the present data would be of interest, and possibly of some use.

To accomplish such an analysis two sets of related data are needed.

[12] It should be recognized, of course, that this is true for the verbs as a whole, but may or may not be true for any individual verb used.

[13] It might also be noted that as part of the pilot study, a group of five sports writers were asked to classify a sub-sample of the verbs of the present study into three categories: verbs which simply denoted victory or defeat; verbs which signified a wide point-spread, and verbs which indicated a narrow margin of victory. The three sets of verbs thus classified were then compared on the actual point-spreads of the games they reported. The differences between these point-spreads were statistically significant and in the predicted direction.

[14] Otto Klineberg, *Social Psychology*, New York: Henry Holt, 1940, pp. 44–46.

[15] Edward Sapir, in *Encyclopaedia of the Social Sciences*, New York: Macmillan, 1933, pp. 155–69.

First, we need some index of the range and frequency of the events being reported. In the present case, this was simply to assess—the "events" were the various point-spreads (we had 40 such classes) and the frequency of each such event was indexed by their respective percent occurrence in our sample of 928 cases.

The second desideratum was for some index of "diversification of verb usage" for each event. A convenient measure here is the *Type-Token Ratio* (TTR).[16] In the present case, the number of types was the number of *different* verbs associated with a particular point-spread, and the number of tokens was the number of cases, or the frequency, of that point-spread event.[17] Generally, then, the TTR can have a range of $1/n$ to 1.00, where $n =$ number of cases or tokens. The larger the TTR, i.e., as the TTR value approaches 1.00, the greater the diversification in verb usage.

FIGURE I

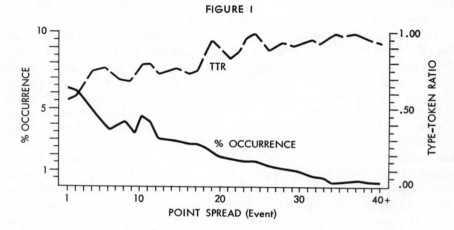

Thus, for each of 40 events it was possible to obtain measures of both the relative frequency of each event and the degrees of verb usage per event. Both these data are presented in Figure 1.[18] The hypothesis to be tested with these data was simply that *the more frequent the occurrence of* an event, the greater the diversity of verb usage, with the correlation coefficient between the two measures being the appropriate statistic.

When such a correlation was actually computed, the results not only

[16] See George A. Miller, *Language and Communication*, New York: McGraw-Hill, 1951, pp. 122–24.

[17] For example, given a particular point-spread occurring, say 10 times, if there was only one verb used in all 10 cases, TTR $= 1/10$ or 0.10; if 10 different verbs were used, TTR $= 10/10$ or 1.00; if seven different verbs were used, TTR $= 7/10$ or 0.70.

[18] In both cases, the curves were "smoothed" by the method of "running averages." See J. P. Guilford, *Fundamental Statistics in Psychology and Education*, New York: McGraw-Hill, 1942, pp. 23–24.

failed to confirm the hypothesis but indicated quite the contrary. The obtained Pearson product-moment correlation coefficient was —0.88, a highly significant but negative r. In other words, the greater the percent occurrence of the event, the smaller the verb diversification (i.e., a greater redundancy of use), and vice versa. This finding is contrary to the expected, and also provides a clue to part of the encoding behavior of the sports writer: As the event he is reporting becomes less frequent and hence more unique, it becomes a "richer" event for him and his description of the event tends toward accounting for the uniqueness in terms of different, less common terms.[19] This is an entirely plausible behavior, and is probably characteristic not only of the sports writer. But even for the sports writer, it remains an interesting speculation for the present.

Discussion

What other discussion does such a study merit?

For one thing, the relatively unambiguous nature of the findings is a rare enough occurrence in communication research. This can be largely traced to the unambiguous, highly objective nature of the variables under consideration, along with the simple and direct methodology of analysis. There was no question whatsoever about either of the variables being analyzed—the verbs studied were the actual words (and not, for example, classifications of verbs) used in the stories; the point-spreads also involved no element of individual decision. Similarly, the analysis of these data in the main parts of the investigation—that reported in Phases II and III—was as simple and straightforward as one could hope for. Probably the least satisfactory part of the study is that contained in Phase I, and this mainly due to the highly abritrary, subjective nature of the classifications. All of which raises the question of whether there are not other, perhaps more significant variables that are equally amenable to objective assessment and to direct analysis.

Within the sports writing area itself, several additional problems present themselves for further research. Similar analysis can be conducted for different sports events, both to investigate the generality of the phenomenon evidenced in the present research and to detect differences between these sports. Similarly, analysis of other language classes would seem a profitable line of inquiry; for example, an investigation of the adjectives used in sports reporting might prove even more interesting than that for verbs. There also are some interesting nuances of sports writing that could be investigated. The *New Yorker* article on baseball verbs touched on one such factor, that dealing with the special case of reporting of home team vs. visiting team victories and losses:

[19] It is of some interest to note that by far the greater proportion of the verbs cited earlier as lacking correspondence to standard dictionary definition were used to reflect games with higher point-spreads, i.e., the more unique events.

If the home team is on the short end of the score, certain laws of mutation apply. 'Shade' becomes 'squeak by.' For 'outslug' put 'win out in sloppy contest.' By a judicious exploitation of 'bow' the home team, while losing, can be given the active position in the sentence and an appearance of graciousness as well.[20]

We did start some exploration of this phenomenon with our present data but did not complete it. What little evidence we did gather does indicate some interesting variations of verb usage.

Also of interest might be conducting similar studies dealing with the connotative aspects of the words used. It is clear that the selection of sports verbs and adjectives is not based solely on the objective content of the event (e.g., point-spread, etc.) but also to convey part of the color and emotion of the contest. There are techniques available today (e.g., the semantic differential) to index such connotations, and studies of selection and effect are quite feasible.

Not least, of course, researches similar to the one reported and suggested here, could and probably should be conducted with other parts of the newspaper, and other media as well. What we are suggesting here is not so much replications of such studies but rather research on the two main aspects of this investigation: the basis of selection of terminology by the professional communicator—his encoding decisions, if you will—and the fidelity of his communication activity in terms of eliciting the desired denotative and connotative meanings in his intended audience.

One thing we hope this research will not lead to is a practice that has been adopted by at least one sports editor who had available to him some of the findings of the present study. His reaction was to circulate a memo to his staff—largely composed of part-time, relatively untrained help, it must be admitted—containing a list of "appropriate" verbs for different ranges of point-spreads. It is fine and dandy to have one's research have some "practical" applications, but not at the sake of stereotyping and restricting the writer's range and freedom of expression.

[20] New Yorker, June 21, 1958, p. 21.

the spectatorial forms

REUEL DENNEY

For all life is a game. . . . PLOTINUS

Spectator and Participant

To play golf, tennis, baseball, or what you will in childhood or maturity engages one in a series of deep and persisting identifications. To play is to belong to some kind of group of more or less definable social and age status. Within this playing group, many aspects of the nonplaying role are "suspended." Some players display one kind of personality on the field and another off it. The artificial time and space limits of the Game permit fluid interpersonal experience that would never occur so rapidly and with so much permutation in "real life." Error and recovery from error, for example, are possible within a single inning of a baseball game. The mere physical objectification of "in" and "out," "batter" and "fielder," "winner" and "loser," occurs in terms of a social rhythm perceptible to all players and shared by all in a system of expectations.

A general childhood experience with the Game is regarded in America as a skeleton key to the secrets of society. Considering that the nation has often been defined as a nation of spectators, the overlap in spectator and participant roles is high. The overlap probably provides one of the symbolic centers of that American tendency to emphasize mutuality and interchange of roles at the expense of their complementary separation. The interesting thing in a rich society such as ours is that many sports consumers can be classified readily as spectators and performers. (Sports such as mountain-climbing and skin-diving, of course, do not involve much spectatorship.) And though the ethos of the spectators is closely related to the ethos of the player, it is less tangible, less certain.

In the 1920s Ernest Hemingway began to work out a code for spectators as one of his themes. In much of his work he presumes that his readers feel guilty and unsure of themselves in a spectator's role. To them he suggests that there are good and bad spectators and that they have different points of self-reference in relation to sports and to the competitors in the sports. An important quality of this self-reference allows the spectator to perform some quasi-ritualistic act in which he acknowledges the vicariousness of his experience and at the same time resists envy or fear of the competitor's situation. Why this should have turned up as a major motif has been explained

• From *The Astonished Muse*, by Reuel Denney. Chicago: University of Chicago Press, 1957, Chapter 6, pp. 121–137. Copyright © 1957 by the University of Chicago Press.

often enough in terms of Hemingway as a personality. This does less than justice to the social environment of the 1920s and to his understanding of it.

It could be argued that the crisis of spectator ethos in the 1920s was part of American feeling because of the international dilemma of the time. Isolation and intervention are crucial political magnifications of the theme of spectatorship and participation; and in World War I the United States began to suffer new ambiguity and self-doubt about its relation to the world. The experience was made personally and historically concrete in the lives and deaths of Americans who sealed a new culture contact with Europe during the war. The people of the 1920s began to question the traditional American ideals of individualism and detachment. They asked whether detachment, spectatorship, "keeping one's powder dry," might not be degradations of an obsolete ideal. They were facing, among other things, the specialization of sports, the industrial expansion of sports, and the consumption of sports by a population seeking at once to escape an old morality and to find a new morality, in play.

Of all the social scenes in which the spectatorial crisis could find a symbolic reference, the world of sports presented the most generally known, fertile, universal and organically interrelated universe of terms. Some observers, like Ring Lardner, found it compelling to explore the locker-room dimension of reality. His stories were stories of working stiffs in baseball uniforms that only required a few moral and pathetic mud-spots on them to look like a clown's attire. Some found it meaningful to explore the relation between the small-business purveyor of sports, such as the fishing or hunting guide, and his clientele. This is one of the crucial role relationships from which Hemingway develops his dialectic of work and play. The 1920s can be characterized, among other things, as the decade in which Americans thought more and made more discoveries about the spectator-audience relationship than in any period before or since. This tends to be obscured by more recent writing which perhaps overemphasizes the self-destructive exhibitionism and voyeurism that haunted some of the famously creative lives of the period.

Amateur and Professional

The specialization of sports may be documented in two ways: by observing the business methods necessary to a university's department of athletics; by observing the decline of interest in sports activities among younger Americans. The business methods have already been commonly observed. The fan in the stadium on Saturday knows that contemporary football requires comptrollers, personnel directors, public relations counselors, and so on. Depending on the size of the athletic department's business, a few men or many perform these functions. The decline of interest among young Americans has not been so much observed or so well understood, but it is a fact.

Some of those who have observed the fact associate it with the low marks on physical aptitude scored by American youngsters as compared with European ones. Whether or not that is a legitimate association, many young athletes from Europe and "lesser developed" areas of the world undeniably look healthier than American youngsters of the same age. In general, the American standard of living and nutrition, which is two or three times higher than that of other countries, produces the pastiest lot of children in the world. Doubtless, American inferiority results partly from overconsumption of milk, a food overrated by Americans and popular in the United States chiefly because of its importance to immigrants as a symbol of class status. But milk is not the only potion that threatens the health of young Americans. "Toughness" and athletic skill are profoundly and widely confused with one another; individual sports like tennis, suitable to urban dwellers, are slighted; and old-fashioned moralizing, muscle-building ideas of physical education prevail in the schools.

It can be interpreted in various ways, then, that recent research directed by Eugene Gilbert shows that interest in active sports declined among young people between 1951 and 1956. It would be rash to associate the decline with the hashed and rehashed problem of physical softness in America; it might mean simply that young people have found other and more interesting things to do. Socially compulsive participant sports have been in the past producers not only of physical fitness but also of that mental unfitness which we find in the marginal participant who later becomes a moralizing or bloodthirsty or vainglorious spectator. Precisely because it is very hard to prove that sports, as contrasted with a physically active life of work and play, are crucial to health or hardiness, it is important to detect in sports-mindedness a desire to feed the sources of 100 percent Americanism, spectator benches, and the star system of the Big Game.

Industrial sports cannot generally create basic traits in our culture, but they can serve to confirm what we admire and what we dislike in the culture. To the degree that big sports pander to a taste for violence, they may encourage it as well as rechannel it. To the degree that they build the entertainment system rather than individual participation, they may distort our ideals of human growth in a free society. The debauching of colleges by "hardheaded" alumni pressure groups may lead to conditions not so different from gangster control of unions.

For who denies that American sports are specialized, centered on the "star" system? We see also that the public supporting sports suffers contradictions, inconsistencies, and uncertainties about amateur and professional status. There are three standards of sports participation available in the United States today.

The first and most powerful, the one supported by the most massive forces in the culture at large, is the business standard. By this standard, the ultimate goal of any athletic ability is to provide sports entertainment for cash. There is clearly nothing wrong with this standard except when, as in any other kind of business, it becomes disconcertingly illegal, as, for example, the purchase of college basketball teams for the benefit of gamblers. Players in a variety of sports ranging from bowling to baseball consider themselves as members of the general American "farm system" that provides stars to the commercial circuit. Their major problem, for years, has been to decide how much they wanted to bargain as a group with their employers or their sponsors and how much they wanted to bargain individually, as stars. The tendency in recent years has been to extend the claims of the proletarians in the wage-bargaining process. Professional football and baseball are the highest developments, probably, of this system.

The second most powerful standard of participation involves social class and has two major variants. The form of participation defended by Avery Brundage of the Olympic Committee and the American Lawn Tennis Association is the participation of the amateur gentleman. This standard prescribes that the athlete's family may buy his practice time and coaching for him but that it is quite unthinkable for anyone else to buy it for him. The important thing is that the athlete should be free from school or employment duties which would hamper his development as a great contender. The second variant is the upwardly mobile standard of the "nongentleman" and is represented best by the subsidized college football player. According to this standard, athletic ability is the commodity that must be marketed in order to complete an education, rise in the world, and overcome the disadvantages of a poor social start in the world. Rising in the world fits very well with the dominant business values of society in the United States, but completing an education does not. The "mobility" standard and the more traditional standard of Brundage both have roots in a theory of the relation between sports and social class. Where the standards conflict, we must hope that Brundage's standard will not be routed. At the same time we must hope that Brundage's standard will be applied with more social and cultural sophistication than it has been in the past.

The third, and less important, standard of participation is the type indorsed by the educational community. Here, participation is based on bona fide registration as a student, passing marks of studies, and certain controls over compensation which pretend to resemble the ironclad standard of amateurism espoused by Brundage. The educational standard is caught squarely between the two class variants mentioned and, at the same time, stands in conflict with the values of the business system. College football is so much larger, as an industry, a career, and a way of life, than most organized sports in the United States that it naturally becomes a major scene of conflict among all these approaches to what organized sports should be in America.

It might be well to point out that there are cross-cultural implications in all this. The American sports code is largely an adaptation of the British code, and America is one of the two English-speaking countries in the world that have carried the cultural context of sports to a keener degree of social intensity than Britain herself. Australia leads the world in the degree to which its sports interests and sports organizations reflect the total social and political ideals of the nation. Sport in Australia is virtually the invisible government of an egalitarian semi-socialistic community based on generations of lower-middle-class immigration from the old country. The development of mass sports and spectacle sports is not out of balance with the development of individual sports, and there is no professional-amateur friction to speak of. Any Australian in sport is believed by his countrymen to be a sort of gentleman to begin with, deserving all the support he can get from the rest of the gentlemen, even if it amounts to providing him with a welfare state and fringe benefits. All this results in part from the ethnic and linguistic consistency of the Australian population, which in turn creates the image of a whole social group going up the social scale all together. In the United States, the greatest complication of sports standards has arisen from the rapid inflow of non-English-speaking immigrant groups.

Yet the United States, along with Canada, deserves to be classed near Australia as one of the countries that has continued the British tradition of associating sports closely with the whole class and political texture of the society and especially its nineteenth-century revolution of making sports available to the rising middle class. In the English-speaking industrial democracies "youth movements" tend to be contained within the ethos of a sporting world associated with industrialism and high consumption; the absence of such connections is one of the things that makes "youth movements" in other countries, especially the Latin and Oriental countries, so utterly different. The ethos of sports for the young, of course, is closely related in highly industrial countries with mass educational opportunity and especially the growth in numbers of secondary school students and college students. The older British ideal of sport tends to hold more in English-speaking countries where sex segregation is practiced in schools, and it tends to decline sharply in countries emphasizing coeducational practice, chiefly the United States.

In comparison with Britain and Australia, the cultural meaning of American sports occupies a tense position between those two. Britain is able to maintain its amateur traditions because its class revolution has proceeded at an orderly pace since the 1880s. Australia is able to maintain a commercial concept of the amateur because it has judged that all of its sportsmen and spectators are gentlemen, and what gentlemen decide about sports, no matter what they decide, is correct by definition. The egalitarian traditions of the Labor party in Australia create the context in which aid to a young athlete is nothing more or less than *noblesse oblige*. The United States gyrates nervously between these two alternative class perspectives of sport because it is not sure what relation it wants to hold as between the athletic organizations and the class system as a whole. We lack the desire to take the Australian way; it would seem socialistic and patronizing to us. We reject the British way because it seems to us unfit for society such as ours in which social mobility proceeds at a faster pace, for more people in a greater variety of social circumstances. We cannot, of course, accept the Latin and Oriental standards of sport, which are still based, except in the "revolutionary" countries where sport is likely to be an industrial display, on a clear-cut difference between master and slave.

Sports opportunities in the United States today, especially in higher-cost individual sports such as tennis, are unequally distributed. The country can afford to support both the spectator system and the participant system, but today the spectator system still serves to mask the deficiency of the participant system. It might cease to do so as soon as it had to pay part of the bill. That is to say, despite our resources and the millions we spend on an athletic star system, many children, especially among minority groups, are growing up with few sports opportunities.

Given this desideratum, it would be wise to define every athlete as professional from the outset and then—only then—to establish certain forms qualifying him for amateur status for a particular event in a particular sport. The first rule of such events would be that no athlete could compete as an amateur in his major sport; for that sport, of course, is the one in which he is professional. The second rule would be that a portion of the income tax paid by sports corporations, including colleges, and by athletes, including college athletes, go to a national Amateur Committee charged with promoting sports for participants without "earning" power in sports.

If the United States is to build the participant system from the receipts of the spectator system, however, and especially if it is to avoid welfare-state sports, the American corporation and the American labor union must work out new ways to stimulate the spirit of amateurism. So far they have lagged. Business stumbled into subsidization of sports more or less accidentally and has not taken stock of the cultural implications. Labor unions seem too sleepy to care.

Meanwhile, the sports industry even tries to dominate its consumers into a sort of "yellow-dog" contract of spectatorship. In the previous chapter we noted critic John Crosby saying indirectly that football is "so different from [what it was in] the old days." He appears to belong to a relatively small group of sophisticates who can afford to wish for the old game that presented a clear-cut, sportsmanlike ideal and that introduced no ambiguities of subsidies, scholastic qualifications, and big-university politics. His view is perhaps the view of the demanding man who wants his entertainment to remain entertainment. To demonstrate a quite different approach to the question of sports spectatorship, we may quote from an article about sports in general: "America is becoming a nation of bad sports. It's about time we stopped coasting on our reputation and looked at the facts. The blunt truth is that Gus H. Fan is proving himself to be a rowdy, unruly, brawling pain in the neck. . . ."

This is the statement with which a writer known as Adie Suehsdorf opens an article entitled "Are Americans Bad Sports?" in *This Week*, a magazine that often prints such articles dealing with the art of consuming mass entertainment. The purpose of this article is to raise standards of sportsmanship in American mass-attended sports.

The article gives four reasons for bad sportsmanship, i.e., verbal and physical violence of an exaggerated character, at mass sports. The first is ignorance of the game on the part of a new class of consumers who do not know the rules. The second is that the games are too complex. The third is that betting money is involved. The fourth is that people seem more interested in identifying with a winner than in enjoying the game as a spectacle.

Let us consider reasons for bad sportsmanship not included by Suehsdorf, excluded really, because he sides with the industry against the consumer:

First, management has favored a situation in which players fight against rules and umpires, as, for example, the modern wrestling card that always includes at least one "dirty" bout. Management hopes thereby to show a genuine contest despite dishonesty in some respects, in some areas, at some time, in the history of most mass-entertainment sports. The audience in turn likes a genuine contest—even if it must be between player and referee—because it senses a lack of "fair contest" in big sports.

Second, management itself, in its function prior to the actual contest, is often committed to unfair practice. Many boxers, for example (and this is reflected in other popular media), are managed by gangsters.

Third, what management considers as unwarranted violence on the part of spectators is often an effort at participation, however foolish. Audience violence is a response to player violence sponsored by management as a promotional device.

However, even staying within Suehsdorf's reasons for bad sportsmanship—ignorance, complexity, betting, and anxiety to win—and ascribing truth to them, we see an authoritarian formula of consumership. The consumer, according to this formula, must be blamed for the consumption patterns imposed on an entertainment management that itself changed the pattern of the sports. The article suggests two methods for improving the situation: more police in stadiums, more education for sports consumers. Their essential onesidedness is revealed in the fact that the first leads theoretically to a situation where a crowd would be required to keep silent while watching a "fixed" game and the second leads theoretically to a situation where a spectator would spend time in night school learning how the mass-entertainment industries want him to respond to the sports for which he pays.

On the other hand, the sports public often responds with an ugly eagerness to the promotion of sports sadism and masochism. Perhaps it even brings to the sports arena—from the depths of American feeling—a brutishness that reminds us of lynch law, Texan male compulsives, and child-hating antivivisectionists. Slaps on the wrists of venal promoters are less likely to improve conditions than is a change of heart in the public itself. The spectator needs a code.

The Code of the Spectator

These comments on the spectator in sports may remind the reader that the audience of a TV show and the spectator of a sports event have been treated here as if they were members of the same species. Yet aren't they

different creatures, in many important senses? And if so, what are the differences? Some answers to this can be suggested by considering the different
standards of spectatorial perception that are associated with audiences for
fictions (movies and TV), audiences for contests (a wrestling match), and
audiences for performances (popular singers).

It is well known that a content-analysis of the characters, actions, symbols, and meanings of the products of popular culture, such as the movie, does
not tell us what the "real life" of the audience is. In fact, the characters,
actions, symbols, and meanings that occur in movies are there *because* they do
not exist in real life. Comparisons between actuality and fiction ought to be
made. We are beginning to realize that such comparisons are constantly being
applied to a wide range of symbolic activities and that the so-called problem
of "movie realism" is only a special case of a general question.

Suppose we were to set up a scale of entertainment products ranging
from those products in which realism is an issue only in a minor degree,
such as music, to those in which it is an issue to a major degree, say movies.
Discussions of realism in music tend to be discussions between disputants who
disagree with each other about the degree to which they hear, or permit,
progammatic elements in their favorite music. Most contributors to it
appear to be aware of the ambiguities involved. Discussions of realism in
movies, on the other hand, often tend to be arguments between disputants
who, although they define social reality differently, agree in thinking that
the attribution of some such realism to any and all movies is the best way
of beginning to criticize them. Between music and movies, however, there
is a range of products for which realism is also applied as a standard.

Closest to the movies in this respect is the field of sports. The TV broadcasting of boxing and wrestling induces a heavy investment of audience
attitudes centered on criteria of realism. The realism in these exhibitions is
expressed in the notion that, ideally, the contest enacted and portrayed
should be a real contest with fair rules. In general, attitudes toward the reality
of the contest becomes, for the audience, the test of different levels of competence in viewing the contest. The viewer who is unaware that the wrestler
dramatizes his triumphs and despairs as a part of the box-office appeal is
dismissed as unsophisticated by the audience-in-the-know. At the same time,
other sports tend to be arranged in a rank order according to the general
public belief as to the possibility of the "fix." Wrestling appears to occupy
the bottom of this rank order, and probably professional baseball, if we disregard the factor of the farm system, appears to occupy the top of the rank
order. Horse racing appears to fall in between these two, along with other
major professional sports.

Wrestling is an especially interesting example of the public's problems in
search of realism. Because the public believes that wrestling is often "fixed,"
it protects itself from cynicism about the matter by preferring to view the
sport as drama rather than as a contest. It is willing to give up the sense of
pure competition between equalized or handicapped contestants in order to

pay attention to a drama of alternative scenes of dominance and submission. One gets the idea that audience interest is concentrated not so much on the indeterminant moments of the contest, in which neither contestant is ahead, as on the moments in which one contestant is very much ahead. The price paid for this view of the sport is that the audience loses competence in some other sense. Strictly speaking, it loses competence in the judgment of the real hurts suffered by real wrestlers in their stunt-man approach to a spectacle performance of fictional violence.

The question might be asked whether a plainly fictional contest whose major rule is to have the rules broken constitutes a problem in realism for the audience. Apparently it does. Conversations about wrestling seem to involve two claims on the part of the participants: (1) the claim that they can recognize situations when the "fix" is upset by the "real" and (2) the claim that they can distinguish a normal amount of villainous rule-breaking from an abnormal and indecent amount of villainous rule-breaking. The first claim, that the "fix" can be distinguished from the "real," is clearly untenable. The same audience cannot pretend to itself at one and the same time that wrestlers are great actors in their line—and not great actors. Probably social perception of wrestling works the other way, that most injured wrestlers leave the ring with injuries unperceived by the audience. The second claim, that there is a line separating "too much" from "enough" rule-breaking is a highly tenable claim. Audiences do develop keen discriminations of this sort; in this respect the audience' "realism" is at its height.

Given the etiquette of any sport, the audience is involved in the competitive state of the struggle and the fairness or unfairness of the application of the rules. The audience claims to know a practical, if not formal, norm. With both movies and sports events, the audience possesses a practical norm which it resents being flouted by the demands of fiction.

The problem of realism has been approached in terms of realism in fiction and realism in contests that have become fictions. We can generalize the problem of realism to make it include the realism of performance. Thus, most cases of ordinary people calling a movie unrealistic center about the acting. Story structure is not really perceived at all; the question is whether, given the story situation, the characters behave as expected or desired.

It is important to the popular audience to feel competent in the judgment of singers. In recent years, the performances of popular singers have been described as being "sincere" or "commercial." In this polarity, "sincere" may mean any one or all of the following: (1) The singer reflects in artistic performance well-known biographical aspects of himself. (2) The singer dramatizes a widely diffused social role. (3) The singer identifies with the audience. (4) The singer is self-stimulated by his own performance to such a degree that he becomes a person making a true statement. (5) The singer employs a new style that, because of its apparent informality or its intensity, achieves the appearance of personalization. (The artist appears to dominate convention and make it his own.) Claims to this sort of competence on the part of audiences are often challenged on the ground that they are naïve. The audience, it is said, mistakes the well known capacity of the skillful artist to use the most calculated and impersonal means to achieve "personal" effects.

Such an attack on the competence of the audience holds up quite well when it is applied to biographical reflection, role dramatization, or audience identification. By the same token, it does not hold up well if the audience claims to perceive sincerity or some other aspect of realism in cases of self-stimulation or stylistic innovation. Even to want to perceive the self-stimulation of a performing artist is to be in a position of considerable familiarity with his routine work. Such familiarity may be sufficient training (it is certainly the pertinent training) for recognizing moments when a performing entertainer, stimulated by face-to-face contact with his audience, also stimulates himself to new levels of dramatic directness in his handling of expression. Again, when a performer introduces a new expressive style, the audience that calls it real or sincere may be simply making a semantic error. Seeing the inhibitions of an older style fall away, it does not yet perceive the inhibitions of the new style. This recognition does not occur until the new expressive style has been present long enough to expose its own stereotypes.

The basic audience claim to competence in the judgment of a popular singer's performance is a claim that the audience perceives the artist's relation to himself when stimulated by the live audience and that the audience recognizes a shift in expressive styles at the moment the artist is making one of these styles his own. Both claims are reasonable, and in structure they resemble the claims made by all audiences in the performance of all the arts. On the other hand, the popular audience often fails to sort its claims of competence out. Its aesthetic theory is perhaps worse than its aesthetic practice. The measure of competence of the audience for a popular singer might be said to consist, then, of its capacity to outgrow biographical, role-identification theories of the "realism" of singer performances and to concentrate on its other intuitions about such "realism." In general, popular intuition of realism in performance of popular music has outgrown biographical, role-identification theories in the last twenty years or so.

It is true that young fan groups usually repeat all these critical stages in their growth. A new singing star, as he develops a fan group, becomes first an object of biographical interest. (It may be important that he is an Italian from Bridgeport and that in high school he couldn't sing a note.) At a second level it may become more widely felt that his biographical success is in some sense representative. At a third level the singing performer may appear to interact with his audience on the basis of a common though implicit recognition of these images. (Frank Sinatra became, at one stage of his career, almost overskilled in telegraphing to his audience what he thought his audience was about to expect from him.) At a fourth level, the audience discriminates enough to perceive when the performer is "on" and when he is "off" and at this point begins to achieve real competence in criticism. It is only a step from this level to the perception that a singer's appeal is bound up in his showmanlike control of a new expressive style.

The so-called problem of realism in popular culture has been generalized here to include fictions, contests, and performances. It is suggested that each of these forms of entertainment has a problem of realism and that, although each of these so-called problems of realism is stated by the audience to itself in different terms, they have deep common elements. The question is how to define these common elements more exactly.

The answer lies partly in the act of self-reference achieved by the spectator, such an act shaping the response whether he is seeing a movie, watching a game, or listening to a singer. The *kind* of self-reference varies from form to form, and to achieve the appropriate self-reference for each, not confusing it with the others, would be the basis of a spectator's code. The self-reference in the proto-critical movie audience is best expressed in terms of Nelson Foote's assertion that some, if not all, leisure activities depend for their quality on "empathy without loss of integrity." If this rule applies to all leisure, it applies especially well to movie and TV spectatorship, where the popular audience' ideas of realism appear to rise from just such a concern. The self-reference in the wrestling audience is best expressed in terms of David Riesman's assertion that some, if not all, leisure activities depend for their quality on a deliberate decision to sustain ambiguity, to test one's tolerance for ambiguity. The self-reference in the singer's audience is best expressed in terms of John Seeley's notion that leisure activities include "the reduction of self-induced tension."

This is not to suggest that an appropriate ethos for the American spectator has now been worked out. Such an ethos clearly involves more fields than movies, popular singing, and sports, issues other than repressed anxieties about commitment and competition. It relates to the theme often expounded by the European, that the American lacks a certain amount of privacy from *himself*, because he insists on interpreting the Socratic "Know Thyself" in pragmatic terms. American spectatorial tension may be strong because it is a special instance of the general case. The American of the twentieth century is an inveterate and compulsive spectator of himself. And the fact that the mass media have generally been occupied with an extensive attempt to teach people how to behave as spectators suggests that anxiety is still strongly connected with the role.

PART FOUR

sport and small groups

OVERVIEW

The readings presented up to this point have emphasized the relationships among sport, social structure, and culture within large social collectivities. In contrast, the material in this part of the text is focused upon the relationships between sport and social organization within smaller social units. Two approaches are taken; first, the consideration of small groups as *special types of social systems*; and second, the treatment of small groups as *subcultures*.

THE SPORT GROUP AS A MICRO-SOCIAL SYSTEM

With respect to the treatment of small groups as special types of social systems:

> Not only are they micro-systems, they are essentially microcosms of larger societies. They present, in miniature, societal features, such as division of labor, a code of ethics, a government, media of exchange, prestige rankings, ideologies, myths, and religious practices. Through careful examination of these micro-systems, theoretical models can be constructed and then applied to less accessible societies for further test and modification. Small-group research is thus a means of developing effective ways of thinking about social systems in general (Mills, 1967, p. 3).

We observe that it is both interesting and surprising that sociologists have not given more attention to sport groups in view of their professed concern with social systems. For sport organizations such as athletic teams generally meet the most stringent definitional criteria applied to social groups for classification as to being either a formal social organization or social system; in that, they are

349

typically characterized by an unequivocal collectivity identity, a set of rules and informal norms governing conduct, an implicit ideology, a set of interpersonal relationships and interaction patterns among members, a precise membership list, an agenda of activity, and procedures for the recruitment, training and retention of members.[1] However, notwithstanding the relative few sociological studies of sport groups, we believe that the several readings presented in the section which follows are: (1) most suggestive as to how the sociological analysis of sport groups is a profitable means of acquiring a better understanding of the structures and processes underlying the success and survival of social systems; and, (2) well illustrate how significant insights can be gained of the nature of human behavior in sport situations by the consideration of sport groups as microsocial systems.

Following Wiseman we note that ". . . any actual, *i.e.*, empirical, social system consists of (1) individuals who are (2) interacting with others on the basis of a minimal degree of complementary expectations by means of, and according to (3) a shared system of beliefs, standards, and means of communication" (1966, p. 5). Accordingly, there appears in Section One, "Sport and Micro-Social Systems," ten readings which focus on sport teams as social systems and emphasize the social structure dimension of social organization within small groups.

The overriding theme of the articles presented in Section One is "individual adjustment and team effectiveness." For each article portrays in some manner how individuals' needs and goals are reconciled with the "needs" and goals of given social systems through such social processes as communication, cooperation, competition and conflict. In the first article Fiedler presents investigations which tested "the hypothesis that group effectiveness is related to the interpersonal perceptions which members of a group have toward one another." His findings suggest that members of effective (*i.e.*, winning) high school basketball teams prefer highly task-oriented individuals as coworkers whereas members of less successful teams prefer more socially oriented coworkers. In the second reading Myers discusses his analysis of the differential perception members of rifle teams had of teammates in competitive and noncompetitive situations. Results of his study indicate that better individual adjustment is a function of competitive experience and team success. McGrath in the third article also focuses on the effectiveness of rifle teams and reports findings which overlap those of Fiedler and Myers. He found in his investigation that teams composed of members characterized by nonpositive interpersonal relations had significantly better scores and showed more improvement in marksmanship than teams consisting of members characterized by positive interpersonal relations. In the fourth reading Lenk describes his study of an Olympic rowing crew and again shows that intergroup conflicts as contrasted with congeniality among team members is not necessarily detrimental to team effectiveness.

Although the first four readings in the first part of Section One stress the

---

[1] See for example Caplow's definition of a formal social organization, 1964, p. 1.

importance of interpersonal perceptions as a variable influencing individual adjustment and team effectiveness; the final three articles emphasize the importance of formal group structure as a variable affecting personal adjustment and group performance. Klein and Christiansen describe their analysis of the group composition and structure of basketball teams and report that player interaction, as determined by pass frequency, is a function of sociometric choices, achievement orientation, team attractiveness, and anticipation of teammate behavior. In the next reading Grusky discusses the effects of the formal structure of professional baseball teams on managerial recruitment; and presents findings which support the hypothesis that high interactors (infielders and catchers) are more likely to become field managers than low interactors (outfielders and pitchers). The final selection by Blalock sets forth a number of theoretical propositions as to why the degree of occupational discrimination against minority groups is relatively low in professional baseball in comparison with other vocations.

THE SPORT GROUP AS A SUBCULTURE

As well as being treated as micro-social systems, small groups may be analytically dealt with as subcultures. Perhaps the concept of *subculture* is best defined by Gordon, who states that it refers:

> . . . to a sub-division of a national culture, composed of a combination of factorable social situations such as class status, ethnic background, regional and rural or urban residence, and religious affiliation, but *forming in their combination a functioning unity which has an integrated impact on the participating individual* (1947, p. 40).

Section Two—"The Sport Group as a Subculture"—contains a series of three readings which focus on certain sport groups as occupational subcultures. Scott, in a chapter drawn from his book *The Racing Game*, describes the subculture of the jockey's world. In the second article Weinberg and Arond write about the occupational culture of boxers, covering such factors as socialization, social mobility and relationships with trainers, managers and promoters. Third in the series of readings is a light piece by Boroff viewing skiers as a subculture.

the sport group as a micro-social system

assumed similarity measures as predictors of team effectiveness

FRED E. FIEDLER

Small groups of individuals, working as teams, committees, or crews, conduct the overwhelming proportion of the nation's civic, industrial, and military business. The effectiveness with which these groups function is thus of practical as well as of theoretical concern in our society.

This paper reports a series of related investigations which deal with interpersonal relationships within a team as correlates of the team's total effectiveness.

Certain aspects of interpersonal perception have been investigated in previously published studies on therapeutic relationships (3) and interpersonal relations in a social group (5). These studies present techniques for obtaining the so-called "Assumed Similarity (AS) scores," which appear to be correlates of liking and warmth in interpersonal relationships. The present series of investigations relates these interpersonal perception variables to team effectiveness.

• From the *Journal of Abnormal and Social Psychology*, **49** (1954), 381–388. Copyright © 1954 by the American Psychological Association. The research reported here was carried out under Contract N6ori-07135 between the University of Illinois and the Office of Naval Research. The investigations were conducted by a group in which several members of the project staff played a part during various phases. In particular, the writer wishes to express his appreciation to Dr. L. J. Cronbach, then director of the project, and to Messrs. Walter Hartmann, S. A. Rudin, Mrs. Mary E. Ehart, Miss Vivian C. McCraven, and Dr. W. G. Warrington.

A first, frankly exploratory study used fourteen high school basketball teams. The most promising measures which emerged from this study were then validated on a second group of twelve high school basketball teams (6). The hypotheses derived from both studies were later tested on teams which differed markedly from the first group, namely, three- and four-man surveying parties (4).

The First Basketball Study

High school basketball squads are composed of from 9 to 18 players. These are chosen by the coach from a larger pool of interested boys competing for places on the first team. This study was conducted in the Midwest, where basketball is of considerable importance to high school players and coaches and where a large number of teams can be found.

THE INSTRUMENT

The tests used in the basketball study were forced-choice questionnaires. These questionnaires consisted of 100 descriptive statements grouped into 20 blocks of five statements each. An attempt was made to construct the blocks so that, in the main, statements within each block would be equally acceptable to the subjects (Ss), but descriptive of different personality dimensions.

One block of statements is given as an example.

	MOST	LEAST
1a. I find it easy to understand what others are trying to tell me.		
b. People think I am a hard worker.	X	
c. I don't mind losing my temper when provoked.		
d. I like people who don't worry about me.		X
e. People often look to me for leadership.		

In a self-description S would answer these statements by making an X in the left square opposite the statement which S considered *most* characteristic of himself, and an X in the right square opposite the statement he considered to be *least* characteristic of himself.

TEST PROCEDURE AND INSTRUCTIONS.   So-called interpersonal perception scores were obtained by giving each S successively three separate questionnaires containing the same blocks of statements. Players were instructed as follows: (a) "describe yourself," (b) "predict how the person with whom you can cooperate best will describe himself," and (c) "predict how the person with whom you can cooperate least well will describe himself."

In addition to these interpersonal perception tests, players named the three team members—not necessarily the best players—with whom they could cooperate best, and the three with whom they could cooperate least well during games.[1]

INTERPERSONAL PERCEPTION SCORES

Conventional tests are scored by comparing S's response with the "right" response of a key. Our scores are obtained by comparing two questionnaires of the same person. This comparison yields the so-called "Assumed Similarity" measures listed immediately below. Tentative interpretations are provided which are based in part on evidence from previous studies.

table 1

CORRELATIONS BETWEEN THE DEC. 31, 1951
CRITERION AND INTERPERSONAL PERCEPTION
SCORES IN 14 BASKETBALL TEAMS

	CORRELATION (RHO)	
ASSUMED SIMILARITY MEASURE	MEDIAN SCORE IN TEAM AND CRITERION	SCORE OF MOST PREFERRED CO-WORKER AND CRITERION
ASp	−0.25	−0.63 [a]
ASo	−0.03	−0.69 [b]

[a] $p < 0.05$ according to Olds's tables (11).
[b] $p < 0.01$ according to Old's' tables (11).
The large number of exploratory tests run on this first sample does not allow interpretation of signifiance levels. These are here given only as a point of reference.

ASSUMED SIMILARITY SCORES

1. *ASp*—a measure of assumed similarity obtained by comparing (correlating) the S's self-description with his prediction of the self-description of his *positive* choice, the best coworker. High *ASp* appears to be related to personal liking and perhaps warmth for the chosen person (3, 5).[2]

2. *ASn*—a measure obtained by comparing the S's self-description with his prediction of his *negative* choice. A high *ASn* score may, on the basis of the interpretation above, indicate a feeling of personal closeness and warmth for the negative choice.

3. *ASo*—a mesaure obtained by comparing S's prediction for his positive choice with his prediction for his negative choice. This measure is interpreted as "set" to differentiate between people. Since *ASn* and *ASo* are

[1] This paper discusses only procedures pertinent to the present hypothesis. A detailed account of the studies is presented in (2, 6, 7, 9).

[2] AS scores can be computed as correlations or as difference scores. To avoid possible confusion we will in this paper speak of high AS as meaning high assumed similarity, i.e., a high correlation between either the self and the predicted self of another person, or between the predicted self-descriptions of two other persons. In terms of D scores, this would imply small differences between the two descriptions on which AS is based.

highly correlated, we will concern ourselves here only with the scores ASp and ASo.

THE CRITERION

Group effectiveness was measured by proportion of games a team had won. The date used here was December 31, 1951,[3] before many changes in team personnel had taken place and by which time each team had played from eight to twelve games.

In general, small schools are handicapped by having relatively few eligible students. However, teams generally compete with other neighboring schools of comparable size, thus equalizing some of the differences which would favor large schools. The criterion reliability was estimated by comparing the proportion of games a team had won during the first and second halves of the season. At this time it was possible only to estimate reliability for the second sample which was tested with end-of-season criteria. The corrected criterion reliability estimate for these twelve teams was 0.88. The corresponding reliability for the December 31 date could not be computed because too few games had been played, but it is undoubtedly lower (7).

RELATION OF ASSUMED SIMILARITY MEASURES TO BASKETBALL CRITERIA

Our hypothesis states that interpersonal perception scores are related to the proportion of games a team wins. We tested whether team members of an effective team will, on the average, perceive each other differently from members of ineffective teams. Here we correlated the team median of the AS scores with the criterion. As can be seen from the second column in Table 1, correlations between the criterion and median scores are generally near zero.

The group may, however, also express its attitude by the type of person whom most members of a team choose as their best co-worker. In order to get at this attitude we considered only the AS scores of those members of the various teams which had received the greatest number of "best co-worker" votes. As can be seen in Table 1, this procedure suggests that the AS scores of the team's "most preferred co-worker" correlate with the criterion in the negative direction.

In previous studies, high ASp seemed to be related to warm, empathic interpersonal relationships. We expected to find these relationships—hence also high AS—to be prevalent in effective teams. The present findings are thus in the direction opposite to that which was anticipated. They suggest that the most preferred cooperators in effective teams tend to be somewhat less warm and emotionally less involved with persons whom they choose as work companions than is the case of keymen in less effective teams.

---

[3] The original report (5) deals with December 15 as the criterion date. Since some teams had at that time played fewer than 4 games, the December 31 date appears to be a better criterion estimate.

table 2

SECOND STUDY: POINT BISERIAL CORRELATIONS
BETWEEN THE CRITERION AND ASSUMED SIMILARITY
SCORES OF MOST PREFERRED CO-WORKER

ASSUMED SIMILARITY MEASURE	$r_{pt. bis.}$	t	p
ASp	−0.20	0.53	
ASo	−0.58	2.20	0.03

The correlations in Table 1 are, of course, based on a small sample of teams, and on only moderately reliable scores, 0.62 and 0.61 for ASp and ASo respectively (9). In addition, they are the survivors of a considerable number of exploratory measures. A validation attempt, therefore, became essential.

Validation Study on Basketball Teams

The second sample of teams was studied solely for the purpose of testing relationships which were significant at the .05 level in the first study, i.e., on measures ASp and ASo of the most preferred co-worker.

The only major modifications were in the method of choosing teams and testing significance. We selected, toward the end of the season, nine teams which had had a predominantly winning season and nine teams which had had a predominantly losing season, and requested their cooperation.[4] These came from the upper and lower third of a roster of over fifty teams. We tested seven "good" teams and five "poor" teams which agreed to cooperate. Since the teams were dichotomously selected, point-biserial correlations were here used to estimate the degree of the relationship. The significance of the difference between the scores of "good" and "poor" teams was tested by the usual t test; inspection of the data indicated that the conditions for applying a t test were not violated. The small samples and the not very high reliability of the scores suggest caution in interpreting these data.

As can be seen from Table 2, the point biserial correlation between the criterion and ASo of the team's most preferred co-worker is −0.58. We attempted to validate two measures. Only one of these (ASo) reached significance. We are therefore not justified to consider the relation of ASo to team effectiveness in basketball as established. ASp of the teams' most preferred co-workers did not correlate significantly with the criterion even though the correlation is in the anticipated direction. We have plotted the measures

[4] The writer gratefully acknowledges the invaluable assistance received from Clyde Knapp and Harry A. Combes of the University of Illinois.

| Q CORRE-LATIONS | ASp | | Q CORRE-LATIONS | ASo | |
	GOOD TEAMS	POOR TEAMS		GOOD TEAMS	POOR TEAMS
0.55			0.55		
0.50			0.50		
0.45	x	xx	0.45		x
0.40	x	x	0.40		
0.35			0.35		x
0.30	x	x	0.30		
0.25			0.25	x	xx
0.20	x		0.20	x	x
0.15	x	x	0.15	x	
0.10			0.10	x	
0.05			0.05	x	
0.00	x		0.00		
−0.05			−0.05		
−0.10			−0.10	x	

Fig. 1. ASo and ASp of Most Preferred Co-worker Plotted against the Criterion in the Second Sample.

ASp and ASo of the most preferred team members from good and poor teams. (See Fig. 1.)

In addition, we also computed validities for the end of the season when all league games had been played. These validities are generally lower than those of December 31. It is clear from these data that ASp in contrast to ASo is not a promising predictor of team effectiveness (7).

Study on Surveyor Teams [5]

THE HYPOTHESIS

The basketball team studies led to one major hypothesis: *Members of effective teams will prefer co-workers who assume relatively little similarity between the persons whom they choose and those whom they reject as their own co-workers.*

As we interpret high AS to be indicative of warmth toward, and acceptance of, others we also explored whether team effectiveness and congeniality are negatively related.

The following study was designed to test this hypothesis, and to obtain evidence regarding the additional question.

SELECTION OF GROUPS

Student surveying parties work in teams of three to four men. The Ss were 71 civil engineering students taking a required course in surveying. The

[5] The writer is indebted to Prof. M. O. Schmidt, Civil Engineering Department, University of Illinois, whose interest and cooperation made this phase of the study possible.

course consists of two parts. The first part is taught on the university campus on a full-day basis, lasting three weeks; the second part covers five weeks. This is offered at a university-operated surveying camp in northern Minnesota where students concentrate on field problems in relatively difficult terrain. The camp is almost completely isolated and self-contained. Students as well as faculty members eat, sleep, and work there, and students are under practically continuous supervision of their instructors.

ORGANIZATION OF THE COURSE AT CAMP. While at camp, the students were divided into six sections, one instructor remaining in charge of each of the sections throughout the camp period. Each section consisted of three or four parties, and each of the parties consisted of three or four men. A total of twenty-two surveying parties was formed.

DIFFERENCES BETWEEN BASKETBALL TEAMS AND SURVEYING PARTIES. Obviously basketball teams differ in many respects from surveying parties. The differences which we considered among the most important are the following:

a. Basketball teams require physical coordination, relatively little verbal interaction. Surveying is primarily an intellectual task requiring frequent verbal communication.

b. Although basketball squads consist of 9–18 members, the surveying parties in our study were no larger than four men.

c. Basketball teams work under considerable time pressure. Speed in surveying is only of secondary importance.

d. Members of basketball teams are highly identified with the team, and personally involved with their team's success. This identification and involvement is almost completely absent in surveying teams. The students were graded individually, and no benefits were derived from being in a "good" surveying party. This is shown by the fact that none of the students were interested in their instructor's opinion of their *team*.

THE INSTRUMENT

As in the basketball studies, Ss responded to three identical questionnaires, predicting a preferred, and predicting a rejected co-worker. Unlike the forced-choice questionnaires used in the basketball study, the surveyor tests consisted of sixty statements, each of which was to be marked on a seven-point scale ranging from *definitely true* to *definitely untrue*. The statements were pretested on a 180-item questionnaire.[6] Statements were selected on the basis of an item analysis to obtain items with large variances on self-descriptions. Statements such as "I am very discriminating in my choice of friends," "I am not likely to admit defeat," or "when a person is a failure it is his own fault," were used. The instrument presents a considerable improvement over the tests used in the basketball studies. The reliabilities for ASp and ASo are 0.83 and 0.93 respectively (2). In addition, the tests require less time for administration.

By comparing the two tests by means of the statistic D (1), it is pos-

---

[6] We are indebted to Col. R. W. Faubion, Commanding Officer, Det. #3, Human Resources Research Center, Chanute Air Force Base, for permission to pretest this instrument.

sible to obtain a score indicating how similarly any two of the questionnaires have been marked.

TEST PROCEDURE AND INSTRUCTIONS. The instructions and administration of questionnaires followed those of the basketball studies, with a few, relatively minor, exceptions. The Ss could predict their preferred and least preferred persons from among those with whom they had previously worked. These did not have to be persons at the camp. The Ss again completed sociometrics regarding the three persons within their section (10–15 Ss) whom they personally liked most and liked least. They similarly named three Ss whom they preferred most, and the three whom they preferred least as co-workers.

THE CRITERIA OF EFFECTIVENESS

Instructors were asked to rank all teams in their section in terms of the following:

a. *Accuracy* with which surveying jobs were done by various parties.

b. *Speed* with which the jobs were done.

c. *Congeniality* of the teams in terms of lack of conflict and smooth-running field operations.

In addition, students in all sections were asked to "rank all parties in the section from best to poorest." This constitutes our *students' ratings* criterion.[7]

Accuracy is the main criterion in surveying. It was, therefore, the only criterion on which we attempted to validate the hypothesis derived from the basketball study. The one-tailed test of significance was applied, therefore, to the accuracy criterion only. Tests relating to other criteria were exploratory.

Each instructor could rank only the three or four surveying parties in his own section. Ranking of parties from different sections was standardized to permit comparison of all parties. AS scores for all twenty-two teams could then be correlated with the various criteria.

The fact that instructors' frames of reference differ decreases to some extent the criterion reliability. This would tend to obscure any relationships present, and it would increase the probability of accepting the null hypothesis when a true difference exists. Table 3 presents the intercorrelations of the four criteria used in this study for three- and four-man parties.

RELATION OF ASSUMED SIMILARITY MEASURES TO CRITERIA IN SURVEYING

The accuracy criterion. Our major hypothesis states that the assumed similarity of most preferred co-workers in good teams will be relatively low. The preferred co-workers in relatively poor teams will have high ASo scores.

Our population of teams consists of 22 surveying parties, divided into six different sections. This division presents difficulties in statistical treatment

---

[7] Students' ratings of Section V could not be used. The Ss in that section had been in more than one surveying party, and a number of students rated teams other than the main teams rated by the instructor of that section.

of the data since no criterion was available for comparing teams from different sections. We have here tested the hypothesis by two methods.

a. We compare the best and the poorest teams within each of the six sections. We can then ask whether the AS scores of the preferred co-worker in the best team from each section are lower than the AS scores of the preferred co-worker in the poorest team in each section. As the two teams for each section are evaluated by the same instructor, the matched *t* test can here be used. This does, however, reduce to 12 the number of teams (cases) used in the analysis. (See Table 4.) As can be seen in Table 4, ASo differences are significant. ASp shows only a negligible difference.

b. A somewhat more satisfactory indication of the *degree* of relation comes from a second analysis. Criterion ratings were converted to scores, and then correlated with the most preferred co-workers' AS scores, both ASp and ASo.

table 3

INTERCORRELATIONS (r) OF CRITERIA FOR THREE- AND
FOUR-MAN SURVEYOR TEAMS [a]

	ACCURACY	SPEED	CONGENIALITY RATINGS
Speed	0.79		
Congeniality ratings	0.15	0.52	
Student ratings	−0.34	0.15	0.39

[a] (See footnote 7.) Based on N's of 22, except correlations with the student rating criterion in which N's = 18.

Table 4 also presents the *r*'s between the primary criterion, accuracy, and these two AS scores. As can be seen, the hypothesized relationship has been found between the criterion and ASo of the most preferred co-worker.

table 4

COMPARISONS OF AS OF PREFERRED CO-WORKERS IN
TEAMS RATED HIGHEST AND LOWEST IN ACCURACY
(N = 12)

INTERPERSONAL PERCEPTION SCORES	MEAN OF HIGHEST TEAMS [a]	MEAN OF POOREST TEAMS	t	p	r (N = 22)
ASp	12.96	12.24	0.56		
ASo	20.61	15.32	3.30	0.025	−0.51

[a] In terms of D's. A high score indicates *low* assumed similarity.

Hence, persons chosen as most preferred co-workers in effective (i.e., accurate) teams perceive a greater difference between those whom they prefer and those whom they reject as co-workers than keymen in less accurate teams. The findings thus are consistent with the hypothesis induced from the results which were obtained in the study on basketball teams.

THE SECONDARY CRITERIA

No significant relation was found between AS scores and secondary criteria. The relation between AS scores on students' ratings is, however, in the opposite direction of those found for accuracy and other criteria based on instructors' ratings. In other words, the students tended to rate those teams as better in which the preferred co-worker assumed relatively high similarity to his negative choice. This appears to lend some support to the interpretation that preference for a person with high AS is related positively to congeniality within the team. (See Table 3.)

The relation of congeniality and effectiveness was explored by one further step. An Intrateam Preference Index (IPI), defined as an index of congeniality, was devised and correlated with each of our four criterion ratings.

This measure of congeniality is based on the following considerations:

a. Each person had rated the other 10–15 members of his section in terms of how well he liked them as co-workers.

b. A subject worked in a three- or four-man team. He could choose his preferred co-workers within his own three- or four-man team, or he could prefer others in his section who were not in the team.

c. We assume that a team whose members choose one another is more congenial than one whose members reject one another or choose outsiders.

The measure is computed by the formula:

Intrateam Preference Index (IPI) =

$$\frac{\left(\begin{matrix}\text{choices} \\ \text{within}\end{matrix} + \begin{matrix}\text{rejections} \\ \text{without}\end{matrix}\right) - \left(\begin{matrix}\text{choices} \\ \text{without}\end{matrix} + \begin{matrix}\text{rejections} \\ \text{within}\end{matrix}\right)}{nk - n}$$

n = number of men within the team
k = number of choices made by each individual

When this intrateam preference index (IPI) was correlated with our four criterion ratings, the following relationships appeared: The correlation between accuracy and the IPI was negative (-0.23), whereas other criterion ratings correlated positively with the IPI. The highest correlation was found between students' ratings and the IPI (0.37). When we compare the most preferred co-workers's ASo scores of teams considered best and those considered poorest by students, we find higher ASo for teams rated high by students and lower ASo scores (greater perceived difference between most and least preferred work companions) for teams which students rated as poor. This relationship is not statistically significant ($t = 2.24$; $t = 2.57$ is required for significance of 0.05). The direction would tend to indicate, however, along with our other data, that effectiveness and congeniality may be inversely related in informal teams. This finding is in accord with the findings in the preceding basketball study. Moreover, it is supported by the results in Halpin's recent study of air crew leaders (8) and a paper by Schachter, Ellertson, and McBride on experimentally assembled student groups (10). The results are not in agreement with Van Zelst's study on construction workers (11). All in all, these data suggest that further study is needed to determine whether or not effectiveness and congeniality are inversely related.

Discussion

Two interpersonal perception scores on assumed similarity were correlated with the criterion in each study. One relation reaches the prescribed significance level every time. The studies thus support the hypothesis that the interpersonal perception variable ASo plays a part in group effectiveness.

We feel that the present findings serve primarily to emphasize that research on interpersonal perception in task groups is a fruitful area for continued efforts. This discussion will, therefore, be largely concerned with the implications of these findings for further research.

Let us first examine the measure which yielded significant results.

ASo. This score was obtained by comparing S's prediction of his positive choice for work companion with his prediction of his negative choice. It is thus the similarity which S assumes to exist between the person with whom he says he can, and the one with whom he says he cannot cooperate. According to our data, the most preferred co-worker in effective teams tends to perceive these two persons as relatively dissimilar. On the other hand, the most preferred co-worker in ineffective teams tends to perceive these persons as relatively similar. Low ASo (i.e., large perceived difference between most and least preferred work companions) may, therefore, reflect an evaluative critical attitude toward others, as contrasted with warm, empathic interpersonal relations. (Further research is needed to clarify the meaning of this measure.) We have found that ASo tends to correlate positively with reputed therapeutic competence (3); in subsequent studies it was shown that Ss assume significantly more similarity to a person who is liked than to someone who is relatively disliked (5, 6). As ASo and ASn (AS to the least preferred) are highly correlated, we believe that the person with low ASo is relatively unaccepting, and perhaps rejecting, to the person who is not a good work companion.

THE MOST PREFERRED CO-WORKER. Although ASo in key persons appears to measure relevant factors in team effectiveness, it also points to a phenomenon which may be of more general theoretical importance. Only the scores of the most preferred co-workers correlate with the criterion. When we correlated the team's median ASo with the criterion, no significant relationships were found. At present we are inclined to take these results as an indication that members of effective teams use a basis different from that of members of ineffective teams for choosing and rejecting others as cooperators. This interpretation is supported by the positive correlations between ASo of the most and of the second most preferred co-workers in basketball teams (0.63 and 0.27 for the first and second samples, respectively). In light of our current interpretation of ASo, this would mean that members of effective teams prefer highly task-oriented persons as co-workers. Members of relatively ineffective teams list as their most preferred co-workers the more accepting, relationship-oriented team members. ASo in the most preferred team worker is thus possibly an indication of the entire team's attitude toward the task, e.g., an index of the team's morale. Whether or not these relations hold in radically different teams, e.g., formally structured groups, permanent crews, etc., remains to be established.

Summary and Conclusions

The present investigations test the hypothesis that group effectiveness is related to the interpersonal perceptions which members of the group have toward one another.

Interpersonal perceptions were measured by correlating identical questionnaires which subjects were instructed to fill out (a) describing themselves, (b) predicting the responses of their preferred co-worker, and (c) predicting the responses of their rejected co-worker.

The first studies used fourteen high school basketball teams, tested at the beginning of the season. A second sample of seven "good" and five "poor" teams was collected toward the end of the season for the purpose of verifying relations identified in the first study. A third sample consisted of twenty-two surveying teams.

The criterion of basketball team effectiveness was the proportion of games the teams had won (at midseason in the first sample, two weeks before the end of the season in the second sample). The criterion in the surveyor study was the instructor rating on accuracy. There was no correlation between the criterion and the median of any assumed similarity score within a team. The assumed similarity score, ASo, of the team's most preferred work companion was negatively correlated with the criterion in all three samples. The finding supports the hypothesis that ASo of the most preferred co-worker in surveying, and possibly also in basketball, is related to team effectiveness.

The interpersonal perception scores of the chosen person are believed to reflect his outlook on other persons and on the task. Low ASo is thought to reflect lack of emotional involvement with teammates and task-oriented attitudes. The group which chooses a differentiating person as preferred co-worker is thus likely to be more concerned with effective task performance, and correspondingly more successful. Some evidence suggests that the more effective surveying teams tend to be less congenial than relatively ineffective teams.

As in previous studies, we found that Ss assumed greater similarity between themselves and their positive, than between themselves and their negative choices.

REFERENCES

1. Cronbach, L. J., and Gleser, Goldine C., *Similarity between persons and related problems of profile analysis*, Urbana, Ill.: Bureau of Research and Service, Univ. of Illinois, 1952. (Mimeo.) (Tech. Rep. No. 2, Contract N6ori-07135.)
2. Cronbach, L. J., Hartmann, W., and Ehart, Mary E., *Investigation of the character and properties of assumed similarity measures*, Urbana, Ill.: Bureau of Research and Service, Univer. of Illinois, 1953. (Mimeo.) (Tech. Rep. No. 7, Contract N6ori-07135.)
3. Fiedler, F. E., A method of objective quantification of certain counter-transference attitudes, *J. Clin. Psychol.*, 1951, 7, 101–107.
4. Fiedler, F. E., *Assumed similarity measures as predictors of team effectiveness in surveying*, Urbana, Ill.: Bureau of Research and Service, Univ. of Illinois, 1953. (Mimeo.) (Tech. Rep. No. 6, Contract N6ori-07135.)
5. Fiedler, F. E., Blaisdell, F. J., and Warrington, W. G., Unconscious attitudes as correlates of sociometric choice in a social group, *J. Abnorm. Soc. Psychol.*, 1952, 4, 790–796.
6. Fiedler, F. E., Hartmann, W., and Rudin, S. A., *The relationship of interpersonal perception to effectiveness in basketball teams*, Urbana, Ill.: Bureau of Research and Service, Univer. of Illinois, 1952. (Mimeo.) (Suppl., Tech. Rep. No. 3, Contract N6ori-07135.)
7. Fiedler, F. E., Hartmann, W., and Rudin, S. A., *Correction and extension of the relationship of interpersonal perception to effectiveness in basketball teams*, Urbana, Ill.: Bureau of Research and Service, Univer. of Illinois, 1953. (Mimeo.) (Tech. Rep. No. 5, Contract N6ori-07135.)
8. Halpin, A. W., The relation between the crew's perception of the leadership behavior of airplane commanders and superiors' ratings of their combat performance, Paper read at Amer. Psychol. Assoc., Washington, D. C., 1952.
9. Rudin, S. A., Lazar, I., Ehart, Mary E., and Cronbach, L. J., *Some empirical studies of the reliability of social perception scores*, Urbana, Ill.: Bureau of Research and Service, Univer. of Illinois, 1952. (Mimeo.) (Tech. Rep. No. 4, Contract N6ori-07135.)
10. Schachter, S., Ellertson, N., McBride, Dorothy, and Gregory, Doris, An experimental study of cohesiveness and productivity, *Hum. Relat.*, 1951, 4, 229–238.
11. Van Zelst, R. H., Sociometrically selected work teams increase production, *Personnel Psychol.*, 1952, 3, 175–185.

team competition, success, and the adjustment of group members

ALBERT MYERS

There has been considerable speculation among educators, men of letters, and parents about the effect of competition upon interpersonal relationships and adjustment. The rational arguments for and against competition in schools, sports, or the military services are legion. In the foreground of consideration is the problem of the individual's adjustment to his group when more than one group is engaged in interteam competition. Specifically, what effect does intergroup competition have on the individual's psychological well-being and his interpersonal relations with others in the group of which he is a member?

The adjustment of individuals to their groups has been of primary interest in several recent studies by Fiedler and his associates (Alexander and Drucker, 1960; Fiedler, Hutchins, and Dodge, 1959; McGrath, 1962). They have been working on the problem of isolating the antecedent variables which facilitate good group member adjustment. The major emphasis has been upon the interpersonal perceptions of the group members. The present research is an attempt to relate certain situational variables, namely, competition and success, to the group adjustment problem.

Previous research on the effects of competition on adjustment has tended to focus on the competition-cooperation distinction. Thus, Deutsch (1949); Stendler, Damrin, and Haines (1951); Hirota (1951); Mizuhara and Tamai (1952); Blau (1954); Grossack (1954); and Gottheil (1955) all indicated that there is better understanding and positive affect between individuals cooperating with one another than between individuals competing against each other. That is to say, there are better relationships between teammates than between opponents.

In addition to the differential perceptions an individual has of team-

• From the *Journal of Abnormal and Social Psychology*, 65, No. 5 (1962), 325–332. Copyright © 1962 by the American Psychological Association. This investigation was supported by Contract No. DA-49-193-MD-2060, "Interpersonal Perception and the Psychological Adjustment of Group Members," between the Office of The Surgeon General, Department of the Army, and the University of Illinois (Fred E. Fiedler, principal investigator).

Fred E. Fiedler, the author's thesis adviser, and Joseph E. McGrath aided in the design and data collection phase of this experiment. James W. Julian and Scott E. Krueger assisted during data collection and analysis. The writer is especially appreciative of the cooperation which he received from Clair Worthy, Commander of the University of Illinois Army ROTC unit, and his staff. In particular, D. McClelland, W. Hooper, and M. Snoke helped to coordinate the project. E. F. Flanders served as consultant and range safety officer.

mates and opponents, it seems likely that an individual might have different perceptions of teammates in competitive and noncompetitive situations. A competitive situation is probably a more intense social experience than a noncompetitive situation. One important issue to be investigated is whether the intensity of a competitive experience between groups has any systematic effect on the adjustment and interpersonal relations of group members.

A competitive experience immediately implies the existence of potential success and failure. It seems likely that success should make it easier for individuals to interact with each other in a more harmonious fashion while failure should put a strain on interpersonal relationships. The first hypothesis, consequently, is that individuals in successful teams will tend to have more favorable interpersonal perceptions of their teammates than individuals on unsuccessful teams.

It seems possible, however, that success has a much different effect in a competitive situation than in a noncompetitive one. As the goals are assumed to be more important in competition, success should be particularly satisfying and failure should be particularly frustrating. If the favorableness of the perceptions of teammates covaries with the degree to which the individual is rewarded, competition should lead to greater variability of interpersonal perception than noncompetition.

The second hypothesis, therefore, is that success in a competitive situation will generate more favorable perceptions of teammates than success in noncompetitive situations. The third hypothesis is that failure in a competitive situation will tend to generate more unfavorable perceptions of teammates than failure in noncompetitive situations.

Method and Procedure

SUBJECTS

A Men's Recreational Rifle Tournament was organized with the assistance of the Army Reserve Office Training Corps (ROTC) unit at the University of Illinois. Announcements of the tournament were made to freshman and sophomore ROTC students during their regular class period. Of approximately 430 students who registered during the following week, 180 were selected.

DESIGN

Sixty teams, each consisting of three men, were formed. Half of these teams were combined into competitive leagues and half into noncompetitive leagues. There were several major differences in the manner in which the two types of leagues were conducted. All of these were designed to emphasize salient aspects of the competitive and noncompetitive conditions while keeping the information obtained by the subjects, their prospect of success, and the objective reward constant. No individual scores were made available to the subjects. Only team results were reported.

COMPETITIVE LEAGUES. Five separate competitive leagues composed of six teams each were formed. The leagues met one hour a week for five weeks. The first two weeks were devoted to marksmanship, safety instructions, and practice firing. Starting with the third week, each league began a 25-bout round robin schedule. Win-loss records were kept and announced for each team and members of the winning team in each league were promised individual trophies.

In order to facilitate the interteam evaluative aspect of this condition, the experimenter announced the results of each bout and made frequent references to the fact that certain teams were doing well and others badly.

NONCOMPETITIVE LEAGUES. The main experimental purpose in the noncompetitive leagues was to prevent interteam comparisons (i.e., competition). The teams did not compete against each other but against a set of three qualification standards of hard, moderate, and easy difficulty. The teams knew in advance against which standard they were firing on each bout (this is the analogous information of knowing how good your opponent is in the competitive condition). The experimenter announced the results of each bout quietly to each team and never made evaluative statements as to a team's past performance. The subjects were told that all members of teams which "qualified" would receive trophies. Although "qualification" was undefined specifically, the subjects were told that the performance standards were appropriate to their experience. It was emphasized that any number, or none of the teams might win trophies.

The first two weeks of practice firing and orientation were identical to the procedure used for the competitive condition.

ABSENCES

In order to create some pressure for good attendance, penalty scores amounting to 20 percent of an absent member's previous average were added to the team score.

MEASURES

Three different types of measures were collected to assess various aspects of the individual's relationship to his team. They were: The individual's esteem for his teammates, the individual's perceived acceptance of himself by the team, and the individual's perception of who or what was to blame on those bouts on which the team failed.

Esteem for teammates was obtained on scales of the semantic differential type with items used by Fiedler in his work. The subjects were asked to rate each of their teammates on 24 six-point scales. The items were of the form friendly-unfriendly, cooperative-uncooperative. Esteem for a particular teammate was determined by simply summing the assigned scores on the 24 items.

Perceived Acceptance scores were determined as the sum of the subject's responses to five, 16-point questionnaire items which were designed to assess how comfortable and accepted the subject felt in his group.

A multiple-choice item was used on which each subject indicated what he believed to be the reason for failure on those bouts in which his team was unsuccessful. The items reflected extrapunitive, intrapunitive, or impunitive modes of response. For example, he could be extrapunitive by saying that one of his teammates did poorly, or he could be intrapunitive by saying that he did poorly himself, or he could be impunitive by saying that the other team performed very well.

Results

ESTEEM FOR TEAMMATES

A subject's esteem to his group was measured by the average esteem he had for his teammates. A team score for esteem was obtained by averaging the individual scores. Thus, a high team esteem score required that all three members describe each other favorably. Team esteem scores in the intermediate range could be achieved by innumerable combinations of high, medium, and low scores.

The means for team esteem scores in the second and fifth weeks and for the changes between these weeks are presented in Table 1. An analysis

table 1

MEAN ESTEEM FOR WEEK 2 AND 5 AND MEAN CHANGE
BETWEEN WEEKS

CONDITION	N	WEEK 2	N	WEEK 5	N	CHANGE [a]
Competitive level of success						
H	10	107.5	11	118.7 [b]	10	9.1
M	7	113.0	7	112.0	7	−1.0
L	11	105.8	11	104.5	11	−1.3
Average	28	108.2	29	111.7	28	2.5
Noncompetitive level of success						
H	10	107.1	10	110.5	10	3.4
M	7	106.0	7	103.3	7	−2.7
L	10	107.7	12	100.0 [b]	10	−11.7 [b]
Average	27	107.0	29	104.4	27	−4.4

[a] Difference in N and rounding errors account for minor discrepancies in summing and averaging.

[b] Data from three teams were unavailable in Week 2. The change scores are based only on teams for which there were data in Week 5 and Week 2. Two teams, which averaged 120 in the noncompetitive condition with low success were among those missing in Week 2. Their scores are included in the Week 5 data. If they are removed, the low success average drops from 100.0 to 96.0 and the noncompetitive condition average drops to 103.2.

of variance on the change scores summarized in Table 2 showed that there was a significant condition effect ($p < 0.05$), i.e., the competitive teams showed more improvement in team esteem than did the noncompetitive teams. In addition, the high success teams showed an improvement in average esteem during the course of the tournament while the low success teams

table 2

SUMMARY OF ANALYSIS OF VARIANCE OF
ESTEEM CHANGE SCORES

SOURCE	df	MS	F
Conditions (C)	1	60.0	4.95 [a]
Success (S)	2	83.0	6.85 [b]
C × S	2	6.0	
Error	49	12.1	
Total	54		

[a] Significant at 0.05 level.
[b] Significant at 0.01 level.

deteriorated. The difference of these changes was significant at the 0.01 level. The effect of success was also significant when each condition was considered separately. Thus, both the independent variables had a significant effect on the team esteem scores.

These data do not support the hypothesis that the competitive condition should generate greater variability between high and low success teams. The difference between the high and low teams was 10.4 ($p < 0.025$) in the competitive conditions and 16.9 ($p < 0.001$) in the noncompetitive condition. The interaction t test to determine whether there was significantly more variability in esteem scores in the noncompetitive condition was insignificant. Thus, success had a uniform effect on the two conditions. This finding does not suggest that large discrepancies exist between the conditions in the subjective value of success. This notion is supported by data obtained from a questionnaire item. The responses of subjects in the noncompetitive condition indicated that they enjoyed the activity no less than did subjects in the competitive condition.

It is also somewhat unlikely that there were great differences in the subjective probability of success between the two conditions. The teams doing poorly, in both conditions, realized that their chances for a trophy were poor while the better teams generally felt that they had a good chance. Even in the noncompetitive condition where the standard was amibiguous, the trophy oriented attitudes seemed appropriate. It seems, therefore, that the differences in esteem cannot be attributed to differences in task interest or subjective probability of success.

Analysis of the Week 5 data alone showed, as would be expected, the same relationships found in the change data. Both the condition and success variables were significant at the 0.05 level. In addition, the successful competitive teams had significantly higher scores ($p < 0.05$) than the successful noncompetitive teams. Contrary to Hypothesis 3, however, the unsuccessful competitive teams had higher esteem scores than the unsuccessful noncompetitive teams. This difference, however, was not significant.

ESTEEM FOR ABSENT AND PRESENT MEMBERS

The two conditions did not differ in the number of absences; fifteen subjects in the competitive condition and sixteen subjects in the noncompetitive condition were absent in Week 5. This represented an absentee ratio of 17.2 percent and 18.3 percent, respectively. Similarly, twelve competitive teams and eleven noncompetitive teams had no absences throughout the ·entire tournament.

There were twelve teams in each condition with absent members in the last week. If a team had one man absent, each of the present members had an opportunity to rate one absent teammate and one present teammate. Table 3 shows the distribution of scores for present and absent members in

table 3

MEAN ESTEEM GIVEN IN WEEK 5 TO PRESENT MEMBERS AND
ABSENT MEMBERS FOR TEAMS WITH ABSENTEES IN WEEK 5

CONDITION	PRESENT IN WEEK 5	ABSENT IN WEEK 5	AVERAGE
Noncompetitive	112.6	92.8	102.7
Competitive	108.3	109.3	108.8

each condition. Whereas there was virtually no difference between the esteem scores given to absent and present members in the competitive condition, substantial differences were obtained in the noncompetitive condition. In the noncompetitive groups, the present members received an average esteem score of 112.6 while the absent members received a score of 92.8. This difference of 19.8 points had a two-tailed significance of 0.02.

The finding raised the question whether these subjects failed to attend in Week 5 because they were not liked in Week 4 or whether they were liked less in Week 5 because they had been absent in Week 5. The data indicated that those individuals who were absent in Week 5 received an average score of 102.1 in Week 4 and those who were present in Week 5 received an average score of 105.5. The difference between these scores was clearly not significant ($t = 0.48$). The relative change in esteem from Week 4 to Week 5 was, however, significant at the 0.05 level by the Wald-Walfowitz run test. There was, incidentally, no overlap in the distribution. None of the absentees received higher esteem scores in Week 5 while none of the present members received lower scores. The data, thus, indicated that the subjects who were absent in Week 5 in the noncompetitive condition were given low scores because they were absent in Week 5.

PERCEIVED ACCEPTANCE

The esteem data were based upon a monadic judgment by each subject, i.e., the degree to which he liked each of his teammates individually. The five-item questionnaire (Perceived Acceptance) attempted to assess each subject's perception of the dyadic relationship that existed for a subject and his team, considered collectively. The two measures were not, of course, unrelated. They were meant to be two aspects of an individual's adjustment to a group. The correlation between these measures was 0.60.

Because certain items on the questionnaire were irrelevant until the competition began, the questionnaire was not administered until the third week.

The means for the Week 3 and the Week 5 data and the mean differences between weeks are shown in Table 4. As with esteem, the competitive teams tended to score higher (more favorably) than the noncompetitive teams and high success tended to lead to more favorable scores than low success.

table 4

MEAN PERCEIVED ACCEPTANCE IN WEEKS 3 AND 5 AND
MEAN CHANGE BETWEEN WEEKS FOR ENTIRE SAMPLE

CONDITION	N	WEEK 3	N	WEEK 5	N	CHANGE
Competitive level of success						
H	11	58.4	11	64.5	11	6.1
M	7	59.9	7	61.0	7	1.1
L	11	52.6	11	55.2	11	2.4
Average	29	56.7	29	60.1	29	3.4
Noncompetitive level of success						
H	10	55.4	10	55.9	10	0.5
M	7	55.2	7	51.6	7	−3.6
L	12	51.9	12	55.1	12	3.2
Average	29	53.9	29	54.5	29	0.6

An analysis of variance of the Week 5 data, summarized in Table 5, indicated a very strong condition effect. The mean difference of 5.6 in Perceived Acceptance scores between the competitive and noncompetitive teams was significant at the 0.01 level, but there was no over-all effect due to success. The failure to achieve an over-all success effect was obviously attributable to the noncompetitive condition which had very little variation. The mean difference between high and low success teams in the noncompetitive condition was only 0.8.

Success had, however, a significant effect within the competitive condition. The 9.3 difference between the high and low success group means on Perceived Acceptance scores was significant beyond the 0.005 level ($t = 3.10$). The high success competitive groups also scored more favorably than the high success noncompetitive teams ($t = 3.18$, $p < 0.001$). It should be noted, however, that the larger variability in the competitive condition was not due to poor adjustment in unsuccessful teams. The unsuccessful teams had a higher average score than the entire noncompetitive condition. Rather,

table 5

SUMMARY OF ANALYSIS OF VARIANCE FOR PERCEIVED
ACCEPTANCE IN WEEK 5 FOR ENTIRE SAMPLE

SOURCE	df	MS	F
Conditions (C)	1	55	9.65 [a]
Success (S)	2	14	
C × S	2	13.5	
Error	52	5.7	
Total	57		

[a] Significant at 0.01 level.

the variability must be attributed to the extremely favorable scores obtained from the successful competitive teams.

Thus, the second hypothesis, which stated that competitive teams of high success would have more favorable adjustment scores than the noncompetitive teams of high success, was substantiated. The data relating to the third hypothesis, on the other hand, were once again, in the opposite direction. Instead of having lower scores than the noncompetitive teams, the low success competitive teams tended to have higher scores.

Thus, it seems that the competitive group members tended to perceive a far more favorable relationship between their teammates and themselves, while the noncompetitive groups apparently never generated a feeling of acceptance. This is in spite of the fact that the individuals had been together for several weeks and at least some of them had enjoyed success in the task. Although many grew to have high esteem for their teammates (particularly in the high success teams), there seemed to be a surprising inability for these individuals to achieve well-integrated interpersonal relationships. It is interesting to note that the final level achieved by the noncompetitive groups was roughly equal to the precompetition level found for both conditions. Perhaps the interpersonal relationships of noncompetitive group members can best be summarized by saying that they remained strangers to each other.

PUNITIVENESS

Table 6 shows the distribution of punitive choices in Weeks 3 and 5. In Week 3 the distribution of the two conditions were virtually identical. The χ^2 testing the difference between these distributions was only 1.4 which is clearly not significant.

There was a significant difference between the conditions in Week 5 on the use of an item reading "one of my teammates did poorly." This is a personal form of extrapunitiveness. As Table 6 shows under the entry Extrapunitive A, 21 percent of the competitive subjects chose this item while 35 percent of the noncompetitive subjects chose it. The critical ratio of 2.05 was significant at the 0.05 level (Walker & Lev, 1953).

table 6

DISTRIBUTION OF CHOICES FOR PUNITIVE QUESTIONS
IN WEEKS 3 AND 5

WEEK	MODES OF RESPONSE	COMPETITIVE	NONCOMPETITIVE
First week of competition (Week 3)	Extrapunitive A (teammate did poorly)	28%	21%
	Extrapunitive B (poor equipment)	03	03
	Impunitive A (other team performed well; standards too difficult)	22	28
	Impunitive B (bad luck)	12	10
	Intrapunitive (I did poorly)	35	38
		100%	100%
Last week of competition (Week 5)	Extrapunitive A	21%	35%
	Extrapunitive B	00	05
	Impunitive A	35	18
	Impunitive B	10	17
	Intrapunitive	34	25
		100%	100%

This result indicates that the competitive teams were less extrapunitive. The second extrapunitive item (B, poor equipment) suggested the same conclusion, but had too low a response rate for an adequate test. Combining the two extrapunitive items yielded a difference which was significant at the 0.02 level ($CR = 2.38$). The noncompetitive groups were more extrapunitive in general and more extrapunitive towards their teammates in particular.

The competitive subjects chose Impunitive A ("the other team performed very well") more frequently than the noncompetitive subjects. There was, on the other hand, a tendency for the noncompetitive subjects to choose Impunitive B (bad luck) more frequently. Consequently, there was no difference between the conditions in the degree to which they were impunitive when the Impunitive A and Impunitive B scores were added together to form a single impunitive score.

As might be expected from the discussion of the individual items, the simultaneous analysis of all items resulted in a chi square of 8.06 which was significant at the 0.05 level. It was necessary to use only four categories since Extrapunitive B (poor equipment) received a total of three votes. It would be legitimate to add these scores to the Extrapunitive A (teammate did poorly) totals or to drop them completely. The latter method was used here in accord with current statistical theory.

Unsuccessful teams had, of course, many more experiences of failure than successful teams. It might be expected that the amount of extrapunitiveness would increase with the number of failures a team experienced. The point biserial correlation between these variables was, however, only 0.07. Thus, somewhat surprisingly, the amount of extrapunitiveness was essentially a condition effect rather than a function of a team's failure experiences.

Discussion

INTERPERSONAL PERCEPTIONS AND SUCCESS

The data clearly demonstrated that an individual's interpersonal perceptions of his group members is significantly affected by the level of success enjoyed by the group. It is relatively simple for people to be friendly and happy when the situation is rewarding. When, on the other hand, the situation creates disappointment for the individuals, it is presumably far more difficult to maintain harmonious group relations. The present data did not, of course, indicate that the individuals on unsuccessful teams actually behaved in a less friendly manner. It is likely, however, that the less favorable interpersonal perceptions reflect, at least in part, antagonistic interpersonal behavior. It is also possible, although less likely, that the behavior of the subjects on unsuccessful teams was as friendly but that the perceptions of these behaviors were drastically distorted. Additional research is needed to answer this question.

INTERPERSONAL PERCEPTION AND COMPETITION

It was not expected that competition would generate more favorable interpersonal perceptions than noncompetition. Hypothesis 3 predicted that the unsuccessful competitive teams would have very low average Esteem for Teammates and Perceived Acceptance scores. However, the unsuccessful competitive teams tended to have higher scores than the unsuccessful noncompetitive teams. Competition, consequently, led to better team relationships regardless of the level of success.

ADJUSTMENT

The major concern of the present study was with the adjustment of an individual to his group. The criteria were measures of interpersonal perceptions. Good group adjustment should imply more than a general satisfaction with teammates. It should also include an ability of team members to withstand disruptive influences; an ability to function adequately in the face of adversity. These properties are incorporated in Hemphill's (1956) concept of group viscidity, Gross and Martin's (1952) concept of cohesion, and Fiedler et al. (1959) concept of quasi-therapeutic relations.

As indicated in the presentation of the results, the effects of two forms of adversity could be estimated. They were absences and failures. Good adjustment should manifest itself by providing the individuals of a group with the capability of maintaining harmonious group feelings in the face of adversity. The well-adjusted group should not disintegrate or deteriorate in the face of disruptive influences.

The data showed that more deterioration occurred in the noncompetitive condition. Absent members were rated in a significantly less favorable manner and there was significantly more extrapunitive behavior among the noncompetitive teams. These data are interpreted as an indication of poor group adjustment. The subjects in the competitive condition, on the other hand, did not respond intolerantly towards absentees, nor were they very extrapunitive.

In addition, of course, the competitive teams had more favorable scores on the Esteem for Teammates and Perceived Acceptance measures. In fact, the competitive condition had more favorable scores than the noncompetitive condition on every measure and in every situation.

Thus, the conclusion that the members of competitive groups were better adjusted seems valid for the following reasons: They esteemed their teammates more highly, they perceived the relationships between their teammates and themselves as being more favorable, they were more tolerant of teammates who posed an objective threat to success through absenteeism, and they were less extrapunitive towards teammates. That is, they did not hold their teammates responsible for failure.

Competition seemed to have acted as a prophylactic against poor group adjustment. At the same time, it permitted extremely good adjustments for members of groups which enjoyed success. Competition had the important property of drawing teammates together. This unification is commonly described as a reaction to a common enemy. It is possible that a *common evaluator* will provide the same function. Individuals will unite when they are being evaluated as a group.

The existence of an outside evaluator perhaps forces the individual to evaluate all performance on which he feels he is being judged. His individual performance, however, is to some degree confounded with that of the group. The individual must evaluate himself as part of the group and any evaluation of the group is, to some extent, an evaluation of himself. If it is assumed that the individual tries to evaluate himself as favorably as possible then there should be a tendency to evaluate all those elements to which he is connected in favorable manner also. This relationship is frequently seen in situations where people defend the actions of their parents, church, or country. It is not only that they identify themselves with these groups, but, in addition, that an outsider identified the individual as being a member of that group. The contingent relationship which exists between an individual and his group should create pressure on the individual towards perceiving his fellow group members favorably. In addition, this pressure should increase as the evaluation becomes more important to the individual.

It was previously mentioned that this study attempted to relate certain situational variables to Fiedler *et al.* (1959) work on adjustment in groups Fiedler *et al.* have incorporated the concept of quasi-therapeutic relations to refer to those sets of interpersonal behaviors which have a facilitative effect on group adjustment. McGrath (1962) has pointed out that a major portion of these facilitative "behaviors" as judged by teammates are perceptually rather than behaviorally determined.

The present study indicated that the perceptions of individuals could be systematically altered so as to produce groups with greater interteam adjustment. In Fiedler *et al.* (1959) language, competition and success had the property of generating quasi-therapeutic relations between teammates. Then, such so-called quasi-therapeutic relations within groups appear to be a consequence of the group's relation to its external environment, as well as of the interpersonal dynamics within the group itself.

Summary

Sixty three-man teams comprised of 180 ROTC students at the University of Illinois participated in a Recreational Rifle Tournament. Six teams in each of five leagues engaged in a face-to-face, 25-bout, round robin. Thirty other teams fired not against the performance of other teams but for qualification against standards. The first two weeks in the five-week study were devoted to practice firing.

Adjustment of each man to his group was measured by a five-item scale and by scores of esteem for teammates on semantic differential scales. Multiple-choice questions yielded scores of extrapunitive, intrapunitive, and impunitive modes of response. These measures were taken at every firing session.

The findings indicated that better team adjustment was generated by the competitive experience and success in the task. It was also found, contrary to one hypothesis, that the low success competitive teams tended to manifest better adjustment than the low success noncompetitive teams. It was concluded that the competitive experience not only engendered good adjustment under favorable conditions (success) but that it acted as a prophylactic against poor adjustment in unfavorable situations (failure).

Two types of adversity could be identified in the experiment. They were absence of teammates, which caused teams to lose points in the competition, and team failure. In both these situations the members of competitive teams responded in a more tolerant and adaptive manner than did members of noncompetitive teams. This tolerance and the general tendency to have more favorable interpersonal perceptions seemed to justify the conclusions that the competitive condition generated better adjustment of individuals in their teams.

REFERENCES

Alexander, S., and Drucker, E. H., The effects of experimentally modified inter-personal perceptions on social behavior and adjustment, Technical Report No. 9, University of Illinois, Group Effectiveness Research Laboratory, Contract DA-49-193-MD-2060, Project on interpersonal perception and the psychological adjustment of group members, Department of the Army. (Mimeo)

Blau, P., Cooperation and competition in a bureaucracy, *Am. J. Sociol.*, 1954, **59**, 530–535.

Deutsch, M., An experimental study of cooperation and competition upon group processes, *Hum. Relat.*, 1949, **2**, 199–232.

Fiedler, F. E., Hutchins, E. B., and Dodge, Joan S., Quasi-therapeutic relations in small college and military groups, *Psychol. Monogr.*, 1959, **73** (3, Whole No. 473).

Gottheil, E., Changes in social perceptions contingent upon competing or cooperating, *Sociometry*, 1955, **18**, 132–137.

Gross, N., and Martin, W. E., On group cohesiveness, *Am. J. Sociol.*, 1952, **57**, 546–554.

Grossack, M. M., Some effects of cooperation and competition upon small group behavior. *J. Abnorm. Soc. Psychol.*, 1954, **49**, 341–348.

Hemphill, J. K., Group dimensions: A manual for their measurement, *Ohio St. U. Stud. Bur. Bus. Res. Monogr.*, 1956, No. 87.

Hirota, K., Experimental studies of competition, *Jap. J. Psychol.*, 1951, **21** (3/4), 70–81.

McGrath, J. E., The influence of positive interpersonal relations on adjustment and effectiveness in rifle teams, *J. Abnorm. Soc. Psychol.*, 1962, **65**, 365–375.

Mizuhara, T., and Tama, S., Experimental studies of cooperation and competition, *Jap. J. Psychol.*, 1952, **22**, 124–127.

Stendler, C., Damrin, D., and Haines, A. C., Studies in cooperation and competition: I. The effects of working for group and individual rewards on the social climate of children's groups, *J. Genet. Psychol.*, 1951, **79**, 173–197.

Walker, Helen M., and Lev, J., *Statistical Inference*, New York: Holt, 1953.

the influence of positive interpersonal relations on adjustment and effectiveness in rifle teams

JOSEPH E. MCGRATH

The present study is part of a program of research dealing with quasi-therapeutic relations in small work groups. By quasitherapeutic relations we mean supportive interpersonal relations among members of work groups which, like the therapeutic situation, provide an environment that facilitates adjustment of the group member. This study was conducted in the context of a rifle team tournament and involved the experimental assembly of teams on the basis of prior interpersonal relations. How these interpersonal relations affected individual adjustment and marksmanship performance is the central focus of the study.

BACKGROUND

In recent years there has been considerable speculation about the value which psychotherapeutic services have in work relations. In particular, Rogers and his co-workers (1951), Gordon (1951), and the Tavistock Institute in London (e.g., Rice, 1958), have urged the application of psychotherapeutic techniques as a means of improving work performance. The basic assumption has been that secure and anxiety free interpersonal relations will not only aid the individual's adjustment but will also help him to perform with increased efficiency. The strong appeal of this argument has led organizations ranging from Indian textile mills (Rice, 1958) to baseball teams to avail themselves of essentially psychotherapeutic services. More recently, Fiedler, Hutchins, and Dodge (1959) have suggested that it might be possible to reduce the anxiety and to improve the work efficiency of group members by judiciously placing them with others who are basically accepting.

There seems to be considerable evidence that positive interpersonal perceptions within a group lead to good interpersonal relations and facilitate individual adjustment. For instance, Fiedler et al. (1959) studied interpersonal perceptions in a variety of groups, including university dormitory groups, Army tank crews, and antiaircraft crews. Results showed that individuals who perceived others as similar, or who were seen as similar by members of their group, tended to be better adjusted and to improve on personal

• From the *Journal of Abnormal and Social Psychology*, 65 (1962), 365–375. Copyright © 1962 by the American Psychological Association. This investigation was supported by Contract No. DA-49-193-MD-2060, "Interpersonal Perception and the Psychological Adjustment of Group Members," between the Office of The Surgeon General, Department of the Army, and the University of Illinois (Fred E. Fiedler, principal investigator).

adjustment indices over relatively short time spans. From these results, the authors postulated that favorable interpersonal perceptions may lead to "quasitherapeutic" relations within the group, which in turn facilitate individual adjustment. A subsequent investigation by Alexander and Drucker (1960) demonstrated that experimentally induced perceptions of similarity aided the adjustment of group members, while individuals who were seen as dissimilar tended to adjust less well to the group.

However, there is some reason to question the assumption that positive interpersonal relations are necessarily conducive to task efficiency. Fiedler and his co-workers (1958) have shown that psychologically close interpersonal relations between leader and followers in task groups may be detrimental to team performance. Furthermore, while the Fiedler et al. (1959) study suggested that good interpersonal relations aid both individual adjustment and task effectiveness, the findings were based primarily on relationships between interpersonal perceptions and indices of adjustment of the self-report type. A later study by Hutchins and Fiedler (1960) reported slight negative correlations between individual adjustment and effectiveness of antiaircraft artillery crews. A recent review of small group research studies by McGrath and his associates (Altman & McGrath, 1959; Altman & Terauds, 1960; McGrath, 1957; Terauds, Altman, & McGrath, 1960) lent further support to the argument that good interpersonal relations within work groups do not necessarily lead to increased individual task effectiveness. Examination of 250 small group research studies showed very few instances of statistical tests, and no instances of significant relationships, between objectively scored indices of individual performance and measures indicative of good interpersonal relationships.

Thus, while it seems fairly well established that positive interpersonal relationships within a group aid the adjustment of group members, it is by no means clear that such relationships have a correspondingly good effect upon the task performance of individuals. The present study was designed as a specific test of the assumption that a positive interpersonal climate within a small work group will lead to both better adjustment and better individual task performance by its members.

GENERAL APPROACH

Two features of the study are worthy of note. First, the experimental task, rifle marksmanship, offers several advantages. It is intrinsically interesting to young men; it yields objective and highly reliable individual performance scores; and, like tremor and concentration measures, marksmanship is likely to be affected by tenseness and therefore should be sensitive to changes in individual adjustment. Rifle marksmanship performance, however, is essentially a series of independent individual performances. Little or no coordination among team members is required. Thus, it may be less sensitive to differences in interpersonal relations than other more interactive group tasks.

The second notable feature of the study is that teams were experimentally assembled on the basis of the participants' prior interpersonal relations. This procedure enabled us to carry our research on quasitherapeutic relations (Alexander & Drucker, 1960; Fiedler et al., 1959; Myers, 1961) the next logical step forward. It also enabled us to test a key methodological question in that program. The Fiedler et al. postulation of "quasitherapeutic" relations within work groups does not indicate whether such relations arise from perceptual or behavioral characteristics of group members. If A sees Teammate B as a warm, supportive individual, is it because B acts toward A in certain ways or because A tends to perceive such supportiveness in his social environment? The answer to this question was of methodological and substantive significance to the research program.

The study, thus, had two objectives: to assess the effects of positive interpersonal relations on individual adjustment and task effectiveness; and to determine whether the formation of positive interpersonal relations in groups depends primarily on the perceptions or the behavior of group members.

Procedure

The present study took advantage of an ongoing experiment in which 60 three-man teams participated in a five-week rifle marksmanship tournament. This experiment by Myers (1961) investigated the effects which competition and team success had on interpersonal perceptions and on adjustment in three-man rifle teams.[1] The tournament participants were 180 Army ROTC volunteers of varying levels of marksmanship ability, who were organized into three-man teams. Measures of individual adjustment, interpersonal perception, and individual and team marksmanship were obtained during and at the end of the marksmanship tournament.

Responses to a sociometric nomination question and four behavior description items at the end of the regular tournament were used to construct an index of interpersonal relations between teammates. The sociometric nomination question asked which teammate(s), if either, "helped you stay calm and relaxed while shooting." The four behavior description items were: "He was a warm person, easy to talk to"; "He was sort of standoffish" (scored in the reverse direction); "He listened attentively to others"; and, "He was disruptive to the group" (scored in the reverse direction). Participants rated each of their teammates on five-point rating scales. For purposes of team assembly, the nominations and ratings were combined into a single index which gave the sociometric nomination a weight equal to the sum of the four behavior description ratings.

Each man was assigned two scores: the total interpersonal relations

[1] We wish to thank Albert E. Myers for coperation in use of the subject population, and to gratefully acknowledge the assistance of James W. Julian, and Scott E. Krueger, all of the Group Effectiveness Research Laboratory, University of Illinois, in the data collection phase of this study. We are especially appreciative of the cooperation which we received from Clair Worthy, Commander of the University of Illinois Army ROTC unit, and his staff. In particular, D. McClelland, W. Hooper, and M. Snoke helped to coordinate the project. E. F. Flanders served as consultant and range safety officer.

scores which he *gave* to his two tournament teammates; and the total inter-personal relations score which he *received* from his two teammates. The first is a "perceptual index," indicating the extent to which the individual saw others as warm, supportive, and accepting. The second is a "behavior index," which reflects the extent to which others saw him as exhibiting such positive interpersonal behaviors.

New teams were composed by putting together sets of three men who had high scores on the perceptual index but low scores on the behavioral index; sets of three men who had low scores on the perceptual index but high scores on the behavioral index; and sets of three men who had inter-mediate scores on both indices. During the following week (Week 6 of the experiment) these new teams participated in one-hour, six-trial, handicap marksmanship contest for a money prize, and then completed the same battery of questionnaires that had been utilized in the first phases of the rifle team experiment.

The use of intrateam rankings (rather than absolute scores) for reas-sembling teams tended to reduce the average score differences between the three sets of experimental teams. Therefore, only data from the two extreme conditions—high scorers on the behavioral index, and high scorers on the perceptual index—were utilized in the analyses, although the intermediate scoring teams were permitted to participate in the marksmanship contest.

Thirty-five teams (105 participants) were available for the Week 6 experimental sessions. Complete data were obtained for 24 individuals (10 teams) scoring high on the behavior index and 29 individuals (11 teams) scoring high on the perceptual index.[2] All analyses presented in this paper are based on data from these 53 individuals at completion of the regular tournament (Week 5) and in the reassembled teams (Week 6).

MEASURES

MARKSMANSHIP. In both the regular tournament and the reassembled teams a "trial" consisted of a three-round shot pattern by each member of the team. Individual marksmanship scores for a given trial were obtained by measuring the distance between the two most separated rounds of the shot pattern in ⅛-inch units. Individual average marksmanship scores were com-puted for each participant for all trials of Week 5 and for all trials of Week 6.

INTERPERSONAL PERCEPTION TESTS (IPT). The basic form of the in-terpersonal perception tests (IPT) used in this study was a 24-item question-naire similar to the Semantic Differential. Each item consisted of an eight-point scale whose ends were defined by a pair of polar opposites, e.g., Talkative-Not talkative. Individuals were asked to describe themselves or other persons by checking one of the eight spaces on each of the 24 items. IPT responses were obtained for self at the end of the tournament (Week 5) and for each teammate in the tournament teams (Week 5) and in the re-assembled teams (Week 6).

[2] A total of 35 teams (105 men) was available for this experiment. Elimination of the intermediate condition (12 teams, 36 men), absenteeism in the sixth week of the study, plus two individuals who participated in the marksmanship task but did not complete questionnaires, accounts for the attrition down to 53 subjects.

Esteem scores were derived from IPT responses by assigning maximum score (eight points) to the most favorable end of each item and minimum score (one point) to the least favorable end, and then summing scores for all 24 items. The following esteem scores were used: Self-Esteem, Esteem for Teammates (the average of the esteem given to the individual's two teammates), and Esteem Received from Teammates (the average of the esteem scores which the individual received from his two teammates).

POSTMEETING QUESTIONNAIRE. This instrument consisted of eight five-point rating scales and four nomination questions. It was administered each week of the study. Several measures were derived from responses to these questions: *Social Adjustment*, which was operationally defined as the sum of responses to five rating items asking to what extent the individual enjoyed being a member of his team and felt accepted and comfortable in it; *Task Satisfaction*, which was operationally defined as the response to a rating item asking the individual how satisfied he was with his own task performance; *Extrapunitiveness toward Teammates*, which was based on the response to a question asking who or what was to blame when the team did poorly; and *Positive Interpersonal Nominations*, which were the nominations an individual received from his teammates on a question asking which teammate, if either, helped him to remain calm and relaxed while shooting. Responses to the latter measure at the end of the tournament were used as part of the basis for assembly of teams in Week 6. Nominations received in the Week 6 teams were used as one measure of the effect of reassembly.

BEHAVIOR DESCRIPTION QUESTIONNAIRE. This instrument consisted of 25 five-point rating scales asking individuals to describe the behavior of each of their teammates. It was administered in both Week 5 and Week 6. As indicated above, responses to four of these items in Week 5 were used as part of the index of positive interpersonal relations for assembly of Week 6 teams. Responses in Week 5 to those same four rating items were used to obtain two scores for each participant: a *behavioral index of interpersonal relations*, which was operationally defined as the sum of the responses which the individual received from his two teammates on these items; and a *perceptual index of interpersonal relations*, which was operationally defined as the sum of the responses which the individual gave to his two teammates on these four items. In addition, mean ratings given and mean ratings received on each of the 25 items of the Behavior Description Questionnaire were computed for members of the two experimental conditions.

Results

PERCEPTUAL AND BEHAVIORAL INDICES OF POSITIVE INTERPERSONAL RELATIONS

The experimental assembly procedures produced two sets of rifle teams representing two contrasting patterns of interpersonal relations. Members of one set of teams were high on the perceptual index but low on the behavioral index of positive interpersonal relations. That is, they had seen former teammates as warm and supportive but had been judged less favorably by those teammates. Members of the other set of teams showed the obverse pattern;

they had been judged by former teammates as warm and supportive, but had perceived their former teammates less favorably. The first question for analysis was which of the two groups should be considered as representing a positive interpersonal relations condition.

This question was attacked by comparing the relative consistency of ratings *given* to former and new teammates versus ratings *received* from former and new teammates. If group members who are perceived favorably by one set of teammates are also perceived favorably by new teammates, then there is a basis for holding that those judgments are a function of the interpersonal behavior of the persons so rated. On the other hand, if group members who perceive one set of teammates favorably also perceive new teammates favorably, then there is a basis for inferring that those judgments are a function of the perceptual tendencies of the persons making the ratings.

Three sets of data were used to make these comparisons: responses to the interpersonal nomination question, responses to the four interpersonal relations rating items, and responses to all 25 items of the Behavior Description Questionnaire. The first two sets of data were utilized because they paralleled, for the reassembled teams, the measures which formed the basis for team reassembly. The third set of data was used to determine whether responses to the four rating items selected for team reassembly were similar to responses to other types of behavior ratings.

The distribution of choices on the interpersonal nomination question for the reassembled teams is given in Table 1. Thirteen of the 29 members of the group which had scored high on the perceptual index (who had received few but who had given many interpersonal nominations to former teammates) received such nominations from their new teammates. In com-

table 1

POSITIVE INTERPERSONAL NOMINATIONS RECEIVED IN THE REASSEMBLED
TEAMS FOR THE TWO EXPERIMENTAL GROUPS

	RECEIVED POSITIVE INTERPERSONAL NOMINATIONS IN REASSEMBLED TEAMS	DID NOT RECEIVE POSITIVE INTERPERSONAL NOMINATIONS IN REASSEMBLED TEAMS	TOTAL
Members of the Experimental group who *gave* positive interpersonal nominations to regular tournament teammates	13	16	29
Members of the Experimental group who *received* positive interpersonal nominations from regular tournament teammates	4	20	24

Note.—$\chi^2 = 4.76$, $df = 1$, $p < 0.05$.

parison, only four of the 24 members of the group who had scored high on the behavioral index (who had received many but who had given few interpersonal nominations to former teammates) received interpersonal nominations from their new teammates. The chi square for this distribution is significant ($p < 0.05$). Thus, the tendency to give positive interpersonal nominations to teammates was more consistent over team situations than the tendency to receive positive nominations from teammates.

The two experimental conditions did not differ significantly on mean scores for the four interpersonal relations items, for either the perceptual or behavioral indices. However, individuals who had scored high on the perceptual index received higher mean scores (hence, more favorable ratings) than persons who had scored high on the behavioral index for 19 of the 25 items of the Behavior Description Questionnaire. They also gave more favorable ratings on 20 of the 25 items. Both of these distributions departed significantly from chance expectation ($p < 0.05$).

These results support the conclusion that perceptual aspects outweighed behavioral aspects in determining the initial interpersonal relations within the reassembled teams. Thus, while the recipient of positive interpersonal judgments may or may not be in fact ". . . a warm person . . . ," who ". . . listens attentively . . ." it appears that persons who give such positive judgments are prone to see warmth and supportiveness in their social environment.

In view of these findings, the set of teams which was composed of men who had given positive interpersonal nominations and ratings to their former teammates were designated as the Positive Interpersonal Relations (PR) group. Teams composed of men who had given low positive interpersonal relations scores to their tournament teammates were designated as the Nonpositive Interpersonal Relations (NR) group.

MARKSMANSHIP

Marksmanship scores for members of the two experimental conditions prior to reassembly (Week 5) and in the reassembled teams (Week 6) are shown in Table 2 and Figure 1. The two groups did not differ significantly in marksmanship at the end of the regular tournament. In Week 6, however, the NR group had significantly better marksmanship scores than the PR group ($p < 0.01$). Furthermore, the NR group showed significant improvement in marksmanship from Week 5 to Week 6 ($p < 0.01$), while the PR group did not improve. Marksmanship scores were also computed for the last three trials of Week 6, when the pressure of the competition was presumably at its highest and when the effects of interpersonal relations in the new teams had time to become manifest. Here an even larger difference was obtained between the two experimental conditions ($p < 0.01$).

These results clearly call into question the assumption that positive interpersonal relations within a work group lead to increased task effectiveness. Members of the PR group apparently had more favorable interpersonal

table 2

MEAN MARKSMANSHIP SCORES FOR THE
TWO EXPERIMENTAL CONDITIONS [a]

	NONPOSITIVE INTER-PERSONAL RELATIONS GROUP	POSITIVE INTER-PERSONAL RELATIONS GROUP	DIFFERENCE
Mean tournament marksmanship score (Week 5)	7.79	8.52	−.73
Mean marksmanship score in reassembled teams (Week 6)	6.46	8.49	−2.03 [b]
Difference (Week 5 to Week 6)	−1.33 [b]	−0.03	
Mean marksmanship score, last three trials for reassembled teams (Week 6)	5.95	8.19	−2.24 [b]

[a] Marksmanship scores were computed on the basis of scatter of shot pattern. Thus, the lower the score, the better the marksmanship performance.
[b] $p < 0.01$.

relations—at least from the subjective viewpoints of the members—than did members of the NR group. Yet members of the NR group improved in marksmanship in the reassembled teams while members of the PR group did not improve. As the two groups did not differ significantly in marksmanship scores while in their original tournament teams, the data suggest that assembly of the new teams somehow facilitated the marksmanship performance of members of the NR group.

ADJUSTMENT MEASURES

Mean scores for members of the two experimental conditions did not differ significantly on any of a number of self-report measures of adjustment and interpersonal perception, either before or after team reassembly, nor was there evidence for gross relationship between positive interpersonal relations and adjustment. Therefore, to understand better the obtained differences in marksmanship between the two experimental conditions, we turned to correlational analyses of the pattern of relationships within each of the two experimental groups.

CORRELATES OF PERFORMANCE AND ADJUSTMENT

The correlational analyses were designed to discover why reassembly into new teams had a facilitative effect upon the task performance of members in the NR group while apparently having a deleterious effect upon their interpersonal relations. It is one thing to postulate that good interpersonal

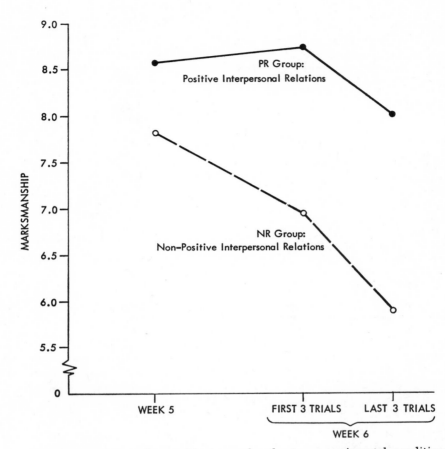

Fig. 1. Average marksmanship scores for the two experimental conditions. (Markmanship is measured in terms of average scatter of three-round shot patterns, in ⅛-inch units.)

relations may or may not lead to effective task performance. It is quite another matter, theoretically, to find that *removal* of supportive teammates leads to an improvement in task performance.

We formulated the general *a posteriori* hypothesis that individuals in the PR group may have had an entirely different orientation toward the team-task situation than did members of the NR group. Specifically, we hypothesized that members of the PR group focused their attention and energies primarily on the social or interpersonal aspects of the team interaction, while members of the NR group concentrated on their own task performance to the neglect of interpersonal relations.

If this hypothesis were true, then adjustment to the team situation should be a function of the individual's own task performance in the NR

table 3

CORRELATIONS WITH MARKSMANSHIP, SOCIAL ADJUSTMENT, AND TASK SATISFACTION

FOR THE TWO EXPERIMENTAL CONDITIONS

	NONPOSITIVE INTERPERSONAL RELATIONS GROUP (N = 24)			POSITIVE INTERPERSONAL RELATIONS GROUP (N = 29)		
	MARKSMAN-SHIP [a]	SOCIAL ADJUSTMENT	TASK SATISFACTION	MARKSMAN-SHIP [a]	SOCIAL ADJUSTMENT	TASK SATISFACTION
Social Adjustment	−0.47 [b]	—	—	0.05	—	—
Task Satisfaction	−0.39	0.45 [b]	—	−0.20	0.40 [b]	0.16
Self-Esteem	−0.04	−0.01	−0.21	0.10	0.48 [c]	0.08
Esteem for Teammates	0.08	0.21	0.32	0.07	0.63 [c]	0.06
Esteem Received from Teammates	−0.20	0.15	0.25	−0.45 [b]	0.04	0.07
Extrapunitiveness toward Teammates	0.05	0.00	0.47 [b]	−0.15	−0.30	0.04
Interpersonal relations ratings given to teammates	0.18	0.55 [c]	0.27	0.01	0.62 [c]	
Interpersonal relations ratings received from teammates	0.21	0.01	0.34	−0.27	−0.06	0.19

[a] Marksmanship is scored in terms of scatter of shot pattern. Thus, a low score means good marksmanship.
[b] $p < 0.05$.
[c] $p < 0.01$.

group but not in the PR group. In contrast, the individual's adjustment to the team situation for members of the PR group should be a function of the individual's social success—how well he liked, and was liked by, his teammates.

This hypothesis was tested by examining the pattern of correlations for performance, adjustment, and interpersonal perception measures within the two experimental conditions (Tables 3 and 4). Diagrams of the pattern of

table 4

PROPORTIONS OF BEHAVIOR RATING ITEMS WHICH HAD POSITIVE
CORRELATIONS WITH MARKSMANSHIP, SOCIAL ADJUSTMENT, AND
TASK SATISFACTION FOR THE TWO EXPERIMENTAL CONDITIONS

	PERCENTAGE POSITIVE CORRELATIONS FOR BEHAVIOR RATINGS GIVEN TO TEAMMATES	PERCENTAGE POSITIVE CORRELATIONS FOR BEHAVIOR RATINGS RECEIVED FROM TEAMMATES
Nonpositive Interpersonal Relations group		
Marksmanship [a]	32	68
Social Adjustment	76 [b]	44
Task Satisfaction	60	68
Positive Interpersonal Relations group		
Marksmanship [a]	52	8 [c]
Social Adjustment	100 [c]	72 [b]
Task Satisfaction	44	72 [b]

[a] Marksmanship is scored in terms of scatter of shot pattern. Thus, a low score means good marksmanship.
[b] $p < 0.05$.
[c] $p < 0.01$.

significant relationships for the two experimental conditions are shown in Figures 2 and 3.

MARKSMANSHIP. In the NR group Marksmanship correlated significantly with both Social Adjustment and Task Satisfaction, which are considered two measures of the individual's adjustment to the team situation. Neither of these relationships held for the PR group. Instead, in the latter group, an individual's marksmanship was related to the favorableness of his teammates' responses to him (esteem received and behavior ratings received).

SOCIAL ADJUSTMENT AND TASK SATISFACTION. Social Adjustment scores and Task Satisfaction were significantly correlated with each other for both groups. In addition, Social Adjustment was significantly related to perceiving teammates as supportive and accepting and to giving favorable behavior ratings to teammates in both experimental groups. However, in the PR group, Social Adjustment was also related to Self-Esteem and Esteem for Teammates, while Task Satisfaction was related to a tendency to receive favorable behavior ratings from teammates. In the NR group, Task Satisfaction was related to a tendency to be extrapunitive toward teammates.

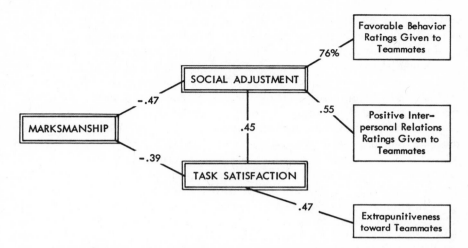

Fig. 2. Diagram of significant relationships for Nonpositive Interpersonal Relations group. (Marksmanship is scored in terms of scatter of shot pattern. Therefore, a low score indicates good marksmanship, and a negative correlation indicates that good marksmanship is associated with a high score on the other variable. Favorable Behavior Ratings Given to Teammates are percentages of 25 BDQ items which correlated in the positive direction with the variable indicated.)

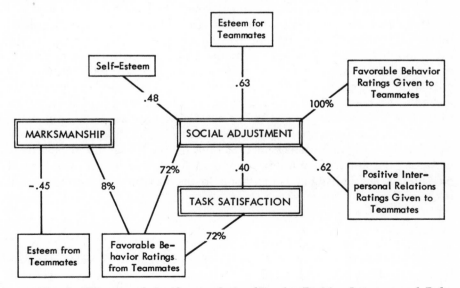

Fig. 3. Diagram of significant relationships for Positive Interpersonal Relations group. (Marksmanship is scored in terms of scatter of shot pattern. Therefore, a low score indicates good marksmanship, and a negative correlation indicates that good marksmanship is associated with a high score on the other variable. Favorable Behavior Ratings Given to Teammates are percentages of 25 BDQ items which correlated in the positive direction with the variable indicated.)

These correlations lend support to the hypothesis that members of the NR group were concerned more with their own task success than with interpersonal relations. In the NR group, both Social Adjustment and Task Satisfaction were related to—and perhaps derived from—success on the task. Those who shot well were satisfied with their own task performance and felt accepted by the group although they did not actually receive more favorable evaluations by teammates). Those who shot poorly responded more negatively to the social situation. In contrast, marksmanship success in the PR group did not increase the individual's felt acceptance (although it actually did earn him more favorable ratings from teammates), and it was not even related to his satisfaction with his own task performance. Rather, in the PR group, the individual's task satisfaction and social adjustment seemed to be closely tied to his social relationships with teammates.

In summary, individuals who perceived supportive, accepting attributes in their former teammates seemed to focus on interpersonal relationships rather than the task activity when placed into new teams. Teams composed of such persons showed good interpersonal relations but no improvement in marksmanship. In contrast, individuals in the NR group, who had not perceived former teammates as supportive, continued to be relatively unresponsive to teammates and they seemed to concentrate on their own task performance. They may, thus, have improved in marksmanship at the cost of less favorable interpersonal relations.

The two contrasting personal orientations which we have here suggested —task success and interpersonal success—are similar to concepts suggested by several other investigators. The pattern of correlations exhibited by the PR group seems fairly close to Parsons and Bales' (1953) integrative pattern, to Bales' (1958) social-emotional pattern, and to Bass' (1961) interaction orientation. The pattern characterizing the NR group, however, seems closer to Fouriezos, Hutt, and Guetzkow (1950) or Bass' self-oriented pattern than to the task orientation described by Parsons, Bales, and Bass. It was individual task success, not team task success, which seemed to be the fulcrum of individual adjustment and interpersonal relations for the NR group in this study. However, this inference must be viewed as highly speculative, since direct measures of the individual's orientation to the situation were not included in the study.

Discussion

Results show that an individual's interpersonal perceptions are relatively consistent from one set of teammates to another, at least within a highly similar team situation. Apparently, as individuals enter new groups, they bring with them a relatively strong set to see others favorably or unfavorably. These perceptual tendencies, rather than the behavior of teammates, tend to determine the initial interpersonal relations in the group.

These findings, especially in conjunction with the Alexander and

Drucker (1960) study, have implications for attempts to construct groups which provide a "quasi-therapeutic" environment for their members. We have shown that interpersonal perceptions which individuals bring with them into new groups are the key to initial formation of positive interpersonal relations. Alexander and Drucker found that interpersonal perceptions can be deliberately altered by experimental means, and that they ultimately aid the adjustment of teammates. At this stage of our knowledge, therefore, it would seem more profitable to attempt the assembly of "quasi-therapeutic" groups by selecting or training group members to perceive teammates in a favorable way rather than by attempting to modify their behavior toward teammates.

The present research shows that we should not expect an invariant pattern of relationships between interpersonal perceptions, adjustment, and task effectiveness. The nature of these relationships depends upon the motivation or orientation of the individual—his "stake in the game." The individual's "success" seems to be crucial to his adjustment in the group situation, but there seem to be at least two different routes to achieve this success. For some individuals, success is defined primarily in terms of effectiveness on the task: task success leads to adjustment and favorable response to teammates. For other individuals, however, personal success in a new team situation seems to be defined in terms of the individual's social relations with his teammates.

In the initial stages of group development, members of the teammate oriented PR group did not seem to have sufficient task motivation for effective task performance. However, they tended to evaluate more favorably those teammates who did well on the task, as evidenced by the correlations between marksmanship and both esteem received and favorable ratings received from teammates. Such favorable evaluation by teammates ought to be a highly desired reward for the teammate oriented person. It may, therefore, be that, over a longer period of time, teammate oriented persons would become more motivated to succeed on the task in order to gain the rewards of increased esteem from teammates.

These findings suggest that attempts to design work groups which will achieve both good member adjustment and effective task performance could best start by assessing the individual's characteristic mode of orientation to the team situation (viz., task success versus interpersonal success) as well as his characteristic ways of responding to his social environment. One type of person may well require a situation which initially provides a substantial degree of task success, while other persons may need an initially rewarding interpersonal situation. Thus, a program for development of quasi-therapeutic and effective groups appears to require a complex set of operations which attack several aspects of the problem simultaneously.

It must be emphasized that some of the findings of this study represent a posteriori hypotheses, and that the above speculations go well beyond our data. Concentrated research efforts specifically designed to test these hypotheses are indicated. Specifically, research is needed to determine the generalizability of these findings to other kinds of populations and group activities.

Research is also needed to identify interaction patterns characteristic of so-called quasi-therapeutic groups. Past efforts to link interpersonal perception to interaction patterns have not been too successful. Nevertheless, this constitutes a logically compelling direction for research, if we are to amplify and extend our knowledge of the nature and effects of interpersonal relations in work groups.

Summary

This study involved the experimental assembly of three-man rifle teams on the basis of prior interpersonal perceptions, and comparison of the interpersonal relations, adjustment, and effectiveness of the assembled teams subsequent to a marksmanship contest. Two types of teams were assembled: teams composed of men who had given favorable ratings to former teammates, termed the Positive Interpersonal Relations (PR) group; and teams composed of men who had not given favorable ratings to former teammates, termed the Nonpositive Interpersonal Relations (NR) group. The NR group had significantly better marksmanship scores and showed significant improvement in marksmanship while the PR group did not improve. The pattern of correlations within each of the two experimental conditions suggested that for members of the NR group success on the task was central to their situational adjustment and interpersonal relations, while for members of the PR group adjustment was related to interpersonal success rather than success on the task.

R E F E R E N C E S

Alexander, S., and Drucker, E. H., The effects of experimentally modified interpersonal perceptions on social behavior and adjustment, Technical Report No. 9, 1960, University of Illinois, Group Effectiveness Research Laboratory, Contract DA-49-193-MD-2060, Project on interpersonal perception and the psychological adjustment of group members, Department of the Army. (Mimeo)
Altman, I., and McGrath, J. E., A conceptual framework for the integration of small group research information, Arlington, Va.: Human Sciences Research, 1959. (HSR-TN-59/1-GN)
Altman, I., and Terauds, Anita, Major variables of the small group field, Arlington, Va.: Human Sciences Research, 1960. (HSR-RR-60/6-GN)
Bales, F., Task roles and social roles in problem-solving groups, in Eleanor E. Maccoby, T. M. Newcomb, and E. L. Hartley (Eds.), *Readings In Social Psychology*, (3d ed.) New York: Holt, 1958, pp. 437–447.
Bass, B. M., Comparison of behavior in groups of self-oriented, interaction-oriented, and task-oriented members, Technical Report No. 25, 1961, Louisiana State University, Contract N7 ONR 35609.
Fiedler, F. E., *Leader Attitudes and Group Effectiveness*, Urbana, Ill.: Univ. Illinois Press, 1958.
Fiedler, F. E., Hutchins, E. B., and Dodge, Joan S., Quasi-therapeutic relations

in small college and military groups, *Psychol. Monogr.*, 1959, **73**(3, Whole No. 473).

Fouriezos, N., Hutt, M., and Guetzkow, H., Measurement of self-oriented needs in discussion groups, *J. Abnorm. Soc. Psychol.*, 1950, **45**, 682–690.

Gordon, T., Group-centered leadership and administration, in C. R. Rogers (Ed.), *Client-Centered Therapy*, Boston: Houghton Mifflin, 1951, pp. 320–383.

Hutchins, E. B., and Fiedler, F. E., Task-oriented and quasi-therapeutic role functions of the leader in small military groups, *Sociometry*, 1960, **23**, 393–406.

McGrath, J. E., A framework for integration of small group research studies: A pilot study, Arlington, Va.: Psychological Research Associates, 1957. (PRA No. 57-20)

Myers, A. E., The effect of team competition and success on the adjustment of group members, Unpublished doctoral dissertation, University of Illinois, 1961.

Parsons, T. C., and Bales, R. F., The dimensions of action-space, in T. C. Parsons, R. F. Bales, and E. A. Shilis (Eds.), *Working Papers in the Theory of Action*, Glencoe, Ill.: Free Press, 1953, pp. 63–109.

Rice, A. K., *Productivity and Social Organization: The Ahmedabad Experiment*, London: Tavistock, 1958.

Rogers, C. R., *Client-Centered Therapy*, Boston: Houghton Mifflin, 1951.

Terauds, Anita, Altman, I., and McGrath, J. E., A bibliography of small group research, Arlington, Va.: Human Sciences Research, 1960. (HSR-RR-60/2-GN)

top performance despite internal conflict: an antithesis to a functionalistic proposition

HANS LENK

As the subtitle suggests, the purpose of this paper is to refute the strict general validity of a thesis that seems to have been taken for granted in micro-sociology and which is also held to be valid in various forms by other sociologists, namely, the proposition: Only small groups, which are low in conflict, or highly integrated can produce especially high performances. It is asserted that a cohesive group is more productive (1). "With generally increasing performances there would be a corresponding increase in orientation to one's partner or fellow group members." "For group achievement, internal competition" would be "inhibitory." "The stronger the intra-group

• Translated by Dr. D. Elisabeth Kenyon from Hans Lenk, "Maximale Leistung trotz innerer Konflikte," in *Kleingruppenforschung und Gruppe im Sport*, *Kölner Zeitschrift für Soziologie und Sozialpsychologie*, **10** (1966), 168–172.

relationships" and group integration, "the greater would be the performance and vice versa" (2). "An organization"—hence also the cooperative characteristic arrangement of a small group—would be "the more successful, the more the informal structure echoes the formal" (3), therefore, the stronger the officially planned cohesiveness manifests itself in the informal structure of relationship.

The antithesis to be advanced here may be surprising, and thus shall be brought out for discussion. The argument is as follows: even violent internal social conflicts in high performing teams of a certain kind need not noticeably weaken their performance capacity, if the team continues to exist despite the conflicts. Indeed, as the conflict develops and becomes more pronounced, even an improved performance can result.

A discussion of the antithesis seems to be especially important. However, in a previous publication with a different title, the precise sociometric data and the matrix and vector analyses have appeared; thus the technical details can be dispensed with here (4).

An unconditional axiom which is characterized by "only" or "all," "every," "always," "imperative," like the thesis to be refuted here, can be denied through the presentation of only one contrary instance. Its negation, a logically equivalent proposition, can already be proved through one single example. The referred to antithesis can be derived easily. If there would be a team that performs at its best despite the deepest of internal conflicts, or whose performance, despite the development of conflict, improves as far as possible, then the antithesis would be proven and, therefore, the original thesis would be clearly refuted, as they are incompatible with each other. The initial sociometrically and participant observed team, the German Olympic Rowing Eight of 1960, showed sharp subgroup conflicts and leadership conflicts which were even commented upon in the press. This was a racing team consisting of athletes from two clubs, four from each.

However, this team came together originally purely out of comradeship, without the cooperation of any official club representative. At that time all the rowers considered the team as a compatible extra unit, between the two clubs. Conflicts did not occur. During the two years in which the team existed, the managing committees of the clubs x and y increasingly introduced club-centered motives into the team. The members of the combined team subsequently split into club cliques, through which conflicts emerged more distinctly. The vast majority of the questionnaire answers traced the division into the two contrary cliques back to the club-centered influence and almost unanimously now considered the joint team a mere service one. Several times conflict almost led to the destruction of the team. By means of sport, within this eight, no performance detriment as a result of the tensions within the group was noticeable. But there should have occurred a performance decrement in comparison with the initial situation (the compatibility and conflictlessness among members from different clubs), as the training regimen and the technical control of the work-outs remained on the same level. At best there could have been only a small performance increase. Actually, the performance did increase and paralleled the sharpness of the conflict during the two years in which the eight existed. Performance was systematically measured using their very frequent training sessions over eight by 560 meters in racing tempo. The team became unbeaten Olympic champions. A sport team, therefore, is able to achieve, in spite of strong internal conflicts, the highest of performances. The conflicts did not noticeably cause any performance decrease.

The second example team, the world champion eight of 1962, was not a combined racing team, but rather a club team. However, there developed within it a complete clique of four rowers in which each man was chosen by each other, thus setting themselves apart from the other rowers. The latter, however, chose members of the clique also. Performance envy or position jealously did not determine their choice. They did not form an anti-clique.

As the emotional unity of a partial group of a social system always creates strong social tensions, indeed, even rejections and animosities from those which are excluded, it can positively be concluded here: the extremely strong formation of the clique could not have occurred as a result of personality evaluations and sympathies. As a matter of fact, the clique consisted of, according to the judgment of the trainer and others, precisely the strongest rowers of the eight. The image of performance capacity of the single rower as judged by the others formed the priority criterion in the top rated team.

A significant curiosity is revealed by the sociogram of the captain's election: a completely symmetrical structure with regard to the two most mentioned rowers. Both were chosen by two others and chose themselves; due to the equally strong leadership polarity the team had a latent leadership conflict. Disagreements—concerning technical questions—would arise if the team's independent decisions would differ from the suggestions of the leading rowers. Like the first one, this second eight also was not able to develop independently and to guide itself. Here, too, only an external authority (such as the coach) could lead the team and keep it together as a unit.

Because of the distinctive leadership dualism and the extremely strong tendency of the clique to separate from the others, one had to predict in 1962 (5), that the team would split into two opposing groups. The aversions would have to be intensified emotionally especially among the leadership polarities, and the team would be exposed to strong leadership fights.

The eight was interviewed a year later (1963) still consisting of the same members. For the non-members of the clique, now disengaged noticeably from it, based upon both the sociometric data and their behavior—twice as emphatic as in 1962—especially in terms of roommate selection, the aversion was five times as great. The non-members of the clique now developed greater unity, the antipathy among themselves had now disappeared in comparison to 1962. They were only one vote short of forming a complete clique.

For instructional-theoretical-mathematical reasons the emotional rejection no doubt stood out at this point as especially clear. The diagram of the rejections forms a subunit—subgroup. Actually in comparison to 1962, two cliques faced each other emotionally now, as it had been predicted on grounds of the sociometric structure and the leadership duality (5). These leadership fights, which now had erupted vehemently, resulted in a considerably more distinct rejection of the two leading persons than in 1962. The team had lost confidence in the 1962 leaders after the conflicts had openly erupted. As the leadership sociogram shows, the team had no internal leadership any longer. It was hierarchically disorganized and was only held together by the outside authority of the coach. Nevertheless, the eight won the European championship during the year of the interview—once more against the strongest opponents of the World Championships of the preceding year. The eight had even become somewhat better in performance measured in terms of training times. The level of performance thus had not suffered from status conflicts and tension between the leadership dualities. As the amount of training and the technical control of the boat had remained the same and only an insignificant increase in muscular strength due to winter training had been achieved, the level performance could, at best, improve insignificantly. This occurred despite the conflicts.

During the following year (1964) a qualifying competition in the single sculls was held for membership in the eight-man crew, resulting in an inner contest being openly generated. Based upon these qualifying tests, two rowers were replaced by two others. The competition in no way inhibited performance; indeed the individual performance of five of the remaining rowers (as measured by their singles time) increased, because they trained even harder before the qualifying test. During that year the team proved to be slightly stronger than the year previous and won the Olympic Silver Medal. Thus internal competition within rowing teams by no means necessarily has an inhibiting effect upon performance as in part the initial thesis suggests.

In comparison to other teams studied, the two teams discussed above, i.e., the eights with the strongest tensions threatening the unity of team, showed retrospectively in four years (that is 1960, 1962, 1963, and 1964) the highest performances in the world.

This, and the fact that the development of conflict went parallel with an optimal improvement of performance, which was the highest attainable, show that the antithesis is correct: even vehement social internal conflicts within top performing rowing teams need not noticeably weaken the strength of the performance at all, when the team continues to exist in spite of conflict (every one of the ambitious members was personally interested in the continuation of the team and the strength of its performance). With the development or intensification of an internal conflict even an increase in performance can occur.

The thesis, namely, that only low conflict groups can achieve high levels of performance, is not generally valid. Its strict general validity proves to be a prejudice (6).

REFERENCES

1. Hare, P., *Handbook of Small Group Research*, Glencoe, Ill.: Free Press, 1962.
2. Lüschen, G., "The Social Function of Modern Sport," in *Krankengymnastik* Jg. 1964, p. 2.
3. Lepsius, R., in R. Konig (ed.), *Soziologie*, Frankfurt, 1958, p. 219. In contrast, R. Konig, "Die Informellen Gruppen im Industriebetrieb," in E. Schnaufer and K. Agthe (eds.), *Organization*, Baden-Baden, 1961.
4. Lenk, Hans, "Conflict and Performance in Top Sport Teams—Sociometric Structures of Competition Eights in Rowing," in *Soziale Welt*, 1964–65, pp. 307–343; "The Racing Community and Group Dynamics," in *Rudersport* 1962, Lehrbeilage I, pp. 5–7.
5. Lenk, Hans, "Sociogram of a Club Eight," in *Rudersport*, 1963, Lehrbeilage, II, pp. 5–7.
6. Moreover, further supporting data based on 26 American high school basketball teams, which obviously do not achieve top level performance, most often lead to rejection of the hypothesis that close relationships among team members would be conducive to winning many games (Fiedler, F. E., *Leader Attitudes and Group Effectiveness*, Urbana, Ill.: University of Illinois Press, 1958, p. 24).

group composition, group structure and group effectiveness of basketball teams

MICHAEL KLEIN AND GERD CHRISTIANSEN

The basketball coach has the following task: from twelve players belonging to one team, five are to be selected and permitted to be on the court at any one time. These groups of five are supposed to represent an optimal combination with regard to their goal, the victory. As a criterion for the decision as to which players shall be placed into a team combination, the coach usually acknowledges the effectiveness of the individual player's per-

• Translated by Dr. D. Elisabeth Kenyon from Michael Klein and Gerd Christiansen, "Gruppenkomposition, Gruppenstrultur und Effektivität von Basketball," in *Kleingruppenforschung und Gruppe im Sport*, Kölner Zeitschrift für Soziologie und Sozialpsychologie, 10 (1966), 180–191.

This investigation was carried out with the friendly financial support of the German Sport Association.

formance, which is determined according to certain indicators. This would, in part, suggest that those five players who hit the basket most often will be combined into a team of five persons. However, certain research results of sociology and social psychology indicate, that the individual performance strongly varies according either to the situation or to the group structure in which it shall be actualized (see 10,16,21,23).

It seems not of primary importance that the combination of a successful team consist of players who achieved a high level of individual performance effectiveness. Rather, it is important to investigate under what conditions the individual characteristics are effectively used to achieve the group goal. Such conditions result first from the group composition, i.e., the internal variation of individual characteristics, and second, out of structural peculiarities of the group.

For investigating the influence of group composition we used achievement motivation of the players as a criterion. That is, in order to actualize the effectiveness, a certain amount of achievement motivation within the team members must be present. We understand the term achievement motivation as a personality variable that expresses the relatively constant need to personally succeed in every game situation independent of the group task. Thus we assume that success of a group is dependent upon a group characteristic that is defined as the average achievement motivation of a particular group.

The average value of our criterion, "achievement motivation" still says nothing about the group as a unit, i.e., the variation of the characteristic within the group. It must be investigated now whether achievement of the group goal is more likely in groups which are homogeneous or heterogeneous with regard to achievement motivation.

M. E. Shaw, R. L. Hoffmann, and N. F. Maier (8,9,10) have found that there is a connection between heterogeneity of certain personality characteristics and efficiency in solving group problems. The results of these investigations lead one to believe that, although a certain level of average achievement motivation must be present, it is not necessary for all members to have equally high levels of achievement motivation.

Within groups which have a homogeneous achievement motivation it is not only important that such groups are composed in certain ways regarding their personal characteristics, it is also important that communication and consensus are present with regard to certain strategies to achieve this goal. The premise for communication and consensus of strategies is a high amount of cohesion within the group (see 2,14). Cohesion is said to be present, when as high as possible a percentage perceives that the group is attractive. Thus "cohesion" would indicate that there are no severe conflicts within the group or contrary opinions about the strategy to achieve goals. This tells nothing about groups which have conflicts in other respects (see 12,13). It is certain only that a positive correlation between cohesion (as an indicator for consensus regarding strategies that achieve the goal of the group) and success of the group exists.

A further structural characteristic of groups which is important for the achievement of a commonly agreed upon group goal, consists of the consensus in the group regarding the distribution of roles, especially status consensus with respect to the member of the group who contributes the most to the achievement of the goal, namely that of the leader ("focused leadership"). The work of C. Heinicke and R. F. Bales (7) supports our assumption that a great amount of "focused leadership" is related to group performance. Where consensus exists in the group concerning the distribution of roles, and especially status consensus concerning the leader, the variable "focused leadership" becomes a measure of the facilitation of the group task, as the team members can concentrate upon achieving the group goal.

Up to this point we have related group characteristics to success, which, with regard to the group goal, required conflictlessness and consensus within this group. On the other hand, it is possible that conflictlessness within the group can relate negatively to success. So, for instance, it is possible that the sociometric structure of friendship relationships conflicts with the optimal communication structure necessary for group success. Although characteristics such as cohesion and status consensus have no direct influence on the course of the ball during the game itself, it is believed of the inter-individual effects of the players have an immediate influence upon the course of the ball in the game and thus an indirect influence upon the success of the team. Within the game there must exist communication nets which distribute the information (here: balls) relevant for a quick and direct achievement of the goal; thus the efficiency of the team becomes possible. The assumption must be examined whether a communication structure for the performance of the group—set-up accordingly to the inter-individual affect relationships—is not optimal.

A communication net is assumed as the theoretical course of the ball which is provided for the group through structural conditions of the game itself (see also 17). In order to exclude these structural conditions of the game, this communication net is established as Basis One. The alterations of the communication course which occurred under the influence of the sociometric influence of the group are normed (standardized) on Element One. Now it must be determined whether the communication net which was established in Element One is the optimum for the group to achieve the goal and whether by this affect structure of the friendship relationships has a negative effect upon the success of the group.

Method

Within two top performing basketball teams each consisting of eight persons, a questionnaire for data concerning personality variables such as aspiration and group variables, such as sociometric structure, cohesion, and "focused leadership," was administered in February 1965, and in February 1966.

Within the first stage of the investigation, pass patterns, score totals, pass failures, and aggressive acts were recorded by the protocol leader for both teams during a total of 1200 game minutes in championship games of the present season or during specially arranged practice or friendship games.

To eliminate the structural conditions of the game (for instance, the fact that the ball distributor or the "post" receives the ball relatively more often—see 17) or instructions of the coach (perhaps the invitations to play more often with a certain person), the recorded data were standardized on Element One; i.e., the observed data were divided by the Basis One expected data.

Within the second stage of investigation which studied seven persons of one of the teams in March 1966, the situation was altered. This particular team was chosen because it was very homogeneous with regard to characteristics such as age and individual achievement and ability. First, there were only two consecutive age groups present within the team; second, the individual ability of the team members with regard to technical skills, shooting accuracy, speed, and physical condition was designated as absolutely equal.

Out of the seven persons in each case three played against three. This procedure can be justified: (a) In such a basketball game there are always only three persons interacting with each other. Every game move can be broken up into all possible combinations of interaction among three persons; (b) game structural conditions are eliminated; (c) the collection of data is simpler and clearer; and (d) this kind of game was already known to the team members through selection courses and regular practice sessions. Of seven persons each was brought together with each other into triads, with each combination playing against each combination. With seven persons this yields 35 combinations and 70 games, of which in fact only 51 could be accommodated; thus the optimal figure of four games for each combination could not be attained. The teams played 41 three-minute games and 10 five-minute games. The games were normed on five minutes.

Before each game every player filled out a short questionnaire to acquire data on the "attractiveness" of the particular combination, "task-related leadership," "prediction of game result," and anticipated conduct of the partners.

The score differences of the games of each combination were totaled. Teams with a positive score difference were called successful teams; those with a negative score difference, unsuccessful teams.

ACHIEVEMENT PERFORMANCE. To measure this variable an aspiration index was used as proposed by L. Worrell (24). The index compares the self-assessment of ability at present with the expected ability in the future. The greater the discrepancy between the two self-assessments of a person, the more likely the assumption is justified that the self-assessment of the future ability is unrealistic. In persons with an exaggerated aspiration level—based upon the Atkinson theory of aspiration level (1)—the tendency to avoid failure is greater than the tendency to achieve success. Thus, herewith a behavioral disposition to achieve little is assessed. A high score on the aspiration scale of Worrell means a low achievement motivation, and a low score, a high achievement motivation. We would like to propose that this aspiration index be used as an indirect method of measuring achievement motivation.

HOMOGENEITY. For each group the difference between the highest and the lowest scores of achievement motivation was found. Thus the range of achievement motivation of the members of the group was used as an indicator of homogeneity. A high score means little homogeneity, and vice versa, a low score, high homogeneity.

FOCUSED LEADERSHIP. It was found by questioning who in the team contributes the most to achieve the goal. The modal value of those most motivated to succeed despite the competition can use their potential ability best. Therefore, we are dealing with persons with a high achievement motivation. Now groups with a common goal, composed of members who show this characteristic to a high degree, should have a positive influence upon success.

Hypothesis: *The greater the average achievement motivation in a basketball team, the more it will be successful in play.*

table 1
AVERAGE TEAM ACHIEVEMENT MOTIVATION AND
TEAM PERFORMANCE

| | AVERAGE ACHIEVEMENT MOTIVATION | |
TEAM PERFORMANCE	HIGH	LOW
High	13	6
Low	5	11
Total	18	17

Table 1 shows that, of the successful teams, the majority have high average achievement motivation, and vice versa, the unsuccessful teams show low average achievement motivation. Therefore, the results point in the expected direction.

The relationship found answers only the question whether the members of basketball teams must have a certain task-specific personality characteristic for group success. But, disregarded here is the fact that in groups with a common goal, different contributions regarding the kind and extent of the activities are expected of the members in order to achieve the group goal. These different "role expectations" possibly demand a different degree of the task-specific personality characteristic. If, in basketball teams, all players have an equally high achievement motivation this might lead to difficulties in a quick and all-accepted role assignment during the game. Thus, the following hypothesis seems to be justified:

Hypothesis: *With regard to achievement motivation, heterogeneous basket-ball teams are more successful than homogeneous teams.*

table 2

COMPOSITION OF THE TEAMS ACCORDING TO ACHIEVEMENT
MOTIVATION AND TEAM PERFORMANCE

TEAM PERFORMANCE	HOMOGENEOUS TEAMS	HETEROGENEOUS TEAMS
High	3	16
Low	13	3
Total	16	19

Table 2 seems to confirm the relation proposed in the hypothesis.

On grounds that groups with high homogeneous achievement motivation show unimpressive group performances, the hypothesis must be modified with respect to the connection between average achievement motivation and team effectiveness. The most effective are probably such teams that do show a high degree of average achievement motivation as a group characteristic but in which the degree of achievement motivation of the individual players varies.

It must be expected now that within those groups with heterogeneity with respect to the task-specific personality characteristic, fewer conflicts concerning the role assignment prevail than in homogeneous groups. From Table 3 it can be gathered that a connection between group composition and consensus concerning role distribution in the group does exist. The consensus about the role distribution in the group is measured here by status consensus concerning the person who contributes most to the achievement of the goal.

table 3

COMPOSITION OF THE TEAMS ACCORDING TO ACHIEVEMENT
MOTIVATION AND STATUS CONSENSUS

STATUS CONSENSUS	HOMOGENEOUS TEAMS	HETEROGENEOUS TEAMS
High	2	14
Low	15	4
Total	17	18

It can be assumed that status consensus about the role distribution facilitates interactions within the group and thus is a prerequisite to the success of the group.

Hypothesis: *Teams with High Status-Consensus Play More Successfully Than Teams with Low Status-Consensus.*

table 4
STATUS CONSENSUS AND TEAM PERFORMANCE

| | STATUS CONSENSUS | |
TEAM PERFORMANCE	HIGH	LOW
High	14	5
Low	2	14
Total	16	19

Status consensus concerning role distribution does not only contribute to a better performance of the group, but also leads to greater cohesion of the group as the study of Heinicke and Bales (7) has shown. This is probably the result of the ease of interactions within the group and the decrease of status conflict (see 5). It can be assumed that under the stated conditions the group is more attractive for the members. Attractiveness of the group is most often used in the literature as a criterion for cohesion.

In groups with a common goal and clear role differentiation with regard to this goal, cohesion facilitates effectiveness of the group, since argument concerning strategies to achieve the goal can be achieved easier in cohesive groups.

Hypothesis: A *Positive Relationship Exists between the Cohesion of a Team and Its Effectiveness.*

table 5
COHESION AND TEAM PERFORMANCE

| | COHESION | |
TEAM PERFORMANCE	HIGH	LOW
High	13	6
Low	7	9
Total	20	15

Summarizing it can be established: the distribution of personality variables in task-oriented groups apparently is not a sufficient prerequisite for achievement of groups. In groups where interactions of the members are the means of achieving a mutual goal, the structure of the group decides whether the individual performances lead to group success or not.

So far no assertions have been made about the sequence of interactions during a game. During the game the course of the ball is the institutionalized form of the course of interaction. In order to be able to give statements about the direct course of the game it is assumed that a team will be more successful the quicker or the more direct the success is sought. It is presumed that for each attack there is an optimal ball course for success. These optimal game moves can be done only if each player has the chance to be given the ball when standing in a favorable position. This assumption is expressed in an hypothesis:

Hypothesis: *Teams are Most Successful When Each Player Gets An Equal Number of Passes*

To test this hypothesis, first of all four variables, yet equally strong team combinations, of one team against different opponents, but equal times against equally strong opponents (team strength measured by league membership and position therein), were evaluated according to distribution of passes and success (score differences) for each sixty game-minutes. A value of 1.0 for the distribution of passes would herein mean an equal distribution.

table 6
DISTRIBUTION OF PASSES AND SUCCESS

	PASSES	SUCCESS
Combination 1	0.87	+18
Combination 2	0.72	+ 8
Combination 3	0.64	+ 5
Combination 4	0.47	−12

Thus it can be determined that different combinations of the same team distribute balls differently wherein that combination which comes closest to the value 1.0 plays the most successfully and that combination which is farthest away from 1.0 plays the most unsuccessfully. In view of this finding, we suggest that different communication stages can be explained by different affect structures within the team combinations, which are operationalized through the sociometric selections. To test the assumption the following hypothesis was formed:

Hypothesis: *Interactions during the game situation (herein defined as passes) appear more often among team members who have elected themselves mutually in a sociometric inventory than among team members who have not elected themselves or have rejected themselves.*

To test this hypothesis three-way combinations were formed during training such that a sociometric couple and an unchosen player were always combined. Passes were then recorded when they originated from one member of the pair. From 1100 observed passes 748 (68 per cent) went to the sociometrically chosen player, and 352 (32 per cent) went to the unchosen player.

Thus it is justified to retain the hypothesis in that form. Yet, if we do not wish to be satisfied with the mere establishment of what was asserted in the hypothesis, we must investigate a few conditions under which alterations appear.

Hypothesis: *Sociometrically rejected team members are given the ball more often than sociometrically isolated ones.*

To test the hypothesis 380 passes in five-member teams were counted in which each two sociometric pairs and one isolate were present. Everyone had the chance to get 76 passes. Eighteen passes or 23.7 per cent of those statistically possible by chance went to the isolates. As a comparison 350 passes in five-member teams which in each case contained two sociometric pairs and one rejected by both pairs, were recorded. Everyone had the chance to get 70 passes. Thirty-four passes or 48.6 per cent of those statistically possible by chance went to the respective rejected players.

Finally, let us investigate whether there are game conditions in which the same team combinations, i.e., a group with a constant affect structure uses different communication paths. We assume that communication paths alter with the difficulty of the given task and thus with the increased performance demand.

Hypothesis: *The Stronger the Opponent, the Less Distribution of Passes Is Determined by Sociometric Choices.*

As a test of the above hypothesis, passes were evaluated in different games; in fact, 400 passes for each category of Table 7. Those data acquired in the training situation are assigned the value of 1 as the expected values. Those passes given to the sociometrically chosen one are those for games against different opponents divided by the expected values. The closer the point value lies to 1.0 the more passes that are given to the sociometrically chosen ones as appeared in training.

Thus, deviations from sociometric preferences do not seem to depend upon the formal importance of the game—also in the training game the goal remains as the victory—but rather upon the strength of the opponent. An exception is the extremely important championship game, which, however, is played only against strong opponents. Victories over strong teams increase the attractiveness of the group certainly more than victories over weak opponents. Summarizing, one can say:

1. "Round about" relationships depending upon the sociometric structure interfere with quick and direct communication flow and thus success.
2. Sociometrically rejected group members who also are chosen by others are more likely to be included in the communication flow than sociometric isolates.
3. High achievement stress on the group weakens those communication paths which are subjectively conditioned in contrast with those objectively conditioned ones.

Summary

In the present study relations were investigated between group variables and the performance of basketball teams in the form of applied social

table 7

DIFFICULTY OF THE OPPONENT AND DISTRIBUTION OF PASSES

Training	TS weak	MS opponent	TS strong	MS opponent	TS far superior opponent	extremely important MS
1.0	0.91	0.89	0.79	0.78	0.70	0.68

(Left scale: 1.0, 0.9, 0.8, 0.7, 0.6)

TS: Training game.
MS: Championship game.

research. The research was based upon published results from small group research. It was possible to determine a positive relationship between achievement and average achievement motivation, heterogeneity of achievement motivation, status consensus, and cohesion of the group. The sociometric structure of the team has an immediate influence upon the communication pathways during the game situation and consequently an indirect influence upon success.

It can be assumed that for each basketball team an optimal five-member combination can be determined. But in addition there is a need for study of the relevant variables with more variable and differentiated groups.

REFERENCES

1. Atkinson, J. M. and C. J. Litwin, "Achievement Motive and Test Anxiety Conceived as Motive to Approach Success and Motive to Avoid Failure," *Journal of Abnormal and Social Psychology*, 60, 1960, pp. 52–63.
2. Berkowitz, L., "Group Standards, Cohesiveness and Productivity," *Human Relations*, 7, 1954, pp. 509–519.
3. Caplow, T., "A Theory of Coalitions in the Triad," *American Sociological Review*, 21, 1956, pp. 489–493.
4. Davol, S. H., "An Empirical Test of Structural Balance in Sociometric Triads," *Journal of Abnormal and Social Psychology*, 59, 1959, pp. 393–398.
5. Festinger, L., S. Schachter and K. Buch, *Social Pressures in Informal Groups*, New York, 1950.
6. Hare, A. P., *Handbook of Small Group Research*, Glencoe, Illinois: Free Press, 1962.
7. Heinicke, C. and R. F. Bales, "Developmental Trends in the Structure of Groups," *Sociometry*, 16, 1953, pp. 7–38.
8. Hoffmann, R. L., "Homogeneity of Member Personality and Its Effects on Group Problem Solvings," *Journal of Abnormal and Social Psychology*, 58, 1961, pp. 27–32.
9. Hoffmann, R. L. and N. F. Maier, "Quality and Acceptance of Problem Solutions by Members of Homogeneous and Heterogeneous Groups," *Journal of Abnormal and Social Psychology*, 62, 1961, pp. 401–407.
10. Homans, G. C., *The Human Group*, New York, Harcourt, Brace & World, 1950.
11. Klein, J., *The Study of Groups*, London, 1956.
12. Lenk, H., "Conflict and Achievement in Top Sport Teams," *Soziale Welt*, 15, 1965, pp. 307–343.
13. Lenk, H., "Maximum Performance in Spite of Inner Conflict," *Kölner Zeitschrift für Soziologie und Sozialpsychologie*, 10, 1966, pp. 168–172.
14. Lott, A. J. and B. E. Lott, "Group Cohesiveness, Communication Level and Conformity," *Journal of Abnormal and Social Psychology*, 62, 1961, pp. 408–412.
15. Roby, T. B. and J. T. Lanzetta, "Work Group Structure, Communication and Group Performance," *Sociometry*, 19, 1956, pp. 105–113.
16. Rohrer, J. H. and M. Sherif, (eds.), *Social Psychology at the Crossroads*, New York, Harper, 1951.

17. Schafer, W. E., "The Social Structure of Sport Groups," *Kölner Zeitschrift für Soziologie*, **10**, 1966, pp. 107–117.
18. Shaw, M. E., "A Note Concerning Homogeneity of Membership and Group Problem Solving," *Journal of Abnormal and Social Psychology*, **60**, 1961, pp. 448–450.
19. Shelley, H. P., "Status Consensus, Leadership and Satisfaction with the Group," *Journal of Social Psychology*, **51**, 1960, pp. 157–164.
20. Shelley, H. P., "Focused Leadership and Cohesiveness in Small Groups," *Sociometry*, **23**, 1960, pp. 209–216.
21. Sherif, M. and C. W. Sherif, *Groups in Harmony and Tension*, New York, Harpers, 1953.
22. Stryker S. and G. Psathas, "Research on Coalitions in the Triad: Findings, Problems and Strategy," *Sociometry*, **23**, 1960, pp. 217–230.
23. Whyte, W. F., *Street Corner Society*, Chicago, Univ. of Chicago Press, 1943.
24. Worrell, L., "Level of Aspiration and Academic Success," *Journal of Educational Psychology*, **50**, 1959, pp. 47–54.

the effects of formal structure on managerial recruitment: a study of baseball organization

OSCAR GRUSKY

A theory of formal structure is presented which examines three interdependent features of positions; spatial location, nature of task, and rate of interaction. A combination of the three attributes provides two types of positions of particular concern, termed high and low interactors. It is assumed that type of position influences the development of varying kinds of role skills. Moreover, possession of key role skills is related to chances for positive career movement in the system. Hence, occupants of certain positions in an organization should be more likely than others to experience upward career mobility. The theory was applied in a preliminary manner to professional baseball organizations and the hypothesis that high interactors (infielders and catchers) would be more likely to become field managers than low interactors (outfielders and pitchers) was supported.

• From *Sociometry*, **26** (1963), pp. 345–353. Copyright © 1963, American Sociological Association, Washington, D.C.

I am grateful to Judith Kairath for doing the coding, to Don Zimmerman for computational work, and the University of California, Los Angeles for research funds. The members, too numerous to name, of the Department of Anthropology and Sociolgy's informal seminar, directed by Joan Moore, were kind enough to criticize an earlier draft of this paper.

The formal structure of an organization consists of a set of norms which define the system's official objectives, its major offices or positions, and the primary responsibilities of the position occupants.[1] Official norms or rules are often of such generality that informal practices inevitably develop as solutions for particular cases. The officially acceptable standards of the present frequently were the unofficial, informal practices of the past. Hence, a fundamental characteristic of formal structures is that they constantly undergo change. At any single point in time the behavior of a position occupant is governed by a combination of official and unofficial standards.[2]

The formal structure, conceived of as the environment within which the informal develops, patterns the behavior of its constituent positions along three interdependent dimensions: (1) spatial location, (2) nature of task, and (3) frequency of interaction. We distinguish between central and peripheral spatial locations, independent and dependent tasks, and frequent and less frequent interpersonal interaction. In accordance with the formulations of Bavelas and Leavitt, central positions are defined as those located close to other positions.[3] Independent tasks are of the kind performed without the necessity of coordination with the activities of other positions. All else being equal, the more central one's spatial location: (1) the greater the likelihood dependent or coordinative tasks will be performed and (2) the greater the rate of interaction with the occupants of other positions.[4] Also, performance of dependent tasks is positively related to frequency of interaction. Combining these three criteria, we define two types of positions in a formal structure, those with high and low interaction potential. We shall refer to *high interactors* and *low interactors*.

In most cases, formal structures are able to maintain themselves despite the fact that succession among position occupants is a continuous process. We assume that both the formal structure and the position occupant mutually

[1] Leonard Broom and Philip Selznick, *Sociology: A Text with Adapted Readings*, 2nd Ed., Evanston, Ill.: Row, Peterson & Co., 1958, pp. 208–213.

[2] Peter Blau and W. Richard Scott, *Formal Organizations*, San Francisco: Chandler Publishing Company, 1962, pp. 5–8.

[3] Alex Bavelas, "Communication Patterns in Task-oriented Groups," *Journal of The Acoustical Society of America*, 22 (November, 1950), pp. 725–730; Harold J. Leavitt, "Some Effects of Certain Communication Patterns on Group Performance," *Journal of Abnormal and Social Psychology*, 46 (January, 1951), pp. 38–50. See also Mark Mulder, "Communication Structure, Decision Structure and Group Performance," *Sociometry*, 23 (March, 1960), pp. 1–14; and Harold Guetzkow and Herbert A. Simon, "The Impact of Certain Communication Nets upon Organization and Performance in Task-oriented Groups," *Management Science*, 1 (April–July, 1955), pp. 233–250.

[4] See Blau and Scott's discussion, *op. cit.*, pp. 126–128. Also, on the relationship between spatial location and liking, see Leon Festinger, Stanley Schachter, and Kurt W. Back, *Social Pressures in Informed Groups*, New York: Harper & Bros., 1950, pp. 33–59. On some effects of type of task, termed degree of "facilitation in role interdependence," see Edwin J. Thomas, "Effects of Facilitative Role Interdependence on Group Functioning," in Dorwin Cartwright and Alvin Zander (eds.), *Group Dynamics*, Second Edition, Evanston, Ill.: Row, Peterson and Co., 1960, pp. 449–471.

influence one another in varying degrees.[5] The particular pattern of characteristics associated with the position a person occupies should affect not only his degree of job satisfaction but also the nature of his career pattern. Hence, Leavitt found that persons occupying central positions were more satisfied and more likely to be selected as leaders than were those in peripheral positions.[6] Our general hypothesis maintains that position in the formal structure of an organization contributes to the development of role skills, which are essential to career movement.[7] As interaction is positively related to liking, high interactors should be selected more often than low interactors as the most respected and popular members of the organization.[8] Also, high interactors should be more likely to learn cooperative social skills and develop a strong commitment to the welfare of the organization. Low interactors should be more likely to focus on individualistic rather than team values and tend to be psychologically distant or aloof. In formal organizations which utilize these or related characteristics as official or unofficial criteria for managerial selection, high interactors should be selected for executive positions more often than low interactors.

We decided to test the managerial recruitment proposition of this theory in an admittedly preliminary and exploratory manner, on baseball teams. Professional sports organizations have a number of unique features which make them useful sources for testing hypotheses of concern to organization theory. For example, they tend to have fairly stable formal structures, are of similar size, keep accurate public records, and utilize relatively objective performance standards.[9] This study examines the relationship between the internal structure of baseball organization and the recruitment of field managers. Specifically, we hypothesized that the occupants of certain key formal positions (infielders and catchers) were more likely than others to become managers.

BASEBALL ORGANIZATION. The playing organization of professional

[5] See Chris Argyris, *Personality and Organization*, Harper & Bros., 1957; Robert K. Merton, *Social Theory and Social Structure*, Revised Ed., Glencoe, Illinois: The Free Press, 1957, pp. 195–206; Leila E. Sussman, "The Personnel and Ideology of Public Relations," *Public Opinion Quarterly*, 12 (Winter, 1948–49), pp. 697–708; and Guy E. Swanson, "Agitation through the Press: A Study of the Personalities of Publicists," *Public Opinion Quarterly*, 20 (Summer, 1956), pp. 441–456.

[6] *Op. cit.* Also, Norman H. Berkowitz and Warren G. Bennis report a positive relationship between the status of the other party and satisfaction with interaction. People receive more satisfaction from interaction with persons of higher status. See "Interaction Patterns in Formal Service-oriented Organizations," *Administrative Science Quarterly*, 6 (June, 1961), pp. 25–50.

[7] A good summary and critique of role skills deemed desirable for business success can be found in Stanley Stark, "Research Criteria of Executive Success," *The Journal of Business of the University of Chicago*, 32 (January, 1959), pp. 1–14.

[8] A number of studies supporting this relationship are discussed in George C. Homans, *Social Behavior: Its Elementary Forms*, New York: Harcourt, Brace and World, Inc., 1961, pp. 181–190.

[9] Some implications of these attributes for sports organizations are discussed in a companion paper on "Managerial Succession and Organizational Effectiveness," *The American Journal of Sociology*, 69 (July, 1963), pp. 21–31.

baseball teams consists of three major interaction units, outfielders, infielders, and the pitcher and catcher.[10] The constituent positions of each unit differ with respect to the attributes of spatial location, type of task, and frequency of interaction.

The outfielders constitute the most isolated unit. They are not only located at a distance from each other but also are far away from the infield.[11] As a result, outfielders probably have the lowest rate of team interaction during the defensive part of the game, although perhaps the highest rate of interaction with the fans.[12]

Field positions in baseball differ considerably with respect to the nature of the primary tasks expected of the occupant. A major dimension is the extent to which the tasks are dependent or independent. Although outfielders do have some dependent functions, for example, when they must throw the ball into the infield to complete a play, independent tasks are more characteristic of their position. In sharp contrast, infielders' functions are predominantly of the dependent type.[13] The third baseman must be able to throw the ball accurately and rapidly to the first baseman and the shortstop must not only field ground balls cleanly but also be able to toss the ball at the proper angle so the second baseman can handle it, pivot, avoid the onrushing runner, and throw quickly to the first baseman.

Because they are densely concentrated close to the center of the game's activity, infielders tend to interact more frequently with each other, rival players, and even the umpires. Their offensive as well as their defensive tasks can be distinguished from that of the outfielders. Where the outfielder is supposed to hit homeruns, an independent function, the infielder is more often expected to hit singles, or bunt, and thereby sacrifice his turn at bat for the team's benefit. It is true that the first baseman, often a converted outfielder, deviates from this overall pattern.

Independent tasks in baseball are more likely to be of the glamorous, heroic type and most frequently are offensive rather than defensive in nature. It is the sluggers who are likely to provide the daily headlines. Where the outfielder is typically expected to excel offensively and not as a fielder, the reverse is the case for the infielder. He is commonly dscribed as a "glove-man."

The third interaction unit, officially called the battery, possesses a num-

[10] The official rules specify that there be nine players but define only the functions of these four. See Hy Turkin and S. C. Thompson, *The Official Encyclopedia of Baseball*, 2nd Revised Ed., New York: A. S. Barnes and Company, 1959, pp. 554–586.

[11] This fact is recognized in a rather amusing fashion by the official rules which define the outfielder as ". . . a fielder who occupies a position in the outfield, which is the area of playing field most distant from home base," *ibid.*, p. 559.

[12] Although not tested in this study, this assumption can be examined empirically. An observer could conceivably take a battery-operated interaction process recorder to a sample of ballgames. Or, of course, a simple interaction matrix could be used.

[13] This statement like many others is based largely on personal observation. As a start, one might utilize box-score data to determine more precisely which positions have the highest proportion of independent and dependent acts.

ber of special characteristics. In general, the catcher's position takes on more of the attributes of the infielder while the pitcher's position resembles that of the outfielder. Two factors are relevant to the classification of the pitcher. First, like the outfielders, his functions are primarily independent. It is not his abilities in team-play that are critical to his success. His offensive tasks are considered of minor importance and are generally of a dependent nature. Second, despite a central location, his interaction rate is severely limited by the fact that he participates in only about one game in four, unless he is a relief pitcher. In the latter case, he typically performs only for a few innings.

Both the spatial location and the dependent nature of the defensive tasks of the catcher place him in a situation of close interdependence and frequent interaction with the infielders. On the other hand, his offensive tasks are frequently of the independent variety. This unique combination, as we shall see, may especially prepare occupants of this position for managerial selection.

As noted earlier, spatial location and nature of task are mutually correlated with frequency of interaction. Applying these criteria, we classify infielders and catchers as *high interactors,* and outfielders and pitchers, *low interactors.* Assuming that the formal characteristics of the position directly affect the nature of the role skills developed by the occupants, then high interactors should be well-liked, more likely to learn cooperative social skills, and should develop a strong commitment to team welfare, whereas low interactors should be less popular, focus more on individualistic rather than team values, and tend to be psychologically distant or aloof.

Elsewhere we have described the major sources of managerial role strain.[14] The considerable discrepancy that exists between the manager's responsibility, and his authority, on the one hand, and the availability of an objective assessment of managerial and team performance to the organization's clientele and higher levels of authority, on the other, combine to lessen the possibility of domination of the players by the occupant of this position. Instead, managerial control in baseball is likely to be based on mutual respect and liking. As interaction is positively related to liking, it is the high interactors whom we would expect to be selected as the most respected and popular. In general, it is this group whose formal position should enable them to develop appropriate managerial skills. Hence, we hypothesized that field managers would be more likely to be recruited from among high than low interactors.

Methods and Findings

A simple random sample was drawn from all players listed in *The Official Encyclopedia of Baseball,* which purports to cover ". . . every man who ever appeared in a regularly scheduled major league game since the birth of professional league play in 1871." [15] From a random start every twentieth

[14] *Op. cit.,* "Managerial Succession and Organizational Effectiveness."
[15] *Op. cit.,* p. 57.

player listed was included in the sample. Of the 465 persons selected, a total of thirteen had been managers. The major sample of field managers was provided from data collected for a previous study. This sample consisted of the total population of field managers of the sixteen professional baseball teams during the periods 1921–1941 and 1951–1958.[16]

Table 1 presents the basic data of the study. The table shows that field managers are almost entirely recruited from among professional players.

table 1

DISTRIBUTION OF MAJOR FIELD POSITIONS OF
MANAGERS AND PLAYERS

POSITION	ALL MANAGERS [a] 1921–41, 1951–58	RANDOM SAMPLE [b]	
		MANAGERS	PLAYERS
Pitcher	6.5%	(2)	38.5%
Catcher	26.2	(5)	11.3
First base	11.2	(1)	4.4
Second base	10.3	(1)	8.2
Third base	13.1	—	4.4
Shortstop	14.0	(1)	8.0
Outfielder	15.9	(1)	22.1
Pinch hitter	—	—	2.9
Non-player	2.8	(2)	—
Not ascertained	—	—	0.2
Totals	100.0%		100.0%
N=	107	(13)	452

[a] Includes all field managers of the sixteen professional baseball teams during the periods indicated.
[b] From *The Official Encyclopedia of Baseball* which covers the 1871–1958 period.

Comparing the larger sample of managers and the players, we find that, as predicted, both pitchers and outfielders were underrepresented among the managerial group, while catchers, first basemen, second basemen, third basemen, and shortstops, were overrepresented. Not a single major position deviated from the expected pattern.

Table 2 combines the positions into two groups, high and low interactors. This table demonstrates: (1) the similarity of the large and small samples of managers with respect to distribution among the two types of positions, (2) strong support for the hypothesis that managers were more likely to have had experience in high than low interaction positions. The hypothesis was supported both when the large sample of managers and the small sample were compared with the random sample of players.

To return briefly to Table 1, we see that this table also suggests that managers were more likely to be recruited from catchers than from any other

[16] *Op. cit.*, "Managerial Succession and Organizational Effectiveness."

table 2

RELATIONSHIP BETWEEN TYPE OF FIELD POSITION AND
MANAGERIAL EXPERIENCE [a]

TYPE OF POSITION	A. ALL MANAGERS [b] 1921–41, 1951–58 (N = 104)	RANDOM SAMPLE [c]	
		B. MANAGERS (N = 11)	C. PLAYERS (N = 438)
High Interactors (Infielders and Catchers)	76.9%	73%	37.4%
Low Interactors (Outfielders and Pitchers)	23.1	27	62.6
	100.0%	100%	100.0%

[a] A × C, Chi Square = 52.92, $df = 1$, $p < 0.0001$; B × C, Chi Square = 4.26, $df = 1$, $p < 0.025$, Yates' correction applied. Values of p are based on one-sided critical region.

[b] Excludes three managers who were not players.

[c] B. excludes two managers who were not players; C. excludes thirteen pinch hitters and one player for whom data were not obtainable.

field position.[17] Where only about 11 percent (11.3 percent) of the random sample of players were catchers, over one-fourth (26.2 per cent) of the large sample of managers had held this position. We noted earlier that the catcher, although identified as a high interactor because of spatial location and defensive tasks, tended also to possess a major attribute of the low interactors in his offensive function. Like the outfielders, he is typically expected to be a slugger. Perhaps this combination of characteristics develops the types of social skills defined as especially appropriate for field managers. As a high interactor, the catcher tends to be in the very center of team action, partici-

---

[17] It is apparent that our theory is a tentative one and that other explanations are equally possible. An anonymous reviewer, for example, suggests as a possible alternative explanation that perhaps there is a norm in professional baseball that catching is the best position for training managers or that persons of managerial potential should be encouraged to become catchers. The theory presented is somewhat more satisfactory than these on several grounds. (1) It explains more. The alternatives above do not explain why infielders are disproportionately more likely than others to become managers. Of course, one might suggest that a norm is the explanation for this also. But then one must explain the genesis of the norm, which could bring you full circle back to the theory presented. (2) It fits in systematically to a comprehensive body of generalizations in the field of organizations. Theory and research by Bavelas, Leavitt, Selznick, Blau and Scott, Homans, and numerous others may be mentioned. (3) It suggests a number of additional empirical propositions. For example, is there a relationship between position played and managerial effectiveness? Is amount of experience as an infielder or number of different positions played a contributory factor affecting managerial recruitment? To what extent does the formal structure influence the development of the informal?

pates directly in the coordination of the efforts of the team, and therefore becomes closely identified with the welfare of the organization as a whole. Also important, however, may be the attitude of psychological remoteness—a trait assumed to be developed primarily among low interactors. It may be that the catcher's characteristically independent offensive performance encourages him to adopt an aloof social style. Homans' formulation suggests the following interpretation.[18] The catcher, because of his key position, earns authority through the acquisition of esteem. He acquires esteem by giving advice which is helpful to others. Hence, he is viewed as someone to be listened to. At the same time, as he is involved in advising and coordinating the efforts of others, the others incur costs in accepting his influence. As a consequence, the others develop mixed feelings toward him. He is esteemed and respected because his advice is personally rewarding as well as contributing to the team's objectives, but, at the same time, he is resented. As Homans further indicates, an aloof social style on the part of the leader tends to be exceedingly helpful to him. This approach and F. Fiedler's supporting research would suggest that all else being equal, managers who had been catchers should be highly effective leaders.[19]

Conclusions

This study has attempted to show the possible effects of formal structure on managerial recruitment patterns. A theory of formal structure was described focusing on three interdependent attributes of positions: spatial location, nature of task, and rate of interaction. Two conditions of interdependency, high and low interaction, were distinguished and seen as affecting the acquisition of role skills which, in turn, influence the recruitment of managers. The theory was applied to baseball organizations and the proposition that occupants of high interaction positions are more likely than those in low interaction positions to become field managers was strongly supported.

It should be pointed out that our discussion omitted the obviously important and perhaps mitigating effects of the informal group structure, assuming that, at least in part, the development of this structure will be influenced by the shape of the formal. Likewise we have been unable to consider the potential influence of personality predispositions on managerial recruitment. It may be, for example, that players with strong needs for affiliation seek infield positions and that these needs are merely reinforced by later experiences. Despite these reservations and others associated with the problem of correlated bias, the data presented may be viewed as tentative support for the theory outlined. It appears that in professional baseball organizations the interactional constraints associated with the type of position occupied as a player are related significantly to chances for obtaining managerial office.

[18] *Op. cit.*, pp. 307–315.
[19] "The Leader's Psychological Distance and Group Effectiveness," in Dorwin Cartwright and Alvin Zander (eds.), *op. cit.*, pp. 586–606.

occupational discrimination:
some theoretical propositions

H. M. BLALOCK, JR.

Historically, most American minorities have entered the labor force at or very near the bottom of the occupational ladder. Prior to the restriction of immigration during the first quarter of the twentieth century, each immigrant group was followed by more recent arrivals to take its place at the base of the pyramid. Therefore as the immigrant group became assimilated and developed industrial skills, while simultaneously losing its visibility as a minority, its relative position generally improved in the expanding economy The Negro has been exposed to a different situation in several important respects. Not only is the economy expanding at a much slower rate, with the major sources of immigration cut off, but the Negro's major handicap— his skin-color—cannot be overcome so readily as language and other cultural characteristics which have given immigrant minorities their visibility. Furthermore, the Northern-born Negro with several generations of urban experience is often more or less automatically classed with more recent Southern migrants of his race. The saliency of skin-color as a characteristic, together with existing prejudices, is sufficiently pronounced to obscure the very real differences between native and migrant Negroes. Thus crimes committed by recent migrants are attributed to the entire group, there being no distinctive label for members of successive generations.

Under these circumstances Negroes face the possibility of becoming a more or less permanent lower-class group. With the exception of occupations which service the minority community, it is certainly conceivable that only the least desirable positions will generally be reserved for such a racial minority. On the other hand there are certain types of occupations which, particularly during periods of labor scarcity, have begun to open up to Negroes. The purpose of the present paper is to examine one of these occupations, professional baseball, in some detail and to list a number of theoretical propositions which are immediately suggested by this analysis.

Let us begin with the assumption that a highly visible minority with an initially low occupational status is at a competitive disadvantage as compared with other persons in the labor force. In a competitive situation, therefore, the minority member will be hired only in the least desirable positions unless he possesses some compensatory advantage over his competitors. We can

• From *Social Problems*, Vol. 9, 1962, pp. 240–247. Copyright © 1962 Society for the Study of Social Problems, Dept. of Sociology and Psychology, Northeastern University, Boston, Mass. This research was carried out while the writer was on a Social Science Research Council Postdoctoral Research Training Fellowship.

distinguish between two general types of such advantages, positive and negative. From the standpoint of the employer, *positive advantages* can be measured in terms of performance per unit of cost; the minority may possess certain special skills or be willing to work for lower wages. Under *negative advantages* we include those factors which would adversely affect the employer should he fail to hire a certain number of minority members, regardless of performance or cost considerations. For example he may lose minority customers, or he may undergo public censure for failing to comply with fair employment practice laws. Or he may be refused government contracts if his policies are obviously discriminatory.

It is of the nature of most negative advantages possessed by Negroes under present circumstances that these advantages diminish in value once a small token minority labor force has been hired. For example, if an employer can point to one or two Negroes in semi-responsible positions, he can usually clear himself of the charge of discrimination. If such Negroes are highly visible to members of the minority (e.g., the Negro personnel man or the salesman in the Negro community), the employer may actually gain favor with the minority group, given the existing level of discrimination by his competitors. Under these circumstances the strength of the negative advantages diminishes with decreasing discrimination, and occupational opportunities for the minority become stabilized at a point where there are a sufficient number of token representatives to relieve pressure on the employer. Further gains for the minority must come at the expense of increased outside pressure on the employer and increased vigilance in locating and demonstrating discriminatory behavior.

If the minority possesses positive advantages, however, an unstable equilibrium situation is likely to prevail once the initial resistance to employment has been broken unless, of course, more powerful counterforces are brought into operation. Thus if Negroes are willing to work for lower wages than whites, and if the efficiency of operation is not impaired by vehement protests and work stoppages on the part of whites, Negroes will be hired in larger and larger numbers until they have saturated the position concerned, until they demand equal wages, or until the opposition of white workers is aroused to the point where the advantage of hiring Negroes at lower wages is effectively counterbalanced.

Perhaps a more interesting illustration of an unstable equilibrium situation produced by a positive advantage has occurred in professional sports, especially in the case of major league baseball. Professional baseball has provided Negroes with one of the relatively few avenues for escape from traditional blue-collar occupations. Why should this be the case? In part, the answer can be given in terms of negative advantages: pressure by the growing number of Negro spectators in franchise cities. But such pressure, alone, would not account for the very rapid gains since World War II.

Negro players were completely excluded from both major leagues prior to 1947. As a result, there built up a pool of first-rate Negro athletes whose abilities were superior to those of many whites of major league caliber. Negroes within such a pool actually possessed a positive advantage over a number of white players. Once the racial barrier was broken when Jackie Robinson joined the Brooklyn Dodgers, there was an almost immediate rush to tap this reservoir of skilled manpower. The result has not been a mere effort to hire a token number of Negroes to warm the benches and to ward off the charge of discrimination, but a genuine integration of Negroes into the major leagues. Many are among the highest salaried athletes in the country, having won at least their share of Most Valuable Player awards and other major honors. This is not to say that Negro players do not face some discrimination on the part of their teammates or that they are completely integrated off the job as well as on the field. But we seem to have in professional baseball an occupation which is remarkably free of racial discrimination. And the change occurred almost overnight.

In order to gain insight into the nature of occupations for which a comparable situation might hold, it will be helpful to analyze the case of professional baseball in some detail. We shall then be in a position to state some theoretical propositions which, hopefully, might apply more generally.

The Case of Professional Baseball

Perhaps the most obvious fact about the baseball profession is its highly competitive nature. Not only is there a high degree of competition among employers for the top athletes, but individual skill is of utmost importance to the productivity of the "work group." [1] Furthermore, skill and performance are easily evaluated. There is a whole series of precise quantitative measures of performance which can be standardized across teams and players—batting averages, slugging averages, home runs, runs batted in, fielding averages, earned run averages, strikeouts, won and lost records, etc. Each player can thus easily be compared with his competitors. There is no question whatsoever as to which batters or pitchers have the best records. In few occupations known to the writer is individual performance so easily evaluated by all concerned, so variable among persons, and so important to the success of the work group.

It is also the case that a high level of performance clearly works to the advantage of one's teammates, both in terms of prestige and income. Although intra-team rivalries inevitably develop, the fact that teammates share in the rewards of outstanding performance tends to channel such competition into more or less good-natured rivalry. No matter how envious they may be, players must outwardly show respect for the batting or pitching star. His performance yields him high status; the higher the productivity, the higher his prestige. This is in marked contrast to situations in which norms develop

[1] Becker theorizes that there should in general be less discrimination in competitive industries than in monopolistic ones. See G. Becker, *The Economics of Discrimination*, Chicago: University of Chicago Press, 1957, Chapter 3.

which regulate output, thereby equalizing the performances of all members and reducing the importance of individual differences in skill.[2]

Because of the highly competitive nature of the occupation and the fact that when performance slips there are numerous other candidates available to take one's place, it would be highly difficult for the work group to develop effective sanctions restricting performance. Nor does high productivity on the part of some individuals mean fewer jobs for others, as in instances where production is limited by consumer demand. Also, there seems to be little or no systematic hostility directed toward the employer as the superordinate agent forcing performance against the will of the players. The norm of high performance is simply part of the game, and it is seldom perceived as a case of employees versus employers.

Players on any one team are not in direct competition with most of their teammates. Although there may be perhaps a dozen or so pitchers in competition for starting positions, the more usual case involves competition among only two or three players who are candidates for a given position. Competition is primarily with a host of more or less anonymous players on other teams or in other leagues. A player knows that if his performance slips he will inevitably be replaced, possibly by someone on his own team but equally as likely by someone else. There is no major hierarchy of positions such that if the top man is replaced, every other person moves up one notch. In effect, this means that one gets ahead on the basis of his own performance alone. He cannot generally rely on moving permanently into a position merely if the performance of his nearest rival is lowered. Nor will it help to place barriers or restrictions in the path of his competitors, unless he can simultaneously handicap a large percentage of these persons. The power position of the individual player is obviously not such that this is possible. His job tenure thus remains inherently insecure. This would seem to be one of the major reasons why the introduction of Negro players did not create an uproar among these professional athletes. Their jobs were threatened, but they had always been threatened, if not by Negroes then by countless others of their own race.[3]

As is true for most other sports, in professional baseball top performance leads to high prestige, income, and acclaim, but it does not imply a corresponding degree of power or control over other players. A team is essentially equalitarian in nature, with persons in authority (coaches, managers) usually being drawn from the ranks of retired rather than active players.[4] There is

[2] Hughes notes a tendency for Negro workers to fail to adhere to norms requiring a restriction of output in part because of the fear that they were being put on trial by management and that greater productivity was required of them as compensation for their minority status. See E. C. Hughes, "The Knitting of Racial Groups in Industry," *American Sociological Review,* 11 (October, 1946), pp. 512–519.

[3] Of course the pool of qualified Negro players was not unusually large. In addition, the norm of good sportsmanship—in part also a resultant of the necessity for regulating competition—undoubtedly worked in favor of nondiscrimination.

[4] The position of team captain seems to be primarily honorific and is often given

thus little or no threat of the Negro teammate becoming the white player's boss, and an additional source of resistance to his employment is thereby removed.

In some occupations workers may successfully prevent the hiring of minority group members by threatening to quit work or even to work for a rival employer. The prestige of major league baseball would seem to be too high, however, for such threats to appear realistic. Nor do league rules permit a player to change jobs by joining a competing team if he happens to object to some of his teammates. His freedom of choice is thus very much limited.[5]

In baseball it is also difficult to control the minority's access to the training necessary for high-level performance. Such skill depends to a large extent on innate abilities which vary considerably from individual to individual. Nor does training in baseball require a college education, as in the case of football, or expensive equipment (as with golf), or access to restricted facilities (golf, swimming). Baseball is almost as much a lower-class as a middle-class sport. Although a long period of training or apprenticeship is required, it is difficult for whites to obtain a monopoly on training facilities, as they have in the case of a number of trades and professions. There are few, if any, trade secrets which are not well known to the public.

Another important factor has worked to the advantage of the Negro in organized baseball. In this profession performance depends only to a slight degree on interpersonal relations and manipulative skills. In contrast, a salesman's performance—also easily evaluated—depends to a large extent on his ability to persuade a prospective client. If the client is prejudiced, the Negro salesman is especially handicapped. Although a particular pitcher may be prejudiced against Negroes, there is little he can do to hamper the performance of the Negro slugger, short of an attempt at foul play. Many of baseball's top performers would never win a popularity contest, but for essentially the same reason the Negro athlete's performance is not as directly dependent upon the good-will of whites as would be the case in most managerial-type positions. We might predict, however, that Negroes will find it much more difficult working into coaching and managerial positions in baseball and will have an exceedingly difficult time obtaining positions in the "front office." [6]

Finally, it may be of some significance that although there is a considerable amount of interaction among players both on and off the field, much of this interaction does not involve the wives and other members of the opposite sex. Players must spend a good deal of the season traveling, eating together, living in hotels, and in general recreating away from their home

---

to a player (usually an infielder) who can best inspire team morale. Authority, however, rests with the coaches and manager.

[5] Such a situation might be contrasted with one involving residential segregation, where whites may readily move away from a neighborhood being invaded by Negroes.

[6] A possible exception, here, would be the star performer who is used by management primarily as a figurehead.

communities. The specter of intermarriage does not so easily arise as would be the case if, for example, a Negro male were hired as a member of an office staff.

Some Theoretical Propositions

The foregoing analysis of professional baseball suggests some general propositions which might apply to other occupations. In listing these propositions, it is necessary to keep in mind that we are assuming other factors to remain constant. In particular, we shall suppose that the prestige-level of the job and general labor market conditions do not vary. It is especially important that the general prestige-level be considered constant since, because of the positive correlation between the competitive nature of an occupation and its prestige, many of these propositions would otherwise seem obviously false.[7] Detailed analyses of other occupations which have suddenly been opened to minority group members should suggest qualifications as well as additional propositions which, hopefully, can then be subjected to empirical testing.

1. The greater the importance of high individual performance to the productivity of the work group, the lower the degree of minority discrimination by employers.
2. The greater the competition among employers for persons with high performance levels, the lower the degree of minority discrimination by employers.
3. The easier it is accurately to evaluate an individual's performance level, the lower the degree of minority discrimination by employers.
4. To the degree that high individual performance works to the advantage of other members of the work group who share rewards of high performance, the higher the positive correlation between performance and status within the group, and the lower the degree of minority discrimination by group members.

   NOTE: It is important, here, that there not be disadvantages of high performance which outweigh the advantages (e.g., where total productivity is limited by consumer demand or where there is extensive hostility toward the employer).
5. The fewer the restrictions placed on performance by members of the work group, the lower the degree of minority discrimination. (Restrictions reduce the minority member's advantage with respect to performance.)

   NOTE: Where high individual performance works to the advantage of the group, restrictions on performance are unlikely. Hence propositions 4 and 5 are closely related.
6. To the degree that a work group consists of a number of specialists interacting as a team and that there is little or no serious competition among these members, the lower the degree of minority discrimination by group members.

---

[7] It is a moot point whether or not it makes sense to conceive of prestige being controlled if competition among employers and importance of individual performance are allowed to vary. However, we shall conceive of comparisons among occupations having roughly the same general prestige.

7. To the degree that a group member's position is threatened by anonymous outsiders rather than other members of his own group, the lower the degree of minority discrimination by group members.

8. To the extent that an individual's success depends primarily on his own performance, rather than on limiting or restricting the performance of specific other individuals, the lower the degree of minority discrimination by group members.

   NOTE: Condition 8 is likely whenever there is intense competition and a large number of potential competitors available outside the work group (e.g., a tenure position at an outstanding university).

9. To the degree that high performance does not lead to power over other members of the work group, the lower the degree of minority discrimination by group members.

   NOTE: Condition 9 is especially likely when there is no hierarchy of power among group members, but where control is exercised by another category of persons altogether.

10. To the degree that group members find it difficult or disadvantageous to change jobs in order to avoid minority members, the lower the degree of minority discrimination by employers.

11. To the extent that it is difficult to prevent the minority from acquiring the necessary skills for high performance, the lower the degree of discrimination. This is especially likely when: (a) skill depends primarily on innate abilities, (b) skill can be developed without prolonged or expensive training, or (c) it is difficult to maintain a monopoly of skills through secrecy or the control of facilities.

12. To the extent that performance level is relatively independent of skill in interpersonal relations, the lower the degree of discrimination. (Lower discrimination is predicted where one works with things rather than where one works with or manipulates persons.)

   NOTE: Proposition 12 is based on the assumption that performance level can be more easily affected by prejudice when such performance depends on interpersonal skills.

13. The lower the degree of purely social interaction on the job (especially interaction involving both sexes), the lower the degree of discrimination.

   NOTE: A high degree of social interaction may not only result in the minority member feeling left out and desiring to leave the job, but it may also affect his performance.

Concluding Remarks

A major question raised by the analysis of professional baseball is that of the typicality of such an occupation. What other occupations have characteristics similar to those of baseball and how many minority group members can be absorbed into these positions? Other entertainment fields immediately come to mind. Competition is intense, box-office appeal is relatively easy to evaluate, and—at least in many types of entertainment—expensive training is less important than talent or native abilities.

Academic and scientific professions also would seem to offer the Negro similar opportunities. Performance is readily evaluated in terms of research contributions or publications and does not depend primarily on interpersonal skills. There is also extensive competition for outstanding personnel, and total productivity is not sharply limited by consumer demand. It is noteworthy that although Negroes have not as yet entered these fields in any numbers, Jews are if anything "overrepresented" in academic and scientific circles. Although there is no question that anti-semitism has proved a handicap, the emphasis within the Jewish subculture given to learning and independent thinking has provided this particular minority with a compensatory positive advantage. Unlike baseball, however, training for academic and scientific careers is both prolonged and expensive. This fact, plus the lack of an intellectual tradition among Negroes, may account for the relatively small number of Negro intellectuals. But with the growing influence of state and national governmental agencies on the hiring of intellectuals (e.g., in large state universities, through military contracts), Negroes should obtain additional leverage which, if added to a greater emphasis on intellectual pursuits, should give rise to increasing numbers of Negro academics.

A large number of white-collar occupations are not of this highly competitive nature, however. Especially on the lower rungs of the white-collar ladder, where a low-status minority might be expected to make its greatest initial gains, many positions are either relatively noncompetitive (e.g., stenographer, sales clerk) or highly dependent upon interpersonal skills (e.g., supervisor, realtor, insurance agent). Furthermore, the Negro finds himself in direct competition with another "minority group," women, entering the lower-level white-collar occupations in ever increasing numbers. Not only are women willing to work for lower salaries, but they constitute a relatively docile labor force. Although labor turnover among females may be high, in many instances such a turnover does not constitute a major problem in positions in which personnel are more or less interchangeable and where performance levels are not highly variable. The fact that heterosexual contacts are frequent in these white-collar occupations further militates against the Negro male.

The number of occupations in which Negroes can make use of important positive advantages may thus be quite limited. If this should be the case, perhaps the best strategy would be to encourage Negroes to seek out those white-collar occupations for which the demand is far greater than the supply because of the hesitancy of majority group members to fill these positions. Well-trained and capable Negroes may find it not too difficult to enter such professions as teaching or social work because of the fact that whites with whom they are competing are far less qualified than themselves. Although such a strategy might appear to involve accepting second-best opportunities, it may also help to reduce the Negro's handicaps in entering a wider range of occupations.

the sport group as a sub-culture

the man on the horse

MARVIN B. SCOTT

Character and Coolness

Worship, as Durkheim has taught us,[1] involves the collective reaffirmation of moral values. Now if we ask where the virtues of moral character—courage, integrity, dignity, and so forth—are reaffirmed in action, we arrive at a curious irony that the race track and not the church is a place of worship.

Attributes of moral character are established only in risk-taking situations: before we are ready to impute to a person the quality of strong character, he must be seen as voluntarily putting something on the line.[2]

At the race track, we find a sphere of life where men are out to establish character, demonstrate virtue, and achieve honor. These men are the jockeys, and while on stage they are putting on the line their money, their reputations, and their lives.

The jockey is one of the few survivals of the traditional concept of "the man of honor"—which interestingly has always been synonymous with "the man on the horse": *cavalier, caballero,* knight.

[1] Emile Durkheim, *The Elementary Forms of Religious Life,* New York: The Free Press of Glencoe, 1957. I am indebted to Erving Goffman for the general point suggested in this paragraph.

[2] This is the central point of Goffman's essay, "Where the Action Is," in *Interaction Ritual,* Chicago: Aldine Publishing Company, 1967.

• Chapter 5 from Scott, Marvin B., *The Racing Game,* Chicago: Aldine Publishing Company, 1968, pp. 25–46. Copyright © by Marvin B. Scott.

Feats of gallantry—or the capacity to follow the rules of decorum when it is costly to do so—are not uncommon at the track. Thus a jockey in a neck-and-neck duel down the stretch has been known to casually hand his whip to a rider who dropped his in the course of the race—and then resume a strenuous hand ride to a winning finish, demonstrating a prideful self-confidence of succeeding though under a handicap.[3]

Integrity, another attribute of moral character, is not mere honesty, but honesty when it is costly to oneself to be honest. An illustration of what I have in mind involves the case of a leading jockey whose license was revoked for betting on mounts other than his own. A wire tap revealed that the jockey had made 27 bets *against* his own mounts, but in eleven of these races he rode the winner.[4] This case dramatically illustrates one of the stable features of horse racing: when a jockey is placed in a situation where he must choose between playing for himself or playing for some other party that employs him, he will opt for the other party. That is, he chooses integrity. Thus we can expect integrity even from a dishonest jockey.

Above all, the jockey with strong character possesses the perceived virtue of coolness. A jockey who possesses this attribute is said to always "keep his cool," "to ride like an ice man," or to have ice in his veins. The ideal horse-jockey combination is a fiery animal and an icy rider.

The cool jockey can wait patiently with a horse in a pocket and get through on the inside, risking the possibility that there will be no opening. Coolness is awaiting far back in the pack, risking the possibility that his horse will not "get up" in time. Coolness is sparing the whip on a front-running horse when another animal has pressed into the lead, risking the possibility that once his horse is passed he will not get started again. All these activities are taken by observers as instances of a jockey's character. In short, moral character is coolness in risky situations.

As mentioned earlier, morning glories are horses that perform well off-stage but fail to demonstrate heart in the heat of competition. The term is also used for jockeys who display all the necessary skills in the morning workouts but lack coolness in the heat of battle. Horsemen believe—no doubt expressing a stereotypical bias—that Negroes lack the moral character necessary for being jockeys, though they are thought to possess a "sweet seat" and "strong hands." (Thus there are many Negro exercise boys, but very few Negro jockeys.) By a kind of self-fulfilling hypothesis, the belief is maintained. When a Negro exercise boy is given opportunities to "don the silks" in the afternoon, he tries so hard to make a good showing that as a result he shows a lack of coolness. Interestingly, in the nineteenth century most jockeys were Negroes, and one of the reputed all-time greats was Isaac Murphy, a Negro. Horsemen acknowledge this, but contend that the style of racing has changed in such a way that qualities are called for today that were less im-

---

[3] For an illustration see Atkinson, *op. cit.*, p. 66.
[4] Tom Ainslie, *Ainslie's Jockey Book*, New York: Trident Press, 1967.

portant in an earlier day, qualities that are captured by the term "coolness."

After a jockey has suffered a serious fall, many players feel they should avoid betting on his later mounts. They feel that he has lost his moral character. Horsemen themselves share this belief and are reluctant to give mounts in important races to jockeys who are making a comeback. Naturally, jockeys fear the physical consequences of a serious spill. But what is not so obvious is that they fear that a spill will cause them to lose their character; similarly, they fear that others will perceive them as losing their character.

What the above discussion has implied and what will now be made explicit is that traits of moral character are generated by social organization.

To begin with a jockey's success depends upon his getting mounts on winning horses. The greenest boy can outride the greatest reinsman—if the former has a superior horse. How, then, does a jockey get the best horses? Simply by having the widest selection of mounts from which to choose. What a jockey wants is a choice between several mounts in a race; he wants to be in demand. And to be in demand he must somehow mobilize his activities so as to *appear* to possess those virtues of character that horsemen deem important for jockeys—integrity, gameness, coolness. In other words, a jockey must commit himself to a line of risk-taking because not to do so would constitute an even greater loss to self.[5]

Becoming a Jockey

To start his career as a jockey, a young man need only convince an employer to take him on. A boy need not ever have been on a horse so long as he meets the physical requirements of size and the psychological requirement of desire.[6]

Once employed he starts as a stable boy—carrying water, mucking stalls, polishing tack, walking hots (horses that are cooled out after working or racing). He also rides about with the horse when shipped and sleeps on straw. Trainers view these demeaning activities as a kind of initiation period. As one put it: "If a boy is willing to travel 300 miles in the back of a van sleeping on piss-soaked straw, or if he wades through a stall full of shit at 5:30 every morning for no pay, you know he wants to be a jock." These activities are known as "learning horse."

The stable boy himself does not think of these activities as particularly

---

[5] Commitment, then, involves some kind of side bet, such as one's reputation. See Howard S. Becker, "Notes on the Concept of Commitment," *American Journal of Sociology*, 66 (July 1960), pp. 32–40.

[6] There is no lower age limit to begin one's career, though most boys are "brought up" (that is, taken on as an apprentice) in their teens. Some boys seek employment after they have passed the legal age when they can quit school. As most of the boy's chores take place from 5 to 9 A.M. and again in the early evening, he may continue with his formal schooling without gross interference with his racing career.

demeaning, so long as it is clear that they are part of the first step of his career. Some fail to get beyond the stage of stable boy and are permanently placed here; others get here as a result of downward mobility (for example, exercise boys who have gone bad). For the young man performing demeaning activities, one of the protective factors to self is age: culturally, we expect boys to engage in dirty work. To distinguish himself from the "failures," the upwardly mobile stable boy will walk about with riding boots (though he is not yet permitted to ride), and during breaks in the routine he will prominently be squeezing rubber balls (as an aid to strengthen his hands for his anticipated future role).

Eventually, the boy is tried on a horse in a workout. If the horse responds to his urging and if the boy follows instructions, he is ready for official apprenticeship. He is placed under contract and apprenticed to the employer for three to five years. The contract, formulated by the Jockey Club, is standard throughout the country. In the contract, the boy pledges to keep the employer's secrets and to obey orders given by his representatives (the trainer). The employer in turn provides room and board, a small salary, and traveling expenses.

Before the boy gets a mount in a race, he will spend months exercising horses. His designation is shifted from stable boy to exercise boy, but he must continue to muck stalls, polish tack, etc. The role of exercise boy is the most prestigious role below the rank of jockey, and is thus a status alternative that cushions the loss of face suffered by a jockey who failed to make the grade.

Horsemen say that the most important reason for exercise boys failing to become jockeys, or for jockeys dropping back to become exercise boys is their inability to make the weight. The interesting questions is why do they fail to make the weight?

To begin with, size (within limits) is no barrier to becoming a jockey; for though it is atypical, jockeys—including some of the leading ones—are as tall as five feet, eleven inches. Although the growing boy cannot control his height, he can control weight, given the desire that he has amply demonstrated in going through the initiation period. My observations and interviews have led me to hypothesize that a boy does not first pick up weight and then have his career blocked. Rather, career opportunities first close up and then he gains weight—though lay beliefs hold the reverse to be the case.[7] The stable boy who finds himself exercising horses for a year or so without getting a mount can see the writing on the wall; the next step in the career ladder is not being opened for him; he sees himself as lacking the skill or character necessary for the competitive scene. By picking up weight, he has a face-saving device for not going on.

[7] It should be emphasized that I am here presenting a tentative hypothesis. Hard data to support the hypothesis is difficult to come by. It would be necessary to obtain weights of the boys and establish correlations (in the statistical sense) between shifts in weight and career events.

Another common instance of sudden weight increase is that of the jockey recently graduated from the apprentice ranks. Until one year from the day he has his first mount or upon winning forty races, whichever is the longer, the apprentice jockey is given what is called a weight allowance or "bug." A five-pound allowance means that any horse ridden by an apprentice will carry five pounds less than that stipulated in the race conditions. As we shall see later, horsemen are hyperconscious of weight and believe that five pounds equal one length—the difference between victory and defeat in most races. Thus a "bug" is likely to get many offers to ride, and having several mounts to choose from in a race will increase his probability of getting hot horses. Frequently the leading jockey at any given meet is a bug, not because of his skill but because of the advantages that come with his weight allowance. But when a jockey loses his bug, suddenly he finds few if any mounts forthcoming. Overnight—at the loss of a bug—the jockey who was yesterday's hottest rider is today's inexperienced kid. At this point, the young jockey begins to pick up weight—which generally is attributed to his being a growing boy.

The acceptable weight for an exercise boy makes face-saving easy for an erstwhile jockey. Although the virtual upper limit for a jockey is 117 pounds, exercise boys can be as heavy as 130. Thus, if a boy weighs 120, he might be continually asked why he doesn't lose weight and get mounts. But if he is over 120, he is considered beyond the point of losing weight; yet he is secure in his position as exercise boy.

If a jockey weighs more than the horse is to carry according to the conditions of the race, the difference is known as "overweight." Bettors believe that "overweight" has a decided effect on the performance of a horse, and information about overweight is taken into account before a final selection is made. Before the first post at all tracks, the overweights of all horses are announced over the public address system. This information is repeated before every race and is also shown in colored-chalk notations on boards located at various places around the track. Some handicapping systems sold to the betting public have as one of the rules: eliminate all horses carrying overweight. Many horsemen share these beliefs about the adverse effects of overweight, and a trainer on some occasions may in fact seek an overweight jockey when he wants his horse to lose.

The overweight limit is five pounds. A pound or two makes a big difference in the mounts a boy can accept. If a horse is scheduled to carry 110 pounds and the jockey scheduled to ride the mount "weighs in" at 116 (his weight and saddle and other gear are included in the weighing), he will be disqualified from riding the horse. A jockey's weight is classified in the following way: a lightweight jockey weighs less than 110 pounds; a middleweight is 110 to 113; and a heavyweight weighs above 113. To lose that extra pound or so before a race, some jockeys go through the process of "wasting," which involves daily sessions in a steam cabinet or sweating between rubber sheets.

Benchmarks in a Rider's Career

A jockey who wins his first race, like a horse, is said to have broken his maiden. The news of a first win is broadcast by the public address announcer, and the crowd cheers the young man; a broken maiden is also a significant item in newspaper sports pages. In the jockey's room, the ritual is to give the boy a cold shower—with his winning silks on.

The second major event in a jockey's career is winning the first handicap or stakes race. A jockey receives 10 percent of the purse for a winning ride. In the heavy-purse stakes and handicap races, of say $100,000, the jockey can earn about $10,000 for a minute's work. But more than money is involved. A race for the big chips poses a real test of moral character. Here coolness is considered to be more crucial than in other races. The winning of the first handicap race is a *rite de passage* where the self-image of one who possesses moral character is dramatically confirmed.

The third important event in the jockey's career is his first bad fall. The significance of this event, as already suggested, is not whether the jockey will be injured badly enough to impede his riding. More important is whether he can—psychologically—ride at all. After a bad spill, some jockeys don't "come back"; they don't feel at home any more on a horse. But to come back after a bad fall and continue to ride with the same success as before fully authenticates one as a jockey in the eyes of horsemen; he has demonstrated the moral attribute of gameness.

In interviewing jockeys (who are difficult to interview in any case, as they are instructed to maintain a distance from strangers who might be prospective conmen or fixers), the most difficult subject to get them to talk about is falls. "We never talk about those things," one rider told me. "It happens, it happens. There's nothing to talk about."

Another jockey who after a fall failed to make a comeback said: "For a while you only get pigs to ride. The trainers with hot horses ain't out to give you a break. Only the gyps like [he mentioned a certain hand-to-mouth trainer] will put you on their plugs. I'm out of the business now. Who wants to get killed riding plugs?"

INCOME AND EXPENSES

Whether they ride plugs or hot mounts, jockey's riding fees are the same. The usual guidelines, as established by the racing associations, are $20 for an unplaced horse, $25 for third, $35 for second, and $50 for first. By tradition, the winning jockey also receives 10 percent of the purse.

Jockeys have many expenses. Except for the silks, they own everything that goes on the horse. A jockey has about $1,000 invested in his "stage clothes": boots, pants, saddles, and other tack.

A much more expensive overhead is the jockey's agent, who receives 20 percent of the earnings—on winning or losing mounts. Jockeys typically do not resent such fees; most believe that their success or failure on the turf depends as much on the agent as anything else. Only occasionally does a jockey refer to his agent as "my pimp." The agent's job is to solicit mounts for the rider. If the boy is hot, the agent has no problem and may insist that a trainer wanting the jockey's services pay a flat fee, usually 10 percent of the purse, win or lose. Usually handling only one jockey, the agent closely identifies with his boy. When discussing the successes or failures of his boy, an agent often refers to him as "I" [8]—"I'm getting nothing to ride these days but cripples," "I was just nosed out on three mounts yesterday," etc.

One aspect of the agent's role is to cool out the losing jockey. When a jockey loses on a favorite, the agent will say that the horse shouldn't have been a favorite; for it wasn't the best horse in the race. If the jockey falls into a slump, the agent will point out the names of all the jockeys who are in a slump, recall the time that some leading jockey had 52 consecutive losers, and expound on a philosophy that deals with the swinging pendulum of luck.

Typically, jockeys don't enter into contracts with agents. The arrangement is based on common understandings. Some jockeys change agents frequently, especially when in a slump, or when they believe that the agent isn't getting enough good mounts. Some agents will go to great lengths to get mounts for their boys, at times going so far as to exercise horses free to establish a relation of indebtedness with trainers. The success of an agent can easily be determined by his demeanor. The agent with the hot boy is quiet, tight-lipped, and noncommittal. The struggling agent is a friendly hail-fellow well met, ready to slap a trainer on the back and offer him a favor. Unless one is aware of the structural elements that determine the agents' "personalities," one might conclude—in observing the same agents over a period of years—that they are a manic-depressive breed.

The jockey's other expense is the valet. The valet is employed by the track, but receives about $5 a mount and $10 a winner from the jockey. At getaway day (that is, the last day of a meet), the jockey customarily gives his valet a bonus of $100 or more, depending on his success. The valets are frequently former jockeys who have grown too big, too old, or too inept to continue as riders. The valets are treated with a good deal of charity; many jockeys feel that "there but for the grace of God. . . ."

About twenty minutes before post time, the jockeys are weighed for the race in the scale room, and the clerk checks the reading against the assigned weight. If the jockey is light, the clerk will tell the valet, "Give him a shade," and if the boy is heavy, the clerk may suggest, "Try a lighter saddle pad." [9]

After being fitted out at the proper weight, the jockey hands his equipment to a valet who goes to the paddock where he assists the trainer in saddling the horse. Later, when the jockey has weighed in after the race, the

[8] Ainslie, *op. cit.*, p. 6.
[9] Atkinson, *op. cit.*, p. 171.

valet takes his equipment and returns it to the jockey's quarters. In his free time, the valet looks after the tack, arranges clothes, helps the jockey dress, etc.

Types of Jockeys

Horsemen recognize three categories of jockeys: "honest boys," "money jocks," and "businessmen."

To get the reputation of an honest boy (most jockeys are so categorized) a jockey must satisfy two conditions: he must accept all mounts offered him, and he must ride in strict accord to instructions.

If a jockey's services are called upon, he must not refuse, lest his reputation as "honest" be damaged. The only legitimate reason for not accepting a mount is to have already accepted a bid to ride some other trainer's horse. Given this cultural expectation, we might expect that all trainers would freely attempt to gain the services of the hottest jockeys, ensuring the best possible chance of their horses finishing in the money. Moreover, we might expect that given a choice between mounts, the jockeys will always choose the hot horse. In actually, trainers will often call upon second-rate jockeys to ride their horses; and jockeys will often choose to ride a second-rate horse. These anomalous choices deserve some explanation.

When a trainer has a horse whose expected performance for a particular event is highly uncertain, often he will prefer to call upon the services of a lesser known jockey. Should he choose a superior jockey and should the horse perform very poorly, then the superior jockey will—when given a choice in the future—choose to ride for another trainer. The trainer's disinclination to ask a hot jockey to ride an uncertain animal has the consequence of resolving the jockey's dilemma: to be "honest" he must accept all mounts—usually on a first-come, first-served basis—but to maintain a good winning record he needs a choice from among *hot* mounts. In sum, trainers in the pursuit of their own self-interest help jockeys maintain their reputation as being both "honest" and "hot."

From time to time, however, a trainer will call upon the services of a hot boy even when he knows for certain that his animal will do little running on a particular day. In the erratic horse's next race, where the winning effort is planned, the trainer may shift to a no-name jockey. This shifting from a hot jockey to a no-name boy is a maneuver to get better odds. The playing public reasons this way: "If hot jock Jones can't bring the animal home, the horse is a nothing." When the horse wins next time at a big price with the no-name jock, the public attributes the victory to some factor of racing luck and not to the manipulations of the man behind the horse. Naturally, the trainer can't pull this maneuver too often, for fear of alienating a good jockey. Moreover, each time the trainer employs this maneuver, he is tacitly indebted to "pay off" the jockey by furnishing him with a hot mount in the future.

As I already suggested, the hot jock will sometimes choose to ride what he takes to be an inferior mount. Such decisions typically involve horses from the leading money-winning stables. The jockey "trades" a bad mount today for a good mount tomorrow. That is, the winning stable, when it has a hot horse, will go back with the boy who is willing to ride those horses whose performance is uncertain.

In general, a type of equilibrium is established whereby the leading trainers get the leading jocks to ride for them, and the leading jocks get the best mounts. But, as I indicated, this state of affairs is the result of many sorts of exchanges and tacit negotiations.

The second criterion of a jock's reputation as "honest"—strictly following instructions of the trainer—can be explained more briefly. Trainers, for reasons that will be made clear later, often have something to gain when their horses lose on a particular occasion. One way of making a horse lose or appear to be off form is to instruct the jockey to run the animal in a manner contrary to the horse's best efforts. If a horse runs best in front, the trainer who wants to lose will instruct the jockey to come from behind; if the horse runs best close to the rail, the trainer will instruct the jockey to keep the horse wide; if the horse responds only to energetic whipping, the trainer will instruct the jockey not to use the whip. The jockey may well realize that the instructions are contrary to the horse's best efforts; he might realize that by *not* following instructions he can win an otherwise losing race. However, he will *not* race in accord with his own best judgment, because what he has at stake is his reputation as an "honest boy."

The second type of jockey—the "money jock"—is not concerned with the number of mounts he receives but with getting the best mounts in the best races. If he had his way, the money jock would accept only mounts in the feature Saturday race. In receiving mounts; his agent is often instructed to demand a flat fee for his services. For instance, the stable demanding the services of the money jock must meet a set fee of, say, $250 (10 percent of the winning share in most ordinary races) on a win-or-lose basis. This demand usually means that the jock will get hot mounts, for owners are slow to put up a win-or-lose fee unless they have a hot horse and expect to win. By getting hot horses, the money jock will be on a mount where he can display his skills and character to best advantage. These are some of the backstage manipulations that make his onstage performance appear so stunning.

Money jocks are preferred by moneyed stables. The leading handicap and stakes horses are to be found in the barns of those owners who regard horse racing literally as a game. Being able to foot the bills, their concern is with the honor that goes with owning (and frequently breeding) the *winner*. Second- or third-place money is seldom a target for these owners.

The characteristic of the money jock is his in-and-out performance. When he is "in," it is frequently because he has—as a consequence of his coolness—staged a ride that saved the horse perhaps as much as five lengths. Many horsemen say that a money jock can give a horse a five-length advantage. They believe the money jock can remain cool in a pocket and plunge through on the inside rail when and if the opportunity comes, rather than taking a horse on the outside where the certainty of racing room may cost a horse five lengths. As one length equals five pounds (by rule of thumb calculation accepted by racing secretaries), the right kind of ride can—in lay theory at least—make up for a deficit of 25 pounds spotted to the opposition. In short, the moneyed stables depend on the money jocks to bring home *first* money.

The third type of jockey—the "businessman"—is a boy who "gets what he can, any way he can," as one observer put it. This is the lay image most spectators have of all jockeys. Even Devereux, in his study of gambling, suggests that because the jockey's racing days are numbered, he will be inclined to conspire with gamblers in their betting coups. By entering into the plans of gamblers by, let us say, pulling a horse on orders (presumably to protect the bookies against a large loss), the jockey can solidify his relations with the gamblers who may be of help to him after retirement.[10]

Devereux's remarks represent an interesting theory of an activity that occurred in a real *past* or a *fictionalized* present. To begin with, jockeys— unlike most other athletes—are neither limited as to age nor do they believe they are. Unlike boxers, baseball players, and football pros who are called old men at 35 and are retired by 40, jockeys have been active and in fact won some of the richest handicap races while in their late fifties; two of the most prominent boys (jockeys are boys at any age) were Pat Remmilard and Johnny Longden, both of whom were racing until their sixtieth years. Asked when jockeys should retire, they respond not by mentioning an age, but say, "When you can't get any more mounts." Second, retirement funds and pension plans (for jockeys disabled in a spill) cushion the pressure of "getting it" while you can. Finally, and most important, the surveillance system (discussed later) of the various racing associations and the severity of sanctions (being ruled off the turf for misconduct) virtually have done away with the "businessman" who has conspired with gamblers to fix a race.

As the term is used today, "businessman" refers to the type of jockey whose overwhelming motivation is the profit motive. This motive is expressed in the jock's assertion, heard in the business world but seldom among the other jocks, "I'm not in business for my health." Further, businessmen believe that, at least for them, the way to make money is by betting on their mounts. So far as possible, businessmen will seek mounts on horses they think are ready to win at a good price.

Among those jockeys who have no agents, by far the largest group are the businessmen. Preferring to hustle their own mounts, they seek out the small-time owner-trainer who stables "platers" (cheap claiming horses). This type of trainer can't pay the win-or-lose fee demanded by the money jocks, nor does he expect to get the hot jocks who are cultivating greener pastures. A more likely choice of rider is the businessman. Moreover, since the owner-

[10] Devereux, *op. cit.*, p. 424.

trainer has to foot all the bills, he finds in the businessman an opportunity to cut corners. Frequently the businessman will exercise horses free or simply wait for payment until the stable is having some success. In exchange, the owner-trainer takes the jockey into his confidence and strategies are worked out together. Although not under contract to the owner-trainer, the jock often will travel the various circuits with him.

The owner-trainer with whom the businessman associates is invariably one who doesn't bet and often has the reputation of being poor but honest. This sets the stage for a mutually advantageous arrangement. A betting trainer would take great pains to conceal his intentions and limit the information flow; for a leak of intentions would affect the odds on the horse, and he wishes to get the most for his betting investment. As the nonbetting trainer has little to lose by revealing his intentions to a jockey (even the nonbetting trainer has *something* to lose by revealing information about his horse, especially in claiming races, as we shall later see), he can get the services of a skillful jockey for little cost: namely, information concerning his intentions.

The businessman is quick to see the advantage in hooking up with the honest trainer. A brief explanation of the problems of putting over a coup will show why this is the case. When betting trainers manipulate horses for the purpose of winning bets, the investigative activities of the racing association quickly get wind of this and place pressure on the stable (just what pressures can be applied will be discussed later). To avoid such investigations, betting stables today engage in *partial* concealment of a horse's true form. A partial concealment, however, implies a partial disclosure of form, which legitimates a horse's winning (that is, nothing is incongruous about a horse winning if it has displayed a recent fair effort). On the other hand, the fact that form has been partly concealed helps assure a fair price (conceived typically at odds of about 4 to 1). Betting stables do not run "in-and-outers" or "sharp wakeups" that pay "boxcar mutuels" (winners with very big payoffs). Thus the gambling stables work to maintain the impression of simon-pure honesty. The known nonbetting, honest trainer, however, can run hot-and-cold horses and win at boxcar mutuels with impunity; officials will take for granted that the erratic performance of his horses is due to low-grade stock, thought to be naturally unpredictable. Also as long as the boxcar mutuels are coming from the horses of honest stables, in-and-out performances are tolerated—indeed, welcome—for they give variety in the payoffs. To the businessman jockey, one or two bets on one or two 40-to-1 shots during a 55-day racing meet are big dividends. Thus the betting jockey prefers to stick with the honest trainer. Indirectly, then, in the manner I have suggested, honesty is in the service of "vice."

When two or three businessmen are in the same race, the scene is set for possible chicanery. One may find here the closest thing to a fixed race, what is called a "jockeys' race." Here two or three boys, surveying the situation in the jocks' room before going to the paddock, will come to an understanding through a kind of tacit bargaining. The conversation among businessmen Tom, Dick, and Harry might run something like this:

Tom: How do you like your mounts today, fellers?

Dick: Well, I have a ready horse, but I'm not going to bet a dime. There's nothing that will keep up with the favorite.

Harry: My horse is pretty fair, too, but no use killing him for show dough. He'll be saved for next week. Think I'll bet him then.

Tom: You know, guys, my horse can turn it on in the stretch. If only something would go with the favorite for a mile and knock the wind out of him! You know, Dick, if your horse went with the favorite for half a mile and then you, Harry, picked him up at the far turn, the favorite would be a dead duck. And if I can get home with Slow Bones, I'll be glad to "save" with you boys.

That is all that need be said. The favorite is knocked out of competition by the top of the stretch, and Tom waltzes home on Slow Bones at 20 to 1. Next time, perhaps it will be Harry's turn to come home first.

A jockeys' race—when it occurs at all—takes place in the last race. One reason for this is that the cheapest race of the day is typically the last race, and here we would be more likely to find two or three businessmen in the same race. Second, the last race is almost always a distance race, at least $1\frac{1}{16}$ miles. The longer distance is necessary for working out a strategy (however vaguely suggested). In a sprint race most of the horses are rushing from start to finish, and strategies to control the pace of the race are not easy to put into operation (unless the planning is highly deliberate and carefully worked out). The most important feature of the last race is that it is the *last* race. At this time the stewards tend to relax their usual vigilance, and the crowd is dispersing and is less likely to shout disapproval at what appears to be a jockeys' race. In fact, many fans assume that the last race will be a jockeys' race and will be stabbing for a long shot to get even on the assumption that a long shot has a better chance in the last race than it would otherwise. And when a long shot does suddenly pop home a winner the crowd—even when they haven't bet on the particular horse—voices a kind of approval. On homeward-bound buses and trains, the conversation will center on how the player bet or almost bet the winning long shot in the last race. On the other hand, a favored horse winning the last race is unpopular; the mass of players are betting long shots to get even. A subtle pressure is exerted on the stewards not to inquire too closely into the last race, as one of their jobs is to keep the public content. A jockeys' race sometimes gives the appearance of a well-rehearsed performance, and yet there is nothing specific to put one's finger on. Nothing is, strictly speaking, illegal.

Another feature of the last race is that the riders, often having only one mount that day, have been sitting in the jockeys' room together for six hours, and as time has passed, eventually have turned their conversation to the race they will run. According to the rules of racing, the jockey—even if he has only one mount—must report to the jockeys' room one hour before the first race, and remain there until riding his last mount of the day. The sheer amount of time jockeys spend together is conducive to "discussing things."

Finally, the businessman is generally better informed than any other type of jockey about the condition of the animal he is to ride and the intentions of the stable. Moreover, as the businessman often has the trainer in his debt, he can get away with not running the race exactly to orders, which in any case will be something like: "You know what the horse can do. Just do your best."

The businessman jockey doesn't see anything wrong with the staging of a race and would probably be mildly shocked if accused of dishonest dealings. The cooperative arrangement is viewed as just another version of the traditional practice of "saving." During a race, a rider may try to make a bargain to share the purse. For instance, two horses may enter the stretch head and head, and one jock will call out: "How about saving?" The other might say: "You're on."

Although the practice of saving is frowned upon officially in most races, it is a mandatory practice among jockeys who ride as an entry in a stakes or handicap race. For example, a stable might enter two (or more) horses in a race, and the jockeys arrange a 60–40 split if one should win.

The bargaining arrangement that occurs among businessmen is to them but a form of the legitimate practice of saving. They legitimate the arrangements they make by referring to it as saving, just as trusted bank employees justify their embezzlement by referring to it as "borrowing." [11]

In sum, an analysis of the deviant practice of the jockeys' race involves the conditions typically thought to be relevant in the analysis of most kinds of deviance.[12] First the *conduciveness* and *opportunity* associated with knowing something about the trainer's intentions and being thrown into interaction together permitting the teaming up in a deviant act; the *strain* placed on the businessman who wins only a few races and has relatively few mounts and must make these count; the *legitimation* of the course of action through a "neutralization technique" [13] of saving; and finally, a *laxity of social control*—characteristic of the last race milieu—on the part of the racing officials.[14]

[11] Donald Cressey, *Other Peoples' Money*, New York: The Free Press of Glencoe, 1953.

[12] Albert K. Cohen, "The Sociology of the Deviant Act," *American Sociological Review*, 30 (February 1965), pp. 9–14.

[13] Gresham M. Sykes and David Matza, "Techniques of Neutralization," *American Sociological Review*, 22 (December 1957), pp. 667–669.

[14] Taken together, these components of a deviant act constitute what Smelser, *op. cit.*, calls a value-added process, which he uses in his explanatory model of all kinds of collective behavior.

Communication Strategies

During a race, the jockeys must keep in mind three separate audiences —the fans, the horsemen and the officials—each of which is demanding a certain kind of performance. The crowd wants an energetic effort; the officials, an honest, free-from-fouling ride; the trainer, a ride to orders. These different audiences frequently make demands at cross purposes. The trainer may instruct the jockey not to press the horse, and this may appear to the crowd as the absence of an energetic ride; and if the horse is heavily bet on, the jockey might be booed. On the other hand, the trainer may give the jockey instructions to get out in front at once, which often involves cutting across the field rapidly and may lead to officials' sanctioning for rough-riding.

Whatever the orders, the jockey must at least *appear* to be riding energetically and cleanly. To bring off these appearances the jockey has developed certain communication strategies—*dramatic accentuation* and *concealment* or a combination of both. (Thus the jockey engages in impression management even in situations of total involvement.)

Dramatic accentuation refers to the exaggeration of an aspect of one's performance. Horsemen sometimes speak of this strategy as riding in the style of Don Meade. In 1930, Don Meade was ruled off the turf for betting on horses other than his own. After several years of applying to be reinstated, he was finally given a license to ride on the strength of a promise that "if they just give me one more chance, they'll see a jockey ride as none had ever ridden in history." To keep his promise he dramatically accentuated an always-trying riding style. "Stigmatized as a jockey who would throw a race, he always pushed his mounts to their utmost, and made a display of this that became part of his characteristic riding style—of shoving a horse. . . ." [15] Today jockeys who think they are under suspicion suddenly adopt the Meade style. To some degree, all jockeys adopt this style to appear honest and energetic. This style, emphasizing the energetic use of hands and legs, does not improve the horse's performance. It is all part of impression management.

Oddly enough, this strategy not only takes in the audience of fans, but also the other jockeys. Some jockeys become specialists in appearing to be working so hard on a horse that the other jockeys in a race may assume that the horse being worked on is tiring fast. The jockey on a front-running mount may begin to wave his elbows furiously (known as "pumping"), and the other jockeys, believing that the horse will soon slow up, will wait before making a move. Suddenly, just as the horse appears to be finished and the other horses make their move, the front horse jumps out to a bigger lead and now is really being pressed by its jockey for the first time. Even when the

[15] Charles B. Parmer, *For Gold and Glory*, New York: Carrick and Evans, 1939, p. 212.

other jockeys suspect that pumping may be a deception, they can never be sure. Hence, at the very least, the strategy undercuts certainty. Although pumping can be used as a strategy to win a race, it is equally serviceable for the jock who has instructions to lose a race. He can save a horse for another race and at the same time give the appearance to the fans and officials of pressing hard.

The example of pumping illustrates that techniques of dramatic accentuation might also serve as a strategy of concealment—one of the strategies that a jockey must learn. Concealment strategies are particularly important in handicap races and trainers will caution riders *not to win by too much*; for an easy win will lead the track handicapper to add extra poundage on the horse in his next outing. If the jockey fails to conceal the true form of a handicap horse, the trainer will mete out sanctions, as Jockey Eddie Arcaro recalls:

> I won the Metropolitan with Third Degree by five lengths. That was a mile race. Handicapper John B. Campbell was so impressed by this performance that he tacked on more weight for Third Degree's Suburban Handicap engagement. That added weight proved to be the difference between victory and defeat. John Gaver [the trainer] gave me hell for that.[16]

A Day in the Life of a Jockey

Unless the jockey exercises horses in the morning or is called upon to have a dry run with a horse in preparation for some big engagement, his working day begins at noon. At that time, he checks into the jockeys' quarters located near the paddock (where the horses will be saddled before each race). By the time the jock arrives, the valets will already have been at work for a few hours, polishing boots and saddles and checking the colors to be worn by the riders. The silks (the shirts that bear the colors of the owner) are brought in from the "color room" and hung on racks in the order of each race and each starting position. When the jocks arrives, he heads straight for the steam room or the whirlpool bath, and then sits down in the locker room to leaf through the *Racing Form* or josh with the valets.

By 12:30, the patrol judge or one of the stewards announces he is going to screen films of the previous day's races. This is known as the jockeys' matinee. Attendance is optional, except for those jockeys who are specifically ordered to attend. From time to time, the judge will stop the film to point out incidents of misconduct, or—in the case of apprentice jocks—he may point out mistakes and offer advice.

Before each race, the jockey's weight is checked in the weighing room. He weighs in wearing his colors, carrying his equipment—and nothing else.

---

[16] Eddie Arcaro, *I Ride to Win*, New York: Greenberg, 1951, p. 39. The strategy of winning by the shortest possible margin is the key deceptive move of the pool room hustler. See Ned Polsky, "The Hustler," in *Hustlers, Beats, and Others*, Chicago: Aldine Publishing Company, 1967.

For example, if he has a cigarette in his mouth, he won't be weighed.

Afterwards, he goes to the paddock where the trainer and sometimes the owner will be waiting in a stall with the same number as the post position of the horse. The horse has already been saddled and either is standing in the stall or is being paraded around the paddock, led by the groom or hot-walker. Now the trainer instructs the jockey: "This horse has been primed for this race; keep him close to the pace and when the early runners fade go to the whip—and come home early."

Parading to the starting gate, the jock looks over at the tote board and see his horse is 3 to 1. He feels a little more confident knowing that so many fans have thought highly of his chances. Also, with all that money riding on him, he knows he must look good. Now he's at the starting gate, and finally, in his stall. All the mounts are in. Some of the boys are chanting: "No chance yet, sir; no chance; no chance, sir." Suddenly all is quiet and the starter presses the button releasing the gate.

It is a close race, but the jock's mount lasts to win. Returning to the winner's circle, he salutes the placing judges with his whip; failing to do so results in a fine. In the winner's circle, he is photographed along with the trainer, the owner and his wife, and friends of the family. Returning to the jockeys' quarters, he can relax if he doesn't ride in the next race. In the jockeys' quarters, he sees some of the other jocks relaxing, watching television, playing cards, pool, or ping-pong. Others are in the heat box or in a bunk bed swathed in rubber sheets.

After his last mount of the day, the jock can leave the jockeys' quarters. He then goes to the club house or turf club where his agent has been playing the horses and talking to the trainers. He consults with the agent as to his future mounts. He stays to watch a race or two, very often as a guest in the private box of one of the owners or trainers. Once the jockey leaves the park, his racing day is over. But the working day is far from over for the trainers and the other men behind the horse.

the occupational culture of the boxer

S. KIRSON WEINBERG AND HENRY AROND

Professional boxers are recruited from among the youth of the lower socio-economic levels. Their changing ethnic composition reflects the ethnic shifts

• From the *American Journal of Sociology*, 57 (1952), 460–469. Copyright © 1952 by the University of Chicago Press.

in the urban lower socioeconomic levels. Fighting is an important road to increased social status, and successful boxers are role-models of the youth. Trainers, managers, and promoters view boxing in different ways from the boxers and frequently affect boxers' careers.

Herein is described the culture of the professional boxer as discovered by personal experience, by reading of firsthand literature, and by interview with sixty-eight boxers and former boxers, seven trainers, and five managers.[1] The aspects covered are recruitment, practices and beliefs, and the social structure of the boxing world.

Recruitment

Professional boxers are adolescents and young men. Nearly all are of low socioeconomic background. Only two of our fighters might possibly have been of middle-class family. Most are immigrants to the city and are children of such. Their residences at the time of becoming boxers are distributed like the commoner forms of social disorganization, being almost all near the center of the city. Nearly all Chicago boxers lived on the Near South and Near West sides. There is an ethnic succession of boxers which corresponds to that of the ethnic groups in these areas. First Irish, then Jewish, then Italian, were most numerous among prominent boxers; now, Negroes (Table 1).

The traditions of an ethnic group, as well as its temporary location at the bottom of the scale, may affect the proportion of its boys who become boxers. Many Irish, but few Scandinavians, have become boxers in this country; many Filipinos, but very few Japanese and Chinese.

The juvenile and adolescent culture of the lower socioeconomic levels provides a base for the boxing culture. Individual and gang fights are encouraged. The best fighter is often the most admired, as well as the most feared, member of a gang. A boy who lacks status tries to get it and to restore his self-esteem by fighting.[2] Successful amateur and professional boxers furnish highly visible role-models to the boys of the slum; this is especially so among urban Negroes at present. Since he has otherwise little hope of any but unskilled, disagreeable work, the boxing way to money and prestige may

---

[1] One of us (Arond) has been a boxer, trainer, and manager. We first determined some common values, beliefs, and practices by a few unstructured interviews. We used the material thus gained to plan guided interviews which would help us sift out what is ethnic from what belongs properly to boxing culture. Mr. Leland White helped in the interviewing.

[2] Some juveniles who fought continually to retrieve their self-esteem and also in sheer self-defense later became boxers. One adolescent who was half-Negro and half-Indian was induced to become a boxer by a trainer who saw him beat two white opponents in a street fight. Another boxer admitted that he fought continually because other boys called him a "sissy." A third boxer fought continually because he was small and other boys picked on him. This compensatory drive among boxers is not unusual.

table 1

RANK ORDER OF NUMBER OF PROMINENT
BOXERS OF VARIOUS ETHNIC GROUPS
FOR CERTAIN YEARS [a]

| | RANK | | |
YEAR	1	2	3
1909	Irish	German	English
1916	Irish	German	Italian
1928	Jewish	Italian	Irish
1936	Italian	Irish	Jewish
1948	Negro	Italian	Mexican

[a] Data tabulated from *World's Annual Sporting Record* (1910 and 1917); *Everlast Boxing Record* (1929); *Boxing News Record* (1938); and *Ring* (1948 and 1949). The numbers in the succeeding years are: 103, 118, 300, 201, and 149. There may be biases in the listings, but the predominance of two or three ethnic groups is marked in all the years. The Irish were very much above others in 1909 and 1916 (about 40 per cent of all boxers listed); in 1948 nearly half of all boxers listed were Negro. The Jews and Italians did not have so marked a predominance.

appear very attractive. As an old-time manager put it, "Where else can a poor kid get a stake as fast as he can in boxing?"

As the ability to fight is a matter of status among one's peers, is learned in play, and is the accepted means of expressing hostility and settling disputes, boys learn to fight early.

One fighter thought of becoming a boxer at the age of ten, because he could not participate in team games as a child; his mother insisted that he had a "bad heart." He stated: "I tried to fight as soon as I got old enough, to be the roughest, toughest kid on the block." He fought so frequently and was arrested so often for fighting that one policeman told him that he might as well get paid for it. At the age of fourteen he participated in fights in vacant lots in the neighborhood. Because of his prowess as a fighter, the other boys in the neighborhood began to respect him more, and he began to associate status with fighting. When he was about seventeen, an amateur fighter told him about a gymnasium where he could learn to become a "ring fighter" instead of a "street fighter." He claimed: "I love fighting. I would rather fight than eat."

Most boxers seem to have been influenced to become "ring fighters" by a boxer in the neighborhood or by a member of the family.[3] One middle-

[3] For the last twenty-five years of boxers, we found the following brother combinations among boxers: 3 sets of five brothers, 5 sets of four brothers, 24 sets of three brothers, and 41 sets of two brothers. We also found sets of father-son combinations. This number, very likely, is less than the actual figures, because some brothers fight as amateurs only and not as professional, and thus their records cannot be traced.

weight champion claimed that he "took after" his brother, followed him to
the gymnasium, imitated him, and thus decided to be a boxer before he was
fifteen years old. Another fighter was inspired by a neighbor and became his
protégé. He continually followed his hero to the gymnasium and learned
to fight himself. Eventually the neighbor induced his manager to take his
protégé into the stable. A third fighter has stated:

> I was twelve when I went to the gym first. If there's a fighter in the neigh-
> borhood, the kids always look up to him because they think he's tough.
> There was an amateur in my neighborhood and he was a kind of hero to all
> us kids. It was him that took me to the gym the first time.

A former welterweight and middleweight champion who has been boxing
since he was eleven years old has written in a similar vein:

> I didn't do any boxing before I left Detroit. I was too little. But I was
> already interested in it, partly because I idolized a big Golden Gloves heavy-
> weight who lived on the same block with us. I used to hang around the
> Brewster Center Gym all the time watching him train. His name was Joe
> Louis. Whenever Joe was in the gym so was I. He was my idol then just like
> he is today. I've always wanted to be like him.[4]

Some managers and trainers of local gymnasiums directly seek out boys
who like to fight and who take fighters as their models. One such manager
says that he sought boys who were considered the "toughest in the block" or
"natural fighters." He would get them to come to the gym and to become
amateur boxers. He entered some in tournaments, from which he received
some "cut," then sifted out the most promising for professional work.

It is believed by many in boxing circles that those in the lower socio-
economic levels make the "best fighters":

> They say that too much education softens a man and that is why the college
> graduates are not good fighters. They fight emotionally on the gridiron and
> they fight bravely and well in our wars, but their contributions in our rings
> have been insignificant. The ring has been described as the refuge of the
> under-privileged. Out of the downtrodden have come our greatest fighters.
> . . . An education is an escape, and that is what they are saying when they
> shake their heads—those who know the fight game—as you mention the
> name of a college fighter. Once the bell rings, they want their fighters to have
> no retreat, and a fighter with an education is a fighter who does not have to
> fight to live and he knows it. . . . Only for the hungry fighter is it a decent
> gamble.[5]

It can be inferred tentatively that the social processes among juveniles
and adolescents in the lower socioeconomic levels, such as individual and
gang fights, the fantasies of "easy money," the lack of accessible vocational
opportunities, and the general isolation from the middle-class culture, are

---

[4] "Sugar Ray" Robinson, "Fighting Is My Business," *Sport*, June, 1951, p. 18.
[5] *Ring*, July, 1950, p. 45.

similar for those who become professional boxers as for those who become delinquents. The difference resides in the role-model the boy picks, whether criminal or boxer. The presence of one or several successful boxers in an area stimulates boys of the same ethnic groups to follow in their footsteps. Boxing, as well as other sports and certain kinds of entertainment, offers slum boys the hope of quick success without deviant behavior (although, of course, some boxers have been juvenile delinquents).[6]

Within the neighborhood the professional boxer orients his behavior and routine around the role of boxer. Usually acquiring some measure of prestige in the neighborhood, he is no longer a factory hand or an unskilled laborer. He is admired, often has a small coterie of followers, and begins to dress smartly and loudly and to conceive of himself as a neighhorhood celebrity, whether or not he has money at the time. Nurtured by the praise of the trainer or manager, he has hopes that eventually he will ascend to "big-time fights" and to "big money." The money that he does make in his amateur and early professional fights by comparison with his former earnings seems a lot to him.

Occupational Culture of the Boxer

The intrinsic occupational culture of the boxer is composed of techniques, illusions, aspirations, and structured roles which every boxer internalizes in some measure and which motivate him both inside and outside the ring. At the outset of his career the boxer becomes impressed with the need for training to improve his physical condition and to acquire the skills necessary to win fights and to avoid needless injury. When he has such status as to be sought out by promoters, he assigns a specified interval for training before the bout. But in the preliminary ranks he must keep himself in excellent physical shape most of the time, because he does not know when he will be summoned to fight. He may be booked as a substitute and cannot easily refuse the match. If he does, he may find it difficult to get another bout. The particular bout may be the chance he has been hoping for. The fighter is warned persistently by tales of the ritualistic necessity of "getting in shape" and of the dire consequences if he does not. "There is no more pitiable sight," stated one boxer, "than to see a fighter get into the ring out of condition."

The boxer comes to regard his body, especially his hands, as his stock-in-trade. Boxers have varied formulas for preventing their hands from excess swelling, from excessive pain, or from being broken. This does not mean a hypochondriachal interest, because they emphasize virility and learn to slough

---

[6] Merton has noted that, while our culture encourages the people of lower standing to orient their conduct toward wealth, it denies them opportunities to get money in the framework of accepted institutions. This inconsistency results in a high rate of deviant behavior (Robert K. Merton, *Social Theory and Social Structure*, Glencoe, Ill.: Free Press, 1949, p. 137).

off and to disdain punishment. But fighters continually seek nostrums and exercises for improving their bodies. One practiced Yogi, another became a physical cultist, a third went on periodic fasts; others seek out lotions, vitamins, and other means of improving their endurance, alertness, and punching power.

"You have to live up to being a fighter." This phrase justifies their deprivations and regulated living. There is also a cult of a kind of persevering courage, called a "fighting heart," which means "never admitting defeat." The fighter learns early that his exhibited courage—his ability, if necessary, to go down fighting—characterizes the respected, audience-pleasing boxer. He must cherish the lingering hope that he can win by a few more punches. One fighter was so severely beaten by another that the referee stopped the bout. The brother of the beaten fighter, a former fighter himself, became so outraged that he climbed into the ring and started to brawl with the referee. In another instance a boxer incurred a very severe eye injury, which would have meant the loss of his sight. But he insisted on continuing to fight, despite the warnings of his seconds. When the fight was stopped, he protested. This common attitude among boxers is reinforced by the demands of the spectators, who generally cheer a "game fighter." Thus the beaten fighter may become a "crowd-pleaser" and may get matches despite his defeat. On the other hand, some fighters who are influenced by friends, by wives, or by sheer experience recognize that sustained beatings may leave permanent injuries and voluntarily quit when they are beaten. But the spirit of the code is that the boxer continue to fight regardless of injuries. "If a man quits a fight, an honest fight," claimed one fighter, "he has no business there in the first place."

Fighters who remain in the sport are always hopeful of occupational climbing. This attitude may initially be due to a definite self-centeredness, but it is intensified by the character of boxing. Boxing is done by single contestants, not by teams. Emphasis is on the boxer as a distinct individual. The mores among boxers are such that fighters seldom admit to others that they are "punchy" or "washed-up." [7] One fighter said: "You can tell another fighter to quit, but you can't call him punchy. If you do, he'll punch you to show you he still has a punch." He has to keep up his front.

Further, the boxer is involved in a scheme of relationships and traditions which focus upon building confidence. The boxing tradition is full of legends of feats of exceptional fighters. Most gymnasiums have pictures of past and present outstanding boxers on the wall, and identification with them comes easy for the incoming fighters. Past fights are revived in tales. Exceptional fighters of the past and present are compared and appraised. Second, the individual boxer is continually assured and reassured that he is "great" and

[7] Because of the changing character of boxing at the present time, promoters or managers may sometimes tell fighters that they are "through"; but fighters, as we have indicated, seldom make these appraisals of other fighters.

that he is "coming up." As a result, many fighters seem to overrate their ability and to feel that all they need are "lucky breaks" to become champions or leading contenders. Many get self-important and carry scrapbooks of their newspaper write-ups and pictures.

The process of stimulating morale among fighters is an integral accompaniment of the acquisition of boxing skills and body conditioning. The exceptions are the part-time fighters who hold outside jobs and who are in the preliminary ranks. They tend to remain on the periphery of the boxing culture and thus have a somewhat different perspective on the mobility aspects of the sport.[8]

As most bouts are unpredictable, boxers usually have superstitions which serve to create confidence and emotional security among them. Sometimes the manager or trainer uses these superstitions to control the fighter. One fighter believed that, if he ate certain foods, he was sure to win, because these foods gave him strength.[9] Others insist on wearing the same robe in which they won their first fight: one wore an Indian blanket when he entered the ring. Many have charm pieces or attribute added importance to entering the ring after the opponent. Joe Louis insisted on using a certain dressing-room at Madison Square Garden. Some insist that, if a woman watches them train, it is bad luck. One fighter, to show he was not superstitious, would walk under a ladder before every fight, until this became a magical rite itself. Consistent with this attitude, many intensify their religious attitudes and keep Bibles in their lockers. One fighter kept a rosary in his glove. If he lost the rosary, he would spend the morning before the fight in church. Although this superstitious attitude may be imported from local or ethnic culture, it is intensified among the boxers themselves, whether they are white or Negro, preliminary fighters or champions.

When a fighter likes the style, punch, or movement of another fighter, he may wear the latter's trunks or one of his socks or rub him on the back. In training camps some fighters make a point of sleeping in the bed that a champion once occupied. For this reason, in part, some take the names of former fighters. All these practices focus toward the perspective of "filling the place" or taking the role of the other esteemed fighter. Moreover, many fighters deliberately copy the modes of training, the style, and the general movements of role-models.

As fighters, in the process of training, become keyed to a finely balanced

---

[8] As the number of local bouts have declined with the advent of television, many preliminary fighters and local club fighters are compelled to work at outside jobs in order to meet their daily expenses.

[9] According to boxing folklore, a former heavyweight champion, Max Baer, was stimulated into action by his trainer who gave him a mixture called "Go Fast," which presumably had the properties of making a "tiger" out of the one who drank it. The suggestive effects of this drink were so great that Baer knocked out his opponent. Thereafter, he demanded it in subsequent fights. This suggestive play also proved effective with a former middleweight champion, Ken Overlin. The drink itself was composed of distilled water and a little sugar.

physical and emotional condition and frequently are irritable, restless, and anxious, they also grow dependent and suggestible. The superstitions and the reassuring statements of the trainer and manager both unwittingly and wittingly serve to bolster their confidence.

Before and during the bout, self-confidence is essential. Fighters or their seconds try to unnerve the opponent. They may try to outstare him or may make some irritating or deflating remarks or gestures. In the ring, tactical self-confidence is expressed in the boxer's general physical condition and movements. His ability to outslug, to outspar, or to absorb punishment is part of his morale. The ability not to go down, to outmaneuver the other contestant, to change his style in whole or in part, to retrieve his strength quickly, or to place the opponent off-balance inevitably affect the latter's confidence. A fighter can *feel* whether he will win a bout during the early rounds, but he is always wary of the dreaded single punch or the unexpected rally.

Boxers become typed by their style and manner in the ring. A "puncher" or "mauler" differs from a "boxer" and certainly from a "cream puff," who is unable to hit hard. A "miller," or continual swinger, differs from one who saves his energy by fewer movements. A "butcher" is recognized by his tendency to hit hard and ruthlessly when another boxer is helpless, inflicting needless damage. A "tanker" is one who goes down easily, sometimes in a fixed fight or "set-up." The "mechanical" fighter differs from the "smart" fighter, for among the "smart" fighters are really the esteemed fighters, those who are capable of improvising and reformulating their style, of devising original punches and leg movements, of cunningly outmaneuvering their opponents, and of possessing the compensatory hostility, deadly impulsiveness, and quick reflexes to finish off their opponents in the vital split second.

Boxers have to contend with fouls and quasi-fouls in the ring. At present, these tactics seemingly are becoming more frequent. They may have to contend with "heeling," the maneuver by which the fighter, during clinches, shoves the laced part of his glove over the opponent's wound, particularly an "eye" wound, to open or exacerbate it, with "thumbing" in the eye, with "butting" by the head, with having their insteps stepped on hard during clinches, with punches in back of the head or in the kidneys, or with being tripped. These tactics, which technically are fouls, may be executed so quickly and so cleverly that the referee does not detect them. When detected, the fighter may be warned or, at worst, may lose the round. The boxers are thus placed in a situation fraught with tension, physical punishment, and eventual fatigue. They may be harassed by the spectators. Their protection consists of their physical condition and their acquired confidence. Moreover, the outcome of the fight is decisive for their status and self-esteem.[10]

---

[10] Some defeated boxers, as a result of physical fatigue and self-recrimination, lapse into a condition resembling combat exhaustion or anxiety. They react by uncontrollable crying spells, tantrums, and random belligerency. The restoration of their confidence is crucial for subsequent fights. Some trainers and managers are quite skilled in accomplishing it.

The boxer's persistent display of aggression is an aspect of status. Thus his aggression becomes impersonal, although competition is intense. Thus two boxers may be friends outside the ring, but each will try to knock the other out in a bout, and after the bout they may be as friendly as competition permits. Furthermore, the injury done to an opponent, such as maiming or killing, is quickly rationalized away by an effective trainer or manager in order to prevent an access of intense guilt, which can ruin a fighter. The general reaction is that the opponent is out to do the same thing to him and that this is the purpose of boxing: namely, to beat the opponent into submission. The exception is the "grudge fight," in which personal hostility is clearly manifest.

In a succession of bouts, if the fighter is at all successful, he goes through a fluctuating routine, in which tension mounts during training, is concentrated during the fight, and is discharged in the usual celebration, which most victorious fighters regard as their inevitable reward. Hence many boxers pursue a fast tempo of living and spend lavishly on clothes, women, gambling, and drink, practices seemingly tolerated by the manager and encouraged by the persons who are attracted to boxers. Many boxers experience intense conflict between the ordeals of training and the pursuits of pleasure.

Social Structure and Social Mobility

Boxers comprise a highly stratified occupation. Rank is determined by their rating in a weight division, by their position in a match, and by their status with stablemates who have the same manager. Annually, for each weight division, fighters are ranked. The champion and about twenty leading contenders are listed on top.[11] The other fighters are listed into "A," "B," and "C" categories. Many local preliminary fighters are not listed. Only the first twenty contenders and the "A" category seem to have any importance. Of 1,831 fighters listed for 1950, 8.8 percent comprised the champion and leading contenders; 16.9 percent were in the "A" category; 74.3 percent were in the "B" and "C" categories.

To determine the vertical mobility of fighters, the careers of 127 fighters were traced from 1938 onward.[12] Of these, 107, or 84.2 percent, remained in the local preliminary or semiwindup category. Eleven boxers, or 8.7 percent, became local headliners, which may be in the "A" category. They had been professional boxers for an average of almost eight years. Eight boxers, or 7.1 percent, achieved national recognition, that is, among the first ten leading contenders. They also had been professionals for an average of almost eight years. One fighter became champion after twelve years in the ring.

The boxers who remain in the sport believe that they can ascend to the top because of the character of the boxing culture, in which the exceptional boxer is emphasized and with whom the aspiring boxer identifies. When the

[11] Data taken from *Ring*, February, 1951.
[12] These computations were made by following the fighters in every issue of *Ring* from 1938 on. This magazine lists all the fights for every month.

boxer ceases to aspire, he quits or becomes a part-time boxer. Yet the aspiring hopes of many boxers are not unfounded, because climbing in the sport does not depend upon ability only and also can be a result of a "lucky break."

Relationships of the Boxer

Boxers live in a wide social milieu of trainers, managers, and promoters. The boxer and trainer usually form the closest relationships in the boxing milieu. At one time, many managers were trainers, too; and a few owners of local gymnasiums still combine these roles, but their number has declined. Furthermore, the relationships between boxer and trainer are becoming increasingly impersonal. Consequently, the careful training and social intimacy which characterized the conditioning of many boxers by trainers in the past has also declined.[13]

Generally, the specialized trainer or trainer-manager represents the authority-figure to the boxer, transmits boxing skills to him, and becomes his anchor point of emotional security. The trainer's relationship with the boxer becomes crucial to his development. The effective trainer polishes his skills, compels him to train regularly, and distracts him from worrying about the fight, and he can control him by withdrawing praise or can restore his morale when he has lost. For example, a trainer reviewed a lost fight to his charge so skillfully that the boxer began to believe that his opponent had won by a few lucky punches. Had he averted these "lucky" punches, the fighter felt that he would have won. His confidence restored, he renewed his training with added vigor and determination.

The trainer may be of distinct help to the boxer during the bout. Frequently his "second," he may advise him of his opponent's weaknesses and of his own faults. In addition, he can be a continuing source of confidence to the fighter. A fighter recalled that before a bout his trainer became ill. He felt alone and somewhat diffident when the fight began. He regained his confidence in the third round, when he felt that his opponent could not hurt him. As the trainer can become so emotionally close to the fighter, he can help or hinder him, depending upon his insight and knowledge of boxing. Though very important to the fighter, the trainer is not a powerful figure in the boxing hierarchy, and some trainers are as exploited as are fighters by the managers.

One boxer has characterized managers as follows: "Some managers are interested in the money first and in the man second; other managers are interested in the man first." Our observations lead us to infer that the vast

[13] "One of the troubles with boxing is what I call assembly line training. There are too few competent trainers and most of them have too many fighters to train. For the most part the boxers look upon training as a necessary evil. . . . [In the past], hours were spent on perfecting a movement—a feint, the proper tossing of a punch, the art of slipping a blow successfully. [This] marked the difference between a skilled craftsman and a lumbering wild-swinging tyro" (Al Buck, "Incompetency the Cause," *Ring*, September, 1950, p. 22).

majority of managers at the present time are in the first category. They regard boxing as a business and the fighter as a commodity and are concerned mainly with making money. To do so, they are compelled to please the promoters and to sell their fighters' abilities to the promoters. Unless the manager is also a trainer, he is not concerned with the techniques of boxing, except to publicize his charge and to arrange matches which will bring the most revenue.

While the boxer devotes his aggressions to training and fighting, the manager slants his aggressions to machinations for better matches and for more money. Having few illusions about the fight business, acquainted with and often accepting its seamier side, he conforms to the standard managerial pattern of having the advantage over "his" boxers in every way. First, managers are organized into a guild, and, though some managers will try to steal boxers from one another, they usually bar fighters who run out on managers.[14] (One boxer, on the other hand, tried to organize fighters into a union. His efforts were squelched quickly, and he was informally blackballed from fighting in New York City.) Second, many managers try to keep their fighters financially and, if possible, emotionally tied to them. Some managers will encourage fighters to borrow money from them and usually will not discourage them from squandering their earnings. One manager stated characteristically: "It's good to have a fighter 'in you' for a couple of bucks." By having fighters financially indebted to them, they have an easy expedient for controlling individuals who are unusually headstrong. Some fighters are in the continual process of regarding every fight as an essential means for clearing their debts.

Legally managers cannot receive more than one-third of the fighters' purses, but many do not conform to this rule. Frequently, they take one-half the purse, or they may put their fighters on a flat salary and get the rest. Some managers tell their preliminary fighters that the purse was less than it was actually and thus keep the rest for themselves.

Furthermore, many managers abuse their fighters so as to make money quickly. They may overmatch them with superior fighters, "rush" them into too many fights, force them to fight when they are out of condition, and hint that the fight is "fixed" and instruct them indirectly to lose. A few managers will match their fighters in another state when they are barred in one state because of injuries; they will obtain matches before the required sixty days have elapsed after their fighters have been knocked out. Fighters may be severely hurt, even ruined, by these tactics.

Some managers, however, are concerned mainly with building up their fighters and doing everything possible to develop their maximum ability; but these managers are in the minority. In short, managers have no informal standards to protect their boxers and are guided chiefly by their own personal considerations in these activities.

[14] The managers' guild also serves in part as a kind of collective protection against promoters.

As many ruthless individuals and petty racketeers who know little about boxing are increasingly drawn into this sport with the prime purpose of making money quickly, boxers tend to have little, if any, protection from managers except that provided by boxing commissions, whose rules can be evaded without difficulty. Moreover, it is extremely difficult for a boxer to climb or get important matches unless he has an effective manager.

The Boxer and the Promoter

The boxer's relationship with the promoter is usually indirect. Yet the promoter is the most influential person in the boxing hierarchy. He is primarily a showman and businessman, emotionally removed from the fighter; and regards him chiefly as a commodity. His aim is to get the most from his investment. Thus the "show" comes first, regardless of the boxer's welfare. To insure his direct control over many boxers, the promoter, who legally cannot be a manager, may appoint one or a series of "managers" as "fronts" and thus get shares of many boxers' earnings, as well as controlling them. Furthermore, he can reduce the amount of the fighter's share because the nominal manager will not bargain for a larger share. In effect, most boxers are relatively helpless in dealing with promoters, especially at the present time, because of the monopolistic character of boxing.

When a potentially good fighter wants to meet leading contenders, the manager may have to "cut in" the promoter or "cut in" some other manager who has connections with the promoter. Thus the mobility of the fighter depends in large part upon the manager's relationship to the promoter. When the manager does not have this acceptable relationship and is unwilling to "cut in" a third party, he will not get the desired matches.[15]

As the promoter is concerned primarily with attracting a large audience, he tries to select and develop fighters who will draw customers.[16] Thus the fighter must have "crowd-pleasing" qualifications in addition to ability. In this connection, the race and ethnic group play a part. A good white fighter is preferred to a good Negro fighter; and in large cities, such as New York and Chicago, a Jewish fighter is considered highly desirable because the majority of fight fans are Jewish and Italian. Despite the efforts of promoters to attract white fighters, especially Jewish fighters, few Jewish fighters have emerged, because the role-models and practices in the local Jewish communities have changed. Even Negro fighters, despite their dominance of the sport in quality

---

[15] E.g., an outstanding light-heavyweight contender is unable to get a title match, although one whom he has defeated will get the match. He was slighted because his manager has not signed with the International Boxing Club. His manager has stated: "The I.B.C. dictates who fights who and when and where. They're big business. But I'll fight; I'm trying to keep the independents [boxers and managers] in business" (*Time*, July 9, 1951, pp. 58–59).

[16] The tastes of contemporary fight fans is directed mainly toward punchers rather than boxers. In the past, clever boxers were highly appreciated.

and quantity of fighters, are increasingly turning to other sports because the role-models are slowly shifting.[17]

The fighter whom a promoter does select for grooming can easily be made mobile once he has shown crowd-pleasing tendencies. He can be, as it were, "nursed" to the top by being matched with opponents who are easy to beat or by meeting "set-ups" who are instructed to lose. Thus he builds up an impressive record and is ready for big-time fights. Hence, it is difficult to tell how competent a fighter is on his early record alone, for his record may be designed for publicity purposes. When a fighter has won all or nearly all of his early matches and then loses repeatedly to leading contenders, he has been "nursed" to the top by the promoter, unless the fighter has incurred an injury in one of his later fights. In these ways the promoter can influence decisively the occupational career of the boxer.

Effect Upon the Boxer

The punitive character of boxing, as well as the social relationships in the boxing milieu, affects the boxer-participants during and after their careers in the ring.

First, the physical effects of boxing, which are intrinsic to the sport, operate to the boxer's detriment. Although boxers may cultivate strong bodies, the direct and indirect injuries from this sport are very high. In addition to the deaths in the ring, one estimate is that 60 percent of the boxers become mildly punch-drunk and 5 percent become severely punch-drunk.[18] The severely punch-drunk fighter can be detected by an ambling gait, thickened or retarded speech, mental stereotypy, and a general decline in efficiency. In addition, blindness and visual deficiency are so pervasive that eye injuries are considered virtually as occupational casualties, and misshaped noses and cauliflower ears are afflictions of most boxers who are in sport for five or more years. Despite these injuries, attempts to provide safeguards, such as headguards, have been opposed by the fans and by many boxers because such devices presumably did not "protect" and did not fit into their conceptions of virility and presumed contempt for punishment.[19]

Second, the boxing culture tends to work to the eventual detriment of the boxer. Many boxers tend to continue a particular fight when they are

---

[17] "In 1937 when [Joe] Louis won the crown from Jimmy Braddock, every Negro boy in all corners of the country worshipped him. Their thoughts centered on boxing and boxing gloves. . . . The boys who once worshipped Louis as boxer have gone daffy about a baseball hero, Jackie Robinson. . . . The eyes of the boys who once looked upon Joe Louis with pride and envy and wanted to emulate him, now are focussed on Jackie Robinson and other top-notch ballplayers" (Nat Loubet, "Jackie Robinson's Rise Blow to Boxing," *Ring*, September, 1950, p. 5).

[18] Arthur H. Steinhaus, "Boxing—Legalized Murder," *Look Magazine*, January 3, 1950, p. 36.

[19] Some precautions have been innovated recently for the boxer's protection, such as the thickness of the padding on the floor of the ring or the absence of protrusions or sharp corners in the ring.

hopelessly beaten and when they can become severely injured. Many boxers persist in fighting when they have passed their prime and even when they have been injured. For example, one boxer, blind in one eye and barred from fighting in one state, was grateful to his manager for getting him matches in other states. Another old-time boxer has admitted characteristically: "It's hard to quit. Fighting gets into your blood, and you can't get it out." Many fighters try to make one comeback, at least, and some fight until they are definitely punch-drunk.

Boxers find further that, despite their success in the sport, their careers terminate at a relatively early age.[20] As their physical condition is so decisive to their role, when they feel a decline in their physical prowess, they tend also to acquire the premature feeling of "being old." This attitude is reinforced by others in the sport who refer to them as "old men," meaning old in the occupation. As boxing has been the vocational medium of status attainment and as they have no other skills to retain that status, many boxers experience a sharp decline in status in their postboxing careers. As an illustration, of ninety-five leading former boxers (i.e., champions and leading contenders), each of whom earned more than $100,000 during his ring career, eighteen were found to have remained in the sport as trainers or trainer-managers; two became wrestlers; twenty-six worked in, "fronted for," or owned taverns;[21] two were liquor salesmen; eighteen had unskilled jobs, most commonly in the steelmills; six worked in the movies; five were entertainers; two owned or worked in gas stations; three were cab-drivers; three had newsstands; two were janitors; three were bookies; three were associated with the race tracks (two in collecting bets and one as a starter); and two were in business, one of them as a custom tailor. In short, the successful boxers have a relatively quick economic ascent at a relatively young age in terms of earning power. But the punitive character of the sport, the boxers' dependence upon their managers, and their carefree spending during their boxing careers contribute to a quicker economic descent for many boxers. Their economic descent is accompanied by a drop in status and frequently by temporary or prolonged emotional difficulties in readjusting to their new occupational roles.[22]

[20] Although the boxing myths emphasize the exceptions who fought past the age of forty—e.g., Bob Fitzsimmons fought until he was about fifty-two—the average fighter is considered "old" after he is thirty years of age. At present, some "old" fighters are still successfully active—e.g., Joe Louis and "Jersey Joe" Walcott, who are thirty-seven years old. In addition to being exceptions, their successful participation in the ring is also a result of the fact that few new heavyweights are entering boxing.

[21] As successful boxers retain a reputation in their respective neighborhoods after they have quit the sport, some businessmen use their names as "fronts" for taverns or lounges. Hence it was difficult to find out whether the boxers themselves owned the taverns. In five cases they did not, although the taverns were in their names.

[22] One former champion said: "I like to hear of a boxer doing well after he leaves the ring. People think all boxers are punchy. We have a bad press. After I left the ring, I had a devil of a time telling people I wasn't punchy." The Veterans Boxing Association, an organization of former boxers, has protested occasionally against radio programs which present what they consider a false stereotype of the former boxer.

a view of skiers as a subculture

DAVID BOROFF

Skiing was once supposed—by sentimentalists—to be the sport of a heroic elite. In a simpler time, when rope tows creaked, the outdoor ideal was untarnished. "It was all fresh air during the day and singing in front of a fire at night," an oldtimer recalled. There were even those who, in Norse fashion, made long cross-country trips on skis. (This has become the fashion again.) But the dynamics of popular sport are irresistible. You start with a Spartan idyll, the sport catches on, and there is an inescapable expansion—and melancholy decline—into crowds, technology, motels.

Ski operators are inclined to be impatient with elitist nostalgia. As the sport gains popularity, the facilities become more lavish—so lavish and so expensive that ever larger crowds become economically imperative. Mt. Snow has led the way with such peripheral things as outdoor swimming and indoor ice skating, saunas—and girl-watching for the predatory. Who has to ski?

Nearly everybody is the answer. For what saves skiing finally is a respect—amounting to reverence—for the sheer skill of the sport. No snobbery is fiercer than that of the *echt* skier. Skiers discuss refinements of technique and equipment with a passion and a minuteness that suggest scholars engaged in esoteric studies.

Technique snobbery is remorseless. The wedelners perform their choreography like movie stars. They come spinning down the mountain with negligent grace and churn into the tow-line in a haughty spume of snow. On the mountainside the serfs laboriously make their way down the slope, picking the easy spots, eying the moguls like enemies. But they, in turn, lord it over the beginners. And even the beginners feel a lofty superiority over the snow bunnies, those fellow-travelers of sport.

Another system of snobbery has to do with where you ski. The farther you go, the more dash you have. The lower Catskills—Grossinger's, the Concord, Davos—are simply out of the question. Skiers love to boast about prodigies of driving that they perform ("We made Stowe in six and a half hours"), and the whole point of a ski weekend is to cram as much as possible into the weekend with the least amount of sleep. The ultimate refinement in this distance steeplechase is the junket to Switzerland—"just for a few days of skiing"—to Chile or even to that final outpost, New Zealand.

The spirit in which you go also yields points in the status rat race. Skiing is big business today, but skiers like to maintain the illusion of a certain nonchalance—Renaissance Italians called it *sprezzatura*, a highly prized quality among courtiers.

Low man on this totem pole is the square who makes arrangements to go on a packaged bus tour, a kind of grubby welfare state in which meals, lodging, and instruction are written into the contract. Bus tours are scorned even by ski operators, a group notable for their magnanimity. The operators' quarrel with bus tours is that they carry their own ski instructors, who allegedly, are uncertified. There are also recurrent reports of ungentlemanly drinking during the day. The package planners have the last word. They argue that skiers should be relieved of the anxieties of travel and lodging. The ski instructors, they insist, are often certified and have the advantage of knowing their students before they teach them. And in this fresh-air democracy, why shouldn't secretaries and salesmen take a crack at skiing?

One would expect that people who make their living from skiing would be free from the status nonsense. But they tend to be as hierarchical as their customers. The pecking order, in ascending order, is the ski bum, ski patrol-man, and ski instructor. The ski bum is really a beatnik with a suntan and an implausible passion for skiing. He—or she—works part-time in a lodge in exchange for board and a season ski pass. He is often a college kid on the lam, a member of that army of restless students who take a semester or year off. Sometimes he is just out of school, determined to squeeze in a full season of skiing before graduate school or career closes in. Ski bums provide a touch of bohemia in a sport which is becoming big business. (There are even ski-bum entertainers whose job it is to sing folk songs in front of the fire.) But, in the end, the Organization will be their undoing. Already, ski operators are nervous about the term ski bums. "Please call them lodge staff," a slope operator suggested primly.

Ski patrolmen, the medical corpsmen of the slopes, are the dray horses of the sport. Brightly costumed, with medical packs bulging around their middle, they maintain safety, take down the injured, and make a final sweep of trails and slopes at the end of the day. They are the beefy cops of the ski area—steady, sturdy, utterly reliable.

But ski instructors are the glamor boys of the sport—the gods of the mountain. Handsomely attired (they must be good-looking and wear stretch pants), deeply tanned, highly visible, they are tirelessly pursued by women. And they must be available. They rotate at ski lodge tables, they talk skiing in the evening, and they must maintain an aura of manly vigor. Soon or late, they begin to believe the legends about themselves.

The reality underneath is somewhat less than glittering. Many ski instructors are just small-town boys who in the summer are prosaic cabinet-makers, construction workers, or telephone linesmen. Recently some professional types have been recruited—engineers, attorneys, and nurses (among the women). Of course, there are the European ski instructors, for some of whom the role of gigolo athlete comes easily. But European instructors are sometimes hired sight unseen—a chancy business. As a result, ski operators

often settle for the kid next door. The result is winter head-turning and summer devaluation.

But even the glamorous winter season has its asperities. Instructors are
expected to turn up in fair weather and foul, sickness or in health. And there
is a curious reversal of the sexual roles of male and female instructors. It is
the men who are courted and petted and spoiled. They are the starlets of the
slopes, and narcissism is a serious occupational hazard. The women, on the
other hand, are like a cartoon version of wartime WACs, hard-bitten, tough,
masculine.

If there is some ambiguity about the life of ski instructors, the ski
towns too are not quite certain whether they are blessed or damned. Wilmington, Vt., near Mt. Snow, is not untypical. Years ago it drowsed all winter
and waited for a small flurry of summer tourists. Now it swings all winter and
people say commiseratingly, "It must be dead here in the summer." And,
along with the skiers, there has been a torrent of dollars. Nevertheless, all is
not well. This old community, which has its origins in the eighteenth century,
finds itself overrun. To many townspeople—flinty Vermonters all—the term
skier means foreigner. The town likes the money but hates the people. Wee
Moran, who runs a ski shop in Wilmington with a Vermonter's crotchetiness,
posted a sign that reads: "Your credit is not good here based on my experience
in the past. If this does not apply to you, I am sure you will not be offended."
And on a blackboard he is prone to write little homilies, e.g., "If you steal
from a crook, you're a clever crook. But if you betray a trust, you're a damned
fool."

As a symptom of change, Wilmington now has an authentic Greenwich
Village type coffeehouse. The proprietor, Phil Capy, is a singer and dancer
with a passion for skiing. During the day, he is a hard-working, paid leader
of the ski patrol at Haystack Mountain. Evenings he runs a small dormitory
for skiers and sings folk songs in the cellar establishment. To some of the
townsmen his coffeehouse is like a hint of Sodom Babylon in its wicked
heyday.

But these are merely the growing pains of a new sport. Skiing has
emerged as one of the country's durable activities, esthetically gratifying,
technically demanding, and bracingly elemental.

The pure mystique of skiing was expressed by a young woman in New
York, dark-haired and intricate of psyche: she was sitting in a lodge feeling
outside. And there were all these tall, handsome blond skiers. And I had
a longing for the blue-eyed and blond-haired.

PART FIVE

further readings in the sociology of sport

supplementary references [1]

Part 2, Section 1: The Sociology of Sport As a Discipline

Cauwels, A., "Introduction a une Sociologie du Sport" (Introduction to a Sociology of Sport), *Sport*, 68–76 (April 1965) (Bruxelles).

Dumazedier, J., "Education Physique, Sport et Sociologie" (Physical Education, Sport and Sociology), *Education Physique et Sport*, 69, 7–10 (1964) (Paris).

Kane, J. E. and C. Murray, "Suggestions for the Sociological Study of Sports," pp. 111–127, in J. E. Kane and C. Murray (eds.), *Readings in Physical Education*, London: Physical Education Association, 1966.

---

[1] The reader's attention is drawn to the existence of more extensive bibliographies containing material of interest to the sport sociologist. Günther Lüschen has prepared a most extensive list for *Current Sociology* (Volume 15, 1968, The Hague, Netherlands, Mouton Publishers); Bryant J. Cratty's recent book, *Social Dimensions of Physical Activity* (Prentice-Hall, 1967) contains a bibliography of 474 entries. References related to the subject of leisure can be found in several sources, including Larrabee and Meyersohn's *Mass Leisure* (Free Press, 1958), Dumazeder's *Toward a Society of Leisure* (Free Press, 1967), and Dulles' *A History of Recreation: America Learns to Play* (Appleton-Century-Crofts, 1965).

In addition to these, there are five volumes scheduled for publication in 1969 that should be of interest to the student of sport sociology. They are: Elliott M. Avedon and Brian Sutton-Smith, *The Study of Games*. New York: Wiley; Robin Herron and Brian Sutton-Smith, *Child Play*. New York: Wiley; Gerald S. Kenyon, ed., *Contemporary Psychology of Sport*, Proceedings of the Second International Congress on Sport Psychology, Washington, 1968; Gerald S. Kenyon, ed., *Some Contemporary Perspectives of Sport Sociology*. Chicago: The Athletic Institute, Proceedings of Symposium on the Sociology of Sport, University of Wisconsin, 1968; and a book of readings by Eric Dunning, Leicester University, to be published in England.

Kenyon, Gerald S., "A Sociology of Sport: On Becoming a Sub-Discipline" in Roscoe C. Brown, Jr., and Bryant J. Cratty, (eds.), *New Perspectives of Man in Action*. Englewood Cliffs, N.J., Prentice-Hall, 1969.

Lüschen, G., "Prolegomena zu einer Soziologie des Sports" (Preliminaries to a Sociology of Sport) *Kölner Zeitschrift für Soziologie und Sozialpsychologie*, **12**, 505–515 (1960).

Magnane, G., *Sociologie du Sport*, Paris: Gallimard, 1964.

Part 2, Section 2: Concepts, Definitions and Classifications

Berne, E., *Games People Play*, New York: Grove Press, 1964.

Caillois, R., *Man, Play and Games* (translated by M. Barash), New York: Free Press, 1961.

Kaplan, M., *Leisure in America: A Social Inquiry*, New York: John Wiley & Sons, 1960.

Piaget, J., *Play, Dreams and Imitation in Childhood* (translated by C. Gattegno and F. M. Hodgson), New York: W. W. Norton, 1951.

Roberts, J. M. and others, "Games in Culture," *American Anthropologist*, **61**, 597–605 (1959).

Sapora, A. V. and E. D. Mitchell, *The Theory of Play and Recreation* (3rd Ed.), New York: Ronald Press, 1961.

Scotch, N. A., "Magic, Sorcery, and Football Among Urban Zulu: A Case of Re-interpretation Under Acculturation," *The Journal of Conflict Resolution*, **5**, 70–74 (1961).

Torkildsen, G. E., "Sport and Culture," M.S. thesis, University of Wisconsin, 1967.

Part 3, Section 1: Sport in Ethnic Cultures

Gini, C., "Rural Ritual Games in Libya," *Rural Sociology*, **4**, 283–299 (1939).

Goellner, W. A., "The Court Ball Game of the Aboriginal Mayas," *Research Quarterly*, **24**, 147–168 (1953).

Hoffman, W. J., "Remarks on Ojibwa Ball Play," *American Anthropologist*, **3**, 133–135 (1890).

Jones, K., "Polynesian Games," M.A. thesis, University of Alberta, 1967.

Roberts, J. M. and others, "Strategy in Games and Folk Tales," *Journal of Social Psychology*, **61**, 185–199 (1963).

Stumpf, F. and F. W. Cozens, "Some Aspects of the Role of Games, Sports, and Recreational Activities in the Culture of Modern Primitive Peoples: the New Zealand Maoris," *Research Quarterly*, **18**, 198–218 (1947).

Stumpf, F. and F. W. Cozens, "Some Aspects of the Role of Games, Sports, and Recreational Activities in the Culture of Modern Primitive Peoples: the Fijians," *Research Quarterly*, **20**, 2–20 (1949).

Sutton-Smith, B., "The Meeting of Maori and European Cultures and its Effects upon the Unorganized Games of Maori Children," *Journal of the Polynesian Society*, **60**, 93–107 (1951).

Part 3, Section 2: Sport in Comparative Perspective

Ahokas, Jaakko, "The Land of Competition: Observations on the Sociology of Games in Finland," *Diogenes*, **26**, 97–106 (Summer, 1959).

Aronson, Sidney H., "The Sociology of the Bicycle," *Social Forces*, **30**, 305–312 (1952).

Boyle, R. H., *Sport—Mirror of American Life*, Boston: Little, Brown & Co., 1963.

Cozens, F. W. and F. S. Stumpf, *Sports in American Life*, Chicago: University of Chicago Press, 1953.

Dulles, F. R., *A History of Recreation* (America Learns to Play) (2nd Ed.), New York: Appleton-Century-Crofts, 1965.

Eyler, Marvin H., "*Origins of Contemporary Sports*," *Research Quarterly*, **32**, 480–489 (1961).

Hayner, N. S., "Mexicans at Play—a Revolution," *Sociology and Social Research* **38**, 80–83 (1953).

McIntosh, P. C., *Sport in Society*, London: C. A. Watts, 1963.

Morton, H. W., *Soviet Sport*, New York: Crowell-Collier, 1963.

Paxon, F. L., "The Rise of Sport," pp. 94–117 in F. L. Paxon, *The Great Demobilization and Other Essays*, Madison: University of Wisconsin Press, 1941.

Seagoe, May V., "Children's Play As an Indicator of Cross-Cultural Differences," *Journal of Educational Sociology*, **36**, 278–283 (1962).

Stone, Gregory P., "American Sports—Play and Display," *Chicago Review*, **9**, 83–100 (Fall, 1955).

Sutton-Smith, B. and B. G. Rosenberg, "Sixty Years of Historical Change in the Game Preferences of American Children," *Journal of American Folklore* (1961).

Wecter, D., "Society and Sport," Chapter XI, pp. 428–457 in D. Wecter, *The Saga of American Society*, New York: Charles Scribner's Sons, 1937.

Weir, L. H., *Europe at Play*, New York: A. S. Barnes, 1937.

Part 3, Section 3: Sport and Social Institutions

SPORT AND ECONOMICS

Andreano, R., *No Joy in Mudville*, Cambridge, Mass.: Schenkman, 1965.

Gregory, P. M., *The Baseball Player: An Economic Study*, Washington, D. C.: Public Affairs Press, 1956.

Mahoney, S., "Pro Football's Profit Explosion," *Fortune*, **70**, 153–155, 218 (1964).

SPORT AND POLITICS

Hanna, W. R., *The Politics of Sport*, New York: American Universities Field Staff, 1962.

Molyneux, D. D., *Central Government Aid to Sport and Physical Recreation in Countries of Western Europe*, Birmingham, England: University of Birmingham, 1962.

SPORT AND RELIGION

Andrus, R., "A History of the Recreation Program of the Church of Jesus Christ of Latter-Day Saints," Ph.D. dissertation, State University of Iowa, 1962.

Postal, Bernard, *Encyclopedia of Jews in Sport*. New York: Block Publishers, 1965.
Ribalow, Harold U., *The Jew in American Sports*. New York: Block Publishers, 1966.
Simonson, T. (ed.), *The Goal and the Glory—America's Athlete's Speak Their Faith*, Westwood, New Jersey: Revell, 1962.

SPORT AND WOMEN

Krotz, L. E., "A Study of Sports and the Implications of Women's Participation in Them in Modern Society," Ph.D. dissertation, Ohio State University, 1958.
Trekell, M., "The Effect of Some Cultural Changes Upon the Sports and Physical Education Activities of American Women—1860–1960," Paper presented at the History and Philosophy Section of the National Convention of the American Association of Health, Physical Education and Recreation, Dallas, Texas, March 18, 1965.
Watts, D. P., "Changing Conceptions of Competitive Sports for Girls and Women in the United States from 1880 to 1960," Ed.D. dissertation, University of California, Los Angeles, 1960.

SPORT AND EDUCATION

Coleman, James, "Adolescent Sub-Culture and Academic Achievement," *American Journal of Sociology*, 65, 337–347 (1960).
Matza, David, "Position and Behavior Patterns of Youth," in Robert E. L. Faris, ed., *Handbook of Modern Sociology*. Chicago: Rand McNally, 1964, pp. 191–216.
Rehberg, Richard A., and Walter E. Schafer, "Participation in Interscholastic Athletics and College Expectations," *American Journal of Sociology*, 73, 732–740 (1968).
Shaw, John H., and Cordts, Harold J., "Athletic Participation and Academic Performance," in Warren R. Johnson, ed., *Science and Medicine of Exercise and Sports*. New York: Harper and Brothers, 1960, pp. 620–630.

Part 3, Section 4: Sport and Social Processes

COMMUNICATION AND SPECTATORSHIP

Bogart, L., "Television's Effects on Spectator Sports," Chapter 9, pp. 162–173, in L. Bogart, *The Age of Television*, New York: Frederick Unger, 1956.
Hastorf, A. H. and H. Cantril, "They Saw a Game: A Case Study," *Journal of Abnormal and Social Psychology*, 49, 129–134 (1954).
Jordon, J., *Long Range Effects of Television on Sports Attendance*, Washington, D. C.: Radio and Television Manufacturers Association, 1950.

DISCRIMINATION

Draper, M., *Sport and Race in South Africa*, Johannesburg: South African Institute of Race Relations, 1963.
Henderson, E. B., *The Negro in Sports*, Washington, D. C.: Associated Publishers, 1969.
Henderson, E. B., and the Editors of *Sport, The Black Athlete—Emergence and Arrival*. Washington, D. C.: Associated Publishers, 1969.

Olsen, Jack, *The Black Athlete—A Shameful Story*. New York: Time, Inc., 1969.
Rosenblatt, Aaron, "Negroes in Baseball: The Failure of Success," *Trans-Action*, **4**, 51–53 (September, 1967), with a reply by Whitehead, **4**, 63–64 (October, 1967).
Thompson, R., *Race and Sport*, London: Oxford University Press, 1964.

SOCIALIZATION

Cowell, C. C., "The Contributions of Physical Activity to Social Development," *Research Quarterly*, **31**, 286–306 (1960).
Helanko, R., "Sports and Socialization," *Acta Sociologica*, **2**, 229–240 (1957).
Kenyon, G. S., "The Contribution of Physical Activity to Social Development," *Report*, Symposium on Integrated Development, Lafayette, Indiana: Purdue University, 1964, pp. 48–54.
Piaget, J., *The Moral Judgment of the Child* (translated by M. Gabain), New York: Free Press, 1965.

SPORT AND SOCIAL CHANGE

AAHPER, *Social Change and Sport*, Washington, D. C.: AAHPER, 1959.
Frohlick, P. E., "Sports and the Community: A Study of Social Change in Athens, Ohio," Ph.D. dissertation, University of Wisconsin; 1952.
Loy, J. W., "A Paradigm of Technological Change in Sport Situations," *International Review of Sport Sociology*, 1:177–194 (1966).

SPORT AND SOCIAL STRATIFICATION

Annarino, Anthony A., "The Contribution of Athletics to Social Mobility," *Proceedings*, 56th Annual Meeting of the College Physical Education Association, New York, 1953, pp. 136–138.
Clarke, A., "The Use of Leisure and Its Relation to Levels of Occupational Prestige," *American Sociological Review*, **21**, 301–307 (1956).
Gerstl, J. E., "Leisure Taste and Occupational Milieu," *Social Problems*, **9**, 56–68 (Summer 1961).
Kenyon, G. S., "The Significance of Physical Activity as a Function of Age, Sex, Education, and Socio-Economic Status of Northern United States Adults," *International Review of Sport Sociology*, **1**, 41–57 (1966).
McIntyre, T. D., "Socio-Economic Background of White Male Athletes from Four Selected Sports at the Pennsylvania State University," M.S. thesis, Pennsylvania State University, 1959.

Part 4: Sport and Small Groups

SECTION 1: SPORT GROUP AS A MICRO-SOCIAL SYSTEM

Emerson, R. M., "Mount Everest: A Case Study of Communication Feedback and Sustained Group Goal-Striving," *Sociometry*, **29**, 213–227 (1966).
Elias, Norbert, and Dunning, Eric, "Dynamics of Group Sports with Special Reference to Football," *British Journal of Sociology*, **17**, 388–401 (1966).
Gamson, William A., and Norman A. Scotch, "Scapegoating in Baseball," *American Journal of Sociology*, **70**, 69–72 (1964), with reply by Grusky, pp. 72–73.

Gordon, Gerald, and Becker, Selwyn, "Organizational Size and Managerial Succession: A Re-examination," *American Journal of Sociology*, 70, 215–222 (1964), with a reply by Grusky, p. 222.

Grusky, Oscar, "Managerial Succession and Organizational Effectiveness," *American Journal of Sociology*, 69, 21–31 (1963).

Kroll, W. and K. H. Peterson, "Personality Factor Profiles of Collegiate Football Teams," *Research Quarterly*, 36, 433–440 (1965).

Kroll, W. and K. H. Peterson, "Study of Values Test and Collegiate Football Teams," *Research Quarterly*, 36, 441–447 (1965).

McGraw, L. W. and J. W. Tobert, "Sociometric Status and Athletic Ability of Junior High School Boys," *Research Quarterly*, 24, 72–80 (1953).

Sherif, M. and others, "Status in Experimentally Produced Groups," *American Journal of Sociology*, 60, 370–379 (1955).

Trapp, W. G., "A Study of Social Integration in a College Football Squad," *Proceedings*, 56th Annual Meeting, College Physical Education Association, Washington, D. C.: 1953, pp. 139–141.

Walters, C. E., "A Sociometric Study of Motivated and Non-Motivated Bowling Groups," *Research Quarterly*, 26, 107–112 (1955).

SECTION 2: SPORT GROUP AS A SUBCULTURE

Boyle, R. H., "A Minority Group: The Negro Baseball Players," in R. H. Boyle, *Sport—Mirror of American Life*, Boston: Little, Brown, 1963.

Kramer, Jerry, *Instant Replay*. New York: World Publishing Co., 1968.

Plimpton, G., *Paper Lion*, New York: Harper & Row, 1965.

Scott, M. B., *The Racing Game*, Chicago: Aldine, 1968.

Stone, Gregory P., and Oldenburg, Roman A., "Wrestling," in R. Slovenko and J. Knight, eds., Motivations in Play, Games and Sports. Springfield, Ill.: Charles C Thomas, 1967, pp. 503–532.

Veeck, Bill (with Ed Linn), *The Hustler's Handbook*. New York: G. P. Putnam's Sons, 1965.

Whyte, W. F., *Street Corner Society*, Chicago: University of Chicago Press, 1955.

references used in introductory statements

Artemov, V., "Physical Education and Leisure," *International Review of Sport Sociology*, 1, 75–84 (1966).

Baltzell, E. Digby, *An American Business Aristocracy*, New York: Collier Books, 1962.

Bendix, R., *Max Weber: An Intellectual Portrait*, Garden City, New York: Doubleday, 1960.

Berne, Eric, *Games People Play*, New York: Grove Press, 1964.

Caillois, Roger, *Man, Play and Games* (translated by Meyer Barash), New York: Free Press, 1961.

Caplow, Theodore, *Principles of Organization*, New York: Harcourt, Brace & World, 1964.

Cowell, C. C., "The Contributions of Physical Activity to Social Development," *Research Quarterly*, 31, 286–306 (May, 1960).

Daniels, A., "The Study of Sport as an Element of the Culture," *International Review of Sport Sociology*, 1, 153–165 (1966).

de Grazia, D., *Of Time, Work and Leisure*, Garden City, New York: Doubleday, 1962.

Dumazedier, Joffre, "The Point of View of a Social Scientist," *Proceedings*, International Conference of the International Council of Sport and Physical Education, Paris, October, 1963, pp. 53–55.

Dumazedier, Joffre, *Toward a Civilization of Leisure*, New York: Free Press, 1966.

Erbach, Günther, "The Science of Sport and Sport Sociology—Questions Related to Development—Problems of Structure," *International Review of Sport Sociology*, 1, 59–74 (1966).

Goellner, W. A., "Court Ball Games of the Aboriginal Mayas," *Research Quarterly*, 24, 147–168 (1953).

Goffman, Erving, *Encounters*, Indianapolis: Bobbs-Merrill, 1961.

Gordon, Milton M., "The Concept of the Sub-Culture and Its Application," *Social Forces*, 26, 40–42 (1947).

Groos, K., *The Play of Animals*, New York: D. Appleton Co., 1898.

Hall, G. S., *Youth*, New York: D. Appleton and Co., 1920.

Hetherington, C. W., "Fundamental Education," *American Physical Education Review*, 15, 629–635 (December, 1910).

Hollingshead, A. B., *Elmtown's Youth*, New York: John Wiley & Sons, 1949.

Horkheimer, M., "New Patterns in Social Relations," *Proceedings*, International Conference of the International Council of Sport and Physical Education, Paris, October, 1963, pp. 23–29.

Howard, G. E., "Social Psychology of the Spectator," *The American Journal of Sociology*, 18, 33–50 (1912).

Huizinga, Johan, *Homo Ludens: A Study of the Play Element in Culture*, Boston: Beacon Press, 1955.

Jones, K., "Polynesian Games," unpublished M.A. thesis, University of Alberta, 1967.

Kane, J. E. and C. Murray, "Suggestions for the Sociological Study of Sport," *Readings in Physical Education*, London: Physical Education Association, 1966, pp. 111–127.

Kukushkin, G. I., "Sociological Research into Physical Culture in the U.S.S.R.," *International Review of Sport Sociology*, 1, 242, 243 (1966).

Larrabee, E. and Meyersohn R., *Mass Leisure*, Glencoe, Illinois: Free Press, 1958.

Lundberg, G., *et al.*, "The Amount and Uses of Leisure," in E. Larrabee and R. Meyersohn, *Mass Leisure*, Glencoe, Illinois: Free Press, 1958.

Magnagne, G., *Sociologie du Sport*, Paris, 1964.

Mead, G. H., *Mind, Self, and Society*, Chicago: University of Chicago Press, 1934.

Mills, Theodore M., *The Sociology of Small Groups*, Englewood Cliffs: Prentice-Hall, 1967.

McDougal, W., *Social Psychology*, Boston: J. W. Luce and Co., 1918.

McIntosh, Peter C., *Sport in Society*, London: C. A. Watts, 1963.

Nash, J. B., "Character Education as an Objective," *Mind and Body*, 38, 497–499 (May 1931).

Natan, A., *Sport and Society*, London: Bowes and Bowes, 1958.

Patrick, G. T. W., "The Psychology of Football," *American Journal of Psychology*, 14, 104–117 (1903).

Piaget, Jean, *Play, Dreams and Imitation in Childhood* (translated by C. Gattegno and F. M. Hodgson), New York: W. W. Norton, 1951.

Salter, M., "Games of the Australian Aborigines," unpublished M.A. thesis, University of Alberta, 1967.

Spencer, H., *The Principles of Psychology*, New York: D. Appleton and Co., 1873, cited by Lehman, H. C. and P. A. Witty, *The Psychology of Play Activities*, New York: A. S. Barnes, 1927.

Stumpf, F. and F. W. Cozens, "Some Aspects of the Role of Games, Sports, and Recreational Activities in the Culture of Modern Primitive People. I. The New Zealand Maoris," *Research Quarterly*, 18, 198–218 (1947).

Tylor, E. B., "On the Game of Pattolli in Ancient Mexico," *Journal of the Royal Anthropological Institute* of Great Britain and N. Ireland, 8, 116–131 (1878).

Veblen, Thorstein, *The Theory of the Leisure Class*, New York: The Modern Library, 1934.

Williams, J. R., "Education through the Physical," *Journal of Higher Education*, 1, 279–282 (May, 1930).

Wiseman, H. V., *Political Systems*, New York: Praeger, 1966.

Wohl, A., "Conception and Range of Sport Sociology," *International Review of Sport Sociology*, 1, pp. 5–17 (1966).

Wolff, K. H., *The Sociology of Georg Simmel*, New York: Free Press, 1964.

Zeigler, Earle F., and King J. McCristal, "The Big Ten Body of Knowledge Project," *Quest*, 9 (1967).

Zetterberg, H. K., *On Theory and Verification in Sociology*, Totowa, N. J.: The Bedminster Press, 1965.